Counseling American Minorities

COUNSELING AMERICAN MINORITIES

SIXTH EDITION

Donald R. Atkinson
University of California, Santa Barbara

Boston   Burr Ridge, IL   Dubuque, IA   Madison, WI   New York
San Francisco   St. Louis   Bangkok   Bogotá   Caracas   Kuala Lumpur
Lisbon   London   Madrid   Mexico City   Milan   Montreal   New Delhi
Santiago   Seoul   Singapore   Sydney   Taipei   Toronto

 **Higher Education**

COUNSELING AMERICAN MINORITIES, SIXTH EDITION

Published by McGraw-Hill, a business unit of The McGraw-Hill Companies, Inc., 1221 Avenue of the Americas, New York, NY 10020. Copyright © 2004 by The McGraw-Hill Companies, Inc. All rights reserved. Previous edition(s) 1998, 1995. All rights reserved. No part of this publication may be reproduced or distributed in any form or by any means, or stored in a database or retrieval system, without the prior written consent of The McGraw-Hill Companies, Inc., including, but not limited to, in any network or other electronic storage or transmission, or broadcast for distance learning.

Some ancillaries, including electronic and print components, may not be available to customers outside the United States.

Domestic   3 4 5 6 7 8 9 0 DOC/DOC 0 9 8 7

ISBN: 978-0-697-36185-1
MHID: 0-697-36185-3

Vice president and editor-in-chief: *Thalia Dorwick*
Publisher: *Stephen D. Rutter*
Special projects editor: *Rebecca Smith*
Marketing manager: *Melissa Caughlin*
Project manager: *Mary Lee Harms*
Manager, new book production: *Sandra Hahn*
Manager, design: *Laurie Entringer*
Cover designer: *JoAnne Schopler*
Cover image: *Corbis*
Associate art editor: *Cristin Yancey*
Associate photo research coordinator: *Natalia Peschiera*
Senior supplement producer: *David A. Welsh*
Compositor: *ElectraGraphics, Inc.*
Typeface: *10/12 Times Roman*
Printer: *R. R. Donnelley/Crawfordsville, IN*

The credits section for this book begins on page C-1 and is considered an extension of the copyright page.

Library of Congress Cataloging-in-Publication Data

Counseling American minorities/ [edited by] Donald R. Atkinson.—6th ed.
    p. cm.
  Includes bibliographical references and index.
  ISBN 0-697-36185-3 (alk. paper)
    1. Minorities—Mental health—United States. 2. Minorities—Counseling of—United States. 3. Cross-cultural counseling—United States. I. Atkinson, Donald R.

    RC451.5.A2C68 2004
    362.2'04256'089—dc21   2003046437

The Internet addresses listed in the text were accurate at the time of publication. The inclusion of a website does not indicate an endorsement by the authors or McGraw-Hill, and McGraw-Hill does not guarantee the accuracy of the information presented at these sites.

www.mhhe.com

Brief Contents

About the Contributors   xxi

Preface   xxv

Part I

RACIAL/ETHNIC
MINORITIES
AND CROSS-
CULTURAL
COUNSELING

1   Defining Populations and Terms   1

2   Within-Group Differences
Among Ethnic Minorities   27

3   Addressing the Mental Health
Needs of Ethnic Minorities   57

Part II

THE AFRICAN
AMERICAN
CLIENT

4   Contextualizing Black
Americans' Health   83

5   The Physical and Mental Health
Needs of African Americans   105

6   African Americans: Treatment
Issues and Recommendations   125

Part III

THE AMERICAN
INDIAN CLIENT

7   Profile of Native Americans   147

8   Physical and Mental Health
Needs of Native American Indian
and Alaska Native Populations   171

9   Treatment Issues for Native
Americans: An Overview
of Individual, Family, and Group
Strategies   193

Part IV

THE ASIAN
AMERICAN
CLIENT

10   Asian Americans: A Practical
History and Overview   217

11   Physical and Mental Health
of Asian Americans   240

12   Treatment Issues with Asian
     American Clients   258

Part V   13   *¡Somos!* Latinas and Latinos
                               in the United States   279
THE HISPANIC
AMERICAN   14   Physical and Mental Health
CLIENT   Concerns of Hispanics   300

                      15   Treatment Issues with Hispanic
                           Clients   317

Part VI   16   Current Issues and Future
                               Directions in Counseling Ethnic
IMPLICATIONS   Minorities   341
FOR MINORITY
GROUP/CROSS-
CULTURAL
COUNSELING

APPENDIX   Cross-Cultural
                               Counseling Competencies:
                               A Conceptual Framework   379

                      Credits   C-1

                      Author Index   I

                      Subject Index   I-12

Contents

About the Contributors   xxi
Preface   xxv

Part I

RACIAL/ETHNIC
MINORITIES
AND CROSS-
CULTURAL
COUNSELING
*Makes a case for
developing cultur-
ally sensitive men-
tal health services
to meet the special
needs of ethnic mi-
norities*

1   Defining Populations and Terms   3

*Defines race, ethnicity, and culture and examines the ap-
propriateness or inappropriateness of other terms associated with ethnic diversity; explains why this book focuses
on African Americans, American Indians, Asian Americans,
and Hispanics*

DEFINING TERMS: RACE, ETHNICITY,
   AND CULTURE   5
   Race: A Valid Construct?   5
      The Biological Definition of Race   6
      Criticisms of the Biological Definition of Race   6
      The Social Definition of Race   8
   Ethnicity and Culture   9
      How is Culture Defined?   9
      Race, Ethnicity, and Culture: Some Conclusions   10
      Culturally Deprived and Culturally Disadvantaged   11

FURTHER DEFINITIONS RELATING TO CULTURE
   AND DIVERSITY   12
   Melting Pot, Acculturation, Assimilation,
      and Cultural Pluralism   12
   Ethnocentrism, Racism,
      and White Privilege   14
   Multicultural Sensitivity
      and Political Correctness   18
   Terms Associated With Specific Ethnic Groups   18

COUNSELING ETHNIC MINORITY POPULATIONS   20
   Cross-Cultural, Multicultural, and Ethnic Minority
      Counseling   21
   The Book's Choice of Populations   22

2   Within-Group Differences Among Ethnic Minorities   27

*Examines the factors that contribute to individual differ-
ences within all ethnic minority groups*

CULTURAL DIFFERENCES WITHIN MAJOR
   ETHNIC GROUPS   29

ACCULTURATION AS A WITHIN-
    GROUP VARIABLE   30
    Early Assimilation Models   30
    Berry's Theories of Psychological Acculturation   31
    Multidimensional and Bicultural Theories
        of Acculturation   34
    Measuring Acculturation   35

RACIAL/ETHNIC IDENTITY DEVELOPMENT AS A
    WITHIN-GROUP VARIABLE   37
    Cross's Model of Racial Identity Development   37
    Helms and the People of Color Racial
        Identity Model   38
    Minority Identity Development Model   39
        Stage One—Conformity Stage   40
        Stage Two—Dissonance Stage   41
        Stage Three—Resistance and Immersion Stage   42
        Stage Four—Introspection Stage   43
        Stage Five—Synergistic Stage   44
        Implications of the MID Model
            for Counseling   44

SOCIOECONOMIC WITHIN-
    GROUP DIFFERENCES   47

CULTURAL MISTRUST AS A WITHIN-GROUP
    VARIABLE   49

3   Addressing the Mental Health
    Needs of Ethnic Minorities   57
Discusses the mental health needs of ethnic minorities and
examines the disparities in mental health services provided
to them in the United States

MENTAL HEALTH NEEDS AMONG
    ETHNIC MINORITIES   58

DISPARITIES IN MENTAL HEALTH SERVICES   61
    Disparities in Access to Mental Health Services   61
        Availability of Mental Health Services   61
        Affordability of Mental Health Services   62

DISPARITIES IN USE OF MENTAL HEALTH SERVICES   63
    Cultural Mistrust   65
    Social Stigma Associated With Mental Illness   65
    Conflicting Views About Psychological Problems   66
    Alternative Sources of Help   68

DISPARITIES IN QUALITY OF TREATMENT   69
    Disparities in Type of Diagnosis   69
    Diagnostic Bias and the *DSM*   71

Disparities in Quality of Intervention   73
Disparities in Mental Health Research   74

SUMMARY   75

Part II

_____

THE AFRICAN AMERICAN CLIENT

Documents the experiences of African Americans, examines their physical and mental health concerns, and discusses treatment issues when working with this population; focuses special attention on physical health concerns that may be a function of lifestyle or oppression and thus subject to improvement through mental health interventions

4   Contextualizing Black Americans' Health   83

Helen A. Neville and Jessica M. Walters, University of Illinois at Urbana-Champaign

Provides a profile of Black Americans and discusses the major social issues affecting this population; describes racial schemas that are somewhat unique to the Black American experience, along with factors that put Black Americans at risk for, or protect them from, physical and mental health problems

DEMOGRAPHY OF BLACK AMERICANS   84

CLASS STRUCTURE   85

EDUCATION   87

INCARCERATION AND THE PRISON
    INDUSTRIAL COMPLEX   87

CURRENT SOCIAL ISSUES   89

PSYCHOLOGICAL PROCESSES: RACIAL SCHEMAS   91
    Racial Identity   92
    Cultural Mistrust   94
    Color-Blind Racial Ideology   95

RISK AND PROTECTIVE FACTORS RELATED
    TO MENTAL AND PHYSICAL HEALTH   96

CONCLUSION   98

EXERCISES   99

5   The Physical and Mental Health Needs of African Americans   105

Lori R. Wicker and Robert E. Brodie II, University of California, Santa Barbara

Discusses the social and cultural factors that affect African American physical and mental health and presents specific physical and mental health problems experienced by African American men, women, and children

PHYSICAL HEALTH   106
    Causal Attributions   106
        Low Socioeconomic Factors   106
        Institutional Racism   107
        Cultural and Lifestyle Factors   108
        Genetic Predisposition   109

Specific Health Needs—Adults   110
   Injuries and Death Resulting From Violence   110
   Cardiovascular Disease   110
   Cancer   110
   Diabetes   111
   HIV/AIDS   111
   Substance Abuse   112
   Organ Donation   112
Specific Health Needs—Youth   112
   Sickle Cell Anemia   113
   Lead Poisoning   113
   Teenage Pregnancy   113

MENTAL HEALTH   114
Causal Attributions   114
   Institutionalized Racism   114
   Socioeconomic Status and Racial/Ethnic Group
      Membership   114
Mental Health Needs   115
   Unhealthy Racial Identity   115
   Unemployment   116
   Educational and Occupational Deficits   116
   Grief and Bereavement   117
Mental Health Needs Specific to Sex and Age   117
   African American Men   117
      Incarceration   118
      Stigma Associated With African American Men   118
   African American Women   119
      Single-Parent Status
         and Economic Hardships   119
      Unavailability of Same-Race Male Partners   119
      HIV/AIDS   119
   Mental Health Needs of Children   120
      Poverty   120
      Educational Attainment   120

CONCLUSION   120

EXERCISES   122

6   African Americans: Treatment Issues
   and Recommendations   125
   Chalmer E. Thompson and Khym Isaac, Indiana
   University—Bloomington
*Reviews research on the treatment of African Americans'
mental health problems and suggests that successful treatment of this population depends on the mental health practitioner's willingness and ability to confront racial issues*

RESEARCH ON TREATMENT ISSUES 126

RACE, CULTURE, AND AFRICAN AMERICANS 131

THE INTERSECTION BETWEEN RACE
AND CULTURE 134

PRACTICE IMPLICATIONS 136

EXERCISES 139

Part III

THE AMERICAN INDIAN CLIENT

Documents the experiences of American Indians, examines their physical and mental health concerns, and discusses treatment issues when working with this population; focuses special attention on physical health concerns that may be a function of lifestyle or oppression and thus subject to improvement through mental health interventions

7   Profile of Native Americans   147

Michael Tlanusta Garrett, Eastern Band of Cherokee, Western Carolina University

Identifies who qualifies as Native American, provides a profile of this diverse population, and discusses cultural values common to the Native American experience; gives special attention to values and lifestyle factors, as well as external social forces, that affect Native American physical and mental health

THE PEOPLE   147
   Who Is Native American: "How Much Are You?"   148
   Terms Applied to Native Americans   149

SURVIVING "HISTORY": SPIRIT NEVER DIES   149

NATIVE TRADITIONS: LIVING THE WAYS   150
   The Tribe/Nation   150
   The Meaning of Family   152
   Wisdom Keepers   152
      Humility   153
      Generosity   153
      Patience   154
      Time   154
      Being   154
   Spirituality and Wellness: Walking in Step   154
      Medicine (Everything Is Alive)   155
      Harmony (Everything Has Purpose)   156
      Relation (All Things Are Connected)   156
      Vision (Embrace the Medicine of Every
         Living Being)   156
   Lessons of the Eagle Feather: Rule of Opposites   157
   Indian Humor: Laughing It Up   157
   Communication Style: Talking the Talk   158

ACCULTURATION: CIRCLES WITH NO BEGINNINGS
AND NO END   158

TRUST VERSUS MISTRUST: AIR OF CRUELTY, WINDS
OF CHANGE   160

SOCIAL SUPPORT SYSTEMS: THE SACRED WEB   161

CURRENT SOCIAL AND POLITICAL ISSUES: CRYING
   FOR A VISION   162
   Identity   162
   Tribal Resources   163
   Treaty Rights   163
   Religious Freedom   163
   Sacred Sites   164
   Repatriation and Reburial   165
   Mascot Issues   165
   Gaming   165
   Cultural Preservation   166

CONCLUSION: MEDICINE BAG   166

EXERCISES   167

8   **Physical and Mental Health Needs
     of Native American Indian
     and Alaska Native Populations**   171
     Roger D. Herring, University of Arkansas—
     Little Rock

Chronicles the physical and mental health problems experienced by Native American Indians, with an emphasis on the causes of death that might be modified through behavioral and social change; examines the successes of existing physical and mental health prevention programs; discusses cultural attributions about the causes of, and solutions to, mental health problems

CURRENT NEEDS: AN OVERVIEW   171

EPIDEMIOLOGICAL DATA   172
   Indian Health Service   172
   Statistical Data   173

PHYSICAL AND MENTAL HEALTH NEEDS   174
      Physical Health   174
      Causes of Death   174
         Breast/Cervical Cancer   174
         HIV/AIDS   174
         Cardiovascular Diseases   175
         Diabetes Mellitus   175
         Maternal/Infant Mortality   175
         General Mortality   176
      Prevention and Treatment Programs   176
         Community Health   176
         Nutrition/Dietetics   176
         Public Health   177
         Dental Services   177

Sanitation   177
Patient Care Statistics   177
Teenage Pregnancy   177
Summary of Health Care   178
Mental Health   178
Nonspecific Mental Disorders   179
Alcohol/Drug Use   179
Suicide   181
Identity Conflicts   181
Summary   182
Cultural Attributions About the Causes
of Psychological Problems   182
Cultural Attributions About the Solutions
to Psychological Problems   183
View of Seeking Mental Health Services   184
Selected Traditional Native Cultural
Healing Beliefs   184
The Four Directions of Existence   185
The Sweat Lodge Ceremony   185
The Vision Quest   186
The Talking Circle   186
Use of Folklore   186

IMPACT OF PSYCHOSOCIAL FACTORS   187

CONCLUSION   188

EXERCISES   189

9   Treatment Issues for Native Americans An Overview of Individual, Family, and Group Strategies   193

Cindy L. Juntunen and Paula M. Morin, University of North Dakota

Provides insight into the reasons why many American Indians are reluctant to use mental health services, including the inherent conflict of values between many traditional healing methods and conventional counseling approaches; suggests more successful treatment approaches for American Indians, such as advocacy and individual, family, and group counseling

NATIVE AMERICAN USE
OF COUNSELING SERVICES   193
Trust   194
Social-Cultural Factors   195
Culture of the Clinician   195
Limited Resources   196

CONFLICTS BETWEEN TRADITIONAL NATIVE
HELPING AND CONVENTIONAL
COUNSELING APPROACHES   196

ISSUES IN DIAGNOSIS AND ASSESSMENT   199

TREATMENT APPROACHES   201
   Advocacy Counseling   201
   Individual Counseling   204
   Family Counseling   206
   Group Counseling   207

CONCLUSION   208

EXERCISES   209

Part IV

THE ASIAN
AMERICAN
CLIENT
Documents the experiences of Asian Americans, examines their physical and mental health concerns, and discusses treatment issues when working with this population; focuses special attention on physical health concerns that may be a function of lifestyle or oppression and thus subject to improvement through mental health interventions

10   Asian Americans: A Practical
     History and Overview   217
     Audrey U. Kim, University of California, Santa Cruz
Sketches the history of immigration by, and discrimination against, Asian Americans; debunks the "model minority" myth while documenting the diversity within the umbrella ethnic group; discusses Asian American cultural values and ethnic identification along with the current status of the group in the United States

IMMIGRATION HISTORY   218
   Early Immigration   218
   1965 Immigration Act   219
   Southeast Asian Immigration   220
   Recent Immigration   221

RACISM AND DISCRIMINATION   222
   Japanese Internment   223
   Employment   224
   Education   226

THE MODEL MINORITY   227
   Education, Occupation, and Income   228
   Implications and Consequences   229

CONCEPTUALIZING IDENTITY   230

CULTURAL VALUES   232

CURRENT STATUS   233

EXERCISES   236

11   Physical and Mental Health
     of Asian Americans   240
     David Sue, Western Washington University
Discusses the barriers to health care among Asian Americans as well as prominent mental health problems and

*mental health practices among this population; examines
the roles of prejudice, acculturation, and socialization in
their use of health care services*

PHYSICAL HEALTH INFORMATION
  ON ASIAN AMERICANS   240
  Barriers to Health Care   241
  Health Practices and Beliefs   242

MENTAL HEALTH   243
  Mental Disorders   244
  Substance Abuse   245
  Biological Factors Associated
    With Substance Abuse   246
  Cultural Influences on Psychopathology   247
  Mental Health Practices and Beliefs   248
  Somatization   248
  Prejudice and Acculturation Conflicts   249
  Family Issues and Problems   250

CONCLUSION   251

EXERCISES   252

12   Treatment Issues with Asian
    American Clients   258
    Bryan S. K. Kim, University of California, Santa
    Barbara
*Documents patterns of mental health utilization among
Asian Americans and examines reasons for underutilization; discusses indigenous healing practices and modified
psychological treatments as alternatives to conventional
approaches to counseling and psychotherapy; offers specific recommendations for providing mental health services
to Asian Americans*

ATTITUDES ABOUT THE SEEKING OF COUNSELING
  SERVICES   259
  Mental Health Service Utilization Patterns   259
  Perceptions of Mental Health Services
    and Providers   259

PSYCHOLOGICAL ASSESSMENT   263

POTENTIAL CONFLICT BETWEEN ASIAN
  AMERICANS' CULTURAL VALUES
  AND CONVENTIONAL COUNSELING   265

INDIGENOUS HEALING PRACTICES
  AS ALTERNATIVE METHODS
  OF MENTAL HEALTH TREATMENT   267

MODIFICATION OF CONVENTIONAL
FORMS OF COUNSELING TO MEET
CULTURAL NEEDS   268

ADDITIONAL SOURCES OF MENTAL
HEALTH SUPPORT   270

TREATMENT RECOMMENDATIONS   271

EXERCISES   272

Part V

THE HISPANIC AMERICAN CLIENT

Documents the experiences of Hispanics, examines their physical and mental health concerns, and discusses treatment issues when working with this population; focuses special attention on physical health concerns that may be a function of lifestyle or oppression and thus subject to improvement through mental health interventions

13   ¡Somos! Latinas and Latinos in the United States   279

Alberta M. Gloria and Theresa A. Segura-Herrera, University of Wisconsin—Madison

Discusses the major demographic, psychological, social, and cultural variables that describe Latinas and Latinos; presents the distinct social and political histories of descendants of Mexican, Cuban, Puerto Rican, Central American, and South American immigrants; discusses specific cultural values that have implications for counseling

DEMOGRAPHIC AND PSYCHOSOCIOCULTURAL
VARIABLES   279
Terminology and Self-Referents   280
Population Estimates   280
Geographic Representation   281
Immigration   281
Generational Status   282
Age   282
Language   283
Employment   283
Income   284
Education   284
Religion and Spirituality   285
Sexuality   286
Phenotype   286

SOCIOPOLITICAL HISTORIES   287
Individuals of Mexican Descent—Mexicanos   287
Individuals of Puerto Rican Descent—
Puerto Riqueños   288
Individuals of Cuban Descent—Cubanos   288
Individuals of Central American Descent—Centro
Americanos   289
Individuals of South American Descent—
Sud Americanos   289

SOCIAL PERCEPTIONS   290
  Media   290
  Economy   290
  Education   291

CULTURAL VALUES   291
  Familismo   292
  Personalismo   292
  Simpatía   292
  Cariño   292
  Respeto   293
  Confianza   293
  Machismo, Hembrismo, and Marianismo   293

¡SOMOS EL PASADO, EL PRESENTE, Y EL FUTURO!
  WE ARE THE PAST, PRESENT, AND FUTURE!   294

EXERCISES   295

14   Physical and Mental Health
     Concerns of Hispanics   300
     José M. Abreu and Hiroshi M. Sasaki, University of
     Southern California
Cites the physical health concerns of Hispanics that result
from lifestyle choices, work-related discrimination, and lack
of proper treatment; discusses in detail the mental health
concerns related to inadequate treatment, acculturative
stress, and refugee status; highlights the mental health problems affecting Hispanic children and youth

PHYSICAL HEALTH CONCERNS   300
  Diabetes   301
  HIV and AIDS   302
  Health Concerns Due to Work-
    Related Discrimination   303
  Other Physical Health Concerns   304
    Cirrhosis   304
    Hepatitis A   304
    Lung Cancer   305
  Unequal Medical Treatment Issues   305

MENTAL HEALTH CONCERNS   306
  Psychiatric Diagnosis and Psychopathology   306
  Sociocultural Factors: Acculturation
    and Acculturative Stress   307
  Children and Youth   309
  Refugees   309
  Culture-Bound Syndromes   310

CONCLUSION   310

EXERCISES   311

**15   Treatment Issues
with Hispanic Clients**   317
José M. Abreu, University of Southern California;
Andrés J. Consoli, San Francisco State University;
and Scott J. Cypers, University of Southern California
Documents mental health utilization patterns among Hispanics and examines reasons for underutilization; presents primary, secondary, and tertiary prevention strategies for physical and mental health problems experienced by Hispanics

MENTAL HEALTH UTILIZATION   317
   Patterns of Utilization Among Hispanics   318
   Reasons for Underutilization   319

TREATMENT ISSUES: PREVENTIVE APPROACH   321
   HIV and AIDS   322
   Diabetes   323
   General Approach to Address Other Concerns   324

TREATMENT ISSUES: SECONDARY
AND TERTIARY APPROACHES   325
   Acculturation, Stress, and Approach to Counseling   325
      Discrimination and Racial Identity   326
      Language Use   327
      Generation Status and Family Structure   328
   Assessment   328
   Culture-Bound Syndromes   330

CONCLUSION   330

EXERCISES   331

Part VI

IMPLICATIONS
FOR MINORITY
GROUP/CROSS-
CULTURAL
COUNSELING
Points up the ability of the mental health professions to serve ethnic minorities

**16   Current Issues and Future Directions
in Counseling Ethnic Minorities**   341
Specifies what the mental health professions are doing and should do to address the special mental health needs of African American, American Indian, Asian American, and Hispanic clients as well as clients from other ethnic minorities

ETHICAL CONSIDERATIONS IN COUNSELING
ETHNIC MINORITIES   341
   Current Ethical Codes   341
   Criticisms of the APA and ACA Ethical Codes   344

ISSUES IN DEFINING AND OPERATIONALIZING
  MULTICULTURAL COUNSELING COMPETENCE   346
  Multicultural Counseling: Competencies
    or Guidelines?   346
  Challenges to Multicultural
    Counseling Competence   349
  Problems With Assessing
    Multicultural Competence   350
  Future of the Multicultural
    Counseling Competence Movement   352

THEORIES AND MODELS THAT GUIDE
  MULTICULTURAL COUNSELING PRACTICE   352
  Helms's Interactional Model   353
  Three-Dimensional Model for Counseling Racial/Ethnic
    Minority Clients   354
    Advocate   358
    Change Agent   358
    Consultant   360
    Adviser   360
    Facilitator of Indigenous Support Systems   361
    Facilitator of Indigenous Healing Methods   361
    Conventional Counselor   362
    Conventional Psychotherapist   363
    Selection of an Appropriate Role   365
  Theory of Multicultural Counseling
    and Therapy   367
  Common Factors Approach
    to Multicultural Counseling   369
    *Common Factors Approach to Counseling and
      Psychotherapy*   369
    EST Versus Common Factors   370
    Common Factors in a Cultural Context   371

CONCLUSION   372

APPENDIX   Cross-Cultural Counseling
                     Competencies:
                     A Conceptual Framework   379

                  Credits   C-1

                  Author Index   I

                  Subject Index   I-12

About the Contributors

José M. Abreu is Assistant Professor of Counseling Psychology at the University of Southern California. He received his Ph.D. in counseling/clinical/school psychology from the University of California, Santa Barbara in 1995. His major research interests are in the area of multicultural counseling, and he teaches a variety of graduate and undergraduate courses that focus on counseling processes, career guidance, and multicultural issues.

Donald R. Atkinson is Professor Emeritus in the combined psychology program (Gevirtz Graduate School of Education) at the University of California, Santa Barbara. He is a coauthor of three books, *Counseling American Minorities: A Cross-Cultural Perspective* (now in its sixth edition), *Counseling Non-Ethnic American Minorities, Counseling Diverse Populations* (now in its third edition), and *Counseling Across the Lifespan,* and author or coauthor of more than 130 journal articles and book chapters, most of which report the results of research on cultural variables in counseling. He is a Fellow in the American Psychological Society and Divisions 17 and 45 of the American Psychological Association, and in 2001 he received the Lifetime Research Award from Division 45 (Society for the Psychological Study of Ethnic Minority Issues). He earned his Ph.D. at the University of Wisconsin–Madison in 1970.

Robert E. Brodie II is a doctoral candidate at the University of California, Santa Barbara in the counseling/clinical/school psychology program. His emphasis is clinical psychology. His areas of specialty are African American mental health, diagnostic bias in the assessment and diagnosis of personality disorders, the delivery of culturally responsive treatments, and psychological and forensic testing.

Andrés J. Consoli is Associate Professor in the Department of Counseling, College of Health and Human Services, at San Francisco State University. He received his *Licenciatura* in clinical psychology from the Universidad de Belgrano, Buenos Aires, Argentina, in 1984. He obtained an M.A. (1991) and a Ph.D. (1994) in counseling psychology from the University of California, Santa Barbara. He specialized in behavioral medicine through a two-year postdoctoral fellowship in the Department of Psychiatry and Behavioral Sciences at Stanford University. He has authored and coauthored several journal articles and book chapters on client-therapist matching, the evolution of psychotherapy, psychotherapy integration, stress and anxiety disorders, and values in psychotherapy.

Scott J. Cypers is a second-year doctoral student in counseling psychology at the University of Southern California. He is interested in therapy process and outcome issues related to depression.

Michael Tlanusta Garrett, Eastern Band of Cherokee, is Associate Professor of Counseling and Head of the Department of Human Services at Western Carolina University. He holds a Ph.D. in counseling and counselor education and an M.Ed. in counseling and development from the University of North Carolina at

Greensboro. His primary research areas deal with wellness, spirituality, acculturation, group techniques, counseling children and adolescents, conflict resolution,
date rape and sexual violence, play therapy, and cultural issues of counseling Native Americans. In addition to numerous articles in the area of multiculturalism, he
has authored the book *Walking on the Wind: Cherokee Teachings for Harmony and
Balance* and coauthored the books *Medicine of the Cherokee: The Way of Right
Relationship* and *Cherokee Full Circle: A Practical Handbook on Ceremonies and
Traditions.*

Alberta M. Gloria is Associate Professor at the University of Wisconsin–
Madison. Her research interests include psychosociocultural factors for Chicano,
Chicana, Latino, Latina students in higher education and issues of cultural congruity
for these students within the academic and cultural environment. Her work has appeared in journals such as *Cultural Diversity and Ethnic Minority Psychology, Hispanic Journal of Behavioral Sciences,* and *The Counseling Psychologist.* She has
served as Secretary and Membership Chair for the Section for Ethnic and Racial Diversity for Division 17 of the American Psychological Association and is currently
the Chair-Elect. She is also the Secretary for the National Latina/o Psychological Association. She was awarded the Women of Color Psychologies Award from Division
35 in 1999 and the Emerging Professional Award from Division 45 in 2002.

Roger D. Herring, Lumbee/Catawba, is Professor of Counselor Education
at the University of Arkansas at Little Rock. He had 20 years of public school education experiences as a teacher, administrator, and counselor prior to entering
higher education. Since that entry, he has published 4 texts, 40 refereed articles,
and 14 book chapters. He has presented at 25 national conferences, 6 regional
conferences, and 21 state conferences and has conducted 16 workshops at various levels. He has also served as editor (JHCEAD), on numerous editorial board
assignments, and on 12 invited book reviews. He has received numerous awards,
including The American Counseling Association's Research Award (1998), The
Association for Multicultural Counseling and Development's Research Award
(1993), The Southern Association of Counselor Education and Supervision's
Outstanding Individual Achievement Award (1992), and 8 Arkansas Counseling
Association Research Awards. His primary research emphasis is multicultural
counseling with ethnic minority youth, emphasizing Native American Indian/
Alaska native adolescents.

Khym Isaac obtained an M.A. in psychology and an M.Ed. in psychological
counseling from Teachers College, Columbia University in 2000. She is currently
pursuing a doctoral degree in counseling psychology at Indiana University. Her
research interests include racial differences in depressive symptoms in daughters
due to their perceived paternal preferences, theory and measures of multicultural
counseling competence, family therapy using the functional family therapy paradigm, the effectiveness of school-based mental health programs, and therapy
process issues between client and therapist.

Cindy Juntunen is Associate Professor and Chair of the Department of
Counseling at the University of North Dakota. She is currently directing an action
research project designed to increase career aspirations and enhance work satisfaction for people moving from welfare to self-sufficiency. She received her Ph.D.

from the University of California, Santa Barbara in 1994. Her research interests include vocational psychology, social action, and counselor supervision. She has published in the areas of career development for women and Native Americans, the school-to-work transition, and counselor supervision.

Audrey Kim is a licensed psychologist at University of California, Santa Cruz's Counseling and Psychological Services. She received her Ph.D. in counseling/clinical/school psychology from University of California, Santa Barbara, where she also taught Asian American Studies. She is committed to research and practice that serves the needs of traditionally underserved or marginalized populations, including Asian Americans and other racial/ethnic minorities. She is a strong believer in the importance of incorporating research into practice and focusing research around clinical applications.

Bryan S. K. Kim is Assistant Professor in the Counseling/Clinical/School Psychology Program in the Department of Education at the University of California, Santa Barbara. He received his Ph.D. from UCSB in 2000. His research focuses on multicultural counseling processing and outcome, the measurement of cultural constructs, and counselor education and supervision. His current research examines the effects of multicultural counseling strategies and client enculturation/acculturation (e.g., cultural values) on counseling process and outcome with Asian Americans. He currently serves on the editional board of *The Counseling Psychologist* and also currently serves as the Finance and Membership Officer of the Asian American Psychological Association and the Treasurer of the Section on Counseling and Psychotherapy Process and Outcome Research in the Society of Counseling Psychology (Division 17) of the American Psychological Association.

Paula M. Morin is a member of the Turtle Mountain Chippewa Tribe and a doctoral student in the counseling psychology program at the University of North Dakota. She is currently working on a dissertation titled "Resiliency and Biculturalism in two Northern Plains Chippewa Tribes." Her research interests lie in the areas of resiliency and coping resources, psychological measures utilized within American Indian populations, and alternative health care delivery systems on the reservation. She has been involved in a revision of an American Indian spirituality instrument and has been published in the area of American Indians and career.

Helen A. Neville, a graduate of the University of California, Santa Barbara, is currently Associate Professor in the Division of Counseling Psychology and the Afro-American Studies and Research Program at the University of Illinois at Urbana-Champaign. Her research has appeared in a wide range of professional journals and focuses on two primary areas: (a) general and cultural factors influencing the stress and coping process, primarily among rape survivors and college students; and (b) racial schemas, including color-blind racial ideology. She has served or is serving on a number of journal editorial boards (e.g., *Journal of Multicultural Counseling and Development* and *Violence Against Women*) and is currently an associate editor of *The Counseling Psychologist.*

Hiroshi M. Sasaki is a second-year doctoral student in counseling psychology at the University of Southern California. His research interests include minority mental health and acculturation; racial, gender, and sexual identity development; stereotype automaticity; and at-risk (especially homeless) youth.

Theresa A. Segura-Herrera is a doctoral student in the Department of Counseling Psychology at the University of Wisconsin–Madison. Her professional and academic areas of interest include the psychological experience of Latino immigration, mental health service delivery and outreach for Latinos, and the experiences of racial and ethnic minorities in higher education. She has coauthored a chapter on the educational experiences of Chicana and Chicano undergraduates for the upcoming *Handbook of Chicano and Chicana Psychology*.

David Sue is Professor of Psychology at Western Washington University and is currently the director of the psychology clinic. He is an associate at the Center for Cross-Cultural Research. He received his Ph.D. in clinical psychology from Washington State University. His research interests revolve around process and outcome variables in cross-cultural counseling, and he has coauthored texts in abnormal psychology and multicultural counseling.

Chalmer E. Thompson is Associate Professor and Director of Training of Counseling Psychology at the Indiana University School of Education in the Department of Counseling and Educational Psychology. She has held prior academic appointments at the University of California, Santa Barbara and the University of Southern California. Her area of research is focused on change processes as related to racial identity development. She is the senior editor (with R. T. Carter) of *Racial Identity Theory: Applications to Individual, Group, and Organizational Interventions* in 1997 (published by Erlbaum). She also directs the Heritage Project, a community-driven, multilevel intervention that is aimed at reversing the adverse effects of racial socialization in students of color.

Jessica M. Walters is currently a doctoral candidate in the Division of Counseling Psychology at the University of Illinois in Urbana-Champaign. Her research interests have focused on two primary areas: sexual harassment and coping with racial stress. Her work examines the effects of sexual harassment, coping styles, and the influence of organizational factors on sexual harassment. In addition, her work investigates race-related stress and its influence on quality of life indicators among Latinos.

Lori R. Wicker is a doctoral candidate in the Counseling/Clinical/School Psychology Program at the University of California, Santa Barbara. Her emphasis is in counseling psychology. Her areas of specialty include the psychological treatment of African Americans, the educational and career development of African Americans, and the delivery of culturally sensitive treatment.

Preface

When I started working on the first edition of *Counseling American Minorities* back in 1976, there was no way I could have known that I would be working on a sixth edition more than 25 years later. In those days my primary concern was finding a publisher who would publish the first edition. Although several books and monographs on counseling Black clients had appeared in the early 1970s (along with a scattering of professional journal articles in the late 1960s and early 1970s), no books had been published that focused on counseling clients from various ethnic groups. There simply was not a broad-based professional awareness of, or interest in, counseling ethnic minorities. In fact, the first two publishers I approached turned down *Counseling American Minorities,* citing concerns about the marketability of a book that focused on disenfranchised groups. After all, the argument went, ethnic minorities were a minority of the population. Furthermore, they were not availing themselves of mental health services; why would educators and practitioners buy a book that addressed the needs of an illusive clientele?

Living in California at the time, it was clear to me and my co-editors of the first edition that ethnic minorities were a rapidly growing segment of the state's population. Furthermore, Census Bureau projections suggested that what we were experiencing in California would be replicated in other states across the nation in the 1980s and 1990s. However, I do not think anyone at that time anticipated just how ethnically diverse the United States would become by the 2000 census, or how diverse it would be projected to become by 2050, based on those 2000 Census Bureau data.

It took more than a decade after the first edition of *Counseling American Minorities* was published for mental health professions to fully embrace the idea that ethnic minorities have special counseling needs, and that their under-utilization of mental health services might be more a function of how the services were offered than reluctance to use them on the part of ethnic minorities. By the 1990s, however, professional organizations had begun incorporating minority mental health services into their ethics codes and accreditation procedures. Multicultural counseling competence became the trendy focus of a growing number of training programs. At the time this sixth edition of *Counseling American Minorities* went to press, I counted 60 books on multicultural counseling in the University of California libraries or on my own bookshelves that had been published since 1980; many of these books were in their second or third edition. Some of these books examine specialty topics within multicultural counseling, such as teenage fathers, gifted youth, older women, career counseling, nutrition and health, and brief psychotherapy.

So why publish another edition of *Counseling American Minorities?* One reason is that a number of academics who train counselors and psychologists keep requesting it. For whatever reason (but I hope it has to do with quality and validity), this book has attracted a loyal following among those who train counselors and psychologists. A second reason is that the book continues to fill a special niche.

Many of the books currently in print that address counseling within a racially/ ethnically/culturally diverse framework do it from one of two perspectives. They either focus on multicultural counseling, in which case they attempt to cover all possible combinations of counselor and client differences, or they focus on one particular racial/ethnic group. Since the first edition, this book has consistently focused on counseling ethnic minorities, with particular attention given to four major ethnic populations, regardless of the counselor's ethnicity. I believe this approach best serves the needs of all counselors and counselors-in-training who want to prepare themselves to work with clients from the largest and most clearly identified ethnic minority groups in the United States. A need still exists for a well-documented book on counseling specific ethnic minority populations.

A major thesis of this edition, like earlier editions, is that culturally sensitive counselors can establish the necessary and sufficient conditions of a productive helping relationship with clients who come from cultural backgrounds different from their own. Although ethnic and cultural similarity between the counselor and client may be highly correlated with counseling success, other attributes (e.g., shared attitudes and values; awareness of one's values, attitudes, and biases; knowledge of the client's culture; use of appropriate counselor roles) also contribute to a productive counseling relationship and may help overcome barriers that can result from ethnic or cultural differences.

The purposes of this edition remain the same as those of the earlier editions. First, the book is intended to sensitize counselors to the life experiences and within-group differences of four ethnic minority groups. It is also my hope and expectation that increased sensitivity to these four populations will generalize to other racial/ethnic minority groups. A second major purpose is to examine how counseling has failed in the past and, despite increased attention to multicultural concerns, continues to shortchange the mental health needs of ethnic minority groups. A third purpose is to suggest new directions for counseling and mental health professionals when they serve ethnic minority clients.

Although this edition of *Counseling American Minorities* continues the tradition of focusing on counseling ethnic minorities, every chapter in the book has been substantially revised. The three introductory chapters, while maintaining many of the same topics from the earlier edition, have been completely updated with new information. Similarly, the last chapter has been completely revised to reflect the latest theory and research on counseling ethnic minorities. However, I am most excited about the changes made to chapters 4 through 15, those chapters that provide information about specific ethnic minority groups. In past editions, reprinted journal articles have been used for these chapters. In this edition, chapters 4 through 15 are all commissioned chapters, written specifically for this book. Furthermore, the chapter authors were selected for their expertise in one of three areas: (a) historical, social, and cultural foundations; (b) physical and mental health concerns; and (c) treatment issues. One chapter in each section addresses each of these areas. This format ensures that the most important topics are covered for each ethnic group and provides a degree of continuity across all four groups that is not found in most books on multicultural counseling (including earlier editions of this book). I hope and trust that readers familiar with the literature on counseling ethnic minorities will find that both the format and content reflect a contemporary view of the field.

Acknowledgments

In addition to the chapter authors, there are a number of people who have contributed to this edition of *Counseling American Minorities* in one way or another. First of all, I want to thank Drs. George Morten and Derald Sue for their assistance with earlier editions of this book. Without their support, the first edition, in particular, might have remained an unrealized dream. I am also grateful for the feedback provided by the following professors, who scrutinized the fifth edition and suggested many of the changes that have guided this revision: John Dillard, University of Louisville; Tarrell Portman, University of Iowa; and Michael Richard, University of South Florida. Finally, I would like to thank the people at McGraw-Hill who contributed to the current edition through their careful editing and thoughtful suggestions.

Part I RACIAL/ETHNIC MINORITIES AND CROSS-CULTURAL COUNSELING

CHAPTER 1 # Defining Populations and Terms

The population of the United States is highly diverse, perhaps more so than at any time in our nation's history. For this reason it is essential that mental health practitioners become sensitive to the needs, values, and beliefs of the many groups who currently reside in the United States. The purpose of this book is to help practitioners achieve this sensitivity. This initial section of the chapter documents the diversification of America. Subsequent sections provide a common language that can be used in discussions of ethnic minority populations and the counseling services provided to them.

Earlier writers referred to the "greening" (Reich, 1970) and the "graying" (Sheppard, 1977) of America to describe the impact of younger and older populations on social and economic institutions in the United States. More recently, Richard Rodriguez (2002) has identified the "browning" of America as yet another change in demographics that has momentous social and economic implications for the country. The browning, or ethnic diversification, of the United States is a function of two major forces: (a) increasing numbers of immigrants from Latin American and Asian countries; and (b) differential birthrates among racial and ethnic groups. Furthermore, data from the 2000 census indicate that the rate of diversification has accelerated in recent years.

Although the largest number of immigrants (8.8 million) entered the United States in the decade between 1901 and 1910, the steadily increasing influx of immigrants since 1970 has resulted in more foreign-born residents in the year 2000 (28.4 million) than at any time in our nation's history (Schmidley, 2001). In that same year, the number of foreign-born and first-generation residents reached the highest number ever, 56 million. Foreign-born and first-generation residents now make up one-fifth of the entire U.S. population, a proportion that is likely to increase as recent immigrants start families and have children of their own.

Prior to 1970, most of the immigrants to the United States came from European countries (e.g., Germany, Italy, Ireland, Great Britain). Although many of these immigrants had to adapt to a new language and new culture, they were, for the most part, assimilated into the mainstream culture within one or two generations. In contrast, the current foreign-born population comes primarily from Latin

America (51%) and Asia (25%). In fact, 9 of the 10 leading countries of foreign birth are located in Latin America or Asia. Mexico alone accounts for more than 25% of the foreign-born population, the largest recorded share of any country since 1890, when Germany accounted for 30% of the foreign-born population. For a number of different reasons to be discussed in chapter 2, assimilation of the new wave of immigrants is progressing at a slower rate than it did for earlier immigrants from Europe.

In addition to a growing number of immigrants from Latin America and Asia, the higher fertility rates for domestic minority and foreign-born women are contributing to the diversification of the U.S. population. Defining fertility rate as "the number of women who reported having a child in the 12-month period ending in June 2000 per 1,000 women [of child bearing age]" (Bachu & O'Connell, 2001, p. 1), the Census Bureau reported fertility rates of 54.6 for Asian and Pacific Islander women, 60 for White non-Hispanic women, 63.2 for Black women, and 80 for U.S.-born Hispanic women. The fertility rate for foreign-born Hispanic women was even higher, at 112 per 1,000 women. In general, foreign-born families have a larger average number of children than "native"-born families (1.25 versus 0.94). Thus, the proportion of children born to foreign-born mothers has been increasing in recent years. In 1980, foreign-born women accounted for 1 in 20 births in the United States: in 2000 they accounted for 1 in 5 births (Schmidley, 2001).

The diversification of the U.S. population is expected to continue well into the twenty-first century. According to the Census Bureau (Grieco & Cassidy, 2001), non-Hispanic Whites made up 69.1% of the total U.S. population in 2000, followed by Hispanics at 12.5%, Blacks at 12.3%, Asian and Pacific Islanders at 3.7%, and American Indians at 0.9%. The Census Bureau predicts that, barring unusual changes in birth and immigration rates, by the year 2025 non-Hispanic Whites will decrease to 62.0% of the population, whereas Hispanics will increase to 18.2%, followed by Blacks at 13.9%, Asian Americans at 6.5%, and American Indians at 1.0% (National Population Projections, 2002). By the year 2050, the Census Bureau projects, non-Hispanic Whites will barely constitute a majority of the population at 52.8%, whereas Hispanics will make up 24.3% of the population, followed by Blacks (14.7%), Asian and Pacific Islanders (9.3%), and American Indians (1.1%). Although official projections provided by the Census Bureau suggest that racial and ethnic minorities will constitute a numerical majority some time after the year 2050, it is important to note that this agency is notorious for undercounting and underprojecting persons of color.

In some states, ethnic diversification is occurring even more rapidly than it is for the nation as a whole. In California, for example, the foreign-born population grew from 1.3 million in 1960 to 8.8 million in March 2000, at which time foreign-born residents made up about one-fourth of the state's population (Schmidley, 2001). The Census Bureau projects that by the year 2025, ethnic minorities will make up about two-thirds of California's resident population (Hispanics, 42%; Asian Pacific Islanders, 18%; Blacks, 7%; Native Americans, more than 1% State Population Projections, 2002).

This diversification trend will have a significant impact on a number of U.S. institutions. For example, ethnic minorities already outnumber European Americans in many school systems around the country, and the percentage of students who are minorities will continue to increase for the foreseeable future. Ethnic minorities will make up a growing percentage of the labor force and, of necessity, will fill more and more jobs from which they have been excluded in the past. As the numbers of ethnic minorities in the workforce increase, their purchasing power will grow significantly and in turn will influence what goods the nation produces and how these goods are marketed. The media and politics in California, New York, Florida, Texas, and many other states are already being heavily influenced by ethnic minority constituencies, a trend that is likely to become more widespread in the future. In fact, it is hard to imagine any aspect of life in the United States that will not be affected at some level by the growing ethnic diversification.

The diversification of the population has important implications as well for counselors, psychologists, and other mental health service providers. These professionals need to increase their cultural sensitivity, knowledge of cultures, and culturally relevant counseling skills in order to meet the needs of a diverse client population. Mental health services need to be structured to ensure that racial and ethnic populations will use and benefit from them. And professional organizations need to press for policies and legislation at the local, state, and national levels that will address discrimination against culturally diverse groups. This book is intended to help train counselors and mental health service providers who can meet these needs. The basic terminology that social scientists use when discussing population diversity is discussed next.

DEFINING TERMS: RACE, ETHNICITY, AND CULTURE

It is particularly important for mental health practitioners to become familiar with terminology relevant to cross-cultural counseling because some clients might interpret the misuse of particular terms as evidence of cultural insensitivity. Practitioners must also recognize that not all terms are universally accepted across or within ethnic minority populations.

Any discussion of the diversity terminology invariably begins with race, ethnicity, and culture. Not only are these terms essential to an understanding of the diverse U.S. population, but they are also three of the most misunderstood and misused words in the English language. Although they are interrelated and are often used interchangeably, they represent unique constructs with varying degrees of validity and utility.

Race: A Valid Construct?

According to the *Oxford Dictionary of Words,* the term *race* first appeared in the English language more than 300 years ago. From its inception, *race* has been one of the most misappropriated terms in the American vernacular (Rose, 1964). There are two general ways of defining race. The first definition is based solely on physical or biological characteristics, whereas the second one is based on social characteristics. The biological definition is presented first because historically it has been more widely used and is more controversial than the social definition.

The Biological Definition of Race   "To the biologist, a race, or subspecies, is an inbreeding, geographically isolated population that differs in distinguishable physical traits from other members of the species" (Zuckerman, 1990, p. 1297). Basic to a biological definition of race is the view that humans can be divided into a set number of genetically determined groups that possess similar physical characteristics. The most commonly accepted categorization divides all humans into three races: Caucasoid, Mongoloid, and Negroid. Physical differences, or *phenotypes,* involving skin pigmentation, facial features, and the color, distribution, and texture of body hair are among the most frequently applied criteria assumed to distinguish these three races. Despite the lack of empirical justification for racial categorization, some social scientists have adopted this biological definition of race; psychologists in particular have been quick to accept a biological view of race.

Criticisms of the Biological Definition of Race   There is little doubt that groups of people do share common physical features and that, given inbreeding, these features can be passed on to subsequent generations. Nevertheless, most anthropologists had rejected the concept of race by the early 1960s, pointing out that all humans belong to a single genus and species, *Homo sapiens.* Furthermore, widely accepted anthropological theory points to the important role that migration, as well as genetics, has played in creating regional differences in human physical characteristics. According to Fish (2002a), anatomically modern humans evolved in Africa about 200,000 years ago; the early evolutionary process resulted in great diversity within this African population. About 100,000 years ago, small groups of humans unrepresentative of that diversity began migrating across the Middle Eastern land bridge and spreading throughout Europe and Asia. More recently (approximately 15,000 years ago), groups from Asia traversed the Bering Strait land bridge and migrated into North and South America. Members of these migrating groups often shared similar physical characteristics that came to be predominant in various regions of the world. Thus, as Fish points out, "we have geographical regions of human variability" (2002a, p. 3) that some social scientists have chosen to label as racial differences. For example, Rushton (1995) defined race as "a geographic variety or subdivision of a species characterized by a more or less distinct combination of traits (morphological, behavioral, physiological) that are heritable" (p. 40).

However, while groups of people sharing similar physical features migrated to separate regions of the world, they carried with them genetic variability that defied the construct of race based on unique genetic ancestry and unique human characteristics. Also, even while groups of people sharing similar physical features were migrating to separate regions, they were procreating with members of other groups in bordering regions who possessed different physical characteristics. This process of genetic intermingling, which created a continuum of physical characteristics, accelerated during the days of colonization and increased exponentially during the twentieth century. As Schaefer (1988) points out, "given frequent migration, exploration, and invasions, pure gene frequencies have not existed for some time, if they ever did" (p. 12). For a thorough and informative analysis of the effects of evolutionary forces on genetic diversity in the human population, refer to Templeton (2002).

There are other problems with the concept of race. For example, there is no biological explanation for why some physical features, such as skin color, have been selected to determine race whereas others, such as eye color, have not. As Zuckerman (1990) suggests, "many of the features are not correlated and none by themselves could furnish an indisputable guide to the anthropologists' definitions of racial groups" (p. 1298). The reality is that a look beneath the superficial characteristics used to categorize racial types reveals more similarities than differences among groups and more differences within racial groups than among them (Littlefield, Lieberman, & Reynolds, 1982). Furthermore, the fact that scientists cannot agree how many races there are—estimates range from 3 to 200 (Schaefer, 1988)—suggests that there is little agreement about which criteria should define race. As a result of these and other concerns, a number of social scientists have urged their colleagues either to redefine the term *race* or to refrain from using the term altogether in their research and writing (Allen & Adams, 1992; Tate & Audette, 2001; Yee, Fairchild, Weizmann, & Wyatt, 1993).

Genetic intermingling is clearly evident in the United States, where the number of "biracial" babies is increasing faster than "monoracial" ones, and this disparity will rapidly increase even if "interracial" marriage rates remain constant (Alonzo & Waters, 1993). This demographic reality moved the Bureau of the Census to provide a "multiracial" option for the first time in the 2000 census. Furthermore, the bureau's classification of "Hispanic" is really "multiracial." The vast majority of Latinos in the United States are indigenous (Indian), mestizo (Indian and Spanish), or mulatto (African and Spanish). People of Mexican origin are indigenous or mestizo, and many also have an African ancestry stemming from the colonial period. When Puerto Ricans, Cubans, Dominicans, and others from the Caribbean are added, the mixture of African, Spanish, and Indian ancestry becomes even more evident (Root, 1992, 1996).

The paradoxical nature of racial categorization is particularly evident with respect to African Americans. The reality is that many African Americans have one or more European American ancestors in their family tree (going back to the days when White slave masters raped Black female slaves with impunity). However, an individual is commonly identified as Black if he or she has *any* African American ancestry. Similarly, for some purposes, an individual is judged to be an American Indian if he or she has at least one grandparent who is American Indian. This method of classifying race in the United States according to ancestry is referred to as *hypodescent*. Hypodescent specifies that racial categories can be arranged in a hierarchy from desirable to undesirable and that children are always assigned the same race as that of the parent of the less desirable race. "One curious result of [hypodescent] is that a white woman can give birth to a black child, but a black woman cannot give birth to a white child" (Fish, 2002b, p. 118).

The Social Definition of Race   Although there is no biological basis for the term *race,* the concept of race has taken on important social meaning in terms of how outsiders view members of a "racial" group and how individuals within a "racial" group view themselves, members of their group, and members of other "racial" groups. These views have resulted in the second, socially based, definition of race. Cox (1948) was among the first to define *race* from a social perspective as "any people who are distinguished or consider themselves distinguished, in social relations with other peoples, by their physical characteristics" (p. 402).

Thus, the term *race* survives despite the lack of a scientific basis because it continues to serve one purpose or another for those who use it. People who subscribe to the superiority of their own race are invested in the term for obvious reasons: It provides a convenient way of maintaining and perpetuating that superiority. For others it provides a convenient way of categorizing people, a way of organizing the world and reducing complexity. For still others, it provides a vehicle for self- and group identity and empowerment, and it is often evoked in reaction to racial discrimination by others. (The concept of racial self-identification is discussed in greater detail in chapter 2.) Helms and her colleagues (Helms, 1996; Helms & Richardson, 1997; Helms & Talleyrand, 1997) have argued that race (or sociorace) remains a useful concept for mental health practitioners precisely because "people are treated or studied as though they belong to biologically defined racial groups on the basis of [racial] characteristics" (Helms & Talleyrand, 1997, p. 1247). Furthermore, the Bureau of the Census continues to use race as a method of categorizing people. The Census Bureau and other federal agencies follow the guidelines put forth by the Office of Management and Budget (OMB) regarding the collection of race and ethnic group information.

> The OMB defines Hispanic or Latino as "a person of Cuban, Mexican, Puerto Rican, South or Central American, or other Spanish culture or origin regardless of race." In data collection and presentation, federal agencies are required to use a minimum of two ethnicities: "Hispanic or Latino" and "Not Hispanic or Latino." Starting with Census 2000, the OMB requires federal agencies to use a minimum of five race categories: White; Black or African American; American Indian and Alaska Native; Asian; and Native Hawaiian and Other Pacific Islander. (Grieco & Cassidy, 2001, pp. 1–2)

In reality, the OMB guidelines provided for a sixth category, Some Other Race. Furthermore, the 2000 census provided 7 Asian and 4 Native Hawaiian and Other Pacific Islander response categories, creating a total of 15 racial response categories. Also for the first time, the 2000 census allowed respondents to select one or more race categories. Given the 6 racial categories, respondents had a total of 57 possible combinations of two, three, four, five, or six races they could designate. Interestingly, only 2.4% of all respondents elected to check two or more racial categories, and almost all (93%) of the 6.8 million respondents who reported multiple racial ancestry indicated exactly two races.

As will become evident later in this chapter, the OMB and Census Bureau policies are inconsistent with emerging practice in the social science literature. As indicated earlier in this chapter, most social scientists are in favor of discarding the term *race* because it has no biological justification (Tate & Audett, 2001). By employing racial categories to collect their data, federal agencies (as well as various other entities, including well-intentioned multicultural researchers) perpetuate a questionable construct. Also, ethnic groups within the Asian (e.g., Chinese, Korean) and Native Hawaiian or Other Pacific Islander (e.g., Native Hawaiian, Samoan) racial categories are treated as racial subcategories, whereas Hispanic and not-Hispanic are treated as the only two ethnic categories. As will be seen in the discussion of ethnicity in the next section, most social psychologists now recognize general ethnic categorization based on continent of ancestry and specific ethnic categorization based on country of ancestry.

Ethnicity and Culture

A review of the literature on ethnicity reveals that this term has three different interpretations (Feagin, 1989). In the broadest sense, *ethnicity* is determined by shared physical *and* cultural characteristics. Thus, Bernal (1990) defines an ethnic group as "a group of individuals who interact, maintain themselves, have some social structure and system of governing norms and values, are biological and cultural descendants of a cultural group, and identify as members of the group" (p. 261). Similarly, according to Nagel (1995) "ethnicity refers to differences of language, religion, color, ancestry, and/or culture to which social meanings are attributed and around which identity and group formation occurs" (p. 443). Because this broad definition includes physical characteristics, *ethnicity* is often used interchangeably with *race.*

The narrowest definition of ethnicity restricts it exclusively to cultural differences. Thus, Barresi (1990) defined ethnicity as referring to "a large group whose members internalize and share a heritage of, and a commitment to, unique social characteristics, cultural symbols, and behavior patterns that are not fully understood by outsiders" (p. 249). An intermediate definition of ethnicity is taken from the Greek root word *ethnos,* originally meaning "nation" (Feagin, 1989). Thus, Schaefer (1988) identified ethnic groups as "groups set apart from others because of their national origin or distinctive cultural patterns" (p. 9). For the purposes of this book, the term *ethnicity* is used to describe differences in national origin (which may or may not involve shared physical features) and cultural factors.

How Is Culture Defined?   For many decades, the study of *culture* was the exclusive domain of cultural anthropologists. More recently, philosophers, psychologists, sociologists, historians, economists, political scientists, linguists, and other academics have begun to focus on this topic. Indeed, not only is the term *culture* used with increasing frequency by social scientists, it is frequently used in the everyday language of the general public as well. *Culture* is now commonly used in reference to the functioning of a specific system or group of people within the larger society that seems far removed from its anthropological roots; two examples are the "culture of psychiatry" or "locker-room culture" (Fernando, 2002).

Although it is a commonly used term, *culture* takes on different meanings in a variety of contexts, prompting Eagleton (2000) to declare that culture is "one of the two or three most complex words in the English language" (p. 1). For many people, including some academics, culture is defined within their own personal and social context. From this perspective culture is, as an Andy Capp cartoon some years ago suggested, something that "my crowd has and yours doesn't have." Culture from this perspective is typically associated with modernity, materialism, and classical music, literature, and paintings (Kuper, 1999).

Most scholars take a broader view of culture, one that accepts the existence of many different forms of culture and that avoids placing these various forms in a hierarchy. Although this more comprehensive view of culture is widely accepted in academic circles, defining specifically what is meant by the term has proved to be a difficult task. Anthropologists, who have struggled with the task longer than any other discipline, have come up with a number of definitions. Two leading anthropologists of the twentieth century, Alfred Kroeber at the University of California, Berkeley and Clyde Kluckhohn at Harvard, attempted to synthesize these numerous attempts into one (somewhat lengthy) definition:

> Culture consists of patterns, explicit and implicit, of and for behavior acquired and transmitted by symbols, constituting the distinctive achievement of human groups, including their embodiments in artifacts; the essential core of culture consists of traditional (i.e., historically derived and selected) ideas and especially their attached values; culture systems may, on the other hand, be considered as products of action, on the other as conditioning elements of further action. (Kroeber & Kluckhohn, 1952, p. 181)

Perhaps the most succinct definition was offered recently by Lefley (2002), who defined culture as "a set of shared beliefs, values, behavioral norms, and practices that characterize a particular group of people who share a common identity and the symbolic meanings of a common language" (p. 4). A safe conclusion that draws on both these definitions is that culture consists of values and behaviors that are learned and transmitted within an identifiable community. It also includes the symbols, artifacts, and products of that community. It is this latter component—the symbols, artifacts, and products—that most people think of when they are asked to describe a culture. Thus, people commonly associate specific food, language, music, art, and rituals with particular cultures. However, it is important to keep in mind that values as well as behaviors are an integral part of culture. It is also important to keep in mind that from a psychological perspective, culture and self are interdependent, that context and person interact to create culture (Segall, Lonner, & Berry, 1998).

Race, Ethnicity, and Culture: Some Conclusions   What conclusions can be made from this examination of the various definitions of race, ethnicity, and culture? First, culture is not the purview of an elite group. Because every society shares and transmits values and behaviors to its members, all social groups have a culture. Second, *race* and *ethnicity* are not interchangeable terms. Rather, *race* refers to (assumed) biological differences, whereas *ethnicity* refers to regional and cultural differences. Third, there is no empirical, biological justification for the concept of race. Fourth, *ethnicity* seems to be a much more useful term because it is descriptive (with regard to nationality or culture) but avoids the problems associated with defining race. *Ethnicity* is clearly preferable to *race* in references to groups of people who are distinguished by their regional ancestry or unique culture. Fifth, the only justification for continuing to use the term *race* in the future is that so much social significance has been attached to its use in the past. As Fenton (1999) suggests:

> The term "ethnic". . . . is not hampered by a history of connotations with discredited science and malevolent practice the way "race" is. [However,] a discourse in which the idea of "race" is present remains a powerful feature of common-sense thinking and of the ordering of social relations. It is this second fact that prevents us from simply abandoning a terminology which includes "race". . . . In the USA in particular we have to accept that we are dealing with a social order which has incorporated, in a pervasive and persistent way, the idea of "racial difference" and that this in many ways matches real divisions and inequalities in the American social structure. (p. 4)

Taking this line of thinking a step further, S. D. Johnson (1990) has pointed out that the only real justification for continuing to use the term *race* is to document the effects of racism and the progress in eradicating it. Rodriguez (2002) expresses it simply but eloquently: "I write about race in America in hopes of undermining the notion of race in America" (p. xi).

It is also important to recognize that individuals of the same regional ancestry may or may not share the same cultural values and behaviors. As Sue and Zane (1987) pointed out, mental health practitioners must "avoid confounding the cultural values of the client's *ethnic group* with those of the *client*" (p. 41). Similarly, Phinney (1996) noted that although psychologists have treated ethnicity as a categorical variable, ethnicity may or may not identify one's culture, identity, and minority status. She points out that "ethnic cultures, rather than unified structures to which one belongs, can be thought of as clusters of dimensions along which individuals or samples vary" (p. 922). The topic of variability within ethnic groups will be touched on in the next section and discussed in greater detail in chapter 2.

Culturally Deprived and Culturally Disadvantaged   Before leaving this discussion of culture, it is important to dismiss two terms, *culturally deprived* and *culturally disadvantaged,* that have been widely used in the past in conjunction with racial and ethnic groups. The term *culturally deprived* implies the absence of culture, a mythical condition that has no relationship to the ethnic groups addressed in this book (or, indeed, to any ethnic group). Notwithstanding the effects of the larger society's culture on racial and ethnic groups through the mass media, the groups discussed in this book clearly possess and transmit their own distinct cultures.

The term *culturally disadvantaged* suggests that the person to whom it is applied is at a disadvantage because she or he lacks the cultural background promoted by the controlling social structure. The use of "disadvantaged" rather than "deprived" is intended to recognize that the individual possesses a cultural heritage, but it also suggests that the culture is not the *right* culture. Although slightly less noxious than *culturally deprived, culturally disadvantaged* still implies a cultural deficiency, whereas the real problem is that the majority culture is viewed as more important than minority ethnic cultures. It is true that a person may be economically disadvantaged because he or she has less money than the average person or is educationally disadvantaged due to inferior formal education. Nevertheless, it is not scientifically valid to suggest that some ethnic groups lack the "right" culture.

Even the more accepted terms *culturally different* and *culturally distinct* can carry negative connotations when they are used to imply that a person's culture is at variance (out-of-step) with the dominant (accepted) culture. The inappropriate application of these two terms occurs in counseling when their usage is restricted to ethnically diverse clients. Taken literally, it is grammatically and conceptually correct to refer to a majority client as culturally different or culturally distinct from the counselor if the counselor is a minority individual.

FURTHER DEFINITIONS RELATING TO CULTURE AND DIVERSITY

The literature on diversity contains a number of terms—in addition to *race, ethnicity,* and *culture*—with which mental health practitioners should become familiar. These terms provide practitioners with insights into the behaviors and values of members of ethnic minority groups who may become clients. They also help clarify the larger social and political processes that affect the status and behaviors of minority ethnic groups within U.S. society. In addition, as has already been noted, some of these terms carry pejorative connotations, and practitioners who inadvertently use them might give the impression of being culturally insensitive.

Melting Pot, Acculturation, Assimilation, and Cultural Pluralism

Throughout the early stages of its development, the United States projected an image of the cultural *melting pot,* a nation in which all nationalities, ethnicities, and races melted into one culture. Many Americans took pride in the melting pot image, and a play by British playwright Israel Zangwill titled *The Melting Pot* enjoyed widespread popularity in this country when it was first performed in 1908. According to the melting pot theory, a new and unique culture continually evolves as each new immigrant group modifies the existing culture (Krug, 1976).

Not everyone in the United States, however, subscribed to the melting pot theory and philosophy. In fact, there was a widespread sentiment that the nation possessed a "true" American culture that was being threatened by the massive influx of "foreign" peoples. As one example, in 1926 Henry Pratt Fairchild, a noted American sociologist, wrote that the melting pot philosophy and unrestricted immigration were "slowly, insidiously, irresistibly eating away the very heart of the United States" (Fairchild, 1926, p. 261). According to Fairchild and others, the "heart of the United States" was an American culture that was based primarily on the values and mores of early immigrants from Northern and Western Europe, principally England, Ireland, Germany, and the Scandinavian countries. Opponents of the melting pot philosophy argued that instead of melting all cultures into one, an effort should be made to "Americanize" all immigrant groups; that is, to force them to relinquish their cultures and adopt the existing American culture. To accomplish this "Americanization," the government established quotas to restrict immigration from those countries whose cultures diverged most from the American culture. The Chinese Exclusion Act of 1882 was the first of a number of federal and state laws that were passed to ensure that certain immigrant groups would have minimal impact on the emerging American culture. Public education, with its universal use of the English language, was viewed as the primary institution for perpetuating the existing American culture (Epps, 1974).

Before this text moves on to a discussion of cultural pluralism, which is an alternative to the melting pot and assimilation philosophies, it is helpful to distinguish between *acculturation* and *assimilation.* Gordon (1964) has defined *acculturation* as one of seven different types of assimilation. Acculturation refers to *cultural assimilation,* or the acquisition of the cultural patterns (e.g., values, norms, language, behavior) of the core or dominant society (the theoretical underpinnings of acculturation will be discussed in greater detail in chapter 2). Assimilation, in contrast, is a broader concept that implies more than the adoption of the dominant culture. It further requires that *structural assimilation* be achieved, or as suggested by McLemore (1983), that "members of the two groups interact with one another as friends and equals and that they select marriage partners without regard to ethnic or racial identities" (p. 35). Even though some immigrants (and their descendants) may desire to become acculturated and may make every effort to adopt the culture of the dominant society, total assimilation may be beyond their grasp because it requires that they be accepted by members of that society. Thus, for some members of ethnic minority groups, assimilation may be a desired but unachievable goal.

For other groups, assimilation may not be a desired goal. Many members of ethnic groups find the cultural assimilation philosophy objectionable because it requires them to relinquish their traditional cultural values and behaviors in favor of those of the dominant culture. With the civil rights movement of the 1960s and 1970s came a growing interest in *cultural pluralism.* According to the theory of cultural pluralism, individual ethnic groups maintain their own cultural uniqueness while sharing common elements of American culture (Kallen, 1956). Cultural pluralism is often likened to a cultural stew in that the various ingredients are mixed together, but rather than melting into a single mass, they remain intact and distinguishable while contributing to a whole that is richer than the parts alone. Cultural pluralism enjoyed some popularity and acceptance during the 1970s, as evidenced by the passage of the Ethnic Heritage Studies Bill by Congress in 1973, which resulted in the establishment of bilingual, bicultural education programs in many metropolitan school districts. Some of the gains in bilingual, bicultural education made in the 1970s were lost in the 1980s and early 1990s as public sentiment and legislative policies swung toward cultural assimilation as a goal. By pure force of numbers, however, the current immigration trend presents a strong argument in favor of continuing or reinstituting bilingual, bicultural programs in the future.

Ethnocentrism, Racism, and White Privilege

Individuals who advocate the assimilation of ethnic minorities into American culture can be said to share a characteristic with individuals who seek to exclude these groups from American society altogether; both are ethnocentric. Sumner (1960) defined *ethnocentrism* as the "view of things in which one's own group is the center of everything, and all others are scaled and rated with reference to it" (pp. 27–28). Individuals who expect racial and ethnic groups to assimilate are in essence saying that the existing U.S. culture is superior to any culture or mix of cultures that could result from the melting pot or cultural pluralism philosophies.

Ethnocentrism is closely related to racism. *Racism* refers to beliefs and practices that accept race as a biological condition and maintain that racial groups other than one's own are intellectually, psychologically, or physically inferior. In a strictly literal sense, racism applies only to racial differences; in common usage, however, the concept has been applied to cultural differences as well.

Jones (1972) identified three types of racism: individual, institutional, and cultural. *Individual racism* involves the personal attitudes, beliefs, and behaviors designed to convince oneself of the superiority of one's race or ethnicity over other races or ethnicities. The widely held (but seldom acknowledged) view among European Americans that African Americans are intellectually inferior is an example of individual racism. *Institutional racism* involves the social policies, laws, and regulations that maintain the economic and social advantage of the racial or ethnic group in power. The use of culturally biased college admission tests is an example of institutional racism. Finally, *cultural racism* involves social beliefs and customs that promote the assumption that the products of the dominant culture (e.g., language, dress, traditions) are superior to those of other cultures. The attitude that Western classical music is superior to Eastern, African, and South American music is an example of cultural racism.

When we think about racism, we generally think about acts of violence or blatant acts of discrimination by clearly racist individuals or White supremacist groups. Because laws have been passed making the more overt forms of discrimination illegal, many people think that racism is a thing of the past. However, acts of violence that are racially motivated still occur, and ethnic minorities still report experiences of discrimination in housing, employment, and education. Furthermore,

> Racism also involves the everyday, mundane, negative opinions, attitudes, and ideologies and the seemingly subtle acts and conditions of discrimination against minorities, namely, those social cognitions and social acts, processes, structures, or institutions that directly or indirectly contribute to the dominance of the white group and the subordinate position of minorities. (Van Dijk, 1993, p. 5)

These subtle acts and conditions of discrimination, which permeate contemporary society (Sydell & Nelson, 2000), are sometimes referred to as the *new racism* or *modern racism*.

> Unlike old style racism, which tends to posit crude notions of "racial" and cultural inferiority, the new racism asserts that differences between groups are simply natural, intractable and non-negotiable, and that for this reason groups are best kept apart. It is proving itself to be a potent means by which dominant groups can discriminate, and yet apparently save face by denying racism. (Henwood, 1994, p. 44)

The new racism is often expressed indirectly, because direct expression of racial bias would be frowned on in a modern, democratic society. An example of the new racism is when European American students assume that different academic standards have been applied to an African American student even though the other students have no direct knowledge of the African American student's academic ability. Another example is a counselor who selectively provides an Asian American student with career information in the sciences because "those are the careers that Asian Americans enter" without first assessing the student's skills and interests.

The effects of racism can also be obvious or subtle. The more obvious effects of racism are the physical and economic harm suffered by ethnic minorities. However, racism has other, less obvious impacts on society. One of the more insidious outcomes of racism is the subtle effect on the thinking of individuals against whom the racism is directed. Through indirect but effective socializing influences, minority group members are taught, and come to accept as "social fact," myriad myths and stereotypes regarding skin color, facial features, and other physical characteristics. These individuals may come to believe that they lack the same potentials and abilities as majority group members. This resulting sense of racial inferiority is sometimes referred to as *internalized racism*. As will be seen in chapter 2, internalized racism can have a profoundly negative effect on the individual's self-esteem and ethnic identification.

Also often overlooked are the effects of racism on the privileged group. As Tatum (1992) has pointed out, racism contributes to a climate in which European Americans feel discomfort or fear in racially mixed settings. Thus, racism restricts the options and experiences of the privileged group as well as those of the oppressed group.

Are mental health providers affected by racism? To answer this question, Tinsley-Jones (2001) conducted 1- to 3-hour interviews with eight licensed psychologists of color that addressed three questions: (a) How had race and ethnicity been manifested in their professional life? (b) How is psychology performing with respect to race and ethnicity? and (c) What changes with respect to race and ethnicity should be made in psychology? On the positive side, interviewees expressed appreciation that the majority of European American psychologists were willing to explore issues of race, ethnicity, and culture, and they viewed the attention to cultural ideas as a healthy trend in the profession. However, they reported some experiences that suggest that modern racism is alive and well in professional psychology. For example, they indicated that they are often viewed as representatives of their race or ethnicity rather than as individuals. Also, they reported sometimes experiencing pressure to constrain signs of their ethnicity or, conversely by virtue of their ethnicity, to confer nonracist stamps of approval on their European American colleagues. The psychologists of color also lamented the lack of attention and progress regarding race and ethnicity issues within the profession in general as well as the lack of adequate conceptual models for providing services to ethnic minority clients. Based on her findings, Tinsley-Jones concluded that "racism is in psychology's midst" (p. 578). She also recommended that "all subtle acts of racism must be challenged, and, of crucial importance, must be challenged by majority culture psychologists" (p. 578).

Many European Americans acknowledge that racism has been a part of this country's history and that racism is still overtly practiced by White supremacist groups, but they reject the idea that they as individuals or the United States as a country could be contributing to the oppression of ethnic minorities. Similarly, most workers in the mental health field find it objectionable to think that we might be contributing directly or indirectly to discrimination against any ethnic population. As suggested earlier in this chapter, however, racism takes many forms. One of the most subtle forms of racism is White privilege. This book focuses on how mental health practitioners can help ethnic minority clients deal with the direct effects of racism; the discussion would be incomplete if it failed to address the indirect effects of racism on European Americans in the form of White privilege.

White privilege refers to the many subtle but pervasive ways in which European Americans experience advantages and entitlements, often without being aware of it, that are not available to ethnic minorities. Peggy McIntosh was one of the first authors to write about the topic. According to McIntosh (1988), "Whites are taught to think of their lives as morally neutral, normative, and average, and also ideal, so that when we work to benefit others, this is seen as work that will allow 'them' to be more like 'us' " (p. 4). In trying to understand why men had such a difficult time accepting the concept of male privilege, McIntosh initiated a self-awareness task of identifying White privilege that she had taken for granted. She generated a list of 46 White entitlements that are not available to her African American coworkers and acquaintances. Ten of these entitlements are listed below to provide examples of White privilege; for a more in-depth discussion, see McIntosh (1988).

1. When I am told about our national heritage or about "civilization," I am shown that people of my color made it what it is.
2. I can turn on the television or open to the front page of the paper and see people of my race widely and positively represented.
3. I can be fairly sure of having my voice heard in a group in which I am the only member of my race.
4. I can go into a book shop and count on finding the writing of my race represented, into a supermarket and find the staple foods that fit my cultural traditions, into a hairdresser's shop and find someone who can deal with my hair.
5. Whether I use checks, credit cards, or cash, I can count on my skin color not to work against the appearance that I am financially reliable.
6. I did not have to educate our children to be aware of systemic racism for their own daily physical protection.
7. I can do well in a challenging situation without being called a credit to my race.

8. I am never asked to speak for all the people of my racial group.
9. If a traffic cop pulls me over or if the IRS audits my tax return, I can be sure I haven't been singled out because of my race.
10. I can be late to a meeting without having the lateness reflect on my race. (McIntosh, 1988, pp. 5–9)

Some of these White privileges are less evident now than when McIntosh wrote her landmark paper, but many are still as pervasive as they were then. For example, many European Americans still choose not to be ethnically or racially categorized, claiming that they are American and that ethnic identification is not important to them. However, being able to make such a claim is further evidence of White privilege because ethnic minorities are not able to deny their ethnic distinctiveness, even if they so desire.

Because all of us feel that we have to work hard to get whatever good things come to us in life and because none of us *feels* privileged, it is difficult for many of us to accept the fact that we are privileged in any way. As the previous list indicates, White privilege involves benefits that millions of Americans take for granted, entitlements that in the ideal world would be available to every person regardless of ethnicity or skin color. Furthermore, not all European Americans benefit equally from White privilege. For example, European American women, sexual minorities, people with disabilities, and poor people do not experience the same entitlements as do nondisabled, heterosexual, wealthy European American men. For all these reasons, it is easy for European Americans to question the concept of White privilege. Yet clearly there are some advantages to which European Americans are entitled solely by virtue of being part of the dominant ethnic group in the United States. Some of these advantages are the result of racial profiling and others are the result of targeted commercialism, but all represent a form of discrimination against ethnic minorities who do not enjoy the same entitlements. Furthermore, to deny White privilege is to deny that ethnic minorities are discriminated against, and denial of discrimination against ethnic minorities is a major component of a racist agenda.

A. G. Johnson (2001) suggests that the first step in reducing or eliminating discrimination against minorities is for European Americans to acknowledge the reality of White privilege. However, most European Americans are reluctant to make this concession because they assume that to do so means accepting personal responsibility for discrimination against minorities. Johnson argues that White privilege exists because "patterns of oppression and privilege are rooted in systems that we all participate in and make happen" (p. 90) and that "we don't have to be ruthless people in order to support or follow paths of least resistance that lead to behavior with ruthless consequences" (p. 92). The key to change is accepting the reality of White privilege and then working to change the system that maintains it.

Mental health service providers can help change the system that oppresses ethnic and other minority groups. However, to bring about systemic change, service providers will need to step outside their conventional roles as counselors and psychotherapists. The roles of change agent and social advocate—helper roles designed to bring about change in oppressive systems—will be discussed in chapter 16 as alternatives to the conventional counseling and psychotherapy roles.

Multicultural Sensitivity and Political Correctness

Acknowledging White privilege can be a starting point for European Americans to engage in the kind of personal exploration of cultural values and biases that all mental health practitioners, regardless of ethnicity, need to undergo to become multiculturally sensitive. In fact, *multicultural sensitivity* can be defined as an awareness of one's attitudes, values, and biases around racial, ethnic, and cultural issues and how they have been shaped by one's own cultural experiences. Multicultural sensitivity also means being sensitive and responsive to how ethnicity and culture have affected clients' attitudes and behaviors. Multicultural sensitivity will be examined in greater detail when multicultural competence is discussed in chapter 16.

Mental health providers are sometimes accused of being overly sensitive to multicultural issues and of engaging in political correctness to show their openness to, and concern for, people who are "different." *Political correctness* was first used in the 1930s by left-wing groups as a form of self-criticism; more recently, however, conservatives have adopted the phrase as a means of discrediting any liberal agenda (Favreau, 1997). *Politically correct* is defined by *Webster's New World College Dictionary* as "conforming to what is regarded as orthodox liberal opinion on matters of sexuality, race, etc., usually used disparagingly to connote dogmatism, excessive sensitivity to minor causes" (Neufeldt, 1996, p. 1045). Unfortunately, as suggested by Stark (1997), " 'Political Correctness' has become a pejorative label—even when used to describe acts of courtesy, respect, fairness, openness, sensitivity to diversity, and responsibility for the consequences of one's behavior" (p. 232). It also serves to trivialize important social issues. By dismissing social initiatives as orthodox liberal dogma, opponents of multicultural education programs, laws against sexual harassment, antidiscrimination measures, and other social programs have been able to subject advocates of these initiatives to ridicule without ever discussing the merits of the social issues involved.

Attempts to arrive at unobjectionable, descriptive terms to apply to ethnic populations are often derided by individuals who are somehow threatened by these efforts as exercises in political correctness. However, because pejorative labels can contribute to negative stereotypes of a group as well as to self-hatred among members of the group, mental health service providers should make every effort to use acceptable descriptors when referring to ethnic populations.

Terms Associated With Specific Ethnic Groups

Social scientists continue to look for appropriate terms to refer collectively to oppressed groups and to ethnic groups in the U.S. population. Authors in the counseling literature have used a number of terms, but unfortunately each term has one or more drawbacks.

Some authors have used the term *minority* to refer to physically or behaviorally identifiable groups that make up less than 50% of the U.S. population. Included in this definition are racial and ethnic minorities, the aged, and people with disabilities. In common usage, however, numerical size alone does not determine minority status. Thus, women as a group are often referred to as a minority. Wirth (1945) has offered a definition of *minority* based on the concept of oppression that is employed in this book. According to Wirth (1945), a minority is

> a group of people who, because of physical or cultural characteristics, are sin-
> gled out from the others in society in which they live for differential and unequal
> treatment, and who therefore regard themselves as objects of collective discrim-
> ination. (p. 347)

This definition allows for a categorization of ethnic groups, plus other groups that are oppressed by society *primarily because of their group membership,* as mi-norities. Examples of nonethnic groups that may be classified as minorities are women, gay men, lesbians, people with disabilities, and older people. Thus, an *ethnic minority* group is an ethnic group that has been singled out for differential and unequal treatment and who regard themselves as objects of collective dis-crimination. In the United States, this definition is applicable to the four racial and ethnic groups that are the focus of this book: African Americans, American Indians, Asian Americans, and Hispanic Americans.

Mental health practitioners often express concern about the appropriateness of terms that are applied to specific ethnic minority groups. Some terms may be accepted in some parts of the country or by some generations within an ethnic mi-nority group but not by others. Furthermore, terms that are used to collectively identify specific ethnic groups are problematic because they fail to recognize eth-nic and cultural differences within the groups.

African American, American Indian, Asian American, and *Hispanic* have emerged in recent years as the standard—although by no means universally ac-cepted—references for the four major racial and ethnic minorities in the United States. As suggested, however, some individuals object to these terms because they are too broad and fail to recognize important ethnic differences that exist within the groups. For example, the term *Asian American* technically includes all Americans who can trace their ancestry to the continent of Asia (including such disparate cul-tural groups as Iranians, Asian Indians, Koreans, and so forth), although common usage is restricted to descendants of Eastern Asian or Pacific Island parentage. To recognize these distinctions, researchers and writers increasingly refer to the spe-cific country of origin or ancestry (e.g., Japanese American, Vietnamese American, Mexican American, Cuban American), particularly when discussing Asian Ameri-can and Hispanic American populations. Similarly, American Indians point out that, depending on how one categorizes tribal affiliations, there are as many as 500 In-dian tribes in the United States. Therefore, any single term that refers collectively to all Indians glosses over the extensive cultural variations within their population.

Similar objections have been raised to other general terms. For example, some individuals who can trace their ancestry to Africa prefer the term *Black* to *African American,* although Ghee (1990) points out that "the term African American is currently being used interchangeably with the term Black and is increasingly being advanced as a self-referent for Americans of African descent" (p. 75). Controversy also exists over the terms *Latino* and *Hispanic* as they apply to people from Central and South America (Hayes-Bautista & Chapa, 1987; Trevino, 1987). The

term *Hispanic* was coined by Washington bureaucrats during the Nixon administration (Rodriguez, 2002), whereas the term *Latino* emerged from within the population to which it was applied. However, some individuals find both terms objectionable because they refer to European countries that conquered and oppressed
the indigenous people of Central and South America. As suggested by Rodriguez,
"Latino commits Latin America to Iberian memory as surely as does Hispanic" (p.
109). A recent PsychInfo search revealed that the term *Hispanic* is used four times
more frequently than *Latino* in professional psychology articles, so the term *Hispanic* will be used most frequently in this textbook. However, be aware that many
people of Central and South American ancestry prefer some other form of ethnic
self-identification (see chapter 13 for further discussion about terms applied to
people who trace their ancestry to Central and South America).

In view of this lack of unanimity regarding racial and ethnic group terminology, it is important that mental health practitioners remain sensitive to their
clients' preferred terms for self-identification. If the issue of race or ethnicity
emerges in counseling, the practitioner may want to ask the client how he or she
self-identifies. In other situations, the terms *African American, American Indian,
Asian American,* and *Hispanic American* are generally acceptable, although every
effort should be made to acknowledge more specific ethnic identities and to recognize individual preferences. These four terms are used in this textbook for the
purpose of organizing discussions of ethnic minority counseling, but it must be
acknowledged that such groupings are an oversimplification, and apologies are
offered to readers who find any of them offensive.

Similar problems arise when referring to the majority group. The term *European
American* is more descriptive than *White, Caucasian American,* and *Anglo American.*
Although *White* and *Caucasian American* are widely used, and at times it is necessary to fall back on them when referencing earlier writings incorporating these terms,
they are objectionable because they assume racial differences that, as was suggested
earlier in this chapter, are questionable constructs. *Anglo American* is the least appropriate term to use for all persons of European ethnic heritage because technically it
refers only to people of English descent (or more distantly, of Germanic descent).
People who trace their ancestry to Italy, France, and the Iberian Peninsula, for example, often object to being called Anglo American. *White* is probably the least objectionable of the three terms, but it is not particularly descriptive. The term *European
American* is used in this book because it is the most consistent with the emerging
trend of identifying the region (or more specifically, country) of ancestry (e.g., African
American, Asian American, Chinese American). Be aware, however, that many (particularly elderly) individuals of European descent object to having *European* inserted
before *American* when they are asked to identify their ethnicity.

COUNSELING ETHNIC MINORITY POPULATIONS

As the title suggests, this is a book about counseling ethnic minority clients. One
of the purposes of this first chapter is to acquaint readers with the basic terms and
definitions that describe ethnic minority populations and their experiences. The

remainder of the chapter defines the terms associated with counseling ethnic minorities and provides a rationale for focusing on African Americans, American Indians, Asian Americans, and Hispanics.

Cross-Cultural, Multicultural, and Ethnic Minority Counseling

Cross-cultural counseling is generally used to refer to any counseling relationship in which two or more of the participants are *ethnically* different. Literally, however, it refers to those counseling relationships in which two or more of the participants are *culturally* different. In this more literal sense, *cross-cultural counseling* could be applied, for example, to a counseling dyad consisting of a low-acculturated Mexican American client and a high-acculturated Mexican American counselor. Cross-cultural counseling also includes situations in which both the counselor and client or clients are ethnic minorities but represent different racial or ethnic groups (African American counselor and Hispanic American client; Asian American counselor and American Indian client; and so forth). It also includes the situation in which the counselor is a racial or ethnic minority person and the client is European American (African American counselor and European American client; Hispanic American counselor and European American client; and so on).

Multicultural counseling has been defined in various ways. Jackson (1995) has defined it as "counseling that takes place between or among individuals from different cultural backgrounds" (p. 3). When *multicultural counseling* is defined this way, the term can be used interchangeably with *cross-cultural counseling*. Others have defined it as any counseling in which the race, ethnicity, or culture of either the mental health practitioner or the client are legitimate topics for consideration and discussion (which basically encompasses all counseling). Currently, some controversy exists concerning which forms of diversity should be included in the term *multiculturalism*. For example, some representatives at the 1999 National Multicultural Conference and Summit proposed that multiculturalism include diversity of race, ethnicity, culture, gender, ability, sexual orientation, and religion (Sue, Bingham, Porche-Burke, & Vasquez, 1999). Because this book focuses on ethnic groups and their cultures, *multicultural counseling* will be defined narrowly as counseling that involves a mental health practitioner and a client from different ethnic cultural backgrounds. Be aware, however, that in other contexts *multicultural counseling* can refer to counseling that involves other forms of diversity.

In order to conduct a successful multicultural counseling program, the mental health practitioner must possess certain professional and personal competencies, including awareness of his or her cultural values and biases, sensitivity toward the client's worldview, and knowledge of culturally appropriate intervention strategies. The appendix at the end of this book provides a detailed account of these competencies.

Ethnic minority counseling refers to any counseling situation in which the client is a member of an ethnic minority group. The purpose of this book is to enhance the ability of mental health practitioners to work with clients from any ethnic minority group, with a particular focus on the four major ethnic populations.

To this end, parts 2 through 5 of this book each address one of the major ethnic populations. Each part includes three chapters that cover specific content that all mental health providers need in order to work with clients from the respective population. The first chapter in each part describes the ethnic minority group, their history in the United States, their cultural features, and their current demographic information. The second chapter identifies the physical and mental health problems experienced by members of this population. Finally, the third chapter examines how mental health providers can help clients address these physical and mental health concerns.

The Book's Choice of Populations

A word needs to be said about the choice of African Americans, American Indians, Asian Americans, and Hispanics as the focus of this book. They are, first of all, the four ethnic groups originally targeted by President Lyndon Johnson for affirmative action and nondiscrimination when he signed Executive Order No. 11246 in 1965. Also, they represent fairly large segments of the population that for some time have been tracked by the Bureau of the Census. However, other ethnic groups also clearly qualify as minorities, that is, have been singled out for differential and unequal treatment. One ethnic group that readily comes to mind is Arab Americans. Arabs have a history of being discriminated against in Europe and the United States, but the frequency and severity of discrimination has intensified since the attack on the World Trade Center and the Pentagon on September 11, 2001. Although Arab Americans represent a small portion of the U.S. population compared to the four ethnic groups covered in this book, mental health workers who deal with this population need to become familiar with Arab Americans' unique experiences and needs. It is hoped that some of the multicultural awareness and sensitivity that mental health professionals gain by reading this book will transfer to their work in counseling Arab Americans as well as members of other ethnic minority groups.

Before this text discusses the specific ethnic populations, it is important to present (a) a better understanding about within-group differences that might affect individual clients and (b) the rationale for altering traditional counseling strategies to address the needs of ethnic minority clients. These two topics are discussed in chapters 2 and 3, respectively.

REFERENCES

Allen, B. P., & Adams, J. Q. (1992). The concept "race": Let's go back to the beginning. *Journal of Social Behavior and Personality, 7,* 163–168.

Alonzo, W., & Waters, M. (1993). *The future composition of the American population: An illustrative simulation.* Paper presented at the winter meeting of the American Statistical Association, Fort Lauderdale, FL.

Bachu, A., & O'Connell, M. (2001). *Fertility of American women: June 2000* (Current Population Reports, P20-534RV). U.S. Census Bureau. Retrieved March 22, 2002, from www.census.gov/prod/2001pubs/p20-543rv.pdf

Barresi, C. M. (1990). *Ethnogerontology:* Social aging in national, racial, and cultural groups. In K. F. Ferraro (Ed.), *Gerontology: Perspectives and issues* (pp. 247–265). New York: Springer.

Bernal, M. E. (1990). Ethnic minority mental health training: Trends and issues. In F. C. Serafica, A. I. Schwebel, R. K. Russell, P. D. Isaac, & L. B. Myers (Eds.), *Mental health of ethnic minorities* (pp. 249–274). New York: Praeger.

Cox, O. C. (1948). *Caste, class, and race.* Garden City, NY: Doubleday.

Eagleton, T. (2000). *The idea of culture.* Oxford, UK: Blackwell.

Epps, E. G. (1974). *Cultural pluralism.* Berkeley, CA: McCutchan.

Fairchild, H. P. (1926). *The melting pot mistake.* Boston: Little, Brown.

Favreau, O. E. (1997). Evaluating political correctness: Anecdotes versus research. *Canadian Psychology, 38,* 212–220.

Feagin, J. R. (1989). *Racial and ethnic relations.* Englewood Cliffs, NJ: Prentice Hall.

Fenton, S. (1999). *Ethnicity: Racism, class, and culture.* New York: Rowman & Littlefield.

Fernando, S. (2002). *Mental health, race, and culture* (2nd ed.). New York: Palgrave.

Fish, J. M. (2002a). A scientific approach to understanding race and intelligence. In J. M. Fish (Ed.), *Race and intelligence: Separating science from myth* (pp. 1–28). Mahwah, NJ: Erlbaum.

Fish, J. M. (2002b). The myth of race. In J. M. Fish (Ed.), *Race and intelligence: Separating science from myth* (pp. 113–140). Mahwah, NJ: Erlbaum.

Ghee, K. L. (1990). The psychological importance of self-definition and labeling: Black versus African American. *Journal of Black Psychology, 17,* 75–93.

Gordon, M. M. (1964). *Assimilation in American life.* New York: Oxford University Press.

Grieco, E. M., & Cassidy, R. C. (2001). *Overview of race and Hispanic origin: 2000.* U.S. Census Bureau. Retrieved February 18, 2002, from www.census.gov/prod/2001pubs/c2kbr01-1.pdf

Hayes-Bautista, D. E., & Chapa, J. (1987). Latino terminology: Conceptual bases for standardized terminology. *American Journal of Public Health, 77*(1), 61–68.

Helms, J. E. (1996). The triple quandary of race, culture, and social class in standardized cognitive ability testing. In D. P. Flanaghan, J. L. Genshaft, & P. L. Harrison (Eds.), *Contemporary intellectual assessment: Theories, tests, and issues* (pp. 517–532). New York: Guilford Press.

Helms, J. E., & Richardson, T. Q. (1997). How "multiculturalism" obscures race and culture as differential aspects of counseling competency. In D. Pope-Davis & H. Coleman (Eds.), *Multicultural counseling competencies: Assessment, education, and training and supervision* (pp. 60–79). Thousand Oaks, CA: Sage.

Helms, J. E., & Talleyrand, R. M. (1997). *Race is not ethnicity. American Psychologist, 52,* 1246–1247.

Henwood, K. L. (1994). Resisting racism and sexism in academic psychology: A personal/political view. *Feminism & Psychology, 4,* 41–62.

Jackson, M. L. (1995). Multicultural counseling: Historical perspectives. In J. G. Ponterotto, J. M. Casas, L. A. Suzuki, & C. M. Alexander (Eds.), *Handbook of multicultural counseling* (pp. 3–16). Thousand Oaks, CA: Sage.

Johnson, A. G. (2001). *Privilege, power, and difference.* Mountain View, CA: Mayfield.

Johnson, S. D., Jr. (1990). Toward clarifying culture, race, and ethnicity in the context of multicultural counseling. *Journal of Multicultural Counseling and Development, 18,* 41–50.

Jones, J. M. (1972). *Prejudice and racism.* Reading, MA: Addison-Wesley.

Kallen, H. M. (1956). *Cultural pluralism and the American idea.* Philadelphia: University of Philadelphia Press.

Kroeber, A. L., & Kluckhohn, C. (1952). *Culture: A critical review of concepts and definitions.* New York: Vintage Books.

Krug, M. (1976). *The melting of the ethnics.* Bloomington, IN: Phi Delta Kappa Education Foundation.

Kuper, A. (1999). *Culture: The anthropologists' account.* Cambridge, MA: Harvard University Press.

Lefley, H. P. (2002). Ethical issues in mental health services for culturally diverse communities. In P. Backlar & D. L. Cutler (Eds.), *Ethics in community mental health care: Commonplace concerns* (pp. 3–22). New York: Kluwer Academic/Plenum Publishers.

Littlefield, A., Lieberman, L., & Reynolds, L. T. (1982). Redefining race: The potential demise of a concept in anthropology. *Current Anthropology, 23,* 641–647.

McIntosh, P. (1988). *White privilege and male privilege: A personal account of coming to see correspondences through work in women's studies.* Working paper no. 189, Wellesley College Center for Research on Women, Wellesley, MA.

McLemore, S. D. (1983). *Racial and ethnic relations in American* (2nd ed.). Boston: Allyn & Bacon.

Nagel, J. (1995). Resource competition theories. *American Behavioral Scientist, 38,* 442–458.

National Populations Projections. (2002). *Projections of the resident population by race, Hispanic origin, and nativity: Middle series.* U.S. Census Bureau, Population Division, Populations Branch. Retrieved February 18, 2002, from www.census.gov/population/projections/nation.html

Neufeldt, V. (1996). *Webster's new world college dictionary* (3rd ed.). New York: Simon & Schuster.

Phinney, J. S. (1996). When we talk about American ethnic groups, what do we mean? *American Psychologist, 51,* 918–927.

Reich, C. A. (1970). *The greening of America: How the youth is trying to make America livable.* New York: Random House.

Rodriguez, R. (2002). *Brown: The last discovery of America.* New York: Penguin Putnam.

Root, M. P. P. (1992). *Racially mixed people in America.* Thousand Oaks, CA: Sage.

Root, M. P. P. (1996). *The multiracial experience.* Thousand Oaks, CA: Sage.

Rose, P. I. (1964). *They and we: Racial and ethnic relations in the United States.* New York: Random House.

Rushton, J. P. (1995). Construct validity, censorship, and the genetics of race. *American Psychologist, 50,* 40–41.

Schaefer, R. T. (1988). *Racial and ethnic groups* (3rd ed.). Glenview, IL: Scott, Foresman.

Schmidley, D. (2001). *Profile of the foreign-born population in the United States: 2000* (Current Population Reports, Series P23-206). U.S. Census Bureau, Government Printing Office. Retrieved February 19, 2002, from www.census.gov/prod/2002pubs/p23-206.pdf

Segall, M. H., Lonner, W. J., & Berry, J. W. (1998). Cross-cultural psychology as a scholarly discipline: On the flowering of culture in behavioral research. *American Psychologist, 53,* 1101–1110.

Sheppard, H. L. (1977). *The graying of working America: The coming crisis in retirement-age policy.* New York: Free Press.

Stark, C. (1997). Academic freedom, "political correctness," and ethics. *Canadian Psychology, 38,* 232–237.

State Population Projections. (2002). *Population projections for states by sex, race, and Hispanic Origin: 1995–2025.* U.S. Census Bureau, Populations Division, Population Branch. Retrieved March 22, 2002, from www.census.gov/population/projections/state/stpjrace.txt

Sue, D. W., Bingham, R. P., Porche-Burke, L., & Vasquez, M. (1999). The diversification of psychology: A multicultural revolution. *American Psychologist, 54,* 1061–1069.

Sue, S., & Zane, N. (1987). The role of culture and cultural techniques in psychotherapy: A critique and reformulation. *American Psychologist, 42,* 37–45.

Sumner, W. G. (1960). *Folkways,* New York: Mentor Books.

Sydell, E. J., Nelson, E. S. (2000). Modern racism on campus: A survey of attitudes and perceptions. *Social Science Journal, 37,* 627–635.

Tate, C., & Audette, D. (2001). Theory and research on "race" as a natural kind variable in psychology. *Theory and Psychology, 11,* 495–520.

Tatum, B. D. (1992). Talking about race, learning about racism: The application of racial identity development theory in the classroom. *Harvard Educational Review, 62,* 1–24.

Templeton, A. R. (2002). The genetic and evolutionary significance of human races. In J. M. Fish (Ed.), *Race and intelligence: Separating science from myth* (pp. 31–56). Mahwah, NJ: Erlbaum.

Tinsley-Jones, H. A. (2001). Racism in our midst: Listening to psychologists of color. *Professional Psychology: Research and Practice, 32,* 573–580.

Trevino, F. M. (1987). Standardized terminology for Hispanics. *American Journal of Public Health, 77(1),* 69–72.

Van Dijk, T. A. (1993). *Elite discourse and racism.* Newbury Park, CA: Sage.

Williams, R. (1983). *Keywords: A vocabulary of culture and society* (2nd ed.). London: Fontana Paperbacks.

Wirth, L. (1945). The problem of minority groups. In R. Linton (Ed.), *The science of man in the world crisis.* New York: Columbia University Press.

Yee, A. H., Fairchild, H. H., Weizmann, F., & Wyatt, G. E. (1993). Addressing psychology's problems with race. *American Psychologist, 38,* 1132–1140.

Zuckerman, M. (1990). Some dubious premises in research and theory on racial differences. *American Psychologist, 45,* 1297–1303.

CHAPTER 2

Within-Group Differences Among Ethic Minorities

In chapter 1, diversification of the United States due to the high immigration and birthrates of ethnic minority groups was discussed. This process of diversification, although accelerated at the current time, is not new. Earlier waves of immigrants from Europe created a tapestry of ethnic and cultural diversity. However, for most families who can trace their ancestors to Europe, these cultural and ethnic differences faded within two or three generations as their families assimilated into the dominant culture through acculturation and interethnic marriages. People of color, however, have often found it difficult to assimilate to the point that interethnic marriages are common, as they now are among descendants of European ethnic groups. For this and other reasons, many individuals and families of African, Asian, Latin American, and Native American background have chosen to maintain their distinct cultural heritage and ethnic identification. By the third decade of the twentieth century, social scientists began to recognize that the assimilation process was not always smooth and predictable, even for those who chose to adopt the dominant culture. It also became evident that not all ethnic groups were equally successful in attaining educational and economic goals.

To explain the differential success rates of the various racial/ethnic groups, researchers began to examine intergroup differences. Research prior to 1970 compared scores of ethnic minority subjects to those of European American subjects on a variety of psychological and behavioral measures. Whether intended or not, this practice assumed that European American performance on these measures represented the norm or desired performance because this group was the most successful in achieving "the American Dream." Deviations from the norm could be used to explain why some ethnic minority groups were not "succeeding." Researchers offered various explanations for the differential performances of minority groups, including the hypotheses that some ethnic groups are genetically inferior to others (racism) and that some cultures are inferior to others (ethnocentrism or cultural racism).

By the 1970s, however, critics of this research methodology and of the genetic and cultural deficit theories were arguing that comparative data had limited usefulness, could be misleading, and in some cases (e.g., use of standardized IQ tests to measure intelligence), were divisive and counterproductive. Rather than comparing the scores of ethnic minorities on behavioral and psychological measures to those of European Americans, these critics argued, social scientists should examine ethnic minority performance within the context of their own culture. For example, tests should be normed for each ethnic group, and individual performance should be contrasted with ethnic group norms rather than with European American norms. As a result, the counseling and mental health literature shifted from studies that compared subjects' responsiveness to counseling across ethnic groups to studies that described responsiveness to counseling within a specific ethnic group.

Studies that described responsiveness to counseling by a single ethnic minority population were useful because they pointed out the need for ethnically similar counselors, culturally sensitive counselors, and culturally compatible counseling strategies. However, they too were misleading because normative responses of individual participants often were generalized to an entire ethnic minority population. By the late 1970s reviewers of this cross-cultural counseling research were arguing that future research with racial/ethnic minorities should include within-group differences as variables of interest. An underlying thesis in these reviews was that mental health practitioners needed to recognize diversity within ethnic groups as well as diversity among ethnic groups when working with an ethnic minority client. In particular, the practitioner needed to understand both the client's cultural heritage and the degree to which the client identified with this heritage. Although each minority group has a unique cultural heritage that makes it distinct from other groups, this distinction has erroneously been interpreted as evidence of *cultural conformity*—a monolithic approach that views all African Americans, American Indians, Asian Americans, and Hispanic Americans as possessing the same group attitudes and behaviors. Clearly, uniformity of attitudes and behaviors is no more true for minority individuals than it is for members of the dominant culture. For example, regarding assimilation, ethnic minority attitudes may vary from desire for total assimilation into the dominant culture to total rejection of the dominant culture and immersion in the minority culture (Parham & Helms, 1981). Each of the major ethnic populations in the United States manifests great diversity, including but not limited to diversity of attitudes, values, behavior, education, income, acculturation, and ethnic identity. By ignoring within-group diversity, researchers promote the view that the group is homogeneous and that modal data from a single sample can be generalized to an entire ethnic group.

It is important for mental health workers to recognize that ethnicity, culture, and minority group status all contribute to ethnic minority experiences (S. Sue, Chun, & Gee, 1995). Ho (1995) argues that to really understand an ethnic minority client, the mental health practitioner must gain insight into the client's internalized culture. Ho is concerned that by stressing cultural differences among ethnic groups, some authors have contributed to overgeneralization and stereotypes about minorities.

This chapter examines a number of variables that account for differences within ethnic groups, with special emphasis on two vital within-group variables, acculturation and racial identity development. To set the stage for discussion of acculturation within specific ethnic groups, the next section focuses on cultural differences that exist within the four major ethnic minority groups covered in this book.

CULTURAL DIFFERENCES WITHIN
MAJOR ETHNIC GROUPS

As suggested in chapter 1, the major ethnic categories of *African American, American Indian, Asian American,* and *Hispanic American* include many cultur- ally diverse groups. Although these four populations have cultural features that distinguish them from one another and from the dominant European American culture, they are all umbrella categories that include many diverse ethnic groups. Mental health practitioners who fail to recognize these cultural differences within the major ethnic categories might appear to minority group clients as "pseu- dosensitive"; that is, knowledgeable about cultural similarities generalizable across the client's umbrella ethnic group but ignorant of the client's specific eth- nic group and culture. This pseudosensitivity may have the same effect on the client as ignoring culture altogether because it communicates a lack of under- standing of the client and the client's culture.

Unfortunately, cross-cultural researchers have contributed to the profession's failure to recognize specific ethnic and cultural differences within a larger um- brella ethnic group. When researchers are unable to find a representative sample of a specific ethnic population, they often lump representatives of diverse groups together to obtain adequate sample sizes for statistical purposes (S. Sue et al., 1995). In addition, researchers sometimes generalize their findings to an entire umbrella ethnic group when these findings are applicable only to one or two spe- cific ethnic/cultural groups (those most readily available to the researcher).

Although a thorough discussion of cultural differences among specific ethnic groups within the general ethnic categories would take up many volumes, we will cite a few examples to make our point. Consider the diverse ethnic groups and cul- tures within the umbrella category of Asian Americans. According to Yoshioka, Tashima, Chew, and Maruse (1981), there are at least 29 distinct Asian American subgroups that differ from one another in language, religion, and values. Within the general category of Asian Americans are ethnic groups whose ancestors for generations were enemies due to ethnic/cultural differences. Even within the more specific ethnic group identified as Chinese Americans there are major cultural dif- ferences between those who have immigrated from Hong Kong, Taiwan, and mainland China. Similar observations can be made about African Americans, American Indians, and Hispanic Americans. For African Americans, within-group ethnic/cultural differences are most evident among those who are recent immi- grants from Africa, the Caribbean, and other parts of the world. However, regional differences that, in effect, constitute cultural differences also exist within African American populations that have resided in this country for generations.

Phinney (1996) has also drawn attention to "the tremendous heterogeneity among members of American ethnic groups":

> Ethnic cultures differ in terms of particular country of origin within a broad cultural group (e.g., Asian Americans of Japanese vs. Korean ancestry), generation of immigration, region of settlement in the United States, socioeconomic status, and community structure. . . . Furthermore, because of their dispersion and mixing with both mainstream American culture and with other ethnic groups in the United States, ethnic cultures are not discrete entities but rather part of a diverse cultural mix. . . . Finally, even if particular subcultures can be described with some accuracy, cultures are not static, but continually evolving and changing. (p. 921)

Even within specific ethnic groups, cultural differences that are not due to acculturation can exist between recent immigrants and those whose ancestors immigrated many generations ago. Cultures in the home country change over time, and the cultural values handed down through four or five generations in this country may be quite different than the cultural values currently practiced in the home country. For example, the cultural values of Japanese Americans whose ancestors immigrated in 1910 may be more similar in some ways to those practiced in Japan in 1910 than to those currently practiced in Japan. Thus, cultural values within an ethnic group may vary due to time of immigration as much as to length of time since immigration, a variable that correlates highly with acculturation.

Acculturation scales provide one measure of cultural differences within ethnic groups. Acculturation is such an important source of cultural differences within ethnic groups that we devote a major portion of this chapter to discussing it and its impact on ethnic minorities.

ACCULTURATION AS A WITHIN-GROUP VARIABLE

According to Olmedo (1979), acculturation is "one of the more elusive, albeit ubiquitous, constructs in the behavioral sciences" (p. 1061). Keefe (1980) suggested that "acculturation is one of those terms all social scientists use although few can agree upon its meaning" (p. 85). However, there is general agreement that acculturation is a process of cultural change that occurs when two or more cultures come into contact with one another (Redfield, Linton, & Herskovits, 1936).

Early Assimilation Models

Although anthropologists became interested in acculturation as early as the 1880s, it was not until the 1920s that they began studying acculturation at the population level in earnest (Berry, 1990). Early anthropological models of acculturation focused on changes in social structure, economic base, and political organization when two cultures came into contact. The assimilation model developed by Park and Burgess (1921), among the first to describe the process of acculturation, was widely accepted by social scientists in the past. This model implied that the United States was a melting pot in which immigrant groups contributed elements of their own culture to an evolving U.S. culture. According to the model, complete assimilation usually occurred within three generations after immigration (Neidert & Farley, 1985).

As suggested in chapter 1, the concept of melting pot acculturation has been criticized for several reasons. First, critics point out that total assimilation has been limited in the past to European immigrants and that people of color are expected to acculturate but are never allowed to assimilate completely (Novak, 1972). Also, most contemporary social scientists describe acculturation in the United States as a unilateral or unidirectional process in which immigrant groups are expected to adopt the dominant culture but contribute little or nothing of their indigenous culture (Kim & Abreu, 2001). Conceptually, then, acculturation involves an unequal status relationship between the majority and minority cultures. For this reason, many persons of color believe that the melting pot concept may actually describe a form of cultural oppression in that ethnic minorities are forced to adopt the ways of the larger society. The melting pot model of acculturation can become a reality only if an equal power relationship exists between the majority and minority cultures.

Another criticism of the Park and Burgess model has to do with its assumption that all immigrants experience the negative effects of being caught between two cultures. Park (1928) coined the term *marginal man* (or more accurately, marginal person) to describe this condition. According to Park (1950), the marginal person lives in a permanent state of crisis due to an internalized cultural conflict. Among the psychological manifestations of this marginal state are "intensified self-consciousness, restlessness, and malaise" (p. 356). Stonequist (1961) expanded upon this concept, suggesting that "the marginal situation produces excessive self-consciousness and race-consciousness" and " 'inferiority complexes' are a common affliction" (p. 148). Contemporary acculturation theorists agree that some immigrants may experience marginalization, but most theorists reject the idea that all immigrants experience the marginal person syndrome. Also, most theorists point out that many immigrants and their descendants achieve a positive, bicultural resolution to acculturation (Berry, 1994).

Finally, the early models have been criticized for conceptualizing acculturation as a unilinear or monocultural process that occurs along a single continuum with the indigenous culture on one end and dominant U.S. culture on the other. According to this model, cultural values and behavior of the indigenous culture are gradually lost while cultural traits of the dominant society are gradually adopted. Increasingly, however, social scientists are recognizing that immigrants can retain values and behavior from their ancestral culture while adopting values and behavior from their culture of residence (Berry & Kim, 1988).

Berry's Theories of Psychological Acculturation

Compared to anthropologists and sociologists, few psychologists have engaged in a sustained program of research related to acculturation. In fact, according to Segall, Lonner, and Berry (1998), "psychology in general has long ignored 'culture' as a source of influence on human behavior and still takes little account of theories or data from other than Euro-American cultures" (p. 1101). One psychologist who has conducted extensive research on acculturation is John Berry. Berry (1990, 1997) makes a distinction between acculturation at the population level, which involves ecological, cultural, social, and institutional changes, and at the individual level, which involves changes in the attitudes and behavior of individuals, also known as *psychological acculturation.* Research on psychological acculturation, initiated in the 1960s, has focused on the process by which individuals change their behavior, identity, values, and attitudes as a result of coming into contact with another culture and as a result of "being participants in the general acculturative changes under way in their own culture" (Berry, 1990, p. 235).

Berry, Trimble, and Olmeda (1986) diagrammed how the process of acculturation operates at both the population and individual levels; their diagram is presented in Figure 2.1. The diagram demonstrates the process and effect of acculturation at a given time. As seen in Figure 2.1, Culture A is the dominant culture and exerts a stronger impact on Culture B and Individual B (from Culture B) than they, in turn, exert on Culture A. Culture B and Individual B also exert an impact on each other. The influence of Culture B on Individual B is referred to as *enculturation,* a process of socializing the individual to his or her indigenous culture that is typically the responsibility of the individual's family. The acculturation and enculturation processes that take place among Culture A, Culture B, and Individual B transform Culture B into Culture B[1] and Individual B into Individual B[1]. If Culture A, Culture B[1], and Individual B[1] remain in contact, then additional changes are likely to occur (Berry, 1990).

Berry and Kim (1988) suggest that individuals have some choice about how to respond to this acculturation process. They have identified acculturation strategies based on "acculturation attitudes" (Berry, Kim, Power, Young, & Bajaki, 1989) that members of acculturating groups hold about accepting the identity, at-

FIGURE 2.1   Framework for Identifying Variables and Relationships in Acculturation Research Psychology of Acculturation

W. J. Lonner and J. W. Berry. *Field Methods in Cross-Cultural Research.* London: Sage © 1986 by Sage Publishers.

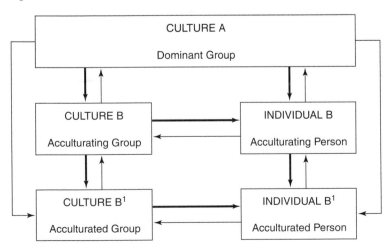

titudes, and behaviors of the cultures involved. Some individuals may choose to give up their identity and the cultural attitudes and behaviors associated with Culture B and embrace those associated with Culture A (assimilation option). Others may choose to maintain their identity and the cultural attitudes and behaviors associated with Culture B while rejecting those of Culture A (separation option). Still others may give up their identity and cultural practices from Culture B while at the same time reject those of Culture A (marginalization option). Some individuals will choose to maintain their identity and many of the cultural practices of Culture B at the same time that they identify with and adopt the attitudes and behaviors associated with Culture A (integration or bicultural option). In general, the integration strategy has been found to produce the most positive adaptation for immigrants (Berry, 1997).

Berry (1994) has identified two basic phenomena that are associated with psychological acculturation. The first is *behavior shift,* the process whereby individuals change their values, attitudes, and behavior. Generally, although not universally, the behavior shift is away from patterns of behavior learned in the indigenous culture and toward those more frequently found in the host culture. The second phenomenon is *acculturative stress,* what some authors refer to as "culture shock" (Oberg, 1954; Winkelman, 1994).

> There is often a particular set of stress behaviors that occur during acculturation, such as lowered mental health status (especially confusion, anxiety, depression), feelings of marginality and alienation, heightened psychosomatic symptom level, and identity confusion. Acculturative stress is thus a phenomenon that may underlie a reduction in the health status of individuals (including physical, psychological, and social aspects). (Berry, 1990, pp. 246–247)

Berry (1990) has identified a number of factors that may influence the degree of acculturative stress experienced by the individual. One such factor is the mode of acculturation experienced by the individual. Berry and Kim (1988) report that people who feel marginalized or separated experience the most stress, those who seek assimilation experience intermediate levels of stress, and those who seek to integrate the two cultures feel the least stress. Another factor is the general tolerance for ethnic diversity in the dominant culture. In general, pluralistic societies, which encourage cultural diversity, have less acculturative stress associated with them than do monistic societies, which discourage diversity. Societies that exclude acculturating groups from full participation may generate more acculturative stress, at least among those who aspire to acculturate.

Berry (1994) makes the important observation that conditions that affect adaptation to acculturation are often under the control of policy makers and health professionals. Bilingual education and bilingual voting ballots are examples of policies that can reduce the stress of acculturation. Similarly, health professionals can reduce the stress associated with acculturation by providing bilingual, bicultural physical and mental health services. Therefore, the probability of successful adaptations can be enhanced through appropriate policy decisions and implementation of appropriate programs for immigrants. Berry (1994) suggests that psychologists can play a role in promoting successful adaptation by addressing these issues through research and by lobbying legislatures regarding social programs that produce successful adaptations.

Multidimensional and Bicultural Theories of Acculturation

In addition to Berry and his colleagues, other psychologists have made important contributions to an understanding of psychological acculturation. For example, Padilla (1980b) was among the first psychologists to develop a model of acculturation and then subject it to empirical verification. He conceptualized a multidimensional model of acculturation for Mexican Americans that consisted of two underlying elements and five dimensions.

> Our model of acculturation involves two essential elements—*cultural awareness* and *ethnic loyalty.* Cultural awareness refers to an individual's *knowledge* of specific cultural material (e.g., language, values, history-art, foods, etc.) of the cultural group of origin and/or the host culture. By loyalty we mean the individual's *preference* of one cultural orientation over the other. (p. 48)

By identifying acculturation as a multidimensional process, Padilla (1980b) drew attention to the fact that the generation since immigration, often used as a unitary measure of acculturation, was not the only dimension that should be taken into account in an assessment level of acculturation. Padilla hypothesized that there were at least five dimensions of acculturation: (a) language familiarity and usage, (b) cultural heritage (knowledge of culture), (c) ethnic pride and identity pride, (d) interethnic interaction, and (e) interethnic distance and perceived discrimination. To test this model of acculturation, Padilla developed a questionnaire that "tapped awareness and loyalty information on the five dimensions of the model" (p. 53) and administered it to Mexican Americans representing a variety of generation levels. After performing a factor and cluster analysis on the data from this study, he concluded that

> Cultural awareness is composed of: respondent's cultural heritage as well as the cultural heritage of the respondent's spouse and parents, language preference and use, cultural identification and preference, and social behavior orientation. Ethnic loyalty consists of: cultural pride and affiliation, perceived discrimination, and social behavior orientation. (p. 81)

Padilla (1980a) suggested that although the acculturation process may be unique to every immigrant group, "many of the psychological processes underlying acculturation are probably similar" (p. 3). Although the acculturation concept can be applied to all ethnic minorities, it seems most applicable to American Indians (not an immigrant group, but definitely a group under constant pressure to acculturate), Asian Americans, and Hispanics. Recently, however, it has been applied to African Americans, even though most African Americans are many generations removed from (involuntary) immigration and despite their long-standing history of helping to shape U.S. culture (Landrine & Klonoff, 1994).

The concept of *biculturalism* is particularly important to current theories of acculturation (Kim & Abreu, 2001). Bicultural socialization can be conceptual-

ized as two continua, one representing involvement (low to high) with the indigenous culture and one representing involvement (low to high) with the dominant culture. According to the bicultural process model of acculturation, the marginal person and the bicultural person respond differently to their socialization in
two cultures. The marginal person feels caught between the conflicting values of
two cultures and consequently feels little commitment to either. In contrast, the
bicultural individual feels committed to both cultures and selectively embraces
the positive aspects of each culture.

De Anda (1984) suggests that six factors contribute to the development of a
bicultural rather than a marginal perspective: (a) degree of cultural overlap between the two cultures; (b) the availability of cultural translators, mediators, and
models; (c) the amount and type of corrective feedback regarding attempts to produce normative behaviors; (d) the compatibility of the minority individual's conceptual style with the analytical cognitive style valued by the dominant culture;
(e) the individual's degree of bilingualism; and (f) the degree of dissimilarity in
physical appearance between the individual and members of the dominant culture. The extent to which these six factors are operating will determine not only
the acculturation attitude that a minority individual will adopt but also the level
of stress he or she will experience as part of the acculturation process.

Measuring Acculturation

In the United States, social scientists have developed numerous scales to measure
acculturation among Hispanic Americans and, to a lesser extent, among other ethnic groups. Kim and Abreu (2001) recently critiqued 33 instruments that measure
acculturation for African Americans, Asian Americans, Hispanics, Native Americans, Native Hawaiians, or all ethnic groups, 23 of which measure Hispanic acculturation. Typically, acculturation measures include items measuring language
usage and preference, ethnic identification, knowledge of culture, and so forth.
Kim and Abreu found that 23 of the 33 instruments they critiqued are still based
on unilinear models of acculturation.

Kim and Abreu (2001) reported a number of other concerns with the instruments they reviewed. Although culture is generally defined to include both values
and behavior (see chapter 1), they found that most of the instruments primarily
measured behavior to the exclusion of values. With regard to psychometric properties, there was no evidence of concurrent or discriminant validity for more than
half of the instruments and no evidence of test-retest reliability for nearly three
quarters of the instruments they reviewed. Kim and Abreu concluded that researchers must develop new measures of acculturation that are based on a bilinear
(or multilinear) model and that place greater emphasis on values acculturation.

Marin (1992) also criticized instruments measuring Hispanic acculturation,
claiming that they (a) lack sound psychometric qualities; (b) rely heavily on language use, dominance, or preference as a valid measure of acculturation; (c) operationalize the measurement of acculturation on a single scale with a different
culture on each end (Marin refers to this as unidimensional measurement; to
avoid confounding this issue with the unidimensional concerns raised by Padilla,

1980b, this method of operationalizing acculturation is referred to as *unilinear measurement* in this book); and (d) fail to include such variables as cognitive style, personality, attitudes, and levels of stress as measures of acculturation. He also criticized researchers for making changes to the wording of items or dropping items on acculturation instruments based on personal preferences and then assuming that the psychometric properties of the original instrument still hold.

A study by Ruelas, Atkinson, and Ramos-Sanchez (1998) provides evidence of the kind of misinterpretation that can occur when an instrument based on a unilinear model is used to measure acculturation. Ruelas et al. administered the ARSMA II (Cuellar, Arnold, & Maldonado, 1995), a multidimensional, bilinear measure of Mexican American acculturation, to 109 Mexican American community college students after exposing them to a counseling vignette. They first examined the relationship between the *combined* ARSMA II scores (which provide a linear measure of acculturation) and participants' perceptions of the counselor's credibility. Counselor credibility ratings were found to be negatively related to linear acculturation: The more acculturated the Mexican Americans were found to be, the lower the credibility ratings they gave the counselor. One could conclude from these results that acquisition of U.S. culture is associated with less positive perceptions of counselor credibility. However, when Ruelas et al. examined scores on the Anglo Orientation Scale and Mexican Orientation Scale independently, they discovered that the loss of Mexican culture, and not the acquisition of Anglo culture, was significantly related to counselor credibility ratings. Had they relied exclusively on unilinear measures of acculturation, they might have concluded erroneously that acquisition of the new culture, rather than the loss of old one, accounts for the significant relationships found.

Unfortunately, using instruments based on a bilinear model of acculturation is no guarantee against misinterpretation of data. Theoretically, the 10 instruments reviewed by Kim and Abreu (2001) that are based on a bilinear model of acculturation should provide a measure of both acculturation and enculturation. Unfortunately, none of them does so adequately because they all primarily measure behavioral acculturation and virtually ignore the important construct of values acculturation.

A recent study by Kim, Atkinson, and Yang (1999) highlights the important role of cultural values in acculturation and enculturation. These researchers developed the Asian Values Scale (AVS), which was then administered, along with the Suinn-Lew Asian Self-Identity Acculturation Scale (SL-ASIA; Suinn, Rickard-Figueroa, Lew, & Vigil, 1987), to 300 Asian American college students. Treating the SL-ASIA as a measure of behavioral acculturation, Kim et al. found that Asian Americans acquired U.S. cultural behaviors more rapidly than they lost their Asian cultural values; that is, they found that behavioral acculturation was occurring more rapidly than values acculturation. Because the SL-ASIA has been so widely used as the sole measure of acculturation in past research, earlier conclusions about the speed at which Asian Americans are acculturating may be misleading. This finding suggests that future research that examines the relationship between acculturation and mental health or counseling process variables should include measures of both behavioral and values acculturation.

Social scientists clearly need to develop bilinear (or multilinear), bidimensional measures of acculturation, that is, instruments that measure adherence to both behavior *and* values for both the new *and* old cultures. Until such instruments are available, social scientists are in danger of misinterpreting rates of acculturation and relationships between acculturation and mental health variables.

RACIAL/ETHNIC IDENTITY DEVELOPMENT AS A WITHIN-GROUP VARIABLE

One of the most promising contributions to the field of multicultural counseling has been theory and research on racial/ethnic/cultural identity development. When George Morten, Derald Sue, and I first published our Minority Identity Development model in the original (1979) edition of this book, we were aware of only three earlier models of identity development, all of which dealt exclusively with Black identity development (Cross, 1971; Jackson, 1975; Vontress, 1971). Since our original edition, however, we have become aware of numerous other models for Black (Gay, 1984), Latino (Ruiz, 1990), White (Helms, 1985, 1990; Ponterotto, 1988), people of color (Helms, 1995), female (Downing & Roush, 1985), homosexual (Cass, 1979; Troiden, 1989), biracial (Poston, 1990), ethnic (Ford, 1987; Smith, 1991), racial/cultural (D. W. Sue & D. Sue, 1990), and general minority identity development (Highlen et al., 1988; Myers et al., 1991). In her book on Black and White racial identity, Helms (1990) listed 11 identity development models for African Americans alone!

Cross's Model of Racial Identity Development

Cross (1970, 1971, 1978, 1991, 1995) is generally credited with founding the first model of Black racial identity development. Cross originally described his model as a "Negro-to-Black Conversion Experience" (1971) and later as a process of psychological nigrescence (1978). The original Cross (1971) model consisted of five stages: preencounter, encounter, immersion, internalization, and internalization-commitment. Blacks at the preencounter stage are "programmed to view and think of the world as being nonblack, anti-black, or the opposite of Black" (Hall, Cross, & Freedle, 1972, p. 159). At the encounter stage, the Black individual becomes aware of what being Black means and begins to validate himself or herself as a Black person. During the immersion stage, the Black person rejects all non-Black values and totally immerses himself or herself in Black culture. In the internalization stage, the Black person gains a sense of inner security and begins to focus on "things other than himself and his own ethnic or racial group" (Hall et al., p. 160). Finally, the internalization-commitment stage refers to Blacks who evidence a sustained commitment to Black culture.

In subsequent writings, Cross (1995) revised his original model based on more recent research findings. Most notably, he suggested that Black self-hatred is not a defining characteristic of the preencounter stage. Although some Blacks at this stage may reject their Black identity, Cross pointed out that self-hatred previously associated with individuals at this stage of identity development has been exaggerated and that "persons in the Pre-Encounter stage hold attitudes toward race that range from low salience or race neutrality, to anti-Black" (p. 98). Cross also modified earlier suppositions that ideological unity is a defining characteristic of the internalization stage, and he suggested that "people in the advanced stages are quite divergent in their ideological perspectives" (p. 97). He also retracted earlier differences in value structures (individualism vs. communalism) between preencounter Black and Blacks in more advanced stages of development. "I now believe that although they hold radically different value orientations, Pre-Encounter persons do not necessar[ily] differ in their value structures from persons in advanced stages of Black identity development" (p. 103). For a recent overview of nigrescence theory and an introduction to the Cross Racial Identity Scale, see Cross, Fhagen-Smith, Cokley, Vandiver, and Worrell (2001).

Helms and the People of Color Racial Identity Model

Janet Helms and her associates have engaged in extensive research and writing on the application of Cross's model to counseling process and outcome (Helms 1984, 1990). Over the years she has modified her interpretation of the model and expanded it to include other ethnic groups. For example, Helms replaced the construct of "stages" with "ego statuses" in order to suggest "dynamic evolution rather than static personality structures or types" (Helms & Cook, 1999). She has also applied her model of racial identity development to both Whites and people of color. According to Helms and Cook (1999), for both Black and White identity development, "the developmental process involves successive differentiations of increasingly more sophisticated racial identity ego statuses whose objective or measurable manifestations are schema or information-processing strategies" (p. 84). For people of color (individuals who can trace some of their ancestry to Africa, Asia, or pre-Columbus America), the central racial identity developmental theme is "to recognize and overcome the psychological manifestations of internalized racism" (p. 189). Helms derived her People of Color Racial Identity (PCRI) model from Cross's (1971) original psychological nigrescence model and the Minority Identity Development model (to be discussed later in this chapter) first published in the 1979 edition of this book.

The PCRI model consists of six statuses: conformity, dissonance, immersion, emersion, internalization, and integrative awareness. In the *conformity* status, individuals tend to devalue their own ethnic group and endorse White standards of merit. Individuals in the *dissonance* status are ambivalent and confused about their commitment to their own socioracial group. Idealization of their socioracial group and denigration of White standards is associated with the *immersion* status. The *emersion* status is associated with a sense of well-being to be a member of one's socioracial group. In the *internalization* status, individuals have a positive commitment to their own socioracial group and respond objectively to White people. Individuals in the *integrative awareness* status value their collective identity but also "empathize and collaborate with members of other oppressed groups" (Helms, 1995). Helms suggests that most people do not express their racial identity in pure forms but more typically have one status that is stronger than others.

A number of studies have been conducted since the early 1980s to determine if Black identity development is related to mental health variables. Much of this research was made possible when Parham and Helms (1981) developed the Black Racial Identity Attitude Scale (RIAS-B) to measure the first four stages of Cross's (1971) model. They and other researchers have used the RIAS-B to examine the relationship between Black identity development and (a) psychological adjustment and (b) counseling process and outcome. Research on psychological adjustment suggests that Black racial identity development is positively related to self-esteem (Phelps, Taylor, & Gerard, 2001), self-concept (Wilson & Constantine, 1999), and self-actualizing tendencies (Parham & Helms, 1985a, 1985b). Black students' value orientations (Carter & Helms, 1987) and cognitive styles (Helms & Parham, 1990) also have been found to be related to Black racial identity development. With regard to research on counseling process and outcome, Black identity development has been found to be associated with, for example, preference for a mental health practitioner of the same race (Helms & Carter, 1991; Parham & Helms, 1981).

In summary, there is empirical support for the concept of Black Racial Identity Development (BRID), and the stages of BRID have been found to be related to counseling process and outcome variables. Future research will likely shed light on the validity of the revised Cross model and the reconceptualized Helms PCRI model. In the meantime, racial identity development continues to serve as an important variable for recognizing within-group differences among ethnic minority groups. For additional discussion about the BRID model, see chapters 4 and 6.

Minority Identity Development Model

Although the Black identity development models pertain specifically to the African American experience, some of the basic tenets of these theories can be generalized and applied to other minority groups because of their shared experience of oppression. Each of the ethnic groups discussed in this book has a unique culture (indeed, within these broad groupings are a number of unique cultures), but they all have been subjected to similar forms of physical, economic, and social discrimination. They share a common experience that affects how they view themselves and others. Researchers have long been aware that minority groups share the same patterns of adjustment to cultural oppression (Stonequist, 1937; Berry, 1965).

Based on views expressed by earlier writers and our own clinical observation that these changes in attitudes and subsequent behavior follow a predictable sequence, my coeditors for the first edition of this book (Drs. George Morten and Derald Sue) and I developed a five-stage Minority Identity Development (MID) model. This model was not intended as a comprehensive theory of personality development but rather as a schema to help mental health practitioners understand minority client attitudes and behaviors within existing personality theories. The MID model defines five stages of development that oppressed people may experience as they struggle to understand themselves in terms of their own minority culture and the oppressive relationship between the minority and majority cultures. Although the MID model describes five distinct stages, the model is more accurately conceptualized as a continuous process in which one stage blends with another and boundaries between stages are not clear.

It was our observation that not all minority individuals experience the entire range of these stages in their lifetimes. Prior to the turbulent 1960s—a decade in which the transition of many individuals through this process was accelerated and, therefore, made more evident—many people were raised and lived their lives in Stage 1. Nor is the developmental process to be interpreted as irreversible. Many minority individuals are socialized by their parents to hold the values associated with Stage 5, but in coming to grips with their own identity, adolescents and young adults often move from Stage 5 to one of the lower stages. Finally, it does not appear that functioning at lower stages of development is a prerequisite to functioning at higher stages. Some people born and raised in a family functioning at Stage 5 appear never to experience a Stage 1 sense of identity. These caveats notwithstanding, the normal and preferred developmental sequence for most minority individuals is from lower stages to higher stages of minority identity development.

Following are descriptions of each stage, and each description contains four corresponding attitudes that may help mental health practitioners to understand behaviors displayed by individuals operating at or near each stage (see Table 2.1). Each attitude is believed to be an integral part of any minority person's identity or of how he or she views (a) self, (b) others of the same minority, (c) others of another minority, and (d) majority individuals.

Stage One—Conformity Stage   Minority individuals in the conformity stage of development exhibit an unequivocal preference for the cultural values of the dominant group over those of their own cultural group. Their views of self, fellow group members, and other minority groups are clouded by their identification with the dominant culture, and they tend to devalue and depreciate themselves on both a conscious and subconscious level. For example, Asian Americans might perceive their physical characteristics as undesirable and their cultural values as a handicap to successful adaptation to the dominant society. In some cases, these negative perceptions can lead to feelings of racial self-hatred (S. Sue & D. W. Sue, 1971).

A. *Attitude toward self: Self-depreciating attitude.* Individuals who acknowledge their distinguishing physical or cultural characteristics consciously view them as a source of shame. Individuals who repress awareness of their distinguishing physical or cultural characteristics depreciate themselves at a subconscious level.

B. *Attitude toward members of same minority: Group-depreciating attitude.* Other members of the minority group are viewed according to the dominant group's beliefs of minority strengths and weaknesses.

C. *Attitude toward members of different minority: Discriminatory attitude.* Other minorities are viewed according to the dominant group's system of minority stratification; that is, those minority groups who most closely re-

TABLE 2.1   Summary of Minority Identity Development Model

Stages of Minority Development Model	Attitudes Toward Self	Attitude Toward Others of the Same Minority	Attitude Toward Others of Different Minority	Attitude Toward Dominant Group
Stage 1— Conformity	Self-depreciating	Group-depreciating	Discriminatory	Group-appreciating
Stage 2— Dissonance	Conflict between self-depreciating and appreciating	Conflict between group-depreciating and group-appreciating	Conflict between dominant-held views of minority hierarchy and feelings of shared experience	Conflict between group-appreciating and group depreciating
Stage 3— Resistance and Immersion	Self-appreciating	Group-appreciating	Conflict between feelings of empathy for other minority experiences and feelings of culturocentrism	Group-depreciating
Stage 4— Introspection	Concern with basis of self-appreciation	Concern with nature of unequivocal appreciation	Concern with ethnocentric basis for judging others	Concern with the basis of group depreciation
Stage 5— Synergetic Articulation and Awareness	Self-appreciating	Group-appreciating	Group-appreciating	Selective appreciating

semble the dominant group in physical and cultural characteristics are viewed more favorably than those who are less similar.

D. *Attitude toward members of dominant group: Group-appreciating attitude.* Members of the dominant group are admired, respected, and often viewed as ideal models. Cultural values and behavior of the dominant society are accepted without question.

Stage Two—Dissonance Stage   The primary feature of this stage is a dissonance created by conflict between negative attitudes adopted in the conformity stage and exposure to positive attitudes about the individual's ethnic group. The movement into the dissonance stage is most often a gradual process, but as Cross (1971) points out, a monumental event such as the assassination of Martin Luther

King, Jr., may propel the Black person into the next stage. Minorities in the dissonance stage begin to experience a breakdown in the denial system they developed in the conformity stage. A Latino who may feel ashamed of his cultural upbringing may encounter a Latina who is proud of her heritage. An African American who may have deceived himself or herself into believing that racial problems are due to laziness, untrustworthiness, or personal inadequacies of his or her group suddenly encounters racism on a personal level.

A. *Attitude toward self: Conflict between self-depreciating and self-appreciating attitudes.* With a growing awareness of minority cultural strengths comes a faltering sense of pride in self. The individual's attitude toward distinguishing physical or cultural characteristics is typified by alternating feelings of shame and pride in self.

B. *Attitude toward members of same minority: Conflict between group-depreciating and group-appreciating attitudes.* Dominant-group views of minority strengths and weaknesses begin to be questioned as new, contradictory information is received. Cultural values of the minority group begin to have appeal.

C. *Attitude toward members of different minority: Conflict between dominant-held views of minority hierarchy and feelings of shared experience.* The individual begins to question the dominant group's system of minority stratification and experiences a growing sense of comradeship with other oppressed people. Most of the individual's psychic energy at this level, however, is devoted to resolving conflicting attitudes toward self, the same minority group, and the dominant group.

D. *Attitude toward members of dominant group: Conflict between group-appreciating and group-depreciating attitude.* The individual experiences a growing awareness that not all cultural values of the dominant group are beneficial to him or her. Members of the dominant group are viewed with growing suspicion.

Stage Three—Resistance and Immersion Stage   In the resistance and immersion stage of development, the minority individual completely endorses minority-held views and rejects the dominant society and culture. Desire to eliminate oppression of the individual's minority group becomes an important motivation of the individual's behavior.

D. W. Sue and D. Sue (1990) believe that movement into this stage occurs for two reasons. First, individuals begin to resolve many of the conflicts and confusions associated with the previous stage. As a result, they develop a greater understanding of societal forces (racism, oppression, and discrimination) along with a realization that they have been victimized by these forces. Second, individuals begin to ask themselves the following question: "Why should I feel ashamed of who and what I am?" The answers to that question evoke both guilt and anger (bordering on rage): guilt that they have sold out in the past and contributed to their own group's oppression, and anger at having been oppressed and brainwashed by the forces in the dominant society.

A. *Attitude toward self: Self-appreciating attitude.* Minority individuals at this stage act as explorers and discoverers of their history and culture, seeking out information and artifacts that enhance their sense of identity and worth. Cultural and physical characteristics that once elicited feelings of shame and disgust at this stage become symbols of pride and honor.

B. *Attitude toward members of same minority: Group-appreciating attitude.* Individuals experience a strong sense of identification with, and commitment to, their minority group as they acquire enhancing information about the group. Members of the group are admired, respected, and often viewed as ideal models. Cultural values of the minority group are accepted without question.

C. *Attitude toward members of different minority: Conflict between feelings of empathy for other minority experiences and feelings of culturocentrism.* The individual experiences a growing sense of camaraderie with persons from other minority groups to the degree that they are viewed as sharing similar forms of oppression. Alliances with other groups tend to be short-lived, however, when their values come in conflict with those of the individual's minority group. The dominant group's system of minority stratification is replaced by a system that values most those minority groups that are culturally similar to the individual's group.

D. *Attitude toward members of dominant group: Group-depreciating attitude.* The individual totally rejects the dominant society and culture and experiences a sense of distrust and dislike for all members of the dominant group.

Stage Four—Introspection Stage   In the introspection stage of development, minority individuals experience feelings of discontent and discomfort with group views rigidly held in the resistance and immersion stage, and they divert attention to notions of greater individual autonomy. Individuals may begin to feel progressively more comfortable with their sense of identity. This security allows them to begin to question the rigidly held belief of the resistance stage that "all Whites are bad." Individuals also feel that too much negativism and hatred directed at White society tend to divert energies from a more positive exploration of identity questions. They also come to realize that the dominant culture contains both positive and negative elements.

As previously mentioned, the introspection stage is characterized by greater individual autonomy. During this stage individuals may begin to experience conflict between notions of responsibility and allegiance to their own minority group and notions of personal autonomy.

A. *Attitude toward self: Concern with basis of self-appreciating attitude.* Individuals experience conflict between notions of responsibility and allegiance to minority group and notions of personal autonomy. They develop self-valuing attitudes that are independent of group identity per se.

B. *Attitude toward members of same minority: Concern with unequivocal nature of group appreciation.* Although attitudes of identification are continued from the preceding resistance and immersion stage, concern begins to develop that not all members of the group manifest positive attitudes and that members of the same minority should be judged on their individual merit.

C. *Attitude toward members of different minority: Concern with ethnocentric basis for judging others.* Individuals experience a growing uneasiness with minority stratification that results from ethnocentrism and begin to place greater value on other groups that experience oppression by the larger society.

D. *Attitude toward members of dominant group: Concern with the basis of group depreciation.* Individuals experience conflict between an attitude of complete distrust for the dominant society and culture and an attitude of selective trust and distrust according to dominant group members' demonstrated behaviors and attitudes. Individuals also recognize the utility of many dominant cultural elements yet are uncertain whether to incorporate such elements into their minority culture.

Stage Five—Synergistic Stage   Minority individuals in the synergistic stage experience a sense of self-fulfillment with regard to cultural identity. They have resolved conflicts and discomforts experienced in the introspection stage and thus enjoy greater individual control and flexibility. They objectively examine the cultural values of other minorities and those of the dominant group, which they accept or reject on the basis of experience gained in earlier stages of identity development. The desire to eliminate all forms of oppression becomes an important motivation for the individual's behavior.

A. *Attitude toward self: Self-appreciating attitude.* Individuals experience a strong sense of self-worth, self-confidence, and autonomy as the result of having established their identity as an individual, a member of a minority group, and a member of the dominant culture.

B. *Attitude toward members of same minority: Group-appreciating attitude.* Individuals experience a strong sense of pride in the group without having to accept group values unequivocally. Strong feelings of empathy with the group experience are coupled with an awareness that each member of the group is an individual.

C. *Attitude toward members of different minority: Group-appreciating attitude.* The individual experiences a strong sense of respect for the cultural values of other groups while acknowledging the individuality of group members. The individual also experiences a greater understanding of and support for all oppressed people, regardless of their similarity or dissimilarity to the individual's minority group.

D. *Attitude toward members of dominant group: Attitude of selective appreciation.* The individual experiences selective trust and liking for members of the dominant group who seek to eliminate repressive activities of the group. The individual also experiences an openness to the constructive elements of the dominant culture.

Implications of the MID Model for Counseling   As previously stated, the MID model is not intended as a comprehensive theory of personality but rather as a paradigm to help mental health practitioners understand their minority clients' attitudes and behaviors. In this respect the model is intended to sensitize practitioners to (a) the role oppression plays in a minority individual's identity development, (b) the differences that can exist among members of the same minority group with respect to their cultural identity, and (c) the potential each minority person has for changing his or her sense of identity. Beyond helping practitioners to understand minority client behavior, the model has implications for the counseling process itself.

The general attitudes and behaviors that describe minority individuals at the conformity stage (e.g., denial of minority problems, strong dependence on and identification with dominant group, etc.) suggest that clients from this stage are unlikely to seek counseling related to their cultural identity. It is more likely that they will perceive problems of cultural identity as problems related to their personal identity. Clients at this stage are more inclined to visit and to be influenced by mental health practitioners of the dominant group than those of the same minority group. Indeed, clients may actively request a White practitioner and react negatively toward a minority practitioner. Mental health practitioners from the dominant group may find the conformist client's need to please and appease a powerful force in the counseling relationship because of the client's strong identification with dominant group members. Attempts to explore cultural identity or to focus on feelings may be threatening to the client because these processes may touch on feelings of racial self-hatred and challenge the client's self-deception ("I'm not like other minorities"). Clients at the conformity stage are likely to present problems that are most amenable to problem-solving and goal-oriented counseling approaches.

Minority individuals at the dissonance stage are preoccupied by questions concerning their concept of self, identity, and self-esteem; they are likely to perceive personal problems as related to their cultural identity. Emotional problems develop when these individuals are unable to resolve conflicts that occur between dominant group views and those of their minority group. Clients in the dissonance stage are more culturally aware than conformity clients and are likely to prefer to work with mental health practitioners who possess a good knowledge of the client's cultural group. Counseling approaches that involve considerable self-exploration appear to be best suited for clients at this stage of development.

Minority individuals at the resistance and immersion stage are inclined to view all psychological problems (whether personal or social) as a product of their oppression. These clients are highly unlikely to seek formal counseling regarding their cultural identity. When they do seek counseling, they generally do so in response to a crisis situation and only accept a mental health practitioner from the same ethnic group. Personal issues are so closely related to ethnic identity development that therapy for these clients often takes the form of exposure to, and practice of, the ways and artifacts of their cultures. Clients at this stage who seek counseling are likely to prefer a group setting. In addition, they respond best to approaches that are more action oriented and aimed at external change (challenging racism).

D. W. Sue and D. Sue (1990) believe that most mental health practitioners find minority clients at this stage difficult to work with. These clients often view the practitioner as a symbol of the oppressive establishment, even if the practitioner is a member of the client's ethnic group. They may direct a great deal of anger and distrust toward the practitioner and challenge the practitioner's racial attitudes and role in society.

Clients at the introspection stage are torn between their preponderant identification with their minority group and their need to exercise greater personal freedom. When these individuals are unable to resolve mounting conflict between these two forces, they often seek counseling. Although introspective clients still prefer to see a mental health practitioner from their own cultural group, they will consider practitioners from other cultures if these practitioners hold worldviews similar to those of their clients and appreciate their clients' cultural dilemmas. Mental health practitioners who use a self-exploration and decision-making approach can be most effective with these clients.

Clients at the synergistic stage of identity development have acquired the internal skills and knowledge necessary to exercise a desired level of personal freedom. Their sense of minority identity is well balanced by an appreciation of other cultures. Although discrimination and oppression remain a painful part of their lives, they have greater psychological resources at their disposal to actively engage the problem. Attitudinal similarity between mental health practitioner and client becomes a more important determinant of counseling success than membership-group similarity.

Racial/ethnic identity development occurs along many dimensions. Although the MID model focuses primarily on the evolution of attitudes, changes also occur in the person's cognitive domain (beliefs), affective domain (feelings), and behavioral domain. These aspects of the human condition may evolve at different rates. For example, a person might exhibit the attitudes but not the behavior of the resistance and immersion stage. The possibility that not all aspects of the person's identity will evolve at an identical rate may be the source of much confusion, especially in situations of assessment. Measures developed to assess the stage of ethnic identification are primarily cognitive and may not adequately tap the affective and behavioral domains.

Although the MID model makes good intuitive and clinical sense, it has yet to be adequately tested empirically. One reason has been the lack of an ethnic identity development instrument that can be used across various ethnic populations. However, generic ethnic identity development scales authored by Phinney (1992) and Luhtanen and Crocker (1992) may facilitate research on the MID model in the future. The fact that scores on the Multigroup Ethnic Identity Measure (MEIM; Phinney, 1992) increased over time for minority students (Perron, Vodracek, Skorikov, Tremblay, & Corbiere, 1998) supports the developmental assumption of the MID model. Studies supporting the construct validity of the Collective Self-Esteem Scale (CSES; Luhtanen & Crocker, 1992) reported in Fisher and Moradi (2001) also lend credibility to the MID model.

As authors of the MID model, George Morten, Derald Sue, and I are perhaps negligent for not having submitted it to empirical verification, but each of us has been occupied with research and writing in other areas. However, the model serves a heuristic function, and hopefully will help the reader distinguish and comprehend intragroup differences that are evident in the chapters to follow.

This concludes our discussion of racial/ethnic identity development. However, there are other factors that contribute to variations within ethnic groups that mental health practitioners should become familiar with in order to understand the behaviors and values of their minority group clients. The remaining sections of this chapter examine two other sources of within-group diversity: socioeconomic differences and cultural mistrust.

SOCIOECONOMIC WITHIN-GROUP DIFFERENCES

Mental health practitioners are generally aware of the socioeconomic differences among ethnic groups. For example, most are aware that among those people 25 years of age or older, fewer African Americans (16.6%) and Hispanics (10.6%) than Whites (28.1%) are college graduates (U.S. Bureau of the Census, 2000). Similarly, most are aware that Blacks and Hispanics have much higher rates of poverty than Whites (20.7%, 19.4%, and 5.7%, respectively, in 2001; U.S. Bureau of the Census, 2002).

Unfortunately, mental health practitioners are less familiar with socioeconomic differences *within* ethnic minority groups. Figures like those in the previous paragraph tend to create a stereotype that all African Americans and Hispanics are uneducated and poor. This stereotype is often reinforced by counseling research that fails to take within-group socioeconomic differences into account as an independent variable. This section briefly documents the range of socioeconomic differences within ethnic groups to dispel the myth that all members of these groups are uneducated and poor (or, in the case of Asian Americans, well educated and rich).

Although, in general, African Americans lag behind European Americans educationally, there is great within-group variation among this population with regard to educational attainment. This variation becomes readily evident in a comparison between the least and most educated members of the population. In 1999, 11.5% of African Americans 25 years and older had less than a high school education. At the same time, however, approximately 16.5% had earned at least a bachelor's degree (U.S. Bureau of the Census, 2000). Similar diversity exists for level of income. Again, the within-group income diversity is most easily represented by a comparison of those at the bottom of the scale to those at the top. In 2001, 20% of African American families had a combined annual income of $14,256 or less (U.S. Bureau of the Census, 2001b), well below the poverty level of $17,960 for a family of four that year. However, the 20% of African American families at the high end of the income scale earned $66,523 or more per year, and the top 5% had annual incomes exceeding $110,977. Although overall incomes for African Americans trail those of European Americans considerably (median family incomes in 2001 were $33,598 for African Americans compared to $57,328 for White non-Hispanics), these statistics demonstrate that some African

American families live in abject poverty while others enjoy moderate to high incomes.

Similar data for Hispanics suggest a wide range of educational and income levels as well. About 43% of Hispanics in 1999 had less than a high school education, while 10.6% had completed college (U.S. Bureau of the Census, 2000). As with African Americans, Hispanic family median incomes ($34,490) trail considerably those of White non-Hispanics ($57,328), but not all Hispanics are poor. The 20% of Hispanic families at the lowest end of the income scale had incomes of $16,000 or less, while the top 20% had incomes of $66,040 or more, and the top 5% of families had combined annual incomes exceeding $113,374 (U.S. Bureau of the Census, 2001b). Income diversity within the Hispanic population is, in part, a function of ethnicity. For example, almost 26% of Puerto Ricans and 24% of Mexican Americans lived in poverty in 1999 compared to 17% of Cuban Americans (Therrien & Ramirez, 2001).

Comparable figures for American Indians are not readily available, but based on more dated reports, this ethnic group appears to be less socioeconomically diverse than African Americans and Hispanics. Nonetheless, there is considerable educational and income diversity within this population as well. Although approximately 34% of American Indians 25 years and over had less than a high school education in 1990, another 9% had completed a bachelor's degree or higher, and more than 3% had a graduate or professional degree (U.S. Bureau of the Census, 1995). The median income for American Indian households for the period from 1998 to 2000 was $31,799 per year. However, based on 1990 census data converted to year 2000 dollars, those households living on reservations earned, on average, more than $11,000 a year less than those living off reservations (DeNavas-Walt, Cleveland, & Roemer, 2001).

The figures for Asian and Pacific Islanders are much different, but again they suggest a great disparity in socioeconomic backgrounds within this umbrella ethnic group. For Asian and Pacific Islanders in 2000, 11.7% of the men and 16.6% of the women ages 25 and over had less than a high school education. At the other end of the educational spectrum, 28.7% of all Asian and Pacific Islanders 25 years of age or older had at least a bachelor's degree (U.S. Bureau of the Census, 2001a). For Asians and Pacific Islanders it is particularly important to recognize that discrepancies in education and income are related to specific ethnic group and recentness of immigration. Regarding the latter variable, those groups who have resided in this country for several generations exhibit higher levels of educational attainment than recent arrivals. For example, although 88% of Japanese Americans had graduated from high school in 1994, only 31% of Hmongs had done so. Further, although approximately 58% of Asian Indians had earned at least a bachelor's degree, only 6% or less of Tongans, Cambodians, Laotians, and Hmongs had graduated from college (U.S. Bureau of the Census, 1995).

Similar within-group variations exist for income levels. In 1999, for example, 13.8% of Asian American and Pacific Islander households had annual incomes below $15,000, while 32.7% had annual incomes of $75,000 or above (U.S. Bureau of the Census, 2001c). Given that one in three Asian American families have annual incomes over $75,000, it is easy to overlook the fact that a sizable percentage—13% in 1998—live in poverty (Humes & McKinnon, 2000). As is the case with education, income levels reflect specific ethnic group and recentness of immigration. On the average, Japanese Americans have the highest median family income level, followed in order by Asian Indian, Filipino, Chinese, Korean, Hawaiian, and Vietnamese.

It is important for mental health practitioners to recognize the impact of poverty on mental health needs. Studies show that being poor relates to a number of mental health outcomes. As one example, low-income people experience more stress than do middle- and high-income people. Also, for ethnic minorities being poor is predictive of a fewer number of treatment sessions and quality of treatment provided (S. Sue, Fujino, Hu, Takeuchi, & Zanbe, 1991). However, it is equally important that mental health practitioners recognize that not all African Americans, American Indians, and Hispanics are poor and not all Asian Americans are well off. Failure to recognize the educated, middle-income background of an African American, American Indian, or Hispanic client or the uneducated, low-income background of an Asian American client can be as culturally insensitive as failing to recognize the client's ethnic background. Psychologists, counselors, and other mental health workers need to be vigilant to stereotypes they may hold of racial/ethnic groups based on their knowledge of socioeconomic differences among these groups.

CULTURAL MISTRUST AS A WITHIN-GROUP VARIABLE

Due to the long and continuing history of European American discrimination against African Americans in the United States, many African Americans are mistrustful of European Americans. Grier and Cobbs (1968) labeled this mistrust "healthy Black paranoia" or "healthy cultural paranoia" to indicate that it is an adaptive response to the centuries of oppression experienced by African Americans. Grier and Cobbs and others point out that psychologists, particularly European American psychologists, often mistake this adaptive response for psychopathology, thus contributing to the overdiagnosis of paranoid schizophrenia among African Americans (Whaley, 2001b).

Objecting to the labeling of an adaptive, healthy response as a form of paranoia, F. N. Terrell and S. Terrell (1981) substituted the less value-laden label of "cultural mistrust." These authors reviewed the literature on Black attitudes toward Whites and concluded that, in general, Blacks are mistrustful of Whites in four areas: (a) educational and training settings, (b) political and legal systems, (c) work and business interactions, and (d) interpersonal or social contexts. To measure cultural mistrust across these four areas, they developed the Cultural Mistrust Inventory (CMI). More recently, Landrine and Klonoff (1996) have developed the Distrust of Whites subscale of the African American Acculturation Scale.

Some studies suggest that cultural mistrust discourages many African Americans from using counseling services provided by European Americans (e.g., Nickerson, Helms, & Terrell, 1994; F. Terrell & Terrell, 1984; Thompson, Worthington, & Atkinson, 1994; Watkins & Terrell, 1988; Whaley, 2001c). After reviewing theoretical and empirical articles on cultural mistrust, Nickerson et al.

(1994) concluded that "the notion that Blacks' mistrust of Whites seems to serve as a significant barrier to the counseling process has theoretical merit," and "it seems reasonable to speculate that Black students' reluctance to seek counseling might be related to their mistrust of White counselors" (p. 379). Whaley (2001b) points out that for some African Americans cultural mistrust may reflect a reaction to an unpleasant or unproductive encounter with a White therapist. For others it may indicate mistrust of an institution established by Whites. In the latter case, the mistrust may generalize to Black mental health practitioners.

In the most extensive review of cultural mistrust research to date, Whaley (2001a) conducted a meta-analysis of 22 studies and found that "the correlations of the cultural mistrust variable with measures of attitudes and behaviors across diverse psychosocial domains demonstrated a medium effect size" (p. 523). Further, he concluded that (a) cultural mistrust is not unique to the mental health setting and presumably reflects a general mistrust of Whites within the Black community, (b) cultural mistrust correlates negatively with age, and (c) the CMI is a valid and reliable measure of cultural mistrust for African Americans. In a subsequent elaboration of his literature review and meta-analysis, Whaley (2001b) concluded that "cultural mistrust has a significant impact on the attitudes and behaviors of African Americans, especially mental health services use" (p. 560).

Whaley (2001a) cited several implications of his meta-analysis. One implication is that mental health practitioners should be willing to address the issue of cultural mistrust when providing mental health services to African American clients. A second is that White mental health practitioners need to realize that they are not viewed as different from other European Americans just because they are working in a mental health setting. A third is that, because mistrust is greater among youths than adults, mental health practitioners "must be willing to explore the potential developmental implications of such differences" (p. 526). Whaley also urged practitioners and researchers to use the total score on the CMI to assess cultural mistrust and not just those subscales that appear to be most relevant to a mental health context.

These theoretically consistent findings suggest that cultural mistrust is an important variable for distinguishing within-group differences among African Americans, one with important implications for mental health practitioners who are providing counseling services for African American clients. Although the construct appears to have similar relevance for other racial/ethnic minority groups, research that extends cultural mistrust to other populations is lacking.

REFERENCES

Berry, B. (1965). *Ethnic and race relations.* Boston: Houghton Mifflin.

Berry, J. W. (1990). Psychology of acculturation: Understanding individuals moving between cultures. In R. W. Brislin (Ed.), *Applied cross-cultural psychology* (pp. 232–253). Newbury Park, CA: Sage.

Berry, J. W. (1994). Acculturation and psychological adaptation: An overview. In A. M. Bouvy, F. J. R. van de Vijver, P. Boski, & P. Schmitz (Eds.), *Journeys into cross-cultural psychology.* Amsterdam: Swets and Zeitlinger.

Berry, J. W. (1997). Immigration, acculturation, and adaptation. *Applied Psychology: An International Review, 46,* 5–68.

Berry, J. W., & Kim, U. (1988). Acculturation and mental health. In P. Dasen, J. W. Berry, & N. Sartorius (Eds.), *Health and cross-cultural psychology* (pp. 207–236). Newbury Park, CA: Sage.

Berry, J. W., Kim, U., Power, S., Young, M., & Bajaki, M. (1989). Acculturation attitudes in plural societies. *Applied Psychology: An International Review, 38,* 185–206.

Berry, J. W., Trimble, J., & Olmeda, E. (1986). The assessment of acculturation. In W. J. Lonner & J. W. Berry (Eds.), *Field methods in cross-cultural research* (pp. 291–324). Newbury Park, CA: Sage.

Carter, R. T., & Helms, J. E. (1987). The relationship between Black value-orientation and racial identity attitudes. *Measurement and Evaluation in Counseling and Development, 19*(4), 185–195.

Cass, V. C. (1979). Homosexual identity formation: A theoretical model. *Journal of Homosexuality, 4,* 219–235.

Cross, W. E., Jr. (1970, April). *The black experience viewed as a process: A crude model for black self-actualization.* Paper presented at the Thirty-fourth Annual Meeting of the Association of Social and Behavioral Scientists, Tallahassee, FL.

Cross, W. E., Jr. (1971). The Negro-to-Black conversion experience: Toward a psychology of Black liberation. *Black World, 20*(9), 13–27.

Cross, W. E., Jr. (1978). The Cross and Thomas models of psychological Nigresence. *Journal of Black Psychology, 5*(1), 13–19.

Cross, W. E., Jr. (1991). *Shades of Black: Diversity of African-American identity.* Philadelphia, PA: Temple University Press.

Cross, W. E., Jr. (1995). The psychology of Nigrescence: Revising the Cross model. In J. G. Ponterotto, J. M. Casas, L. A. Suzuki, & C. M. Alexander (Eds.), *Handbook of multicultural counseling* (pp. 93–122). Thousand Oaks, CA: Sage.

Cross, W. E., Jr. (2001). Nigrescence theory and measurement: Introducing the Cross Racial Identity Scale. In J. G. Ponterotto, J. M. Casas, L. A. Suzuki, & C. M. Alexander (Eds.), *Handbook of multicultural counseling* (2nd ed., pp. 371–393). Thousand Oaks, CA: Sage.

Cuellar, I., Arnold, B., & Maldonado, R. (1995). Acculturation Rating Scale for Mexican Americans–II: A revision of the original ARSMA scale. *Hispanic Journal of Behavioral Sciences, 17,* 275–304.

de Anda, D. (1984). Bicultural socialization: Factors affecting the minority experience. *Social Work, 29,* 101–107.

DeNavas-Walt, C., Cleveland, R. W., & Roemer, M. I. (2001). *Money income in the United States, 2000* (Current population report, P60-213). Washington, DC: U.S. Dept. of Commerce, Economics and Statistics Administration.

Downing, N. E., & Roush, K. L. (1985). From passive acceptance to active commitment: A model of feminist identity development for women. *The Counseling Psychologist, 13,* 695–709.

Fischer, A. R., & Moradi, B. (2001). Racial and ethnic identity: Recent developments and needed directions. In J. G. Ponterotto, J. M. Casas, L. A. Suzuki,

& C. M. Alexander (Eds.), *Handbook of multicultural counseling* (pp. 341–370). Thousand Oaks, CA: Sage.

Ford, R. C. (1987). Cultural awareness and cross-cultural counseling. *International Journal for the Advancement of Counselling, 10*(1), 71–78.

Gay, G. (1984). Implications of selected models of ethnic identity development for educators. *The Journal of Negro Education, 54*(1), 43–52.

Grier, W. H., & Cobbs, P. M. (1968). *Black rage.* New York: Basic Books.

Hall, W. S., Cross, W. E., & Freedle, R. (1972). Stages in the development of Black awareness: An exploratory investigation. In R. I. Jones (Ed.), *Black psychology* (pp. 156–165). New York: Harper and Row.

Helms, J. E. (1984). Toward a theoretical explanation of the effects of race on counseling: A Black and White model. *The Counseling Psychologist, 12,* 153–165.

Helms, J. E. (1985). Cultural identity in the treatment process. In P. Pedersen (Ed.), *Handbook of cross-cultural counseling and therapy.* Westport, CT: Greenwood Press.

Helms, J. E. (1990). *Black and White racial identity: Theory, research, and practice.* Westport, CT: Greenwood Press.

Helms, J. E. (1995). An update of Helms's White and people of color racial identity models. In J. G. Ponterotto, J. M. Casas, L. A. Suzuki, and C. M. Alexander (Eds.), *Handbook of Multicultural Counseling* (pp. 181–198). Thousand Oaks, CA: Sage.

Helms, J. E., & Carter, R. T. (1991). Relationships of White and Black racial identity attitudes and demographic similarity to counselor preferences. *Journal of Counseling Psychology, 38,* 446–457.

Helms, J. E., & Cook, D. A. (1999). *Using race and culture in counseling and psychotherapy: Theory and process.* Boston: Allyn and Bacon.

Helms, J. E., & Parham, T. A. (1990). The relationship between Black racial identity attitudes and cognitive styles. In J. E. Helms (Ed.), *Black and White racial identity: Theory, research, and practice* (pp. 119–131). Westport, CT: Greenwood Press.

Highlen, P. S., Reynolds, A. L., Adams, E. M., Hanley, C. P., Myers, L. J., Cox, C. I., & Speight, S. L. (1988, August). *Self-identity development model of oppressed people: Inclusive model for all?* Paper presented at the meeting of the American Psychological Association, Atlanta, GA.

Ho, D. Y. F. (1995). Internalized culture, culturocentrism, and transcendence. *The Counseling Psychologist, 23,* 4–24.

Humes, K., & McKinnon, J. (2000). *The Asian and Pacific Islander population in the United States* (Current Population Report P20-529). Washington, DC: U.S. Bureau of the Census. Retrieved September 30, 2002, from www.census.gov/prod/2000pubs/p20-529.pdf

Jackson, B. (1975). Black identity development. *MEFORM: Journal of Educational Diversity and Innovation, 2,* 19–25.

Keefe, S. E. (1980). Acculturation and the extended family among urban Mexican Americans. In A. M. Padilla (Ed.), *Acculturation: Theory, models, and some new findings* (pp. 85–110). Boulder, CO: Westview Press.

Kim, B. S. K., & Abreu, J. M. (2001). Acculturation measurement: Theory, current instruments, and future directions. In J. G. Ponterotto, J. M. Casas, L. A. Suzuki, & C. M. Alexander (Eds.), *Handbook of multicultural counseling* (2nd ed., pp. 394–424). Thousand Oaks, CA: Sage.

Kim, B. S. K., Atkinson, D. R., & Yang, P. H. (1999). The Asian Values Scale: Development, factor analysis, validation, and reliability. *Journal of Counseling Psychology, 46,* 342–352.

Landrine, H., & Klonoff, E. A. (1994). The African American Acculturation Scale: Development, reliability, and validity. *Journal of Black Psychology, 20,* 104–127.

Landrine, H., & Klonoff, E. A. (1996). *African American acculturation: Deconstructing race and reviving culture.* Thousand Oaks, CA: Sage.

Luhtanen, R., & Crocker, J. (1992). A collective self-esteem scale: Self-evaluation of one's social identity. *Personality and Social Psychology Bulletin, 18,* 302–318.

Marin, G. (1992). Issues in the measurement of acculturation among Hispanics. In K. F. Geisinger (Ed.), *Psychological testing of Hispanics* (pp. 235–251). Washington, DC: American Psychological Association.

Myers, L. J., Speight, S. L., Highlen, P. S., Cox, C. I., Reynolds, A. L., Adams, E. M., & Hanley, T. C. (1991). Identity development and world view: Toward an optimal conceptualization. *Journal of Counseling and Development, 70,* 54–63.

Neidert, L. J., & Farley, R. (1985). Assimilation in the United States: An analysis of ethnic and generation differences in status and achievement. *American Sociological Review, 50,* 840–850.

Nickerson, K. J., Helms, J. E., & Terrell, F. (1994). Cultural mistrust, opinions about mental illness, and Black students' attitudes toward seeking psychological help from White counselors. *Journal of Counseling Psychology, 41,* 378–385.

Novak, M. (1972). *The rise of the unmeltable ethnics.* New York: MacMillan.

Oberg, K. (1954). *Culture shock.* Indianapolis, IN: Bobbs-Merrill Series in Social Sciences.

Olmedo, E. L. (1979). Acculturation: A psychometric perspective. *American Psychologist, 34,* 1061–1070.

Padilla, A. M. (1980a). *Acculturation: Theory, models, and some new findings.* Boulder, CO: Westview Press.

Padilla, A. M. (1980b). The role of cultural awareness and ethnic loyalty in acculturation. In A. M. Padilla (Ed.), *Acculturation: Theory, models, and some new findings* (pp. 47–84). Boulder, CO: Westview Press.

Parham, T. A., & Helms, J. E. (1981). The influence of black students' racial identity attitudes on preference for counselor's race. *Journal of Counseling Psychology, 28,* 250–257.

Parham, T. A., & Helms, J. E. (1985a). Attitudes of racial identity and self-esteem of Black students: An exploratory investigation. *Journal of College Student Personnel, 26*(2), 143–146.

Parham, T. A., & Helms, J. E. (1985b). Relation of racial identity attitudes to self-actualization and affective states of Black students. *Journal of Counseling Psychology, 32,* 431–440.

Park, R. E. (1928). Human migration and the marginal man. *American Journal of Sociology, 33,* 881–893.

Park, R. E. (1950). *Race and culture.* Glencoe, IL: Free Press.

Park, R. E., & Burgess, E. W. (1921). *Introduction to the science of sociology.* Chicago: University of Chicago Press.

Perron, J., Vondracek, F. W., Skorikov, V. B., Tremblay, C., Corbiere, M. (1998). A longitudinal study of vocational maturity and ethnic identity development. *Journal of Vocational Behavior, 52,* 409–424.

Phelps, R. E., Taylor, J. D., & Gerard, P. A. (2001). Cultural mistrust, ethnic identity, racial identity, and self-esteem among ethnically diverse black students. *Journal of Counseling and Development, 79,* 209–216.

Phinney, J. S. (1992). The Multigroup Ethnic Identity Measure: A new scale for use with diverse groups. *Journal of Adolescent Research, 7,* 156–176.

Phinney, J. S. (1996). When we talk about American ethnic groups, what do we mean? *American Psychologist, 51,* 918–927.

Ponterotto, J. G. (1988). Racial consciousness development among White counselor trainees: A stage model. *Journal of Multicultural Counseling and Development, 16,* 146–156.

Poston, W. S. C. (1990). The biracial identity development model: A needed addition. *Journal of Counseling and Development, 69,* 152–155.

Redfield, R., Linton, R., & Herskovits, M. (1936). Memorandum on the study of acculturation. *American Anthropologist, 37,* 149–152.

Ruelas, S. R., Atkinson, D. R., & Ramos-Sanchez, L. (1998). Counselor helping model, participant ethnicity and acculturation level, and perceived counselor credibility. *Journal of Counseling Psychology, 45,* 98–103.

Ruiz, A. S. (1990). Ethnic identity: Crisis and resolution. *Journal of Multicultural Counseling and Development, 18,* 29–40.

Segall, M. H., Lonner, W. J., & Berry, J. W. (1998). Cross-cultural psychology as a scholarly discipline: On the flowering of culture in behavioral research. *American Psychologist, 53,* 1101–1110.

Smith, E. J. (1991). Ethnic identity development: Toward the development of a theory within the context of majority/minority status. *Journal of Counseling and Development, 70,* 181–188.

Stonequist, E. V. (1937). *The marginal man.* New York: Charles Scribner's Sons.

Stonequist, E. V. (1961). *The marginal man: A study in personality and culture conflict.* New York: Russell and Russell.

Sue, D. W., & Sue, D. (1990). *Counseling the culturally different: Theory and practice.* New York: Wiley.

Sue, S., Chun, C., & Gee, K. (1995). Ethnic minority intervention and treatment research. In J. F. Aponte, R. Young-Rivers, & J. Wohl (Eds.), *Psychological interventions and cultural diversity* (pp. 266–282). Boston: Allyn and Bacon.

Sue, S., Fujino, D. C., Hu, L. T., Takeuchi, D. T., & Zanbe, N. W. S. (1991). Community mental health services for ethnic minority groups: A test of the cultural responsiveness hypothesis. *Journal of Counseling Psychology, 59,* 533–540.

Sue, S., & Sue, D. W. (1971). Chinese-American personality and mental health. *Amerasia Journal, 1,* 36–49.

Suinn, R. M., Rickard-Figueroa, K., Lew, S., & Vigil, P. (1987). The Suinn-Lew Asian Self-Identity Acculturation Scale: An initial report. *Educational and Psychological Measurement, 47,* 401–407.

Terrell, F. N., & Terrell, S. (1981). An inventory to measure cultural mistrust among Blacks. *Western Journal of Black Studies, 5,* 180–184.

Terrell, F., & Terrill, S. (1984). Race of the counselor, client sex, cultural mistrust level, and premature termination from counseling among Black clients. *Journal of Counseling Psychology, 31,* 371–375.

Therrien, M., & Ramirez, R. R. (2001). *The Hispanic population in the United States* (Current Populations Report P20-535). Washington, DC: U.S. Census Bureau. Retrieved September 30, 2002, from www.census.gov/population/socdcmo/hispanic/p20 535/p20-535.pdf

Thompson, C. E., Worthington, R., & Atkinson, D. R. (1994). Counselor content orientation, counselor race, and Black women's cultural mistrust and self-disclosures. *Journal of Counseling Psychology, 41,* 155–161.

Troiden, R. R. (1989). The formation of homosexual identities. *Journal of Homosexuality, 17,* 43–73.

U.S. Bureau of the Census. (1995). *Population profile of the United States: 1995.* Current Population Reports, Series P23-189. Washington, DC: U.S. Government Printing Office.

U.S. Bureau of the Census. (2000). *Educational attainment in the United States: March 2000.* Retrieved September 27, 2002, from www.census.gov/population/socdemo/cducation/p20 536.html

U.S. Bureau of the Census. (2001a). *Educational attainment of the population 25 years and over by sex and race and Hispanic origin: March 2000.* Retrieved September 30, 2002, from www.census.gov/population/socdemo/race/api/ppl-146/tab07.pdf

U.S. Bureau of the Census. (2001b). *Historical income tables—families.* Retrieved September 30, 2002, from www.ccnsus.gov/hhes/income/histinc/incfamdet.html

U.S. Bureau of the Census. (2001c). *Total money income in 1999 of households by type, and race and Hispanic origin of householder: March 2000.* Retrieved September 30, 2002, from www.census.gov/population/socdemo/race/api/ppl-146/tab14.pdf

U.S. Bureau of the Census. (2002). *Historical poverty tables.* Retrieved September 30, 2002, from www.census.gov/hhes/poverty/histpov/hstpov4.html

Vandiver, B. J., Fhagen-Smith, P. E., Cokley, K. O., Cross, W. E., Jr., Worrell, F. C. (2001). Cross's nigrescence model: From theory to scale to theory. *Journal of Multicultural Counseling & Development, 29,* 174–200.

Vontress, C. E. (1971). Racial differences: Impediments to rapport. *Journal of Counseling Psychology, 18,* 7–13.

Watkins, C. E., & Terrell, F. (1988). Mistrust level and its effects on counseling expectations in Black client–White counselor relationships: An analogue study. *Journal of Counseling Psychology, 35,* 194–197.

Whaley, A. L. (2001a). Cultural mistrust and mental health services for African Americans: A review and meta-analysis. *The Counseling Psychologist, 29,* 513–531.

Whaley, A. L. (2001b). Cultural mistrust: An important psychological construct for diagnosis and treatment of African Americans. *Professional Psychology: Research and Practice, 32,* 555–562.

Whaley, A. L. (2001c). Cultural mistrust of White mental health clinicians among African Americans with severe mental illness. *American Journal of Orthopsychiatry, 71,* 252–256.

Wilson, J. W., & Constantine, M. G. (1999). Racial identity attitudes, self-concept, and perceived family cohesion in Black college students. *Journal of Black Studies, 29,* 354–366.

Winkelman, M. (1994). Cultural shock and adaptation. *Journal of Counseling and Development, 73,* 121–126.

Yoshioka, R. B., Tashima, N., Chew, M., & Maruse, K. (1981). *Mental health services for Pacific/Asian Americans.* San Francisco: Pacific Asian Mental Health Project.

CHAPTER 3

Addressing the
Mental Health Needs
of Ethnic Minorities

In the first edition of this book, several authors chastised mental health practitioners for failing to adequately address the mental health needs of ethnic minorities. That same year, based on a review of national data, the Special Populations Task Force of the President's Commission on Mental Health concluded that racial/ethnic minorities "are clearly underserved or inappropriately served by the current mental health system in this country" (Special Populations, 1978, p. 73). Fortunately, much more attention is currently being given to the mental health needs of ethnic minorities. Nevertheless, as this chapter points out, more progress needs to be made.

During the 1970s professional organizations representing mental health practitioners (American Personnel and Guidance Association, now called the American Counseling Association, or ACA) and psychologists (American Psychological Association, or APA) were just beginning to address issues related to ethnic minorities. The ACA became the first of these two organizations to create a division that addressed ethnic minority issues when it established The Association for Non-White Concerns in Personnel and Guidance (later renamed the Association for Multicultural Counseling and Development) in 1972. In 1979 the APA took an important step when it amended its accreditation standards to require formal training in cross-cultural issues (Mio & Morris, 1990). Two years later it revised its ethical guidelines and, in the process, mandated that psychologists receive training in cultural differences. In January 1987 the APA established the Society of Psychological Study of Ethnic Minority Issues (Division 45). Three years later it published *Guidelines for Providers of Psychological Services to Ethnic, Linguistic, and Culturally Diverse Populations* (American Psychological Association, 1990). Most recently, in August 2002 the APA Council of Representatives adopted as policy the Guidelines on Multicultural Education, Training, Research, Practice, and Organizational Change for Psychologists.

The increased attention to ethnic minority issues within ACA, APA, and other mental health organizations can be attributed in part to the political activities of racial/ethnic minority members and their nonminority supporters. For example, in 1969 the Black Student Psychological Association presented a number of demands to the APA Council of Representatives that directed attention to the underrepresentation of ethnic minorities in professional psychology. Also, advocates for racial/ethnic minority issues were active at the 1973 Vail Conference, the 1975 Austin Conference, and the 1978 Dulles Conference, all of which addressed at some level the need to expand the roles of culturally diverse people in psychology (D. W. Sue, 1990). The establishment of Division 45 was the direct result of an intense lobbying effort by ethnic minority members of APA.

Thus, in terms of formalized policy and procedures within professional organizations, much has been accomplished since the 1970s. Unfortunately, however, at the service delivery level there is evidence that much remains to be done. A recent supplement to the Surgeon General's report on mental health noted that although most people with diagnosable mental disorders fail to receive treatment, ethnic minorities in particular experience disparities in mental health services (Department of Health and Human Services [DHHS], 2001). This chapter examines ethnic minority needs for mental health services as well as disparities in mental health services experienced by ethnic minorities.

MENTAL HEALTH NEEDS AMONG ETHNIC MINORITIES

It has been common practice historically to use mental health treatment rates to estimate ethnic minority mental health needs. These estimates in turn have been used for a variety of purposes, including justifying mental health resource allocations and, in some instances, promoting racist views of ethnic minorities and their culture. An example of the latter use of treatment rate is provided by Williams (as cited in Griffith & Gonzalez, 1994), who found data published in the mid-nineteenth century suggesting that Blacks who were freed and living in the northern states had high rates of mental illness. These data were then used to argue that Blacks were incapable of dealing with the stresses of being free and thus were better off in slavery.

Conversely, many mental health providers interpreted the low treatment rates for ethnic minorities from the late nineteenth century through the 1970s as evidence that minorities in general, and Asian Americans and Hispanic Americans in particular, experienced fewer or less severe mental health problems than did European Americans (Jones & Gray, 1986; Leong, Wagner, & Tata, 1995; D. W. Sue, 1994). The conclusion that ethnic minorities had fewer mental health problems in turn was used to justify mental health policies that largely ignored the special psychological needs of ethnic populations (Schwab, as cited in Griffith & Gonzalez, 1994).

More recently, prevalence of mental disorders has been used as a measure of need among ethnic groups. In one of the largest and most scientific attempts to date to determine the actual prevalence rate of mental disorders in the United States, the National Institute of Mental Health sponsored the Epidemiological Catchment Area (ECA) survey in the early 1980s, which assessed the prevalence of 30 major psychiatric disorders through standardized interviews with 20,000 Americans in five states. Some researchers have examined the ECA data and data from other large samples and concluded that racial/ethnic differences exist in the prevalence of mental disorders. For example, Adebimpe (1994) reviewed the ECA data and concluded that "race-related differences were found in rates of alcoholism, phobic disorders, generalized anxiety disorder, and somatization disorder, which were more frequent among blacks, and in obsessive-compulsive disorder, which was less frequent" (p. 27). More recently, Kessler and Zhao (1999) examined data from the National Comorbidity Survey (NCS), a household survey of more than 8,000 people in 34 states and 174 counties conducted in the early 1990s, and concluded that "Blacks . . . have significantly *lower* prevalences of mood disorders, substance use disorders, and lifetime comorbidity than whites," whereas "Hispanics . . . have significantly *higher* prevalences of mood disorders and active comorbidity than non-Hispanic whites" (p. 141; italics added).

In general, however, studies and reviews of research based on ECA and NCS data have concluded that although African Americans report higher levels of symptoms than European Americans do, symptom differences are not maintained when adjustments are made for sociodemographic differences (Jones-Webb & Snowden, 1993; Lefley, 1994). For example, Horwath, Johnson, and Hornig (1994) examined data on 4,287 African Americans and 12,142 White Americans from the ECA survey and concluded that "the lifetime prevalence of panic disorder is similar in white and African-American populations" (p. 60). Similarly, Friedman, Paradis, and Hatch (1994) reported finding that "the presenting symptoms and clinical characteristics of African American and white patients with panic disorder and agoraphobia were very similar" (p. 142). Analyses of ECA data like these led Lefley (1994) to conclude that "although there were significant ethnic differences in prevalence rates for some of these disorders, the differences disappeared when the data were controlled for age, gender, marital status, and most importantly, socioeconomic status" (p. 225).

In reality, socioeconomic status, community context, and other factors may interact with ethnicity to affect mental health needs. Kessler and Neighbors (1986) found strong evidence that race is related to psychological distress at lower income levels but not at higher income levels, suggesting that race and class have interactive effects on distress. Furthermore, psychological stress may be exacerbated or attenuated by the community context. Using ECA data for four metropolitan areas, Schwabe and Kodras (2000) examined the percentage of respondents who reported being distressed (depressed or anxious) by race (Black or White), socioeconomic status, and community context. Consistent with Kessler and Neighbor's findings, Schwabe and Kodras found that when they aggregated the data, distress was greatest among Blacks with the lowest socioeconomic status and that racial disparities attenuated with increases in socioeconomic status. However, they also found that in Baltimore, where Blacks were in the numerical majority, where there was a strong Black political movement, and where there were declining job opportunities for Whites, low-income Whites experienced more distress than low-income Blacks. Their results led them to conclude that

> Race should not be conflated with class nor with culture because there exists no
> distinct, universal white or black culture that produces consistent patterns of
> health and illness across time and place. Rather, race differences in psychological distress across socioeconomic levels appear to be conditioned by the setting

in which blacks and whites live, work, and interact, including economic opportunities, political power, and historical traditions in race relations. (p. 256)

This study helps explain the conflicting findings of earlier studies, which were
often carried out in a single community. It also suggests that it is the stress of feeling disadvantaged and powerless that may promote psychological distress and not
ethnicity per se.

Thus, when adjusted for other contributing factors (e.g., socioeconomic
level, education, urban versus rural setting, incarceration status, substance abuse),
the prevalence of distress and mental illness among ethnic minorities is about the
same as that experienced by European Americans. That was basically the conclusion published in a recent supplement (DHHS, 2001b) to the Surgeon General's
report on mental illness (DHHS, 1999). Summarizing much of the research to
date, the supplement concluded that major mental disorders are found in every
racial and ethnic group and in every region of the world. Furthermore, the report
suggested that when adjusted for other contributing factors, the prevalence of
mental disorders (21%) is similar across racial and ethnic groups in the United
States. In other words, the report is stating that all other things being equal, mental disorders are not a function of race or ethnicity. Only the most ardent racist
would suggest that being African American, for example, *causes* someone to be
mentally ill.

However, other things never are equal. Adjusting for "other contributing factors" tends to mask the fact that ethnic minorities are subjected to a disproportionate share of the conditions that contribute to mental illness. Thus, the supplement to the Surgeon General's report (DHHS, 2001b) pointed out that ethnic
minorities are overrepresented in populations that are vulnerable to mental health
problems; in particular, they are overrepresented at the lower income levels. Furthermore, living at or below poverty level subjects many ethnic minorities to other
stressors that contribute to mental health problems. The supplement's executive
summary (DHHS, 2001a) states that

> Ethnic and racial minorities in the United States face a social and economic en-
> vironment of inequality that includes greater exposure to racism, discrimination,
> violence, and poverty. Living in poverty has the most measurable effect on the
> rates of mental illness. People in the lowest strata of income, education, and oc-
> cupation (known as socioeconomic status) are about two to three times more
> likely than those in the highest strata to have a mental disorder. (p. 8)

Thus, even though ethnicity is not directly related to mental illness, the fact
that ethnic minorities are "overrepresented among the conditions thought to generate susceptibility to, or prolong the effects of, mental illness, such as poverty,
racism, homelessness, incarceration, substance abuse, and poor access to health
care" (National Advisory Workgroup, 2001) means that a disproportionate share
of ethnic minorities experience mental health concerns. And most important, the
2001 supplement to the Surgeon General's report concluded that compared to
White Americans, ethnic minorities experience disparities in the mental health
services that they receive.

DISPARITIES IN MENTAL HEALTH SERVICES

According to the Surgeon General (DHHS, 2001), the disparities in mental health services experienced by ethnic minorities are evident in the following areas: mental health services accessibility, mental health services utilization, quality of treatment, and mental health research. This remainder of this chapter addresses these disparities.

Disparities in Access to Mental Health Services

Access to mental health services is a function of the availability and affordability of services. Availability of mental health services includes factors such as proximity of the services, nearness of the services to public transportation, and appropriateness of services. Appropriateness refers to the availability of mental health service providers who speak the client's language, are aware of and knowledgeable about cultural issues, can provide unbiased service, and can offer culturally relevant interventions.

Availability of Mental Health Services   As suggested, availability of appropriate mental health services is one component of accessibility. It is also the component of availability that has received the most attention by critics of mental health services for ethnic minorities. Appropriate mental health services for ethnic minorities are provided by language appropriate, culturally sensitive, multiculturally competent mental health practitioners. S. Sue and Zane (1987) pointed out that "the single most important explanation for the problems in service delivery (for ethnic minorities) involves the inability of therapists to provide culturally responsive forms of treatment" (p. 37).

For some ethnic minority clients, culturally responsive treatment needs to be provided by an ethnically similar mental health practitioner. In an extensive review of process and outcome research, Atkinson and Lowe (1995) found "substantial evidence that treatment outcomes are enhanced by matching therapist and client on the basis of language and ethnicity" (p. 397). Even when language is not an issue, there is overwhelming evidence that ethnic minorities prefer to work with an ethnically similar practitioner. For example, Atkinson and Lowe found that "Other things being equal, ethnic minority participants prefer an ethnically similar counselor over an ethnically dissimilar counselor" (p. 392). A study by Blank, Tetrick, Brinkley, Smith, and Doheny (1994) reinforced this conclusion. These researchers found that ethnically similar case manager and client dyads resulted in more total client visits than did ethnically dissimilar dyads. American Indians who want to see an ethnically similar psychiatrist, for example, could face a major accessibility problem: There are only 1.5 American Indian/Alaska Native psychiatrists per 100,000 members of this population (DHHS, 2001). When culturally appropriate programs are not offered, ethnic minority clients will not avail themselves of mental health services even if these services are publicly supported.

On a more positive note, evidence suggests that when ethnicity-specific mental health programs are made available to ethnic minority communities, members of those communities make use of them. According to Takeuchi, Sue, and Yeh (1995):

> ethnicity-specific mental health programs . . . typically involve the recruitment of ethnic personnel, modifications in treatment practices that are presumably more culturally appropriate, and development of an atmosphere in which services are provided in a culturally familiar context. Most are located in communities with relatively large ethnic populations and serve a predominantly ethnic clientele. (p. 638)

To determine if ethnicity-specific mental health programs have more positive effects than mainstream mental health programs for ethnic minority clients, Takeuchi et al. (1995) examined the return rates, total number of treatment sessions, and therapist ratings at termination for African Americans, Asian Americans, Mexican Americans, and Whites using Los Angeles County Department of Mental Health services over a 6-year period ending in 1988. The results indicated that ethnic minority clients involved in ethnicity-specific mental health programs are more likely to continue beyond one session and to stay for more total sessions than those ethnic minority clients involved in a conventional mental health programs. This finding has major implications for ethnic minority clients because treatment outcomes tend to improve with length of treatment.

Interestingly, culturally appropriate treatment provided in a culturally familiar context was apparently a more important determinant of use than having an ethnically similar mental health practitioner. For the most part, participation in an ethnicity-specific program produced a higher return rate and more total number of treatments regardless of whether clients were ethnically matched with their practitioner.

There is also evidence that ethnic minorities are more likely to utilize mental health services when these minorities constitute a majority of the clients being served. Snowden and Hu (1996) examined the records of approximately 25,000 clients using a large, ethnically diverse mental health system over a 3-year period. The proportion of ethnic minorities in a program was found to be a significant predictor of utilization; that is, the greater the proportion of minorities in the program, the longer minorities utilized the services offered by the program. Presumably, a mental health system with a high proportion of minority clients develops a minority-oriented atmosphere, which in turn promotes favorable utilization patterns.

Affordability of Mental Health Services   Affordability of mental health services refers to both the cost of the services and the ability to pay for them. During the 1980s and early 1990s, the provision of psychological services became increasingly privatized. The cost of private mental health services is prohibitive for those on low incomes; indeed, middle-class families often must rely on their insurance plans to pay for physical and mental health care. According to the Surgeon General's Report on Mental Health (DHHS, 2001), poverty disproportionately affects ethnic minorities. Citing 1999 Census Bureau data, the report indicated that whereas only 8% of Whites are poor, 11% of Asian Americans and Pacific Islanders, 23% of Hispanics,

24% of African Americans, and 26% of American Indians and Alaska Natives have incomes below the poverty level. Compounding this problem is the fact that many ethnic minority individuals hold unskilled, temporary jobs that provide no health insurance. According to a recently released report by the U.S. Census Bureau (2001), Hispanics (66.8%) were the least likely ethnic minority group to be covered by health insurance in 2001, followed by American Indians and Alaska Natives (72.9% based on a 3-year average), Blacks (81.0%), and Asians and Pacific Islanders (81.8%). In contrast, 90.0% of Whites had insurance coverage in 2001.

These data help explain why many ethnic minorities do not receive mental health services to address their psychological problems. Ethnic minorities with low incomes who do not have mental health coverage through an insurance policy, who do not have surplus financial resources for mental health services, and who do not qualify for Medicare generally cannot afford private mental health services and therefore must look to public (government-sponsored) or nonprofit mental health services for help with psychological problems. For example, Rosenheck and Fontana (1994) reported that

> Black veterans and Mexican Hispanic veterans were significantly less likely than white veterans to have used non-VA mental health services or self-help groups, after adjusting for health status and other factors. [However,] there were no differences between ethnocultural groups in use of VA mental health services. (p. 685)

Unfortunately, however, public mental health services are often stretched to the point that the quality of services are diminished. Public agencies, like county and community mental health centers, are often faced with diminished funding from local, state, and federal governments at the same time that they have to provide services to severely disabled individuals who in the past would have been cared for in state hospitals. As a result, many community and county mental health agencies, by necessity, have had to restrict their services to providing medication-based or crisis-oriented interventions for people with chronic mental disorders. Furthermore, Gottesfeld (1995) contends that mental health services are underused by minority clients because

> public and nonprofit organizations have no financial incentives to retain minority mental patients. Funding does not depend on retention and usually there is a waiting list of patients to replace those who drop out. Incentives for mental health organizations to make changes to retain minority patients do not seem to exist at the present time. (p. 210)

In conclusion, then, a disproportionate share of ethnic minorities cannot afford private mental health services, and appropriate public mental health services are often not available.

Disparities in Use of Mental Health Services

Research consistently has provided evidence that racial and ethnic minorities utilize mental health services differently than European Americans do. A pattern of underutilization of outpatient services has been documented for African Americans.

In his review of studies based on data from the Epidemiological Catchment Area survey, Adebimpe (1994) found that fewer Blacks than Whites who met diagnostic criteria for depression sought help in the 6-month period before the study. Similarly, Greene, Jackson, and Neighbors (1993) found that older African Americans are more likely than their younger counterparts not to seek any help, either formal or informal, for serious personal problems. Furthermore, they discovered that a substantial percentage of older African Americans did not utilize any type of help. "When faced with a serious crisis, they have no access whatsoever to outside sources of assistance" (p. 197).

Differential utilization rates have been documented for other ethnic groups as well. Cheung and Snowden (1990) reviewed data from community-based surveys of mental health use and concluded that compared to Whites: (1) Asian Americans and Latinos are underrepresented, (2) African Americans are underrepresented in some surveys and overrepresented in others, and (3) little is known about Native American use rate. In a major study that sampled more than 1.2 million federal employees and their families, Padgett, Patrick, Burns, and Schlesinger (1994) found that Black and Hispanic women were less likely to use outpatient mental health services than White women, even after controlling for socioeconomic and other factors. A more recent study by Alvidrez (1999) reinforced this finding: European American women were much more likely than African American women or Latinas to have seen a mental health professional in the past for a personal or emotional problem. In his review of research on Asian American use of inpatient and outpatient mental health services, Leong (1994) concluded that "studies of Asian-American clients in both mental health hospitals and community mental health centers have found that they tend to have a lower rate of utilization of mental health services" (p. 83) than other ethnic groups.

In addition, there is evidence that when racial/ethnic minorities make an initial contact with a mental health service they are less likely than their European American counterparts to return for subsequent counseling (Barnes, 1994). S. Sue, Fujino, Hu, Takeuchi, and Zane (1991), examining data from the Los Angeles County mental heath system, found that African Americans average fewer sessions and terminate outpatient services sooner than European Americans do. A recent large-scale study by Edlund et al. (2002) using data from the National Comorbidity Survey (NCS) and the Mental Health Supplement to the Ontario (Canada) Health Survey (OHS) suggests that ethnic minorities may drop out sooner than White Americans and Canadians. Edlund et al. examined the dropout patterns for the 830 respondents in the NCS and 431 respondents in the OHS who had been in treatment for problems with emotions, nerves, mental health, or use of alcohol or drugs during the 12 months prior to being interviewed. *Dropout* was defined as terminating treatment for reasons other than symptom improvement. After controlling for country, types of disorders, number of visits, and provider profiles, Edlund et al. found that factors such as income, urbanicity, gender, education, and race had no significant effect on dropout rates in general (i.e., dropping out of treatment prematurely). By controlling for number of visits, however, they found that ethnic minorities may drop out after fewer sessions than do European Americans (i.e., ethnic minorities have fewer sessions than European Americans before they terminate prematurely).

Taken as a whole, the research on minority utilization of mental health services suggests that "minority group members, especially Latinos and Asian Americans, are underrepresented in outpatient care" and that "African Americans . . . [are] . . . more likely than other ethnic groups to use psychiatric emergency services and to experience psychiatric rehospitalization" (Snowden & Hu, 1997, p. 237). Even though accessibility is probably the major impediment to ethnic minority use of mental health services, cultural barriers may also reduce utilization. These barriers include mistrust, social stigma attached to mental illness, conflicting views about the causes of and solutions to mental problems, and alternative sources of help.

Cultural Mistrust   Cultural mistrust (discussed in greater detail in chapter 2) is an understandable deterrent to utilization of mental health services. Government institutions such as the Bureau of Indian Affairs, U.S. Department of Health, and the criminal justice system have a long history of discriminating against ethnic minorities. Can anyone familiar with the Tuskegee Experiment, in which the progress of untreated syphilis was studied among Black men without fully informed consent, be surprised that many African Americans are mistrustful of health services that claim to look out for their welfare? After reviewing the research on cultural mistrust, Whaley (2001) found a general mistrust of White Americans and the institutions run by White Americans within the Black community. This mistrust can generalize to Black and other ethnic minority service providers as well.

Social Stigma Associated with Mental Illness   The review of research by Leong et al. (1995) suggests that in some cultures there is a stigma against seeking professional help for psychological problems that may hinder ethnic minority use of mental health services. This stigma has been found among African Americans (Neighbors, Caldwell, Thompson, & Jackson, 1994), Asian Americans (D. W. Sue, 1994), and Hispanic Americans (Leong et al., 1995). For example, Nickerson, Helms, and Terrell (1994) reviewed several studies that examined African American opinions about mental illness and found evidence that, compared to Whites, Blacks tend to stigmatize and reject those with mental illness, avoid the label of mental illness, and have more negative attitudes about the efficacy of psychotherapy.

The need to preserve family honor is a cultural value that may deter some ethnic minorities from seeking professional mental health services. D. W. Sue (1994) points out that

> In traditional Asian families, much stress is placed upon bringing honor to the family name and maintaining a good reputation through public consumption . . . Behaviors such as failure in school, delinquency, vocational problems, or mental illness may bring shame, disgrace, and dishonor to the family name . . . As a result, the family system exerts great pressures to keep such things hidden from public view, and thus may result in the low usage of clinical services. (p. 293)

Similarly, Esquivel and Keitel (1990) noted that "in some cultures it is a dishonor for the family to have a child with an emotional problem" (p. 215). Lefley (1994) points out that some observers have suggested that as a result of cultural values Hispanic and Asian American families may keep family members experiencing psychological distress at home longer and "present them for hospitalization at an advanced stage of illness, when they might require longer hospital stays" (p. 226).

Asian Americans in particular may find that the need to express emotions or relate intimate information to a mental health practitioner conflicts with their traditional cultural values. In some Asian American communities, the expression of emotions may be considered inappropriate or a sign of unacceptable instability. In these communities, denial of psychological problems may produce somatic symptoms or physical solutions. For example, D. W. Sue (1994) pointed out that

> the manner of symptom formation and expression among Asians seems influenced by cultural values as well. . . . Asians are more likely to express psychological conflicts somatically and to present their problems in a much more symbolic and circuitous manner than their White counterparts. (p. 293)

Lippincott and Mierzwa (1995) reviewed the research on Asian and Asian American mental health and stated that "a common trait among those studied whose cultural background was Asian appeared to be their tendency, when seeking help, to present somatic complaints in place of psychological complaints" (p. 201). Thus, many traditional ethnic minorities will seek help from medical practitioners when they are experiencing psychological problems.

The idea that stigma and values in an ethnic culture can contribute to underutilization of mental health services is often referred to as *cultural barrier theory* (Leong et al., 1995). Cultural barrier theory is frequently used to explain Hispanic and Asian American underutilization of mental health services and suggests that values in their respective cultures undermine both the seeking of help and the counseling process.

If the cultural barrier theory is valid, then there should be a positive relationship between acculturation and attitudes toward mental health practitioners and services. However, recent research suggests that the opposite may be true for Mexican Americans. For example, Ruelas, Atkinson, and Ramos-Sanchez (1998) found a negative relationship between acculturation and ratings of counselor credibility and cross-cultural competence among this group. Furthermore, they concluded that the loss of Mexican American culture, not the acquisition of European American culture, accounted for less favorable counselor ratings. Subsequent research by Ramos-Sanchez (2000), Ramos-Sanchez, Atkinson, and Fraga (1999), and Fraga (2003) found that endorsement of Mexican values in general and *personalismo, respeto,* and religiosity in particular was associated with positive attitudes toward counselors and satisfaction with counseling. Perhaps future research on cultural barrier theory will substantiate what seems to be obvious, that all cultures include some values that encourage, and some values that discourage, positive attitudes toward mental health services and providers.

Conflicting Views about Psychological Problems   The beliefs about the causes of, and solutions to, psychological problems held by mental health practitioners often conflict with those held by ethnic minority clients. With respect to the causes of psychological problems, mental health practitioners make varying attributions depending on the personality and counseling theories to which they subscribe. These causal attributions include such varying etiologies as irrational thinking, operant and classical conditioning, incongruence between self-concept and experience, existential crisis, traumatic events in early childhood, fixation on ego stages, dysfunctional family system, and so on. Causal attributions for psychological problems held by ethnic minorities are usually a function of the beliefs from their indigenous culture, their current culture, or some combination of both (Koss-Chioino, 2000). Often the etiology beliefs from indigenous cultures are based on violations of cultural norms or supernatural dictates. For example, some American Indians believe individuals can bring on mental illness by ignoring cultural values and norms (LaFromboise, 1998). Traditional Chinese medicine teaches that people become mentally ill because of the imbalance of cosmic forces and lack of willpower (Hahn, 1995). Traditional Hispanics attribute many psychological symptoms to physical and metaphysical causes (Rivera, 1988), such as an imbalance of hot and cold humors and a spell cast by an evil-eye.

Closely related to beliefs about the causes of mental disorders is the definition of what constitutes mental disorder. The heavy emphasis on individualism in Western cultures permeates every aspect of mental health services, including how mental illness is defined, and often comes into conflict with the collectivistic values of many ethnic minority clients. According to van Uchelen (2000), "many of the conceptual and methodological tools of our trade encode and reproduce the prevailing ideology of individualism of Western society" (p. 66). Indeed, individualistic values are so pervasively imbedded in Western psychology that it is difficult to think of psychological phenomena from a collectivistic viewpoint. As a result, mental health theorists, researchers, and practitioners are constantly looking at collectivistic processes through an individualistic lens, which often distorts those processes. As an example of the distortion that can result, van Uchelen points to the theory and research on locus of control:

> The underlying assumption of locus of control is that the individual is taken as the fundamental unit of reference or agent to which locus of control beliefs pertain. To the extent that a person holds an independent view of self, the assumption of the self as an autonomous agent and source of control is not problematic. . . . However, when the self is seen in interdependent terms, it is no longer accurate to view the autonomous individual as the unit to which the experience of power and control pertain. . . . A collectivistic conceptualization of control would allow us to use an interdependent view of a person who experiences and realizes power in the context of relationships within the collective. (p. 69)

This kind of bias in basic theory and research seriously affects definitions of mental health and mental illness. From the perspective of Western psychology, the mentally healthy person is independent and autonomous and exercises control over his or her environment. Van Uchelen (2000) points out that the inability to function autonomously and live independently is actually a common measure of mental illness in Western societies. In contrast, many collectivist cultures actually promote interdependence and communal living. Similarly, beliefs held by mental health practitioners and ethnic minority clients about how psychological problems can be resolved often clash. The current major effort within professional psychology to identify empirically supported treatments (ESTs) clearly places the emphasis on specific treatments (frequently, treatments based on cognitive behavior theory) that are found to be effective with specific psychological problems (Crits-Christoph, 1998). In validating ESTs, researchers make every effort to isolate the effects of the treatment and to rule out the effects of client characteristics, therapist characteristics, and relationship variables. However, there is substantial evidence that client, therapist, and relationship variables account for much more of the variance in therapy outcome than do treatment variables (Wampold, 2001).

The merits of the EST movement aside, the belief held by mental health practitioners that only treatments based on Western psychological principles are effective often conflicts with beliefs held by ethnic minority clients about how psychological problems are solved. To demonstrate the nature of this conflict, Atkinson, Bui, and Mori (2001) cited the hypothetical (but culturally valid) example of a 62-year-old Hmong woman who is referred to a mental health practitioner by her medical doctor because she is acutely depressed after being diagnosed with breast cancer. Through an interpreter the woman reveals that she is sad about the cancer but depressed because her placenta is buried in Cambodia and, according to Hmong beliefs, upon her death her soul is likely to wander naked and alone throughout eternity if it cannot find her "placental jacket." Without the placental jacket, her soul will not be able to find her ancestors, a prerequisite to her being reborn as the soul of a new baby. The woman believes she can only be assisted by a *txiv neeb* (Hmong shaman), who will negotiate with the spirits to ensure that her soul finds her placenta after death. The mental health practitioner believes that the woman needs to be treated with cognitive therapy, a well-established EST for depression. It seems clear that this clash in beliefs is likely to lead to early termination of therapy. As Wohl (1995) points out, "if the explanatory models of the clinician and the patient are far apart and the distance between them is not negotiated, treatment will flounder" (p. 81).

Alternative Sources of Help   Some African Americans, American Indians, Asian Americans, and Hispanic Americans make use of informal help or folk healers when they experience psychological distress (Adebimpe, 1994; Greene et al., 1993; Koss-Chioino, 2000; Leong et al., 1995). Ethnic minorities may seek alternative sources of help because of the stigma attached to seeking professional psychological help. They may also use alternative sources of help for psychological problems because they lack trust in conventional mental health services and service providers. For example, Leong et al. (1995) found that African Americans often prefer parents, relatives, neighbors, and friends as sources of help because they distrust professional help sources.

The desire to see a healer who shares their cultural beliefs about the causes of, and cures for, psychological problems is another important reason why some ethnic minority persons seek out folk healers to address these problems (Esquivel & Keitel, 1990). In her discussion of ethnomedical systems employed by African Americans, American Indians, Asian Americans, and Hispanic Americans, Koss-Chioino (1995) suggested that "all ethnic groups have transferred to the United

States many or all of their main beliefs and practices connected to healing" (p. 145). Chung and Lin (1994) reviewed research on refugees from Southeast Asia and concluded that "most Southeast Asian refugees are unfamiliar with Western mental health concepts, and are still deeply influenced by a multitude of indigenous cultural beliefs and practices that significantly affect the symptom presentation, conceptualization, and the help-seeking behavior of this group" (p. 109). In their review of research on help-seeking attitudes among ethnic minorities, Leong et al. (1995) found that Hispanic Americans often prefer family, folk healers, clergy, and general medical providers as alternatives to professional mental health service providers because of shared beliefs about the causes and cures of mental problems.

Although people in all four ethnic groups discussed in this book may make use of folk healers to some extent, there are conflicting data about the proportion that actually see folk healers for physical or mental health problems. For example, Rivera (1988) reviewed research on Mexican American use of *curanderos* (folk healers) and found that studies conducted in the 1960s reported widespread use (20–25% actually using *curanderos;* 50–60% believing in them), whereas studies conducted in the 1970s and 1980s reported very low use (less than 10% actually using *curanderos*). In his own survey of 128 Hispanic women living in the Denver, Colorado, area, Rivera found that 23% of the respondents had received treatment from a folk healer. He concluded that "Curanderismo is still part of Hispanic health care beliefs and practices, even among people born mostly in the United States and speaking English at home" (p. 239).

As ethnic immigrants acculturate, the likelihood that they will begin seeking help from professional mental health services presumably increases. However, the use of alternative sources of help may continue for many generations, despite increasing acculturation among later generations. Based on data from the California Southeast Asian Mental Health Needs Assessment Project, Chung and Lin (1994) concluded that for most ethnic groups from Southeast Asia, "there was a dramatic change from prominently utilizing traditional medicine in their home country to a higher usage of mainstream service in the United States . . . [but] . . . regardless of the significant increase in the use of Western medicine, traditional medicine continued to be important for all five Southeast Asian refugee groups after resettlement" (p. 109).

Disparities in Quality of Treatment

Disparities in the quality of treatment received by ethnic minorities as opposed to European Americans typically involve disparities in the type of diagnosis, the quality of intervention, or both. This section addresses these topics in that order.

Disparities in Type of Diagnosis   With regard to type of diagnosis, a number of reviews of research have concluded that African Americans, in particular, are overdiagnosed for some mental disorders and underdiagnosed for others. For example, Snowden and Cheung (1990) found that African Americans are more likely to be diagnosed as schizophrenic and less likely to be diagnosed as having an affective disorder than are Whites. Similarly, in their review of research on anxiety disorders among African Americans and non-African Americans, Paradis, Hatch, and Friedman (1994) found that African Americans are underdiagnosed with anxiety disorders and overdiagnosed with schizophrenic disorders. Leo, Narayan, Sherry, Michalek, and Pollock (1997) found that (a) African Americans were most likely to be referred for evaluation of psychosis; (b) Caucasians were most likely to be referred for suicide assessment; (c) African Americans were most likely to be given a psychotic diagnosis, specifically schizophrenia and dementia; and (d) Caucasians were most likely to be diagnosed with a mood disorder, especially depressive disorders. In a more recent review, Baker (2001) reported that psychotic disorders are diagnosed more often, and affective disorders less often, among African Americans than among European Americans.

These disparities in diagnosis may be due to a number of factors. It is possible, for example, that African Americans simply do not seek professional help for depression or anxiety as often as European Americans do. Another possibility is that there are cultural differences in how symptoms of mood disturbances are expressed. If this possibility is true, then mental health practitioners may be ignoring or misperceiving symptoms manifested by African Americans as psychotic symptoms. Still another possibility is that disparities in diagnosis (at least with regard to paranoia) are the result of adaptations African Americans have made to a history of discrimination. Justifiable mistrust by African Americans of education, the government, and other institutions is sometimes misdiagnosed as paranoia. Whaley (1998) examined the research on paranoia among Blacks and concluded that the overdiagnosis of paranoia may in part reflect patterns of behavior that are normative among African Americans. More specifically, Whaley argued that the overdiagnosis of paranoia among Blacks is the result of failure on the part of mental health professionals to recognize (a) the continuum of severity inherent in paranoia, (b) the oppressive conditions that can elicit paranoid reactions, (c) the manifestation of paranoid symptoms as a feature of depression, and (d) the protective function of cultural mistrust.

Most troubling, however, is the possibility that disparities in diagnosis are due to racial/ethnic biases that are built into diagnostic instruments or that are held by mental health professionals. An example of racial/ethnic bias inherent in diagnostic instruments was provided by Ramirez et al. (2001), who reviewed 18 studies that examined the performance across ethnic groups of cognitive screening measures used to diagnose dementia. Several of the more commonly used screens (e.g., Mini-Mental State Exam, Orientation-Memory-Concentration Test, Mental Status Questionnaire) "yielded relatively higher false positive ratios for Blacks and/or Latinos than they did for Whites" (p. 110) and "underestimated the cognitive capacities of Blacks and Latinos (as compared to Whites)" (p. 111).

Diagnostic bias among mental health professionals is more difficult to prove and decidedly more difficult to accept, especially by those accused of being biased. Abreu (2001) reviewed the research on diagnostic bias and concluded that clinical studies consistently report negative biases toward ethnic minority clients, whereas experimental analogue studies (the purposes of which are usually transparent and do not correct for social desirability responses) consistently find no evidence of bias. The obvious basis for diagnostic bias is racism, and not many mental health professionals want to believe that their clinical judgments are being influenced by racism. However, the activation of racial stereotypes need not be deliberate in order to bias the diagnosis of ethnic minority clients. As Abreu points out, psychotherapist bias in diagnosis and treatment may be explained by automatic, unconscious processes in social perception. Furthermore, his review of studies that controlled for social desirability and examined unconscious processes revealed that therapists do invoke racial stereotypes when making clinical judgments.

Diagnostic Bias and the DSM   Mental health practitioners are primed by the *Diagnostic and Statistical Manual of Mental Disorders (DSM)* to diagnose client problems as mental disorders that reside in the individual and to largely ignore the external forces that can produce and exacerbate psychological problems. The *DSM* arguably exerts greater influence on mental health practice in general and psychotherapy practice in particular than any other publication. Social workers, counselors, psychologists, psychiatrists, and other mental health professionals working in private and public mental health settings all rely on the current edition of the *DSM* (*DSM-IV-TR* as of this printing) to make clinical diagnoses and to justify insurance reimbursement or expenditure of public funds. Various editions of the *DSM* have consistently categorized and described disorders from an intrapsychic perspective, in that each disorder is assumed to reside within the individual. In the *DSM-IV-TR,* in fact, every effort was made to avoid any reference to disorder etiology, with particular effort made to discount external influences. This bias is clearly evident in the following definition of mental disorders stated in the manual:

> In DSM-IV, each of the mental disorders is conceptualized as a clinically significant behavioral or psychological syndrome or pattern that occurs in an individual and that is associated with present distress (e.g., a painful symptom) or disability (i.e., impairment in one or more important areas of functioning) or with significantly increased risk of suffering death, pain, disability, or an important loss of freedom. In addition, this syndrome or pattern must not be merely an expectable and culturally sanctioned response to a particular event, for example, the death of a loved one. *Whatever its original cause, it must currently be considered a manifestation of a behavioral, psychological, or biological dysfunction in the individual. Neither deviant behavior (e.g., political, religious, or sexual) nor conflicts that are primarily between the individual and society are mental disorders unless the deviance or conflict is a symptom of a dysfunction in the individual.* (American Psychiatric Association, 1994, xxi–xxii; italics added)

Thus, although many mental health professional organizations have made great strides toward recognizing the important role of culture and discrimination in the identification and assessment of client mental health problems, virtually all diagnoses of mental disorders continue to be made on the basis of dysfunction within the individual.

In all fairness, it should be recognized that psychosocial and environmental problems can be recorded on Axis IV and that ethnic and cultural considerations were acknowledged for the first time in the fourth edition of the *DSM*. However, discrimination, one of the major psychosocial and environmental stressors for ethnic minorities, is not listed as an option for Axis IV, and only Axis I and II are considered mental disorders. Furthermore, although cultural elements were introduced for the first time in the *DSM-IV,* changes that had been proposed by a workgroup sponsored by the National Institute of Mental Health (NIMH) that "challenged universalistic nosological assumptions and argued for the contextualization of illness, diagnosis and care were minimally incorporated and marginally placed" (Mezzich et al., 1999, p. 457). The steering committee for the NIMH Group on Culture, Diagnosis, and Care (consisting of 50 cultural experts, both clinicians and scholars) made the following observation about the intrapsychic focus of the *DSM-IV* and its predecessors:

> The DSM has traditionally concentrated on pathology conceptualized as rooted and fixed in the biological individual. This ignores the way in which many psychiatric problems are not only substantially more prevalent among individuals facing social disadvantage but, in important ways, constituted by those same economic, family, social, and cultural predicaments. (Mezzich et al., 1999, p. 461)

Mezzich et al. went on to make the following scathing denunciation of the *DSM-IV:*

> Some of the major biases of DSM-IV concern ontological notions of what constitutes a real disease or disorder, epistemological ideas about what counts as scientific evidence, methodological commitments to how research should be conducted, and pragmatic considerations about the appropriate uses of the DSM. Contrary to its frequent portrayal as an atheoretical, purely descriptive nosology based on scientific evidence, the DSM is a historical document with a complicated pedigree and many theoretical notions expressed in its structure and content. Most of the disorders of the DSM are syndromes in search of underlying pathological mechanisms or course trajectories that would make them more bona fide diseases. (p. 461)

Thus, the argument has been made that intrapsychic and methodological biases are built into the *DSM-IV.* However, there is also some evidence that the personality disorder criteria used in the *DSM-IV* may be ethnically biased, contributing to the disparities in diagnosing that were presented earlier in this chapter. Iwamasa, Larrabee, and Merritt (2000) had undergraduate college students sort criteria for Axis II personality disorders by ethnicity. Individual criteria for each of the personality disorders were placed on 3 by 5 in. cards and student sorters were told that the criteria on the cards represented personality characteristics. The students were then instructed to place each card with the ethnic group (African American, Asian American, European American, Latino, Native American) they felt most possessed the characteristic. The students applied a disproportionate share of the antisocial and paranoid criteria to African Americans, schizoid criteria to Asian Americans, schizotypal criteria to Native Americans, and avoidant, borderline, dependent, histrionic, narcissistic, and obsessive-compulsive criteria to European Americans (Latinos did not receive a disproportionate share of any Axis II criteria). As Iwamasa et al. suggest, participants may have sorted the criteria on the basis of negative stereotypes associated with each ethnic group. It is also possible, however, that the personality disorders "include characteristics that actually are more common among some ethnic groups than others" and that "the DSM PD criteria include characteristics that some ethnic groups perceive as culturally appropriate and not pathological" (p. 292). To the extent that this latter explanation is operational, it is clear that future iterations of the DSM need to reduce ethnic bias and to put even more emphasis on the role of culture in diagnosing mental disorders.

Disparities in Quality of Intervention   Treatment bias is also possible in the types of interventions people receive. According to D. W. Sue (1994), "multicultural specialists have repeatedly pointed out that traditional forms of counseling and therapy are Eurocentric and perhaps inappropriate and antagonistic to the lifestyles and cultural values of various minority groups" (p. 293).

Treatment bias may begin operating at the point at which people enter the mental health system. Takeuchi and Cheung (1998) examined data from 9,184 African American, Asian American, Mexican American, and White clients seen in Los Angeles County mental health facilities between 1983 and 1988. The purpose of their study was to look at the relationship between severity of psychological disorder and type of referral, that is (a) self-referral, (b) family or friends, (c) health agency, (d) social service agency, and (e) legal authority. They found that African American men, regardless of disorder, entered the mental health system through the legal system more often than any other ethnic/gender group did, which supports the hypothesis that "people with less power are more likely than the powerful to be coercively placed in psychiatric care" (p. 149). This finding contrasted with that of White men and women, who came into the mental health system via informal or self-referrals for minor problems and via coercive referrals for severe disorders. Asian Americans, in general, were more likely than other groups to enter the system through interpersonal referrals (family/friends or social service).

Disparities in types of referral may help explain disparities in the type of setting in which treatment is received. In reviewing research on the relationship between race and use of inpatient mental health services, Snowden and Cheung (1990) found a history of Black overrepresentation in mental hospitals dating back to 1914. They also reviewed 1980 and 1981 survey data from the National Institute of Mental Health and found that African Americans and American Indians are more likely, and Asian Americans/Pacific Islanders less likely, to be hospitalized than Whites. Examining only involuntary psychiatric hospitalization (which constitutes 29% of all psychiatric hospitalization), Rosenstein, Milazzo-Sayre, MacAskill, and Manderscheid (1987) found that non-Whites are 3.5 times more likely than Whites to receive involuntary criminal commitment and 2.4 times more likely to receive involuntary noncriminal commitment. African American overrepresentation among involuntary commitments may be particularly acute in public psychiatric hospitals (Cannon & Locke, 1977; Snowden & Cheung, 1990). Snowden and Cheung suggest that racial differences in public hospitalization rates may be due to socioeconomic differences, cultural differences in the seeking of help, and diagnostic biases on the part of referring psychologists and psychiatrists.

Of particular concern is the possibility that ethnic minorities receive less expensive, time-intensive, and effective forms of treatment. An early review of research by Abramowitz and Murray (1983) revealed that ethnic minorities receive "less preferred" forms of treatment than do European American clients. More recently, Leo et al. (1997) conducted a retrospective review of psychiatric consultations completed for African American and Caucasian patients in a tertiary-care hospital who were 65 or older. The researchers found that Caucasians were more likely to be referred for psychiatric consultation, whereas African Americans were more likely to receive recommendations involving legal measures (e.g., guardianship). Similarly, Kales et al. (2000) examined the records of 23,718 older veterans from Veteran's Administration medical centers across the United States to determine inpatient and outpatient utilization by ethnic group and type of disorder (cognitive disorders, mood disorders, psychotic disorders, substance abuse disorders, anxiety disorders, and all other disorders). After adjusting for age, medical comorbidity, and psychiatric comorbidity, the researchers found no differences in inpatient utilization by ethnicity. For outpatient utilization, however, they found that African American veterans with psychotic disorders had significantly fewer psychiatric visits than did Caucasians with psychotic disorders.

On a more positive note, evidence suggests that when ethnicity-specific programs are made available they provide superior and preferred forms of treatment for ethnic minority clients. For example, Snowden and Hu (1997) examined ethnic differences in patterns of service utilization among 4,000 clients with serious impairments (dementia, delirium, schizophrenia, affective disorder, "other psychosis," or personality disorder) in two West Coast counties. At the time of the study, the two counties had varying histories of specialized minority-oriented programming. In the county that made extensive use of contracts—many of which were with minority providers—and other specialized programs for minorities, ethnic minority clients were more likely than White clients to receive case management, individual treatment, and medication and less likely than White clients to be hospitalized. The reverse was found in the county that had very few specialized minority-oriented programs. Snowden and Hu concluded that "the pattern of findings suggests but does not definitively prove that as ethnic minority groups are more likely to utilize outpatient services and programs supporting community living, they are less likely to use emergency services and inpatient care" (p. 244).

Disparities in Mental Health Research

According to the National Advisory Mental Health Council Workgroup on Racial/Ethnic Diversity in Research Training and Health Disparities Research (2001):

> There exist . . . a paucity of empirical data that describe the impact and effects of mental disorders on our Nation's racial/ethnic minority groups, defined in this report as African Americans, American Indians/Alaska Natives, Asian/Pacific Islanders, and Hispanics. Members of these groups remain underrepresented or unreported in most studies of mental illness, although they are overrepresented among the conditions thought to generate susceptibility to, or prolong the effects of, mental illness. (p. 1)

The invisibility of ethnic minorities in mental health research was documented in the 2001 supplement to the Surgeon General's Report on Mental Health (DHHS,

2001b). This report examined research since 1986 that has evaluated the efficacy of treatments for bipolar disorder, major depression, schizophrenia, and attention deficit/hyperactivity disorder. Almost 10,000 people had participated in these studies, but no information on race or ethnicity was available for nearly half of them (4,991). For another 7% of participants ($N = 656$), ethnic minorities were all lumped together in a "nonWhite" category. For the remaining 47% of participants ($N = 4,335$), data on ethnicity were available but indicated that very few minorities (561 Blacks, 99 Hispanics, 11 Asian American/Pacific Islanders, 0 American Indians/Native Alaskans) were included in research on empirically supported treatments. Furthermore, not a single study analyzed treatment efficacy by ethnicity or race.

S. Sue, Chun, and Gee (1995) have proposed a number of reasons why psychotherapy researchers have not addressed ethnicity as a research variable, including the researchers' lack of interest in ethnicity, a lack of funding for ethnicity-related research topics, and the view that only massive social and political change could address the needs of ethnic minorities. More recently, S. Sue (1999) has expressed concerns not only with the paucity of psychological research on ethnic minority populations but also with the lack of funding for such research and with the unevenness and low quality of the research that has been conducted. S. Sue suggests that problems with ethnic minority research start with the bias within the research establishment in favor of internal validity over external validity. He argues that although the scrutiny given threats to internal validity by editors and reviewers when they review manuscripts for publication is appropriate, equal rigor should be given to threats to external validity. As indicated in the analysis of empirically supported treatment research that was mentioned earlier in this chapter, this lack of emphasis on external validity has the effect of discouraging ethnic minority research.

> Because much psychological research is not based on ethnic minority populations, it is unclear whether a particular theory or principle is applicable to all racial groups, whether an intervention has the same phenomenological meaning for different cultural groups, or whether measures of questionnaires are valid for these populations. (S. Sue, 1999, p. 1074)

Furthermore, S. Sue (1999) suggests, as long as the bias in favor of internal validity prevails, mainstream research will not be compelled to examine the generality of theories, interventions, or questionnaires. In order to address the problems with ethnic minority research, S. Sue recommends that the research community (a) place greater demands on external validity while it maintains high standards for internal validity, (b) accept a wider range of research designs as legitimate research methodologies (e.g., qualitative as well as quantitative research designs), and (c) pay greater attention to cultural variables that might account for ethnic differences found in ethnic minority research.

SUMMARY

Although studies that control for sociodemographic data have found that mental illness is not related to ethnicity per se (why would mental health professionals even suspect that such a relationship exists?), the fact remains that a disproportionate share of ethnic minorities are affected by the conditions that contribute to mental illness. Thus, ethnic minorities are as likely, or even more likely, to need mental health services than European Americans are. However, the Surgeon General has documented disparities in mental health services experienced by ethnic minorities in the following areas: mental health services accessibility, mental health services utilization, quality of treatment, and mental health research. These disparities result from a number of factors, most of which can be traced to racial/ethnic discrimination in one form or another. They also exist despite efforts by professional psychological organizations to eliminate discrimination against, and raise sensitivity to, ethnic minorities. It seems clear that much needs to be done if the disparities in mental health services are to be eliminated in the future.

REFERENCES

Abramowitz, S. I., & Murray, J. (1983). Race effects in psychotherapy. In J. Murray & P. R. Abramson (Eds.), *Bias in psychotherapy* (pp. 215–255). New York: Praeger.

Abreu, J. (2001). A didactic resource for multicultural counseling trainers. *The Counseling Psychologist, 29,* 487–512.

Adebimpe, V. R. (1994). Race, racism, and epidemiological surveys. *Hospital and Community Psychiatry, 45,* 27–31.

Alvidrez, J. (1999). Ethnic variations in mental health attitudes and service use among low-income African American, Latina, and European American young women. *Community Mental Health Journal, 35,* 515–530.

American Psychiatric Association. (1994). *Diagnostic and statistical manual of mental disorders* (4th ed.). Washington, DC: Author.

American Psychological Association. (1990). *Guidelines for providers of psychological services to ethnic, linguistic, and culturally diverse populations.* Washington, DC: Author.

Atkinson, D. R., Bui, U., & Mori, S. (2001). Multiculturally sensitive empirically supported treatments—An oxymoron? In J. G. Ponterotto, J. M. Casas, L. A. Suzuki, & C. M. Alexander (Eds.), *Handbook of multicultural counseling* (pp. 542–574). Thousand Oaks, CA: Sage.

Atkinson, D. R., & Lowe, S. M. (1995). The role of ethnicity, cultural knowledge, and conventional techniques in counseling and psychotherapy. In J. G. Ponterotto, J. M. Casas, L. A. Suzuki, & C. M. Alexander (Eds.), *Handbook of multicultural counseling* (pp. 387–414). Thousand Oaks, CA: Sage.

Baker, F. M. (2001). Diagnosing depression in African Americans. *Community Mental Health Journal, 37,* 31–38.

Barnes, M. (1994). Clinical treatment issues regarding Black African-Americans. In J. L. Ronch, W. Van Ornum, & N. C. Stilwell (Eds.), *The counseling sourcebook: A practical reference on contemporary issues* (pp. 157–164). New York: Crossroad.

Blank, M. B., Tetrick, F. L., Brinkley, D. F., Smith, H. O., & Doheny, V. (1994). Racial matching and service utilization among seriously mentally ill consumers in the rural south. *Community Mental Health Journal, 30,* 271–281.

Cannon, M. S., & Locke, B. Z. (1977). Being black is detrimental to one's mental health: Myth or reality? *Phylon, 38,* 408–428.

Cheung, F. K., & Snowden, L. R. (1990). Community mental health and ethnic minority populations. *Community Mental Health Journal, 26,* 277–291.

Chung, R. C., & Lin, K. (1994). Help seeking among Southeast Asian refugees. *Journal of Community Psychology, 22,* 109–120.

Crits-Christoph, P. (1998). Training in empirically validated treatments. In K. S. Dobson & K. D. Craig (Eds.), *Empirically supported therapies: Best practice in professional psychology* (pp. 3–25). Thousand Oaks, CA: Sage.

Department of Health and Human Services. (1999). *Mental health: A report of the Surgeon General.* Rockville, MD: Author.

Department of Health and Human Services. (2001a, August 26). Mental health: Culture, race, and ethnicity (executive summary)—A supplement to mental health: A report of the Surgeon General. Rockville, MD: Author. Retrieved October 7, 2002, from www.surgeongeneral.gov/library/mentalhealth/cre/execsummary-1.html

Edlund, M., Wang, P. S., Berglund, P., Katz, S. J., Lin, E., & Kessler, R. (2002). Dropping out of mental health treatment: Patterns and predictors among epidemiological survey respondents in the United States and Ontario. *American Journal of Psychiatry, 159,* 845–851.

Esquivel, G. B., & Keitel, M. A. (1990). Counseling immigrant children in the schools. *Elementary School Guidance and Counseling, 24,* 213–221.

Fraga, E. (2003). *The relationship among perceived client-counselor ethnic similarity, perceived Hispanic cultural value similarity, and counseling process and outcome variables.* Unpublished doctoral dissertation, University of California, Santa Barbara.

Friedman, S., Paradis, C. M., & Hatch, M. L. (1994). Issues of misdiagnosis in panic disorder with agoraphobia. In S. Friedman (Ed.), *Anxiety disorders in African Americans* (pp. 128–146). New York: Springer.

Gottesfeld, H. (1995). Community context and the underutilization of mental health services by minority patients. *Psychological Reports, 76,* 207–210.

Greene, R. L., Jackson, J. S., & Neighbors, H. W. (1993). Mental health and help-seeking behavior. In J. S. Jackson, L. M. Chatters, & R. J. Taylor (Eds.), *Aging in Black America* (pp. 185–200). Newbury Park, CA: Sage.

Griffith, E. E. H., & Gonzalez, C. A. (1994). Essentials of cultural psychiatry. In R. E. Hales, S. C. Yudofsky, & J. A. Talbott (Eds.), *The American Psychiatric Press textbook of psychiatry* (2nd ed., pp. 1379–1404). Washington, DC: American Psychiatric Press.

Hahn, R. A. (1995). *Sickness and healing: An anthropological perspective.* New Haven, CT: Yale University.

Horwath, E., Johnson, J., & Hornig, C. D. (1994). Epidemiology of panic disorder. In S. Friedman (Ed.), *Anxiety disorders in African Americans* (pp. 53–64). New York: Springer.

Iwamasa, G. Y., Larrabee, A. L., & Merritt, R. D. (2000). Are personality disorder criteria ethnically biased? A card-sort analysis. *Cultural Diversity and Ethnic Minority Psychology, 6,* 284–296.

Jones, B. E., & Gray, B. A. (1986). Problems in diagnosing schizophrenia and affective disorders among blacks. *Hospital and Community Psychiatry, 37,* 61–65.

Jones-Webb, R. J., & Snowden, L. R. (1993). Symptoms of depression among Blacks and Whites. *American Journal of Public Health, 83,* 240–244.

Kales, H. C., Blow, F. C., Bingham, C. R., Roberts, J. S., Copeland, L. A., & Mellow, A. M. (2000). Race, psychiatric diagnosis, and mental health care utilization in older patients. *American Journal of Geriatric Psychiatry, 3,* 301–309.

Kessler, R. C., & Neighbors, H. W. (1986). A new perspective on the relationships among race, social class, and psychological distress. *Journal of Health and Social Behavior, 27,* 107–115.

Kessler, R. C., & Zhao, S. (1999). Overview of descriptive epidemiology of mental disorders. In C. S. Aneshensel & J. C. Phelan (Eds.), *Handbook of the sociology of mental health* (pp. 127–150). New York: Kluwer Academic/Plenum Publishers.

Koss-Chioino, J. D. (1995). Traditional and folk approaches among ethnic minorities. In J. F. Aponte, R. Young Rivers, & J. Wohl (Eds.), *Psychological interventions and cultural diversity* (pp. 145–163). Boston: Allyn and Bacon.

Koss-Chioino, J. D. (2000). Traditional and folk approaches among ethnic minorities. In J. F. Aponte & J. Wohl (Eds.), *Psychological interventions and cultural diversity* (2nd ed., pp. 149–166). Boston: Allyn and Bacon.

LaFromboise, T. (1998). American Indian mental health policy. In D. R. Atkinson, G. Morton, & D. W. Sue (Eds.), *Counseling American minorities* (5th ed., pp. 137–158). Boston: McGraw-Hill.

Lefley, H. P. (1994). Service needs of culturally diverse patients and families. In H. P. Lefley & M. Wasow (Eds.), *Helping families cope with mental illness* (pp. 223–242). Chur, Switzerland: Harwood Academic Publishers.

Leo, R. J., Narayan, D. A., Sherry, C., Michalek, C., & Pollock, D. (1997). Geropsychiatric consultation for African-American and Caucasian patients. *General Hospital Psychiatry, 19,* 216–222.

Leong, F. T. L. (1994). Asian Americans' differential patterns of utilization of inpatient and outpatient public mental health services in Hawaii. *Journal of Community Psychology, 22,* 82–96.

Leong, F. T. L., Wagner, N. S., & Tata, S. P. (1995). Racial and ethnic variations in help-seeking attitudes. In J. G. Ponterotto, J. M. Casas, L. A. Suzuki, & C. M. Alexander (Eds.), *Handbook of multicultural counseling* (pp. 415–438). Thousand Oaks, CA: Sage.

Lippincott, J. A., & Mierzwa, J. A. (1995). Propensity for seeking counseling services: A comparison of Asian and American undergraduates. *Journal of American College Health, 43,* 201–204.

Mezzich, J. E., Kirmayer, L. J., Kleinman, A., Fabrega, H., Parron, D. L., Good, B. J., Lin, K., & Manson, S. M. (1999). The place of culture in DSM-IV. *The Journal of Nervous and Mental Disease, 187,* 457–464.

Mio, J. S., & Morris, D. R. (1990). Cross-cultural issues in psychology training programs: An invitation for discussion. *Professional Psychology: Theory and Practice, 21,* 434–441.

National Advisory Mental Health Council Workgroup on Racial/Ethnic Diversity in Research Training and Health Disparities Research. (2001). *An investment in America's future: Racial/ethnic diversity in mental health research careers.* Washington, DC: National Institute of Mental Health. Retrieved from www.nimh.nih.gov/council/diversity.pdf

Neighbors, H. W., Caldwell, C. H., Thompson, E., & Jackson, J. S. (1994). Help-seeking behavior and unmet need. In S. Friedman (Ed.), *Anxiety disorders in African Americans* (pp. 26–39). New York: Springer.

Nickerson, K. J., Helms, J. E., & Terrell, F. (1994). Cultural mistrust, opinions about mental illness, and Black students' attitudes toward seeking psychological help from White counselors. *Journal of Counseling Psychology, 41,* 378–385.

Padgett, D. K., Patrick, C., Burns, B. J., & Schlesinger, H. J. (1994). Women and outpatient mental health services: Use by Black, Hispanic, and White women in a national insured population. *Journal of Mental Health Administration, 21,* 347–360.

Paradis, C. M., Hatch, M., & Friedman, S. (1994). Anxiety disorders in African Americans: An update. *Journal of the National Medical Association, 86,* 609–612.

Ramirez, M., Teresi, J. A., Silver, S., Holmes, D., Gurland, B., & Lantiqua, R. (2001). Cognitive assessment among minority elderly: Possible test bias. *Journal of Mental Health and Aging, 7,* 91–118.

Ramos-Sanchez, L. (2000). *The relationship between acculturation, specific cultural values, gender, and Mexican Americans' help-seeking intentions* (Doctoral dissertation, University of California, Santa Barbara, 2000). *Dissertation Abstracts International—B 62/03,* 1595. Retrieved October 29, 2002, from http://wwwlib.umi.com/dissertations/search

Ramos-Sanchez, L., Atkinson, D. R., & Fraga, E. D. (1999). Mexican Americans' bilingual ability, counselor bilingualism cues, counselor ethnicity, and perceived counselor credibility. *Journal of Counseling Psychology, 46,* 125–131.

Rivera, G. (1988). Hispanic folk medicine utilization in urban Colorado. *Sociology and Social Research, 72,* 237–241.

Rosenheck, R., & Fontana, A. (1994). Utilization of mental health services by minority veterans of the Vietnam era. *The Journal of Nervous and Mental Disease, 182,* 685–691.

Rosenstein, M. J., Milazzo-Sayre, L. J., MacAskill, R. L., & Manderscheid, R. W. (1987). Use of inpatient services by special populations. In R. W. Manderscheid & S. A. Barrett (Eds.), *Mental health, United States, 1987* (DHHS Publication No. ADM 87-1518). Washington, DC: U.S. Government Printing Office.

Ruelas, S. R., Atkinson, D. R., & Ramos-Sanchez, L. (1998). Counselor helping model, participant ethnicity and acculturation level, and perceived counselor credibility. *Journal of Counseling Psychology, 45,* 98–103.

Schwabe, A. M., & Kodras, J. E. (2000). Race, class, and psychological distress: Contextual variations across four American communities. *Health, 4,* 234–260.

Snowden, L. R., & Cheung, F. K. (1990). Use of inpatient mental health services by members of ethnic minority groups. *American Psychologist, 45,* 347–355.

Snowden, L. H., & Hu, T. (1996). Outpatient service use in minority-serving mental health programs. *Administration and Policy in Mental Health, 24,* 149–159.

Special Populations Task Force of the President's Commission on Mental Health. (1978). *Task panel reports submitted to the President's Commission on Mental Health: Vol 3.* Washington, DC: U.S. Government Printing Office.

Sue, D. W. (1990). Culture-specific strategies in counseling: A conceptual framework. *Professional Psychology: Research and Practice, 21,* 424–433.

Sue, D. W. (1994). Asian-American mental health and help-seeking behavior: Comment on Solberg et al. (1994), Tata and Leong (1994), and Lin (1994). *Journal of Counseling Psychology, 41,* 292–295.

Sue, S. (1999). Science, ethnicity, and bias: Where have we gone wrong? *American Psychologist, 54,* 1070–1077.

Sue, S., Chun, C., & Gee, K. (1995). Ethnic minority intervention and treatment research. In J. F. Aponte, R. Young Rivers, & J. Wohl (Eds.), *Psychological interventions and cultural diversity* (pp. 266–282). Boston: Allyn and Bacon.

Sue, S., Fujino, D. C., Hu, L., Takeuchi, D. T., & Zane, N. W. S. (1991). Community mental health services for ethnic minority groups: A test of the cultural responsiveness hypothesis. *Journal of Consulting and Clinical Psychology, 59,* 533–540.

Sue, S., & Zane, N. (1987). The role of culture and cultural techniques in psychotherapy: A critique and reformulation. *American Psychologist, 42,* 37–45.

Takeuchi, D. T., & Cheung, M. (1998). Coercive and voluntary referrals: How ethnic minority adults get into mental health treatment. *Ethnicity and Health, 3,* 149–158.

Takeuchi, D. T., Sue, S., & Yeh, M. (1995). Return rates and outcomes from ethnicity-specific mental health programs in Los Angeles. *American Journal of Public Health, 85,* 638–643.

U.S. Census Bureau. (2001). *Health insurance coverage: 2001.* Retrieved October 9, 2002, from www.census.gov/hhes/hlthins/hlthin01/hlth01asc.html

van Uchelen, C. (2000). Individualism, collectivism, and community psychology. In J. Rappaport & E. Seidman (Eds.), *Handbook of community psychology* (pp. 65–78). New York: Kluwer Academic/Plenum Publishers.

Wampold, B. E. (2001). *The great psychotherapy debate: Models, methods, and findings.* Mahwah, NJ: Erlbaum.

Whaley, A. L. (1998). Cross-cultural perspective on paranoia: A focus on the Black American experience. *Psychiatric Quarterly, 69,* 325–343.

Whaley, A. L. (2001). Cultural mistrust and mental health services for African Americans: A review and meta-analysis. *The Counseling Psychologist, 29,* 513–531.

Wohl, J. (1995). Traditional individual psychotherapy and ethnic minorities. In J. F. Aponte, R. Young Rivers, & J. Wohl (Eds.), *Psychological interventions and cultural diversity* (pp. 74–91). Boston: Allyn and Bacon.

Part II THE AFRICAN AMERICAN CLIENT

CHAPTER 4 # Contextualizing Black Americans' Health

Helen A. Neville and Jessica M. Walters, University of Illinois at Urbana-Champaign

Today most whites appear to believe that racial discrimination is no longer a significant factor . . . [and] that racial differences in jobs, income, and housing [are] not "mainly due to discrimination." (Sears, Hetts, Sidanius, & Bobo, 2000, p. 12)

The substantial white consensus on the decline of racism is not based on empirical evidence. On the contrary, research shows that black men and women still face extensive racial discrimination in all arenas of daily life . . . Recent in-depth studies have documented continuing antiblack discrimination, ranging from blatant acts reminiscent of the legal segregation period to subtle and covert forms that have flourished under the conditions of segregation. The belief in the declining significance of race cannot be reconciled with the empirical reality of racial discrimination. (Feagin & Vera, 1995, p. 4)

We begin this chapter with quotes from leading race scholars to underscore that although gains have been made in the social, economic, and political life of Black Americans, racism persists and continues to structure the lived experiences of individuals in this country. We do not mean that Black Americans are completely shaped by these external factors. Nor do we mean that Black Americans do not resist racism and are not working toward eliminating the barriers that impede individual and collective progress. We simply mean that racism continues to thrive in the United States, and consequently, Black people still face and resist racial oppression in multiple arenas.

Most of the public discourse on Black Americans centers on the ill effects of racism as manifested in the persistent educational and wealth gaps between Blacks and Whites, the political underrepresentation of Black communities, and the overrepresentation of Blacks among the poor and working classes. Often overlooked within these forums are discussions of the risk and protective factors that influence Black Americans' mental and physical health—the factors that may negatively impact Black Americans' health, such as racism in access to and quality of health care, as well as the factors within the Black American community that can promote better health outcomes, such as support from the church or other community institutions.

The purpose of this chapter is to provide a snapshot of the external and internal forces that shape Black Americans' health and to lay the groundwork for the reader to contextualize related treatment issues. The seven sections of the chapter are designed to underscore the link between macrolevel factors, such as the political economy and race relations at a given historical moment, and research and practice in counseling and applied psychology. Also, an underlying thread throughout the sections is consideration of the tension between external forces (e.g., racial oppression) and internal forces (i.e., agency) in shaping one's individual and group level health. Specifically, in the first section, we describe the demography of Black Americans using information from the most recent census data as a way to provide the parameters of the population. Next, we highlight the class positions and the education situation of Blacks in the United States. This information sets the stage for an understanding of core social, economic, and political issues faced by Black Americans as outlined in the fourth section. In our last two sections, we focus on issues most directly related to psychological processes, namely the development and expression of racial schemas, and to risk and protective factors related to health.

Throughout the chapter we highlight the modal experiences of Black Americans, but at the same time we try to accentuate within-group differences, especially as they relate to the intersection between race, class, and gender. Although the focus of the chapter is on Blacks as a racial group, much of the research and examples provided are drawn from studies completed on African Americans, an ethnic group within the Black population. We thus caution the reader to not overgeneralize the material presented here to other Black ethnic groups in the United States (e.g., Nigerian, Haitian, Puerto Rican, Cuban, etc.).

DEMOGRAPHY OF BLACK AMERICANS

Proportional to the total population, the Black population in the United States has remained stable over the past few decades, and little proportional population growth is projected in the future. Similar to previous census reports, 2000 census data indicates that 12.9% of people in the United States (or 34.7 million) reported being Black or African American, of which about .6% indicated that they were Black as well as one or more other races. The Black population is expected to grow only marginally in the next decade, in which it will rise less than a percentage point to 13.3%. Currently, the population is roughly distributed evenly between females (52%) and males (48%); nearly one third of the population is under 18 (31%) and only 8% are over 65. The Black population is distributed across the union, with a little more than half (54%) concentrated in the South; the remaining population is primarily represented in the Midwest (19%) or Northeast (18%), with only about 10% living in the West. About 60% of Black Americans live in 10 states: New York, California, Texas, Florida, Georgia, Illinois, North Carolina, Maryland, Michigan, and Louisiana. There are 13 states that constitute less than 3% of the total Black population in the United States: Hawaii, New Mexico, Oregon, Utah, Wyoming, Idaho, Montana, Iowa, South Dakota, North Dakota, New Hampshire, Maine, and Vermont (U.S. Census Bureau, 2001a).

Clearly, the roots of the majority of Black Americans have been well planted in the United States for centuries as a result of the forced slave trade. However, there is ethnic and national diversity among Black individuals in this country that results from more recent immigration. According to 2000 census data, at least 5% of Blacks in the United States reported roots in non-Hispanic West Indies countries, of which 33% were from Jamaica. Another 4% of Blacks (1,422,006) in the United States reported ancestry from sub-Saharan Africa, which includes approximately 10% who have Nigerian ancestry. And nearly 3% of Black individuals (1,035,683) reported having "Hispanic" origins. Although only a small percentage of individuals born outside the United States have immigrated from Africa or the West Indies, it is projected that by the year 2025 a little over one fifth (21%) of the new immigrants in the country will be Black (U.S. Census Bureau, 2001a).

CLASS STRUCTURE

Class is a critical factor influencing the life chances and health conditions of Black Americans, yet it is an understudied phenomenon in applied psychology. There are numerous complex sociological theories that define class. For the purposes of this chapter, class is defined as "a social category referring to social groups forged by interdependent economic and legal relationships, premised upon people's structural location within the economy—as employers, employees, self-employed, and unemployed, and as owners, or not, of capital, land, or other forms of economic investments" (Krieger, Williams, & Moss, 1997, p. 345). We use this definition partly because it situates class within a social relations perspective that "correspondingly helps explain generation, distribution, and persistence of—as well as links between—myriad specific pathways leading to social [and racial] inequalities in income, wealth, and health" (Krieger et al., 1997, p. 346). To be consistent with this interpretation, we use income, poverty, unemployment, and wealth as proxies for class structure among Black Americans.

Although there has been a reduction in the income gap between Black and White Americans over the past decades, a significant difference still exists between the individual and household income of these two groups. For example, consistent census data suggest that the median Black American family household income is typically around 60% of White family households ($35,080 vs. $55,051 in 2000). The income gap is complicated by the intersection among race, gender, and family constellation. According to the 2000 census, Black women householders who lived alone had the lowest average earnings ($15,508); they earned 85%, 69%, and 53% of what their White women, Black men, and White men counterparts earned, respectively (U.S. Census Bureau, 2001b).

In 2001, nearly one quarter (22.7%) of Blacks lived at or below the poverty line, and they overwhelmingly resided in racially segregated neighborhoods; this figure is approximately 3 times greater than the poverty rate for White Americans (7.8%) and more than twice that of Asian Americans (10.2%). Among those Blacks who live in poverty, single mothers have one of the highest poverty rates in the country. In 2001 their poverty rate was estimated at approximately 35%; in other words, more than one third of single Black mothers live at or below the poverty line. Not surprisingly, then, a staggering number of Black children live in poverty. Data suggest that upwards of 30% of Black children under the age of 18 were living in poverty in 2001 (U.S. Census Bureau, 2001c).

There are a number of ways that readers can misinterpret these figures. One way is to assume that Black people living in poverty are poor because they do not work. This assumption simply is not accurate. A significant percentage of Black people who are poor can be classified as the working poor—these are individuals who work at low-paying jobs or are unable to find full employment; often these workers are single mothers with part- or full-time employment who are trying to provide for the needs of their families. In 2000, Black women were classified as working poor (11.4%) nearly three times more than was the White labor force (4%) and two times more than Black men were (5.6%; Bureau of Labor Statistics, 2000). Also, sometimes people overgeneralize the statistics; they assume that because Black people are overrepresented among the poor, the majority of Black people are poor. The statistics that we have presented challenge this misperception. Although there is a high level of poverty among Black Americans, the majority of Black Americans do not live in poverty.

Like the poverty rates, the unemployment rates for Black Americans are significantly higher than for their White counterparts. Even during robust economic times, Black Americans have significantly higher unemployment rates. "The standard 2-to-1 ratio of black to white unemployment has remained virtually unchanged for the past 40 years" ("Don't Count on a College Diploma," 1998, p. 16). In 2000 Black Americans were right on target with this trend: In general they had twice the unemployment rate of White Americans (the rate typically hovered around 9% vs. 4%). The intersection between race and age widened this gap. For Black youth between the ages of 16 to 19, unemployment rates soared at least as high as 29% in 2000, compared to nearly 12.7% for their White counterparts (Bureau of Labor Statistics, 2000).

Another important index of class is the level of wealth accumulated. By wealth we mean, quite simply, how much people are worth, their net assets. Wealth factors include whether an individual owns a home and the value of the home, has stocks or bonds, and has a savings account and the amount of the savings. Not only is wealth accumulated through individual hard work, but it is accumulated intergenerationally; thus, wealth (like poverty) is inherited. For example, when young couples buy their first home, they often do so with assistance from their parents, either as a loan or a gift. Through this simple transference of wealth, the young couple now has an opportunity to begin to develop financial equity. Oftentimes, this opportunity would not have been possible if not for parental assistance. Another example of intergenerational transference of wealth is parents who send their children to college, especially elite, prestigious colleges and universities.

The gap in wealth between Black and White Americans is startling. Across the board, White individuals have greater wealth as evidenced in home ownership (11.4% vs. 79.4% in 2000; U.S. Census Bureau, 2001b) and in the enormous difference in net worth. White American families' net worth is more than 8 times that of Black American families; the median net worth (minus home equity) of Black Americans has been reported as 1% of that of White American families (School of Cooperative Individualism, 1999). Wealth clearly affects access to the best schools and colleges, health care, and other necessities of life.

EDUCATION

According to the American Council on Education (2002), the enrollment of racial and ethnic minorities in higher education increased by over 48% between 1990 and 1999. That significantly more Blacks and Latinos are entering college is definitely cause for celebration. Unfortunately, though, huge enrollment and graduation gaps persist in spite of the gains. There are significant differences in the percentage of college graduates and the meaning of a college degree between Black and White Americans. In the late 1990s around 34% of Black men and between 43% and 45% of Black women were participating in higher education (American Council on Education, 2002). Census 2000 data indicate that 15.5% of Black Americans are college graduates (about equal numbers of men and women); this figure contrasts to 27.7% of Whites and 42.4% of Asian Americans who are college graduates. The 2-to-1 unemployment ratio between Black and White Americans that we mentioned earlier holds true for college graduates as well. Although Black American college graduates' unemployment rate is typically about half that of their high school counterparts, it is still twice that of White American college students. In fact, the unemployment rate of Black American college graduates is generally equivalent to the unemployment rate of White high school graduates ("Don't Count on a College Diploma," 1998).

In terms of secondary education, the good news is that the majority of Black youth graduate from high school, typically over 73% of Black females and a little over 70% of Black males (U.S. Census Bureau, 1999). The bad news is that many Black youth living in racially segregated communities attend inferior schools that are underresourced. Analyses of available census data suggest that urban school districts receive about 12% less funding for each child compared to nonurban, predominantly White school districts. In addition, school districts with predominantly racial minority children don't have the same access to computers and the buildings have more structural defects than do school districts with predominantly White students ("The Myth That Black and White Schools," 1998).

INCARCERATION AND THE PRISON
INDUSTRIAL COMPLEX

By now most people have heard the oft-cited statistic that there are more Black men involved in the penal system (in prison or jail or on parole) than there are Black men in higher education. This issue clearly is a major social concern that is much deeper and complex than a mere statistic can reveal. The following quote from the Human Rights Watch (2000) report on racial disparities in the penal system underscore the issues at hand. Specifically, this quote from the report identifies the factors that account for the rise in racial disparities in arrests and sentencing of offenses and in the increasing browning of American prisons:

> The single greatest force behind the growth of the U.S. prison system since the mid-1980s has been the national "war on drugs." Spearheaded by major federal drug policy initiatives that significantly increased penalties for drug offenses and markedly increased federal funds for state anti-drug efforts, federal and state measures to combat drugs have concentrated on criminal law enforcement rather than prevention and treatment (Part IV, ¶1) . . . The impact of incarceration as a weapon in the war against drugs has fallen disproportionately on black Americans. Blacks are overrepresented in U.S. prisons relative to their proportion of the population and . . . relative to their rates of drug offending. Whites, conversely, are significantly underrepresented. The disproportionately high percentage of blacks among those admitted to state prison on drug charges is cause for alarm (Part VI, ¶1) . . . But the disparity in the rates at which black and white men over the age of eighteen are sent to prison on drug charges is nothing short of a national scandal. The drug offender admissions rate for black men ranges from 60 to a breathtaking 1,146 per 100,000 black men. The white rate, in contrast, begins at 6 and rises no higher than 139 per 100,000 white men (Part VI, ¶3) . . . Nationwide, the rate of drug admissions to state prison for black men is thirteen times greater than the rate for white men. In ten states black men are sent to state prison on drug charges at rates that are 26 to 57 times greater than those of white men in the same state. (Part VI, ¶4)

This quote clearly delineates the negative consequence of the "war on drugs" launched under the Ronald Reagan presidency. What it doesn't capture is the negative impact that the disproportionate incarceration of Black Americans has on the health and development of families and communities. Employment possibilities, participation in the polity, and opportunities to parent and provide for children are all connected to one's involvement (or not) in the prison system.

In the prison discourse, the experiences of women are often assigned to the margins, if they are mentioned at all. Women have been negatively influenced by the "war on drugs" as well. Although women make up only about 7% of the overall prison population (San Francisco NOW, 2002), a tremendous increase in women prisoners has taken place over the past decade and a half, corresponding to the "war on drugs" campaign. Black women, like their Black male counterparts, are grossly overrepresented within the prison population; although Black women are approximately 12% of the woman population, they are more than 50% of women prisoners. From 1986 to 1991, Black women's drug offense incarceration rate at the state level rose 828%, compared to increases of 241% and 328% in White and Latina women, respectively (Bush-Baskette, 1998). Mary Frances Berry (1999), historian and chairperson of the U.S. Commission on Civil Rights, sums up the crisis best: "If society had wanted to use the legal system to make war on poor Black women and children, it could have chosen no better weapons than the shameful 'war on drugs' " (p. 194).

The hypercriminalization of Black Americans is not simply a consequence of the "war on drugs"; instead, it is part of a larger macrolevel process commonly referred to in the prison activist literature as the prison industrial complex (PIC; e.g., Goldberg & Evans, 1998). Scholars and activists such as Angela Davis have been at the forefront of the prison abolitionist movement and have been raising public consciousness of the PIC. The PIC quite simply is the interconnection between private business and government interests for the purpose of social control and profit. Not only do private prisons profit from crime, but so, too, do businesses that make money from prison labor or from supplying prisons with equipment and services. The Prison Activist Resource Center (2002) defines the PIC as more "than prisons and the business and transnational corporations that profit by running, and supplying prisons, and by employing prisoners. The PIC may be thought of as the entire apparatus of internal state repression, which includes increasingly militarized police forces . . . It includes repressive laws, obscenely long sentences, state executions, judges who hand down discriminatory sentences along racial and political lines, and mandatory minimum sentencing laws . . . It includes an expanding prison culture: cop shows, court TV, films which glamorize or trivialize prison life" (p. 1). Scholars and activists place the prison system into the larger political economy and have created powerful arguments that connect the criminalization of politically disempowered groups to the profit of businesses and multinational corporations. Thus, the overrepresentation of Black Americans in prison is a social problem not only because of the stress it places on the health and development of families and communities across the country but also because it is a manifestation of a larger system of racial-class oppression.

CURRENT SOCIAL ISSUES

What accounts for the social and economic gaps between Black and White Americans? Two popular perspectives in the social science literature that help explain racial disparities in the United States are captured in the victim blame–system blame paradigm. According to the victim blame perspective, Black Americans are overrepresented among the poor, have greater college dropout rates, are overrepresented in the prison population, and so on primarily because of factors internal to the Black community. Individuals who adopt a victim blame perspective attribute social and economic disparities primarily to stereotypic beliefs that they hold about Black Americans (e.g., Blacks do not work hard, are lazy, have dysfunctional families, are violent, etc.). On the other hand, individuals who adopt a system blame perspective attribute racial disparities primarily to factors external to the Black community (e.g., racial oppression, class exploitation, sexism, and their intersections).

Our interpretation of these racial disparities is based on a system blame perspective in which we contend that the current sociopolitical and economic issues facing Black Americans are rooted in the intersection between the U.S. political economy and a history of racial oppression. A number of wide-ranging and comprehensive books explore the interconnections between multiple systems of oppression on Black American's lived experiences, including *Economics of Racism* (Perlo, 1996), *White Racism* (Feagin & Vera, 1995), *White Supremacy and Racism in the Post–Civil Rights Era* (Bonilla-Silva, 2001), and *Black Feminist Thought*

(Collins, 1990). We believe that Black Americans are not achieving at the same rate as White Americans not because they are lazy but rather because they have been locked out through complex (and sometimes hidden) systemic ways.

A brief exploration of the racial disparities in health elucidates the influence of multiple levels of oppression on individual and group experiences. Under President Bill Clinton, the Office of Minority Health (OMH) in the Department of Health and Human Services identified six major areas of health disparities in the United States: infant mortality, cancer screening and management, heart disease, diabetes, HIV infection/AIDS, and immunizations. Building on the OMH findings, the recent Healthy People 2010 (2002) report revealed some disturbing racial disparities in health. For example, according to data outlined in the report, Black infant mortality is more than twice that for Whites, and Black men are twice as likely to contract prostate cancer as White men are.

In some cases, Black Americans have a lower or similar incidence of a disease compared to their White counterparts, but because of poor health care coverage or racialized practices in the medical field, the progression of the disease is different. For example, breast cancer is more prevalent in White women, but Black, Asian American, Latina, and Native American women are more likely to die from the disease (American Cancer Society, 2000). Studies have also indicated that physicians' decision making can be subconsciously influenced by racial and gender biases. In an analogue study, Schulman and colleagues (1999) found differences in physicians' recommendations for how to manage chest pain. Women and Blacks were less likely to be referred for cardiac catheterization than were men and Whites; Black women were significantly less likely to be referred for catheterization than were White men. In other examples from the medical literature, African American patients, compared to their White counterparts, have been found to face greater barriers in obtaining necessary surgical treatments for serious medical conditions such as heart disease (Hannan et al., 1999) and lung cancer (Bach, Cramer, Warren, & Begg, 1999). Wicker and Brodie (chap. 5) also elaborate on the link among racism, class, and health in the physical and mental health needs of African Americans.

The data on health disparities illustrate that disparities in Black Americans' lived experiences are not caused by any factors within the Black community. Black women are not dying from cancer at a higher rate than White women because they are lazy, they are dying because as a group they are not receiving the same level of medical care. This different level of care may be due to race-class-gender barriers in their seeking medical assistance early, to the quality of care they receive once they seek assistance, or to a combination of the two.

In addition to health, economic, and education disparities and to hypercriminalization, Black men and women today, especially poor and working-class Black Americans, face a number of related social issues:

- Lack of a living wage, which is necessary to adequately feed, clothe, and shelter a family
- Limited quality health care coverage (especially for families who are among the working poor)

- Lack of culturally relevant and responsive teaching practices in urban and predominantly Black schools
- Increased disparities in access to computers and technology
- Racial profiling
- Racial or gender harassment on the job
- Exclusion or marginalization from the polity

Clearly, this list is not exhaustive. Instead, it provides some key areas of disparities that could be addressed by mental health workers working together with community members. Although racial disparities exist, Black Americans have always struggled against racial oppression as manifested in social and economic inequities. Currently, important Black institutions are working to enhance the quality of education being provided to Black youth; to end racial profiling practices within law enforcement; to decrease the technological divide; and to improve the physical and mental health of the community. National organizations such as the Black Radical Congress, the National Association for the Advancement of Colored People, and the Black Women's Health Project along with countless local institutions, including churches and youth-oriented organizations, are all working together to make systemic changes in laws and institutional practices and to promote individual and community agency so that people can make better lives for themselves and the community in which they live.

PSYCHOLOGICAL PROCESSES: RACIAL SCHEMAS

We have centered our discussion thus far on the influence of macrolevel systems on Black Americans' lived experiences. To contextualize the experiences of Black Americans, it was necessary to first outline how distal systems such as the political economy shape individual and community experiences and opportunities. These larger systems influence and are influenced by micro- and individual-level systems, which in turn help shape individual behavior. In this section, we describe key race-related individual-level processes, especially as they relate to health.

A little over 30 years ago, William Cross (1971) introduced his nigrescence, or the Negro to Black Conversion, model. As one of the first psychological models of racial identity, his early work radically transformed how applied psychologists thought about race and within-group differences among Black Americans. Nigrescence provided a framework for psychologists to conceptualize the ways in which Black Americans may differ in the saliency and "sense" of blackness, which in turn has been found to have implications for health outcomes. Since Cross's seminal publication, scholars have extended, revised, and created new models of racial identity to describe the multiple ways in which Black individuals come (a) to understand themselves as racial beings in a racially hierarchical society, and (b) to develop a positive racial group concept within this context. In fact, nigrescence and its various branches are the most widely cited and researched black racial identity theories in the social science literature. More recently, scholars also have begun to examine other dimensions of racial beliefs among Black Americans to further capture the varied ways in which people make sense of and process racial information.

The purpose of this section is to describe a number of racial schematic paradigms in the literature and to provide empirical support for the models. By racial schemata we mean the psychological processes that individuals use to encode, retrieve, and make meaning of race and racism. Because of space constraints we have delimited our discussion to three topics: an outline of two racial identity models (i.e., Helms's and Cross's models); cultural mistrust; and color-blind racial ideology. Other racial schematic models in the literature that are not covered in this chapter include the Multidimensional Inventory of Black Identity and corresponding theory (Sellers, Rowley, Chavous, Shelton, & Smith, 1997), African Self-Consciousness (Baldwin, 1981), collective self-esteem (Luhtanen & Crocker, 1992), and ethnic identity models (e.g., Phinney, 1992).

Racial Identity

Drawing on Cross's nigrescence conceptualization, Janet Helms developed a racial identity model that initially applied to Black Americans (Helms, 1990) and that later extended to racial minorities more generally (Helms, 1995). From Helms's perspective, racial identity reflects how individuals come to understand themselves as racial beings within a racially stratified society. Helms developed parallel theories for Whites and for racial minorities. Thus, one theory was designed to describe the process for those individuals who benefit from the racial hierarchy (i.e., Whites), and the other theory applied to those who experience oppression within the hierarchy (i.e., racial minorities). For our purposes, we will describe the latter model only as it applies to Black Americans.

Helms's (1995) model consists of a rearticulation of Cross's five basic racial identity stages (or statuses, as redefined by Helms) that describe the multiple attitudes, beliefs, and behaviors Black Americans use to develop a positive racial identity. Individuals endorse attitudes and beliefs reflective of each of the statuses simultaneously, but depending on social context and life experience, individuals typically have stronger inclinations that reflect one status. The five strategies of Helms's racial identity model are as follows:

1. *Conformity* (formally referred to as preencounter) reflects an internalization of dominant White middle-class beliefs about what being Black means in society. Individuals operating in this status have a restricted dichotomous view of race in which that which best approximates white or Whites is right and good and that which represents black or Blacks is negative. Conformity attitudes also reflect the dominant ideology that race is unimportant.
2. *Dissonance* (formally referred to as encounter) is captured by a disruption in an individual's beliefs about race; a person operating in this status struggles between countering internalized negative beliefs about Blackness and trying to explore a personal definition of what it means to be Black. Race and racism are now coming into the individual's radar.
3. *Immersion/Emersion* portrays the processes of completely immersing oneself into Blackness and then emerging from these beliefs to the adoption of more flexible views on race. Attitudes and beliefs in this status are the oppo-

site of those in conformity status; now, black is perceived as good and white as bad. Individuals operating in this status present a heightened awareness of race and racism in multiple situations. Their understanding of what it means to be Black is externally defined.

4. *Internalization* reflects an internalized definition of what it means to be Black. Individuals who operate in this status recognize the influence of race and racism but also begin to acknowledge other social identities in their lives (e.g., gender, sexual orientation). This status represents a shift from an external definition of a racial self to an internal one.

5. *Internalization Commitment* is similar to internalization, except that individuals who operate in this status incorporate a more multicultural perspective in which they have internalized a positive racial identity. They have also begun to build coalitions with and make connections to individuals from other oppressed groups.

The empirical research to date has provided strong support for the first four statuses of the model (the fifth status is not measured by the widely used Racial Identity Attitudes Scale developed by Janet Helms and Thomas Parham; see Helms, 1990, for a description). Thus, there is now mounting documentation of the link between racial identity attitude and mental health, generally suggesting that greater internalization of a positive racial identity is related to increased psychological well-being and more effective coping skills among African Americans. Conversely, limited awareness of and comfort with one's racial identity is related to lower psychological well-being and greater psychological distress (see Neville & Lilly, 2000, for a review). More specifically, *conformity* attitudes have been found to be related to greater perceived stress, self-derogation, and suppressed anger. *Internalization* attitudes, on the other hand, have been found to be related to greater problem-solving efficacy, increased self-esteem, and positive identification with one's ethnic origin (see Fischer & Moradi, 2001, for a review).

Cross's nigrescence model had originally been designed to describe the varied levels of Black consciousness during the civil rights and black power movements. William Cross (1995) and colleagues (e.g., 2001; Vandiver, Cross, Worrell, & Fhagen-Smith, 2002) have revised the earlier nigrescence model to better reflect the nuances of Black identity in the current racial climate. Cross and Vandiver (2001) summarized the revised model and introduced a new measurement to assess the revised nigrescence theory: the Cross Racial Identity Scale (CRIS). The new theory includes a reinterpretation and extension of Cross's five original stages (preencounter, encounter, immersion-emersion, internalization, and internalization-commitment) and a redefinition of racial identity to reflect the degree to which individuals identify racially as Black and their willingness to engage in problems facing the Black community and in Black American culture. The key difference in the revised model is the identification of racial identity subtypes. For example, the revised model considers three preencounter subtypes; each of these subtypes, or exemplars, reflect a low degree of racial saliency or importance of race to one's identity, but they differ in the degree of expressed racial hatred. The extended model now includes eight identity types captured in the following exemplars:

1. *Preencounter assimilation* represents a nonengagement in race and Blackness. This type of person adopts a raceless identity and often views self as an American and an individual.
2. *Preencounter miseducation* reflects an internalization of negative racial stereotypes of Blacks as a people. This type of person is able to separate his or her personal identity from that of other Blacks.
3. *Preencounter (racial) self-hatred* depicts a person with deep-seated hatred for Blackness and loathes being Black. Needless to say, such an individual avoids connections with Black activities and Black American culture.
4. *Immersion-emersion anti-White* represents an intense connection to what is Black and an intense hatred for Whiteness and everything that it represents.
5. *Immersion-emersion intense Black involvement* captures individuals who adopt an almost cultlike connection to and commitment to anything representing Blackness.
6. *Internalization nationalist/Afrocentric* describes a person who adopts an Afrocentric approach to self and others and is committed to Black issues.
7. *Internalization biculturalist* refers to an individual who engages in both mainstream culture and Black American issues and culture.
8. *Internalization multiculturalist inclusive* captures a person who acknowledges his or her multiple identities and is committed to and engages in Black issues.

Most of the empirical studies on the CRIS to date have focused on establishing the content, construct, convergent, and divergent validity of the scale. Initial data, however, support a link between racial identity types and psychological well-being. Specifically, greater endorsement of the preencounter self-hatred type has been found to be related to decreased self-esteem (Vandiver et al., 2002). Also, research suggests that the exemplars can be characterized by two higher order factors: prediscovery and discovery. Prediscovery types include the three preencounter exemplars and thus reflect individuals who have not begun to explore the meaning and importance of race in their lives. Conversely, the discovery higher order factor reflects an internalized racial identity and includes the internalized multiculturalist inclusive, internalized Afrocentric, and immersion-emersion anti-White exemplars.

Cultural Mistrust

The external forces described earlier in this chapter coupled with individual personal and racial experience influence the development of an individual's racial identity. This identity, in turn, is linked to mental health functioning among Black Americans. Cultural mistrust is another racial schematic structure that is shaped by both systemic racial oppression and individual experiences and that also impacts Black American health-related processes. Generally, cultural mistrust refers to a healthy distrust of potentially threatening environments and systems. More specifically, cultural mistrust is the suspicion or mistrust that some Black Americans have of majority institutional structure (e.g., police, education, work, politics and law) as well as of interpersonal situations with Whites as a result of a history of racial oppression in the United States. Levels of expressed cultural mistrust can help explain why some Black Americans may avoid interpersonal contacts with Whites or may choose to not seek counseling or assistance from the police after a violent crime. Cultural mistrust can impact individual and group level decisions and activities in myriad ways.

Since Terrell and Terrell's seminal work in 1981, cultural mistrust has emerged as an important within-group variable to help explain the varied perspectives of Black Americans, especially perspectives associated with counseling-related processes. Recently, Whaley (2001) quantitatively reviewed 22 studies that used the Cultural Mistrust Inventory, the primary scale used in the literature to assess cultural mistrust. Findings from this meta-analysis suggest that African Americans' mistrust of broader majority White institutions is transferable to the therapy context as well. It is rare for individuals to be able to compartmentalize racial distrust in just one domain; thus, individuals who are distrustful of the law enforcement or of the education system because they represent predominantly White institutions are also likely to distrust most institutional structures that are perceived to be White, such as counseling and psychotherapy. Specific research on the topic has found that higher levels of cultural mistrust are related to lower satisfaction with medical care (LaVeist, Nickerson, & Bowie, 2000), lower positive attitudes toward the seeking of help for a mental health concern at a predominantly White clinic (Nickerson, Helms, & Terrell, 1994), lower self-disclosure in a counseling situation even with a Black mental health practitioner (Thompson, Worthington, & Atkinson, 1994), and more negative initial evaluations of a White practitioner (Watkins, F. Terrell, & S. L. Terrell, 1989).

Color-Blind Racial Ideology

Outside of racial identity and cultural mistrust theories, there is very little research on within-group differences among African Americans with respect to racial beliefs or racial schemas. Racial identity focuses on the degree to which individuals understand themselves as racial beings within a hierarchal social structure, and cultural mistrust centers on distrust of these structures. Little is known about other aspects of racial beliefs, such as potential differences in Black Americans' understanding and awareness of racism, or Black Americans' multiple racial ideologies and the cognitive filters that they adopt to perceive the social world.

Color-blind racial beliefs have emerged as a new construct that has implications for an understanding of racial ideologies of individuals across racial and ethnic backgrounds. Essentially, a color-blind racial framework is a contemporary set of beliefs that serves to minimize, ignore, or distort the existence of race and racism. At its core is the belief that racism is a thing of the past and that race and racism no longer play a significant role in current social and economic realities. Color-blind racial ideology differs from racial identity in that the latter is concerned with how a person makes psychological meaning out of being Black. Color-blind racial ideology, on the other hand, is more concerned with how aware a person is of external factors (i.e., the existence of institutional racism).

Most of the research on color-blind racial ideology has linked higher levels of denial of racism to increased racial prejudice and intolerance among Whites. For example, Neville, Lilly, Duran, Lee, and Browne (2000) found that higher color-blind racial beliefs among a predominantly White sample were related to greater negative racist beliefs against Blacks, to racial and gender intolerance, and to the belief that society is fair and just (i.e., just world belief hypothesis).

Emerging theoretical and empirical research examines the implications of the adoption of color-blind racial ideology for Black Americans. Initial data suggests that Black Americans who have greater levels of denial and distortion of racism are more likely to internalize negative racial messages, adopt antiegalitarian beliefs, and blame Black people themselves for social and economic inequities (Neville, Coleman, Falconer, & Holmes, 2002). In essence, to adopt a color-blind racial perspective is to adopt a belief system that, if acted upon, can counter one's individual and group survival. For example, individuals who deny the existence of racism may be more likely to support legislation that limits racial representation in areas such as education. Also, individuals who fail to perceive racism in their own environment may lack psychological preparation to deal with racism once it is acknowledged. A number of narratives have demonstrated how some "color-blind" Black professionals have become overwhelmed with high levels of racial stress once they realized that race and racism do matter, including Cose's (1993) *The Rage of a Privileged Class* and Barrett's (1999) *The Good Black: A True Story of Race in America.*

In this section, we explored three domains of racial schemas, or ways in which Black Americans process and make meaning of racial information within the current social structure. The interconnected domains of racial identity, cultural mistrust, and color-blind racial ideology have implications for psychological adjustment (primarily racial identity attitudes) as well as health-related behaviors and political choices. More research is needed to establish a link between racial schemas and physical health issues, especially help-seeking behaviors, medical compliance, physical health symptoms, and how medical professionals respond to and treat Black patients.

RISK AND PROTECTIVE FACTORS RELATED TO MENTAL AND PHYSICAL HEALTH

Up to this point, our primary discussion has been the ill effects of racial oppression on Black Americans, whether they are manifested in social and economic disparities or on individual-level psychological processes. In this section, we provide a framework for the reader to contextualize Black American health, taking into consideration the issues that threaten health as well as those that promote health. Using a risk-protective paradigm, we outline key macro- and individual-level factors that (a) pose as risk factors to the development and progression of psychological and physical health and (b) protect individuals from the development of psychological distress and physical disease, primarily related to stress and at-risk circumstances. In Clark, Anderson, Clark, and Williams's (1999) path-breaking *American Psychologist* article, they proposed a contextual model to examine the biopsychosocial effects of racism on Black Americans. Within this model they implicitly consider both risk and protective factors that influence health.

Clark and colleagues (1999) theorized that the physical and mental health outcomes of Black Americans are manifoldly determined by internal and external forces. Black Americans are faced with complex environmental stimuli on a daily basis; these stimuli can be people's living conditions, their interactions with individuals or institutions, or any aspect of their environment that may be a source of chronic and acute stress. These stimuli might represent sources of general stress that most people may encounter, or they may be related to race and racism. An individual's evaluation of whether an environmental stimuli is a source of general or racial stress is moderated by a host of individual variables related to that person's constitutional factors (e.g., skin tone, family history of disease), sociodemographic factors (e.g., class background), and psychological and behavioral factors (e.g., personality, self-concept). Clark and colleagues further argue that there is a link between perceptions of racism or general stressor and health outcomes. However, this relationship is attenuated by the types of coping responses used by an individual to deal with the stressors and also by an individual's psychological and physical stress reactions (e.g., anger, resentment, hostility).

As a way to synthesize and extend both the risk-protective and the biopsychosocial models, we outline here some key factors that have been found to increase disease and distress and some factors that promote well-being and health. Clearly, macrolevel systems influence the type and quality of health care provided to communities and individuals as well as the nature and progression of disease and distress. For example, the intersection between racism and class exploitation plays a role in the type of health risks that poor and working-class Black individuals confront and also the type of health care coverage and treatment provided. At the same time, larger Black institutions, through such tools as lobbying, education and training, community outreach, advocacy, and so on, are trying to counter these negative forces and to create conditions that enhance the health of Black Americans.

For more than two decades the Black Women's Health Project (BWHP), for example, has diligently worked to enhance the health status of African American women. The organization's education, outreach, and research efforts have gained national attention. BWHP has received federal funding for important research investigations, including projects that evaluate the effectiveness of weight and obesity reduction health programs and decrease domestic violence in African American communities. BWHP also works collaboratively with other organizations (e.g., the National Coalition for Health and Environmental Justice) to address the root causes of critical health concerns. The Association of Black Psychologists (ABPsi) is another national organization that has worked since the late 1960s to improve access to and quality of mental health services for African Americans. ABPsi has been involved in important struggles related to African American health, including AIDS/HIV and K-12 education work. To find out more about or to get involved in health activism, please visit the Black Women's Health Project's website at www.blackwomenshealth.org or the Association of Black Psychologists' website at www.abpsi.org.

Micro systems such as family and community involvement have a more direct impact on psychological and physical health of African Americans than do macro systems. Clearly, family and community interactions can be a source of both tremendous stress and tremendous support. Micro systems have the potential to buffer the effects of racism-related stress and other types of stress on health. Family, church, and social organizations are central to the Black American community; they foster community and social involvement and consequently promote psychological well-being and health (Snowden, 2001). These various social networks provide a supportive atmosphere that exerts a protective influence against the development of poor health. For example, individuals under stress may find that their social support networks keep them from developing stress-related symptomatology. Social embeddedness is one form of social support; it refers to a network of friends, relatives, and community. Black Americans often rely on these social support systems to help them deal with daily life stressors. These social support networks enhance well-being through their protective effects and their connectedness and fellowship.

We have already identified individual-level processes, such as personal social class, racial identity, and cultural mistrust, that influence health outcomes. Other individual-level processes, such as personality and coping style, serve as protective factors in the development of disease and distress. The importance of religiousness among African Americans has also been shown to be particularly helpful protective mechanism. Some research findings indicate that Black Americans rely on religiousness to cope with stressful life events more so than do White Americans (e.g., Bourjolly, 1998). More important, research suggests that religious involvement in turn is related to psychological well-being (Levin & Taylor, 1998) and physical health (Hill & Butler, 1995). In a recent investigation, Bowen-Reid and Harrell (2002) examined the harmful effects of racist experiences on physical and mental health and examined the moderating effects of spirituality. They found that individuals with a religious commitment suffered less somatic and psychological distress. In sum, the research on micro and individual protective mechanisms suggests that Black Americans receive support from their social networks and utilize various coping strategies to deal with daily life stressors. The quantity and quality of social relationships and interactions within organizations, church, and the community have an important bearing on the amount of stress that Black Americans may perceive in their environments and, moreover, on decreasing the likelihood that life stressors will adversely affect their overall health.

CONCLUSION

In this chapter, we have provided information about the demography, class, and educational background of Black Americans as a way to contextualize their mental and physical health. We have explained how racial oppression interfaces with other forms of oppression to influence the lived experiences of Black American men and women, and we have shown that individual and collective factors such as racial schemas and community outreach can potentially enhance health as well.

Exercises

1. In groups of three or four, design a social justice action project that addresses a specific social injustice concerning Black Americans in your community (e.g., department, campus, neighborhood, city). To create your project plan, answer the following questions:
   (a) Why have you selected this specific social injustice?
   (b) What organizations or individuals in the community are working on the targeted injustice?
   (c) How can you work with that organization or individual on the project?
   (d) What are the potential goals of your project?
   (e) What are your steps to achieve these goals? (Remember, it is essential to work collaboratively with others who are already organizing around this issue. Why reinvent the wheel?)
   (f) How would you evaluate the effectiveness of your social justice action project?

2. Read this case summary about Lana Thompson, and answer the following questions:
   (a) What additional information would you like to obtain from Lana and why?
   (b) What are Lana's presenting concerns, and what potential factors influence these concerns?
   (c) What are some potential intervention strategies that would address Lana's concerns?

Lana Thompson is a 22-year-old sophomore at Summerville University, a predominantly White 4-year institution. Lana is the youngest of three children and the first and only person in her family to attend college. Her parents are both African American and were high school sweethearts. Her mother works in retail at a department store in her hometown, and her father works at the post office. There does not appear to be any psychopathology in her immediate family (e.g., alcohol dependence, depression, etc.). Summerville University is approximately 110 miles from her parents' home and the predominantly Black community in which she was raised. Lana is embarrassed by her only brother, who is in prison for a drug-related crime; she prefers not to talk about him or the fact that he is in prison. After working for three years in retail upon graduating from high school, Lana decided to enroll in college and major in business; she said she wants to get more out of her life than her parents have. She explicitly stated that she wanted to "get out of that ghetto." Lana is coming to counseling because she has been tired lately and has been unable to concentrate on her schoolwork. She has one or two close friends on campus, but she feels as though she cannot connect with others because she is slightly older than most of her fellow students. Lana indicated that she particularly feels alienated in her business classes, even though she has made numerous gestures to befriend her classmates. She is thinking about changing her major, but she is uncertain of her options. Because Lana is not receiving a scholarship, she is working more than 30 hours a week to make ends meet.

REFERENCES

American Cancer Society. (2000). *Cancer facts and figures 2000.* Retrieved October 3, 2002, from www.cancer.org/downloads/STT/F&F00.pdf

American Council on Education. (2002). *Students of color make enrollment and graduation gains in postsecondary education according to ACE's annual status report.* Retrieved October 3, 2002, from www.acenet.edu/news/press_release/2002/09september/OMHE.report.html

Bach, P. B., Cramer, L. D., Warren, J. L., & Begg, C. B. (1999). Racial differences in treatment of early-stage lung cancer. *New England Journal of Medicine, 341,* 1198–1205.

Baldwin, J. A. (1981). Notes on an Africentric theory of Black personality. *Western Journal of Black Studies, 5,* 172–179.

Barrett, P. M. (1999). *The good Black: A true story of race in America.* New York: Dutton.

Berry, M. F. (1999, October). The forgotten prisoners of a disastrous war. *Essence,* p. 194.

Bonilla-Silva, E. (2001). *White supremacy and racism in the post-civil rights era.* Colorado: Lynne Rienner.

Bourjolly, J. N. (1998). Differences in religiousness among black and white women with breast cancer. *Social Work in Health Care, 28,* 21–39.

Bowen-Reid, T. L., & Harrell, J. P. (2002). Racist experiences and health outcomes: An examination of spirituality as a buffer. *Journal of Black Psychology, 28,* 18–36.

Bureau of Labor Statistics. (2000). *Report on the youth labor force.* U.S. Department of Labor. Retrieved October 3, 2002, from www.blws.gov/opub/rylf/pdf/rylf2000.pdf

Bureau of Labor Statistics. (2002). *A profile of the working poor, 2000.* U.S. Department of Labor. Retrieved October 3, 2002, from www.bls.gov/cps/cpswp2000.pdf

Bush-Baskette, S. R. (1998). The war on drugs as a war against Black women. In S. I. Miller (Ed.), *Crime control and women: Feminist implications of criminal justice policy* (pp. 113–129). Thousand Oaks, CA: Sage.

Clark, R., Anderson, N. B., Clark, V. R., & Williams, D. R. (1999). Racism as a stressor for African Americans: A biopsychosocial model. *American Psychologist, 54,* 805–816.

Collins, P. H. (1990). *Black feminist thought: Knowledge, consciousness, and the politics of empowerment.* New York: Routledge, Chapman, and Hall.

Cose, E. (1993). *The rage of a privileged class.* New York: HarperCollins.

Cross, W. E., Jr. (1971). The Negro-to-Black conversion experience. *Black World, 20,* 13–17.

Cross, W. E., Jr. (1995). The psychology of Nigrescence: Revising the Cross model. In J. G. Ponterotto, J. M. Cases, L. A. Suzuki, & C. M. Alexander (Eds.), *Handbook of multicultural counseling* (pp. 93–122). Newbury Park, CA: Sage.

Cross, W. E., Jr., & Vandiver, B. J. (2001). Nigrescence theory and measurement: Introducing the Cross Racial Identity Scale (CRIS). In J. G. Ponterotto, J. M. Cases, L. A. Suzuki, & C. M. Alexander (Eds.), *Handbook of multicultural counseling* (2nd ed., pp. 371–393). Newbury Park, CA: Sage.

Don't count on a college diploma to reduce the Black-White unemployment gap. (1998, Spring). *Journal of Blacks in Higher Education,* 16–17.

Feagin, J. R., & Vera, H. (1995). *White racism.* New York: Routledge.

Fischer, A. R., & Moradi, B. (2001). Racial and ethnic identity: Recent developments and needed directions. In J. G. Ponterotto, J. M. Cases, L. A. Suzuki, & C. M. Alexander (Eds.), *Handbook of multicultural counseling* (2nd ed., 341–370). Newbury Park, CA: Sage.

Goldberg, E., & Evans, L. (1998). *The prison industrial complex and the global economy.* Berkeley, CA: Agit.

Hannan, E., L., van Ryn, M., Burke, J., Stone, D., Kumar, D., Arani, D., Pierce, W., Rafii, S., Sanborn, T. A., Sharma, S., Slater, J., & DeBuono, B. A. (1999). Access to coronary artery bypass surgery by race/ethnicity and gender among patients who are appropriate for surgery. *Medical Care, 37,* 68–77.

Healthy People 2010: A systematic approach. (2002). Retrieved on January 21, 2003 from www.healthypeople.gov/Document/html/uih/uih_bw/uih_2.htm

Helms, J. E. (Ed.). (1990). *Black and White racial identity: Theory, research, and practice* (pp. 9–47). New York: Greenwood.

Helms, J. E. (1995). An update of Helms's White and people of color racial identity models. In J. G. Ponterotto, J. M. Cases, L. A. Suzuki, & C. M. Alexander (Eds.), *Handbook of multicultural counseling* (pp. 93–122). Newbury Park, CA: Sage.

Hill, P. C., & Butler, E. M. (1995). The role of religion in promoting physical health. *Journal of Christianity, 14,* 141–155.

Human Rights Watch. (2000). *Punishment and prejudice: Racial disparities in the war on drugs.* Retrieved on January 21, 2003, from www.hrw.org/reports/2000/usa

Krieger, N., Williams, D. R., & Moss, N. E. (1997). Measuring social class in U.S. public health research: Concepts, methodologies, and guidelines. *Annual Review of Public Health, 18,* 341–378.

LaVeist, T. A., Nickerson, K. J., & Bowie, J. V. (2000). Attitudes about racism, medical mistrust, and satisfaction with care among African American and White cardiac patients. *Medical Care Research and Review, 57,* 146–161.

Levin, J. S., & Taylor, R. J. (1998). Panel analyses of religious involvement and well-being in African Americans: Contemporaneous versus longitudinal effects. *Journal for the Scientific Study of Religion, 37,* 695–709.

Luhtanen, R., & Crocker, J. (1992). A collective self-esteem scale: Self-evaluation of one's social identity. *Personality and Social Psychology, 71,* 512–526.

Murry, V. M., & Brody, G. H. (1999). Self-regulation and self-worth of Black children reared in economically stressed, rural, single-mother-headed families: the contribution of risk and protective factors. *Journal of Family Issues, 20,* 458–484.

The myth that Black and White schools are equally funded. (1998, Winter). *Journal of Blacks in Higher Education,* 17–18.

Neville, H. A., Coleman, M. N., Falconer, J. W., & Holmes, D. (2002, August). *Color-blind racial attitudes and false psychological consciousness among African Americans.* Poster session presented at the annual meeting of the American Psychological Association, Chicago, IL.

Neville, H. A., & Lilly, R. L. (2000). The relationship between racial identity cluster profiles and psychological distress among African American college students. *Journal of Multicultural Counseling and Development, 28,* 194–208.

Neville, H. A., Lilly, R. L., Duran, G., Lee, R. M., & Browne, L. (2000). Construction and initial validation of the Color-Blind Racial Attitudes Scale (CoBRAS). *Journal of Counseling Psychology, 47,* 59–70.

Nickerson, K. J., Helms, J. E., & Terrell, F. (1994). Cultural mistrust, opinions about mental illness, and Black students' attitudes toward seeking psychological help from counselors. *Journal of Counseling Psychology, 41,* 378–385.

Perlo, V. (1996). *Economics of racism in the U.S.A.: The roots of inequality.* New York: International Publishers.

Phinney, J. S. (1992). The Multigroup Ethnic Identity Measure: A new scale for use with diverse groups. *Journal of Adolescence, 13,* 171–183.

Price, R. H., Choi, J. N., & Vinokur, A. D. (2002). Links in the chain of adversity following job loss: How financial strain and loss of personal control lead to depression, impaired functioning, and poor health. *Journal of Occupational Health Psychology, 7,* 302–312.

Prison Activist Resource Center. (2002). *The World Trade Organization and the prison industrial complex.* Retrieved November 10, 2002, from www.globalexchange.org/wto/prisons.html

San Francisco NOW. (2002). *Women in Prison Task Force.* Retrieved on January 21, 2003, from www.sfnow.org/womeninprisons.php

School of Cooperative Individualism. (1999). *Wealth distribution statistics as reported by the United Nations Development Program.* Retrieved October 3, 2002, from www.cooperativeindividualism.org/wealth_distribution

Schulman, K. A., Berlin, J. A., Harless, W., Kerner, J. F., Sistrunk, S., Gersh, B. J., Dube, R., Taleghani, C. K., Burke, J. E., Williams, S., Esenberg, J. M., Escarce, J. J., & Ayers, W. (1999). The effects of race and sex on physicians' recommendations for cardiac catheterization. *The New England Journal of Medicine, 25,* 618–626.

Sears, D. O., Hetts, J. J., Sidanius, J., & Bobo, L. (2000). Race in American politics: Framing the debate. In D. O. Sears, J. Sidanius, and L. Bobo (Eds.), *Racialized politics: the debate about racism in America* (pp. 1–43). Chicago: University of Chicago.

Sellers, R. M., Rowley, S. A. J., Chavous, T. M., Shelton, J. N., & Smith, M. A. (1997). Multidimensional Inventory of Black Identity: A preliminary investigation of reliability and construct validity. *Journal of Personality and Psychology, 73,* 805–815.

Snowden, L. R. (2001). Social embeddedness and psychological well-being among African-Americans and Whites. *American Journal of Community Psychology, 29,* 519–536.

Terrell, F., & Terrell, S. L. (1981). An inventory to measure cultural mistrust among Blacks. *Western Journal of Black Studies, 5,* 180–184.

Thompson, C. E., Worthington, R., & Atkinson, D. R. (1994). Counselor content orientation, counselor race, and Black women's cultural mistrust and self-disclosures. *Journal of Counseling Psychology, 41,* 155–161.

U.S. Census Bureau. (1999). *Educational attainment in the United States.* Retrieved October 3, 2002, from www.census.gov/prod/2000pubs/p20-528.pdf

U.S. Census Bureau. (2001a). *The Black population: 2000.* Retrieved October 3, 2002, from www.census.gov/prod/2001pubs/c2kbr01-5.pdf

U.S. Census Bureau. (2001b). *Money income in the United States: 2000.* Retrieved October 3, 2002, from www.census.gov/prod/2001pubs/p60-213.pdf

U.S. Census Bureau. (2001c). *Poverty in the United States: 2000.* Retrieved October 3, 2002, from www.census.gov/prod/2001pubs/p60-214.pdf

Vandiver, B., Cross, W. E., Jr., Worrell, F., & Fhagen-Smith, P. E. (2002). Validating the Cross Racial Identity Scale. *Journal of Counseling Psychology, 49,* 71–85.

Vandiver, B., Fhagen-Smith, P. E., Cokley, K. O., Cross, W. E., Jr., & Worrell, F. C. (2001). Cross's nigrescence model: From theory to scale to theory. *Journal of Multicultural Counseling and Development, 29,* 174–200.

Watkins, C. E., Terrell, F., & Terrell, S. L. (1989). Cultural mistrust and its effects on expectational variables in Black client–White counselor relationships. *Journal of Counseling Psychology, 36,* 447–450.

Whaley, A. L. (2001). Cultural mistrust and mental health services for African Americans: A review and meta-analysis. *Counseling Psychologist, 29,* 513–531.

CHAPTER 5

The Physical and Mental Health Needs of African Americans

Lori R. Wicker and Robert E. Brodie II, University of California, Santa Barbara

In exploring the physical and mental health needs of African Americans, mental health practitioners must have an understanding of the environmental context in which many African Americans exist and how environmental factors can affect the expression, interpretation, and prevalence rates of physical and mental illness. However, mental health professionals working with African American clients should not take a negative perspective of the African American client and community while reading the information presented in this chapter. The African American family and community are extremely adaptive and resilient, given the myriad effects of personal discrimination and institutionalized racism. When working with African American clients, the professional should take care to emphasize the strengths of the clients and their community and to assess behaviors associated with socioeconomic status as potentially adaptive for an individual living in an adverse situation.

To begin this process, clinicians need to think in a culturally responsive manner, that is, they should actively integrate culture into all phases of the therapeutic process (Smith & Celano, 2000), from initial client contact to the termination phase. Clinicians must become aware of the fact that a client's racial/ethnic group membership and socioeconomic status may have an effect on the presentation of mental illness, the clinician's perception and judgments about the client, and subsequent interactions with the client, including diagnosis and recommended treatment plan. A culturally responsive professional who works with African American clients needs an accurate understanding of the African American family; its African roots, historical development, and contemporary expressions; and its impact on the psychological development and socialization of its members (Parham, White, & Ajamu, 1999).

In this chapter we include an overview of the physical and mental health needs of African Americans, information on the factors that attribute to their physical and mental health needs, and an outline of the specific physical and mental health needs of African American adults and children. We conclude the chapter with a discussion of the implications of the physical and mental health needs of African Americans for counseling.

PHYSICAL HEALTH

On the basis of the health literature and statistical rates of physical problems that afflict the African American population, it is clear that African Americans suffer from a higher rate of morbidity and have higher rates of mortality than Whites do. In many cases, African Americans also suffer from a higher rate of morbidity and mortality than do Hispanics/Latinos/Chicanos and Asian Americans (Sylvester, 1998). Specifically, African Americans have a higher incidence of hypertension, diabetes, AIDS, physical injuries by firearms, infant mortality, homicide, sickle cell disease, obesity, and asthma, and higher death rates resulting from heart disease, stroke, and cancers (National Center for Health Statistics, 2001; U.S. Census Bureau, 2000). Furthermore, according to Washington (1997), sexually transmitted diseases independent of HIV as well as tuberculosis and arthritis are prevalent causes of morbidity within the African American community that may be overlooked because they are not among leading causes of mortality. African Americans also have a high incidence of dental problems such as early tooth loss, greater tooth decay, and periodontal disease (Jones-Wilson & Mabunda, 1997).

In order to fully understand why African Americans have higher morbidity and mortality rates than other ethnic groups, researchers have investigated various factors associated with these racial differences. Findings indicate that differences in morbidity and mortality rates between African Americans and Whites are decreased when socioeconomic status is controlled for, yet in many cases African Americans still have higher rates of morbidity and mortality compared to Whites (Ostrove, Feldman, & Adler, 1999). Low socioeconomic status is in part a contributing factor to increased morbidity and mortality among African Americans, but the difference in morbidity and mortality may also be accounted for by factors that are related to institutional racism, culture and lifestyle, and genetic predisposition. A relationship between the health and the socioeconomic status of African Americans has also been found with regard to mental illness and will be further explored in the mental health section of this chapter.

Causal Attributions

Physical health problems among African Americans are often caused by low socioeconomic status, institutional racism, cultural and lifestyle factors, and genetic predisposition. The following sections consider each of these causal attributions.

Low Socioeconomic Status   The higher rate of morbidity and mortality among African Americans is partly explained by their low socioeconomic status. As a result of economic hardship, African Americans are less likely to be able to afford the resources associated with good health and more likely to be exposed to factors associated with poor health.

Low-income African Americans are less likely to have access to resources that facilitate good health and health care practices. For example, they are less likely to have medical insurance. In 1999, 19.4% of African Americans under the age of 65 years were without health care coverage, compared to 14.7% of Whites (National

Center for Health Statistics [NCHS], 2001). Thus, statistics suggest only about a 5% difference between the number of African Americans who have health insurance and the number of Whites. However, an additional, more critical factor may be that a substantial number of African Americans are underinsured, such that their copayment is beyond what they can afford (Sylvester, 1998). Many African Americans work in low-paying and low-prestige jobs that do not offer complete medical coverage. Without adequate health care coverage, African Americans are at risk for decreased physical health. They are less likely to have annual checkups, take part in preventative screening, and purchase needed medications and are more likely to seek health care from an emergency room or hospital clinic only when they have become severely ill (Sylvester, 1998). Additionally, socioeconomic status can affect nutritional and exercise habits. Individuals with low socioeconomic status are more likely to purchase foods that are less expensive but not as nutritious (e.g., canned produce vs. fresh produce). They are also less likely to belong to health clubs or gyms, which decrease the likelihood of exercise. Notably, children from families with low socioeconomic status are also at risk for receiving inefficient medical care and poor nutrition (Sylvester, 1998).

Low-income African Americans are more likely to be exposed to environmental factors that are associated with decreased health. They are more likely to live in impoverished neighborhoods that have high rates of crime and violence (Reed, Darity, & Roberson, 1993). Thus, they are at increased risk of injury and death due to violence. Furthermore, individuals with low-socioeconomic status are more likely to work in low-status jobs that may involve a high amount of physical labor; hence, they are at increased risk for job-related accidents and physical problems (e.g., back injury). These jobs may also involve exposure to occupational hazards, waste materials, and toxins, which over time can have negative health effects (Robinson, 1989, as cited by Jackson and Sellers, 1996).

Institutional Racism   As a result of their minority status within the United States, African Americans are detrimentally affected by institutionalized racism. Specifically, the formal practices, traditions, customs, and behaviors that are ingrained in the country's societal framework are oftentimes harmful to African Americans and deny them the same opportunities that other racial groups have. Because of institutionalized racism, African Americans have experienced discrimination in the quality of education their children receive as well as in areas such as employment and salary practices, access to medical care, housing, and the criminal justice system. These factors contribute in part to the increased rate of morbidity and mortality among African Americans.

Several instances of institutional racism are related to residential racial segregation. As a result of residential segregation, first initiated after the abolition of slavery and further compounded by the National Housing Act of 1934 as part of Franklin Delano Roosevelt's New Deal, African Americans are most highly concentrated in urban inner cities and metropolitan areas. These areas have higher levels of air pollution, poorer air quality, and higher numbers of toxic waste dumps, all of which have been associated with a higher prevalence of asthma and respiratory problems among African Americans living in these areas (Jackson &

Sellers, 1996). The buildings in these cities tend to have high levels of lead, which results in a higher prevalence of lead poisoning among African American children (Jackson & Sellers, 1996). Additionally, billboards that promote use of alcohol and tobacco as well as liquor stores that provide access to them are more prevalent in urban inner cities than in other areas (Jackson & Sellers, 1996; Reed et al., 1993). The greater number of billboards and liquor stores in predominately African American communities attests to the large amount of money invested in increasing the likelihood that African Americans will purchase and consume alcohol and cigarettes.

Other forms of institutional racism that have a negative impact on the physical health of African Americans are related to the medical field and medical professionals. It appears that less research may be conducted on those diseases and conditions that primarily affect African Americans. For example, Reed et al. (1993) noted that sickle cell anemia in African Americans has a prevalence 6 times greater than does diabetes in the general population, but it receives minimal societal attention. Additionally, African Americans may receive substandard medical attention. Many low-income African Americans rely on state or county medical facilities, where medical care may be delayed or negligible because of overcrowding and a high patient-to-doctor ratio. Furthermore, the medical profession does not appear to be adequately transmitting information regarding the awareness of symptoms and the positive effects of treatment for various health conditions and diseases to the African American communities. For example, Gregg and Curry (1994) found that African American women in their study felt that the adverse effects of chemotherapy and surgery were greater than the benefits, such that, once diagnosed with cancer, a person would live a less painful and longer life without the treatment.

Cultural and Lifestyle Factors   Cultural and lifestyle factors may contribute in part to the higher rates of mortality and morbidity among African Americans. First, culturally related nutritional habits—such as high consumption of fried foods, high consumption of meats (particularly those with high fat content), high use of salt and fat products (i.e., butter, lard) in the preparation of foods, and the popularity of desserts among African Americans—results in a diet that is high in fat, sugar, and sodium and low in fiber. This type of diet does not facilitate good health and has been associated with the development of cardiovascular diseases (e.g., coronary artery disease, stroke, and high blood pressure), cancers (e.g., colon, breast, and prostate), and diabetes (McGinnis, as cited by Washington, 1997). Second, such a diet is associated with obesity, and obesity is directly related to heart disease, cancer, and diabetes. Third, very few African Americans engage in physical activity and regular exercise. In 1998, 33.8% of African Americans reported that they did not engage in any physical activity, and only 30.1% reported engaging in some type of physical activity on a regular basis (U.S. Census Bureau, 2000). A sedentary lifestyle and lack of exercise has been associated with a higher prevalence of heart disease and colon cancer (Washington, 1997).

The failure to engage in preventive care such as self-examinations and screenings and the failure to follow through with doctors' recommendations are additional factors that contribute to the high rates of mortality and complications from physical ailments that African Americans experience. Failure to engage in preventive care is in part a result of limited access to health care. Additionally, because the Africentric worldview endorses an external locus of control over an internal locus of control, many African Americans may feel that their health is primarily determined by factors outside their control rather than by health behavior and practices that are in their control. In fact, Gregg and Curry (1994) found that many low-income African American women felt that the development of cancer had little to do with lifestyle but was more determined by destiny or the will of God. Similarly, a person's success in overcoming cancer was more likely to be attributed to God than to treatment such as chemotherapy. Ascribing the outcome of health to external factors may decrease African Americans' perceived need to alter eating and lifestyle habits, because these habits presumably do not determine the status of their health.

Further extensions of worldview, such as orientation of time, might also explain why some African Americans do not engage in preventive care. Many African Americans with an African worldview have a strong orientation for the past and present but not for the distant future (Parham et al., 1999). Thus, altering dietary habits or obtaining routine screenings in order to identify and prevent a physical ailment that may develop in the future is inconsistent with their lack of focus on the future (Sylvester, 1998).

Worldview beliefs and cultural and lifestyle behaviors can have a direct effect on African American children. As discussed by Jackson and Sellers (1996), the family is the primary place from which individuals receive information about health and health behaviors and is the primary transmitter of culturally related attitudes, values, and behaviors. Thus, African American children are likely to engage in the same cultural and lifestyle behaviors that African American adults do and thereby are likely to experience the same negative impacts on health.

Genetic Predisposition   African Americans have a genetic predisposition for several health conditions that may contribute to higher rates of morbidity and mortality. African Americans are more likely than Whites to have sickle cell anemia. Sickle cell anemia (which is discussed in greater detail later in this chapter) is an inherited disease that originally developed as the body's natural defense mechanism against malaria. Hence, sickle cell anemia is a geographical disease that is more common in individuals who are from or whose ancestors are from countries where malaria is prevalent, such as Africa. Because sickle cell anemia and sickle cell trait (presence of the recessive gene) are only transmitted genetically, African Americans are the primary group of individuals within the United States who have the health condition.

African Americans are also disproportionately affected by tuberculosis. Research has shown that African Americans are more likely to contract an initial infection, although they do not seem to develop the disease at a higher rate than other individuals (Washington, 1997). Contraction of tuberculosis is associated with poverty, poor housing, and poor health care (Taylor & Katz, 1996), which may also explain the higher prevalence of tuberculosis among African Americans.

Specific Health Needs—Adults

African Americans have a shorter life expectancy than Whites do. Specifically, in 1999 the average life expectancy for African Americans was 71.4 years (67.8 years for men and 74.7 years for women). Comparatively, the average life expectancy for Whites was 77.3 years (74.6 for men and 79.9 for women; Anderson & DeTurk, 2002). Additionally, African Americans are more likely to die from health conditions and diseases such as cancer; their infant mortality rate is almost 3 times that of Whites; and because of high homicide rates, the death rate of African American adults between the ages of 25 and 55 is double the death rate of Whites in the same age group. The primary cause of death for African Americans aged 45 and under is accidents, including homicide; infant mortality is the second highest cause of death (Reed et al., 1993).

Injuries and Death Resulting From Violence   Injuries and death resulting from violence (i.e., firearms) are a significant cause of morbidity and mortality among African Americans. In 1999, African American men were injured by firearms at a rate of 37.3 (per 100,000 persons) and died as a result of homicide by firearms at a rate of 29.5 (Hoyert et al., 2001). Comparative rates for White males were 16.3 and 3.5, respectively. Although African American women have a much lower injury and death rate due to firearms, their rates are still significantly higher than the rates of White women. In 1999, African American women were injured by firearms at a rate of 4.6 and died as a result of homicide by firearm at a rate of 3.8 (Hoyert, Arias, Smith, & Murphy, 2001). Comparative statistics for White women were 2.8 and 1.0, respectively. Furthermore, these rates may be higher than the statistics indicate. Washington (1997) notes that many injuries among African Americans due to violence may go unreported because many African Americans are uninsured and therefore may seek treatment from emergency rooms (for which statistics are not reported) and because individuals who fear repercussions from the criminal justice system may not seek medical treatment. These high rates of violent injury and death are caused in part to the struggle over limited resources among low-income African Americans. The scarcity of resources often results in criminal activity (i.e., theft, drug sales), which frequently leads to violence.

Cardiovascular Disease   African Americans have extremely high rates of cardiovascular disease (e.g., coronary artery disease, stroke, and high blood pressure). Furthermore, they have disproportionately high rates of death from cardiovascular disease, which may be attributed to socioeconomic factors (e.g., lack of access to medical treatment and medication), institutionalized racism (e.g., substandard treatment), or cultural and lifestyle factors (e.g., sustained diet that is high in fat and cholesterol). Heart disease is the primary cause of mortality among African Americans, and stroke mortality is 65% higher in African Americans than in Whites (Sylvester, 1998).

Cancer   African Americans are diagnosed with cancer at higher rates and die from cancer more frequently than do individuals from other ethnic/racial groups.

According to the *SEER Cancer Statistics Review, 1973–1999* the three most frequently diagnosed cancers and types of cancer deaths in the period from 1988 to
1992 for African American men and White men were prostate, lung and bronchus,
and colon and rectum (Ries et al., 2002). However, the incidence rates for African
American men with respect to the cancers were greater than the incidence rates for
White men. African American men were diagnosed with prostate cancer at a rate
of 180.6, lung and bronchus cancer at a rate of 117.0, and colon and rectum cancer at a rate of 60.7; comparative rates for White men were 137.9, 79.0, and 57.6,
respectively (rates are average annual per 100,000). Similarly, the number of
deaths caused by these cancers was higher for African American men compared to
White men. African American men died from prostate cancer at a rate of 53.7, lung
and bronchus cancer at a rate of 105.6, and colon and rectum cancer at a rate of
28.2; comparative rates for White men were 24.4, 74.2, and 23.4, respectively.

For African American and White women, the three most frequently diagnosed cancers and types of cancer deaths in the period from 1988 to 1992 were
breast, colon and rectum, and lung and bronchus (Ries et al., 2002). African
American women were diagnosed more frequently with colon and rectum cancer
and with lung and bronchus cancer than were White women. African American
women were diagnosed with breast cancer at a rate of 95.4, colon and rectum cancer at a rate of 45.5, and lung and bronchus cancer at a rate of 44.2; comparative
statistics for White women were 115.7, 39.2, and 43.7. Furthermore, African
American women had a higher death rate from breast cancer and from colon and
rectum cancer than White women did. African American women died from breast
cancer at a rate of 31.4, colon and rectum cancer at a rate of 20.4, and lung and
bronchus cancer at a rate of 31.5; comparative statistics for White women were
27.7, 15.6, and 32.9.

Cancer is the second leading cause of death among African Americans. The
high mortality rate from cancer is largely attributed to the fact that African Americans are often diagnosed with cancer in later, more advanced stages of the disease, when treatment is less effective (Washington, 1997).

Diabetes   Diabetes is much more prevalent among African Americans than
Whites. Based on statistics that began in 1996, 199.1 of every 1,000 African
Americans report having diabetes, in contrast to only 87.5 of every 1,000 Whites
(Adams, Hendershot, & Marano, 1999). Thus, African Americans develop diabetes at twice the rate that Whites do. Furthermore, African Americans have a
higher death rate (4.2%) from diabetes than do Whites (2.6%; Anderson, 2001).
African Americans are also more likely than Whites to experience complications
as a result of diabetes, such as heart disease, stroke, kidney failure, blindness, and
the need for amputation of the legs or feet (Jones-Wilson & Mabunda, 1997; Reed
et al., 1993).

HIV/AIDS   The HIV/AIDS epidemic is spreading to the African American population at alarming rates, particularly among women and children. Of the reported
AIDS cases for men in the years from 1985 to 2000, 34.2% were African American men and 49.2% were White men (NCHS, 2001). At first glance, this statistic

suggests that the disease is more prevalent among White men; however, because African American men only make up about 6% of the population, a 34.2% report rate is disproportionably high. Most disturbing is the fact that, of reported AIDS cases among women during these same years, 60% were African American women, and of the reported AIDS cases among children, 61.3% were African American children (NCHS, 2001). Comparative figures for White women and White children were 22.8%, and 18.3%, respectively.

Substance Abuse   Although statistics indicate that alcohol consumption is less prevalent among African Americans than among Whites (U.S. Census Bureau, 2000), an indication of the rate of illegal drug dependence among African Americans was not found. Regardless of the rate, substance abuse appears to be having severe detrimental effects on the African American population. According to Washington (1997), from 1985 to 1992, African Americans in California had a higher than average rate of drug-related deaths. Additionally, many African American children are being born with physical, mental, and cognitive impairments because their mothers have used substances while pregnant (Washington, 1997).

Organ Donation   African American individuals who need organ transplants are more likely to suffer from increased morbidity and are more susceptible to death than are Whites. Organ transplants are thought to be more successful when the donor is the same race as the recipient. Unfortunately, the rate of organ donation among African Americans is lower than the demand for organ transplants among African Americans. African Americans who need transplants experience long waits for compatible organs; many African Americans never receive organs; and African Americans experience higher costs for organ transplants due to the low supply and high demand. The higher costs of the transplants make it difficult for African Americans to obtain complete coverage by insurance companies (Jones-Wilson & Mabunda, 1997).

Specific Health Needs—Youth

Sadly, there is a high death rate (deaths per 100,000) among African American youth, particularly infants. In 1999, the death rate for African American children under 1 year of age was 1,551.1, for children aged 1 to 4 years it was 58.9, and for children aged 5 to 14 years it was 28.7 (Minino & Smith, 2001). Comparative death rates for White youth in the same age groups were 572.7, 29.7, and 17.5, respectively. Disturbingly, the infant mortality rate of African American babies is almost 3 times higher than the rate for White babies. The high rate of infant mortality has been associated in part with the fact that African American women are more likely to give birth to babies with low birth weights. These babies are then at increased risk for sudden infant death syndrome, respiratory syndrome, infections, and injuries. However, even African American babies that are of normal weight have a greater risk for death (Reed et al., 1993).

Like African American adults, African American teens experience high death rates from homicide and cardiovascular disease. African American adolescents are 5 times more likely to die from homicides and are twice as likely to die from heart and congenital defects as White teenagers are (Taylor & Katz, 1996).

Sickle Cell Anemia   One out of every 400 African American babies is born with sickle cell anemia, a genetic disease, and 1 out of every 10 is born with sickle cell trait (a recessive form of the disease in which the individual is only a carrier and experiences no symptoms of the disease). Sickle cell causes a portion of an individual's red blood cells, which are normally circular shaped, to be sickle shaped. This abnormality in the shape of the red blood cell can affect circulation throughout the body. The active period of sickle cell anemia is referred to as a "crisis." During a crisis, the sickle-shaped cells cluster together and block the passage of oxygen through that portion of the body. This blockage may cause the individual to experience fever, severe pain, loss of appetite, weakness, and sometimes a decrease in white blood cell count. At present, there is no cure for sickle cell disease, and in rare cases complications from sickle cell may result in a shorter life span.

Lead Poisoning   Fifty percent of urban children are affected by lead poisoning. Because a high number of African American children live in urban areas, they are disproportionately affected by lead poisoning. Very few children are exposed to an intoxicating level of lead that causes severe illness; however, the majority of children affected by lead poisoning suffer some degree of irreversible neurological damage, which can have a negative affect on academic achievement and behavior (Reed et al., 1993). Specifically, the effects of lead poisoning include decreased intelligence, developmental delays, behavioral disturbances, decreased stature, and anemia (Murphy, 1991, as cited by Reed et al., 1993). One source of lead poisoning to which children are commonly exposed is in the paint used on the walls of homes and schools. Lead in the paint can become particularly problematic because of the exorbitant costs associated with removing the old leaded paint and repainting with lead-free paint.

Teenage Pregnancy   There is a high rate of pregnancy among African American teens between the ages of 15 and 19, much higher than the rate of teenage pregnancy among Whites. According to the U.S. Census Bureau (1997), the birthrate in 1996 among African American teens was 91.4 per 1,000; comparatively, the birth rate among White teens was 48.1 per 1,000. Teenage pregnancy oftentimes has negative consequences both for the children born to young teen mothers and for the mothers themselves. First, many of the young mothers have to rely on Medicaid, and they may receive delayed and less than adequate prenatal care, which increases the risk for low birth weight and infant mortality (Taylor & Katz, 1996). Second, because many teen mothers are poor and unemployed, their children are likely to live in poverty and are susceptible to the negative health risks associated with poverty. Third, the teen mothers are less likely to complete high school, and their low levels of educational attainment limit their occupational skills.

MENTAL HEALTH

Although African Americans experience more physical illness than Whites, the literature suggests that African Americans experience mental illness proportional to Whites. Because the life experiences of African Americans as a minority group are vastly different from the life experiences of Whites, however, the conditions that contribute to mental illness among African Americans are unique. In this section, we discuss these unique conditions. But first, we explore how the mental health needs of African Americans are impacted by discrimination and racism on an institutional level and by racial/ethnic group membership and socioeconomic status.

Causal Attributions

Mental health problems experienced by African Americans are often attributed to institutional racism and low socioeconomic status. The following sections explore both these factors.

Institutionalized Racism   Institutionalized racism results in increased psychological distress for African Americans and increased physical, social, emotional, and economic hardship. Klonoff, Landrine, and Ullman (1999) indicated that increased experience with racial discrimination and stressful events was associated with psychiatric symptoms among African Americans. Furthermore, Klonoff et al. indicated that, for African Americans, racial discrimination was the best predictor of psychiatric symptoms in general and somatization and anxiety in particular. The ramifications of institutionalized racism specific to the mental health of African Americans are evidenced in African Americans' lower utilization rates of mental health services and their high rate of misdiagnosis by mental health professionals (which can lead to inadequate treatment).

The effects of institutionalized racism are widespread and can have deleterious effects on African Americans at a systemic level. The effects are seen in the types of mental health issues that African Americans as a whole present with. Furthermore, there are unique mental health needs and circumstances that affect men, women, and children differently.

Socioeconomic Status and Racial/Ethnic Group Membership   African Americans are disproportionately represented in the lower socioeconomic status group, and research indicates that there is a correlation between socioeconomic status and diagnosed mental health (Schulz et al., 2000). Individuals with lower socioeconomic status tend to have higher rates of mental illness than do individuals with higher socioeconomic status. For example, Ostrove et al. (1999) found that African Americans and Whites with lower levels of education, income, and wealth reported more depressive symptoms than did those with higher levels of education, income, and wealth. This higher rate of mental illness can be attributed to the stressors that are associated with poverty, such as financial problems, unemployment, residence in neighborhoods that have high rates of violence and crime, and poor access to health care.

Further, within the African American community, a negative stigma exists around the notion of mental illness. It is typically more acceptable for individuals to have physical illness than mental illness. Thus, acknowledgment of psychological problems and the attainment of mental health treatment is seldom openly encouraged and supported. Additionally, because of culturally insensitive treatment, many African Americans do not continue with psychotherapy through the elimination of their presenting issue. African Americans often terminate therapy early (as soon as after the first session). Both these issues contribute to the underutilization of mental health services by African Americans. As a result, many mental illnesses among African Americans go undiagnosed and untreated. Consequently, once African Americans do present in therapy, the initial illness may have progressed to a more severe form of the disorder, and the clinicians' interpretation may be that African Americans in general exhibit more severe pathology.

A variety of factors affect the mental health needs of African Americans— for example, race, social class, sex, and age. Mental health professionals should consider all these factors when providing mental health services. Specifically, clinicians should recognize that the mental health needs and experiences of the African American female may differ significantly from those of the African American male and also from the African American child or elder. In the following sections we outline needs that are salient to the African American community as a whole and then address needs that are specific to African American males, females, and children.

Mental Health Needs

Historically, African Americans have underutilized mental health services. Consequently, once they do enter treatment, their mental illness has progressed to a more severe and debilitating state. African Americans are also more often misdiagnosed (clinicians tend to underdiagnose depression and overdiagnose schizophrenia and schizoaffective disorders), and they are frequently diagnosed as exhibiting more severe mental illness than their White counterparts (Adebimpe, 1981; Cornelius, Fabrega, Cornelius, Mezzich, & Maher, 1996).

The expression of mental illness in African Americans does not always manifest in traditional symptomatology, and mental health practitioners should be aware that African Americans have a tendency to somatize, that is, express their psychological problems in a physical form. As a result, African Americans may seek treatment for physical complaints when they are actually suffering from a psychological issue such as depression; the underlying psychological issue is then likely to go untreated (Adebimpe, 1997).

Unhealthy Racial Identity   The development of a healthy racial identity, or a racial identity that is in cohesion with the community in which one lives, is a factor that clinicians should be aware of when working with African Americans and all ethnic minorities. How a person perceives himself or herself in reference to the dominant group and society in general (the Euro-American culture) and to his or her own ethnic group can provide clinicians with pertinent information regarding that individual's psychological well-being. If the client's racial identity or view of himself or herself is in contradiction with the culture in which he or she exists, the client may have potential issues that need to be addressed. For example, if an African American client is living in an ethnically homogeneous African American community but does not particularly identify with being African American or share a African American identity, that client may experience conflicted feelings about the people he or she lives with, which may result in social isolation and depression. Conversely, an individual who heavily identifies with the African American culture but who is living or going to school in an area predominated by Whites may also suffer from social isolation and feelings of depression. A more thorough discussion of the Nigrescence Racial Identity model, which proposed a set of racial identity stages that African Americans experience, can be found in chapters 2 and 4 of this book as well as in Helms (1990) and Parham et al. (1999).

Williams and Williams-Morris (2000) discuss the psychological impact of internalized racism on African Americans and how internalized racism may affect racial identity. They define internalized racism as the "acceptance, by marginalized racial populations, of the negative societal beliefs and stereotypes about themselves" (p. 255). The authors propose that African Americans are made to feel worthless and powerless through the combined effects of economic hardship and the belief that African Americans are inferior. They cite multiple studies that suggest that, for African Americans, there is a relationship between internalized racism and alcohol consumption, psychological distress, depression, and lower self-esteem and less ego identity.

The idea of internalized racism closely parallels the concept of self-hatred, which has been vehemently rejected by Parham et al. (1999). These authors state that the notion of self-hatred implies "that African American people look to Whites, and White America, as their only source of validation and emulation" (p. 41) and disregards the notion that African American people may define themselves through traditional aspects of the African American identity and culture. Regardless of whether mental health professionals choose to put credence into the self-hatred paradigm, they should be aware that the impact of long-standing institutionalized racism has had deleterious effects on the racial identity of African Americans.

Unemployment   Many African Americans experience negative effects from unemployment, such as social isolation, financial problems, and lack of meaning to life. In fact, Ostrove et al. (1999) found a significant relationship between employment status and health in both African American and White individuals. Those individuals who were employed reported less depression and better physical health than did those individuals who were unemployed. This relationship was stronger for African Americans than for Whites.

Educational and Occupational Deficit   There is a tremendous need within the African American community for intervention with regard to education and career development. Continued low levels of education and career development are primary sources of continued poverty. As we have already pointed out in this chapter, poverty is related to a host of aversive physical and mental problems. Thus, critical interventions are needed in order to improve the quality of the primary and secondary education that African Americans are receiving, to increase the level of postsecondary education that African Americans are achieving, and to further facilitate career development.

Clinicians also must be able to assess the social experiences of those African Americans who have achieved higher educational and occupational status. Because of the limited number of African Americans who occupy a higher socioeconomic status, many highly educated and professional African Americans experience difficulty establishing social networks and relationships with other African Americans within their socioeconomic group. This situation may result in feelings of isolation and limited social support.

Grief and Bereavement   Grief and bereavement issues may be particularly prevalent among the African American community. As we discussed in the physical health section, African Americans have disproportionately high rates of death from cardiovascular disease and cancer; the mortality rate of young African American men is extremely high; and the infant mortality rate is disturbingly high. Further, many African Americans who are living in low socioeconomic areas laden with crime and violence may witness criminal and violent incidents, which can have an adverse psychological impact (Williams & Williams-Morris, 2000).

Mental Health Needs Specific to Sex and Age

Mental health professionals will find that some African American mental health needs are specific to sex and age. In the following sections, we discuss the mental health needs specific to men, women, and children, respectively.

African American Men   Psychological research has not paid adequate attention to the social and economic difficulties experienced by African American males or the effects of these difficulties on their psychological functioning. Thorn and Sarata (1998) have stated that the plight of African American men should be studied and understood as distinct from that of African American women and other ethnic groups. In the extant literature regarding African American men, African American males are being referred to as an endangered species (Parham & McDavis, 1987). Evidence for this assertion is that the mortality rate for African American male babies is greater than that for African American female babies. Furthermore, African American males between the ages of 15 and 25 have the highest mortality rate of any ethnic-by-sex group. They are most likely to die as victims of homicide, suicide, and drug use (Baker & Bell, 1999). And finally, the African American community is losing large numbers of African American males to incarceration in state and federal penal institutions.

African Americans are afflicted with increased psychological distress that results from the high prevalence of crime and violence in low socioeconomic neighborhoods. African American males are being incarcerated at an alarming rate.

Currently, more African American men are incarcerated than attend college, and African American men make up 45% of the male prison population (Thorn & Sarata, 1998). The effects of the large numbers of African American men being incarcerated are systemic and detrimental to the individual, the family, and the community as a whole.

Incarceration   Incarceration effects on individual offenders include having to cope with the harsh conditions of imprisonment, with the strain of separation from family and friends (Williams & Williams-Morris, 2000), with the stigma associated with being incarcerated, and with difficulties readjusting to society after being released. Once an African American male enters the criminal justice system, a cycle begins that is difficult to change. After he is released from prison, he may have a difficult time reestablishing himself back into the community. Because of stigmatization, as well as his low educational and skill levels, he may have trouble finding employment. As a result, many ex-convicts relapse into criminal activity as a means to support themselves and their family (King, 1993). The high recidivism rate of African American males is further complicated by their tenuous interactions with the criminal justice systems. African American men are frequently ignorant of their rights in legal matters, and because of their low socioeconomic status, they are not able to hire adequate legal representation. Consequently, African American males may be encouraged to accept legal pleas that will shorten their initial sentence but that may not be in their best interest in the long run.

The incarceration of the African American male has negative impacts on his family. Specifically, the absence of the father from a family can result in loss of economic, social, and emotional support. The need to rely solely on the income of the mother can result in a significant economic strain. Additionally, the children in the home will not benefit from the direct guidance of a male figure throughout their development. This absence may have a stronger impact on male children, because male role models and socialization activities with fathers have greater salience to male children's development.

The incarceration of the African American male also has negative impacts on the community. Most crime and violence within the African American community is Black on Black crime. Consequently, because of the high recidivism rate of individuals released from prison, unfortunate repercussions occur in the community in which convicts are released.

Stigma Associated with African American Men   An additional mental health need of African American men is related to their tendency to be perceived as more aggressive, intimidating, lazy, cognitively deficient, and prone to violence than are men from other racial/ethnic groups. These perceptions result in increased incidents of discrimination toward African American men and increased interpersonal difficulties throughout their social and work life. Mental health professionals who believe these perceptions of African American men will be unable to establish rapport with the African American male client, and effective treatment will be difficult, if not impossible.

African American Women   Many African American women experience increased psychological distress as a result of their single-parent status, economic hardships, unavailability of same-race male partners, and threat of HIV/AIDS.

Single-Parent Status and Economic Hardships   The majority of African American households are single parent and female headed. Many of these households occupy low socioeconomic or poverty-level status. Single parenting combined with economic hardship results in emotional and psychological distress for the mother and, ultimately, for the children.

Coiro (2001) reports that low-income mothers of children may be at particular risk for depression. The types of life stressors reported by the women included (a) having trouble finding a place to live, (b) having a relative or close friend in jail, and (c) having someone close who died or was killed. Further, the results indicated that many of the women did not seek mental health services because they did not recognize that their depression was a treatable disorder. In these situations, the depression of the mothers, combined with the stressor of poverty, has a negative impact on the children as well.

Unavailability of Same-Race Male Partners   The great disparity between the number of eligible African American females and eligible African American males means that many African American women will be unable to establish an intimate relationship with a same-race male. Several factors contribute to this disparity: (a) a high mortality rate of African American men due to homicide, (b) a high incarceration rate of African American men, (c) a percentage of African American men who are gay, and (d) a percentage of African American men who marry non–African American women. Furthermore, as was discussed in chapter 4, many more African American women than men are attending college. Therefore, African American women are less likely to be able to establish a relationship with an African American man who holds the same level of education.

The unavailability of African American men as lifetime partners can result in loneliness for African American women. It is also related to the increased stress that African American women experience when they have to raise their children without the social, emotional, and financial support of a father.

HIV/AIDS   The high rates of diagnosed HIV and AIDS in the African American community result not only in physical and medical concerns but in mental health concerns as well. Because of the required HIV testing of women during pregnancy, many African American women are finding out for the first time that they are infected with HIV and that their unborn child is infected as well (Miles, Gillespie, & Holditch-Davis, 2001). This news is undoubtedly emotionally devastating for these women. Furthermore, once the child is born, the women are faced with the emotional stress of nurturing a child who suffers from the physical symptoms of HIV. These mothers are highly concerned about their child's future health status and are presumably experiencing some feelings of guilt. In addition to this psychological distress, the mothers are processing their own diagnosis and struggling with their own physical symptoms (Miles et al., 2001).

Mental Health Needs of Children   African American children have special
mental health needs due to poverty and low levels of educational attainment.

Poverty   Poverty has been shown to have a negative effect on the mental
health of children. Samaan (2000) reviewed the results of various studies that investigated the effects of poverty on the mental health of a racially diverse sample
of children and concluded that children from lower socioeconomic backgrounds
were at increased risk for mental health problems compared to children from
higher socioeconomic backgrounds. Specifically, McLeod and Shanahan's study
(as cited in Samaan, 2000) indicated that children who lived in poverty were at
increased risk for depression and antisocial behaviors and that increased poverty
over time (5 years) was associated with increased levels of antisocial behavior. A
caveat to the McLeod and Shanahan study is that although we use the term antisocial because it was the term used in the study, we caution that the environmental context in which the "antisocial" behavior took place may not have been considered. What was determined in the study to be antisocial behavior actually may
have been adaptive behavior given the home life situation of the child.

Similarly, the results of Costello, Farmer, Angold, Burns, and Erkanli (as
cited by Samaan, 2000) indicated that children of lower socioeconomic status
were 3 times more likely to have a comorbid emotional and behavioral condition
than were children of higher socioeconomic status. Costello et al. also compared
prevalence rates of psychiatric conditions and comorbidity between African
American children and White children. The results of their study indicated that
African American children had a higher prevalence rate of enuresis as compared
to White children, but prevalence rates of all other psychiatric disorders and comorbidity were similar among African American children and White children.

Educational Attainment   African American children may have an educational disadvantage because of the disparity in resources and quality of teachers
found in the predominantly African American neighborhoods and schools compared to those found in the predominantly White neighborhoods and schools. The
disparity in education is not limited to resources; rather, it is sometimes reflected
in achievement and educational placement. When African American children
enter the educational system, they possess cognitive, sensory, and motor skills
that are equal to those of their White age-mates. However, academic achievement
levels for African American children, compared to White children, decrease with
the length of time they stay in school. Further, African American children are 3
times more likely than their White counterparts to be labeled as educable mentally retarded and to be enrolled in remedial classes, and they are half as likely to
be enrolled in gifted classrooms (Kunjufu, 1985).

CONCLUSION

Throughout this chapter, we have outlined the physical and mental health needs
most salient to African Americans as well as the critical factors that contribute to

these needs. Although African Americans are exhibiting great resiliency in response to the multiple hardships they encounter on a macro and micro level, there is a great need for intervention from mental health professionals.

Psychologists need to provide psycho-education to help African Americans improve their physical health. African Americans can benefit from information that emphasizes the importance of preventive care such as cancer and diabetes screenings and the importance of safe sex practices, and they can benefit from information that demystifies the negative perceptions that many African Americans have regarding medical care. African Americans can also benefit from psycho-education programs that focus on healthy eating and lifestyle habits. Research has indicated that churches provide an ideal setting for this type of psycho-education (Turner, Sutherland, Harris, & Barber, 1995). Psychologists, particularly those working in medical settings, can serve as liaisons between African Americans and medical health professionals to facilitate increased communication between the two. Finally, the frequency of homicide and injury due to violence among adults and children suggests a need for intervention programs designed to provide viable alternatives to violent and criminal behavior, such as after-school programs, job skills training programs, and anger and stress management groups.

Psycho-education appears to be a critical need with respect to mental health as well. African Americans can benefit from information regarding the symptoms of psychological distress as it occurs in adults as well as in children. Furthermore, African Americans need to be made aware of the types of treatment available, and they need increased access to psychological treatment. Given the likelihood that African Americans may not be able to afford the typical costs of psychological services and may not have medical insurance that covers mental health treatment, psychologists may want to consider offering their services pro bono or on a sliding fee scale in the local African American communities. The experiences of African Americans imply a tremendous need for support groups, particularly for single mothers, children and spouses of incarcerated men, and African American males.

Finally, we as mental health professionals have the power to lobby against the various forms of institutionalized racism discussed in this chapter. Mental health professionals can advocate for increased equality with regard to the health care, education, and employment of African Americans and other minority groups. Additionally, mental health professionals can lobby against the disproportionate inclusion of alcohol and tobacco billboards and liquor stores in the African American communities.

Exercises

1. T. D. is a 39-year-old African American male who has been referred to therapy after being charged with domestic violence. Mr. D. is in his second marriage, his first marriage having ended in divorce, and he is the father of two children (one child from the first union and one child from the union with his current wife). The child from his previous marriage lives with his ex-wife; Mr. D. lives with his wife, their child, and her child from a previous union. He works as an independent laborer, but he has difficulty finding work because he is not a member of the local union. He has been denied membership to the union because years ago he was convicted of a felony for distribution of an illegal substance. His intermittent work opportunities result in a severe financial strain for the family. When asked about the domestic violence charge, he stated, "I didn't hit her; I just pushed her away kind of hard. I didn't mean to, but she kept complaining about money and about me getting a job again. I'm trying, but she doesn't seem to understand."
   a) What are some of the environmental and sociopolitical factors that are affecting this client and his relationship?
   b) How would you best facilitate a safe therapeutic environment for this client that would allow him to invest in therapy and eventually make progress?
   c) How might your beliefs and values interfere with your ability to establish an effective working relationship with this client?

2. Ms. H. is a 27-year-old African American single mother seeking therapy. When asked what brought her in, she replied, "The school psychologist who works with my 9-year-old son said I should look into therapy because it would be a good way to help me deal with my stress." Ms. H. went on to explain, "I'm a single parent and it's hard. My son is failing school, he's constantly being suspended for fighting, and I don't know what to do. Recently, I started working a second job, so when I come home I'm exhausted. I have no time for myself. I just feel like my life is falling apart. Over the last two years I have gained 40 pounds, I can't seem to make a relationship work, and I'm starting to have all kinds of health problems that I've never had before, like high blood pressure."
   a) How might the client's physical health be impacted by her mental health?
   b) What are some potential barriers that may interfere with this client's ability to continue with treatment?
   c) How might the client's presenting issues be affecting her interactions with her son?

REFERENCES

Adams, P. F., Hendershot, G. E., & Marano, M. A. (1999). Current estimates from the National Health Interview Survey, 1996. *Vital Health Statistics Series, 10*(200), 1–212. Hyattsville, MD: National Center for Health Statistics.

Adebimpe, V. R. (1981). Overview: White norms and psychiatric diagnosis of Black patients. *American Journal of Psychiatry, 138*(3), 279–285.

Adebimpe, V. R. (1997). Mental illness among African Americans. In I. Al-Issa & M. Tousignant (Eds.), *Ethnicity, immigration, and psychopathology* (pp. 95–105). New York: Plenum Press.

Anderson, R. N. (2001). Deaths: Leading causes for 1999. *National Vital Statistics Report, 49*(11), 1–88. Hyattsville, MD: National Center for Health Statistics.

Anderson, R. N., De Turk, P. B. (2002). United States life tables, 1999. *National Vital Statistics Report, 50*(6), 1–39. Hyattsville, MD: National Center for Health Statistics.

Baker, F. M., & Bell, C. C. (1999). Issues in the psychiatric treatment of African Americans. *Psychiatric Services, 50*(3), 362–368.

Coiro, M. J. (2001). Depressive symptoms among women receiving welfare. *Women and Health, 32*(1/2), 1–23.

Cornelius, J. R., Fabrega, H., Cornelius, M. D., Mezzich, J., & Maher, P. J. (1996). Racial effects on the clinical presentation of alcoholics at a psychiatric hospital. *Comprehensive Psychiatry, 37*(2), 102–108.

Gregg, J., & Curry, R. H. (1994). Explanatory models for cancer among African-American women at two Atlanta neighborhood health centers: The implications for a cancer screening program. *Social Science and Medicine, 39*(4), 519–526.

Helms, J. E. (1990). *Black and white racial identity: Theory, research, and practice.* New York: Greenwood Press.

Hoyert, D. L., Arias, E., Smith, B. L., Murphy, S. L. (2001). Deaths: Final data for 1999. *National Vital Statistics Report, 49*(8), 1–114. Hyattsville, MD: National Center for Health Statistics.

Jackson, J. S., & Sellers, S. L. (1996). African-American health over the life course. In P. M. Kato & T. Mann (Eds.), *Handbook of diversity issues in health psychology* (pp. 301–317). New York: Plenum Press.

Jones-Wilson, F. C., & Mabunda, L. M. (1997). The family. *Reference Library of Black America, 3,* 583–609.

King, A. (1993). African-American males in prison: Are they doing time or is the time doing them? *Journal of Sociology and Social Welfare, 20*(4), 9–27.

Klonoff, E. A., Landrine, H., & Ullman, J. B. (1999). Racial discrimination and psychiatric symptoms among blacks. *Cultural Diversity and Ethnic Minority Psychology, 5*(4), 329–339.

Kunjufu, J. (1985). *Countering the conspiracy to destroy Black boys.* Chicago, IL: African American Images.

Miles, M. S., Gillespie, J. V., & Holditch-Davis, D. (2001). Physical and mental health in African American mothers with HIV. *Journal of the Association of Nurses in AIDS Care, 12*(4), 42–50.

Minino, A. M., & Smith, B. L. (2001). Deaths: Preliminary data for 2000. *National Vital Statistics Report, 49*(12), 1–40. Hyattsville, MD: National Center for Health Statistics.

National Center for Health Statistics. (2001). *Health, United States, 2001.* Hyattsville, MD: Public Health Service.

Ostrove, J. M., Feldman, P., & Adler, N. E. (1999). Relations among socioeconomic status indicators and health for African-Americans and whites. *Journal of Health Psychology, 4*(4), 451–463.

Parham, T. A., & McDavis, R. J. (1987). Black men, an endangered species: Who's really pulling the trigger? *Journal of Counseling and Development, 66*(1), 24–27.

Parham, T. A., White, J. L., & Ajamu, A. (1999). *The psychology of Blacks: An African centered perspective.* Upper Saddle River, NJ: Prentice Hall.

Reed, W., Darity, W., & Roberson, N. (1993). *Health and medical care of African Americans.* Westport, CT: Auburn House.

Ries, L. A. G., Eisner, M. P., Kosary, C. L., Hankey, B. F., Miller, B. A., Clegg, L., & Edwards, B. K. (Eds.). (2002). *SEER Cancer Statistics Review, 1973–1999.* National Cancer Institute, Bethesda, MD. Retrieved September 2, 2002, from seer.cancer.gov/csr/1973_1999/

Samaan, R. A. (2000). The influences of race, ethnicity, and poverty on the mental health of children. *Journal of Health Care for the Poor and Underserved, 11*(1), 100–110.

Schulz, A., Williams, D., Israel, B., Becker, A., Parker, E., James, S. A., & Jackson, J. (2000). Unfair treatment, neighborhood effects, and mental health in the Detroit metropolitan area. *Journal of Health and Social Behavior, 41*(3), 314–332.

Smith, G. G., & Celano, M. (2000). Revenge of the mutant cockroach: Culturally adapted storytelling in the treatment of a low-income African American boy. *Cultural Diversity and Ethnic Minority Psychology, 6*(2), 220–227.

Sylvester, J. L. (1998). *Directing health messages toward African Americans: Attitudes toward health care and the mass media.* New York: Garland.

Taylor, D. A., & Katz, P. A. (1996). Health and related services available to black adolescents. In M. Kagawa-Singer et al. (Eds.), *Health issues for minority adolescents* (pp. 36–79). Lincoln: University of Nebraska Press.

Thorn, G. R., & Sarata, B. P. V. (1998). Psychotherapy with African American men: What we know and what we need to know. *Journal of Multicultural Counseling and Development, 26*(4), 240–253.

Turner, L. W., Sutherland, M., Harris, G. J., & Barber, M. (1995). Cardiovascular health promotion in north Florida African-American churches. *Health Values, 19*(2), 3–9.

U.S. Census Bureau. (1997). *Statistical abstract of the United States: 1997* (117th ed.). Springfield, MA: National Technical Information Service.

U.S. Census Bureau. (2000). *Statistical abstract of the United States: 2000* (120th ed.). Springfield, MA: National Technical Information Service.

Washington, E. A. (1997). *The health status of African Americans in California.* Woodland Hills, CA: California Endowment and California Healthcare Foundation.

Williams, D. R., & Williams-Morris, R. (2000). Racism and mental health: The African American experience. *Ethnicity and Health, 5*(3–4), 234–268.

CHAPTER 6 African Americans: Treatment Issues and Recommendations

Chalmer E. Thompson
and Khym Isaac, Indiana University–
Bloomington

What do African American clients need from mental health practitioners? Like all people who seek or require the services of mental health practitioners, African American clients need professionals who can help reduce or eliminate the problems that prevent them from living fulfilling lives. They need practitioners who can also competently assess the extent and severity of their dysfunction, capitalize on the resources that facilitate treatment interventions, and embrace the strengths and resiliencies that have benefited the clients in the past. In this chapter we examine how and why these needs are not always realized when African Americans are involved in treatment. We also present a conceptual explanation of why disturbing trends in treatment outcomes occur when practitioners work with African Americans and how the trends can be reversed.

When discussing treatment, we believe that identifying any population on the basis of the shared racial and cultural heritage and experiences of its members necessitates consideration of *how* this heritage and collection of experiences are linked to psychological functioning and treatment experiences. Consequently, our goal in this chapter is to place race and culture at the focus of our discussion, first by scrutinizing the phenomenon of racism in general and then describing its impact on treatment. Race, described here as a "knowledge system" (Smedley, 1993), is laden with perversities in how people come to perceive others who are both different from and similar to themselves. Race also influences relational processes whereby assumptions about people and their relative worth as humans enter into the therapy. We describe aspects of the racial experiences of African Americans specifically and the kinds of relational processes that can emerge when they are involved in therapy. We also address how the constructs and models presented by Neville and Walters (see chapter 4) are associated with these relational processes and with processes of dehumanization. We later reintroduce culture and explain how both race and culture converge to influence treatment-related issues such as the decision to pursue treatment and the therapy process.

Our writing of this chapter is governed by philosophical hermeneutics and thus the assumption that human interactions are coconstructed within local realities—such as families, school settings, communities—and in turn are influenced

125

by and influence broader ecological contexts (e.g., Foucault, 1987). These contexts include sociopolitical structures such as racism, class exploitation, sexism, and heterosexism that are frequently ignored or minimized. Psychology is not immune from this proclivity toward omitting or reducing the impact of sociopolitical structures from conceptualizations about human development and functioning, decision making, and psychotherapy practice (e.g., Bulhan, 1985; Cushman, 1995). In drawing from philosophical hermeneutics, we emphasize the dynamic and fluid construction of counseling inclusive of the impact of sociopolitical structures. We closely examine racism as an influence of relational processes and show how mental health practitioners, in assuming the role of authority in treatment, can learn to approach rather than avoid issues of race and racism and to position themselves advantageously in "working through" the difficult issues that pertain to the client, the practitioner, and the therapy process. We believe that this working-through process is crucial to the promotion of mental health of African Americans and all persons in society as they engage dynamically in the construction of realities.

We begin by briefly reviewing the research on African American clients/patients and the variables that appear to relate to the decision to pursue treatment and to therapy process and outcome.

RESEARCH ON TREATMENT ISSUES

Research has shown that African Americans have profited from certain types of psychological treatment. In comparative studies, psychological treatments have been found to be at least as effective for African Americans as they are for Whites—the racial group often used in the comparisons. For example, cognitive-behavioral therapy has been shown to be equally effective in reducing anxiety among African Americans and Whites (Friedman, Paradis, & Hatch, 1994; Treadwell, Flannery-Schroeder, & Kendall, 1995). Studies by Rosenbeck and Fontana (1994) and Zoellner, Feeny, Fitzgibbons, and Foa (1999) found that African Americans and White Americans responded similarly to treatment for posttraumatic stress disorder. Although these studies may be accompanied by the interest of the researchers to test whether or not the delivery of treatment is dispensed equitably by race or that the treatment is effective across the two racial groups, other studies based on noncomparative analyses have concentrated on the effectiveness of certain treatment protocols when African American patients were involved. Hence, in a sample of predominantly Black older medical patients, Lichtenberg, Kimbarow, Morris, and Vangel (1996) found behavioral treatment to be generally effective. In a study consisting largely of African American patients who were severely mentally ill, Baker and Bell (1999) documented increased levels of adaptive functioning following the patient's participation in an intensive psychosocial rehabilitation program. Evidence suggests affirmative responses, at least in relation to behaviorally oriented programs of treatment, to the questions Do African Americans profit from standardized treatment protocols? and Is there racial equity in the delivery of treatment? (U.S. Surgeon General's Report, 2001).

But studies also have shown that African Americans have not profited from treatment (U.S. Surgeon General's Report, 2001). For example, Chambless and Williams (1995) found that Blacks were less responsive than Whites to a behavioral treatment for agoraphobia. Although similar to Whites in their responses to psychotherapy and medication for depression, African Americans were found to have less improvement in their ability to function in the community (Brown, Shear, Schulberg, & Madonia, 1999). One might surmise from the outcomes of both these studies that the relative lack of response by African Americans can be attributed to some deficiency in African American patients in the sample, to the delivery of the treatment, or both.

However, we argue that the researchers' omission of variables about aspects of race and culture leads primarily to *speculations* of how race and culture configure into these findings rather than to more sound conclusions about their role in treatment outcomes. Stated another way, and in concurrence with Betancourt and Lopez (1993), Helms, (1992, 1994), and Miller (1999), it would seem that direct investigations about race and culture would optimally yield explanations about how these constructs pertain to issues of treatment. By directly studying race and culture through the use of measures and interviews, researchers can acquire useful knowledge about, for instance, whether the treatment succeeds or fails to succeed as a result of the practitioner's addressing the cultural needs of the client, or whether the practitioner translates treatment in ways that are racially responsive to the client.

Furthermore, some findings are troubling because they suggest that African Americans have not received the care they need when they have sought mental health services. According to the U.S. Surgeon General's Report (2001), studies have shown that African Americans were found to be less likely than White Americans to receive appropriate care for depression and anxiety, with *appropriate care* being defined as care that adheres to official guidelines based on evidence from clinical trials. In a large study that examined a representative national sample, evidence indicated that African Americans are diagnosed accurately less often than Whites when they are suffering from depression and are seen in primary care or when they are seen for psychiatric evaluation in an emergency room (Strakowski et al., 1997). This study is supported by other research that has found clinician bias in the diagnosis of schizophrenia, with African Americans being overdiagnosed as schizophrenic in comparison to Whites (e.g., Neighbors & Jackson, 1996; Baker & Bell, 1999). In a very recent study, Trieweiler et al. (2000) found that well-trained clinicians not only were more likely to make clinical and research-based diagnoses of schizophrenia for African Americans than for Whites, but also had applied different decision rules to African American and White patients in judging the presence of schizophrenia.

We remind readers again that the reasons for these findings are left to speculation, but perhaps many readers have already surmised (as have the researchers) that these practitioners acted more favorably toward White patients than Black clients because of race and culture. These conclusions are likely to be reached because of what researchers know from past research on psychotherapy treatment (see chapter 3) and from other sources (e.g., personal experiences, critical examinations of media representations, scholarship from outside psychology, literary references and narratives, etc.). Although psychological researchers have certain knowledge about these experiences, they have generally resisted the study of race and culture in treatment outcome (see Martín-Baró, 1994; Fish, 2002; Thompson, in press b). Their resistance suggests that the effect of race (in particular) on practitioners' treatment decisions and clients' treatment responsiveness has been viewed as political and, by implication, outside the realm of legitimate science (e.g., Cushman, 1995).

Another unfortunate result of the absence of research on race and culture is the continuing uncertainty about whether there can be optimism in the prospect that African Americans will perceive psychological treatment as a viable option for meeting their mental health needs. One way of discerning whether African Americans generally are disposed to mental health services is to examine utilization rates. In their review of the literature on psychological research of non-White racial/ethnic groups, Sue, Zane, and Young (1994) concluded that African Americans tended to *overutilize* services relative to other racial/ethnic groups, including Whites. This conclusion would certainly lead to some optimism about the willingness of African Americans to seek formal mental health services, but in the studies reviewed by Sue et al., there are ample data that either refute the conclusion or reveal certain "twists" in the findings relative to treatment outcomes (see also Snowden, 1999).

For example, Sue, Fujino, Hu, Takeuchi, and Zane (1991) found that among thousands of clients who used outpatient services in the Los Angeles County mental health system, African Americans overutilized services in comparison to Asian, Mexican, and White Americans, yet they exhibited less positive treatment outcomes than the other groups. Padgett, Harman, Burns, and Schlesinger (1994) investigated the utilization rates from a large, racial/ethnic female sample who had visited an outpatient facility at least once since 1983. Findings from this study showed that even after controlling for the effects of low socioeconomic status, insurance coverage, and other sociodemographic factors, there remained racial/ethnic differences among the sample. White women were consistently higher users of mental health services, whereas African American women were least likely to seek treatment compared to White and Hispanic women. Diala et al. (2000) analyzed responses of Whites and African American women and men who participated in another national survey and found that African Americans used mental health services less than Whites. The researchers also found that African Americans had more positive attitudes than Whites toward seeking mental health services prior to their visits, but were less likely to use the services. In addition, they found that Blacks had less positive attitudes than Whites after utilization. Bosworth et al. (2000) monitored the mental health service utilization of 526 women at the Durham (North Carolina) VA Medical Center and found that African American women often expressed a greater need for mental health services than Whites but that both groups tended to use the services equally. And in a nationwide study involving interviews with Black adults who participated in the National Survey of Black Americans (NSBA), Neighbors and Jackson (1996) uncovered extremely low usage of the mental health services; only 9% of subjects reported that they had sought the help of a community mental health center, psychiatrist, or psychologist. Neighbors and Jackson also discovered that mental health usage was low even among subjects who believed that their problems were particularly burdensome.

These findings are not encouraging, and psychological researchers still have only a foggy idea about why and under what conditions African Americans view psychological treatment as a viable option for meeting their mental health needs. For example, African Americans may seek mental health services that emphasize medicinal treatment over psychotherapy so that their contact with mental health practitioners will be relatively minimal. Given the many nuances related to help seeking, we believe that an alternative to examining trends in African Americans' help seeking behaviors is to investigate aspects *about* African Americans and the local realities that hinder or facilitate the help seeking. The following are examples of questions that might be addressed through research. How might African American utilization patterns differ in communities where there are few African Americans relative to non–African Americans versus settings where African Americans predominate? How might utilization patterns differ in clinics where there are virtually no African American staff members on site versus clinics where African Americans are amply staffed at all occupational levels? How might utilization patterns differ among mental health facilities based on what the grapevine has to say about the quality of treatment provided Blacks by each facility? How might utilization be affected by the interaction of these contextual factors with individual factors such as prior hospitalization, cultural mistrust, embarrassment over the need for treatment, and gender-related beliefs about self-reliance and privacy of personal issues?

Furthermore, when studying help-seeking behaviors among Blacks, researchers need to take into account the availability and reliability of informal sources that help Blacks meet mental health needs. In their research of Black women who took part in a nationwide study, Mays, Caldwell, and Jackson (1996) discovered that severity of the problem, degree of religiosity, and geographic residence related significantly to the type of services used by Black women. The researchers found also that women who lived in the U.S. South were less likely to use private therapists than were women in other parts of the country.

Knowledge about the local realities in which African Americans seek or fail to seek help will also reveal useful data about *when* treatment is sought and *what* alternatives to formal treatment are considered. Some African Americans become involved in formal treatment only when there is a crisis (e.g., U.S. Surgeon General's Report, 2001). Others consult religious institutions as a valuable resource (e.g., Williams, Griffith, Young, Collins, & Dodson, 1999). Resilience and the forging of social ties have enabled many African Americans to overcome adversity and to maintain a high degree of mental health. Taylor, Hardison, and Chatters (1996) write that almost 85% of African Americans have described themselves as "fairly religious" or "very religious" and that prayer is among their most common coping responses.

How race and culture relate to these help-seeking behaviors or how they play roles in help-seeking decisions is also unclear. However, some evidence suggests that racial-cultural factors may lead African Americans to positive decisions about seeking help. Boesch and Cimbolic (1994) surveyed 182 directors of counseling centers at Black and non-Black universities and found that the percentage of Black students receiving emotional or social counseling at centers with at least one Black counselor was more than double that at centers with no Black counselors. Several studies have focused attention on Black clients' preference for Black mental health practitioners (see chapter 3). Sue et al. (1994) concluded in their research review that African American clients generally prefer African American practitioners. In a more recent study by Okonji, Ososkie, and Pulos (1996), 120 African American Job Corp students watched one of four videotapes that showed either reality therapy or person-centered therapy conducted by an African American or a European American male counselor. Results indicated a preference for reality therapy and the African American male counselor.

A growing number of studies are including measures of racial identity attitudes, cultural mistrust, and color-blind ideology, three constructs that are based on formulations specifically about the experiences of race and racism. As Neville and Walters noted in chapter 4, racial identity development attitudes have been shown to be related to treatment issues, such as African Americans' preference for Black therapists, psychological functioning, and the quality of treatment process. The study of cultural mistrust and color-blind ideology has also shown to be useful to practitioners as they explain treatment issues to African Americans. We contend that this body of research on the influence of racism on different treatment-related processes and outcomes has important implications for future research, especially when it is folded into holistic conceptualizations about client assessment, therapy process, and explanations about therapy outcome (see chapter 4; Whaley, 2001). In other words, investigators who concentrate their gaze on racial issues do so for the purpose of informing practice and ensuring that clients are perceived as whole beings. With further research on racial identity, cultural mistrust, and color-blind ideology, mental health practitioners can learn a great deal more about the relevance of race to African American help-seeking and therapeutic outcomes.

Before turning to our next section, we address briefly the dearth of studies on counseling or psychotherapy process that include examinations of racial and cultural issues. In their review of the research on therapy process of actual therapy cases, Hill and Nutt Williams (2000) discovered no studies that addressed the potential patterns that can occur in the process of actual therapy sessions when issues of race and culture are addressed. We believe that studies of this sort can glean valuable knowledge about some of the dynamics that are occasioned when practitioners of different races and African American clients coconstruct the therapy process (see Thompson, in press a; Thompson & Neville, 1999). In other words, investigations into the contexts in which therapy occurs can reveal crucial data on how the practitioner and client work to negotiate the meaning of race and culture in this relationship. Perhaps one barrier to this research is that investigators must imagine what this process would look like: For what mental health purposes would practitioners working with African American clients raise issues of race or culture? In what direction would these practitioners be headed? We examine these issues next by addressing the phenomenon of race and its relationship to culture.

RACE, CULTURE, AND AFRICAN AMERICANS

If mental health professionals were able somehow to extract out race from culture and momentarily erase away other political structures that intersect with these constructs, such as sexism, heterosexism, and class exploitation, they may well begin to imagine just how relatively straightforward and uncomplicated cultural learning absent of race can be. Culture would be constructed merely as a way in which people function in the world, how they make sense of their surroundings— the material and spiritual—and how they relate to and create rituals with others at different ecological levels, such as with their families, communities, and neighboring communities. When race is subtracted from culture, people will still make cultural appraisals and judgments about who is better or worse. But these manifestations would occur without the institutional force that promotes differential and unfair treatment of people based largely on superficial characteristics (e.g., Thompson & Neville, 1999). Overlooked as well would be the conditioning that people of all races experience in the United States to marginalize the perspectives of people of color while making central the perspectives of Whites, a conditioning that ultimately marginalizes all human worth.

In a race-free world, the practitioners' efforts to communicate and develop relationships with persons from a different culture would require practitioners to gain exposure to people within that particular culture, to abide by rules or roles that shape interactions and relationships, and more than likely, to learn the language or dialect in order to communicate. Practitioners would need to learn about the barriers that prevent them from relating effectively with their culturally different client. On the other side of the equation are the clients whose culture is different from the practitioners' culture and who would need to be open to any efforts to establish communication. The client would need to believe that he or she can receive some effective help from the culturally different practitioner, perhaps by acknowledging transcultural characteristics that can promote growth and problem resolution.

Adding racism and other structures of disadvantage back into the cultural fold creates a reality that is morally more complicated. With the addition of race, culture now is besieged with human actions in which people are appraised and differentially treated by virtue of superficial stimuli like skin color and dialect. These actions are met with reactions, and eventually, there evolves sets of beliefs about people that stir fear and hatred between different groups or that promote a sense of hesitancy about open communication and meaningful dialogue. Racism is based on distortions in reality and promotes stereotypes about people that must be constantly disproved. To cast *any* group as possessing certain innate characteristics relative to other groups is to segment off qualities of individuals and reduce their humanity. This reduction of humanity applies in both the inferior-designated and superior-designated groups.

Added back is an ideology of race, a structural and largely unchanging constant (e.g., Davis, 1991) that originated by humans who arranged themselves and others into categories that varied from "better" to "worse." For African Americans, consignment was decidedly in the lower rungs of the human hierarchy as established by Europeans, who placed themselves at the highest rung. Because they were perceived as savages during the importation to the United States and other countries and as subhumans relative to Whites during generations of enslavement and because they have been subjected to poor and inferior treatment, violent attacks, and a string of injustices since their emancipation, African Americans have been well-ensconced in a system of dehumanization based on race. Other racial groups have been and continue to be deeply ensconced in this system (see Takaki, 1993).

The moral component of racism lies in its impact on the lives of all people who operate within the structure and who are conditioned to conform to a status quo that minimizes a reality of racism. We contend that some people across racial groups are quite conscious of this conformity, and, indeed, knowingly participate and influence disparities in access and treatment. Some people are not entirely conscious of their conformity or participation, but when the clues of this unfair structure are surfaced, they also may be unwilling to resolve the dissonance they experience. They may elect instead to avoid the moral struggle of discerning why certain people are treated poorly and unfairly.

Thompson (in press a) contends that an examination of relational nuances of racism reveals a two-pronged conditioning process. The two prongs operate simultaneously, though people are not always conscious of this fact. In this process, people in American society learn to (1) diminish, appropriate, or cast as negative or inferior the perspectives and worldviews of historically marginalized people, such as people of color, and (2) establish as "standard," credible, superior, or innocent the perspectives and worldviews of dominant groups, such as Whites. When either point of the prong is tested, the people who try to engage meaningfully in dialogue can fall into certain entrapments that close down productive communication.

We illustrate these processes in the following example. Walter White (1893–1955) was a prominent figure in the National Association for the Advancement of Colored People (NAACP) who frequently wrote newspaper articles about the egregious acts of racial hatred and violence committed by White people toward Black people. According to biographer Waldron (1978), W. White attempted to stir the consciousness of (especially White) readers by encouraging his readers to examine their participation in racism and in their failure to work against this social disease. A woman once wrote the following to W. White in response to one of his articles: "Your 'Color Lines' article is bitter, but you do realize, I think, that white people are very cruel to other white people too! I know that!" (Waldron, 1978, p. 19). In examining this response, we will assume that the woman who wrote W. White is racially White. We'll call her Ms. Jones.

By reporting that Whites also treat other Whites cruelly, Ms. Jones may be assuming that Mr. White is preoccupied with the issue of racial cruelty of Blacks by Whites and ignorant of more universal cruelty. But her statement about the cruelty of Whites by Whites is not parallel to W. White's reports. His reports address how Whites behave cruelly to Blacks because of race. One can infer from Ms. Jones's statement that the matter of Whites mistreating other Whites *because* they are White is probably not true; rather, Whites treat other Whites cruelly for nonracial reasons. Perhaps another way of restating what Ms. Jones may have intended is that "people treat each another cruelly." Other examples of this universalizing of Whites in response to painful racial stimuli are presented in contemporary examples by Ancis and Syzmanski (2001).

In her attempt to universalize cruelty, Ms. Jones minimizes the profundity of Mr. White's descriptions and probably does so to personally ward off the reality of racism. Consequently, although Mr. White wrote about rampant acts of cruelty that took place during his time, including the lynching of entire families in the South, this reality is treated as minimally horrific in Ms. Jones's response. We propose that by trying to neutralize the impact of Mr. White's message in her mind, Ms. Jones is also trying to neutralize herself as a White person and, by association, other Whites like herself. Perhaps another strategy Ms. Jones could have used would have been to identify a certain group of Whites as perpetrators of racism and therefore still absolve herself and "normal" Whites.

On the other side of the interaction is Mr. White, whose race is *essentialized* by his being African American and by his writing about racism. The topic of racism becomes *neutralized* within this engagement with Ms. Jones because, when the referent group-ness of the dominant group is erased or muted, then racism itself is altogether questioned. It becomes the messenger who is questioned and suspected of ill-will, ignorance, or preoccupation.

In reflecting on this essentialism-neutralism bind, we propose that in a recursive helix, interactions between African Americans (whose experiences are essentialized and often diminished because they are "raced") and Whites (whose experiences and perspectives are removed from the phenomenon of systematic racism) perpetuate the dehumanization that began with the need to see the *other* as segmented, childlike, or less than human. African Americans who feel a need to voice the dehumanization they experience and to talk about this aspect of reality can be quieted by accusations of preoccupation or exaggeration. Whites can harbor attitudes and express views about these presumed preoccupations and can ascribe negative qualities onto African Americans (often privately with other Whites) whom they perceive as opportunistic or whiney.

But the evolution of these interactions alone does not account for the current climate in which people generally avoid talking meaningfully about race yet concur that there is "something" about the environment that seems patently amiss. We suggest that the distances, discomfort, and codification that are created when people resist talking openly about race also relate to the psychological investment that people have in the status quo. For some Whites who interact with African Americans, this investment is racial entitlement within the existing status quo. For some African Americans who interact with African Americans, this investment is associated with the "bargains" that have helped them to elevate their status along the racial hierarchy. Interest in a shared humanity and in the creation of community and equity are absent when people operate with these investments and when they generally employ color-blind ideology as a strategy for coping with racism (see Neville, Worthington, & Spanierman, 2001).

Reducing African Americans solely as *racial* beings is a dehumanizing process because it evokes conflict and unresolved injustices while it diminishes other human qualities about the person. Whites can become neutralized in this configuration and thus removed from affairs related to racism. And because this disengagement does little to dissipate the problem, Whites may receive reactions from Blacks that also are dehumanizing. For example, Blacks can grow to mistrust Whites and the systems that support an ideology of racism. On the other hand, people with low cultural mistrust are likely to be conditioned to believe in Whites' neutralization and in the essentialism of race for Blacks. As a consequence, low-mistrust people may idealize Whites (and other racial/ethnic groups) because they see them as disengaged from a painful past and from coeval manifestations of racism. This disengagement can seem liberating, but it is still fictitious because Whites are not disengaged from racism. The tendency to perceive Whites as such without truly getting to know individuals is also to divest Whites of human qualities and thus to dehumanize Whites.

Blacks may also try to avoid associating with other Blacks on the basis of social class, skin color, or ethnicity. This avoidance is an attempt to disconnect their selves from the weighty robe of race and to be free to be perceived as more than "just" African American. We propose that internalized racism is borne out of the dehumanizing, cyclical structure of racism. When and if Blacks eventually become aware of the extent to which racism affects their lives and the world around them, they may elect to align themselves with other Blacks for the sole purpose of gathering strength. However, these alliances may have to do more with racial affiliation than with culture.

Essentialism-neutralism is a bind that limits humans from engaging in authentic interactions. Efforts variously to neutralize or essentialize others reflect needs to shift the burden of the pathology of racism from place to place rather than work through the problems inherent in the pathology. We believe that this bind is addressed in racial identity theories, whereby individuals form perceptions about themselves and others simultaneously and often in conflict with the notion that all people share a common humanity. Liberation from this bind is reflected when the person operates principally in the advanced status of racial identity development (see Helms, 1995).

However therapy relationships are configured—whether they consist of White practitioners with Black clients, Black practitioners with Black clients, or Native American practitioners with Black clients—there is a need for the practitioners to consider their positioning within the hierarchy, including the ways in which they have benefited from racial privilege or have tried to elevate their status within other structures of disadvantage. It is important to this self-assessment that practitioners determine the extent to which they have resisted conformity and have strived to act on behalf of equality and moral advancement. Individuals rarely operate at either pole and, therefore, need to acknowledge the complexities inherent in this development.

THE INTERSECTION BETWEEN RACE AND CULTURE

African American culture consists of a constellation of behaviors, practices, and beliefs that have evolved through the generations. These behaviors, practices, and beliefs include but are not limited to rhythm, call-and-response, improvisation, oral traditions, and spontaneity (Jones, 1997); strong familial elements, including fictive kinship, or the inclusion of nonfamily members who are treated like blood relatives (e.g., Baker & Bell, 1999; Boyd-Franklin, 1989; White, 1991); and vibrancy, which creates individual style, spirituality, and movement (Boykin, 1983). The configuration of African American culture is also an amalgamation of influences that includes the adoption of practices, values, and beliefs that originate from Europe. Ostensibly, the influences of African American culture on White culture are clear, but these influences are not always acknowledged in society.

Against this backdrop, African-descended people can internalize the belief that their ancestry is vacuous, primitive, and inferior to White ancestry and culture. This perception is built not only on a relative absence of and distortion of knowledge about African culture but also on incomplete and distorted knowledge about European or White culture (e.g., Ben-Jochannan & Clarke, 1991; Franklin & Moss, 2000; Woodson, 1990). The two-pronged process again is summoned as it relates to the relationship between racism and culture: Racism influences the appraisal not only of humans but also of the culture of "others," which is seen as segmented from or inferior to the overarching culture that both the dominant and subordinate groups have variously constructed. Concomitantly, the cultural influences of the dominant group are perceived as superior. Another important aspect of this process is that when the culture of the other is perceived negatively or inferior or even essentialized to explain behaviors and actions of members of the other, it diminishes the influence of this culture to the dominant culture. Influence is perceived as minimal, and in many cases, the culture of the other is appropriated (e.g., Thompson & Neville, 1999). Fortunately, many African Americans have made efforts to carry forward the tradition of African culture and history in formal and informal settings (e.g., Beauboeuf-Lafontant & Augustine, 1996; hooks, 1994). These histories can also help all Americans restore an aspect of their selves. On an extreme end of healthy pride is romanticism governed by selective attention to reality and knowledge. Some people can romanticize Africa when they feel dejected and angry about racism in American society.

People of all races who believe that African culture is either nonexistent or inferior to White or to universal culture have colluded with the institutional structures that reinforce these ideas. We propose that when history about African culture and African American culture is restored, people can learn to appreciate the humanity of those from the past. We believe that the disconnection between this history and African Americans in contemporary society relates to a sense of dispossession. Stated another way, when the lives of Africans who helped build this nation and who struggled to survive amid horrific treatment are disregarded, so too is their humanity. Shrugging off the humanity of Africans is to internalize erroneous beliefs about the separation of the past from the present and to perceive Africans as unnecessary and disposable (see also Freire, 1972). We believe this dissociation and suppression of history has bearing on how African Americans learn to make decisions about their perceptions of themselves, other African Americans, and non–African Americans as constituents of shared communities.

Although encouraging African American clients to appreciate their culture and to do so realistically appears anathema to therapy, we believe that this strategy can be especially valuable to clients who harbor internalized racism and who feel dispossessed about their lives and outlook for the future.

PRACTICE IMPLICATIONS

Omi and Winant (1986) observed that racial categories and the meaning of race are given *concrete expression* by the specific social relations and historical context in which they are embedded. To us, the words "concrete expression" imply that practitioners need to listen to clients who are willing to talk about their racial experiences in order to understand the impact of racism on their clients' psychological functioning. However, there are prohibiting factors related to this quest for understanding. For one, people generally do not discuss racial issues to the full extent of its definition and meaning. Morrison (1992) proposes that *not* talking about race is considered in some circles as a "liberal, polite gesture," whereby codes are used to infer race. Furthermore, some people may have tendencies to talk meaningfully about race either in racially segregated circles or within circles where persons have similar views about race.

There are cues to understanding how African Americans feel about themselves and other African Americans racially. For example, African American clients may talk openly about their association with a Black college, religious institution, or organization. A male African American client who seems happy to meet his Black mental health practitioner can show this pleasure by the way he shakes hands, uses Black English, or drops some hint of his association to a local Black church. These cues are indications that could lead to the conclusion that these clients are comfortable around African Americans and may have positive feelings about their Africanness. Still, these hypotheses would have to be confirmed. As they do with all assessments, practitioners need to gather other sources of data rather than draw conclusions too quickly about the person.

But these data represent only one aspect of racial identity assessment. Practitioners need data about the other aspect, about how African Americans perceive non–African Americans, to make firmer decisions about this development. Conducting a racial assessment need not involve direct questions about how the person perceives himself or herself racially. Indeed, in light of a climate in which meaningful racial "talk" can be tense and elicit suspicions from the client, it is likely that the practitioner will need to develop ways to assess the client's level of comfort in discussions of race issues. Some very subtle ways are to merely insert a question of clarification about an issue ("You mentioned earlier that you were raised in a sheltered environment. Tell me more." And if race still is not raised, "Was this neighborhood primarily African American, White, mixed?") These inserted questions can be a valuable way to convey to the client that matters of race are an aspect of the counseling.

We assert that mental health practitioners need to resist the assumptions that quickly propel their assessment of African American clients in flat and unnuanced ways. They should resist the urge to neutralize their clients. At the same time, they need to halt their inclinations to essentialize their client. Seeing the client as human requires not only an ongoing reflection about one's "position," however unintentional, within the communities in which one lives but also a reflection of the position of others in similar and neighboring communities.

Therapy that enfolds an understanding of the dialectical relationship between the client and practitioner by race entails a sensibility toward interpersonal processes. According to Teyber (2000), the interpersonal process of therapy assumes that people derive an understanding of their selves and their world based on their interactions with others. Teyber does not address the issue of how this derived understanding emerges in regard to race. However, Thompson (in press b) proposes that the marriage between interpersonal processes and liberation psychology can be crucial to examinations of the racialized aspects of the practitioner-client relationship. Liberation psychology is defined as the study of the human condition inclusive of a reality of social injustice and inequality.

The convergence between liberation psychology and interpersonal processes is an attempt to address moral and political aspects of the client's life and of the therapist-client interaction. Consider how qualities of the practitioner, client, and communities invoke potential strains or facilitations in the relationship in each of the following scenarios.

1. A Caribbean American female mental health practitioner, age 43, who is a first-generation American and identifies herself primarily as working class, is paired with a 32-year-old African American female client whose family has lived in New York City for as long as the eldest in her family can remember. The client lives in the Bronx, where there have been recent tensions between Caribbean immigrants and native Black New Yorkers.

2. The mental health practitioner is a White American female, age 60, whose ethnic roots are only vaguely traced to Italy, Poland, and Sweden but whose family identifies as White. She lives in a poor neighborhood with other Whites and is paired with an African American female client, age 20, who lives in a suburban White community just 15 miles outside Atlanta, Georgia, that is known among other African Americans as the "vanilla suburbs." The client prefers to identify herself as "American," provides little information about her family, and phenotypically (e.g., skin color and hair texture) appears to have African ancestry.

3. The mental health practitioner is an African American male, age 50, who received his doctorate from an Ivy League university and is now working in a small Midwestern college town in the midst of a career transition. He and his family are originally from (and primarily still reside in) a wealthy and primarily Black community in Washington, D.C. He is seeing an African American male client, age 40, who is a townie in the Midwestern community, in which only 4% of the population is Black and over 92% of the town is White. The client is from a working-class background. Both practitioner and client are aware of African American ancestry dating back to slavery.

In each of these scenarios, the mental health practitioner and the client are described not only by race but also by the region of the country in which they live and work, their ages, and other qualities that can influence their perceptions of one another. These data are presented to suggest that both practitioner and client are likely to form appraisals about each other based on physical cues such as appearance, language or dialect used, and clothing. The practitioner has additional data from which to appraise the client that informs his or her perceptions or judgments about the client. For example, the practitioner and client in Scenario 1 may have ample contact with people of the other's racial and ethnic group. However, these contacts may not involve close friendships but, instead, brief interactions in adjacent neighborhoods, especially if the presence of Caribbean people in the neighborhood is relatively recent. In Scenario 3, the practitioner and client may attend the same church, but interactions beyond the church are generally limited to persons of all races who share similar socioeconomic backgrounds.

Like any of the myriad aspects of counseling, the racial aspects of counseling require mental health practitioners to attend to the readiness of the client in terms of when and how matters of race are to be addressed. The following guidelines are for practitioners as they think about their roles as therapists with African American clients.

1. We believe that an important aspiration for mental health practitioners is to consider each and every person as possessing equal worth. This aspiration may be spiritual or moral. The practice of this aspiration can be realized in a progressive relationship of racial identity interaction (Helms, 1995), whereby race is used as a path to examine some of the sociopolitical forces that influence development and interpersonal functioning. In the progressive interaction of Helms' (1995) interaction model, the therapist operates with the assumption that sociopolitical forces divide people from forming meaningful relationships and from developing in psychologically healthy ways. Reinforcing higher status racial identity and attending to lower status helps create movement in this important development.
2. Race and culture are highly intertwined. However, racism is one form of oppression that attempts to dictate how people ought to appraise and treat others relative to human worth. Gaining an appreciation of the drama of race within local and national contexts is essential to an understanding and appreciation of how that drama can be resisted and worked through in counseling.
3. The proneness toward elevating the self is probably related to the desire for approval, a sense of belonging and affiliation, and love. The need for belongingness can translate into processes of dehumanization. To defuse these tendencies, we recommend that therapists engage with one another in moral dialogues that center on race as well as on the other structures of disadvantage, such as sexual orientation, sexism, and class exploitation.
4. Psychotherapy can involve the engagement of moral dialogues, with the practitioners attuning to issues of community- versus self-interest, justice, truthfulness, and commitment. The practitioner strives to realize these goals through caring, courage, and prudence (see Doherty, 1995).

Finally, mental health practitioners recognize that change does not occur in a vacuum. They should optimize treatment by considering resources outside traditional therapy, such as spiritual leaders and community agencies. Agency heads need to examine the racial dynamics in the communities where they serve. Ensuring that Blacks and other members in the community are represented throughout positions in the agency would seem crucial to the creation of a climate that is conducive to African Americans. These efforts are likely to be more long term and can require the assistance of community members to play a role in the development of the agency. But we hope we have also made it clear that physical representation of staff at these agencies is limiting if there is no similar effort to ensure that all staff members are committed to competent service. We believe that mental health practitioners should make efforts to offer professional expertise to both remedial and preventive efforts.

Exercises

1. Refer back to the scenarios presented in this chapter, and insert a description of yourself in the place of the counselor. Describe yourself not only racially and culturally, but also according to your sexual orientation, age, social class, degree of proficiency in spoken English, religious preference, and other characteristics that can provoke impressions of your sociopolitical "position." We encourage creativity: Feel free to add characteristics to the client descriptions that will enhance both similarities and differences between you and the clients.

2. When inserting yourself into each of the scenarios in this chapter, imagine where you would live and how your neighborhood would be comprised demographically by age, race, and social class in particular. Also imagine how likely it would be to see your client occasionally on the street, at the supermarket, or at civic or religious events. Perhaps you and your client are likely to attend the same religious institution or fraternize at similar social gatherings. Or there is the likelihood that you live in the same city but reside in different communities.

   a) What are some of the probable racial dynamics in the setting in which you and your client share, and how might these dynamics influence the client's expectations of you in the therapy?

   b) To what extent does your client appear to be culturally tied to his or her African ancestry?

   c) How can your relationship with your client influence his or her racial identity development?

REFERENCES

Ancis, J., & Syzmanski, D. (2001). Awareness of White privilege among White counseling trainers. *The Counseling Psychologist, 29,* 548–569.

Baker, F. M., & Bell, C. C. (1999). Issues in the psychiatric treatment of African Americans. *Psychiatric Services, 50,* 362–368.

Beauboeuf-Lafontant, T., & Augustine, D. S. (Eds.). (1996). *Facing racism in education* (2nd ed.). Cambridge, MA: Harvard Educational Review (Reprint Series No. 21).

Ben-Jochannan, U., & Clarke, J. H. (1991). *New dimensions in African history.* Trenton, NJ: African World Press.

Betancourt, H., & Lopez, S. R. (1993). The study of culture, ethnicity, and race in American psychology. *American Psychologist, 48,* 629–637.

Boesch, R., & Cimbolic, P. (1994). Black students' use of college and university counseling centers. *Journal of College Student Development, 35,* 212–216.

Bosworth, H. B., Parsey, K. S., Butterfield, M. I., McIntyre, L. M., Oddone, E. Z., Stechuchak, K. M., & Bastian, L. A. (2000). Racial variation in wanting and obtaining mental health services among women veterans in a primary care clinic. *Journal of the National Medical Association, 92,* 231–236.

Boyd-Franklin, N. (1989). *Black families in therapy: A multisystems approach.* New York: Guilford.

Boykin, A. W. (1983). The academic performance of Afro-American children. In J. T. Spence (Ed.), *Achievement and achievement motives* (pp. 320–371). San Francisco: W. H. Freeman.

Brown, C., Shear, M. K., Schulberg, H. C., & Madonia, M. J. (1999). Anxiety disorders among African-American and white primary medical care patients. *Psychiatric Services, 50,* 407–409.

Bulhan, H. A. (1985). *Frantz Fanon and the psychology of oppression.* New York: Plenum.

Chambless, D. L., & Williams, K. E. (1995). A preliminary study of the effects of exposure in vivo for African Americans with agoraphobia. *Behavior Therapy, 26,* 501–515.

Cushman, P. (1995). *Constructing the self, constructing America: A cultural history of psychotherapy.* Reading, MA: Addison-Wesley.

Davis, F. J. (1991). *Who is Black? One nation's definition.* University Park: Pennsylvania State University.

Diala, C., Muntaner, C., Walrather, C., Nickerson, K. J., LaVeist, T. A., & Leaf, P. J. (2000). Racial differences in attitudes toward professional mental health care and in the use of services. *American Journal of Orthopsychiatry, 70,* 455–464.

Doherty, W. J. (1995). *Soul searching: Why psychotherapy must promote moral responsibility.* New York: Basic.

Fish, J. (2002). *Race and intelligence: Separating science from myth.* Mahwah, NJ: Erlbaum.

Foucault, M. (1987). *Mental illness and psychology.* Berkeley: University of California.

Freire, P. (1972). *Pedagogy of the oppressed.* New York: Herder and Herder.

Franklin, J. H., & Moss, A. A., Jr. (2000). *From slavery to freedom: A history of African Americans* (8th ed.). Boston: McGraw-Hill.

Friedman, S., Paradis, C. M., & Hatch, M. (1994). Characteristics of African-American and white patients with panic disorder and agoraphobia. *Hospital and Community Psychiatry, 45,* 795–803.

Helms, J. E. (1992). *A race is a nice thing to have: A guide to being a White person or understanding the White persons in your life.* Kansas City: Content Communications.

Helms, J. E. (1994). How multiculturalism obscures racial factors in the psychotherapy process. *Journal of Counseling Psychology, 41,* 162–165.

Helms, J. E. (1995). An update of Helms's White and People of Color racial identity models. In J. Ponterotto, J. M. Casas, L. A. Suzuki, & C. M. Alexander (Eds.), *Handbook of multicultural counseling.* Thousand Oaks: Sage.

Hill, C. E., & Nutt Williams, R. (2000). The process of individual therapy. In S. D. Brown and R. Lent (Eds.), *Handbook of counseling psychology* (pp. 670–710). New York: Wiley.

hooks, bell. (1994). *Teaching to transgress: Education as the practice of freedom.* New York: Routledge.

Jones, J. M. (1997). *Prejudice and racism* (2nd ed.). New York: McGraw-Hill.

Lichtenberg, P. A., Kimbarow, M. L., Morris, P., & Vangel, S. J. (1996). Behavioral treatment of depression in predominantly African-American medical clients. *Clinical Gerontologist, 17,* 15–33.

Martín-Baró, I. (1994). *Writings for a liberation psychology.* Cambridge, MA: Harvard University.

Mays, V. M., Caldwell, C. H., & Jackson, J. S. (1996). Mental health systems and service utilization of help-seeking among African American women. In H. W. Neighbors & J. S. Jackson (Eds.), *Mental health in Black America* (pp. 161–176). Thousand Oaks, CA: Sage.

Miller, J. G. (1999). Cultural psychology: Implications for basic psychological theory. *Psychological Science, 10,* 85–91.

Morrison, T. (1992). *Playing in the dark: Whiteness and the literary imagination.* Cambridge, MA: Harvard University.

Neighbors, H. W., & Jackson, J. S. (1996). *Mental health in Black America.* Thousand Oaks, CA: Sage.

Neville, H. A., Worthington, R. L., & Spanierman, L. (2001). Race, power, and multicultural counseling psychology: Understanding White privilege and color-blind racial attitudes (pp. 257–288). In J. G. Ponterotto, J. M. Casas, L. A. Suzuki, & C. M. Alexander (Eds.), *Handbook of multicultural counseling.* Thousand Oaks, CA: Sage.

Okonji, J. M. A., Ososkie, J. N., & Pulos, S. (1996). Preferred style and ethnicity of counselors by African American males. *Journal of Black Psychology, 22,* 329–339.

Omi, M., & Winant, H. (1986). *Racial formation in the United States: From the 1960s to the 1980s.* New York: Routledge Kegan Paul.

Padgett, D. K., Harman, C. P., Burns, B. J., & Schlesinger, H. J. (1994). Women and outpatient mental health services: Use by Black, Hispanic, and White women in a national insured population. *Journal of Mental Health Administration, 21,* 347–360.

Rosenbeck, R., & Fontana, A. (1994). Utilization of mental health services by minority veterans of the Vietnam era. *Journal of Nervous and Mental Disease, 182,* 686–691.

Smedley, A. (1993). *Race in North America: Origin and evolution of a worldview.* Boulder, CO: Westview.

Snowden, L. R. (1999). African American service use for mental health problems. *Journal of Community Psychology, 27,* 303–313.

Strakowski, S. M., Hawkins, J. M., Keck, P. E., McElroy, S. L., West, S. A., Bourne, M. L., Sax, K. W., & Tugrul, K. C. (1997). The effects of race and information variance on disagreement between psychiatric emergency service and research diagnoses in first-episode psychosis. *Journal of Clinical Psychiatry, 58,* 457–463.

Sue, S., Fujino, D. C., Hu, L., Takeuchi, D., & Zane, N. (1991). Community mental health services for ethnic minority groups: A test of the cultural responsiveness hypothesis. *Journal of Consulting and Clinical Psychology, 59,* 616–624.

Sue, S., Zane, N., & Young, K. (1994). Research on psychotherapy with culturally diverse populations. In A. E. Bergin & S. L. Garfield (Eds.), *Handbook of psychotherapy and behavior change* (4th ed.; pp. 783–817). New York: Wiley.

Takaki, R. (1993). *A different mirror: A history of multicultural America.* Boston: Little Brown.

Taylor, R. J., Hardison, C. B., & Chatters, L. M. (1996). Kin and nonkin as sources of informal assistance. In H. W. Neighbors & J. S. Jackson (Eds.), *Mental health in Black America* (pp. 130–160). Thousand Oaks, CA: Sage.

Teyber, E. (2000). *Interpersonal process in psychotherapy: A relational approach* (4th ed.). Belmont, CA: Wadsworth/Thomson Learning.

Thompson, C. E. (in press a). Awareness and identity: Foundational principles in multicultural counseling. In T. Smith (Ed.)., *Practicing multiculturalism and affirming diversity.* New York: Prentice Hall.

Thompson, C. E. (in press b). Psychological theory and culture: Implications for practice. In R. T. Carter (Ed.), *Handbook of racial-cultural psychology.* New York: Wiley.

Thompson, C. E., & Neville, H. A. (1999). Racism and mental health. *The Counseling Psychologist, 27,* 155–223.

Treadwell, K. R. H., Flannery-Schroeder, E. C., & Kendall, P. C. (1995). Ethnicity and gender in relation to adaptive functioning, diagnostic status, and treatment outcome in children from an anxiety clinic. *Journal of Anxiety Disorders, 9,* 373–384.

Trierweiler, S. J., Neighbors, H. W., Munday, C., Thompson, S. E. Binion, V. J., & Gomez, J. P. (2000). Clinician attributions associated with diagnosis of schizophrenia in African American and non-American patients. *Journal of Consulting and Clinical Psychology, 68,* 171–175.

U.S. Surgeon General's Report. (2001). *Mental health: A report of the Surgeon General.* U.S. Department of Health and Human Services, Office of the Surgeon General, SAMHSA. Retrieved from http://www.mentalhealth.org/cre/ch3

Waldron, E. E. (1978). *Walter White and the Harlem Renaissance.* Port Washington, NY: Kennikat.

Whaley, A. L. (2001). Cultural mistrust of White mental health clinicians among African Americans with severe mental illness. *American Journal of Orthopsychiatry, 71,* 252–256.

White, J. L. (1991). Toward a Black psychology. In R. L. Jones (Ed.), *Black psychology* (3rd ed.; pp. 3–13). Berkeley, CA: Cobb and Henry.

Williams, D. R., Griffith, E. E. H., Young, J. L., Collins, C., & Dodson, J. (1999). Structure and provision of services in Black churches in New Haven, Connecticut. *Cultural Diversity and Ethnic Minority Psychology, 5,* 118–133.

Woodson, C. G. (1990). *The mis-education of the Negro.* Trenton, NJ: Africa World Press.

Zoellner, L. A., Feeny, N. C., Fitzgibbons, L. A., & Foa, E. B. (1999). Response of African American and Caucasian women to cognitive behavioral therapy for PTSD. *Behavior Therapy, 30,* 581–595.

Part III   THE AMERICAN
            INDIAN CLIENT

CHAPTER 7 # Profile of Native Americans

Michael Tlanusta Garrett, Eastern Band of Cherokee, Western Carolina University

Ezigaa and I were standing on the lakeshore one fine ricing morning. It was cool but the bright sun was warming things up nicely. The overnight dew was leaving the plants. We were watching my two sons, Jim and Joseph. They were using my canoe to go out and harvest rice. I got profound when I realized I had seen four generations of Anishinaabeg harvesting rice. I decided to give my grandson a quiz.

"Ezigaa, who made that rice?"

"The Creator," he answered.

"What about the water, who made the water?"

"The Creator," the four-year-old boy said.

"How about those ducks, who made them?"

"The Creator," he said.

"Who made Ezigaa?" I asked.

"The Creator."

I thought my grandson had been paying attention. I was not prepared some time later when he asked, "Grandpa, who made the Creator?"

—JIM NORTHRUP (1997, pp. 48–49)

THE PEOPLE

Native Americans consist of approximately 2.4 million self-identified people with a population that is steadily growing (U.S. Bureau of the Census, 2001). Although this number represents only 1% of the total population of the United States, Native people have been described as representing "fifty percent of the diversity" in our country (Hodgkinson, 1990, p. 1). Across the United States, there are more than 557 federally recognized tribes/nations (220 of which reside in Alaska), approximately 150 tribes in the process of petitioning the government for federal recognition, and approximately 30 state-recognized tribes (Russell, 1997). Given the wide-ranging diversity of this population, it is important to understand that the term *Native American* encompasses the vastness and essence of tribal traditions represented by hundreds of Indian nations. Navajo, Catawba, Shoshone, Lumbee,

Cheyenne, Cherokee, Apache, Lakota, Seminole, Comanche, Pequot, Cree, Tuscarora, Paiute, Creek, Pueblo, Shawnee, Hopi, Osage, Mohawk, Nez Perce, Seneca—these are but a handful of the hundreds of Indian nations that exist across the United States.

Native Americans represent a wide-ranging diversity illustrated, for example, by approximately 252 different languages (Thomason, 1991). At the same time, a prevailing sense of "Indianness" based on common worldview and common history seems to bind Native Americans together as a people of many peoples. Although acculturation plays a major factor in Native American worldview, there tends to be a high degree of psychological homogeneity, that is, a certain degree of shared cultural standards and meanings based on common core values that exist for traditional Native Americans across tribal groups (Choney, Berryhill-Paapke, & Robbins, 1995; DuBray, 1985; M. T. Garrett, 1999a).

Because approximately 78% of the Native American population resides in urban areas and only 22% of the total population of Native people live on reservations, the degree of traditionalism versus the degree of acculturation to mainstream American values and cultural standards for behavior is an important consideration in counseling Native people (Heinrich, Corbine, & Thomas, 1990; Russell, 1997). Native Americans come from different tribal groups with different customs, traditions, and beliefs; they live in a variety of settings including rural, urban, or reservation (J. T. Garrett & M. T. Garrett, 1994). Cherokees and Navajos are both Native Americans, but their regional cultures, climatic adaptations, and languages differ greatly. However, part of what they share in common is a strong sense of traditionalism based on basic cultural values and worldview.

In order to better understand how to provide Native clients with culturally responsive services in the counseling process, mental health professionals must enter the world of a Native client. The purpose of this chapter is to offer an overview and understanding of this population by discussing terminology, historical context, traditional Native values and worldview, acculturation, discrimination, social support systems, current socioeconomic conditions, and current social and political issues within the Native community as they relate to counseling for Native American clients.

Who Is Native American: "How Much Are You?"

The term *Native American* is often used to describe indigenous peoples of the Western hemisphere in an effort to provide recognition—viewed by many as long overdue—of the unique history and status of these people as the first inhabitants of the American continent. The U.S. Bureau of Indian Affairs (1988) legally defines a Native American as a person who is an enrolled or registered member of a tribe or whose blood quantum is one fourth or more, genealogically derived from Native American ancestry. Native nations across the country set differing criteria for blood quantum—from the Cherokee Nation of Oklahoma, which enrolls members with blood quantum as little as $\frac{1}{512}$, to the Ute Nation of Utah, which requires a minimum blood quantum of $\frac{5}{8}$ for tribal membership; most tribes/nations require $\frac{1}{4}$ blood quantum (Russell, 1997). The U.S. Bureau of the

Census (2001), meanwhile, relies on self-identification to determine who is a Native person. Oswalt (1988) points out, however, that "if a person is considered an Indian by other individuals in the community, he or she is legally an Indian . . . [in other words], if an individual is on the roll of a federally recognized Indian group, then he or she is an Indian; the degree of Indian blood is of no real consequence, although usually he or she has at least some Indian blood" (p. 5).

Terms Applied to Native Americans

Among some of the terms used historically or currently to refer to Native people are: *American Indian, Alaskan Native, Native people, Indian, First American, Amerindian, Amerind, First Nations people, Aboriginal people,* and *Indigenous people.* The term *Native American* or *Native people* (and sometimes *Indian*) will be used here to refer generally to those Native people indigenous to the United States who self-identify as Native American and maintain cultural identification as a Native person through membership in a Native American tribe recognized by the state or federal government or through other tribal affiliation and community recognition.

SURVIVING "HISTORY": SPIRIT NEVER DIES

Many authors have described the deliberate attempts throughout U.S. history by mainstream American institutions such as government agencies, schools, and churches to destroy the Native American institutions of family, clan, and tribal structure, religious belief systems and practices, customs, and traditional way of life (Deloria, 1988; Locust, 1988; Reyhner & Eder, 1992). Deloria (1988, p. 166) commented, "When questioned by an anthropologist on what the Indians called America before the White man came, an Indian said simply, Ours." Characterized by institutional racism and discrimination, dominant culture has had a long history of opposition to Native cultures, and its attempts to assimilate Native people have had a long-lasting effect on the cultures and Native people's way of life (Deloria, 1994).

It was not until 1924 that the U.S. government recognized the citizenship of Native Americans—no longer a threat to national expansion—through passage of the Citizenship Act (Deloria, 1988). In addition, Native Americans were not granted religious freedom until 1978 (I was eight years old), when the American Indian Religious Freedom Act was passed (overturning the Indian Religious Crimes Code, passed by Congress in 1889), which guaranteed Native people the constitutional right to exercise their traditional religious practices for the first time in a century (Loftin, 1989). On a more personal note, every time I see a $20 bill, I am reminded of the betrayal of my tribe by the government back in 1838 when Andrew Jackson (depicted in all his glory on the $20 bill) signed off on an illegal act that forced the removal of over 16,000 Cherokees from parts of North Carolina, South Carolina, Tennessee, and Georgia to the Oklahoma territory (M. T. Garrett, 1998).

In more recent times, massive efforts to "civilize" Native people—such as the government-supported, church-run boarding schools and the relocation programs of the 1950s—have created a historical context in which generational trauma and cultural discontinuity continues to affect Native people of all ages (Hirschfelder & Kriepe de Montano, 1993). During all these incidents, the Bureau of Indian Affairs, a division of the Department of Interior charged with carrying out the government-to-government relationship between the federal government and Native tribes, has not always sought to include Native people in the management of their own affairs. In some instances, the Bureau of Indian Affairs has simply served to perpetuate the policies of assimilation that have divided, oppressed, and impoverished generations of Native people (Deloria, 1988).

These are but a few examples of historical factors that have affected Native Americans psychologically, economically, and socially for generations. However, it important to not lose sight of the most important considerations for counseling Native people based on this information: trust versus mistrust. From both a historical and contemporary perspective, oppression is and continues to be a very real experience for Native people. What has provided a foundation for both the symbolic and literal survival of Native people has been the ability to be resilient while we attempt to maintain the traditions of our ancestors.

NATIVE TRADITIONS: LIVING THE WAYS

Several authors have described common core values that characterize Native traditionalism across tribal nations (Heinrich et al., 1990; Little Soldier, 1992; Thomason, 1991). Some of these Native traditional values (see Table 7.1) include the importance of community contribution, sharing, acceptance, cooperation, harmony and balance, noninterference, extended family, attention to nature, immediacy of time, awareness of the relationship, and a deep respect for elders (Deloria, 1994; Dudley, 1992; Dufrene, 1990; Four Worlds Development Project, 1984; J. T. Garrett & M. T. Garrett, 1994, 1996; M. T. Garrett, 1996a; Heinrich et al., 1990; Herring, 1999; Plank, 1994; Red Horse, 1997). All in all, these traditional values show the importance of honoring, through harmony and balance, what Native people believe to be a very sacred connection with the energy of life; this is the basis for a traditional Native worldview and spirituality across tribal nations.

The Tribe/Nation

Traditional Native people experience a unique relationship between themselves and the tribe. In a very real sense, Native American individuals are extensions of their tribal nation—socially, emotionally, historically, and politically. For many Indian people, cultural identity is rooted in tribal membership, community, and heritage. Many Native nations are matriarchal/matrilineal or matriarchal/patrilineal, but there are those that follow patriarchal/patrilineal ways too (or other variations of gender dominance and tracing of family heritage); dominance and heritage, in turn, affect not only communal and social structure and functioning but

TABLE 7.1   Comparison of Cultural Values and Expectations

Traditional Native American	Contemporary Mainstream American
Harmony with nature	Power over nature
Cooperation	Competition
Group needs more important than individual needs	Personal goals considered important
Privacy and noninterference; try to control self, not others	Need to control and affect others
Self-discipline both in body and mind	Self-expression and self-disclosure
Participation after observation (only when certain of ability)	Trial and error learning, new skills practiced until they are mastered
Explanation according to nature	Scientific explanation for everything
Reliance on extended family	Reliance on experts
Emotional relationships valued	Concerned mostly with facts
Patience encouraged (allow others to go first)	Aggressive and competitive
Humility	Fame and recognition; winning
Win once, let others win also	Win first prize all of the time
Follow the old ways	Climb the ladder of success; importance of progress and change
Discipline distributed among many; no one person takes blame	Blame one person at cost to others
Physical punishment rare	Physical punishment accepted
Present-time focus	Future-time focus
Time is always with us	Clock watching
Present goals considered important; future accepted as it comes	Plan for future and how to get ahead
Encourage sharing freely and keeping only enough to satisfy present needs	Private property; encourage acquisition of material comfort and saving for the future
Speak softly, at a slower rate	Speak louder and faster
Avoid singling out the listener	Address listener directly (by name)
Interject less	Interrupt frequently
Use fewer "encouraging signs" (uh-huh, head nodding)	Use verbal encouragement
Delayed response to auditory messages	Use immediate response
Nonverbal communication	Verbal skills highly prized

Source: M. T. Garrett, 1999b.

also family/clan structure and functioning. The extended family (at least three generations) and tribal group take precedence over all else. The tribe is an inter-dependent system of people who perceive themselves as parts of the greater whole rather than a whole consisting of individual parts. Likewise, traditional Native people judge themselves and their actions according to whether they are bene-fiting the tribal community and its continued harmonious functioning.

In mainstream American society, worth and status are based on "what you do" or "what you have achieved." For Native Americans, "who you are is where you come from." Native Americans essentially believe that "If you know my family, clan, tribe, then you know me." As a result, traditional Native people might be likely to describe some aspect of their family or tribal heritage when asked to talk about themselves.

The Meaning of Family

It has been said that about the most unfavorable moral judgement an Indian can pass on another person is to say he acts as if he didn't have any relatives (DuBray, 1985). Upon meeting for the first time, many Indian people will ask, "Where do you come from; who's your family? Who do you belong to? Who are your people?" The intent is to find out where they stand in relation to this new person and what commonality exists. In fact, these questions are a simple way of building bridges—or recognizing bridges that already exist but are as yet unknown. Family may or may not consist of blood relatives. It is common practice in the Indian way, for instance, to claim another as a relative, thereby welcoming him or her as real family. From that point on, that person is a relative and that is that. After all, family is a matter of blood and of spirit.

Wisdom Keepers

Native elders are the keepers of the sacred ways, as protectors, mentors, teachers, and support givers, regardless their "social status." Native communities honor their Indian elders, the "Keepers of the Wisdom," and consider those elders as highly respected people because of their lifetime's worth of wisdom and experience. Elders have always played an important part in the continuance of the tribal community by functioning in the role of parent, teacher, community leader, and spiritual guide (M. T. Garrett & J. T. Garrett, 1997). To refer to an elder as Grandmother, Grandfather, Uncle, Aunt, Old Woman, or Old Man is to refer to a very special relationship that exists with that elder through deep respect and admiration.

In the traditional way, the prevalence of cooperation and sharing in the spirit of community is essential for harmony and balance. It is not unusual for a Native child to be raised in several different households over time. This movement is generally not because no one cares enough to keep them around very long or because Native American people are lazy and irresponsible, but because it is considered both an obligation and a pleasure to share in raising and caring for the children in one's family. Grandparents, aunts, uncles, and other members of the community are all responsible for the raising of children, and they take this responsibility very seriously.

In the traditional way, elders direct young children's attention outward to the things with which they coexist (trees, plants, rocks, animals, elements, the land) and to the meaning of these things. They show the children the true relationship that exists among all things and the ways in which to honor this relationship. In this way, children develop a heightened level of sensitivity for everything of which they are a part and that is a part of them, for the circular (cyclical) motion and flow of life-energy, and for the customs and traditions of their people.

A very special kind of relationship based on mutual respect and caring takes place between Indian elders and Indian children as each child moves through the Life Circle from "being cared for" to "caring for," as Red Horse (1980) puts it. With increase in age comes an increase in the sacred obligation to family, clan, and tribe. Native American elders pass down to the children the tradition that their life-force carries the spirits of their ancestors. With such an emphasis on connectedness, Native traditions revere children, not only as ones who will carry on the wisdom and traditions but also as "little people" who are still very close to the spirit world and from whom we have much to learn. Brendtro, Brokenleg, and Van Bockern (1990, p. 45) relate a story shared with them by Eddie Belleroe, a Cree elder from Alberta, Canada:

> In a conversation with his aging grandfather, a young Indian man asked, "Grandfather, what is the purpose of life?" After a long time in thought, the old man looked up and said, "Grandson, children are the purpose of life. We were once children and someone cared for us, and now it is our time to care."

Humility   In the Native traditional way, people are important and unique as individuals but are also part of the Greater Circle of Life. As Native people come to view themselves in relation to the Greater Circle, they begin to view their actions or intentions in terms of how these actions affect the Circle, whether it be the family, clan, tribe, community, or universe. From a Native traditional perspective, one of the greatest challenges in life is to recognize our place in the universe and to honor this place always. Modesty and humility are essential to a harmonious way of life in which the emphasis is placed on relation rather than domination. Individual praise should be welcomed if it has been earned, but this praise need not be used to bolster a person into thinking or acting as though he or she is greater than any other living thing in the Circle.

Boasting of one's accomplishments and loud behavior that attracts attention to oneself are discouraged in the traditional way, where self-absorption and self-importance brings disharmony on oneself and one's family. In the Circle, the group must take precedence over the individual, and the wisdom of age takes precedence over youth, though it does not make anyone better or more worthy than anyone else. Many times, a traditional Native person may drop his or her head and eyes, or at least be careful not to look into the eyes of another, as a sign of respect for any elder or other honored person. No one is worthy of staring into the eyes of an elder or looking into the spirit of that honored person. This gesture also signifies that a person does not view himself or herself as better than anyone else.

Generosity   Traditional Native views concerning property accentuate the underlying belief that "whatever belongs to the individual also belongs to the group," and vice versa. It should come as no surprise to see Indian people sharing or giving their "possessions" away to others in certain circumstances. Generosity is considered a sign of wisdom and humility.

Traditional Native people are accustomed to cooperating and sharing. As a result, they participate well in group activities that emphasize cooperation and group harmony. Individual competition for the sake of beating others or showing others up is highly frowned on in Native American culture. Many Indian people do very poorly in activities that emphasize competition among individuals. However, activities (especially sports) that emphasize intergroup competitions can be quite lively, to say the least, but all in good fun. The idea of seeking group harmony through cooperation and sharing takes precedence above all else.

Patience   Everything has its place. Very often, it is simply a matter of time before a person recognizes where and how things fit together. In Native traditions, there is a sacred design to the world in which we live, to the process of life itself. And very often it is not a matter of whether "things" fall into place, but whether our capacity for awareness and understanding of "things" falls into place. It is important that we learn through careful observation, listening, and patience as well as asking questions or thinking things through. Everything offers us a valuable lesson, from all our surroundings to each of our experiences. It takes time and a special kind of willingness or openness to receive all the lessons that are offered to us throughout life.

Time   Life offers us opportunities to think in terms of what is happening now, to be aware of what is taking place all around us, to focus on current thoughts, ideas, feelings, and experiences. Where we are *is* where we have come from and where we are going. We do not always have to live by the clock. Mother Earth has her own unique rhythms that signal the beginnings and endings of things. Again, we need only observe and listen quietly to know when it is time. So-called Indian time says that things begin when they are ready and things end when they are finished.

Being   Native tradition ("the Medicine Way") emphasizes a unique sense of being that allows us to live in accord with the natural flow of life-energy. Being says, "It's enough just to be; our purpose in life is to develop the inner self in relation to everything around us." Being receives much of its power from connectedness. Belonging and connectedness lie at the very heart of where we came from, who we are, and to whom we belong. True being requires that we know and experience our connections and that we honor our relations with all our heart.

Spirituality and Wellness: Walking in Step

Different tribal languages have different words or ways of referring to the idea of honoring a person's sense of connection, but the meaning is similar across nations in its reference to the belief that human beings exist on Mother Earth to be helpers and protectors of life. In Native communities, it is not uncommon, as an example, to hear people use the term *caretaker*. Therefore, from the perspective of a traditionalist, to see one's purpose as that of caretaker is to accept responsibility for the gift of life by taking good care of that gift, the gift of life that others have received, and the surrounding beauty of the world in which we live (J. T. Garrett, 2001).

More or less, the essence of Native American spirituality is about "feeling" (Wilbur, 1999a, 1999b). The feeling of connection is something that is available to all of us, though experienced in differing ways. It is important to note that the spiritual beliefs of Native Americans depend on a number of factors that include level of acculturation (traditional, marginal, bicultural, assimilated, pantraditional); geographic region; family structure; religious influences; and tribally specific traditions (for further discussion of levels of acculturation, see J. T. Garrett

& M. T. Garrett, 1994; M. T. Garrett & Pichette, 2000; LaFromboise, Coleman, & Gerton, 1993). However, it is possible to generalize, to some extent, about some of the basic beliefs that characterize Native American traditionalism and spirituality across tribal nations. The following, adapted from Locust (1988, pp. 317–318), elaborates on a number of basic Native American spiritual and traditional beliefs:

1. There is a single higher power known as Creator, Great Creator, Great Spirit, or Great One, among other names (this being is sometimes referred to in gender form, but does not necessarily exist as one particular gender or another). There are also lesser beings known as spirit beings or spirit helpers.
2. Plants and animals, like humans, are part of the spirit world. The spirit world exists side by side with, and intermingles with, the physical world. Moreover, the spirit existed in the spirit world before it came into a physical body and will exist after the body dies.
3. Human beings are made up of a spirit, mind, and body. The mind, body, and spirit are all interconnected; therefore, illness affects the mind and spirit as well as the body.
4. Wellness is harmony in body, mind, and spirit; unwellness is disharmony in mind, body, and spirit.
5. Natural unwellness is caused by the violation of a sacred social or natural law of Creation (e.g., participating in a sacred ceremony while under the influence of alcohol or drugs, or having had sex within four days of the ceremony).
6. Unnatural unwellness is caused by conjuring (witchcraft) from those with destructive intentions.
7. Each of us is responsible for our own wellness by keeping ourselves attuned to self, relations, environment, and universe.

This list of beliefs in Native American spirituality crosses tribal boundaries but is by no means a comprehensive list. It does, however, provide a great deal of insight into some of the assumptions that may be held by a traditional Native client. In order to better understand what it means to "walk in step" according to Native American spirituality, it is important to discuss four basic cultural elements: Medicine, Relation, Harmony, and Vision (M. T. Garrett & Wilbur, 1999).

Medicine (Everything Is Alive)   In many Native American tribal languages (e.g., in Cherokee), there is no word for religion because spiritual practices are an integral part of every aspect of daily life, which is necessary for the harmony and balance, or wellness, of individual, family, clan, and community (M. T. Garrett & J. T. Garrett, 2002; M. T. Garrett, J. T. Garrett, & Brotherton, 2001). Healing and worship are considered as one and the same. For Native American people, the concept of health and wellness is not only a physical state but a spiritual one as well. "Medicine," as a Native concept, implies the very essence of our being, or life force, which exists in all creatures on Mother Earth (J. T. Garrett & M. T. Garrett, 1996). In the traditional way, Medicine can consist of physical remedies such as herbs, teas, or poultices for physical ailments, but Medicine is simultaneously something much more than a pill you take to cure illness, get rid of pain, or correct a physiological malfunction. Medicine is everywhere. It is the very essence of our inner being; it is that which gives us inner power.

Harmony (Everything Has Purpose)   Every living being has a reason for being. Traditional Native Americans look upon life as a gift from the Creator. As a gift, it is to be treated with the utmost care out of respect for the giver. Native Americans live in a humble way and give thanks for all the gifts that they receive every day, no matter how big or small. Native American spirituality often places great emphasis on the numbers four and seven. The number four represents the spirit of each of the directions—east, south, west, and north, usually depicted in a Circle. The number seven represents the same four directions as well as the upper world (Sky), lower world (Earth), and center (often referring to the heart, or sacred fire) to symbolize universal harmony and balance (visualized as a sphere). In the traditional way, we seek to understand what lessons are offered to us by giving thanks to each of the four directions for the wisdom, guidance, strength, and clarity that we receive. Not every tribe practices the directions in this way, but almost all tribes have some representation of the four directions as a circular symbol of the harmony and balance of mind, body, and spirit with the natural environment (and spirit world).

Relation (All Things Are Connected)   Central to Native American spiritual traditions is the importance of "relation" as a total way of existing in the world. The concept of family extends to brothers and sisters in the animal world, the plant world, the mineral world, Mother Earth, Father Sky, and so on. Respect for Medicine also means that we practice respect for the interconnection that we share. Across tribal nations, there are certain natural or social laws that must be observed out of respect for relation. These laws often point to restrictions on personal conduct regarding such things as death, incest, the female menstrual cycle, witchcraft, certain animals, certain natural phenomena, certain foods, marrying into one's own clan, and strict observance of ceremonial protocol (Locust, 1988). In general, a rule of thumb in Native tradition is that we (a) never take more than we need, (b) give thanks for what we have or what we receive, (c) take great care to use all of what we do have, and (d) give away what we do not need (or what someone else may need more than us).

Vision (Embrace the Medicine of Every Living Being)   Across tribal nations, many different ceremonies are used for healing, giving thanks, celebrating, clearing the way, and blessing (Lake, 1991). Among the various traditions, a few examples of ceremonies include sweatlodge, vision quest, clearing-way ceremony, blessing-way ceremony, pipe ceremony, sunrise ceremony, sundance, and many, many others (Heinrich et al., 1990; Lake, 1991). One of the functions of ceremonial practice is to reaffirm our sense of connection with that which is sacred. In American mainstream ideology, the purpose of life consists of "life, liberty, and the pursuit of happiness." From a traditional Native perspective, a corollary would be, "life, love, and the pursuit of wisdom." Understanding one's vision is understanding the direction of one's path as a caretaker who moves to the rhythm of the sacred heartbeat. As Black Elk, Oglala Lakota Medicine Man, put it, "the good road and the road of difficulties, you have made me cross; and where they cross, the place is holy" (cited in M. T. Garrett, 1998, p. 85).

Lessons of the Eagle Feather: Rule of Opposites

Eagle feathers are considered to be infinitely sacred among Native Americans, who make use of the feathers for a variety of purposes, including ceremonial healing and purification. Eagle Medicine represents a state of presence achieved through diligence, understanding, awareness, and a completion of "tests of initiation" such as the vision quest (M. T. Garrett & Osborne, 1995) or other demanding life experiences. Highly respected elder status is associated with Eagle Medicine and the power of connectedness and truth. It is through experience and patience that this Medicine is earned over a lifetime. And it is through understanding and choice that it is honored. This old anecdote probably best illustrates the lessons of the eagle feather:

> Once while acting as a guide for a hunting expedition, an Indian had lost the way home. One of the men with him said, "You're lost, chief." The Indian guy replied, "I'm not lost, my tipi is lost."

The Eagle feather, which represents duality, tells the story of life. It tells of the many dualities or opposites that exist in the Circle of Life, such as light and dark, male and female, substance and shadow, summer and winter, life and death, peace and war (M. T. Garrett & Myers, 1996). The Eagle feather has both light and dark colors, dualities and opposites. Though a person can make a choice to argue which of the colors is most beautiful or most valuable, the truth is that both colors come from the same feather, both are true, both are connected, and it takes both to fly (J. T. Garrett & M. T. Garrett, 1996). The colors are opposite, but they are part of the same truth. The importance of the feather lies not in which color is most beautiful but in the discovery and acceptance of what the purpose of the feather as a whole may be. In other words, there is no such thing as keeping the mountains and getting rid of the valleys; they are one and the same, and they exist because of one another. As one elder puts it:

> The Eagle feather teaches about the Rule of Opposites, about everything being divided into two ways. The more one is caught up in the physical, or the West, then the more one has to go in the opposite direction, the East, or the spiritual, to get balance. And it works the other way too—you can't just focus on the spiritual to the exclusion of the physical. You need harmony in all Four Directions. (J. T. Garrett, 1991, p. 173)

Indian Humor: Laughing It Up

Contrary to the stereotypical belief that Indian people are solemn, stoic figures poised against a backdrop of tepees, tomahawks, and headdresses, the truth is, Indian people love to laugh (J. T. Garrett & M. T. Garrett, 1994; Maples et al., 2001). As a matter of fact, humor is a critical part of the culture, especially around mealtime. It is amazing to watch the transformation that occurs when people come together around food and really begin to open up. In Indian country, mealtime is sometimes the worst time to try to eat, because everyone (yourself included) is laughing so hard, cutting up, sharing side-splitting stories, and teasing each other. Moreover, many tribal oral traditions emphasize important life lessons through the subtle humor expressed in the stories. So often, it is the arrogant, manipulative, vain, clownlike figure of Rabbit or Possum or Coyote or Raven (the character depends on the tribe, but is always the one who thinks he or she knows it all) who ends up learning a hard lesson in humility in the end, much to the amusement of others and maybe as a reminder to others (J. T. Garrett & M. T. Garrett, 1996; M. T. Garrett, 1998; Herring, 1994).

Native people live for laughter, which plays a very important role in the continued survival of the tribal group. After all, laughter relieves stress and creates an atmosphere of sharing and connectedness. As George Good Striker, Blackfoot elder, puts it, "Humor is the WD-40 of healing" (cited in M. T. Garrett, 1998, p. 137).

Communication Style: Talking the Talk

Native interaction style emphasizes nonverbal communication over verbal communication. Moderation in speech and avoidance of direct eye contact are nonverbal communicators of respect for the speaker, especially if it is a respected elder or anyone in a position of authority (M. T. Garrett, 1996b). Careful listening and observation are exercised in order to understand more of what is meant and less of what is actually said. Storytelling is commonly used to communicate feelings, beliefs, and the importance of experience (M. T. Garrett & J. T. Garrett, 1997). The use of oral recitation emphasizes the need for listeners to be silent, patient, and reflective. In an attempt to be respectful of harmony, traditional Indian people practice self-discipline through silence, modesty, and patience. Direct confrontation is avoided because it disrupts the harmony and balance that are essential for good relations. Native Americans believe that there are more effective ways to deal with discrepancies and dissatisfaction. Cooperation and sharing, as a reflection of harmony, are an important part of interactions with others. Individuals in mainstream culture are rewarded for being outgoing and assertive. Such behaviors as asking questions, interrupting, speaking for others, telling others what to do, or arguing are fairly common in mainstream society. These behaviors severely contradict what traditional Native people have been taught are respectful and appropriate ways of interacting with others (M. T. Garrett, 1995).

ACCULTURATION: CIRCLES
WITH NO BEGINNINGS AND NO END

Although many of the core traditional values permeate the lives of Native Americans across tribal groups (see Table 7.1), Native Americans are not a completely homogeneous group; they differ greatly in their level of acceptance of and commitment to specific tribal values, beliefs, and practices (J. T. Garrett & M. T. Garrett, 1996). Native individuals differ in terms of their level of acculturation, geographic setting (urban, rural, or reservation), and socioeconomic status (M. T. Garrett & Pichette, 2000; Herring, 1996). The following levels of acculturation, defined as "the cultural change that occurs when two or more cultures are in persistent contact" (Garcia & Ahler, 1992, p. 24), have been identified for Native Americans:

1. *Traditional*—May or may not speak English, but generally speak and think in their native language; hold only traditional values and beliefs and practice only traditional tribal customs and methods of worship.
2. *Marginal*—May speak both the native language and English; may not, however, fully accept the cultural heritage and practices of their tribal group nor fully identify with mainstream cultural values and behaviors.
3. *Bicultural*—Generally accepted by dominant society and tribal society/nation; simultaneously able to know, accept, and practice both mainstream values and behaviors and the traditional values and beliefs of their cultural heritage.
4. *Assimilated*—Accepted by dominant society; embrace only mainstream cultural values, behaviors, and expectations.
5. *Pantraditional*—Have made a conscious choice to return to the "old ways"; are generally accepted by dominant society, but seek to embrace previously lost traditional cultural values, beliefs, and practices of their tribal heritage; therefore, may speak both English and their native tribal language. (cited in M. T. Garrett & Pichette, 2000, p. 6)

These five levels of acculturation represent a continuum along which any given Native American individual may fall (see Figure 7.1). The most popular and most

FIGURE 7.1   The acculturation continuum

Source: M. T. Garrett & Pichette, 2000.

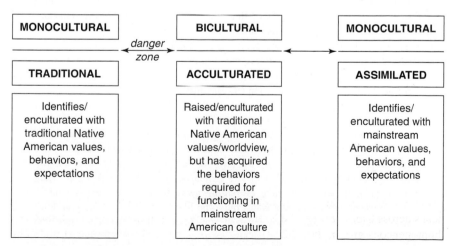

deceiving means of determining a person's "Indianness" and degree of traditionalism comes not only from ethnic heritage and blood quantum but also from his
or her life experiences and life choices (J. T. Garrett & M. T. Garrett, 1994).

TRUST VERSUS MISTRUST:
AIR OF CRUELTY, WINDS OF CHANGE

Mental health practitioners are trained professionals who encourage clients to tell
their story, make sense out of their story, and actively create their story through
intentional living. In working with Native clients, practitioners must also understand the influence of oppression on a Native client's experience and must assess
the extent to which the process of acculturation has affected the client's cultural
identity (M. T. Garrett & Pichette, 2000). Oppression and experiences with discrimination are and continue to be a very real part of the Native experience in this
country. In the following text, a Navajo elder describes her first experiences in
school, which took place more than 40 years ago; she was unable to speak any
English and had never left the reservation before she attended boarding school at
the age of seven:

> It was the first time I've seen a brick building that was not a trading post. The
> ceilings were so high, and the rooms so big and empty. It was so cold. There was
> no warmth. Not as far as "brrr, I'm cold," but in a sense of emotional cold. Kind
> of an emptiness, when you're hanging onto your mom's skirt and trying hard not
> to cry. Then when you get up to your turn, she thumbprints the paper and she
> leaves and you watch her go out the big metal doors. The whole thing was cold.
> The doors were metal and they even had this big window with wires running
> through it. You watch your mama go down the sidewalk, actually it's the first
> time I seen a sidewalk, and you see her get into the truck and the truck starts
> moving and all the home smell goes with it. You see it all leaving.
>
> Then the woman takes you by the hand and takes you inside and the first
> thing they do is take down your bun. The first thing they do is cut off your hair,
> and you been told your whole life that you never cut your hair recklessly because
> that is your life. And that's the first thing them women does is cut off your hair.
> And you see that long, black hair drop, and it's like they take out your heart and
> they give you this cold thing that beats inside. And now you're gonna be just like
> them. You're gonna be cold. You're never gonna be happy or have that warm
> feeling and attitude towards life anymore. That's what it feels like, like taking
> your heart out and putting in a cold river pebble.
>
> When you go into the shower, you leave your squaw skirt and blouse right
> there at the shower door. When you come out, it's gone. You don't see it again.
> They cut your hair, now they take your squaw skirt. They take from the begin-
> ning. When you first walk in there, they take everything that you're about. They
> jerk it away from you. They don't ask how you feel about it. They never tell you
> anything. They never say what they're gonna do, why they're doing it. They
> barely speak to you. They take everything away from you. Then you think,
> mama must be whackers. She wants me to be like them? Every time you don't
> know what they're doing, they laugh at you. They yell at you. They jerk you

around. It was never what I wanted to be. I never wanted to be like them. But my mom wanted me to be like them. As I got older, I found out that you don't have to be like them. You can have a nice world and have everything that mama wanted, but you don't have to be cold. (McLaughlin, 1994, pp. 47–48)

SOCIAL SUPPORT SYSTEMS: THE SACRED WEB

In addition to contemporary counseling interventions and treatment modalities, mental health practitioners can incorporate tribal-specific interventions as appropriate to meet the cultural, spiritual, personal, or career needs of specific Native clients. To help practitioners in their collaboration with Native clients in the counseling process, the following practical recommendations are offered; they draw on the natural support systems that exist within Native culture and traditions (M. T. Garrett & Carroll, 2000):

- *Sociodemographics*—Native clients can reconnect with a sense of purpose by finding ways to combat the high rates of unemployment, inadequate housing, low educational levels, poverty-level incomes, isolated living conditions. Participation in community-wide volunteer programs to help those in need has proved to be a successful part of healing for many Indian people.
- *Physiology*—Native people should be encouraged to get regular physical checkups and have blood tests done in order to monitor any difficulties regarding blood sugar or any other physiological difficulties.
- *Historical context*—A critical component of counseling could include a psychoeducational piece or dialogue designed to provide insight about historical factors such as exploitation of Native people through discrimination, assimilation through boarding schools and relocation programs, or disruption of traditional cultural and familial patterns. This approach could provide important topics for discussion as well as help Native clients explore their own level of cultural identity development.
- *Acculturation/identity*—Native clients can be assisted with an exploration of personal cultural identity and career issues through a focus on the cultural themes of belonging, mastery, independence, and generosity. Clients can be asked the following general questions for each of the four respective areas: (a) Where do you belong? (b) What are you good at; what do you enjoy doing? (c) What are your sources of strength; what limits you? (d) What do you have to offer or contribute?
- *Isolation/social connections*—Participation in social events such as family gatherings and powwows, to name but a couple, allows Native clients to experience social cohesion and social interaction in their communities. Moreover, some Native clients can benefit from a sense of reconnection with community and traditional roles. This reconnection could be and has been accomplished through the revival of tribal ceremonies and practices (e.g., talking circles, sweat lodges, powwows, peyote meetings, and so on), which reestablish a sense of belonging and communal meaningfulness for Native

people and allow them to "return to the old ways" or at least integrate many of these ways into modern-day life, even in urban settings.

- *Generational splits*—Native clients of all ages can benefit from acting as or learning from elders who serve as role models and teachers for young people. This approach has become more commonly practiced by tribal nations across the country in therapeutic programs as well as in the schools.
- *Coping mechanisms*—Native clients can learn other methods of dealing with stress, boredom, powerlessness, and the sense of emptiness associated with acculturation and identity confusion. Consultation with or participation of a Medicine person (i.e., traditional Native healer) may prove very helpful.
- *Noninterference*—The avoidance behavior that community members engage in so as to maintain the cultural value of not imposing their will on another may be destructive to an individual Native client and must be addressed with the client as well as with community members. Carol Attneave's (1969, 1985) Network Therapy has been very effective with Indian clients; it offers a way for practitioners to work with an individual in both family and community contexts.

CURRENT SOCIAL AND POLITICAL ISSUES: CRYING FOR A VISION

In addition to the reality of the many difficulties that Native people face in this day and age, there are social and political issues that create both problems and opportunities for Native people. In this section, the issues of blood quantum, resources, treaty rights, religious freedom, mascots, gaming, and cultural preservation are discussed.

Identity

Indian people have mixed intertribally for eons and interracially for at least the last 500 years, which has resulted in many generations of mixed-blood Indian people (Russell, 1997). Native people are the only ethnic minority group that actually has to prove their cultural identity through blood quantum, and they carry an "Indian card" to prove that they are what they say they are. For some Native people, this need for proof is yet another form of oppression, whereas for others, it is just a normal part of everyday life and, for some, a source of pride in tribal membership. According to Russell (1997), at least 98% of the Native population is tribally mixed, and approximately 75% are also racially mixed. These days, the term *full blood* is used to refer to those Native people who consider themselves to be 100% of one tribe. However, in reality, the term probably has more to do with spiritual and traditional lifestyle than to physiological heritage per se. Among some of the long-term ramifications for Native people on this issue are the continuing dilution of blood quantum and the survival of urban Indians. Blood quantum causes much division and controversy in Indian communities and, in some cases, leads to social and economic inequities. Although some tribes have modified their enrollment criteria to incorporate members who possess heritage from more than one tribe, no tribe allows enrollment in more than one tribe. The reality is that some people are going to be excluded who should be included, and some people will be included who should be excluded.

Tribal Resources

There are more than 311 federally recognized reservations in the United States, totaling approximately 55 million acres; 11 million acres (20%) within reservation boundaries are owned by non-Indians. This land base provides many Native nations with an array of resources from which to benefit the people and also with a number of challenges in how to maintain, protect, or expand that land base. According to Russell (1997), these resources include 44 million acres in range and grazing land, 5.3 million acres of commercial forest, 2.5 million acres of crop area, 4% of the U.S. oil and gas reserves, 40% of the U.S. uranium deposits, 30% of western coal reserves, and $2 billion in trust royalty payments. It is an interesting irony that some of the most desolate reservations have become valuable resources as a result of minerals, environmental resources, and locale.

Treaty Rights

Another issue faced by many tribes/nations is that of treaty rights. Two controversial examples include the fishing rights of Native people in the Pacific Northwest and in the Great Lakes area of Michigan, Minnesota, and Wisconsin. In both instances, tribes have resorted to "fish-ins" that defy state law but are in accordance with Indian treaty rights with the U.S. government. One of the most controversial topics to hit the media in recent times is the whaling rights of tribes in the Pacific Northwest. Strong opposition has come from state agencies, non-Native fishers, conservationists, and environmentalists and has only added to the strain already placed on tribes by an increased influx of people, more industry, and more recreation in many of those areas.

Religious Freedom

As was mentioned earlier in this chapter, passage of the American Indian Religious Freedom Act of 1978 guaranteed religious freedom for Native people in this country for the first time in a century. However, two U.S. Supreme Court rulings severely limited the religious rights that the law was enacted to protect. First, in *Lying, Secretary of Agriculture, et al. v. Northwest Indian Cemetary Protective Association, et al.* (1988), the Supreme Court ruled in favor of allowing the U.S. Forest Service to pave a stretch of road through an area that was held as sacred by the Karok, Yurok, and Tolowa tribes of northern California. This decision was made in spite of the fact that even the U.S. Forest Service's expert witness concluded that the road would destroy the religion of those three tribes. Second, in *Employment Division of Oregon v. Smith* (1990), the Supreme Court denied Alfred Smith, a Native drug rehabilitation counselor, unemployment benefits because he had been discharged from his position for "misconduct." Smith had attended a meeting of the Native American Church where he used peyote during prayer. Peyote, a sacred, hallucinogenic cactus "button," is used in the Native American Church as a sacrament in much the same way that the Catholic Church uses wine during holy communion. However, the Court failed to recognize and uphold the use of peyote as an integral part of that Native spiritual tradition. So alarmed were both the Native and Judeo-Christian communities that coalitions were formed to restore religious freedoms through legislative means, and those efforts are continuing to this day.

Sacred Sites

Traditional Native practices are inseparably bound to the land and natural formations that exist in whatever geographic location that tribe occupies. Native people have sacred places and go to these sacred places to pray, fast, seek visions, conduct ceremonies, receive guidance from spirit guides, and teach youth the traditional ways. Many physical conditions such as tree spraying and logging, dams, fencing, road building, mining, hydroelectric plants, urban housing, tourism, and vandalism inextricably affect sacred sites. Unfortunately, many of the sacred sites revered by Native people are not under their control but instead are under the control of federal agencies intent on using the land for the purpose of tourism development, clear-cutting, and uranium mining. Some sacred sites are listed here:

- Blue Lake, New Mexico (preserved), sacred to the Taos Pueblo
- Kootenai Falls, Montana (preserved), sacred to the Kootanai Indians of Montana, Idaho, and British Columbia
- Mount Adams, Washington (preserved), sacred to the Yakima
- Badger-Two Medicine, Montana (endangered), sacred to the Blackfeet, threatened by companies wanting to drill for oil and gas
- Canyon Mine, Arizona (endangered), sacred to the Havasupai, threatened by uranium mining that is permitted by the U.S. Forest Service
- Medicine Wheel, Wyoming (endangered), sacred to the Arapaho, Blackfeet, Crow, Cheyenne, Lakota, and Shoshone, threatened by proposed measures by the U.S. Forest Service to develop the area as a tourist attraction and promote logging activities in the vicinity
- Mount Graham, Arizona (endangered), sacred to the San Carlos Apache, threatened by construction of a seven-telescope observatory
- Celilo Falls, Oregon (desecrated), sacred to the Umatilla, Nez Perce, Yakima, and Warm Springs Indians, flooded by the Dalles Dam in 1957
- Rainbow Natural Bridge, Utah (desecrated), sacred to the Navajo, Paiute, and Pueblos, destroyed by completion of the Glen Canyon Dam on the Colorado River in 1963 and the rising of Lake Powell
- San Francisco Peaks, Arizona (desecrated), sacred to the Apaches, Hopis, Navajos, and Zunis, destroyed by the development of the Snow Bowl, a portion of the peaks used for downhill skiing

Many of these sites are cornerstones of Native religious traditions and cannot be substituted. Therefore, many legal efforts are being undertaken by tribes across the country to protect and preserve not only the sacred sites on which their culture is based but also their very way of life passed down through generations.

Repatriation and Reburial

Among the many sacred sites disturbed or destroyed by such things as erosion and flooding, plowing, urban development, road building, land clearing, logging, and vandalism have been the ancient graves of Native people. Perhaps worst of all has been the desecration of Native graves by pothunters and vandals who loot for objects that are valued in national and international markets. Grave desecration and looting of Native graves reached its peak in the 1980s. Outraged by such disregard and violations of sacred areas, Native American nations demanded the immediate return of all that was rightfully theirs, including skeletal remains, burial goods, and sacred objects. In the end, Native people have persevered through the passage of critical legislation that now protects Native gravesites from looting and provides Native people with legal means for reclaiming both remains and sacred objects. Many of these remains and objects have been ceremonially returned to their original sites when possible under the careful guidance and blessing of tribal elders and Medicine people.

Mascot Issues

As many tribes/nations continue to move toward increased sovereignty, land and natural resources are only part of the problem. A constant source of controversy between Native and non-Native has been the mascot issue. Sports teams across the country have been challenged to do away with stereotypical, racist images of Native people as mascots. A few examples include the Atlanta Braves, the Washington Redskins, the Cleveland Indians, the Florida State University Seminoles, and too many others to list here. For the most part, these images tend to fall into one of two categories: the hostile, warlike Indian or the dopey, clownlike figure with headdress, big nose, red skin, big lips, and other stereotypical features. Native people in many places have become increasingly outspoken, demanding the same respect both socially and legally that is paid to other cultural groups in the United States.

Gaming

When people think of Indians these days, the cultural perception that comes to mind is gaming. Casinos and bingo halls have sprung up like wildfire in Indian country, and in most cases, Native nations are having to deal with increased capital in a short period of time and the challenges that accompany it. Northrup (1997, p. 226) jokingly replies to the question, "why do you call it a Rez instead of a reservation? Because the White man owns most of it." The popular perception by non-Native people is that Indians are getting filthy rich off per capita checks, that is, the varying amounts of money that are distributed to tribal members as corporate partners, more or less, with tribally owned casinos and bingo halls. The truth is that these per capita amounts for many tribes are small amounts, are usually distributed maybe once or twice per year, and in most cases, have done little to alleviate already high rates of unemployment for Native people across the country. When asked the unemployment rate on the reservation, Northup (1997, p. 215) replies, "I don't know, that's not my job." He goes on to comment, "Gambling has done a lot for us in the last decade. . . . it has brought our Rez unemployment rate from 80% all the way down to 50%." Although the gaming industry has become a major source of income and economic development for many Native nations, the challenge at this point is how to maintain that investment and how to plan for the future so that the growth continues and the people continue to benefit.

Cultural Preservation

Increased sovereignty for Native nations also means increased control over the way that cultural resources are maintained and preserved. In many Native nations and communities across the country, huge efforts are being made to preserve culture through programs both in and outside the schools that teach youth such things as traditional arts and crafts, the language, ceremonies and prayers, songs and chants, and dance. Many of these programs began as remedial efforts in residential youth treatment centers and sobriety programs for all ages. As the efficacy of such programs has become evident, their popularity has grown. This move toward cultural preservation is a far cry from the efforts of the mainstream only one or two generations ago to "civilize Indians" through mandated, church-run, government-supported Indian boarding schools whose primary objective was to strip Native youth of any cultural foundation. Although Native people still face many difficulties—whose origins lie in the cultural genocide of the past and the resulting cycle of oppression and poverty that Native people have faced now for hundreds of years—winds of change have crossed the land. With the surge in cultural pride, one of the biggest challenges for Native people today is to eliminate infighting and to find a common vision that will carry the people safely and successfully into the future generations.

CONCLUSION: MEDICINE BAG

When I was a young boy, my father used to tell me an old Cherokee story that was passed from generation to generation in our tribe. It was said that during certain times of the year, the Medicine men and women would gather up in the mountains to seek the Medicine together. The Medicine, of course, has a very broad meaning that includes anything in the physical, mental, spiritual, or natural/environmental aspects of life. For many evenings, these people would dance and use their rattles and drums, would sing old chants and songs from days gone by, and would share stories of their experiences and journeys during that year. They all knew that they were there for a purpose and that during the last evening of their ceremony together, the "spirit people" would place something very special in their Medicine bag. It might be something specific, or it might be something broad. It might be something they had learned, such as a new use for an herb or plant; it might be a story that could be used; it might be a special stone; or it might even be some new ability or healing power with which to help those in need. Whatever it was, it was put there for a very special purpose—to bring about harmony and balance in their world. And so, it is good. Hoyona.

Exercises

1. Tara is a Choctaw ninth grader who attends public school just off the reservation. She is very bright but reserved, and she is frequently made fun of by other kids because she is overweight. Recently, her grades have begun to drop significantly, and she has been getting into fights with other kids. Her family has expressed concern over Tara's lack of friends in the school, and they are thinking about pulling her out of the school and enrolling her instead in the reservation school system. Prior to now, Tara had talked about her hopes of being the first in her family to attend college and had wanted to study either fine art or business. Lately, she has said that she just wants to "go home."

   a) How would you develop rapport with Tara in order to provide effective therapeutic intervention? How might you include and draw upon Tara's family as both a personal and cultural resource for her?

   b) Would you consider conducting a suicide assessment with Tara? If so, how might you go about it in a way that would be culturally responsive?

   c) How would you characterize Tara's cultural identity and level of acculturation at this point? What could you do to help her develop positive cultural identity that would help her meet her goals?

2. Will is a Seneca man in his mid 50s who lives in a urban setting. He is divorced and has two children from that marriage that he sees sporadically. Will is very talkative and doesn't hesitate to describe his experience in Indian boarding school until age 11 or his participation in Indian activist groups during the 1970s, 1980s, and early 1990s. It is apparent that one thing that continues to haunt him is his experience as a special forces operator during the Vietnam war, though he rarely discusses this. He has been sober now for more than 9 years and recently has begun to work closely with Native youth as a mentor in the local urban Indian center. Though he says he was not involved much in cultural things when he was young, he has found that his talent and involvement as a respected traditional dancer on the local powwow circuit has helped him maintain his sobriety. Because of the recent death of his father, however, with whom he was very close, Will has been questioning what he should do next.

   a) How would you earn Will's trust? Furthermore, what issue would you choose to address first with Will, and how would you approach it in a way that would be culturally responsive to him?

   b) Where does Will seem to be on the acculturation continuum, and how might that impact your approach to counseling with him?

   c) Given what you know about Will right now, how are your life experiences and worldview similar to or different from his?

REFERENCES

Attneave, C. L. (1969). Therapy in tribal settings and urban network intervention. *Family Process, 8,* 192–210.

Attneave, C. L. (1985). Practical counseling with American Indian and Alaska Native clients. In P. Pedersen (Ed.), *Handbook of cross-cultural counseling and therapy* (pp. 135–140). Westport, CT: Greenwood.

Brendtro, L. K., Brokenleg, M., & Van Bockern, S. (1990). *Reclaiming youth at risk: Our hope for the future.* Bloomington, IN: National Education Service.

Choney, S. K., Berryhill-Paapke, E., & Robbins, R. R. (1995). The acculturation of American Indians: Developing frameworks for research and practice. In J. G. Ponterotto, J. M. Casas, L. A. Suzuki, & C. M. Alexander (Eds.), *Handbook of multicultural counseling* (pp. 73–92). Thousand Oaks, CA: Sage.

Deloria, V., Jr. (1988). *Custer died for your sins: An Indian manifesto.* Norman: University of Oklahoma Press.

Deloria, V., Jr. (1994). *God is red.* Golden, CO: Fulcrum.

DuBray, W. H. (1985). American Indian values: Critical factor in casework. *Social Casework: The Journal of Contemporary Social Work, 66,* 30–37.

Dudley, J. Iron Eye. (1992). *Choteau Creek: A Sioux reminiscence.* Lincoln: University of Nebraska Press.

Dufrene, P. M. (1990). Exploring Native American symbolism. *Journal of Multicultural and Cross-Cultural Research in Art Education, 8,* 38–50.

Four Worlds Development Project. (1984). *The sacred tree: Reflections on Native American spirituality.* Wilmot, WI: Lotus Light.

Garcia, R. L., & Ahler, J. G. (1992). Indian education: Assumptions, ideologies, strategies. In J. Reyhner (Ed.), *Teaching American Indian students* (pp. 13–32). Norman: University of Oklahoma Press.

Garrett, J. T. (1991). Where the medicine wheel meets medical science. In S. McFadden (Ed.), *Profiles in wisdom: Native elders speak about the earth* (pp. 167–179). Santa Fe, NM: Bear and Company.

Garrett, J. T. (2001). *Meditations with the Cherokee: Prayers, songs, and stories of healing and harmony.* Rochester, VT: Bear and Company.

Garrett, J. T., & Garrett, M. T. (1994). The path of good medicine: Understanding and counseling Native Americans. *Journal of Multicultural Counseling and Development, 22,* 134–144.

Garrett, J. T., & Garrett, M. T. (1996). *Medicine of the Cherokee: The way of right relationship.* Santa Fe, NM: Bear and Company.

Garrett, M. T. (1995). Between two worlds: Cultural discontinuity in the dropout of Native American youth. *The School Counselor, 42,* 186–195.

Garrett, M. T. (1996a). "Two people": An American Indian narrative of bicultural identity. *Journal of American Indian Education, 36,* 1–21.

Garrett, M. T. (1996b). Reflection by the riverside: The traditional education of Native American children. *Journal of Humanistic Education and Development, 35,* 12–28.

Garrett, M. T. (1998). *Walking on the wind: Cherokee teachings for harmony and balance.* Santa Fe, NM: Bear and Company.

Garrett, M. T. (1999a). Soaring on the wings of the eagle: Wellness of Native American high school students. *Professional School Counseling, 3,* 57–64.

Garrett, M. T. (1999b). Understanding the "Medicine" of Native American traditional values: An integrative review. *Counseling and Values, 43,* 84–98.

Garrett, M. T., & Carroll, J. (2000). Mending the broken circle: Treatment and prevention of substance abuse among Native Americans. *Journal of Counseling and Development, 78,* 379–388.

Garrett, M. T., & Garrett, J. T. (1997). Counseling Native American elders. *Directions in Rehabilitation Counseling: Therapeutic Strategies with the Older Adult, 3,* 3–18.

Garrett, M. T., & Garrett, J. T. (2002). Ayeli: Centering technique based on Cherokee spiritual traditions. *Counseling and Values, 46,* 149–158.

Garrett, M. T., Garrett, J. T., & Brotherton, D. (2001). Inner circle/outer circle: Native American group technique. *Journal for Specialists in Group Work, 26,* 17–30.

Garrett, M. T., & Myers, J. E. (1996). The rule of opposites: A paradigm for counseling Native Americans. *Journal of Multicultural Counseling and Development, 24,* 89–104.

Garrett, M. T., & Osborne, W. L. (1995). The Native American sweat lodge as metaphor for group work. *Journal for Specialists in Group Work, 20,* 33–39.

Garrett, M. T., & Pichette, E. F. (2000). Red as an apple: Native American acculturation and counseling with or without reservation. *Journal of Counseling and Development, 78,* 3–13.

Garrett, M. T., & Wilbur, M. P. (1999). Does the worm live in the ground? Reflections on Native American spirituality. *Journal of Multicultural Counseling and Development, 27,* 193–206.

Heinrich, R. K., Corbine, J. L., & Thomas, K. R. (1990). Counseling Native Americans. *Journal of Counseling and Development, 69,* 128–133.

Herring, R. D. (1994). The clown or contrary figure as a counseling intervention strategy with Native American Indian clients. *Journal of Multicultural Counseling and Development, 22,* 153–164.

Herring, R. D. (1996). Synergetic counseling and Native American Indian students. *Journal of Counseling and Development, 74,* 542–547.

Herring, R. D. (1999). *Counseling with Native American Indians and Alaska Natives: Strategies for helping professionals.* Thousand Oaks, CA: Sage.

Hirschfelder, A., & Kreipe de Montano, M. (1993). *The Native American almanac: A portrait of Native America today.* New York: Macmillan.

Hodgkinson, H. L. (1990). *The demographics of American Indians: One percent of the people; fifty percent of the diversity.* Washington, DC: Institute for Educational Leadership.

LaFromboise, T. D., Coleman, H. L. K., & Gerton, J. (1993). Psychological impact of biculturalism: Evidence and theory. *Psychological Bulletin, 114,* 395–412.

Lake, M. G. (1991). *Native healer: Initiation into an ancient art.* Wheaton, IL: Quest Books.

Little Soldier, L. (1992). Building optimum learning environments for Navajo students. *Childhood Education, 68,* 145–148.

Locust, C. (1988). Wounding the spirit: Discrimination and traditional American Indian belief systems. *Harvard Educational Review, 58,* 315–330.

Loftin, J. D. (1989). Anglo-American jurisprudence and the Native American tribal quest for religious freedom. *American Indian Culture and Research Journal, 13,* 1–52.

Maples, M. F., Dupey, P., Torres-Rivera, E., Phan, L. T., Vereen, L., & Garrett, M. T. (2001). Ethnic diversity and the use of humor in counseling: Appropriate or inappropriate? *Journal of Counseling and Development, 79,* 53–60.

McLaughlin, D. (1994). Critical literacy for Navajo and other American Indian learners. *Journal of American Indian Education, 33,* 47–59.

Northrup, J. (1997). *The rez road follies: Canoes, casinos, computers, and birch bark baskets.* New York: Kodansha International.

Oswalt, W. H. (1988). *This land was theirs: A study of North American Indians* (4th ed.). Mountain View, CA: Mayfield.

Plank, G. A. (1994). What silence means for educators of American Indian children. *Journal of American Indian Education, 34,* 3–19.

Red Horse, J. G. (1980). Indian elders: Unifiers of families. *Social Casework, 61,* 490–493.

Red Horse, J. G. (1997). Traditional American Indian family systems. *Families, Systems, and Health, 15,* 243–250.

Reyhner, J., & Eder, J. (1992). A history of Indian education. In J. Reyhner (Ed.), *Teaching American Indian students* (pp. 33–58). Norman: University of Oklahoma Press.

Russell, G. (1997). *American Indian facts of life: A profile of today's tribes and reservations.* Phoenix, AZ: Russell.

Thomason, T. C. (1991). Counseling Native Americans: An introduction for non-Native American counselors. *Journal of Counseling and Development, 69,* 321–327.

U.S. Bureau of the Census. (2001). *2000 census counts of American Indians, Eskimos, or Aleuts and American Indian and Alaska Native areas.* Washington, DC: Author.

U.S. Bureau of Indian Affairs. (1988). *American Indians today.* Washington, DC: Author.

Wilbur, M. P. (1999a). The rivers of a wounded heart. *Journal of Counseling and Development, 77,* 47–50.

Wilbur, M. P. (1999b). Finding balance in the winds. *Journal for Specialists in Group Work, 24,* 342–353.

CHAPTER 8   # Physical and Mental Health Needs of Native American Indian and Alaska Native Populations

Roger D. Herring, Lumbee/Catawba, University of Arkansas–Little Rock

This chapter addresses the physical and mental health needs of the indigenous peoples of the continental United States—Native American Indians and Alaska Natives. Other Western hemispheric indigenous peoples such as Hawaiians, natives of Guam (Chamorro), Samoans, and Puerto Ricans are not indigenous to this continent and are not included in this discussion. Many of the cultural values and belief structures of Alaska Natives are analogous to those of the Native American Indians of the lower states. Similarly, many of the counseling endeavors and strategies discussed in chapter 9 of this text may be adapted to address the physical and mental health concerns of both groups. Generally, when one addresses a particular Native individual or nation (e.g., Sioux or Cherokee), the best practice is to use the specific label used by this individual rather than a more general term. However, in the context of this chapter, the adjective *Native* will be used rather than the terms *Native American Indian* and *Alaska Native* in reference to both groups. Ethnic-specific referents will be used when the discussion or example warrants such specificity.

This chapter includes an overview of the physical and mental health needs of Native peoples, data on contributing factors to their physical and mental health needs, and information on specific physical and mental health concerns among these populations. Discussion will also be presented regarding causation and attribution relative to these terms. A brief discussion of several implications for counseling with these populations concludes this chapter.

CURRENT NEEDS: AN OVERVIEW

Contemporary Natives are experiencing very similar physical and mental health needs in both Alaska and the lower 48 states. Tribal autonomy and financial settlements have considerably enhanced these people's lives, yet conditions continue to remain deplorable for many. The negative impact of historical and contemporary discriminatory policies and practices on Native entities has devastated their standard of living and created major cultural conflicts (as summarized in chapter 7 of this text).

In addition, Native peoples have been further affected by recent national economic cycles. Between 1980 and 2000, their unemployment rate increased 12.6%. This rate averages 46% and ranges from a high of more than 80% on some reservations to a low of 0% in the more prosperous tribes (Herring, 1999, 2002). By almost all economic indicators of poverty, Native peoples can be classified as the "poorest of the poor" in this nation. Poverty and prolonged unemployment have combined with substandard housing, malnutrition, inadequate health care, shortened life expectancy, and high suicide rates to affect and limit opportunities for educational attainment (LaFromboise, 1998). To further complicate matters, most Natives feel that they have no choice or control in their lives.

Through centuries of conquest, cultural extermination, genocide, and coercive assimilation, Native peoples have experienced the most pervasive physical, economic, political, and cultural discrimination in this nation's history. The best way to keep people down is to deny them the means of improvement and achievement and to deny them equal opportunities. Racism in the United States began for economic reasons that spread into societal aspects of colonial America. For slavery to exist and hence to continue as a source of free labor, a concerted effort had to take place to dehumanize Native peoples (Pewewardy, 1997). The perpetrators of slavery went to great lengths—employing false scientific facts, religious teachings, the media, gross misconceptions and illustrations, and rumors—to disprove Native humanity.

Environmental variables also can be very influential in the physical and mental development and socialization of Native individuals. It is critical that health care professionals be aware of how Natives' cultural backgrounds contribute to their perceptions of their problems. Although it is unwise to stereotype Natives because of their heritage, it is useful to assess how the environmental context interacts with Natives' needs.

EPIDEMIOLOGICAL DATA

This section of the chapter provides important information about two topics related to physical and mental health data on Native people—the Indian Health Service (IHS) and the efficacy of statistical data regarding Natives.

Indian Health Service

The IHS, an agency within the Department of Health and Human Services, is responsible for providing health services to federally recognized Native nations and tribes. The provision of health services to Native entities evolved from a special relationship between the federal government and Native nations and tribes. This government-to-government relationship is based on Article I, Section 8, of the

U.S. Constitution and has been given form and substance by numerous treaties, laws, Supreme Court decisions, and executive orders.

The IHS is the federal health care provider and health advocate for Native people, and its goal is to raise their health status to the highest possible level. The mission is to provide a comprehensive health services delivery system for Natives with opportunity for maximum tribal involvement in developing and managing programs to meet their needs. The IHS has developed and operated a health services delivery system designed to provide a broad-spectrum program of preventive, curative, rehabilitative, and environmental services. The operation of the IHS health services delivery system is managed through local administrative units called service units. A service unit is the basic health organization for a geographic area served by the IHS program. A few service units cover a number of small reservations; some large reservations are divided into several service units. The service units are grouped into larger jurisdictions of cultural, demographic, and geographic management, which are administered by area offices. Service areas are also available in urban areas that include a large number of federally recognized Native peoples (i.e., tribal enrollment cardholders).

Statistical Data

The statistical data regarding Native physical and mental health needs that are used in this chapter are from the Indian Health Service (IHS, 2002a, 2002b) unless otherwise cited. These rates have been adjusted for the miscoding of the "Native" category on death and medical records. This adjustment is necessary because on death certificates, ethnic group status is usually recorded by the funeral director, who may or may not query the family members of the decedent. Likewise, the ethnic group status may not appear on the birth certificate. In the following statistics, if either the mother or the father or both parents were recorded as Native American Indian or Alaska Native on the birth certificate, the birth is considered a Native birth. In addition, most IHS data reflect 3-year averages because of the limited number of Native people compared to the total U.S. population.

As of 2000, the IHS service population was 1.51 million. Since 1990, the IHS population has been increasing at a rate of about 2.3% per year, excluding the impact of new tribes. The largest percentage of the 2000 service population, 21%, is located in the Oklahoma City area, followed by the Navajo area with 15%. More than 605,000 Natives reside in the Urban Indian Health Programs service area. Of these, 35% reside within urban programs that offer limited health care, 32% in comprehensive primary care programs, 26% in referral programs, and 7% in demonstration programs.

The Native population is younger than the U.S. general population, according to the 2000 census. The Native birthrate for 1994–1996 of 24.1 births per 1,000 population was 63% greater than the U.S. general population birthrate for 1995 of 14.8. For Natives, 33% of the population was younger than 15 years, and 6% was older than 64 years. For the U.S. general population, the corresponding values were 22% and 13% respectively. Seventeen percent of Native males were under age 15, and 16% of Native females were in this age group. The

Native median age was 24.2 years, compared with 32.9 years for the U.S. general population.

According to the 2000 census, 65.3% of Natives age 25 and older residing in the current reservations are high school graduates or higher, compared with 75.2% for the U.S. general population. For those with a bachelor's degree or higher, the percentages are 8.9 and 20.3 respectively. These data greatly influence the employability of Native individuals. For Native males age 16 and older residing in current reservations, 16.2% are unemployed, compared to 6.4% for the U.S. general population. For females, those percentages are 13.4 and 6.2 respectively.

Native peoples also have lower incomes than the general population. In 1999, Natives residing in the current reservations had a median household income of $19,897 compared with $30,056 for the U.S. general population. During this same time period, 31.6% of Natives lived below the poverty level, in contrast to 13.1% for the U.S. general population. These statistics certainly imply a more focused endeavor to alleviate the numerous health care needs of Native populations.

PHYSICAL AND MENTAL HEALTH NEEDS

The physical and mental health needs of Native populations, historically and contemporarily, reflect much higher percentages when compared to the rates of the U.S. general population. Although not the focus of this chapter, the effects of history and environment heavily influence the delivery of physical and mental health services to Native populations. Other cultural variables include familialism, sharing and the concept of time, cooperation, nonverbal communication, and within-group differences.

Physical Health

The following discussions of selected physical health needs attest to the drastic results from a history of discrimination, oppression, genocide, and socioeconomic inequities.

Causes of Death   Although not the only indicator of physical health, causes of death provide some evidence of health problems that need to be addressed.

Breast/Cervical Cancer   For Native decedents of all ages in 1994–1996, female breast cancer was the third leading cancer death cause and cervix uteri was the 14th. When only Native female cancer deaths are ranked, female breast cancer moves to second and cervix uteri moves to seventh. In 1994–1996, 3.7 times as many deaths were due to female breast cancer than to cervix uteri (253 to 69).

HIV/AIDS   The intergenerational memory of the effect of disease on Native people helps support a climate of suspicion around contemporary issues such as HIV/AIDS (Native American Leadership Commission on Health and AIDS, 1994). Some Native peoples fear that HIV/AIDS will have an even more devastating effect on their communities than did previous historical epidemics of smallpox, measles, and cholera, which were deliberately spread by both the British and Americans (Stiffarm & Lane, 1992).

Native deaths from HIV infection have not reached the level experienced in the general population. However, the rate of HIV infection is increasing more rapidly for Natives than for other ethnic groups. Since 1987–1989, the Native rate has increased 417%, whereas since 1988, the rate for all ethnic groups has increased 129%. Native males more often die from HIV infection than do Native females. The peak age-specific death rate for Native males in 1994–1996 (27.7 for age 35 to 44 years) was 4.3 times the Native female peak rate (6.5 for age 25 to 34 years).

Cardiovascular Diseases   Deaths due to cardiovascular diseases have been decreasing in the U.S. general population at a greater rate than in the Native population. Since 1973, the age-adjusted heart disease rate for the U.S. general population has decreased 43% and the cerebrovascular diseases rate has decreased 58%. The comparable percentage decreases for the Native population since 1972–1974 are 4% and 35% respectively. Natives died from diseases of the heart in 1994–1996 at an age-adjusted rate (156.0 per 100,000) that is 13% higher than for the general population in 1995 (138.3 per 100,000). A similar relationship also exists for deaths due to cerebrovascular diseases. The Native rate of 30.5 per 100,000 in 1994–1996 was 14% higher than the general population rate of 26.7 per 100,000 in 1995.

Native males are more likely to die from heart disease than are Native females; their age-specific death rate was higher for all age groups in 1994–1996, except for age groups 1 to 4 and 15 to 24. However, for cerebrovascular diseases, the age-specific death rates were relatively close for Native males and females. For both conditions for males, the death rate increased with age, starting with age groups over 4 years.

Diabetes Mellitus   The rate of diabetes deaths has been increasing in both the Native and general populations. Since 1981–1983, the Native age-adjusted diabetes death rate has increased 93%, compared to 39% for the general population. This rate is much higher within some regions, such as the Southwest. In 1994–1996, the Native age-adjusted rate (46.4 deaths per 100,000 population) was 3.5 times the 1995 general population rate of 13.3 deaths per 100,000.

For both Native females and males in 1994–1996, the age-specific diabetes mellitus rate generally increased with age. The Native female rate (nonzero rates) was greater than the Native male rate, except for age groups 25 to 34 years and 35 to 44 years.

Maternal/Infant Mortality   For the Native population, 46% of mothers were under age 20 when they had their first child, and 21% were at least age 25. Fortunately, the maternal mortality rate for Native females dropped from 27.7 (per 100,000 live births) in 1972–1974 to 6.1 in 1994–1996, a decrease of 78%. Also, the Native infant mortality rate has decreased 58% since 1972–1974. However, the infant mortality rate in 1994–1996 was still 22% greater than the rate for the U.S. general population in 1995 (i.e., 9.3 deaths per 1,000 live births compared to 7.6). The two leading causes for Native infant deaths were sudden infant death syndrome (SIDS) and congenital anomalies. For the general population, the two leading causes were congenital anomalies and disorders related to short gestation and low birth weight.

Native infants are more likely to die during the postneonatal period (28 days to under 1 year) than the neonatal period (under 28 days). The reverse is true for the U.S. general population. In 1994–1996, the Native postneonatal mortality rate was 7% greater than the Native neonatal mortality rate (i.e., 4.8 versus 4.5 per 100,000). In contrast, the general population's neonatal mortality rate in 1995 was 81% greater than its postneonatal mortality rate, 4.9 to 2.7 per 100,000.

General Mortality   The leading causes of death for Native decedents of all ages residing in the IHS service area per 100,000 population (1994–1996) were diseases of the heart (133.5) followed in order by malignant neoplasms (94.4), accidents (86.8), diabetes mellitus (36.3), chronic liver disease and cirrhosis (28.8), cerebrovascular diseases (27.8), pneumonia and influenza (22.2), suicide (18.3), pulmonary diseases (15.4), and homicide (14.9). However, the cause of death rankings differed by sex. For Native males, the top two causes were diseases of the heart and accidents. For Native females, the top two causes were diseases of the heart and malignant neoplasms.

In 1994–1996, the Native (IHS service area) age-adjusted death rates for the following causes were considerably higher than those for the general U.S. population: alcoholism (627% greater), tuberculosis (533% greater), diabetes mellitus (249% greater), accidents (204% greater), suicide (72% greater), pneumonia and influenza (71% greater), and homicide (63% greater).

Prevention and Treatment Programs   The IHS has developed a number of prevention and treatment programs to address the health problems experienced by Native people. The following section provides data on some of the more prominent programs and suggests areas in which more preventive efforts are needed.

Community Health   The IHS Injury Prevention (IP) program organizes a wide variety of projects to address major health problems. Exemplary projects are: child passenger protection, roadway and roadside hazard identification, safety belt use promotion, deterrence of drinking and driving, drowning prevention, smoke detector usage, helmet use, and injury prevention campaigns. The IP program has contributed to a 32% decline in hospitalizations for injuries and poisonings since 1987.

Nutrition/Dietetics   The nutrition and dietetics program reported more than 87,000 patient and client contacts during 1998. Nearly one-half (46%) were in a hospital setting, followed by ambulatory clinics (34%) and community settings (20%). Nearly 73% of the contacts were for clinical nutrition counseling and 20% were for health promotion. Of the clinical nutrition counseling contacts, the majority were for general nutrition (36%) and diabetes (32%). The number of patient and client contacts reported by the nutrition and dietetics program has decreased 77% since 1993, which does not necessarily reflect a decrease in total workload.

Public Health   More than 321,000 public health nursing visits were recorded in 1998. The most frequent program areas addressed during these visits were health promotion and disease prevention (43%), morbidity (16%), and child health (8%). The visits were concentrated in two age groups: children under 5 years of age (20%) and adults over the age of 64 (16%). Female visits outnumbered male visits by 51%.

Dental Services   On reservations, 1,025 community water systems existed in 1998. Of this number, 276 water systems delivered fluoride for the entire year; of those systems, 76 were in compliance. Optimally fluoridated systems provide the dental benefits of this safe and cost-effective public health measure to more than 40% of the Native population. Increasing the number of optimally fluoridated water systems is a high priority for the IHS Dental and Office of Environmental Health and Engineering programs.

Since 1986, a dramatic increase has occurred in dental sealant usage. The number of sealants placed in 1998 is almost double the number placed in 1986. Dental sealants can prevent up to 100% of dental decay. Dental sealants are plastic coatings applied to the chewing surfaces of teeth. They are applied to children's teeth when they first erupt into the mouth at about the age of 6 and 12 years. Given the high rate of dental disease among the Native population, dental sealants are one of the best preventive methods available today.

Sanitation   Since 1960, more than 230,000 Native homes were funded by IHS for the provision of sanitation facilities. These services included water and sewerage facilities, solid waste disposal systems, and technical assistance to establish and equip operation and maintenance organizations for new, rehabilitated, and existing homes. Although many improvements have been witnessed, numerous Native communities and families remain without indoor plumbing and without adequate sewage facilities.

Patient Care Statistics   In 1997, about 85,000 Native individuals were admitted to IHS, tribal, and general hospitals. The leading cause of hospitalization was obstetric deliveries and complications of pregnancy and puerperium. The total number of ambulatory medical visits was more than 7.3 million in 1997, an increase of more than 1,500% since 1955. The leading cause was supplementary classification categories (e.g., child well care, examinations, tests, and follow-ups). The number of dental services increased nearly 1,100% (from less than 0.2 million in 1955 to about 2.1 million in 1998).

Teenage Pregnancy   Whereas teenage mothers account for 12% of all births among European Americans, comparable proportions among Native teenagers range from 18% to 25%, depending on the research effort. Teenage pregnancy and parenthood are associated with educational setbacks, unemployment, family problems, and welfare dependency (Herring, 1997a, 1997b). Given the lack of role models, skills, and self-confidence necessary to pursue alternative paths, many Native female youth, especially those from families with low socioeconomic status, may actively seek the traditional role of mother as the only rite of passage by which to enter into adult womanhood (Rivers & Morrow, 1995).

Summary of Health Care   The physical health status of Native individuals poses significant concerns. Native life expectancy is about 8 years less than that of European Americans. Many Native individuals live in poverty (27% of the total population; 31% of the elderly), according to U.S. Census Bureau (2000) reports. Native peoples are 10 times more likely than European Americans to develop diabetes. In addition, other health problems include injuries from accidents, tuberculosis, liver and kidney disease, high blood pressure, pneumonia, and malnutrition (U.S. Bureau of the Census, 2000).

Health education and professional counselors need to focus their efforts on the prevention and management of chronic illnesses and conditions in this population. Disease patterns in Natives have followed several trends, including a shift from acute, infectious diseases to those of a more degenerative type (Baruth & Manning, 2003). Many Native individuals rarely see a physician, primarily because of isolation and lack of transportation. Traditional rites of folk healing and the spiritual aspect of disease also have deterred reliance on a strictly scientific medical community (Baruth & Manning, 2003).

Physical and mental health professionals need to become aware of the tragic living conditions that exist for Natives on and off reservations (Herring, 1999). Inadequate nutrition, substandard housing, unemployment, illiteracy, poverty, sanitation, and physical health services are pervasive. Health professionals working with Native clients and counselees "regardless of lifespan stage, must understand their cultural characteristics and worldviews and then plan counseling interventions that will be effective with, and 'make sense' to, these clients" (Baruth & Manning, 2003, p. 171).

Mental Health

Several issues affect the nature of psychiatric epidemiological data: "a lack of uniformity in the definition of mental problems or psychiatric disorders across epidemiological studies; a lack of cultural validity in most epidemiological studies; and biases in reporting the epidemiology" (Paniagua, 1994, p. 101). Collected data are translated into prevalence and incidence scores. When these scores are reported, however, biases may occur. Practitioners must determine whether errors exist in the reporting of data. Paniagua (1994, p. 101) offered three guidelines (modified for this subject) for a quick screening of epidemiological data collected with Native groups.

1. Identify the sample (number of Native individuals) from which the data were collected.
2. Determine the population (i.e., total number in the entire population) from which the sample was selected to reach conclusions regarding the represen-

tativeness of the sample (e.g., is the sample of Native individuals representative of all Native peoples?)
3. Read the study's conclusions in words rather than in complex statistical procedures.

An example of bias in the collection of physical and mental health epidemiological data is provided by Thompson, Walker, and Silk-Walker (1993). Data from the IHS "are widely quoted as being representative of all Indians" (p. 199). A major bias in the reporting of such data is that the IHS only recognizes Native individuals living on 32 reservations, omitting Natives from state and other reservations and those living in urban areas. When the diversity of Native peoples is not considered, the resulting data distorts the strengths and challenges they face (Lum, 2003).

Nonspecific Mental Disorders   During the fiscal year 1997, the 10 leading causes of hospitalization for Native patients were ranked. Nonspecified mental disorders (i.e., vague, ambiguous, or undiagnosable presenting symptoms) ranked according to age group in the following manner:

Age	Rank	% combined	% male	% female
5–14	9th	7.6	5.5	9.8
15–24	4th	4.3	10.2	2.8
25–44	4th	10.0	12.3	8.8
45–54	9th	11.1	10.8	11.3
55–older	10th (all other)			

During the same time period, the 10 leading causes of ambulatory medical clinical impressions for patients (i.e., walk-in patients) were ranked. Nonspecified mental disorders ranked according to age group in the following manner:

Age	Rank	% combined	% male	% female
5–14	8th	21.4	20.7	22.0
15–24	9th	22.2	24.9	21.0
25–44	6th	6.1	7.6	5.4
45–54	8th	4.5	4.6	4.4
55 older	10th (all other)			

The 15 to 24 age group appears to be the most vulnerable age group in both nonspecific mental disorders and ambulatory medical clinical impressions. The data certainly indicate that Native adolescents and young adults need multiple interventions to offset the threats of mental disorders. The correlation between mental disorders and substance abuse may also be an influencing factor.

Alcohol/Drug Use   Another excellent example of the distortion of data exists in the research on Native peoples and the use of alcohol. Notwithstanding that substance use and abuse is a critical mental health concern, considerable differences exist in alcohol use of individuals from different Native nations or tribes, between

men and women, and among age groups. Many Natives do not drink or only drink
moderately. Abstinence is high among certain tribes such as the Navajo (Myers,
Kagawa-Singer, Kumanyika, Lex, & Markides, 1995). For example, an estimated
60% of Navajos abstain from alcohol, whereas greater than 80% of Utes and Ob-
jiwas have used alcohol (Taylor, 2000).

Unfortunately, when researchers generalize report findings about drinking
and Natives, the diversity of alcohol use and abuse is omitted. Lum (2003) states
the case more emphatically:

> if researchers continue to treat indigenous people as a monolithic group, they
> will contribute to stereotypical images—in this case, the perception that alcohol
> presents a widespread problem for all Native people. This stereotype of the
> drunken Indian perpetuates the belief that indigenous people are biologically
> predetermined to alcoholism and that they are helpless, hopeless, passive vic-
> tims. (p. 202)

Beyond the stereotypes, three factors need to be recognized in this problem.
First, physiological studies have indicated a genetic factor for some forms of substance abuse. Second, sociological research has demonstrated the influences of
such factors as family patterns and parenting styles, poverty, unemployment, and
cultural genocide. Third, psychological factors (e.g., self-concept and self-esteem,
or ethnic and personal identity development) have been found to play a role.

Substance abuse continues as a mental health concern faced by Native peoples. They are considerably more likely to die of alcohol-related causes than the
general U.S. population. In IHS hospitals approximately 21% of hospitalizations
are for alcohol-related problems ("Alcohol-Related Hospitalizations," 1992). In
Alaska, 32% of Natives of childbearing age reported heavy drinking, which is responsible for the disproportionately high percentage of cases of fetal alcohol syndrome reported in this population ("Prevalence and Characteristics of Alcohol
Consumption," 1994). In addition, drug abuse and dependence are very high
among young Native clients.

In one survey, up to 70% of Native adolescents in an urban school setting
were involved in drug and alcohol abuse (Red Horse, 1982). Alcohol use is associated with fighting, vandalism, and delinquency (Manson, Tatum, & Dinges,
1982). The use of illicit substances is related to the 50% dropout rate from school
by Native youth (Beauvais, Chavez, Oetting, Deffenbacher, & Cornell, 1996). In
a more recent study, Taylor (2000) investigated self-efficacy and alcohol use in
114 Native adults. He investigated three myths about alcohol use and abuse: the
"firewater myth" (p. 153) that portrays rapid intoxication from small amounts of
alcohol by Natives who then become boisterous and raucous; the myth that alcoholism rates are inordinately high among all Native peoples; and the myth that alcohol use and abuse are the primary causes of numerous other physical and mental difficulties that Native peoples currently encounter.

From the results of this study, Taylor (2000) surmised that two types of alcohol users exist in Native communities. The anxiety alcohol users comprise
nearly 25% of Natives who are chronic alcoholics; this type is more likely to be
older and unemployed and to exist marginally. The recreational alcohol users tend

to be episodic binge drinkers and are often young Native adults. Alcohol has had devastating effects on some Native communities and is often linked to other social problems such as violence, suicide, and sexual abuse (Bachman, 1992).

For people accepted into the IHS substance abuse treatment program, most initial contacts are for alcohol addiction only. However, the number of contacts involving other drugs has been increasing. In 1997, the total alcohol-related discharge rate (first diagnosis) for IHS and tribal direct and contract general hospitals was 28.1 per 10,000 user population aged 15 years and older. This rate is 1.6 times the rate of 17.6 for U.S. general short-stay hospitals. The rates for discharges with first-listed diagnosis of alcoholism for persons 15 years old and older were 8.6 for alcoholic psychosis, 14.1 for alcoholism, and 5.3 for chronic liver disease and cirrhosis.

Also, the age-adjusted drug-related death rate for Natives residing in the IHS service area increased from 3.4 deaths per 100,000 population in 1979–1981 to 8.4 in 1994–1996. The 1994–1996 rate is 65% higher than the U.S. general population of 5.1% for 1995. The age-specific drug-related death rate (1994–1996) for Native males peaked at 31.7 per 100,000 for age group 35 to 44 years. The peak Native male rate was 2.4 times the peak Native female rate of 13.0 per 100,000.

Suicide   Natives have the highest rate of completed suicide of any ethnic group, especially on certain reservations (Herring, 1999). This suicide epidemic is thought to be the result of alcohol abuse, poverty, boredom, and family breakdown. Adolescence to adulthood is the time of greatest risk for suicide (EchoHawk, 1997). The age-adjusted suicide death rate per 100,000 for Natives decreased 29% from a high (22.5) in 1975–1977 to a low (16.0) in 1984–1986. Since then, however, the rate has increased 21% to 19.3 in 1994–1996. The 1994–1996 rate is 72% higher than the U.S. general population.

The age-specific suicide death rate (1994–1996) for Native males was higher for all age groups in comparison with Native females. The Native male rate peaked at 66.7 deaths per 100,000 population for age group 25 to 34 years. Suicide is also the second leading cause of death for Native youth, with 23.6 deaths per 100,000 in the 15 to 19 year age group.

Identity Conflicts   Ethnic identity is conceptually separate from personal identity and ethnicity. Ethnic identity is thought to be achieved through a process of crisis (exploration of alternatives) followed by commitment (decisions that reflect personal investment (Phinney & Alipuria, 1990). One simple approach that mental health practitioners can use to operationalize ethnicity is to ask individuals what they consider their ethnic group to be. The situation of Native individuals, however, is more complex. Native individuals have to prove who they are. This proof may be either a certain blood quantum percentage or a tribal enrollment card. The biethnic or multiethnic status of Native individuals reduces their chances of establishing their ethnic identity.

The most viable causation for ethnic identity among Native peoples is the degree of acculturation. The federal government and military went through a period in which the aim was to acculturate the Native populations. The ultimate goal was to absorb the "Indian problem" into the dominant culture.

Native peoples represent a range of orientation from pantradition to acculturated. English or Spanish maybe a second language for many. Several studies have provided consistent evidence that the degree of acculturation is related to how Native individuals, especially Native youth, perceive and respond to helping services (Herring, 1999). These studies suggest that less acculturated Native individuals are more likely to trust and express a preference for, and a willingness to see, an ethnically similar professional. In addition, less acculturated Native individuals have expectations for nurturance and expert techniques to facilitate the session.

A study by Portman (2001) examined the gender role identity attributes of Native women compared with a predominantly White female group. This investigation used the short form of the Beta Sex Role Inventory. Results reflected a significant difference on the masculine subscale between the two groups, with Native women having higher scores. One implication of the study's results is an apparent tendency for Native women to classify themselves as psychologically androgynous.

Dana (1998) documented the cultural competence that a health care professional needs in order to provide adequate, credible, and potentially beneficial services for multicultural individuals. He presented a model for effective culture-specific services that emphasizes the use of cultural and ethnic identity information to increase the accuracy of diagnoses.

Summary   Despite the considerable progress made over the past two decades in the addressing of health concerns of Native peoples, their overall health care lags well behind that of other ethnic groups in the United States (Portman, 2001). Solutions to the numerous mental concerns confronting Native individuals must be sought cooperatively by clients, counselees, and helping professionals. Providing effective mental health interventions to such a diverse and challenged population requires appropriate cultural training and experience if counseling interventions are to be culturally effective (Baruth & Manning, 2003). Perhaps, according to Baruth and Manning,

> one of the most significant problems for American Indians is the collection of destructive stereotypical images that are often perpetuated in literature and in the media. These stereotypes can potentially influence the decisions of counselors and the career and employment aspirations of their clients. Clients and counselors must strive to overcome the negative stereotypes that continue to thwart American Indian progress. (p. 168)

Cultural Attributions About the Causes of Psychological Problems

Culture-specific disorders are known as cultural-bound syndromes in the literature. Simons and Hughes (1993) preferred the term *cultural-related syndromes,* because many have been observed across different cultures. Health care professionals should have some familiarity with cultural-related syndromes shared by Native clients. For example, pantraditional or traditional Native clients may report that their weakness, loss of appetite, and fainting are the result of the action of witches and evil supernatural forces. Such verbalizations would be interpreted as schizophrenia by a helping professional unfamiliar with the effect of ghost sickness among Native peoples. However, if the Native client is not pantraditional or traditional and this belief is not shared by family members, these and similar presenting symptoms are probably not a culturally supported belief (Westermeyer, 1993).

Examples of cultural-related syndromes that helping professionals may find in traditional Native clients include the following (Simons & Hughes, 1993):

- Ghost sickness (weakness or dizziness resulting from the action of witches or evil forces)
- Wacinko (feelings of anger, withdrawal, mutism, or suicide resulting from reaction to disappointment and interpersonal problems)

Traditional Natives of the Southwest may also display cultural-related syndromes that are associated with Mexican Americans. Their long history of interactions with Mexicans and Mexican Americans has had considerable influence on Native cultures in that region. These syndromes include the following:

- *Ataque de nervios* (out-of-consciousness state resulting from evil spirits)
- *Mal puesto* (hex root-work and voodoo death; unnatural diseases and death resulting from the power of people who use evil spirits)
- Wind and cold illness (a fear of the cold and the wind; feeling a weakness and susceptibility to illness resulting from the belief that natural and supernatural elements are not balanced)

Much has been written about the use of alcohol as a tool of oppression. From an attribution perspective in particular, the use of alcohol historically as a way to cheat Native peoples of their land and other natural resources is often cited. The drinking of alcohol may have been initially incorporated into cultural practices in that it was seen as an activity of sharing, giving, and togetherness (Swinomish Tribal Mental Health Project, 1991). Turning down an offered drink is an act of individual autonomy and disruptive to group harmony. Other explanations have focused on the release of feelings of frustration and boredom and on allowing Natives to express emotions that are normally under control; drinking of alcohol as a social event; and the acceptance of drinking in many tribal groups (Anderson & Ellis, 1995). Substance abuse is often related to low self-esteem, cultural identity conflicts, lack of positive role models, abuse history, social pressures to use substances, hopelessness about life, and a breakdown in the family (Swinomish Tribal Mental Health Project, 1991).

Cultural Attributions About the Solutions to Psychological Problems

A number of Native cultural value and belief systems can affect the process and, subsequently, the results of psychological interventions. However, the Native perspective of mental health services and degree of acculturation tempers all helping endeavors. In the following sections, Native attitudes about seeking conventional mental health services will be presented first, followed by traditional beliefs about healing and use of folklore.

View of Seeking Mental Health Services   Effective helping with Native individuals must recognize their varied orientations to mental health professionals. Research indicates that all pantraditional and most traditional Native adults seldom look to the mental health services of the dominant culture as a means of improving their chosen way of life (LaFromboise, 1998). In addition, many Native adults recognize the need for professional aid only when Native community-based helping networks are unavailable or undesirable (Herring, 1999). Such reluctance to use professional counseling may also be attributable to older Native adults' memories of frequent negative and tragic interactions with non-Native people. Furthermore, many Native individuals believe that mental illness is a justifiable outcome of human weakness or the result of avoiding the discipline necessary to maintain cultural values and community respect (Herring, 1999). Native youth are also socialized to these traditional beliefs.

Native individuals who do avail themselves of mental health services often express concern about how conventional Western psychology superimposes biases onto their problems and molds their behavior is a direction that conflicts with Native cultural lifestyle orientation (LaFromboise, 1998). This incompatibility between conventional counseling approaches and indigenous approaches constitutes a cultural variance that may hinder effective counseling by the unknowing helping professional.

Selected Traditional Native Cultural Healing Beliefs   Native peoples often view the world in a more holistic manner than do European Americans (Heinrich et al., 1990). The traditional way emphasizes the need to seek harmony within oneself, with others, and with one's surroundings (Garrett, 1996). Garrett and Wilbur (1999) described several basic Native spiritual and traditional beliefs, adapted from Locust (1988) and cited in Baruth and Manning (2003, p. 163):

1. A single higher power exists and is known by names such as Creator, Great Creator, Great Spirit, or Great One, among other names. Lesser beings are known as spirit beings or spirit helpers.
2. Plants and animals are part of the spirit world, existing conjointly with and intermingling with the physical world.
3. Traditional Natives believe that human beings are comprised of a spirit, mind, and body, all of which are interconnected; therefore, illness affects the mind, spirit, and body.
4. Wellness is harmony in body, mind, and spirit; unwellness is disharmony in mind, body, and spirit.
5. Natural unwellness is caused by a violation of a sacred social and natural law of creation (e.g., participating in a sacred rite while intoxicated).
6. Unnatural wellness is caused by conjuring (witchcraft) from those with destructive intentions.

7. Each individual is responsible for his or her own wellness by being attuned to self, relations, environment, and universe (Locust, 1988; Garrett & Wilbur, 1999)

Healing is a powerful, culturally endorsed ritual. If the Native client trusts the healer and shares the same cultural myths, healing is better achieved (Hammerschlag, 1988).

If a Native individual develops a state of disharmony with nature, he or she needs to consult with a Native healer. The healer will suggest multiple strategies for the individual to regain harmony. For illustrative purposes, selected healing practices will be briefly considered: the four directions of existence, the sweat lodge ceremony, the vision quest, and the talking circle. This list is not intended to be exhaustive; rather, it provides examples found among most tribal entities, except where noted.

The Four Directions of Existence   Most Native people have learned the traditional way of keeping in step with nature by listening, by asking permission, by practicing patience, and by giving thanks (Garrett, 1996). The professional might incorporate this technique of seeking harmony by asking the client to answer the following questions, as posed by the four directions, and to balance the answers in whatever way is comfortable (adapted from Garrett & Garrett, 1996):

Who or what am I a part of; where do I belong? East is the direction of the path of the spiritual and is associated with the color red. The term spirit refers to an active flow of energy that connects all things to the universal spirit. Spiritual refers to a teaching that is embedded in cultural values. Both terms can be referred to differently in ceremonies and traditional teachings.

What do I have to contribute or share? North is the direction of the Mental Path—the direction of learning and sharing—symbolized by the colors white or blue. The mental aspect is considered an integral part of the physical aspects of a person. Mental medicine teaches that individuals have to understand all things in nature to understand themselves. One challenge is to find "helpers" on Earth who can provide calmness when the natural environment is not present.

What do I enjoy doing or do well? The direction of south is the nature path, where the spirit is transformed into a human. The color of the south is usually white to represent purity or green to represent plants. Individuals who seem to best fit in the direction of the south seek to retain or regain their innocence. They enjoy games and focus on peaceful thoughts and caring for animals and others.

What are my strengths; what limits me? The physical path is the direction of the west, usually associated with the color black. The west is often related to endurance, physical beauty, competition, and introspection. The west can be thought of as a direction of adolescence and learning how to best utilize an individual's physical gifts.

The Sweat Lodge Ceremony   The sweat lodge ritual is a widely accepted and widely practiced tradition that serves to purify those undergoing any sort of healing or transformation (Lake, 1991). The following description of this ceremony is adapted from Heinrich and associates (1990), as drawn from sources representing several tribes and nations: Sioux, Menominee, Winnebago, Crow, Cheyenne, and Inuit. A primary purpose of this ritual is to prepare a male Native youth for his vision quest, which will immediately follow. The steam symbolizes Native peoples' ascending prayers to the Great Spirit. The sweat is created by four separate inclusions of hot stones, representing the four directions. The medicine man inside the lodge assists the youth with his prayers, which provide spiritual guidance, and places the youth's body and mind in the proper state for the real test—the vision quest. The sweat lodge ceremony honors the process of growth and healing that is so central to the practice of group counseling (Garrett & Osborne, 1995).

The Vision Quest   This description of the vision quest is adapted from several sources (Heinrich et al., 1990; Herring, 1999). Upon emerging from the sweat lodge, the youth makes another prayer and offers tobacco to the four directions, again asking help in his endeavor. He is now ready for that important experience—his vision quest, that is, his search for a sign or signs that will lead him on the path he is to follow for the rest of his life. The youth is taken to a remote and isolated area set aside for just this purpose. He will be left alone for four days and nights without food or water. His time will be spent in reflection and prayer. His fasting will allow his mental capabilities to be more attentive to the natural world, to be directed toward and singularly focused on his relationship with the universe and his role in it. Some one event or series of events, whether it takes place in a dream state or in full consciousness, will reveal to this youth a real element of the future he must follow.

The Talking Circle   Native peoples have long used the talking circle to celebrate the sacred interrelationship that is shared with one another and with the world. Garrett and Osborne (1995) described this process in this way:

> The idea of council or "The Talking Circle" permeates the traditions of Native Americans to this day in the sense that it symbolizes an entire approach to life and to the universe in which each being participates in the Circle and each one serves an important and necessary function that is valued no more or no less than that of any other being. By honoring the Circle, we . . . honor the process of life itself, of which we are a part, and the process of growth that is an ever-flowing stream in our human nature. (p. 33)

If the participants become inconsiderate of one another's right to dialogue, a talking stick is used. The group member with the talking stick is the only person who can speak. Control of the group and interaction of all members is thus ensured.

Use of Folklore   A thorough knowledge of the oral literature of traditional Native peoples can enhance the helping professional's understanding of their verbal and nonverbal communications. Oral literature reflects the client's culture and can provide a glimpse into the problems faced by the client as well as the problem-solving skills that are available. Native folklore communicates their appreciation of and relationship to the Earth and its animals. These beliefs are passed generationally through experience and storytelling. Native folk tales are meant to teach as well as to entertain. Bruchac (1991) wrote that if children misbehave, they will be told a story rather than punished because "striking a child breaks that child's spirit, serves as a bad example and seldom teaches the right lesson, but a story goes into a person and remains there" (p. i).

The Chiricahua and Mescalero Apache use folklore as a group-supported means of expressing and transiently resolving repressed and unresolved infantile conflicts (Boyer, 1979). Apache folklore is also used as a complement to the defensive and adoptive functions of individual dreams, fantasies, and daydreams. "While the Apache youth of today do not know the details of the traditional stories, legends, and myths, their educational and mystical qualities continue to be transmitted and the role of folklore continues to be of great importance in socialization" (Boyer, 1979, p. 51).

IMPACT OF PSYCHOSOCIAL FACTORS

Health care professionals must understand how sociocultural and ethnic group contexts influence the development of mental health problems in Native peoples, especially Native youth. Concurrently, the negative influences of these problems on Native youths' development must be understood. Some researchers contend that the common element among Native youth at risk for future psychological maladjustment is the maintenance of a foreclosed or diffused identity status. In addition, cultural marginality and the stress associated with acculturation result in heightened anxiety, lowered self-esteem, and aggressive acting out or withdrawal behavior, which can contribute to such problems as substance abuse, academic underachievement or dropping out, teenage pregnancy, delinquency, suicide, and homicide (Rivers & Morrow, 1995).

Before working with Native clients, health care practitioners must be aware of their own cultural biases (Sue & Sue, 1999). It is also important that they be aware of how cultural influences have shaped their perception of what is "right" or "wrong" in parent-child relationships. Natives are more indulgent and less punitive to their children than are parents from other ethnic groups (MacPhee, Fritz, & Miller-Heyl, 1996). It is also important to avoid stereotypes of what an individual Native is like. Instead, health care professionals need to respond to the individual and to identify and explore his or her values. Many Natives adhere completely to mainstream values; others, especially those near reservations, are more likely to hold to traditional values (Sue & Sue, 1999, p. 283). Issues of ethnic differences between the helping professional and the client or counselee should be explored indirectly, the client's or counselee's value structure should be identified, and possible issues of cultural conflict and identity should be investigated. Basic need may have to be addressed first. Problems resulting from poverty (e.g., food, shelter, child care, and employment) should be discussed along with possible solutions.

Can the current counseling skills that most helping professionals have learned be appropriate in their work with members of the Native population? Controversy surrounds the answer to this question. Confusion exists over attempts to develop ethnic-specific approaches with Native clients and counselees. Native individuals respond best to cooperative approaches that offers a combination of client-centered and behavioral approaches. Allow the client to express his or her view of the goals for counseling. Most important, it is crucial that the mental health professional remember to respond to the Native client as an individual (Sue & Sue, 1999).

CONCLUSION

This chapter addresses the physical and mental health concerns of Native American Indian and Alaska Native populations. A review of the literature suggests that health care interventions with Native populations can pose various areas of bias. To appreciate why Native groups may have difficulties with the components of mainstream society and why such difficulties could increase bias in the helping interventions of these groups, try to picture yourself as a Native who is attempting to deal with the elements of mainstream society. For example, could you name the location and the building you are in after you have experienced a panic or shock attack in an unfamiliar city?

Such is the case of an Alaska Inuit or Hunkpapa Sioux who is transported from his or her natural surroundings to a modern, urban setting. Such is the case of a traditional Cherokee or Lummie, with limited standard English proficiency, who is interviewed by an European American psychologist for presenting problems of ghost sickness.

The challenges to Native peoples continue as conservative, reactionary Americans try to deny these people their inherent right to traditional means of subsistence such as fishing, whaling, and gathering medicines (Lum, 2003). Native peoples also face challenges when they try to make a living in more modern ways but within a context of sovereignty (Weaver, 2000). Economic development is also a challenge (as well as a hope) as Natives search for opportunities to be self-sustaining without compromising their own well-being (Lum, 2003). Through culturally congruent helping endeavors, health care professionals can demonstrate respect for Native values, traditions, and spiritual beliefs systems. "Once both clients and professionals are able to get past the stereotypes they hold of each other, it will be possible for them to work together in healthy, productive ways within a climate that respects indigenous cultures" (Lum, 2003, p. 216).

Exercises

---

1. Michael Redhorse is a Native American Indian student in an urban junior high school. His school has a small number of Native American Indian youth who were moved from reservations to the city so that their parents could find better employment opportunities. Michael is an academically and artistically talented sophomore who informs his counselor that he is returning to the reservation to live with his grandparents. Michael believes that his return to the reservation will, for all practical purposes, end his formal education. However, he feels an intense need to become immersed in his tribal culture and artwork.
   a) What is the presenting issue?
   b) What will be the goal of counseling?
   c) How might Michael's Native American Indian community facilitate his decision making?

   Adapted from Herring (1997a, 1997b) and Sodowsky and Johnson (1994).

2. Will is a 28-year-old gay Cherokee male. He is originally from a small town in northwest Arkansas. His parents were reared there after his ancestors escaped from the Trail of Tears death march that was intended to resettle peaceful Cherokee tribes people from the Carolinas to Oklahoma after the U.S. government had stolen their lands. Will is the youngest child of parents who are now in their late 60s. He attended a large state university in California on an Indian scholarship and completed his undergraduate degree in social work. Will has spent the last 10 years living in San Francisco, where he moved when he found out that he was HIV seropositive. He has a fairly extensive network of friends and lives with his partner of eight years. Will has worked in several social work agencies but is currently unemployed because six months ago he had become symptomatic with recurring pneumocystis. He is now taking a combination of medications that seem to have the pneumonia under control, and he is ready to return to work. He has come to see a career counselor at the One-Stop Center in his city because he is not sure that he can work a full 40-hour week and because as a social worker he is burned out by having to listen to other people's problems as well as deal with his own. He is at a loss as to what to do.
   a) As a counselor at the One-Stop Center, what are your first impressions of Will?
   b) Relying on your initial impressions, what advice would you give to Will?
   c) What role will Will's ethnicity play in your interventions?

REFERENCES

Alcohol-related hospitalizations—Indian Health Service and Tribal Hospitals, United States, May 1992. (1992). *MMWR—Morbidity and Mortality Weekly Report, 41,* 757–760.

Anderson, M. J., & Ellis, R. (1995). On the reservation. In N. A. Vacc, S. B. DeVaney, & J. Wittmer (Eds.), *Experiencing and counseling multicultural and diverse populations* (3rd ed., pp. 179–198). Bristol, PA: Accelerated Development Press.

Bachman, R. (1992). *Death and violence on the reservation.* New York: Auburn House.

Baruth, L. G., & Manning, M. L. (2003). *Multicultural counseling and psychotherapy: A lifespan perspective* (3rd ed.). Upper Saddle River, NJ: Pearson Education.

Beauvais, F., Chavez, E. L., Oetting, E. R., Deffenbacher, J. L., & Cornell, G. R. (1996). Drug use, violence, and victimization among white American, Mexican American, and American Indian dropouts, students with academic problems, and students in good academic standing. *Journal of Counseling Psychology, 43,* 292–299.

Boyer, L. B. (1979). *Childhood and folklore: A psychoanalytic study of Apache personality.* New York: The Library of Psychological Anthropology.

Bruchac, J. (1991). *Native American stories.* Golden, CO: Fulcrum.

Dana, R. H. (1998). *Understanding cultural identity in intervention and assessment.* Thousand Oaks, CA: Sage.

EchoHawk, M. (1997). Suicide: The scourge of Native American people. *Suicide and Life Threatening Behavior, 27,* 60–67.

Garrett, J. T., & Garrett, M. (1996). *Medicine of the Cherokee: The way of right relationship.* Santa Fe, NM: Bear & Company.

Garrett, M. T. (1996). "Two people": An American Indian narrative of bicultural identify. *Journal of American Indian Education, 36*(1), 1–21.

Garrett, M. T., & Osborne, W. L. (1995). The Native American sweat lodge as metaphor for group work. *Journal for Specialists in Group Work, 20,* 33–39.

Garrett, M. T., & Wilbur, M. P. (1999). Does the worm live in the ground? Reflections on Native American spirituality. *Journal of Multicultural Counseling and Development, 27*(4), 193–206.

Hammerschlag, C. A. (1988). *The dancing healers: A doctor's journey of healing with Native Americans.* New York: HarperCollins.

Heinrich, R. K., Corbine, J. L., & Thomas, K. R. (1990). Counseling Native Americans. *Journal of Counseling and Development, 69*(2), 128–133.

Herring, R. D. (1997a). *Counseling diverse ethnic youth: Synergetic strategies and interventions for school counselors.* Fort Worth, TX: Harcourt Brace.

Herring, R. D. (1997b). *Multicultural counseling in schools: A synergetic approach.* Alexandria, VA: American Counseling Association.

Herring, R. D. (1999). *Counseling with Native American Indians and Alaska Natives: Strategies for helping professionals.* Thousand Oaks, CA: Sage.

Herring, R. D. (2002). Will: The case of the "Fancy Dancer." In S. G. Niles, J. Goodman, & M. Pope (Eds.), *The career counseling casebook: A resource for practitioners, students, and counselor educators* (pp. 142–146). Tulsa, OK: National Career Development Association.

Indian Health Service. (2002a). *Regional differences in Indian health.* Washington, DC: Author.

Indian Health Service. (2002b). *Trends in Indian health.* Washington, DC: Author.

LaFromboise, T. D. (1998). American Indian mental health policy. In D. R. Atkinson, G. Morten, & D. W. Sue (Eds.), *Counseling American minorities* (5th ed., pp. 137–158). Boston: McGraw-Hill.

Lake, M. G. (1991). *Native healer: Initiation into an ancient art.* Wheaton, IL: Quest Books.

Locust, C. (1988). Wounding the spirit: Discrimination and traditional American Indian belief systems. *Harvard Educational Review, 58,* 315–330.

Lum, D. (Ed.). (2003). *Culturally competent practice: A framework for understanding diverse groups and justice issues* (2nd ed.). Pacific Grove, CA: Thompson–Brooks/Cole.

MacPhee, D., Fritz' J., & Miller-Heyl, J. (1996). Ethnic variations in variations in personal social networks and parenting. *Child Development, 67,* 3278–3295.

Manson, S. M., Tatum, E., & Dinges, N. G. (1982). Prevention research among American Indian and Alaska Native communities: Charting further courses for theory and practice in mental health. In S. M. Manson (Ed.), *New directions in prevention among American Indian and Alaska Native communities* (pp. 1–61). Portland: Oregon Health Sciences University.

Myers, H. F., Kagawa-Singer, M., Kumanyika, S. K., Lex, B. W., & Markides, K. S. (1995). Panel III: Behavioral risk factors related to chronic diseases in ethnic minorities. *Health Psychology, 14,* 613–621.

Native American Leadership Commission on Health and AIDS. (1994). *A Native American leadership response to HIV and AIDS.* New York: American Indian Community Home.

Paniagua, F. A. (1994). *Assessing and treating culturally diverse clients: A practical guide.* Thousand Oaks, CA: Sage.

Pewewardy, C. (1997, January 13–20). Melting pot, salad bowl, multicultural mosaic, crazy quilt, orchestra or Indian stew: For native peoples, it's your choice! Or is it? *Indian Country Today,* p. A7.

Phinney, J. S., & Alipuria, L. L. (1990). Ethnic identity development and psychological adjustment in adolescence. In A. R. Stiffman & L. E. Davis (Eds.), *Ethnic issues in adolescent mental health* (pp. 53–72). Newbury Park, CA: Sage.

Portman, T. A. A. (2001). Sex role attributions of American Indian women. *Journal of Mental Health Counseling, 23*(1), 72–84.

Prevalence and characteristics of alcohol consumption and fetal alcohol awareness—Alaska, 1991 and 1993. (1994). *MMWR—Morbidity and Mortality Weekly Report, 43,* 3–6.

Red Horse, J. (1982). Family structure and value orientation in American Indians. *Social Casework, 61,* 462–467.

Rivers, R. Y., & Morrow, C. A. (1995). Understanding and treating ethnic minority youth. In J. F. Aponte, R. Y. Rivers, & J. Wohl (Eds.), *Psychological interventions and cultural diversity* (pp. 164–180). Boston: Allyn and Bacon.

Simons, R. C., & Hughes, C. C. (1993). Cultural-bound syndromes. In A. C. Gaw (Ed.), *Culture, ethnicity, and mental illness* (pp. 75–93). Washington, DC: American Psychiatric Press.

Sodowsky, G. R., & Johnson, P. (1994). World views: Culturally learned assumptions and values. In P. Pedersen & J. C. Carey (Eds.), *Multicultural counseling in schools: A practical handbook* (pp. 59–80). Needham Heights, MA: Allyn and Bacon.

Stiffarm, L. A., & Lane, P., Jr. (1992). The demography of Native North America: A question of American Indian survival. In M. A. Jaimes (Ed.), *The state of Native American genocide, colonization, and resistance* (pp. 23–25). Boston: South End Press.

Sue, D. W., & Sue, D. (1999). *Counseling the culturally different: Theory and practice* (3rd ed.). New York: Wiley.

Swinomish Tribal Mental Health Project. (1991). *A gathering of wisdoms.* LaConner, WA: Swinomish Tribal Community.

Taylor, M. J. (2000). The influence of self-efficacy on alcohol use among American Indians. *Cultural Diversity and Ethnic Minority Psychology, 6*(2), 152–167.

Thompson, C. L., Walker, R. D., & Silk-Walker, P. (1993). Psychiatric care of American Indians and Alaska Natives. In A. C. Gaw (Ed.), *Culture, ethnicity, and mental illness* (pp. 189–243). Washington, DC: American Psychiatric Press.

U.S. Bureau of the Census. (2000). *Statistical abstracts of the United States: 2000.* Washington, DC: Government Printing Office.

Weaver, H. N. (2000). Activism and American Indian issues: Opportunities and roles for social workers. *Journal of Progressive Human Services, 11*(1), 3–22.

Westermeyer, J. J. (1993). Cross-cultural psychiatric assessment. In A. C. Gaw (Ed.), *Culture, ethnicity, and mental illness* (pp. 125–144). Washington, DC: American Psychiatric Press.

CHAPTER 9 # Treatment Issues for Native Americans: An Overview of Individual, Family, and Group Strategies

Cindy L. Juntunen, University of North Dakota, and Paula M. Morin, Turtle Mountain Band of Chippewa, University of North Dakota

The need for improved counseling and mental health services for Native Americans is readily apparent. Several significant mental health concerns exist within the Native American population, including high rates of depression, suicide, substance use, and post-traumatic stress syndrome (Indian Health Services, 2001). In fact, the Indian Health Services (IHS) reports that mental health concerns account for more than one third of the demand for services from IHS facilities. However, there is a serious lack of resources for meeting these needs. Furthermore, an astounding lack of attention is paid to Native American issues in the professional counseling and psychological literature, which further impairs the ability of professionals to offer high-quality and culturally relevant services.

The lack of both clinical services and empirical research highlights the necessity of attending to the mental health concerns of Native Americans. In this chapter, we review issues related to counseling and treatment of emotional and mental health concerns of Native American clients. To begin with, we review Native American perceptions and use of counseling and mental health services. This review is followed by a discussion of ways in which traditional Native healing approaches and conventional counseling might conflict. Finally, in the majority of the chapter, we address issues of treatment and assessment, paying specific attention to attempts to integrate conventional and indigenous treatment strategies.

NATIVE AMERICAN USE OF COUNSELING SERVICES

Very little information exists about the help-seeking behaviors of Native Americans (J. L. Johnson & Cameron, 2001). However, the Surgeon General's report of 2001 (U.S. Department of Health and Human Services, 2001) does state that Native

193

Americans, like other ethnic and racial minority groups in the United States, are likely to seek mental health services at a lower rate than are White Americans. J. L. Johnson and Cameron have identified four barriers to help-seeking behavior by Native Americans: trust, social-cultural factors, the culture of the clinician, and limited resources. These barriers interact in several ways, but each presents particular issues for counseling.

Trust

A major contributor to the experience of Native Americans is the historical and present-day battering of the Indian culture by dominant society. Historically, genocide was the method of cultural devastation, exemplified by the phrase "the only good Indian is a dead Indian" (Heinrich, Corbine, & Thomas, 1990). Although the policy of physical genocide ceased, ongoing attempts to either erase or usurp the Native culture continue to serve as a form of cultural genocide. From forcing children into boarding schools to maintaining the use of Native American images as athletic mascots, many attempts have been and continue to be made to minimize the Native American identity.

The oppression that results from centuries of prejudice and abuse impact the Native American people as a whole as well as the individual Native American client. In the words of one Native American participant in a qualitative study:

> When I look at the recent violations that Indian people as a nation have succumbed to, it is like any other kind of violation. I compare it to being violated verbally, emotionally, and sexually. You feel that you are nothing, that you caused it, and you're the lowest of the lowest. If you're an Indian person, it's just around you all the time. Your perpetrators are still there around you, reminding you that you're a dirty person and that it's not good to be who you are. (Milbrodt, 2002, p. 26)

The non-Indian mental health practitioner needs to recognize that he or she might be representing an oppressive society in the counseling session. It is no wonder, then, that mistrust can be a primary issue for practitioners, particularly dominant-culture practitioners, to address when working with Native American clients (see chapter 7). Native American clients may have a very legitimate concern that therapy will change them into something they are not, perhaps even fearing that they will be changed or taught to be "White."

Mental health practitioners can, however, work to foster trust by becoming familiar with and actively integrating Native values, such as those delineated by Garrett (see chapter 7), into their conceptualization of and work with the client. Specifically, practitioners need to learn about the values and traditions of the tribe or nation with which a client is affiliated (C. A. Johnson & Johnson, 1998; Malone, 2000) and not assume that all values ascribed to Native Americans (including those discussed later in this chapter) are of equal salience to individuals from differing tribes or nations. It is important to seek out reliable sources for such information and not depend on stereotypes and popular media that tend to portray Native Americans either from a deficit model or as a romanticized historic symbol. Attneave (1982) pointed out that among the most offensive things mental health practitioners can do is try to connect to Native clients around "novels, movies, a vacation trip, or an interest in silver jewelry" (p. 57) or allude to having a distant, romantic Native American ancestor. Such efforts to demonstrate understanding are more likely to make the client feel that the practitioner perceives them as part of a category rather than an individual.

Social-Cultural Factors

Issues of acculturation are likely to impact both the response to and relevance of counseling and psychotherapy. Depending on their relative commitment to traditional Native cultures and the dominant culture, clients may both seek and respond to help quite differently. J. L. Johnson and Cameron (2001) suggest that help-seeking behavior can be affected by four types of acculturation (as proposed by Berry & Kim, 1988). Individuals who value traditional culture and reject dominant culture are likely to seek help from traditional, Native health care sources. Those who assimilate to the dominant culture are more likely to pursue conventional Western mental health care and may not be receptive to traditional cultural or spiritual practices. Integrated individuals, those likely to value both their Native American culture and aspects of the dominant culture, may be more likely to integrate traditional and Western sources of help. Finally, some individuals may be *deculturated,* rejecting both traditional and dominant culture. Deculturated individuals may not seek help from either source.

   In the following sections, we present a variety of interventions, some of which are part of conventional Western psychology, others that are specific to indigenous cultures, and a number that attempt to integrate the two. It is essential that practitioners develop a thorough understanding of both the cultural background and acculturation of the client before making decisions about which type of treatment strategies to use in order to maximize the cultural and personal relevance of counseling.

Culture of the Clinician

J. L. Johnson and Cameron (2001) suggest that clinicians who are not themselves Native American may be more likely to "ignore symptoms that American Indians deem important, or are less likely to understand the American Indian's fears, concerns, and needs" (p. 216). However, little information is available to indicate whether Native American clients have a clear preference for Native American mental health practitioners. Some studies conducted with students suggest that Native American students, particularly female students, have a preference for counselors of the same ethnicity (BigFoot-Sipes, Dauphinais, LaFromboise, Bennett, & Rowe, 1992; M. E. Johnson & Lashley, 1989), particularly when the presenting concern is personal rather than vocational (Haviland, Horswill, O'Connell, & Dynneson, 1983). In a recent study that involved female participants living in reservation communities, Bichsel and Mallinckrodt (2001) found that women generally preferred a counselor of the same ethnicity and sex who used a nondirective style. Participants with a high commitment to Native culture (more traditional) also placed a high value on cultural sensitivity, endorsing a culturally sensitive Anglo counselor over a culturally insensitive Native American coun-selor. This difference was not noted among participants with a high commitment to Anglo culture. This study presents interesting implications for mental health practitioners and reinforces the need for practitioners to attend to acculturation and its potential interaction with their own sensitivity to cultural differences.

Limited Resources

The final barrier to help-seeking that was identified by J. L. Johnson and Cameron (2001) is the limited resources available to Native American populations, many of whom live in fairly isolated, rural communities. The IHS is the primary re-source for many Native Americans, particularly those living on or near reserva-tion lands, and IHS mental health services are significantly understaffed (IHS, 2001). In our region (the Northern Plains), many IHS facilities utilize "rent-a-doc" systems, wherein professionals are contracted to work at the IHS for any-where from a weekend or two to several years. Many of these professionals are non-Indian, and some are not interested or invested enough to learn about the cul-ture of the tribe. There is very little continuity in the client's care, and services are at times inadequate and underused. Further, access to IHS can be challenging in very rural areas, where lack of transportation, poverty, and other barriers can con-tribute to underutilization.

    Although the individual mental health practitioner may not be able to directly impact the availability of mental health resources for any given community, prac-titioners can help to better meet the needs of Native Americans by forming rela-tionships with other sources of help, including natural or informal helpers who are part of the community (Waller & Patterson, 2002). Particularly, practitioners can make a point of learning about and coordinating services with trusted healers or elders in the community to facilitate a more integrated service delivery system and meet the needs of a larger clientele with a relatively small number of providers. Further, alternative methods of service delivery might be considered. If clients have difficulty accessing mental health services, it may be appropriate to develop field mental health services in which professionals go to the client rather than requiring the client to come to the professionals. Field mental health services could result in earlier intervention or prevention, could cut down on the ratio of crisis visits in which clients only seek help when absolutely essential, and could ultimately provide better care with less personal and economic cost.

CONFLICTS BETWEEN TRADITIONAL NATIVE HELPING AND CONVENTIONAL COUNSELING APPROACHES

At a fundamental level, psychological treatment approaches are "derived from and serve to affirm the values of American culture. They are not value-free but are infused with the individualistic philosophy and priorities of the dominant culture" (LaFromboise, Trimble, & Mohatt, 1998, pp. 163–164). Further, these values differ from traditional Native values in a number of important ways. Garrett has provided a thorough overview of the values most relevant to Native Americans in chapter 7. In the following sections we discuss those values that have particular potential for conflict with conventional counseling, including relying on extended family, valuing group needs above individual needs or goals, limiting verbal interaction, sharing, and focusing on the present rather than future or past. Individual and tribal differences exist in terms of these values; they cannot be assumed to be universal. However, as noted by Garrett, the values listed herein are likely to be endorsed by a majority of Native Americans and are worthy of consideration by mental health practitioners who work with Native American clients.

Conventional counseling typically emphasizes the experience of the individual, and the therapeutic relationship is a one-to-one bond between clinician and client. This approach is inconsistent with the Native American value of self in relation to extended family and community. A mental health practitioner who is unaware of the importance of extended family and community to Native Americans may view the Native client as enmeshed or overly dependent on others. However, in a recent survey of American Indian family caregivers, respondents identified the importance of extended family as a primary value that providers needed to respect (Garwick & Auger, 2000). It is important that practitioners recognize the valued role of extended family in order to not treat family relationships as an indicator of pathology or diagnostic symptom purely because they differ from the Western emphasis on the nuclear family. Further, treatment decisions can be improved by enlisting the support of the extended family. Traditionally, Native Americans first seek help among family and friends (Garwick & Auger, 2000; Sutton & Broken Nose, 1996; Waller & Patterson, 2002). According to Sutton and Broken Nose, "The Indian Way consists of families working together to solve problems" (p. 33). Mental health practitioners can increase both trust and credibility as helpers by working in conjunction with the family and can also enhance the potential for effective change by including the family as a support and change agent for the client.

Like family relationships, the connection to the larger community is a vital aspect of Native American life (see chapter 7). In a recent qualitative study regarding career development (Juntunen et al., 2001), the majority of the participants indicated that their decisions about work and careers had been influenced by the needs in their local tribal communities. In some cases, respondents had selected a college major or job strictly on the basis of what would be most helpful to their home communities. The authors noted that this choice reaffirmed the value of community and that counselors needed to be cautious not to infer a lack of autonomy or decision-making ability for the individual client. Given the socioeconomic factors that contribute to mental health concerns for Native Americans (see chapters 7 and 8), attending to career and employment issues may have a significant impact on improved mental health. A connection between work and community may lead to greater work satisfaction, improved job attainment and retention, and greater resources to contribute to improved health.

Differences in verbal and nonverbal activity between conventional counseling and traditional Native American interaction patterns can also provide an opportunity for conflict if a mental health practitioner does not take them into consideration. In a study of communication styles on the Wind River Reservation in Wyoming, S. A. Lee (1997) provided several recommendations for non-Native mental health practitioners: Don't stare, listen well, explore emotions gently, and explore spirituality only after establishing trust. These recommendations were based on participant experiences that indicated that, compared to non-Native clients, Native clients were more comfortable with silence and less likely to maintain prolonged eye contact. Native clients were also described as expressing emotion with more subtlety and restriction than non-Native clients, which supported similar conclusions by other authors (J. T. Garrett & Garrett, 1994; Garwick & Auger, 2000; Thomason, 1991). Native American individuals might also use a less direct style of communication; they may utilize a story or a more circular train of thought to express an idea, compared to the more linear, direct expression of ideas consistent with the dominant culture. This approach can be confusing and even frustrating to practitioners who are unfamiliar with this communication style. In the words of my (Paula Morin's) father, Native American clients might be more likely to "climb the hill sideways." Indirect communication does not mean that a client is avoiding an issue; he or she may simply be getting to it in a different fashion.

Sharing is a very important value, particularly for more traditional Native American clients (see chapter 7; see also Sue & Sue, 1999). Many Native Americans are not connected to material objects, and they will willingly pass them on when the appropriate time comes or when another has need. Although mainstream treatment relationships and interventions do not advocate sharing between mental health practitioner and client, respecting this value can help strengthen the counseling relationship. Collateral relationships are important to Indians, and the therapeutic relationship is a personal one. By sharing, the Native American client is saying "I accept you" or "I want this relationship to work." This symbol of acknowledgment of the relationship may be at odds with the boundaries set between clients and clinicians in conventional psychotherapy (Willging, 2002). However, if a clinician can respect the therapeutic value of sharing, it becomes apparent that such sharing can come in many different forms that do not necessarily present ethical dilemmas: sharing a personal story, small material things or items from nature, or relevant books or articles. Even having beverages available in one's office can be an acknowledgment of the value of sharing.

Differences in time orientation, with a Native American emphasis on the present moment rather than on the future or even the past, can present some conflict with treatment from various theoretical perspectives. For example, some authors have suggested that psychodynamic and person-centered approaches are less preferred than approaches that emphasize the present and promote problem-solving and social skills (LaFromboise et al., 1998; Trimble & LaFromboise, 1987). Further, a long-term commitment to psychotherapy is not necessarily consistent with traditional approaches to healing, which frequently revolve around ceremonies that are either single events or a short series of events (Willging, 2002). Finally, at the session level of the counseling process, the use of 50-minute hours and strict adherence to the boundaries and limits imposed on the counseling relationship by time may be at odds with the Native American belief that things occur as they are meant to occur and are not dictated by the time on the clock.

When considering possible ways that Native American values and conventional counseling strategies might clash, mental health practitioners should keep in mind the importance of acculturation. Some of these potential conflicts may be more likely for clients who identify with traditional Native ways and not as much of an issue for clients who are more bicultural. However, an awareness of the potential for conflict, combined with a thorough understanding of the client's relative acculturation, can help mental health practitioners make informed decisions about both diagnosis and treatment.

ISSUES IN DIAGNOSIS AND ASSESSMENT

The lack of empirical support for assessment strategies and limited evidence of validity for use with Native American clients is, frankly, a professional disgrace. Native Americans are frequently not represented in normative samples for assessment instruments, and when they are included their numbers are so low as to make any intertribal generalization impossible. For example, the normative sample for the MMPI-2, one of the most widely used assessment instruments for all populations, included 77 Native Americans, all from a single region of the United States (Butcher, Dahlstrom, Graham, Tellegen, & Kaemmer, 1989). This small sample did score higher than European Americans on most of the clinical scales, but there is no clear analysis of what these differences might mean or how they should be interpreted (Allen, 1998).

The literature search that we conducted for this chapter identified only a very small number of studies addressing assessment with Native Americans. However, Allen's (1998) review of current assessment research strategies does provide useful information and ideas for improving personality assessment with Native American clients. Allen identifies three potential alternatives that may improve assessment techniques for Native Americans: developing and validating instruments that tap indigenous categories of mental health and illness; operationalizing acculturation variables that are likely to affect assessment results; and evaluating the use of picture-story tests.

In support of the first alternative, developing instruments to tap indigenous categories of mental illness, Allen (1998) cites a series of studies that have considered the cultural variation in the description and experience of depression. Allen reviewed several studies that looked at the Center for Epidemiological Studies Depression (CES-D) scale, in each of which Native American sample responses demonstrated factor structures that differed from European American samples and from each other. Based on these studies, Allen suggested that the structure of depression might differ for Native Americans relative to European Americans and might also differ across tribal and geographic differences within the Native American population. Allen also reported on a study by Manson (1994), in which both a Native and a European American sample were asked to group depression and anxiety symptoms using a Q-sort procedure. There were clear and consistent differences between these two groups, suggesting that both Native Americans and European Americans shared intragroup schemas for depression and anxiety but that they differed significantly from each other. Allen concluded that

> studies of depressive symptoms among American Indians and Alaska Natives, using diverse methodological approaches, all converge on a similar finding. The research raises serious questions about the universality of the construct of depression, as operationalized through Western psychiatric conceptualizations, when used with Indian people. (p. 25)

Allen suggests, therefore, that it is better to develop and validate new instruments for assessment of depression more appropriate to the culture, because the current instruments appear to be measuring something other than what was intended within the Native American population.

Allen (1998) also suggests that models of cultural identity, or acculturation, can contribute to an understanding of personality assessment for Native Americans. Certainly, the variables that contribute to acculturation are likely to have an effect on mental health issues; they may impact the assessment of mental health concerns or decisions about treatment. The consideration of cultural identity in conjunction with personality assessment might allow for a more comprehensive understanding of the constructs relevant to effective assessment with Native Americans.

Finally, picture-story tests may provide more culturally relevant options for personality assessment. For example, Dana (as cited in Allen, 1998) developed a set of cards based on thematic apperception tests (TAT) for Lakota adults in order to meet the needs of tribal providers. Several of the cards maintained the original TAT themes depicted by Murray (1943), whereas others were created to portray themes of particular cultural relevance to the Lakota people. Noting that several picture-story tests have been developed for specific Native nations, Allen suggests that such projective instruments may be adapted to be more culturally relevant while maintaining some of the interpretive value that they are assumed to have for dominant-culture clients.

An assessment completed with interviews and diagnostic evaluation is easily as subject to bias as formal assessment instruments are perhaps even more so. Diagnostic decision making often incorporates psychological or psychiatric terms that might have limited relevance or meaning to traditional Native American clients (Norton, 1999). As we noted in this chapter's discussion about communication style differences, emotions might be expressed differently in line with cultural norms. Specifically, it is not uncommon for Native Americans to express distress in terms of impaired social relationships rather than in terms of internal emotional states such as depression or anxiety (Norton, 1999).

Cultural context as well as the cultural identity of the individual client must be taken into account through all stages of assessment. However, C. A. Johnson and Johnson (1998) caution that cultural context should not be used to normalize behaviors that are likely to create problems for the individual. They warn that mental health practitioners can sometimes get caught up in the idea of respecting culture, or even romanticizing culture, to the point that they dismiss real mental health concerns as being a function of cultural norms. At this extreme, cultural sensitivity becomes a hindrance to clients' receiving the best possible treatment.

TREATMENT APPROACHES

Empirical support for treatment efficacy or effectiveness with Native American clients, like empirical support for assessment, is virtually nonexistent. In fact, J. L. Johnson and Cameron (2001) report that there has never been a major psychotherapy outcome study that addresses Native American response to treatment.

Despite this lack of systematic outcome research, individual researchers and clinicians are studying various approaches to service provision with Native American clients, and a small body of literature is beginning to emerge. Although many of the findings have not been replicated, the ideas and studies presented in the following sections provide some suggestions and guidance for mental health practitioners working with Native American clients.

As we noted earlier in this chapter, the history of oppression of Native American people is present in the counseling relationship, and the clinician needs to be constantly aware of this presence. The experience of oppression can be a difficult one for dominant-culture practitioners to grasp. However, imagine putting a mouse into a maze and monitoring its efforts to find the reward at the end. Consider what might happen if each time the mouse found a viable route, you picked it up and placed it at another dead end. If you were to keep moving the mouse repeatedly, and the mouse only very occasionally got the reward it sought, one of two things might happen: The mouse might adapt and become expert at finding viable routes quickly, or the mouse might give up and become despondent.

This external control of the mouse's experience—where rules are changed without notice, rewards are removed and controlled by others, and the needs of the mouse are treated as inconsequential—is a tiny reflection of the historical experience of Native Americans in the United States. For many Native Americans, the history of oppression has contributed to resilience and adaptability; for others, it has contributed to hopelessness, pain, and depression; and of course many others experience some combination of these consequences. When the client enters the clinician's office, the clinician must be able to respect that experience and use the knowledge of it to help the client, not reject it out of resistance to being considered part of an oppressive system. The mental health practitioner's own attitudes toward that history of oppression and own willingness to recognize it as real will allow him or her to provide services that are both culturally sensitive and relevant for the client. Once able to acknowledge that oppression, the practitioner may initiate action to counteract it. In fact, Lewis and Arnold (1998) suggest that clinicians need to accept a "responsibility for social action" (p. 51) in response to oppression, effectively becoming agents of social change. Advocacy counseling is one method mental health practitioners can use to foster such change.

Advocacy Counseling

Advocacy counseling, also known as a social action or social justice approach to counseling, is that which "expand[s] the practice of counseling from its traditional focus on the intrapsychic concerns of clients to a broader focus on the many extrapsychic forces that adversely affect the emotional and physical well-being of people" (Kiselica & Robinson, 2001, p. 387). C. C. Lee (1998) suggests that advocacy counseling helps clients "challenge institutional and social barriers that impede academic, career, or personal-social development" (pp. 8–9).

Advocacy counseling can be particularly relevant when practitioners work with clients who are dealing with issues related to oppression. Lewis and Arnold (1998) suggest that mental health practitioners can engage in four activities that will serve to counter oppression: address the tendency of the counseling profession to collude with oppression; support community empowerment efforts; engage in political advocacy; and emphasize the social action agenda of professional organizations.

The mental health professional can collude with oppression as a function of the agencies in which counseling occurs, including those in which counseling may be mandatory, such as criminal justice, welfare, and government or social service agencies. The nature of health care, with its reliance on insurance reimbursements and managed care, can at times be damaging to clients. Mental health practitioners can be aware of these examples and seek ways to "interrupt oppressive processes . . . when [they] speak up on behalf of their clients" (Lewis & Arnold, 1998, p. 58) and challenge the bureaucracy and dominant-culture norms that can function to control rather than empower clients.

Empowerment of community efforts, such as the development or expansion of indigenous health care efforts, can also counteract oppression by increasing the amount of control that individuals in a community have over their environments and resources. Mental health practitioners, because of the nature of their work, are frequently aware of the concerns that are common in a community, so they can help activate community members to seek systemic solutions to such concerns. Lewis and Arnold (1998) point out that counselors can use their interpersonal and organizational skills to participate in community action efforts as long as they are cautious that they do not assume control of such social action.

Involvement in political advocacy can serve the needs of clients, because many political issues are directly linked to the well-being of oppressed groups. Individual clinicians might join groups that are challenging public policies that impact, for example, poverty, educational access, or mental health care access. An example of this activism can be found in protests against the use of Native American athletic mascots that are currently being conducted around the country and in which many mental health practitioners are individually involved. Practitioners might also join together to advocate for change at the institutional or legislative level. In a related fashion, Lewis and Arnold (1998) suggest that mental health practitioners might look to professional organizations, such as the American Counseling Association, to identify ways in which they can move beyond efforts to educate members about issues of multiculturalism and oppression and begin to engage in social action.

A commitment to advocacy or social action counseling carries with it some challenges. It can be a significant personal and professional risk to take a public stance and advocate for oppressed clients (Grieger & Ponterotto, 1998). Mental health practitioners who engage in advocacy run the risk of offending colleagues and employers, being less popular, and being identified as troublemakers or malcontents. The willingness to take on such risks requires a strong commitment to social change as well as several professional and personal qualities. Kiselica and Robinson (2001) identify six attributes or skills necessary to engage in advocacy counseling: the capacity for commitment and an appreciation for human suffering; excellent nonverbal and verbal communication skills; the ability to see issues in the context of multiple systems; skills in individual, group, and organizational interventions; knowledge and ability to use the media and related technology, such as the Internet; and the assessment and research skills necessary to evaluate advocacy initiatives.

Advocacy can play an important role in mental health care for Native Americans. As noted by both Garrett (chapter 7) and Herring (chapter 8), Native Americans as a group have experienced, and continue to experience, the effects of oppression in a variety of ways, including limited appreciation for indigenous values, social and political factors that contribute to pervasive poverty, and limited access to health care. Particularly, Herring notes several health and mortality concerns of relevance to Native Americans. Two of these, cardiac disease and diabetes mellitus, represent a significant portion of the physical health concerns of Native Americans, and behavioral health factors, such as diet and exercise, contribute to both of them. With a traditional counseling perspective, the response to these issues might focus largely on the need for the individual to change his or her eating and exercise behaviors. Counseling might focus on issues related to compliance with medical orders, strategies for proper health and diet choices, or behavioral reinforcers for exercise. An advocacy counselor may well attend to these issues. However, he or she would also be attending to environmental factors that could be contributing to the health risk. For example, how regularly does the client have access to physical health care? Is there a primary physician available to follow the client's changing health needs, or is this a community served by a series of physicians providing short rotations of care to IHS clinics? Does the physician communicate in language that is culturally appropriate for the client? The answers to questions such as these might encourage the mental health practitioner to challenge the quality of health care services available to the community, engage other community members in that effort, and assist in a community empowerment plan to improve health care services. Similarly, it would be important to consider the impact of external forces on diet decisions. For example, in the Northern Plains many Native American families have relied on government subsidies of food, programs in which tribal communities receive commodities such as cheese and canned meats. Frequently, these foods are high in starch and sugar content and have the potential to contribute to both weight and blood sugar concerns. The counselor advocate might become more informed about this system, determine the relative benefits and risks of it, and work with other professionals to create change, if such change would improve the health resources of clients in the community. In fact, some community activists have analyzed the nutritional content of such foods in the last few years, and change is slowly occurring. Canned meat, for example, has been largely exchanged for frozen meats of various types and quality. Nonetheless, commodity food supplies are not on par with food available in the average grocery store in terms of nutritional value, and foods essential to restricted diets (low-fat, low-salt, or sugar-free, for example) are virtually unavailable.

Advocacy counseling can provide several avenues for responding to the needs of underserved clients, including members of racial/ethnic minority groups. Mental health practitioners who are aware of their potential to act as agents of social change may be more able to both identify and provide services that are culturally relevant at the individual, family, group, and organizational level.

In addition to advocacy counseling, several efforts to increase the cultural relevance of counseling and psychotherapy have been proposed for individual, family, and group counseling. Further, a number of specific presenting issues—including substance abuse, depression and suicide, and career development—have received some concentrated attention. In the following sections we address strategies for individual, family, and group counseling and note application to specific presenting issues as they emerge.

INDIVIDUAL COUNSELING

As we have already mentioned in this chapter, individual counseling is not necessarily consistent with the traditional values of Native American culture. Further, Trimble and LaFromboise (1987) have pointed out that Native Americans may simply lack awareness of counseling and the role it might play. Therefore, both clinician and client may have mismatched expectations when a counseling relationship is initiated. Discussing these expectations and allowing the client to decide between alternatives for approaching the therapeutic work may increase the initial trust and form a foundation for a therapeutic relationship.

M. T. Garrett and Myers (1996) discuss the application of the *rule of opposites* to counseling. Using the symbol of the circle, which is central to Native American values and spirituality, the rule of opposites recognizes that there are two opposing points to each issue as well as a continuum of points around the circle. Any decision or situation has at least two sides that might be accepted or chosen. For example, Peregoy (1999) mentions the high incidence rates of alcoholism and surmises that some Natives may use drinking to deal with painful emotions that potentially arise from boredom and frustration. Drinking alcohol is a negative option, basically a detrimental coping skill. Using the rule of opposites, the mental health practitioner can help the client look to the opposite side of the circle, to see that there are also positive methods to express emotions. For example, the practitioner might consider that, within the American Indian population, art and music are very popular as expressions of emotions. Dufrene and Coleman (1993) add that art and music, including traditional dance, are actually true forms of positive expression–positive coping skills in which many American Indians are interested and participate.

Yet another expression of emotion and healing comes from American Indian humor (Maples et al., 2001). Humor can serve several different purposes for Native Americans. One of the major purposes is reaffirming the sense of connectedness to the group, tribe, community, and family. Mental health practitioners might find it appropriate, once a trusting relationship is established, to join in humor with a client, thereby expressing acceptance and a sense of alliance with the client.

Spirituality is an important aspect for mental health practitioners to consider in counseling with Native American clients, particularly if the practitioner is working in conjunction with tribal healers or elders, who may involve the client in ceremonies and spiritual traditions. However, S. A. Lee (1997) cautions that it is important that the practitioner not push for details about spiritual ceremonies or expect clients to discuss their spirituality before a level of therapeutic trust is established. Further, the non-Native clinician must respect the sacred nature of healing ceremonies and both discuss and participate in them only as appropriate for a given tribal community.

The vision quest is a spiritual ceremony that might be integrated creatively into individual counseling (Heinrich et al., 1990). The vision quest, "like psychotherapy, is a transforming ritual" (Hammerschlag, as cited in Heinrich et al., p. 128); it has been used historically as a rite of passage for boys and young men who seek religious renewal. The vision quest consists of a sacred sweat followed by a period of isolation during which a vision is sought and, ultimately, by reintegration into the community (for a more complete description, see Heinrich et al.). The vision quest is suggested for integration with psychotherapy when the goal is to help the client find a sense of purpose and meaning (Heinrich et al.).

The use of spiritual sweats has been supported by other providers as well. For example, the Wyoming State Hospital has constructed a sweat lodge on its property, and sweats are integrated into the hospital's work with Native American patients (Tolman & Reedy, 1998). Following the construction of the sweat lodge and training by staff in Native American chemical dependency counseling, the hospital noted both an increase in referrals of Native American patients and a decrease in the length of stay for Native American patients. Tolman and Reedy report that within "less than a 2-year span from the start of the Sweat Lodge, all Native American patients who had been labeled previously as 'chronic' due to the nature of their illnesses were discharged to less restrictive settings" (p. 387).

Mohatt and Varvin (1998) present a very interesting case study in which they integrated conventional psychological and psychiatric treatment with a sweat lodge ceremony conducted by a Lakota medicine man and medicine woman. The researchers conclude that the two systems can be complementary but that potential areas of conflict must be addressed. However, with the combination of "good doctors" (p. 94) from both traditional Native and psychological healing traditions, their client was able to achieve and maintain mental health. (See the Mohatt and Varvin article for a comprehensive example of the conceptualization of culture as part of diagnosis, treatment, identity, and explanation of mental illness.)

Inclusion of a vision quest or other comparable spiritual experience into counseling presents a challenge to dominant-culture counselors, who will need to struggle with the meaning of the experience. Practitioners will find such a professional exercise more demanding than adjusting communication patterns or reading about tribal history. However, integrating such practices and working collaboratively with the Native healers who would lead the client through such a transformation has the potential to dramatically increase the impact of counseling. Heinrich and colleagues (1990) raise an important question:

> The counselor can make adjustments in the technical aspects of the craft of counseling, but is this sufficient? Counselors must affirm that minority cultures are not inherently inferior and that they possess values and meanings that are, at least in some dimensions, superior to those of the dominant culture. In addition, counselors must be invested in learning, intellectually and affectively, a new language

of culturally relevant metaphors that will, at least temporarily, alter their perceptions of what is real and what is possible. (p. 132)

Family Counseling

Family therapy offers many benefits for culturally relevant counseling. The systemic nature of family work and its emphasis on relationships is consistent with
traditional Native American orientation toward life (Sutton & Broken Nose,
1996). Attneave (1982) indicated that through family therapy, clients are seeking
a "restoration of a sense of innate worth and goodness, a restoration of feelings
of adequacy and of the fit of person, place, and family" (p. 82), all crucial to improved mental health and supported by the process of family therapy.

Involvement of family, even when the emphasis for treatment might be on an
individual, is quite natural among Native American clients (C. A. Johnson &
Johnson, 1998). The concept of family may involve a significant number of extended family members, including relatives that dominant-culture practitioners
might refer to as cousins, aunts, and uncles. Traditionally, family is a significant
source of support among Native Americans, and having a family involved in therapy supports the entire therapeutic process. For example, family support has been
identified as instrumental in the commitment to sobriety (J. Johnson & F. Johnson, as cited in McCormick, 2000), with almost half of respondents identifying
that family was the primary cause for sobriety. Additionally, family support has
been integrated into a reasons-for-living assessment and intervention for suicide
prevention among Native youth (Graham, 2002), demonstrating that a positive
way to connect to family members may help in the prevention of suicide attempts.

Despite the immense traditional value placed on family, Native American
families may struggle to remain intact. Governmental policies in North America,
both in the United States and Canada, "all but eliminated family and community
from involvement in child rearing" (Coleman, Unrau, & Manyfingers, 2001, p.
52). As such, Native American families may suffer both a psychological and
physical parental loss that extends across several generations (Christensen &
Manson, 2001).

In order to address this parental loss, Christensen and Manson (2001) suggest that mental health practitioners use the framework of adult attachment in
work with families. They acknowledge that attachment cannot be understood
without attending to the larger cultural context, but they suggest that it may be a
"starting point for understanding the dynamics of mental health for American Indian families in that . . . it takes into account important cross-generational conti-
nuities" (p. 1462). The authors further assert that Native American parents may
need to attend to their own healing, using the attachment framework, before any
family healing can occur. To demonstrate this model, the authors present three
family case studies that provide good examples of the integration of family history, adult attachment, and cultural factors.

Coleman and her colleagues (2001) have suggested strategies that social
workers can use to make Family Preservation Services (FPS) more appropriate
for Native American families. FPS is designed to prevent children from unneces-

sarily being removed from homes and placed into foster care. Native children are removed from their home at a rate much higher than their representation in the population, yet FPS has never prioritized Native families for services. In response, Coleman et al. (2001) suggest several steps that FPS programs can take. First, at the time of hire, FPS should assess whether potential workers have an honest interest in accepting and learning about Native culture. Second, FPS workers must be willing to challenge their own ethnocentric beliefs and receive training on how to do so as an ongoing part of their practice. Third, workers must be willing to collaborate with traditional healers, elders, and community members as well as extended family. Fourth, FPS workers must recognize and understand support systems to which the family has access. Fifth, the teaching skills that FPS workers use as part of their program must be adapted to Native culture. Sixth, FPS training must include cultural knowledge across a wide range of values, communication patterns, and belief systems. Finally, the agencies that oversee FPS interventions must take responsibility for supporting workers in obtaining the appropriate preparation to provide culturally relevant interventions.

In this comprehensive review of the potential for FPS to have a positive impact for Native American families, Coleman and her colleagues (2001) have provided a model for facilitating change at both the individual and agency level in order to provide better services to families and children. This excellent model places the responsibility for change on systems rather than on the backs of individuals and families.

Group Counseling

Group counseling approaches can be integrated with traditional healing practices, including talking circle (Heilbron & Guttman, 2000) and sweat lodge (Colmant, 1999; M. W. Garrett & Osborne, 1995). The group, which is structured typically in a circle, is consistent with the spiritual healing symbol of the circle or wheel and fosters a nonhierarchical relationship that allows for openness among participants.

In a group for First Nations women, Heilbron and Guttman (2000) integrated several symbolic traditional symbols and ceremonies. The group began with a purification ceremony that was conducted by a First Nations member of the group. A traditional prayer summoned the Creator to give the group strength, and a traditional symbol (in this case, an eagle feather) was passed from person to person as each spoke. This approach was integrated with cognitive therapy techniques. Heilbron and Guttman report that group members appeared to benefit from the integrated group in several ways. Sharing the traditional ceremony reaffirmed the women's ability to explore their lives in their own cultural context, and the spiritual framework of the group increased the value of participation. Heilbron and Guttman note that the non-Native counselor might be either a full participant or an observer of the group, depending on the wishes of the participants. It is again essential that the mental health practitioner attend to cultural norms about non-Native individuals participating in spiritual events. For example, the eagle feather used by this group has utmost sacred value to many Native American tribes, and its use would be interpreted very differently by different individuals. A non-Native clinician should never try such a technique without consulting or collaborating with a tribal elder or healer.

Network therapy is a form of intervention that integrates indigenous problem-solving strategies into counseling, and it sometimes involves very large groups who serve as a support network (LaFromboise et al., 1998). It is quite informal and nonhierarchical, and it relies on the larger community to support change for a given client or group of clients. Network therapy uses the group to bring about therapeutic change or to deal with a crisis; the mental health practitioner serves primarily as a catalyst who conducts the process. Although the network therapy approach is not strictly group counseling in that it may be brought to bear on the concerns of an individual client, it has potential application for a group process.

Finally, some specific attention has been paid to the use of group counseling strategies for treatment of substance abuse. One discussion is the relative merit of Alcoholics Anonymous (AA) among Native American communities. There are some concerns that the tenets of AA are inconsistent with Native values, including the very basic value of keeping private concerns private (Larvie, cited in Milbrodt, 2002). Further, Watts and Gutierres (1997) point out that AA places responsibility for the addiction on the shoulders of the addict, whereas more traditional Native American beliefs place responsibility on the larger family or community system. Nonetheless, others argue that the group support of AA can be valuable, particularly if the group is modified to meet the needs of the given community. Milbrodt argues that "in designing substance abuse prevention programs, counselors must ensure that their plan allows the community to function as a whole" (p. 39). M. T. Garrett and Carroll (2000) point out that several components of AA, including spirituality, unity, service, and recovery are consistent with the Native American values of spirituality, living in harmony, and place in community.

CONCLUSION

There is increasing evidence that the traditional values and belief systems of Native American culture can be effectively integrated with conventional counseling in order to provide improved mental health service. However, much of the current information regarding treatment and assessment issues for Native Americans is based on theory, has limited empirical support, and is reliant on single studies with little replication or demonstrated generalized validity. There is a critical need for additional research and case studies to support these efforts, and mental health professionals have an obligation to ensure that such research is completed and disseminated.

In this chapter, we have provided several ideas and guidelines for mental health practitioners working with Native American clients. Clearly, the values, worldview, and belief systems of Native American culture have much to contribute to healing and wellness. Respecting these contributions, and respecting the unique cultural identity of each Native American client, will improve every mental health practitioner's ability to provide effective and relevant mental health care.

Exercises

1. Mary is an American Indian graduate student in her second year of a counseling psychology doctoral program. She is involved in her fieldwork at a state mental health facility. She has been assigned a young American Indian female client who suffers from depression triggered by her husband's infidelity. Mary is being supervised by a female psychologist of European descent. During the processing of Mary's initial session with this American Indian client, Mary is questioned about what the supervisor sees as her reluctance to confront the client about her submissiveness to her husband. Mary is confused by the question because confrontation did not seem appropriate in the session. Mary felt that direct confrontation may have been disrespectful at the time and that when confrontation was needed, there would be a more tactful, respectful way to go about it. When Mary explained to her supervisor that she did not feel comfortable approaching the client with direct, hard confrontation during that session and perhaps in any subsequent sessions, the supervisor's response was, "Oh, that is just because of your culture."

   a) What values might be contributing to the disparity between Mary's impression and the impression of her supervisor?

   b) What issues might you expect to emerge in the future if this discrepancy is not resolved? What responsibility does the supervisor have to resolving this situation? What responsibility does Mary have to resolving this situation?

   c) What are some issues that you might consider important in working with the client in this situation? How would you assess for depression or other emotional health concerns?

2. Jack is a 34-year-old Native American man who has been referred to counseling by his physician. Jack has been feeling "ill at ease" for several weeks, and notes that his stomach has been upset and he has had frequent headaches. Because of these problems, he went to the physician for a medical checkup, but no physical cause for his concerns could be identified. During this visit with his physician, Jack revealed that he had recently lost his parents in a car accident, and his comment triggered the referral to your office. Jack denies any feelings of depression or anxiety. However, he does report that he has a hard time sleeping, does not spend as much time with friends or family as he used to, and feels as if his life is without purpose. Jack is divorced and lives alone. He has two children but does not see them very often. He used to be an active participant in local community events and was a well-known grass dancer in his younger adulthood. He seldom attends such events now and hasn't been to a pow-wow for more than a year.

   a) What kind of assessment strategies would you use to understand Jack's current concerns? What information would you collect, and what initial conceptualization might you form?

   b) Once your assessment is complete, what kind of treatment options might be most appropriate for Jack? Are there traditional healing strategies that you might consider? If so, how would you determine whether these would be appropriate?

c) Assuming that you are able to integrate traditional healing approaches with your counseling, how would you go about doing this? Who would you consult, what resources would you obtain, and what role would you play in the process?

REFERENCES

Allen, J. (1998). Personality assessment with American Indians and Alaska natives: Instrument considerations and service delivery style. *Journal of Personality Assessment, 70,* 17–42.

Attneave, C. (1982). American Indians and Alaska Native families: Emigrants in their own homeland. In M. McGoldrick, J. K. Pearce, & J. Giordano (Eds.), *Ethnicity and family therapy* (pp. 55–83). New York: Guilford Press.

Berry, J. W., & Kim, R. (1988). Acculturation and mental health. In P. R. Dasen, J. W. Berry, & N. Sartorius (Eds.), *Health and cross-cultural psychology: Toward application* (pp. 207–236). Thousand Oaks, CA: Sage.

Bichsel, R. J., & Mallinckrodt, B. (2001). Cultural commitment and the counseling preferences and counselor perceptions of Native American women. *The Counseling Psychologist, 29,* 858–881.

BigFoot-Sipes, D. S., Dauphinais, P., LaFromboise, T. D., Bennett, S. K., & Rowe, W. (1992). American Indian secondary school students' preferences for counselors. *Journal of Multicultural Counseling and Development, 20,* 113–122.

Butcher, J. N., Dahlstrom, W. G., Graham, J. R., Tellegen, A., & Kaemmer, B. (1989). *Minnesota Multiphasic Personality Inventory 2 (MMPI-2): Manual for administration and scoring.* Minneapolis: University of Minnesota Press.

Christensen, M., & Manson, S. (2001). Adult attachment as a framework for understanding mental health and American Indian families. *American Behavioral Scientist, 44,* 1447–1465.

Coleman, H., Unrau, Y. A., & Manyfingers, B. (2001). Revamping Family Preservation Services for Native families. *Journal of Ethnic and Cultural Diversity in Social Work, 10,* 49–68.

Colmant, S. A. (1999). Using the sweat lodge ceremony as group therapy for Navajo Youth. *Journal for Specialists in Group Work, 24,* 55–73.

Dufrene, P. M., & Coleman, V. D. (1993). Art and healing for Native American Indians. *Journal of Multicultural Counseling and Development, 21,* 143–154.

Garrett, J. T., & Garrett, M. W. (1994). The path of good medicine: Understanding and counseling Native American Indians. *Journal of Multicultural Counseling and Development, 22,* 134–144.

Garrett, M. T., & Carroll, J. J. (2000). Mending the broken circle: Treatment of substance dependence among Native Americans. *Journal of Counseling and Development, 78,* 379–387.

Garrett, M. T., & Myers, J. E. (1996). The rule of opposites: A paradigm for counseling Native Americans. *Journal of Multicultural Counseling and Development, 24,* 89–104.

Garrett, M. W., & Osborne, L. W. (1995). The Native American sweat lodge as metaphor for group work. *Journal for Specialists in Group Work, 20,* 33–39.

Garwick, A., & Auger, S. (2000). What do providers need to know about American Indian culture? Recommendations from urban Indian family caregivers. *Families, Systems, and Health, 18,* 177–189.

Graham, T. L. C. (2002). Using reasons for living to connect to American Indian healing traditions. *Journal of Sociology and Social Welfare, 19,* 55–75.

Grieger, I., & Ponterotto, J. G. (1998). Challenging intolerance. In C. C. Lee & G. R. Walz (Eds.), *Social action: A mandate for counselors* (pp. 17–50). Alexandria, VA: American Counseling Association.

Haviland, M. G., Horswill, R. K., O'Connell, J. J., & Dynneson, V. V. (1983). Native American college students' preference for race and sex and the likelihood of their use of a counseling center. *Journal of Counseling Psychology, 30,* 267–270.

Heilbron, C. L., & Guttman, M. A. J. (2000). Traditional healing methods with First Nations women in group counselling. *Canadian Journal of Counselling, 34,* 3–13.

Heinrich, R. K., Corbine, J. L., & Thomas, K. R. (1990). Counseling Native Americans. *Journal of Counseling and Development, 69,* 128–132.

Indian Health Services. (2001). Mental health services. Retrieved September 12, 2002, from http://www.ihs.gov/adminmngrresources/budget/old_site/cj2002/svcs web docs/mental health services.doc

Johnson, C. A., & Johnson, D. L. (1998). Working with Native American families. In H. P. Lefley (Ed.), *Families coping with mental illness: The cultural context—New directions for mental health services* (pp. 89–96). San Francisco: Jossey-Bass.

Johnson, J. L., & Cameron, M. C. (2001). Barriers to providing effective mental health services to American Indians. *Mental Health Services Research, 3,* 215–223.

Johnson, M. E., & Lashley, K. H. (1989). Influence of Native Americans' cultural commitment on preferences for counselor ethnicity and expectations about counseling. *Journal of Multicultural Counseling and Development, 17,* 115–122.

Juntunen, C. L., Barraclough, D. J., Broneck, C. L., Seible, G. A., Winrow, S. A., & Morin, P. (2001). American Indian perspectives on the career journey. *Journal of Counseling Psychology, 48,* 274–285.

Kiselica, M. S., & Robinson, M. (2001). Bringing advocacy counseling to life: The history, issues, and human dramas of social justice work in counseling. *Journal of Counseling and Development, 79,* 387–397.

LaFromboise, T. D., Trimble, J. E., & Mohatt, G. V. (1998). Counseling intervention and American Indian tradition: An integrative approach. In D. R. Atkinson, G. Morten, & D. W. Sue (Eds.), *Counseling American minorities* (5th ed., pp. 159–182). Boston: McGraw-Hill.

Lee, C. C. (1998). Counselors as agents of social change. In C. C. Lee & G. R. Walz (Eds), *Social action: A mandate for counselors* (pp. 3–14). Alexandria, VA: American Counseling Association.

Lee, S. A. (1997). Communication styles of Wind River Native American clients and the therapeutic approaches of their clinicians. *Smith College Studies in Social Work, 68,* 57–81.

Lewis, J. A., & Arnold, M. S. (1998). From multiculturalism to social action. In C. C. Lee & G. R. Walz (Eds.), *Social action: A mandate for counselors* (pp. 51–66). Alexandria, VA: American Counseling Association.

Malone, J. L. (2000). Working with aboriginal women: Applying feminist therapy in a multicultural counselling context. *Canadian Journal of Counselling, 34,* 33–42.

Manson, S. M. (1994). Culture and depression: Discovering variations in the experience of illness. In W. J. Lonner & R. S. Malpass (Eds.), *Psychology and culture* (pp. 285–290). Boston: Allyn and Bacon.

Maples, M. F., Dupey, P., Torres-Rivera, E., Phan, L. T., Vereen, L., & Garrett, M. T. (2001). Ethnic diversity and the use of humor in counseling: Appropriate or inappropriate? *Journal of Counseling and Development, 79,* 53–79.

McCormick, R. M. (2000). Aboriginal traditions in the treatment of substance abuse. *Canadian Journal of Counselling, 34,* 25–32.

Milbrodt, T. (2002). Breaking the cycle of alcohol problems among Native Americans: Culturally-sensitive treatment in the Lakota community. *Alcoholism Treatment Quarterly, 20,* 19–44.

Mohatt, G. V., & Varvin, S. (1998). Looking for "a good doctor": A cultural formulation of the treatment of a First Nations' woman using western and First Nations methods. *American Indian and Alaska Native Mental Health Research, 8,* 83–100.

Murray, H. A. (1943). *Thematic Apperception Test manual.* Cambridge, MA: Harvard University Press.

Norton, I. M. (1999). American Indians and mental health: Issues in psychiatric assessment and diagnosis. In J. M. Herrera & W. B. Lawson (Eds.), *Cross cultural psychiatry* (pp. 77–85). New York: Wiley.

Peregoy, J. J. (1999). Revisiting transcultural counseling with American Indians and Alaskan Natives: Issues for consideration. In J. McFadden (Ed.), *Transcultural counseling* (2nd ed., pp. 137–170). Alexandria, VA: American Counseling Association.

Sue, D. W., & Sue, D. (1999). *Counseling the culturally different* (3rd ed.). New York: Wiley.

Sutton, C. T., & Broken Nose, M. A. (1996). American Indian families: An overview. In M. McGoldrick, J. Giordano, & J. K. Pearce (Eds.), *Ethnicity and family therapy* (2nd ed., pp. 31–44). New York: Guilford Press.

Thomason, T. C. (1991). Counseling Native Americans: An introduction for non-Native American counselors. *Journal of Counseling and Development, 69,* 321–327.

Tolman, A., & Reedy, R. (1998). Implementation of a culture-specific intervention for a Native American community. *Journal of Clinical Psychology in Medical Settings, 5,* 381–392.

Trimble, J. E., & LaFromboise, T. (1987). American Indians and the counseling process: Culture, adaptation, and style. In P. Pedersen (Ed.), *Handbook of cross-cultural counseling and therapy.* New York: Praeger.

U.S. Department of Health and Human Services. (2001). *Mental health: Culture, race, and ethnicity—A supplement to mental health. A report of the Surgeon General.* Rockville, MD: U.S. Department of Health and Human Services, Substance Abuse and Mental Health Services Administration, Center for Mental Health Services.

Waller, M. A., & Patterson, S. (2002). Natural helping and resilience in a Dine' (Navajo) community. *Families in Society: The Journal of Contemporary Human Services, 83,* 73–84.

Watts, L. K., & Gutierres, S. E. (1997). A Native American–based cultural model of substance dependency and recovery. *Human Organization, 56,* 9–18.

Willging, C. E. (2002). Clanship and *K'e:* The relatedness of clinicians and patients in a Navajo counseling center. *Transcultural Psychiatry, 39,* 5–32.

Part IV THE ASIAN AMERICAN CLIENT

CHAPTER 10 # Asian Americans: A Practical History and Overview

Audrey U. Kim, University of California, Santa Cruz

According to the 2000 U.S. Census, there were almost 12 million Asian Americans in the United States, comprising 4.2% of the population (U.S. Bureau of the Census, 2002b). The U.S. Census uses the term *Asian* to refer to people with origins in East Asia, Southeast Asia, or the Indian subcontinent. The three largest reported Asian ethnic groups—Chinese, Filipinos, and Asian Indians—account for almost 60% of Asian Americans, followed by Korean- and Japanese-Americans (U.S. Bureau of the Census, 2002b). Although Asian Americans currently comprise a relatively small percentage of the general population, they are one of the fastest growing groups in this country. Between 1990 and 2000, while the general population grew at a rate of 13%, the Asian American population increased by 72% (U.S. Bureau of the Census, 2002b). Thus, by 2010, the Asian American population is expected to double, and it is the fastest growing racial group in the country (Zia, 2000). Because the majority of Asian Americans reside in large metropolitan areas, they generally make up a larger population in the cities than the 5% of the population that they represent nationwide.

The term *Asian American* is a broad umbrella term that includes diverse Americans of Asian ancestry. For example, the language, culture, history, and religion of the Philippines are very different from those of Japan. Some Asian groups, including the Chinese and Japanese, have a long history of immigration to the United States that dates back to the late nineteenth century; in contrast, other Asian groups, such as Southeast Asians, are relative newcomers to the United States. Furthermore, within a specific ethnic group, there is significant variability in terms of education, class, and acculturation level. For example, affluent Asian Indian entrepreneurs in Silicon Valley may have little in common with Asian Indian cabdrivers in New York City, even though they belong to the same ethnic group and speak the same language.

At the same time, regardless of their differences, Asian Americans also share some commonalities. For example, many Asian Americans adhere to Confucian or collectivist values. Moreover, regardless of ethnicity, Asian Americans share similarities in terms of how and why they came to the United States and how they have been received by the larger American society. Asian American immigrant experiences resemble those of their European counterparts; however, as people of color with distinct physical features, they continue to be perceived as foreigners who can never be completely absorbed into American society (Chan, 1991). In many respects, the experiences of Asian Americans have been similar to those of other American ethnic minorities.

In recent years, Pacific Islanders have at times been included with Asian Americans for demographic purposes. However, given the breadth of this topic, this chapter focuses only on Asian Americans. This chapter is intended to provide the health care professional with a brief practical overview to better understand the history and background of the Asian American client. Topics to be covered include immigration history and adjustment to the United States, experiences of discrimination, issues of employment and education, identity issues, cultural values, and the current status of Asian Americans.

IMMIGRATION HISTORY

Asian immigration to the United States can be divided into four themes: early immigration, the 1965 Immigration Act, Southeast Asian immigration, and recent immigration.

Early Immigration

Contrary to popular perceptions, there has been a long history of Asians in the United States. For example, scholars have noted that as early as the sixteenth century, Chinese shipbuilders accompanied the Spanish to Baja California, and by the eighteenth century, descendants of Filipino sailors who had worked on the Manila galleons could be found on the Louisiana coast (Chan, 1991; Fong, 2002). Between 1848 and 1924, hundreds of thousands of immigrants from China, Japan, the Philippines, Korea, and India journeyed to the United States to seek a better life and to escape political and economic turmoil in their home countries— much like their European counterparts. At first, America welcomed this cheap source of labor from Asia. However, as waves of anti-Asian sentiment swept through this country, Asian groups, one by one, were eventually barred from entering the United States.

Thousands of Chinese men provided the backbone of the workforce that built the transcontinental railroad; many even died performing this backbreaking and dangerous work. Yet, characteristic of how the contributions of Asian Americans have so often been forgotten or overlooked, no Chinese were invited to the jubilant opening ceremonies; in fact, they were not even allowed free transport to return to their homes in California (Chan, 1991; Takaki, 1989)! By the 1870s, as more European Americans had settled in California, Chinese and other Asians found that they were increasingly restricted to menial, low-status jobs. Thus, many found work in agriculture while others opened small businesses or worked as domestic servants. During the latter part of the nineteenth century, some Chinese workers also went to Hawaii to labor on the sugar plantations. However, by

1882, anti-Chinese hostility had intensified sufficiently so that Congress responded with passage of the first Chinese Exclusion Act, which suspended the entry of Chinese workers into the United States.

The early histories of other Asian groups parallel that of Chinese workers. Japanese, Filipinos, Koreans, and Asian Indians were recruited to work on the Hawaiian sugar plantations and on Californian farms and orchards as well as in Alaskan canneries. However, especially in times of economic hardship, Asian Americans became easy scapegoats and targets of hostility. As anti-Asian sentiment spread, Japanese were barred from entering the United States by the Gentlemen's Agreement (1907), and finally, with the 1924 Immigration Act, all Asian immigration was in effect halted. However, because the Philippines became a territory of the United States in 1898, Filipinos were considered U.S. "nationals" and were exempt from these restrictions until the 1934 Tydings-McDuffie Act. The first group of Filipinos consisted of students on government scholarships ("pensionados") as well as privately funded students; however, most of these young men were unable to complete their studies and instead became agricultural laborers or domestic servants.

Many of these early Asian immigrants lived in "bachelor societies" because of restrictive immigration policies, uneven sex ratios, and antimiscegenation laws. Small numbers of Asian women were able to immigrate during these early years. However, it was not until after World War II that significant numbers of Asian women were allowed to enter the United States, resulting in rising numbers of Asian American families and children and a growing Asian American population. Specifically, under the terms of the 1945 War Brides Act and the 1952 McCarran-Walter Act, Asian women were able to immigrate to the United States as wives of veterans. Interestingly enough, Asian American veterans were initially excluded from the War Brides Act, and it had to be amended in 1947 to include veterans of Asian ancestry.

World War II was also a turning point for Asian Americans in other ways. After the Japanese attack on Pearl Harbor, Americans of Japanese ancestry were branded as security threats and forced to leave their homes and relocate to concentration camps for the duration of the war. Ironically, attitudes toward other Asian American groups generally improved during the war, partly because many Asian countries were allies of the United States in the war (Chan, 1991). For example, Chinese Americans were able to find skilled and professional work in war-related industries that had previously been closed to them. After World War II, as it competed with the communist bloc for power and influence, the United States opened its doors a crack to Asian immigrants who could offer scientific and technical expertise. Later, as Japan became one of its most stable allies in Asia during the cold war, the reputation of Japanese Americans in the United States also improved.

1965 Immigration Act

The political climate of the cold war made it difficult for the United States to maintain its overtly racist immigration policies. This political climate, in addition to other sociopolitical factors such as the civil rights movement and specialized labor needs, helped bring about passage of the 1965 Immigration Act, which abolished the system of "national origins" that had been used to severely restrict the numbers of immigrants from Asia. Instead, the 1965 act implemented a system based on preferences that favored family reunification and immigrants with professional skills. Although far from the intentions of the framers of this legislation, the 1965 Immigration Act resulted in the large-scale immigration of Asians to the United States and has shaped Asian American communities today.

Immigration from Asia can best be understood in terms of push and pull factors as well as in the context of global economic restructuring (Fong, 2002; Ong, Bonacich, & Cheng, 1994). With the passage of the 1965 Immigration Act, the United States was partly trying to attract immigrants with scientific and technical knowledge who could help to win the cold war. At the same time, the United States was faced with a shortage of health care workers. During this same period, educated professionals in Asia were finding that they could not find commensurate work in their home countries because of economic conditions, and thus immigration offered an attractive alternative. Many of those emigrating from Asia also came from countries with close connections to the United States, such as the Philippines and Korea, and were somewhat familiar with American culture and indeed attracted by it. Thus, compared to the earlier waves of Asian immigrants, those coming in the 1960s and 1970s were generally from more educated, middle-class, and urbanized backgrounds and were coming as family units with the intention to settle permanently rather than as sojourners (Chan, 1991; Fong, 2002).

However, like their earlier counterparts, these recent Asian immigrants found that their status remained contingent on the fluctuating demands of the U.S. economy. Thus, by the late 1970s, Congress had responded to the depressed economy by amending the 1965 act and restricting the immigration of professionals. Again, by the late 1990s, Asian immigrants were being recruited to serve as "high-tech temps" and were granted entry into the United States on temporary visas (Zia, 2000). The general perception is that immigrants from Asia and elsewhere have come to this country to take advantage of economic opportunities and take jobs away from "native" Americans. However, the history of Asian immigrants shows otherwise; immigrants have often been recruited to fill important economic niches and have provided a valuable labor supply in times of need. Scholars have also referred to this phenomenon as a "brain drain," acknowledging that the U.S. economy has benefited from the educational investment provided by the home countries of these immigrant workers.

Southeast Asian Immigration

By the late 1970s, the numbers of Asian professionals immigrating to the United States had experienced a relative decline; in contrast, during this same period, large numbers of Southeast Asian refugees began to enter the United States. Many of these people from Vietnam, Cambodia, and Laos had not intended to immigrate to the United States. Rather, they were refugees from countries devastated by wars in which the United States had played a major role. By 1965, the United States had become enmeshed in the politics of Southeast Asia in an effort to combat communism. President Lyndon Johnson authorized the use of American combat troops and launched a bombing campaign in Vietnam that ravaged the country. However, this war to "contain" communism quickly infected other parts of Southeast Asia, including Cambodia and Laos, devastating these regions and the lives of these peoples.

When Saigon fell in 1975, high-ranking Vietnamese military and government personnel, most with close ties to the U.S. military, were evacuated and brought to resettle in the United States. This first wave of Southeast Asian refugees was generally comprised of the urban elite and middle class, who were somewhat westernized. The second wave of refugees who came to the United States between 1978 and 1980 was a more socioeconomically diverse group that also included people from Laos and Cambodia. This second wave also included those who had suffered in work camps and had otherwise been persecuted by the new communist governments. In 1975, Cambodian communists, known as the Khmer Rouge, gained control of Cambodia and began a systematic genocide of its own people. It is estimated that 1 million to 3 million Cambodians out of a population of 7 million died during the Khmer Rouge regime as a result of starvation, disease, and execution. In 1978, Vietnam invaded Cambodia and established a new government, but the Cambodian people continued to suffer and refugees began to flee the country to nearby Thailand. Communists also came to power in Laos and began a massive bombing campaign against the Hmong, an ethnic minority group that had assisted U.S. forces in the Vietnam war.

Many of these second-wave refugees from Vietnam, Cambodia, and Laos fled to Thailand and the Philippines and were often stranded in refugee camps for years until they were authorized entry by the United States or another receiving country. The third wave of Southeast Asian refugees came after 1980 and continues to this day. This group consists primarily of relatives of those who are already resettled in the United States, children of American soldiers (Amerasians), and survivors of political work camps (reeducation camps). Mutual assistance associations, which are community organizations staffed by coethnics, have been instrumental in helping many Southeast Asian refugees with resettlement and adjustment to the United States. It is important to recognize that the United States has taken in these refugees not only out of humanitarian concern but also as an acknowledgment that U.S. foreign policy and military actions in Southeast Asia are largely responsible for the displacement of these people.

Recent Immigration

Since the late 1970s, most Asian immigrants have come to the United States through family reunification rather than the professional preferences of the 1965 Immigration Act. The proportion of professionals has declined to less than 20%, and the percentage coming through family reunification (i.e., chain migration) has increased to more than 80% of all quota immigrants (Chan, 1991). In part, this change is due to the amendments passed in the late 1970s that restricted professionals from entering. Also, as economies in Asia have improved, the push factors for potential emigrants have not been as strong. Thus, in recent years, it has been the more economically disadvantaged in Asia who have been the most likely to immigrate to the United States. Moreover, the United States has opted to issue more temporary work visas to fill labor shortages. For example, during the Silicon Valley boom, large numbers of foreign high-tech specialists were recruited to work temporarily in the United States; of these special H1-B visa holders, 44% were Indian and 9% were Chinese (Zia, 2000). In addition, more Asian parents have begun to send their children to the United States for high school or college because of the intense academic pressure and competition at home. These youths, known as "parachute kids," sometimes come to live on their own or with relatives; in other cases, a parent may accompany them while they complete their studies. According to the U.S. Immigration and Naturalization Service (n.d.), Asians comprised 31% of the total immigrant population in 2000. Of these immigrants from Asia, only 22% were admitted under employment-based preferences, while 31% came under family-sponsored preferences and another 38% were admitted as immediate relatives of U.S. citizens.

One of the ways in which Asian Americans are diverse is their history in the United States: how and why an individual's family came to the United States. Such factors are important for health care professionals to consider when they work with Asian American clients. Thus, a Japanese American client who is fourth generation (i.e., great-grandparents were immigrants) and whose family experienced internment might have a very different sense of self and have different counseling needs than does a recent Asian Indian immigrant. Even various recent groups who have come to the United States have important differences. For example, the Hmong have historically relied on oral tradition and did not use a written language until recently. Thus, a health care practitioner might need to approach therapy very differently when working with an older Hmong client who lives in a rural area with extended family members than when working with a college-educated Taiwanese immigrant from the city.

RACISM AND DISCRIMINATION

Throughout their history, Americans of Asian ancestry as well as Asian immigrants have experienced hostility from the people and government of the United States in various forms, including prejudice, economic discrimination, political disenfranchisement, physical violence, social segregation, and incarceration as well as the immigration exclusion that has already been discussed in this chapter (Chan, 1991). For example, Chinese miners in the nineteenth century were routinely preyed on by robbers or driven off their claims by European American miners who realized that the Chinese enjoyed no protection under the law (Chan, 1991). Since Asian immigrants could not become naturalized citizens, they also could not vote and thus had no political power. In contrast to their popular image as passive and subservient, Asian Americans did make valiant efforts to stand up to oppression through legal means. However, the courts repeatedly determined that Asians were ineligible for naturalized citizenship. Asian Americans who were not citizens were also prohibited from owning land, although some did manage to circumvent these restrictions by transferring ownership to their American-born children.

Asian Americans also experienced various forms of social segregation. For example, antimiscegenation laws kept them from marrying outside their race. Because the early waves of Asian immigrants had consisted primarily of single men, these prohibitions had severe psychological and sociological implications for Asian communities. It was not until 1948 that antimiscegenation statutes were deemed unconstitutional in California and not until 1967 that all such laws were removed in the United States (Chan, 1991). American-born youth also experienced social segregation. For example, in the 1920s Survey of Race Relations directed by sociologist Robert E. Park, researchers noted that Asian American youth were forced to sit at the back of movie theaters and were barred from public recreational facilities such as swimming pools. Those who participated in high school athletics were often restricted to segregated teams (Fisk University Social Science Institute, 1946).

Japanese Internment

One of the most overt and striking examples of discrimination in recent history is the internment of more than 110,000 Japanese Americans during World War II. Although the order to relocate Japanese Americans on the West Coast was touted as a military necessity, evidence suggests that this was not the real reason and that racist resentment and animosity were the driving forces (Chan, 1991). In fact, U.S. government intelligence failed to find any evidence of Japanese American disloyalty. Moreover, even though the United States was also at war with Germany and Italy, only Americans of Japanese ancestry were singled out for this kind of discrimination. Advisors to the Justice Department explained that while German and Italian-Americans could be monitored, "the Occidental eye cannot rapidly distinguish one Japanese resident from another" (Chan, 1991, p. 124). It is also interesting to note that although Hawaii was in as much danger of being attacked as the West Coast was, Japanese Americans in Hawaii were not interned, because evacuating the 150,000 Japanese Americans there, who comprised 37% of the islands' population, would have crippled the state's economy. Historian Ronald Takaki (1989) alludes to the true motives behind the push for internment when he quotes the Grower-Shipper Vegetable Association from the *Saturday Evening Post:*

> We've been charged with wanting to get rid of the Japs for selfish reasons. We might as well be honest. We do. It's a question of whether the White man lives on the Pacific Coast or the brown man. They came into this valley to work, and they stayed to take over. . . . If all the Japs were removed tomorrow, we'd never miss them in two weeks, because the white farmers can take over and produce everything the Jap grows. (p. 389)

The experience of internment has left a tragic mark for Japanese Americans and continues to have impact today. When the order for internment was issued, Japanese Americans on the West Coast were forced to sell their property and goods at a fraction of their value; it is estimated that they suffered economic losses of more than $400 million (Fong, 2002). They were then sent to crude, makeshift camps with armed guards and barbed wire for the duration of the war. Two thirds of those interned were actually U.S. citizens; many had lived only in the United States and had little knowledge of or connection to Japan. Inside these camps, family and social structures fell apart. The status and authority of fathers, who were no longer breadwinners, began to disintegrate, while their sons acquired more independence and power. Children were no longer allowed to attend Japanese language schools and were instead encouraged by their European American teachers to become more Americanized. At the end of the war, Japanese American internees were discharged into a hostile society that still saw them as the enemy. It was difficult for many to reestablish their lives—socially and psychologically as well as economically—outside the barbed wire fences.

The experience of internment also drove a deep wedge between those who were proud of their Japanese heritage and resented the internment, and those who desperately wanted to be accepted as Americans. These issues became especially pronounced when the U.S. government required interned Japanese Americans to sign loyalty oaths forswearing allegiance to the Japanese emperor. Bitter divisions broke out within families and within the community about how to answer these questions, partly because answering implied that one held such allegiance in the first place. In the end, the majority complied with the loyalty tests. During this time, Japanese Americans were also being recruited to serve in the military in segregated units. Many resented being asked to serve a country that had imprisoned them and their families, whereas others saw this service as an opportunity to prove their loyalty as Americans. In the end, 23,000 Japanese Americans served in the U.S. military during World War II, and the 442nd Nisei Regimental Combat Team distinguished itself as the most highly decorated unit in the U.S. military for its size and length of service.

The Civil Liberties Act was finally passed in 1988; it provided an official apology as well as financial redress for surviving Japanese Americans who had been interned during World War II. However, this act cannot dissolve the schisms that developed during the internment and that still remain in the Japanese American community. Moreover, the intense pressures put on Japanese Americans in the camps to acculturate have left an imprint on the community; some researchers have noted that Japanese Americans tend to be more acculturated than other Asian American groups (see Nagata, 1998). During this time, other Asian Americans felt little sense of kinship with the Japanese Americans who were interned. Instead, they were careful to differentiate themselves. For example, shopkeepers put up signs proclaiming "We are not Japanese" or individuals wore buttons stating "I am Chinese." It was not until the Asian American movement in the 1960s that Americans of diverse Asian ancestries began to recognize commonalities in their histories and experiences.

Employment

The stories of Japanese internment or Asian exclusion laws may now seem distant because overt forms of discrimination based on race are no longer legal in the United States. However, Asian Americans continue to experience various forms of prejudice, discrimination, and racism. For example, Asian Americans, like other peoples of color, share an ongoing history of discrimination with regard to employment. Asian workers were originally recruited to this country for difficult and backbreaking jobs that could not otherwise be filled and were routinely paid less than White workers. As Asians gravitated toward urban centers, they found limited opportunities for employment; most jobs were menial, low-status jobs. Many Chinese men, for example, ended up opening laundries. Contrary to popular perception, this was not because washing clothes was traditionally a male occupation in China but because this was one of the few occupations that the host society deemed appropriate for them (Siu, 1987). Second-generation Asian Americans did not fare much better. Born and raised in the United States and educated in American schools, they expected to enjoy all the rights and privileges of citizenship. However, because of the prejudice they faced in American society, even those with college degrees found it difficult to practice their professions outside their ethnic enclaves.

Compared to the earlier waves, Asian immigrants since 1965 have generally come with higher levels of educational and professional skills; yet they too have experienced discrimination in the workforce. Some Asian immigrants have been unable to transfer their professional and educational backgrounds to commensurate jobs in the United States because of difficulties with licensing requirements and language barriers as well as overt forms of prejudice and discrimination. Thus, some Asian immigrants have experienced a downward mobility from the status of a professional in their home country to a small business owner in the United States (e.g., Carino, Fawcett, Gardner, & Arnold, 1990; Min, 1995). Whereas the American public might see small business ownership as evidence that these immigrants have achieved the "American Dream," these mom-and-pop shops are in reality a disguised form of cheap labor in which many businesses fail and others stay afloat by extracting long hours of unpaid labor from family members (Light & Bonacich, 1988; Fong, 2002). Even those immigrants who have managed to maintain their professional status have found discrimination in other forms. For example, many immigrant physicians were only able to find work in less desirable subspecialties or settings (Takaki, 1989).

Compared to earlier periods in the United States when Asian Americans were restricted from certain occupations or forbidden to practice professions outside ethnic enclaves, today the professional and occupational status of Asian Americans seems to have improved. However, Asian Americans today continue to experience discrimination that is more subtle, that takes the form of the glass ceiling or discrepancies in promotions and salaries. Although Asian Americans in the school setting are perceived to be achievement oriented, hard working, and eager to learn, in the workplace they are viewed as passive, unassertive, and too technically oriented and as having poor social skills or leadership potential (Fong, 2002). Along these lines, the Federal Glass Ceiling Commission released a report in 1995 that noted that of the top 1,000 industrial firms and 500 largest businesses in the United States, only 3% of senior managers were people of color. Like other peoples of color, Asian Americans have pushed up against this glass ceiling, which, though invisible, is a real barrier to positions in upper management. In her detailed study of Caucasian, African American, and Asian American engineers, sociologist Joyce Tang (2000) found that both Asian Americans and African Americans were significantly disadvantaged in terms of career mobility and that they lacked equal access to management positions. Even in Silicon Valley, where Asian Americans comprise 30% of high-tech professionals, a Pacific Studies Center study found that Whites held 80% of managerial positions whereas Asian Americans held just 12.5% (Abate, 1993, cited in Fong, 2002).

Asian Americans also experience discrimination in the government and public sectors, as shown by Kim and Lewis's (1994) comparison of Asian Americans to non-Hispanic Whites in federal government. These researchers found in 1992 that even though Asian Americans had higher median education than did White males, they held lower-level positions, and that White males were twice as likely as Asian American males to hold supervisory positions. Likewise, the relative status of Asian American women with regard to mean grade and supervisory status declined between 1978 and 1992 even though Asian American women generally had higher levels of education than did their White counterparts. In response to criticism that these findings might be related to Asian American immigrants' lack of fluency in English, Lewis and Kim (1997) reexamined and expanded their study. They analyzed a sample of male military veterans in federal employment, because veterans are generally native or near-native speakers of English. However, the results of this analysis showed that the employment grade gap actually tripled in size!

It is not surprising, then, that there are also significant discrepancies between Asian Americans and Whites in terms of salaries for comparable jobs. In their analysis of salaries among scientists and engineers, Ong and Blumberg (1994) found a consistent pattern in which median salaries of Asian Americans were significantly lower (up to 10%) than were those of non-Hispanic Whites with the same level of education. This pattern was also found in a National Science Foundation (2000) study of Asian American and White scientists and engineers between the ages of 40 and 49, a period in which workers are generally in their professional prime. The results of this study indicated that the median salary for Asian Americans was $50,000 versus $60,000 for Whites. More recently, a task force study of Lawrence Livermore Laboratory examined claims of racial bias in hiring, salaries, and promotions and found an average difference of nearly $1,000 *per month* between Asian American and White workers (Tansey, 1999).

Education

In addition to discrimination in the workforce, Asian Americans have a history of suffering discrimination with regard to education. For example, Chinese children in San Francisco were kept in segregated schools until the 1930s, and Chinese children in Mississippi were not allowed into White schools until 1950 (Chan, 1991). Although overt segregation in schools may no longer be an issue, there have been allegations in recent years about informal quotas used to control the numbers of Asian Americans in elite colleges and universities (Takagi, 1992). For example, in 1983, Asian American students at Brown University observed a disturbing trend: Although the admit rate for Asian Americans to Brown in 1975 had been 44%, by 1983 this figure had gone down to just 14%, even though in this same time period the number of Asian Americans applying to Brown had increased eightfold (Asian American Students Association of Brown University, 1983, cited in Fong, 2002). Similar patterns were observed at other Ivy League universities as well as at the University of California campuses, where admit rates for Asian American applicants were lower than for White students and where the academic qualifications of Asian Americans who were granted admission were found to be higher than those of White students (Takagi, 1992). None of these universities admitted to any wrongdoing, but some did acknowledge that there might be a problem in how Asian American applications were being evaluated.

These controversies still have not been completely resolved; these are complicated issues that cannot be determined merely through statistical analyses (Min, 1995). In fact, some of the discrepancies in admit rates for Whites and Asian Americans were eventually explained by the preferential treatment shown to athletes and children of alumni, the majority of whom are White. However, these investigations also revealed some of the hostilities and biases against Asian American students. Asian American students were commonly stereotyped as "nerds" who negatively impacted other students by raising class curves and taking precious spots away from other groups (Takaki, 1989). In their research, Bunzel and Au (1987) discovered various types of racial stereotyping among college administrators who perceived Asian American students to lack appreciation for a well-rounded liberal education, to be too career oriented, and to lack interest in public service. Some officials have made the argument that Asian Americans are overrepresented in higher education compared to their numbers in the general population. However, this argument is applied selectively; for example, children of alumni are also overrepresented on college campuses compared to the general population, but this inequality is rarely acknowledged as a problem. In prior decades, this rationale was used to limit the number of Jewish students at elite institutions. Moreover, the argument betrays a lack of appreciation for the social, economic, and ethnic diversity among Asian Americans (Fong, 2002).

THE MODEL MINORITY

In a racial tapestry in which the Black-White paradigm dominates, Asian Americans have occupied an ambiguous status in American society. They have been lauded as the "model minority," a term that was first coined in the mid-1960s by journalists who praised the academic achievements and economic successes of Asian Americans. It is no coincidence that this characterization of Asian Americans first appeared at a time when other racial/ethnic minority groups were calling for government action to remedy the long-standing history of racism and discrimination in this country. By holding up Asian Americans as the model minority, the implicit message was that if other minority groups would only emulate the successful strategies of Asian Americans, they too could achieve the American Dream! However, by ignoring important socioeconomic realities, this seemingly complimentary stereotype has had an insidious impact on Asian Americans. For one, it has fueled competition and resentment and has driven a wedge between Asian Americans and other racial/ethnic communities, as noted in a 1992 report by the U.S. Commission on Civil Rights. This report also stated that the model minority myth glosses over serious social and economic problems faced by some Asian Americans. This myth also distracts attention from the continuing overt as well as subtle forms of racial discrimination faced by Asian Americans, and it places extreme pressure on Asian American youth to succeed in school.

Education, Occupation, and Income

When data about Asian American education, employment, and income is examined in detail, the gleaming image of the model minority loses its luster and reveals a more complex and diverse reality. For example, according to 1999 census figures, 42% of Asian Pacific Americans 25 years of age and over have completed at least four years of college education compared to 28% of non-Hispanic Whites (Fong, 2002). However, when data for various subgroups (i.e., sex, ethnicity) are analyzed, a less uniform pattern emerges. For example, less than 4% of Cambodian, Laotian, and Hmong women reported completing college compared to 66% of Asian Indian men. Thus, data indicate that while some Asian Americans are highly educated, others are not, and it is important for counselors and educators not to make inaccurate assumptions about Asian Americans' access to or level of education.

Similarly, there is significant diversity in terms of occupational status and income level among Asian Americans. For example, a report by the U.S. Bureau of the Census (2000) showed that compared to non-Hispanic Whites, a larger percentage of Asian Pacific Islanders were represented in both managerial/professional occupations and in service occupations. Ong and Hee (1993) found that 12% of Asian American men earned less than $6 per hour compared to 9% of non-Hispanic White men, and that 20% of Asian American men earned incomes less than $15,000 per year compared to 14% of non-Hispanic White men. Asian American women seemed to fare somewhat better than non-Hispanic White women; 21% (versus 22% of non-Hispanic White women) earned less than $6 per hour, and 39% (versus 41% of non-Hispanic White women) earned less than $15,000 per year. Thus, it is important to recognize the diversity in occupational and economic status among Asian Americans, especially with respect to factors such as gender.

Reports of median family income can present a misleading picture of the economic status of Asian Americans. The majority of Asian Americans tend to live in urban areas that have high costs of living, whereas European Americans reside in regions throughout the country with variable costs of living. Fong (2002) notes that when median incomes are analyzed for Asian Americans and European Americans in five large cities (Chicago, Houston, Los Angeles, New York, and San Francisco), they show that Asian American median incomes are significantly lower than those of European Americans. In addition, Asian American families tend to have more workers contributing to the household income. Fong points out that according to the 1990 census, Asian Americans were comparable to the general U.S. population in the percentages of households with one worker and two workers. However, there was a much larger gap between the percentages of households with three or more workers. Almost 20% of Asian American households reported having three or more workers, compared to just 13% of the general U.S. population. Again, when subgroups are analyzed, these differences become more marked. For example, almost 52% of Asian Indians reported two-worker households and almost 30% of Filipino Americans stated that there were three or more workers in their household. In addition, the low unemployment figures for Asian Americans can be interpreted as high levels of *underemployment* rather than as an indicator of economic success; many Asian Americans would rather work low-paid, part-time positions than receive public assistance (Chan, 1991)

Fong (2002) suggests that it would be more accurate to examine the per capita income of workers rather than family income to evaluate the economic status of Asian Americans. Given that Asian Americans possess relatively high levels of education and that many reside in expensive urban areas, it would be reasonable to expect relatively high per capita income. However, Ong and Hee's (1993) study found significant disparities between education and income. According to the results of this study, even though they had higher overall levels of education, Asian American men earned less per hour ($15.40 versus $15.90) and reported lower per capita income ($26,760 versus $28,880) than did White men. Although Asian American households may appear to have relatively high median family incomes, this statistic does not take into account the higher levels of education, the number of workers per family, and the regional costs of living. Moreover, a focus on median incomes ignores the significant numbers of Asian American families who are actually living at or below poverty level. According to the U.S. Bureau of the Census (2002a), in 2001, 10.2% of Asian Pacific Islanders lived below the poverty level compared to 7.8% of non-Hispanic Whites.

Implications and Consequences

When the status of Asian Americans is more closely examined, it becomes clear that the image of the model minority is actually an inaccurate one. Even though this "positive" stereotype has been embraced by some Asian Americans, it is ultimately a damaging and harmful myth. When all Asian Americans are considered to be affluent and well educated, the needs of those who do not fit this profile are neglected, and social services and public resources are not accessible to them. The myth of the model minority can also damage the psyche of individual Asian Americans by setting unrealistic expectations. It puts undue pressure on Asian American youth to succeed academically, and it ignores the realities of racism and discrimination faced by Asian Americans in the workplace. Not all Asian American youths are valedictorians of their high schools and headed to Ivy League universities; for example, among some Southeast Asian communities, many youths are joining gangs and dropping out of high school, but these problems are not given sufficient attention and resources from the larger society.

Moreover, what must it be like emotionally and psychologically for an Asian American who has a learning disability when he is constantly presumed to fit the model minority image? How does an Asian American middle manager make sense of the fact that she cannot get promoted beyond the glass ceiling? When institutional and societal barriers are not recognized, it becomes easier for individuals to internalize blame for not fitting into the model minority image.

The myth of the model minority can also create false hopes for Asian Americans of being accepted by the larger society as an "honorary" White American. There is a general belief that Asian Americans have not been persecuted like other racial/ethnic minorities, even though history has proven otherwise. The reality is that Asian Americans have encountered the same kinds of persecution as other people of color, yet Asian Americans have often been neglected in the Black/White paradigm of race in America. Moreover, when Asian Americans are held up as a model minority, they are being used as scapegoats and as buffers between the haves and the have-nots. One striking example of this situation took place during the Los Angeles riots of 1992, when economic frustrations and rage against the White police officers who had beaten Rodney King were instead channeled toward Korean American merchants. People who characterize Asian Americans as a model minority are in fact reinforcing the image of America as an egalitarian society in which any individual can succeed if he or she just works hard enough. According to this viewpoint, those people who have not achieved the American Dream are themselves at fault. Thus, this myth of Asian Americans as a model minority has been used to chastise other racial/ethnic minority groups. At the same time, many marginalized Americans have come to resent Asian Americans, who are lauded as shining examples of the American Dream.

CONCEPTUALIZING IDENTITY

Although identity is a complex construct for all individuals, it may be particularly so for certain Asian Americans. Although it is beyond the scope of this chapter to provide a detailed discussion, it must be noted that for some Asian Americans, other identities such as gender and sexual orientation may be as important and salient as ethnic/racial identity, and that these multiple identities can intersect in rich and complex ways. Some Asian Americans identify not only with an ancestral Asian culture or the dominant European American culture but also with other ethnic minority cultures as well. For example, a Filipino American who grew up in an African American neighborhood might identify strongly with African American culture and self-identify in that way. In addition, the term *1.5 generation* is used to refer to those immigrants who were born elsewhere but raised primarily in the United States. Many 1.5-generation Asian Americans find themselves straddling and mediating between two cultures. Increasing numbers of Asian Americans are also multiracial and often identify with two or more cultures or racial identities. In fact, it is estimated that one in four Asian American children is multiracial (Zia, 2000). However, these individuals have often been forced to choose one racial category; it was not until 2000 that the U.S. Bureau of the Census allowed respondents to mark more than one ethnic or racial category. Whereas multiracial Asian Americans have generally grown up in the United States, Amerasians are mixed-race Asians who were born in Asia; many of them are children of U.S. military men. Finally, adoptees comprise another distinct and growing group of Asian Americans. Significant numbers of Asian orphans have been adopted by American families. Estimates indicate that almost 100,000 Korean children have been adopted by American families since the 1950s; in recent years, many children from China have also been adopted (Fong, 2002). Some Asian Americans have also had the experience of returning to the country of their ancestry and realizing that they are outsiders in that culture as well. The experience of not fitting into a category, of not being fully accepted as American or Asian can be difficult and confusing for many Asian Americans, who are then left to carve out for themselves what their ethnic identity means to them.

For all Asian Americans, experiences with racism can impact how they feel about their ethnic identity (Uba, 1994). Racism can cause some individuals to distance themselves from their ethnic identity and even internalize negative feelings about their ethnic group. Conversely, some people can respond to racism with an increased sensitivity to even subtle forms of racism (Chan, 1991). The preponderance of stereotypes and membership in a devalued group can also make it difficult for Asian Americans and other ethnic minorities to develop positive identities (Spencer & Markstrom-Adams, 1990). In her recent analysis of Asian American psychology, Laura Uba (2002) observes the common conflation of race and nationality. Asian Americans, even those without any accent, are routinely asked "Where are you from?" When they answer, for example, "Chicago" or "San Francisco," the response is inevitably "No, where are you *really* from?" Such questions indicate not only ignorance about the difference between a person's ethnicity and nationality, but also how Asian Americans continue to be perceived as the "other" and how they are not accepted as "real" Americans (Uba, 2002). A Japanese American who is fourth generation and has never been to Japan may be expected to speak the language and be knowledgeable about Japanese history. In contrast, few people would expect a third-generation French American to speak French and know details about the French Revolution. Moreover, few Americans of European descent have been told to "go back where you came from," but that statement is familiar to many Asian Americans.

Asian Americans are a diverse group, comprised of people from various national origins, ethnic groups, languages, religions, socioeconomic backgrounds, and immigration histories. To this day, many Asian Americans prefer to identify themselves in terms of their specific ethnic group rather than as "Asian American." For example, Chinese Americans who speak Cantonese and those who speak Mandarin identify with different regions of China and speak different dialects. There are also ethnic Chinese whose families have resided in other countries for generations. Thus, for example, a health care practitioner might work with an ethnic Chinese client from Vietnam who may self-identify as Chinese, Vietnamese, and American. Even immigrants from the same ethnic background may have historical conflicts that influence how they view each other. For example, a Vietnamese American who was a member of the Viet Cong and a Vietnamese American who was a South Vietnamese military official may harbor negative feelings toward one another even though they share language, culture, and values. Asian Americans also vary in terms of their generational status. A person who was born in Asia and immigrated to the United States as an adult is considered first generation and may even self-identify as Filipino or Korean rather than Filipino American, Korean American, or Asian American.

In recent decades, there has been a growing consciousness of a pan-Asian ethnic identity. During the 1960s and the civil rights movement, some Asian Americans began to recognize that they shared a common struggle with other racial minorities and that Asian immigrants as a group had common interests and experiences that transcended cultural differences and animosities based on historical conflicts in Asia (Zia, 2000). In describing the panethnic movement, Espiritu (1992) notes that external factors can facilitate the forging of alliances among diverse groups. Espiritu points out that in earlier years, the Bureau of the Census tried to lump all Asian groups together into one homogeneous category; Census Bureau categories have often been arbitrary and inconsistent, reflecting administrative needs rather than meaningful cultural and racial differences acknowledged by the group. Ironically, Asian American activists had to respond as a unified voice in order to express their unique identities and to demand a more detailed and accurate count of Asian American subgroups. Asian American activists have also come to understand the advantages of being counted together as a larger group in order to gain political power and recognition, and with it, the distribution of state resources. In addition, the recent surge in anti-Asian sentiment and violence has helped unify Asian American groups across ethnic, class, generational, and political divisions in order to forge this pan-Asian consciousness.

CULTURAL VALUES

Health care professionals who work with Asian American clients need some understanding of Asian cultural values. Kim, Atkinson, and Yang (1999) empirically identified 14 Asian value domains and then discussed their applications to counseling in a follow-up article (Kim, Atkinson, & Umemoto, 2001). These researchers caution that Asian Americans comprise an extremely diverse group and that there are significant differences within Asian ethnic groups. Thus, some of the cultural values that the researchers identified may not be applicable to a specific Asian culture or to an individual client. The full articles provide a detailed discussion of Asian cultural values; they are briefly reviewed here as an overview of Asian American experiences and perspectives. Kim and his colleagues (1999) state that traditional Asian Americans emphasize collectivism (i.e., importance of group over individual interests and goals), maintenance of interpersonal harmony, reciprocity, and placing other's needs ahead of one's own. The authors note the importance of family, filial piety, respect for elders, conformity to family and social norms, and deference to authority figures. In addition, the authors point out that Asian Americans value self-control, self-effacement, and avoidance of family shame and that individuals are expected to resolve their own psychological problems. The researchers also note that many Asian Americans place an emphasis on educational and occupational achievement.

Many Asian immigrants come from societies in which education is a primary vehicle for upward mobility and social status. For example, in some countries, such as China or Korea, even peasants could aspire to wealth and status for themselves and their families by passing difficult university and government entrance exams. Many Asian immigrants have experienced various forms of discrimination and racism in the workforce and have come to view education as one protective buffer. Even those Asian immigrants who were professionals in their home countries have often found their careers impeded by discrimination or language barriers. As a result, some of these parents have come to view scientific and technical careers as safer avenues for their children. Indeed, data indicate that one factor that allows Asian Americans to maintain some economic parity with White Americans is their higher levels of education. Many Asian immigrants have come to the United States specifically so that their children can have better futures. Many Asian immigrants think in terms of the family unit rather than individuals, and Asian parents are often willing to make extreme sacrifices for their children, with the expectation that the children will reciprocate by achieving academic and occupational "success" and taking care of their parents later on. Thus, Asian American parents may expect to have a say in their children's choice of a college major, occupation, and even marriage partner.

Although traditional, individualistic models of psychotherapy emphasize the importance of differentiating from one's parents and making one's own choices, health care practitioners need to be sensitive to the cultural values that may oblige Asian American clients to consider the needs and wishes of their parents when making individual choices. For example, practitioners may encounter young Asian Americans who feel significant pressure from their parents to excel academically or to choose specific majors or careers. Practitioners should also be mindful of how religious values may intersect with Asian American cultural values. For example, Catholicism is important to many Americans of Vietnamese and Filipino descent and may impact their worldview and the ways in which they approach counseling. On a related note, ethnic churches have provided an important social support for many Asian Americans (e.g., Korean Americans).

CURRENT STATUS

In addition to understanding the history of Asian Americans in the United States, mental health professionals must be knowledgeable about the current status of Asian Americans. To this day, Asian Americans are plagued by pernicious stereotypes that impact not only how others see them but also how they feel about themselves. Jessica Hagedorn, a prominent Asian American writer, comments on these stereotypes:

> Suzie Wong. Flower Drum Song. Dragon Lady. Madame Butterfly. China Doll. Tokyo Rose. Fu Manchu. Charlie Chan. Mr. Moto. Ming the Merciless. Little Brown Brother. Savage. Mysterious. Inscrutable. Sinister. Exotic. Submissive.

Diminutive. Indolent. Insolent. Sexless. Sexy. Mail Order Bride. Model Minority.
I could go on and on, listing familiar and not so familiar stereotypes, drawing
from the abundant arsenal of dehumanizing images that assault us daily in America, as we sleep and read, as we eat, work and study. (cited in Zia, 2000, p. 135)

Asian women are often stereotyped as submissive geishas or dragon ladies. Asian
men are commonly portrayed as sinister martial arts masters or as emasculated
geeks. Such caricatures lead many Asian Americans to internalize their feelings
of embarrassment or shame (Zia, 2000). Moreover, the media's blending of Asian
identities contributes to the general perception that all Asians are the same. A
striking example of such generalization was Disney's high-budget production of
Mulan, which features Chinese soldiers dressed in Japanese samurai uniforms
(Zia, 2000). It is no wonder, then, that Asian Americans are commonly identified
as members of another Asian ethnic group or that the public has trouble differentiating between Americans of Asian descent and Asian nationals.

Perhaps the most famous and tragic case of mistaken identity was that of Vincent Chin. In 1982, at the height of the economic recession in Detroit's auto industry, a young Chinese American man, Vincent Chin, was viciously beaten and
killed by two disgruntled unemployed auto workers. These men assumed Vincent
to be Japanese and blamed him (as the symbol of the Japanese auto industry) for
taking away their jobs. These two killers pleaded guilty to manslaughter; a Michigan judge initially sentenced each to three years of probation and $3,780 in fines
and court costs. However, both men were subsequently acquitted. The murder of
Vincent Chin and the lenience of the sentences shocked and mobilized Asian
Americans all over the country. For many, it confirmed the sense that Asian Americans were truly second-class citizens who could not count on protection under
the law, and it emphasized the importance of panethnic political activism.

Since then, Asian American activists have called for law enforcement agencies to maintain statistics on reported cases of hate bias incidents and for stronger
penalties against those convicted of hate-related crimes. The 1999 audit by the
National Asian Pacific American Legal Consortium documented 486 incidents of
anti-Asian violence, up from 429 incidents in 1998. Even when racial epithets are
hurled at Asian Americans before a physical attack, law enforcement officials are
wary of acknowledging these as hate crimes; moreover, the media rarely cover
such stories. In short, Asian Americans who are the targets of verbal or physical
harassment often find it difficult to get officials to take such threats seriously and
to acknowledge that these attacks are *racially* motivated (Fong, 2002; Zia, 2000).
Moreover, since September 11, there has been a resurgence of violence against
Asian Americans; in particular, South Asians, who have been mistaken for Middle Easterners, have been repeatedly harassed and attacked throughout the country. Perhaps not surprisingly, law enforcement and the press have been relatively
quiet and unresponsive to such incidents. Is this unresponsiveness related to the
image of Asian Americans as a model minority and as honorary Whites who have
not suffered like other people of color have?

In addition to being victims of hate crimes, Asian Americans have been subject to other forms of renewed suspicion and hostility by the American public,
even prior to September 11. As Asian economies have prospered, some Ameri-

cans have come to resent Asian Americans, who represent the dreaded Asian "invader." In the late 1980s, New Yorkers bemoaned the Japanese buyout of Rockefeller Center. However, Mitsubishi's "buyout" of Rockefeller Center represented only 14% ownership of the property. In fact, two thirds of the foreign investment in the United States came not from Asia but from Europe, but European investment did not elicit the same kinds of fearful responses (Zia, 2000).

Similarly, the political activities of Asian Americans have been unduly scrutinized. In 1996, Asian American political activists launched a vigorous political fund-raising campaign in an effort to gain more recognition from the Clinton administration. During this period, Asian American donors were accused of trying to influence U.S. policy and even spying for China. In the end, a small number of Asian Americans were found guilty of campaign finance violations. However, the transgressions of a few were generalized to the entire Asian American community. Meanwhile, similar violations by others (e.g., Dole fund-raiser Simon Fireman, German Thomas Kramer) were only cursorily reviewed by the press; certainly, these Americans were not suspected of being foreign spies. Helen Zia (2000) describes a sense of déjà vu for some Asian Americans:

> The willingness of people to associate Americans of Asian descent with spying, corruption, "dual loyalties," and other sundry un-American acts was reminiscent of the war hysteria of the 1940s, when all Japanese American families on the West Coast had their household cameras and maps confiscated and Japanese American farmers were accused of planting their crops in patterns that would aid Japanese airplanes in case of an air attack. The Asian Americans who came to the United States after the 1965 Immigration Act got a first hand lesson in how quickly today's model minority could become tomorrow's demon despised. (pp. 299–300)

Another story emblematic of the current status of Asian Americans is that of Dr. Wen Ho Lee. In March 1999, Dr. Lee, a Taiwanese-born U.S. citizen, was fired from his job as a research scientist at Los Alamos Nuclear Laboratory after he was accused of giving U.S. nuclear weapon secrets to China. Dr. Lee was never formally charged with espionage; however, he was imprisoned for nine months, where he was subjected to intimidation, harassment, and a grueling government investigation that ultimately failed to build a credible case against him. Timothy Fong (2002) notes:

> The Wen Ho Lee case shows how racial profiling against Asian Americans comes from a severe lack of understanding and only serves to create conflicting images of visibility and invisibility for Asian Americans in the minds of many in the United States today. Asian Americans are visible only in such stereotypes as "perpetual foreigners," "overachievers," and the "model minority." This often leads to irrational thoughts, acts, and resentment. (p. 3)

As long as Asian Americans are identifiable by their distinct non-European phenotype, they will continue to be subject to scrutiny in times of economic or political instability. Health care professionals, like other Americans, may assume that Asian Americans are a generally affluent and educated group that has not experienced significant discrimination like other minority groups. However, history and current data indicate otherwise. Practitioners must recognize not only that Asian American clients and their ancestors have endured a history of racism and discrimination but also that these practices are still occurring. Mental health professionals can help their Asian American clients work through their internal issues and can help them understand the external and societal factors that contribute to psychological distress.

Exercises

1. You are a therapist at an HMO, and a Cambodian American woman in her 30s has been referred to you by her physician. She is complaining of a long-standing history of headaches and stomach problems, but her doctor has been unable to identify any medical conditions. The client reports that she always feels stressed and that she frequently has nightmares and difficulty sleeping. You find out that this woman was born in Cambodia and fled the country in the early 1980s with her family. The client currently works for county social services but also helps manage her family's sandwich shop. The client notes that she always feels tired at work and is frustrated and bored by her job. The client is unsure why her doctor has referred her for counseling.
    a) How might this client's experiences in Cambodia and migration to the United States affect her present condition?
    b) What are the various issues and stressors in this client's life?
2. You are a counselor at a large public university. A Korean American male undergraduate has been referred to you by the residential college staff for alcohol violations. The client is sullen and states that he just doesn't feel very motivated about school and would rather party with his friends. He says that he used to get As and Bs but then stopped trying to excel in school because he felt that nothing he ever did seemed good enough for his parents. The client notes that his parents are disappointed that he is going to the state school and are hoping that he will at least get a degree that will ensure a stable career. The client says that the only thing he is remotely interested in are his film classes, but his parents have threatened to cut off his tuition if he continues to take these "frivolous" classes.
    a) How might you help this client resolve some of the conflicts between him and his family?
    b) What sociocultural issues do you need to consider in order to understand this client's situation?

REFERENCES

Bunzel, J. H., & Au, J. K. D. (1987, Spring). Diversity or discrimination? Asian Americans in college. *The Public Interest, 87,* 56.

Carino, B., Fawcett, J., Gardner, R., & Arnold, F. (1990). *The new Filipino immigrants to the United States: Increasing diversity and change* (East-West Population Institute Paper Series No. 115). Honolulu: East-West Center Population Institute.

Chan, S. (1991). *Asian Americans: An interpretive history.* New York: Twayne.

Espiritu, Y. L. (1992). *Asian American panethnicity: Bridging institutions and identities.* Philadelphia: Temple University Press.

Federal Glass Ceiling Commission. (1995, March). *Good for business: Making full use of the nation's human capital.* Retrieved November 12, 2002, from http://www.dol.gov/asp/programs/history/reich/reports/ceiling.pdf

Fisk University Social Science Institute. (1946). *Orientals and their cultural adjustment: Interviews, life histories, and social adjustment experiences of Chinese and Japanese of varying backgrounds and length of residence in the United States.* Nashville, TN: Fisk University Social Science Institute.

Fong, T. P. (2002). *The contemporary Asian American experience: Beyond the model minority myth.* Upper Saddle River, NJ: Prentice-Hall.

Kim, B. S. K., Atkinson, D. R., & Umemoto, D. (2001). Asian cultural values and the counseling process: Current knowledge and directions for future research. *Counseling Psychologist, 29,* 570–603.

Kim, B. S. K., Atkinson, D. R., & Yang, P. H. (1999). The Asian Values scale: Development factor analysis, validation, and reliability. *Journal of Counseling Psychology, 46,* 342–352.

Kim, P. S., & Lewis, G. B. (1994, May–June). Asian Americans in public service: Success, diversity, and discrimination. *Public Administration Review, 54,* 285–290.

Light, I., & Bonacich, E. (1988). *Immigrant entrepreneurs: Koreans in Los Angeles, 1965–1982.* Berkeley: University of California Press.

Min, P. G. (1995). Korean Americans. In P. G. Min (Ed.), *Asian Americans: Contemporary trends and issues* (pp. 199–231). Thousand Oaks, CA: Sage.

Nagata, D. K. (1998). Internment and intergenerational relations. In L. C. Lee & N. W. S. Zane (Eds.), *Handbook of Asian American psychology* (pp. 433–456). Thousand Oaks, CA: Sage.

National Asian Pacific American Legal Consortium. (1999). *Audit of violence against Asian Pacific Americans.* Retrieved November 15, 2002, from http://www.napalc.org/literature/annual_report/1999.html

National Science Foundation. (2000). *Women, minorities, and persons with disabilities in science and engineering: 2000.* Retrieved October 10, 2002, from www.nsf.gov/sbe/srs/nsf00327/

Ong, P., & Blumberg, E. (1994). Scientists and engineers. In P. Ong (Ed.), *The state of Asian Pacific America: Economic diversity, issues, and policies* (pp. 177–179). Los Angeles: LEAP Asian Pacific Public Policy Institute and UCLA Asian American Studies Center.

Ong, P., Bonacich, E., & Cheng, L. (1994). *The new Asian immigration in Los Angeles and global restructuring.* Philadelphia: Temple University.

Ong, P., & Hee, S. J. (1993). Work issues facing Asian Pacific Americans: Labor policy. *The state of Asian Pacific America: Policy issues to the year 2020* (pp. 11–24). Los Angeles: LEAP Asian Pacific American Public Policy Institute and UCLA Asian American Studies Center.

Siu, P. P. C. (1987). *The Chinese laundryman: A study in social isolation.* New York: New York University Press.

Spencer, M., & Markstrom-Adams, C. (1990). Identity processes among racial and ethnic minority children in America. *Child Development, 61,* 290–310.

Takagi, D. (1992). *The retreat from race.* New Brunswick, NJ: Rutgers University Press.

Takaki, R. (1989). *Strangers from a different shore.* Boston: Little, Brown.

Tang, J. (2000). *Doing engineering: The career attainment and mobility of Caucasian, Black, and Asian American engineers.* Boulder, CO: Rowman and Littlefield.

Tansey, B. (1999, December 24). Nine Asians at lab file bias claim. *San Francisco Chronicle,* A3.

Uba, L. (1994). *Asian Americans: Personality patterns, identity, and mental health.* New York: Guilford Press.

Uba, L. (2002). *A postmodern psychology of Asian Americans.* Albany: State University of New York Press.

U.S. Bureau of the Census. (2000). *The Asian and Pacific Islander population in the United States: Population characteristics, March 1999.* Washington, DC: Government Printing Office.

U.S. Bureau of the Census. (2002a, September). *Poverty in the United States: 2001.* Retrieved November 15, 2002, from http://www.census.gov/prod/2002pubs/p60-219.pdf

U.S. Bureau of the Census. (2002b). *The Asian population: 2000.* Retrieved November 10, 2002, from http://www.census.gov/prod/2002pubs/c2kbr01-16.pdf

U.S. Commission on Civil Rights. (1992). *Civil rights issues facing Asian Americans in the 1990s.* Washington, DC: Government Printing Office.

U.S. Immigration and Naturalization Service. (n.d.). *Immigrants year 2000* (Advance Report to be published in *2000 Statistical Yearbook of the Immigration and Naturalization Service*). Retrieved November 12, 2002, from http://www.ins.usdoj.gov/graphics/aboutins/statistics/IMM00yrbk/IMM2000.pdf

Zia, H. (2000). *Asian American dreams: The emergence of an American people.* New York: Farrar, Straus, and Giroux.

CHAPTER 11 # Physical and Mental Health of Asian Americans

David Sue,
Western Washington University

The term *Asian American/Pacific Islander* (AA/PI) refers to approximately 28 Asian and 19 Pacific Islander groups that represent a wide array of cultures and languages (National Women's Health Information Center, 2002). National baseline data on AA/PI health issues are lacking. Physical and mental health statistics that do exist are often aggregated or combine the groups, subsequently ignoring the major differences that exist in the various subgroups subsumed under the heading of Asian and Pacific Islander. Sampling problems render interpretations problematic from the findings of national surveys and the surveys of the different AA/PI groups. Sample sizes are often too small for reliable conclusions or tend to focus on Asian Americans residing in high-density areas, which therefore limits generalization of the findings (National Center for Health Statistics, 1997). In addition to the between-group differences, there are large within-group differences that also influence physical and mental health issues and concerns. Although the majority of Asian Americans are recent immigrants or refugees, some come from families who have been in the United States for four or five generations and may be quite acculturated.

With these limitations in mind, I will first present the data on the health of the Asian American population and the possible impact of cultural values and beliefs as well as societal factors. Second, the mental health of Asian Americans will be considered in the context of biological, cultural, and societal influences.

PHYSICAL HEALTH INFORMATION ON ASIAN AMERICANS

In general, the AA/PI population would appear to be quite healthy. Asian American women and men have the highest life expectancy of any ethnic or racial group in the United States. However, when the data are disaggregated by specific AA/PI subgroup, wide discrepancies are found. The life expectancy of the following groups are as follows: Samoan (74.9 years), Native Hawaiian (77.2 years), Filipino (81.5 years), Japanese women (84.5 years), and Chinese women (86.1

years; National Women's Health Information Center, 2002). In fact, the age-adjusted death rate for Native Hawaiians is nearly twice that for the general population (Department of Health and Human Services [DHHS], 2002).

Many health conditions appear to disproportionately impact some AA/PI groups. Tuberculosis is one of the most serious problems facing the Asian American population compared to other racial groups in the United States. It is 13 times more common among Asian populations—especially those from Cambodia, China, Laos, Korea, India, Vietnam, and the Philippines—than among Whites. Hepatitis B, an inflammation of the liver, is 25 to 75 times more common among Samoans and immigrants from Cambodia, Laos, Vietnam, and China than among Whites. Asian American women are at particular risk for osteoporosis because of their relatively lower bone mass and density, smaller frames, and lower intake of calcium compared to other groups. Native Hawaiian women have the highest breast cancer death rate of any racial/ethnic group in the United States (National Women's Health Information Center, 2002). Cervical cancer incidence rates among Vietnamese women are nearly 5 times those of White women (Miller et al., 1996). Asian/Pacific Islander males, especially Vietnamese Americans, have the highest rate for liver cancer. The incidence rate for stomach cancers in both men and women is especially high among Korean, Vietnamese, Japanese, Alaska Native, and Hawaiian populations (National Cancer Institute, 2002). Acculturation to U.S. lifestyles is related to higher health risk factors for chronic diseases such as heart disease, diabetes, and cancers (Penn et al., 2000). For example, Asian American women born in the United States have a 60% higher risk of developing breast cancer than do Asian American women born in Asia (Ziegler et al., 1993).

Barriers to Health Care

Access to reliable and consistent health care is sometimes limited because of cultural and language differences as well as social and other barriers. The majority of Asian Americans are immigrants or refugees, and problems occur over their facility with English. Many are linguistically isolated. If residing in the United States illegally, they may not seek medical care for fear of deportation. Poverty or the lack of medical insurance may also prevent the seeking of treatment. In 1998 and 1999, nearly 21% of the AA/PI population was without health insurance compared to 11% of White Americans (U.S. Census Bureau, 2000b). The overall poverty rate is about 10.3% for AA/PI families versus 5.5% for Whites. However, even higher rates of poverty are found among Vietnamese, Hmong, Cambodian, and Laotian American populations (U.S. Census Bureau, 2000a).

The lack of knowledge of the risk factors related to diseases may also be a problem for specific groups of Asian Americans. In one study of Southeast Asian populations in Ohio, 94% did not know what high blood pressure is, nor did they know what could be done to prevent heart disease (Tamir & Cachola, 1994). Knowledge of hepatitis B, its treatment, and prevention among Cambodian American women in Seattle, Washington, was generally inaccurate. For example, the majority did not know that asymptomatic individuals could spread the disease.

More than two thirds of those women who were thought to be susceptible had not been vaccinated (Taylor, Jackson, Chan, Kuniyuki, &Yasui, 2002). Lack of knowledge can also result in failure to participate in screenings. The fact that Vietnamese women have a high rate of cervical cancer, nearly 6 times that of non-Latino Whites, may be due in part to low rates of cancer screening. According to the American Cancer Society (2002), only 67% of Asian/Pacific Islander women 18 years or older, versus 80% of White women the same age, have had a Pap test within the past three years. The lack of screening is higher among Southeast Asian groups. In a study of Vietnamese women living in Massachusetts, only about 50% reported having had a Pap test (Yi, 1994). In addition, Southeast Asian women tend to have more severe cervical cancer cases because of late diagnoses and are less likely to follow up with treatment (Carey & Gjerdingen, 1993). On average, Asian American and Pacific Island women also have significantly lower breast cancer screening rates than the national average (American Cancer Society, 2002).

Health Practices and Beliefs

Health practices and beliefs range from Asian Americans who are well acquainted with and accepting of Western-style views of health and sickness to those with traditional cultural beliefs and practices. Among Southeast Asian groups such as the Mien, Hmong, and Vietnamese, health and religion are intertwined (Ethnomed, 2001). Sickness is believed to come from the wrath of the gods. In this belief system, the physician is a priest who negotiates with the gods to reduce the sickness. Many Asian groups also employ a medicinal system based on Chinese medicine. In this system, living things are composed of four basic elements: air, fire, water, and earth, each with the associated characteristic of cold, hot, wet, and dry. This hot-cold belief is common to many Vietnamese regardless of educational status or occupation. Illness may be attributed to organic or physical problems; an imbalance of yin and yang; an obstruction of *chi* (or life energy); failure to be in harmony with nature; punishment for immoral behavior (in this or past lives); or a curse placed by an offended spirit. Most Vietnamese believe in organic causes of illness unless there is an obvious upset of supernatural forces, whereas most Hmong believe minor illness is organic but serious illness is supernaturally caused. Some Asian groups believe that Asians have different physiologic constitutions than Caucasians do and that Western medicines are "hot" and too potent for Asian physiology. In the hot-cold theory, illness is caused by an alteration in the natural balance between hot and cold elements in the universe. To restore balance and harmony, the intake of drugs, herbs, and foods is adjusted. Western medicines are considered hot, and herbal remedies are believed to have cooling properties. Because of these beliefs, there may be high levels of noncompliance with Western medications (Chen & Hawks, 1995). Asians often dilute prescribed medication or discontinue it when taking herbal medications. In one sample, a large percentage of Southeast Asian Americans reported using traditional health practices and medicines (69% of women and 39% of men). This use can be a problem because health insurance does not generally cover culturally accepted medical practices such as acupuncture and herbal medications (Buchwald, Panwala, & Hooton, 1992).

Among some Vietnamese who were interviewed regarding health practices and impediments to care, Jamin, Yoo, Moldoveanu, and Tran (1999) found the following health beliefs and reactions. To the Vietnamese, waiting to be seen in county facilities is considered degrading and an insult to pride. A Vietnamese would rather pay more money to be courteously and promptly treated by the physician. Many Vietnamese also show differences in receptivity to types of treatment. In terms of medical practices, most were willing to take medications in pill form, but only 30% were willing to take injections. There is a strong aversion to any procedure that punctures the skin. For example, only 7% believed amniocentesis was safe. More than one third believed that the chances of being cured of cancer were poor or impossible. There was also fear of certain screening tests. Some women believe a PAP smear would ruin their virginity or cause harm. Thus, traditional beliefs about health practices and illnesses can interfere with appropriate health care.

A recent national survey of adults 18 years and older regarding health care quality, "Quality of Health Care for Asian Americans" (Hughes, 2002), reported the following:

- In general, Asian Americans are less satisfied than other Americans are with health services. They expressed less confidence in their physicians and expressed more discontent about not being treated with dignity and respect than did other ethnic groups. Twice as many Asian Americans (11%) as the overall population (5%) reported that the physician did not understand their culture and background and that they would receive better treatment if they were of a different ethnicity.
- Overall satisfaction with medical services differed among the subgroups. Slightly more than one quarter of Chinese and Koreans were "very satisfied" with their health care versus nearly three quarters of Japanese.
- Preventive care was also lower among Asian Americans. Only 41% indicated having a physical exam during the past year and 70% indicated having their blood pressure checked, compared to 48% and 79% respectively of the overall population.
- 38% of Vietnamese and 36% of Japanese use herbal medicines; 24% of Koreans often use acupuncture, and 14% of Chinese consult with traditional healers.

The findings indicate that Asian Americans do not perceive the medical profession to be receptive to or understanding of cultural differences; this perception serves as a barrier for preventive care and health screenings.

MENTAL HEALTH

The report from the Surgeon General titled "Mental Health: Culture, Race, and Ethnicity" (DHHS, 2001) concluded that rates of mental illness among Asian and Pacific Islanders are not sufficiently studied to permit firm conclusions about overall prevalence. In addition, self-report data might be suspect because of the strong stigma involved in the admission of mental illness among this population. Because of the relatively low numbers of Asian Americans included in the surveys, the results are often aggregated, which masks between-group differences. Few epidemiological investigations of mental health in Asian populations exist.

Mental Disorders

Zhang and Snowden (1999) examined the ethnic differences in lifetime prevalence of major mental disorders in five communities in the United States. Some ethnic differences between Asian Americans and Whites were found. Asians had significantly lower rates of schizophreniform disorder and of manic and bipolar disorders. They also reported lower rates of drug and alcohol abuse and dependence and lower rates of panic disorder and somatization. Rates that were similar to Whites were found in major depression, dysthymia, obsessive-compulsive disorder, and phobia and anorexia nervosa. However, the samples from the five communities were not strictly representative of the U.S. population.

Some surveys have been done on specific locations or with specific populations. In a study of the prevalence of depression in the city of Seattle, Asian Americans had a prevalence rate that was slightly higher than for Whites but lower than that of African Americans and Hispanic Americans (Noh & Avison, 1996). Asian American women have the highest suicide rates among women ages 15 to 24 and over age 65 (O. M. Lum, 1995). Asian Americans also report higher levels of social anxiety than White Americans do (Okazaki, Liu, Longworth, & Minn, 2002).

Southeast Asian refugees are considered a high-risk group because many may have been exposed to catastrophic environmental stressors such as torture, combat, witnessing the death of family members and relatives, and forcible detainment in harsh refugee camp conditions. The major concerns of a group of Southeast Asian refugees in the United States involved: (a) being separated from or the death of loved ones, (b) marital and family problems, (c) worries about the future, (d) English proficiency difficulties, and (e) job dissatisfaction. Nearly 25% had made suicide attempts and complained about the changes in the behavior of their children (L. T. Nguyen & Henkin, 1983). High rates of post-traumatic stress disorder, somatization, and depression have been found in this population (Chun, Eastman, Wang, & Sue, 1998; Frye & D'Avanzo, 1994). Unfortunately, because of problems such as the shame and stigma attached to mental illness, lack of financial resources, and the limited number of bilingual providers, AA/PI populations have very low mental health utilization rates. In many cases, those who do come in for treatment show high levels of disturbance. These high levels may result from the delay in services until problems become very severe (Surgeon General's Report, 1999).

Asian American adolescents appear to be encountering problems in adjustment that may be due to acculturation conflicts. Asian American females seem to be particularly at risk for depression. A national survey of boys and girls attending 265 public, private, and parochial schools (Schoen et al., 1997) reported that among girls in grades 5 through 12, Asian American girls had the highest rate of depressive symptoms (30%), compared to 27% of Hispanic girls, 22% of White girls, and 17% of Black girls. In the same study, Asian American boys were more than twice as likely as White boys to report that they had been physically abused (17% vs. 8%) and three times more likely to report being sexually abused (9% vs. 3%). Nearly one quarter of Asian American boys reported not feeling safe in their neighborhood versus 10% of White boys, and 29% did not feel safe in their schools versus 15% of White boys (Shoen, Davis, Des Roches, & Shekhdar, 1998). The findings are troubling because adolescence is an important formative period. Indeed, depression and physical abuse are related to risky behaviors and poor mental health. The results would seem to indicate that instead of being a model minority, Asian American adolescents should be considered an at-risk population.

Substance Abuse

Asian/Pacific Islander Americans as a group have very low rates of substance abuse but there are significant differences in use among the subpopulations. Pacific Islanders have illicit drug rates equivalent to or higher than the other racial groups. In a survey of substance use, AA/PI youth smoked cigarettes at half the rate of White youth, although those who do smoke consume more cigarettes per day than any other group. The reported rates of alcohol use among Asian American youth showed a deep decline from 1999 to 2000 from 11.8% to 7.1%. No other group showed such a decline (the White rate, 18.4%, actually went up in that period). Marijuana use also dropped, from 5.8% to 2.5% from 1999 to 2000 for AA/PI group members, whereas it increased for Whites and Native Americans (7.8% and 19.9% respectively; "Asian/Pacific Islander Americans and Substance Abuse," 2002). However, of those who drink habitually, Asians drink more than any other ethnic group.

The data on substance use and abuse must be viewed with caution. There may be major differences in usage among older adult, younger American-born, immigrant, and refugee populations. Many of the studies regarding substance use sampled populations in Hawaii. The generalizability of the findings to mainland Asian populations might be limited. Native Hawaiians tend to have higher rates of drinking among Asian groups. In Mainland studies, Chinese men reported the least drinking and Japanese men the most. Among women, Filipinos reported the lowest drinking levels and Japanese women reported the most (Zane & Huh-Kim, 1999).

In general, Asian and Pacific Islander adolescents constituted about 2% of all admissions to substance abuse treatment facilities in 1999; they made up about 4% of the U.S. population. A study of Asian and Pacific Islander adolescents in substance abuse treatment revealed the following information: (1) The number of AA/PI admissions increased by 52% from 1994 to 1999; (2) about three quarters of Asian and Pacific Islander adolescent admissions were first-treatment episodes; (3) marijuana was the primary substance for AA/PI adolescents entering treatment, followed by alcohol and stimulants; (4) nearly three times as many AA/PI adolescents reported daily usage of stimulants as compared to the total youth treatment population (11% vs. 4%; Substance Abuse and Mental Health Services Administration, 2002).

Biological Factors Associated With Substance Abuse

Some researchers believe that there is a biological basis for the relatively low rate of substance abuse among Asian American populations. In most Asian cultures, the overall prevalence of alcohol-related disorders appears to be relatively low.

> The low prevalence rates among Asians appear to relate to a deficiency, in per-haps 50% of Japanese, Chinese, and Korean individuals, of the form of aldehyde dehydrogenase that eliminates low levels of the first breakdown product of alco-hol, acetaldehyde. When the estimated 10% of individuals who have a complete absence of the enzyme consume alcohol, they experience a flushed face and pal-pitations that can be so severe that many do not subsequently drink at all. Those 40% of the population with a relative deficiency of the enzyme experience less intense flushing but still have a significantly reduced risk of developing an Al-cohol Use Disorder. (American Psychiatric Association, 2000, p. 219)

The ALDH2*2 genetic variant that affects the metabolism of acetaldehyde is believed to be responsible for the low degree of alcohol abuse. The gene variant is found most commonly in people of Asian descent. It is estimated that 5% of northern Asians (Chinese, Japanese, and Korean) inherit two ALDH2*2 allele, while about 35% inherit one. The remaining 60% do not have this genetic varia-tion. ALDH2*2 homozygous individuals are highly reactive to alcohol; they ex-perience facial flushing as well as tachycardia, hypotension, or nausea after in-gesting even a moderate amount. Those who inherit only one allele show more reaction to alcohol than those without this genetic variant (McCarthy, Wall, Brown, & Carr, 2000). The possession of the ALDH2 is associated not only with the development of alcohol-related behavior but with other substance use such as tobacco as well, because the use of alcohol may be an important step to the use of other substances (Wall, Shea, Chan, & Carr, 2001).

Although the ALDH2 genetic variance may account in some degree for lower levels of alcohol abuse and dependence in Asian populations, it is estimated that 60% do not have this genetic variation. Strong cultural restraints in Asian cultures also militate against excessive drinking and public displays of drunkenness, which could also account for lower rates of alcohol consumption. Alcohol con-sumption among Asians is also related to generational status in the United States; third- and fourth-generation Americans report more drinking than do the first and second generations. Attitudes about alcohol consumption as well as cultural pre-scriptions appear to be important in moderating the drinking pattern of Asian Americans (D. Sue, 1987).

Investigators have also posited the possibility of neurological differences be-tween Asian and Caucasians; they point to the lower dosages needed for a treat-ment response to the antipsychotic medication haloperidol (Lin et al., 1989), the antianxiety medication alprazolam (Lin et al., 1988), and the tricyclic antidepressants (Lin, Poland, & Lesser, 1986). Such differences are presumed to be related to susceptibility to mental disorders. Although such studies, along with the ALDH2 genetic variation, may demonstrate some psychobiological differences between Asians and Caucasians, the findings are limited in support of a biological perspective. Instead, a number of studies indicate the importance of environmental and cultural stressors (culture conflicts, language problems, prejudice and discrimination, poverty, and trauma) that produce increased risk for psychopathology (Chun et al., 1998).

Cultural Influences on Psychopathology

Culture influences the manifestation of psychopathology. The existence of culture-bound syndromes point to the lack of correspondence between indigenous labels and established diagnostic categories and can lead to missed diagnosis or misdiagnosis (Lin & Cheung, 1999). Thus, mental health problems may be underestimated in Asian American populations. Culture shapes the experience and expression of psychopathology by supplying specific content to thought and feelings that are manifested as maladaptive cognitions and emotional distress. Culture-bound syndromes refer to recurrent, locality-specific patterns of aberrant behavior. They are considered to be a subset of folk illness and may not fit into contemporary diagnostic and classification systems such as the *DSM*. The following list provides examples of culture-bound syndromes (Aderibigbe & Pandurangi, 1995; Castillo, 1997; American Psychiatric Association, 2000):

- *Taijjin Kyofusho*. In this common form of social phobia in Japan and Korea, the individual exhibits extreme anxiety about the possibility of offending others through attributes such as eye contact, having an offending odor, or having unpleasant or misshapen physical features. This disorder is somewhat similar to social phobia or body dysmorphic disorder. However, the main focus is the fear of being offensive to others. The fear can be interpreted as a pathological amplification of the cultural concerns about the self in social interactions and the importance of harmonious social interactions. The disorder is included in the *Japanese Diagnostic System for Mental Disorders.*
- *Latah*. This disorder is characterized by sudden fright, followed by an altered mental state; socially inappropriate, obscene, or blasphemous speech; or command or automatic obedience. It is common in Malaysia and Indonesia and has characteristics similar to the dissociative disorders.
- *Koro*. This disorder is characterized by episodes of sudden and intense anxiety accompanied by palpitations, sweating, and faintness involving fear that the penis (or, in females, the nipples) will recede into the body and possibly cause death. It has some features similar to depersonalization, panic, and atypical somatoform disorder. It is found primarily in Malay and southern China.
- *Amok*. Amok is a dissociative-like state characterized by outbursts of unrestricted violence that are associated with homicidal attacks. It is generally precipitated by perceived slights or insults. It is attributed indigenously to

interpersonal conflict, intolerably embarrassing or shameful situations, or loss of honor. It is most prevalent among males from Malaysia or Indonesia and may be related to a brief psychotic reaction.

- *Hwa-Byung.* Hwa-byung is a Korean folk syndrome that is characterized by prominent anxiety, somatoform, and mood symptoms such as insomnia, fatigue, panic, fear of impending death, palpitations, heat sensation, flushing, dysphoria, and generalized aches and pains. The condition is common, especially among less educated, middle-age Korean women. It is attributed to the suppression of anger by wives who are unable to express the emotion directly to the husband or mother-in-law.

- *Shenjing shuairuo* ("neurasthenia"). This disorder is characterized by physical and mental complaints involving fatigue, dizziness, headaches, or other pain. Gastrointestinal problems and sexual dysfunction are also expressed. The diagnosis is included in the *Chinese Classification of Mental Disorders* and closely resembles the *DSM-IV* category of mood disorders.

Mental Health Practices and Beliefs

In the Philippines, psychological problems are attributed to a weak soul, spirits, or hot-cold imbalances. Such attributions have been found among Filipino college students in Hawaii, who attributed the cause of depression to bad luck or a weak soul, whereas their Caucasian counterparts were more likely to endorse physical causes such as heredity, viruses, or diet (Edman & Johnson, 1999). Among older Cambodians in America, strong emotional disturbances are usually attributed to possession by malicious spirits, bad karma from misdeeds during past lives, or a "bad seed" from family inheritance. Because of the negative connotations, mental illness is commonly denied and feared. Emotional problems are therefore presented as physical issues (Ethnomed, 2001).

However, psychosocial stressors are also accepted by some Asians as the cause of emotional disturbances. In a study of 108 residents of Chinatown in San Francisco, 30% believed that mental disorders were caused by pressures and problems, 20% attributed such problems to personality, 8% to neglect, and 5% to a combination. The remaining one third did not identify any cause. Japanese American college students were more likely to attribute mental illness to social causes (problems with others or interpersonal difficulties) than were their White counterparts (Narikiyo & Kameoka, 1992). Thus, the conception of mental illness varies according to the specific group studied and the degree of acculturation of the population. In a study by Ying, Lee, Tsai, Yeh, and Hwang (2000), the conception of depression by Chinese American college students was more similar to that of White Americans than was found in the general Chinese American community.

Somatization

It is believed that mental health issues are often not diagnosed in Asian American populations because emotional problems are presented through physical symptoms. In many Asian cultures, mind and body are integrated with each other, whereas in Western societies the mind and body are seen as separable. In general, non-Western cultures experience emotional stressors and mental illness through bodily complaints (somatopsychological), and Westerners tend to experience physical complaints as psychological (psychosomatic). In the early 1900s, the concept of neurasthenia was introduced in China and was described as *shenjing shuairuo,* or neurological weakness (see the section in this chapter titled "Cultural Influences on Psychopathology"). By the 1980s, up to 80% of psychiatric patients in mainland China were diagnosed as suffering from neurasthenia (Parker, Gladstone, & Chee, 2001). This culture-bound mental disorder is considered the Chinese version of depression. It fits the Chinese view of disease causation on the basis of a disharmony of vital organs and the imbalance of *qi,* or vital energy. The disorder is viewed as the imbalance of yin and yang, resulting in the disturbance of the normal functioning of vital fluids and visceral systems.

Because Chinese medicine is organ oriented, patients often describe their mental problems as related to the functioning of the organs. "Hasty organ" refers to an internal organ that is overwhelmed with some urge, loses its stability, and thus causes the person to become irritable and explosive. "Elevated liver fire" is seen as a cause for agitation and tension, and emotion is related to the circulation of vital air in the body, which diminishes when one is in a sorrowful or depressed mood (Kung, 2001; S. Lee, 1993). Studies of the Chinese American community (Ying, 1988) indicate that many individuals continue to hold a somatopsychological conception of depression. The clinical picture of emotional disturbances may involve physical complaints of dizziness, headache, and poor concentration. Instead of complaints of depression or anxiety during emotional disturbances, the client may report somatic problems such as feelings of fatigue, restlessness, and disturbances in sleep or appetite (S. Lee, 1993; D. W. Sue & Sue, 2003; Toarmino & Chun, 1997). Even Southeast Asian refugees experiencing psychotic episodes have described their symptoms in terms of somatic complaints (S. D. Nguyen, 1985).

Prejudice and Acculturation Conflicts

Asian Americans still face discrimination and racism that impact mental health. Although many are fourth- or fifth-generation Americans, they are often still considered foreigners. In a recent national survey (Committee of 100, 2001), negative attitudes toward this group were still found. For example, nearly one third of those surveyed thought that Chinese Americans would be more loyal to China than to the United States, and about half believed that Chinese Americans would pass secret information to China. About one quarter of those surveyed would disapprove if someone in their family married an Asian American, and 17% would be upset if a substantial number of Asian Americans moved into their neighborhood.

The lack of full acceptance and exposure to Western standards and norms has had an impact on Asian American adjustment. Among many Asian American women, the model of female beauty is the White, Western woman. Several studies have reported that Asian American women are less satisfied with their racially defined features and report lower self-esteem than their Caucasian counterparts (Mintz & Kashubeck, 1999). South Asian women report wanting to be lighter in skin color (Sahay & Piran, 1997). There is also a rising incidence in the number of Asian American women seeking treatment for eating disorders (Park, 2000). Resolution of ethnic identity is also related to mental health. Those who are marginalized (low identity and low acculturation) report significantly greater numbers of stressors than do individuals with a bicultural or traditional orientation (Lieber, Chin, Nihira, & Mink, 2001).

Family Issues and Problems

Because of the model minority stereotype, the issue of domestic violence among Asian American families has seldom been raised. In addition, few official reports may be made by Asian Americans because of the stigma attached to admitting problems within the family. It is difficult to determine the extent of the problem because no nationwide samples have been obtained, so problems in generalization can occur in studies of specific samples. However, some of the available statistics are disturbing.

In a study of domestic violence in the Washington, DC, Maryland, and Virginia areas (Preisser, 1999), 484 battered Asian women and children sought services in 1996. The cases of domestic violence were reported in nearly all Asian ethnic groups, with the majority of clients identified as Korean, Vietnamese, South Asian (Indian, Pakistani, Bangladeshi, Sri Lankan, and Nepali), and Chinese. Estimates of the number of families encountering domestic violence may be underestimated because of impediments such as the lack of familiarity with language, transportation, location, and availability of services. Nearly half the battered clients spoke little or no English. Interpreters were especially needed for Korean and Vietnamese victims. There is also a stigma of being abused, and victims often have limited economic resources. Victims often feel extremely isolated and helpless. Because of the collectivistic orientation, disruptions in family life may be perceived as the wife's failure. A woman who reports abuse may be cut off from a group cultural life that is vitally important. Laotian and Cambodian women are the most subservient to their husbands (J. L. Lum, 1999). Huisman (1996) found that although the victim's extended family sometimes acted to protect the victim, more often they maintained the status quo and sometimes even contributed to the violence.

In another study (Song, 1996) that involved interviews with 150 immigrant Korean women, 60% reported being battered, with more than one third reporting that the abuse occurred at least once a month. Most of the victims preferred to solve the problem of abuse through the passage of time, keeping the problem in the family, and praying rather than through talking to friends or relatives or seeking professional help. Most of the abused women believed that seeking help outside the family or from formal sources would shame them in front of their neighbors and relatives. The cases of abuse may be related to the stresses of immigration and adjustment. The abuse frequency was higher and more severe during the first 3 to 5 years of residency in the United States. Of the men who were abusive, 58% had taken jobs that were at a lower employment level than they held prior to immigration which may have been a stressor given that traditional Asian culture emphasizes honoring a hierarchical structure and avoiding the loss of face.

The number of reported cases of child abuse among Asian Americans appears to be increasing (Coalition for Asian American Children and Families, 2002). Vietnamese immigrants frequently report problems such as intergenerational conflict and difficulty in disciplining their children. The children adopt Western values and styles and may challenge parental authority. Vietnamese-born students reported a lower quality of parental relationships and less social integration than American-born Vietnamese students. Vietnamese-born male students were at particular risk for poor paternal relationships (Dinh, Sarason, & Sarason, 1994). Because of the acculturation conflict, it is not uncommon for Asian American students to attribute psychological stress to their relationship with their parents. Children are expected to conform to family expectations, and if they don't, the resulting conflicts can contribute to problems such as adjustment disorders, low self-esteem, anxiety, depression, and abuse (R. M. Lee, Choe, Kim, & Ngo, 2000).

In a study of undergraduates conducted at the University of British Columbia, the Asians (45% recent immigrants, 26% long-term immigrants, and 29% born in Canada) were more likely than their Caucasian counterparts to report physical and emotional abuse and neglect in their families (Meston, Heiman, Trapnell & Carlin, 1999). Compared to European American families, parent-adolescent conflicts in Chinese American families were more highly correlated with school misconduct, antisocial behavior, and at-risk behaviors (smoking, drinking alcohol; R. M. Lee et al., 2000). For some immigrant adolescents who become alienated either through problem with schools, society, or family conflicts, gangs may furnish a sense of belonging. It is difficult to obtain representative statistics on gang membership. However, it is estimated that of the more than 2,000 gang members in the metro Denver area, 300 of them are Asian. Two of the Vietnamese gangs are the Asian Pride and Viet Pride. The three Hmong gangs are called the Oriental Ruthless Boys (ORBs), the Asian Crips (ACs), and the Masters of Destruction (MODs; Emery, 2000). Thus, societal issues and acculturation conflicts in some Asian American families may contribute to a breakdown in family relationships and to dysfunctional behaviors.

CONCLUSION

Because of the lack of national baseline data, the aggregation of Asian American groups, and the study of only specific Asian populations, the state of the physical and mental health of these populations is not clear. As a group, Asian Americans appear to be a relatively healthy group; however, specific subgroups, particularly the Southeast Asians, appear to be doing less well. Rates of screening and preventive care appear to be impacted by both cultural health beliefs and a view that the medical profession may not be responsive to the cultural background of Asian Americans. Mental health needs of these populations may be underestimated because of cultural issues involving the stigma and shame of the admission of mental illness as well as undiagnosed cultural expressions or forms of psychopathology. Biological factors may be involved in low levels of substance abuse, especially in alcohol use. However, cultural constraints on the consumption of alcohol also clearly play a role. Recent studies of adolescents show an alarmingly high rate of depression among Asian American females and high rates of physical abuse in Asian American males. These findings may be a result of culture conflict with the dominant society and acculturation differences with parents. Indeed, within the "model minority," the incidence of low self-esteem among children and adolescents and reports of domestic violence and child abuse appear to be increasing.

Exercises

1. You are asked to do an epidemiological study on the prevalence of mental disorders in Asian Americans.
   a) Identify the shortcomings of present research.
   b) Address these shortcomings in your research design.
   c) How might you consider the impact of culture-bound syndromes in designing your research?
2. The data seem to indicate that Asian Americans underutilize physical health screening and physical exams.
   a) Identify the possible reasons for the underutilization.
   b) How could utilization and screening rates be improved at the individual, system, and cultural levels?

REFERENCES

Aderibigbe, Y. A., & Pandurangi, A. K. (1995). The neglect of culture in psychiatric nosology: The case of culture bound syndromes. *International Journal of Social Psychiatry, 41,* 235–241.

American Cancer Society. (2002). *Cancer prevention and early detection: Facts and figures 2002.* Atlanta, Georgia: American Cancer Society.

American Psychiatric Association (2000). *Diagnostic and statistical manual of mental disorders* (4th ed., text revision). Washington, DC: American Psychiatric Association.

Asian/Pacific Islander Americans and substance abuse. (2002). *Prevention, 5,* 1–2.

Buchwald, D., Panwala, S., & Hooton, T. M. (1992). Use of traditional health practices by Southeast Asian refugees in a primary care clinic. *Western Journal of Medicine, 156,* 507–511.

Carey, P., & Gjerdingen, D. K. (1993). Follow-up of abnormal Papanicolaou smears among women of different races. *Journal of Family Practice, 37,* 583–587.

Castillo, R. J. (1997). *Culture and mental illness.* Pacific Grove, CA: Brooks/Cole.

Chen, M. S., & Hawks, B. L. (1995). A debunking of the myth of healthy Asian Americans and Pacific Islanders. *American Journal of Health Promotion, 9,* 261–268.

Chun, K. M., Eastman, K. L., Wang, G. C. S., & Sue, S. (1998). Psychopathology. In L. C. Lee & N. W. S. Zane (Eds.), *Handbook of Asian American psychology* (pp. 457–484). Thousand Oaks, CA: Sage.

Coalition for Asian American Children and Families. (2002). *Asian American myths and facts.* New York: Author.

Committee of 100. (2001). *American attitudes toward Chinese Americans and Asian Americans.* New York: Author.

Department of Health and Human Services. (2001). *Mental health: Culture, race, and ethnicity.* Rockville, MD: Office of the Surgeon General.

Department of Health and Human Services. (2002). *HHS fact sheet on Asian American and Pacific Islander issues.* Retrieved November 16, 2002, from http:/www/aapi.omhrc.gov/2pgAAPI/whatsnew2.htm

Dinh, K. T., Sarason, B. R., & Sarason, I. G. (1994). Parent-child relationships in Vietnamese immigrant families. *Journal of Family Psychology, 8,* 471–488.

Edman, J. L., & Johnson, R. C. (1999). Filipino American and Caucasian American beliefs about the causes and treatment of mental problems. *Cultural Diversity and Ethnic Minority Psychology, 5,* 380–386.

Emery, J. (2000, August 20). Misplaced loyalty: Asian gangs lure teens to life of crime. *Denver Post,* L1.

Ethnomed. (2001). *Ethnic medicine information from Harborview Medical Center.* Seattle: University of Washington.

Frye, B. A., & D'Avanzo, C. (1994). Themes in managing culturally defined illness in the Cambodian refugee family. *Journal of Community Health Nursing, 11,* 89–98.

Hughes, D. L. (2002). *Quality of health care for Asian Americans* (Publication No. 525). New York: The Commonwealth Fund.

Huisman, K. A. (1996). Wife battering in Asian American communities. *Violence Against Women, 2,* 260–283.

Jamin, D., Yoo, J.-H., Moldoveanu, M., & Tran, L. (1999). Vietnamese and Armenian health attitudes survey. *Journal of Multicultural Nursing and Health, 5,* 6–13.

Kung, W. W. (2001). Consideration of cultural factors in working with Chinese American families with a mentally ill patient. *Families in Society, 82,* 97–107.

Lee, R. M., Choe, J., Kim, G., & Ngo, V. (2000). Construction of the Asian American Family Conflict Scale. *Journal of Counseling Psychology, 47,* 211–222.

Lee, S. (1993). The prevalence and nature of lithium noncompliance among Chinese psychiatric patients in Hong Kong. *Journal of Nervous and Mental Disease, 181,* 618–625.

Lieber, E., Chin, D., Nihira, K., & Mink, I. T. (2001). Holding on and letting go: Identity and acculturation among Chinese immigrants. *Cultural Diversity and Ethnic Minority Psychology, 7,* 247–261.

Lin, K.-M., & Cheung, F. (1999). Mental health issues for Asian Americans. *Psychiatric Services, 50,* 774–780.

Lin, K.-M., Lau, J. K., Smith, R., Phillips, P., Antal, E., & Poland, R. E. (1988). Comparison of alprazolam plasma levels in normal Asian and Caucasian male volunteers. *Psychopharmacology, 96,* 365–369.

Lin, K.-M., Poland, R. E., & Lesser, I. M. (1986). Ethnicity and psychopharmacology. *Culture, Medicine, and Psychiatry, 10,* 151–165.

Lin, K.-M., Poland, R. E., Nuccio, I., Matsuda, K., Hathue, N., Su, T., & Fu, P. (1989). A longitudinal assessment of haloperidol doses and serum concentrations in Asian and Caucasian schizophrenic patients. *American Journal of Psychiatry, 146,* 1307–1311.

Lum, J. L. (1999). Family violence. In L. C. Lee & N. W. S. Zane (Eds.), *Handbook of Asian American psychology* (pp. 505–526). Thousand Oaks, CA: Sage.

Lum, O. M. (1995). Health status of Asians and Pacific Islanders. *Clinical Geriatric Medicine, 11,* 53–67.

McCarthy, D. M., Wall, T. L., Brown, S. A., & Carr, L. G. (2000). Integrating biological and behavioral factors in alcohol use risk: The role of ALDH2 status and alcohol expectancies in a sample of Asian Americans. *Experimental and Clinical Psychopharmacology, 8,* 168–175.

Meston, C. M., Heiman, J. R., Trapnell, P. D., & Carlin, A. S. (1999). Ethnicity, desirable responding, and self-reports of abuse: A comparison of European- and Asian-ancestry undergraduates. *Journal of Consulting and Clinical Psychology, 67,* 139–144.

Miller, B. A., Kolonel, L. N., Bernstein, L., Young, J. L., Jr., Swanson, G. M., West, D., Key, C. R., Liff, J. M., Glover, C. S., & Alexander, G. A. (Eds.). (1996). *Racial/ethnic patterns of cancer in the United States 1988–1992.* Bethesda, MD: National Cancer Institute.

Mintz, L. B., & Kashubeck, S. (1999). Body image and disordered eating among Asian Americans and Caucasian college students: An examination of race and gender differences. *Psychology of Women Quarterly, 23,* 781–796.

Narikiyo, T. A., & Kameoka, V. A. (1992). Attributions of mental illness and judgments about help seeking among Japanese-American and White American students. *Journal of Counseling Psychology, 39,* 363–369.

National Cancer Institute. (2002). *Cancer health disparities.* Bethesda, MD: National Cancer Institute.

National Center for Health Statistics. (1997). *Impact on Asian or Pacific Islander (API) health research.* Washington, DC: Centers for Disease Control and Prevention.

National Women's Health Information Center. (2002). *Asian American and Pacific Islander women's health.* Washington, DC: Department of Health and Human Services.

Nguyen, L. T., & Henkin, L. B. (1983). Change among Indochinese refugees. In R. J. Samada & S. C. Woods (Eds.), *Perspectives in immigrant and minority education.* New York: University Press of America.

Nguyen, S. D. (1985). Mental health services for refugees and immigrants in Canada. In T. C. Owen (Ed.), *Southeast Asian mental health: Treatment, prevention, services, training, and research* (pp. 261–282). Washington, DC: National Institute of Mental Health.

Noh, S., & Avison, W. R. (1996). Asian immigrants and the stress process: A study of Koreans in Canada. *Journal of Health and Social Behavior, 37,* 192–215.

Okazaki, S., Liu, J. F., Longworth, S. L., & Minn, J. Y. (2002). Asian American–White American differences in expressions of social anxiety: A replication and extension. *Cultural Diversity and Ethnic Minority Psychology, 8,* 234–247.

Park, E. (2000). Starving in silence: Eating and body image disorders plague young Asian and Asian American women. *AsianWeek, 21,* 17–20.

Parker, G., Gladstone, G., & Chee, K. T. (2001). Depression in the planet's largest ethnic group: The Chinese. *American Journal of Psychiatry, 158,* 857–864.

Penn, N. E., Kramer, J., Skinner, J. F., Velasquez, R. J., Yee, B. W. K., Arellano, L. M., & Williams, J. P. (2000). Health practices and health-care systems among cultural groups. In R. M. Eisler & M. Hersen (Eds.), *Handbook of gender, culture, and health* (pp. 105–138). Mahwah, NJ: Erlbaum.

Preisser, A. B. (1999). Domestic violence in South Asian communities in America: Advocacy and intervention. *Violence Against Women, 5,* 684–699.

Sahay, S., & Piran, N. (1997). Skin-color preference and body satisfaction among South Asian–Canadian and European-Canadian female university students. *Journal of Social Psychology, 137,* 161–171.

Schoen, C., Davis, K., Collins, K. S., Greenbert, L., Des Roches, C., & Abrams, M. (1997). *The Commonwealth Fund Survey of the health of adolescent girls.* New York: The Commonwealth Fund.

Schoen, C., Davis, K., Des Roches, C., & Shekhdar, A. (1998). *The health of adolescent boys: Commonwealth Fund Survey findings.* New York: The Commonwealth Fund.

Song, Y. I. (1996). *Battered women in Korean immigrant families.* New York: Garland.

Substance Abuse and Mental Health Services Administration. (2002). *The DASIS report: Asian and Pacific Islander adolescents in substance abuse treatment, 1999.* Rockville, MD: U.S. Government Printing Office.

Sue, D. (1987). Use and abuse of alcohol by Asian Americans. *Journal of Psychoactive Drugs, 19,* 57–66.

Sue, D. W., & Sue, D. (2003). *Counseling the culturally diverse* (4th ed.). New York: Wiley.

Surgeon General's Report. (1999). *Mental health: A report of the Surgeon General.* U.S. Department of Health and Human Services. Washington, DC: U.S. Government Printing Office.

Tamir, A., & Cachola, S. (1994). In N. W. S. Zane, D. T. Takeuchi, & K. N. J. Young (Eds.), *Confronting critical health issues of Asian and Pacific Islander Americans* (pp. 209–247). Thousand Oaks, CA: Sage.

Taylor, V. M., Jackson, J. C., Chan, N., Kuniyuki, A., & Yasui, Y. (2002). Hepatitis B knowledge and practices among Cambodian American women in Seattle, Washington. *Journal of Community Health, 27,* 151–163.

Toarmino, D., & Chun, C.-A. (1997). Issues and strategies in counseling Korean Americans. In C. C. Lee (Ed.), *Multicultural issues in counseling* (2nd ed., pp. 233–254). Alexandria, VA: American Counseling Association.

U.S. Census Bureau. (2000a). *The Asian and Pacific Islander population in the United States: March 2000 (update).* U.S. Department of Commerce. Washington, DC: U.S. Government Printing Office.

U.S. Census Bureau. (2000b). *Health insurance coverage.* U.S. Department of Commerce. Washington, DC: U.S. Government Printing Office.

Wall, T. L., Shea, S. H., Chan, K. K., & Carr, L. G. (2001). A genetic association with the development of alcohol and other substance use behavior in Asian Americans. *Journal of Abnormal Psychology, 110,* 173–178.

Yi, J. K. (1994). Factors associated with cervical cancer screening behavior among Vietnamese women. *Journal of Community Health, 19,* 189–200.

Ying, Y. (1988). Depressive symptomatology among Chinese-Americans as measured by the CES-D. *Journal of Clinical Psychology, 44,* 739–746.

Ying, Y.-W., Lee, P. A., Tsai, J. L., Yeh, Y.-Y. & Huang, J. S. (2000). The conception of depression in Chinese American college students. *Cultural Diversity and Ethnic Minority Psychology, 6,* 183–195.

Zane, N. W. S., & Huh-Kim, J. (1999). Addictive behaviors. In L. C. Lee & N. W. S. Zane (Eds.), *Handbook of Asian American psychology* (pp. 527–554). Thousand Oaks, CA: Sage.

Zhang, A. Y., & Snowden, L. R. (1999). Ethnic characteristics of mental disorders in five U.S. communities. *Cultural Diversity and Ethnic Minority Psychology, 5,* 134–146.

Ziegler, R. G., Hoover, R. N., Pike, M. C., Hildsheim, A., Nomura, M. M. Y., West, D. W., Wu-Williams, A. H., Kolonel, L. N., Horn-Ross, P. L., Rosenthal, J. F., & Hyer, M. B. (1993). Migration patterns and breast cancer risk in Asian American women. *Journal of the National Cancer Institute, 85,* 1819–1827.

CHAPTER 12 ## Treatment Issues with Asian American Clients

Bryan S. K. Kim, University
of California, Santa Barbara

Asian Americans comprise one of the fastest growing ethnic groups in the United States (U.S. Bureau of the Census, 2002). As of 2000, there were nearly 12 million Asian Americans living in the United States, representing an increase of 72% since 1990 (U.S. Bureau of the Census, 2002); these figures include multiracial Asian Americans, a category that was not used in the 1990 census. This growth in population size has brought increased attention to the psychological needs of Asian Americans. Leong, Wagner, and Tata (1995), after a review of relevant literature, stated:

> studies have shown a great need for [psychological] services among Asian Americans to deal with a variety of problems including academic, interpersonal, health/substance, abuse, dating, bicultural and biracial issues, family difficulties due to emerging cultural differences, marginality, difficulties relating within various subgroups, and the experience of racism. (p. 428)

To understand how best to meet these needs, mental health practitioners must be familiar with a range of issues related to counseling and psychotherapy with Asian Americans.

This chapter provides an overview of psychocultural issues related to Asian Americans and offers suggestions on ways that mental health practitioners can effectively serve this population. Specifically, the chapter presents information related to (1) attitudes about the seeking of mental health services, (2) psychological assessment, (3) potential areas of conflict between Asian Americans' cultural values and conventional approaches to counseling and psychotherapy, (4) indigenous healing practices as alternative methods of mental health treatment, (5) modification of conventional forms of counseling and psychotherapy to meet cultural needs, and (6) additional sources of mental health support. The chapter concludes with specific treatment recommendations based on extant theory and research on mental health services for Asian American clients.

Throughout the chapter, particular attention will be placed on issues of acculturation and enculturation, because most counseling theory and research with Asian Americans have shown that these constructs are important for this population (Atkinson, Morten, & Sue, 1998). In particular, adherence to Asian cultural values, a dimension of enculturation, will be highlighted in the chapter. Multicultural counseling theorists and researchers have pointed out that cultural values are an important factor to consider when mental health practitioners work with Asian American clients (Atkinson, Morten, & Sue, 1998; D. W. Sue & Sue, 1999).

ATTITUDES ABOUT THE SEEKING
OF COUNSELING SERVICES

Asian American attitudes about the seeking of counseling services are reflected in their patterns of mental health utilization and their perceptions of mental health services and providers.

Mental Health Service Utilization Patterns

As a result of the increased attention to psychological needs of Asian Americans, a number of research studies have examined Asian Americans' use of psychological services to determine whether their utilization rate has been similar to that of other racial and ethnic groups. In general, the results have shown that Asian Americans' rate of mental health service utilization has been less than expected. Snowden and Cheung (1990), based on a review of 1980 and 1981 nationwide survey data from the National Institute of Mental Health, found that Asian Americans had the lowest rates of admission into hospitals for mental health concerns among all racial and ethnic groups. Research studies using local samples also found underutilization of psychological services by Asian Americans living in California (S. Sue, Fujino, Hu, Takeuchi, & Zane, 1991) and Hawaii (Leong, 1994; S. Sue & Morishima, 1982).

Interestingly, Snowden and Cheung (1990) also found that Asian Americans in state and county mental hospitals required longer stays than all other ethnic groups, and those in Veterans Administration and private hospitals required longer stays than European Americans did. However, for other Asian American clients, there appears to be an increased tendency for premature termination from service. For example, S. Sue (1977) reported that 50% of Asian American clients failed to return for services after the initial intake interview, whereas the initial dropout rate for European Americans was 30%.

Perceptions of Mental Health Services and Providers

An initial glance at these findings might lead to the impression that Asian Americans tend not to experience psychological problems in comparison to other groups, and if they do, the problems tend to be minor in nature with only a few exceptions that require extensive treatment. However, these possibilities have been dispelled by multicultural counseling scholars who noted that there are no particular reasons why Asian Americans, in comparison to other groups, should have decreased incidences of psychological problems (Atkinson, Morten, & Sue,

1998; D. W. Sue, 1990). Rather, given the minority status of this group and related experiences of racism, it seems reasonable to expect that the need for psychological services among Asian Americans is greater than it is for European Americans (Leong et al., 1995).

Hence, a more plausible explanation for these findings is that some other within-group or outside-group factors limit Asian Americans' use of Western-based psychological services. One possibility is that there may be readily available therapeutic systems within Asian American communities, such as a network of family members, respected elders, and indigenous healers, who can help individuals with psychological difficulties (Atkinson, Morten, & Sue, 1998; D. W. Sue & Sue, 1999). In terms of outside-group factors, multicultural counseling scholars have suggested that mainstream psychological service providers may lack cultural relevancy, sensitivity, and competency that may discourage Asian Americans from seeking help from them (Atkinson, Morten, & Sue, 1998; D. W. Sue & Sue, 1999).

Although the presence of these factors is certainly plausible (and will be further discussed later in the chapter), recent theoretical and research work has focused on two other within-group factors. These factors are (1) Asian Americans' lack of familiarity with conventional Western forms of helping, and (2) Asian cultural norms that discourage Asian Americans from seeking help from others. A within-group variable that reflects one's familiarity with U.S. cultural norms in general, and Western forms of helping specifically, is *acculturation.* Originally theorized by Berry (1980) as an index of within-group heterogeneity, acculturation refers to the process of adaptation to the cultural values, behavior, knowledge, and identity of the dominant culture (B. S. K. Kim & Abreu, 2001). Multicultural counseling scholars have suggested that among Asian Americans who are not familiar with U.S. cultural norms (i.e., low level of acculturation), counseling and other forms of conventional psychological service may appear foreign, not credible, and even threatening (Atkinson, Morten, & Sue, 1998; D. W. Sue & Sue, 1999).

In contrast to the concept of acculturation, a within-group variable that reflects adherence to Asian cultural norms is *enculturation* (B. S. K. Kim & Abreu, 2001). First defined and used by Herskovits (1948), enculturation is an index of within-group heterogeneity and refers to the process of socialization to the norms of one's indigenous culture, including the salient values, ideas, and concepts (Berry, Poortinga, Segall, & Dasen, 1992; Segall, Dasen, Berry, & Poortinga, 1990). Hence, enculturation is different from acculturation in that the context for the former process is the home (minority) culture, whereas the context for the latter process is the host (dominant) culture (Berry et al., 1992; Segall et al., 1990). Recently, enculturation has been defined as the process of retaining one's indigenous cultural values, behaviors, knowledge, and identity (B. S. K. Kim & Abreu, 2001). Multicultural counseling scholars have suggested that Asian Americans who are highly enculturated may feel ashamed about having psychological problems and revealing their problems to mental health practitioners or other individuals outside their family (Atkinson, Morten, & Sue, 1998; D. W. Sue, 1990).

Based on these ideas about acculturation and enculturation vis-à-vis underutilization of Western-based psychological services, multicultural counseling researchers have conducted studies on two attitudinal constructs related to help seeking: attitudes toward the seeking of professional psychological help (Atkinson & Gim, 1989; Tata & Leong, 1994), and willingness to see a counselor for specific types of problems (Atkinson, Lowe, & Matthews, 1995; Gim, Atkinson, & Whiteley, 1990). In research studies that examine the relationship between Asian American acculturation and attitudes toward the seeking of professional psychological help (Atkinson & Gim, 1989; Tata & Leong, 1994), the results have consistently indicated that less acculturated Asian Americans tend to have less favorable attitudes toward the seeking of professional psychological services than do the more acculturated Asian Americans. Hence, these findings support the notion that Asian Americans' underutilization of psychological services is related to their lack of familiarity with Western norms.

However, the support for this notion about the lack of familiarity toward Western forms of helping becomes less clear when the construct of willingness to see a counselor is also considered. Surprisingly, studies that examine the relationship between Asian Americans' willingness to see a counselor and their acculturation level (e.g., Gim et al., 1990) have shown that less acculturated Asian Americans tend to have *greater* willingness to see a counselor than do their more acculturated counterparts. While recognizing the need for more research on the relationship between acculturation and willingness to see a counselor, Gim et al. (1990) and Atkinson, Whiteley, and Gim (1990) tried to make sense of this finding by speculating that less acculturated Asian Americans, although they may hold negative attitudes toward seeking professional psychological help, may be willing to seek help from a counselor when they acknowledge the need for help. The authors reasoned that perhaps Asian cultural values, particularly *deference to authority figures,* may cause Asian Americans to ascribe increased credibility to trained professionals such as counselors. Although this conjecture on the influence of Asian values is an interesting one, it is tentative at best because it assumes that low acculturation is synonymous with high adherence to Asian cultural values.

Recognizing the possibility that high adherence to Asian cultural values (high cultural values enculturation) may not be equivalent to low acculturation, multicultural counseling researchers have made recent efforts to directly examine the relationship between enculturation and help-seeking attitudes. Although research bearing on this issue is limited, a study by B. S. K. Kim and Omizo (in press) provided some initial data. The authors investigated the relationships among Asian American college students' adherence to Asian cultural values, their attitudes toward seeking professional psychological services, and their willingness to see a counselor. Adherence to Asian values was measured by the Asian Values Scale (B. S. K. Kim, Atkinson, & Yang, 1999), which measures dimensions such as *collectivism, conformity to norms, emotional self-control, family recognition through achievement, filial piety,* and *humility.* The results showed that increased adherence to Asian cultural values was associated with both less positive attitudes toward seeking psychological help and less willingness to see a counselor, after the researchers accounted for the effects of related demographic variables (age, gender, generation since immigration, and previous counseling experience). The results also showed that attitudes toward the seeking of professional psychological help was a significant mediator on the relationship between adherence to Asian cultural values and willingness to see a counselor in general and for personal problems and health problems in particular. That is, one's adherence to Asian cultural values was associated with one's attitudes toward the seeking of professional psychological services, which, in turn, was related to one's willingness to see a counselor for both general and specific concerns. Hence, when adherence to Asian cultural values is directly assessed, the results support the idea that underutilization of psychological services is related to high adherence to Asian cultural norms.

In summary, research findings regarding acculturation, enculturation, and help-seeking attitudes lend some support to the notion that Asian Americans' underutilization of psychological services is due to (1) a lack of familiarity with Western forms of helping, and (2) Asian cultural values that discourage Asian Americans from seeking help. The findings suggest that Asian Americans who are not familiar with Western norms tend to have less positive attitudes toward the seeking of professional psychological help and that those who are enculturated to Asian cultural norms tend to have both less positive attitudes about seeking help and less willingness to see a counselor.

Based on these findings, a number of clinical implications can be formulated. First, given the lack of positive attitudes toward seeking professional psychological help by many Asian Americans (i.e., individuals with high enculturation or low acculturation), mental health practitioners need to conduct more outreach services. Perhaps educative materials developed specifically for an Asian American audience and describing the potential benefits of psychological services can be disseminated. In addition, materials designed to eliminate or cope with the stigma surrounding psychological problems could be developed and distributed. The involvement of Asian American professionals may be helpful in efforts to enhance the credibility of these outreach efforts.

Second, administrators of mental health agencies should consider hiring Asian American clinicians in an attempt to increase utilization rates. This suggestion is especially appropriate if the agencies are located in communities with large groups of Asian Americans. In a similar vein, administrators should consider offering workshops to their staff members to educate them about counseling issues salient to Asian American clients. Perhaps multicultural counseling experts can be brought in to conduct these workshops and to discuss ways in which staff members can be more culturally relevant, sensitive, and effective with these clients.

Third, when Asian Americans enter treatment, mental health practitioners may need to attend to issues of shame and embarrassment, especially with individuals whose values and behaviors reflect high enculturation and low acculturation. If mental health practitioners suspect that the clients are embarrassed about their need for counseling, the practitioners should help the clients figure out effective ways to cope with these feelings. A secondary positive outcome for practitioners who engage in this process is that the clinicians may gain a great deal of information about clients' cultural norms and beliefs, which subsequently can benefit the counseling process. In addition to this direct intervention to decrease the sense of shame and embarrassment, a potentially useful strategy is to assign the clients to an ethnically similar practitioner. Having a practitioner with a similar ethnic background may lead clients to have a greater appreciation for the normality and benefits of the help-seeking endeavor. However, some Asian American clients with an ethnically similar clinician might feel an increased sense of shame and embarrassment because they may be sensitive to the fact that an "in-group" person will be learning about their problems.

PSYCHOLOGICAL ASSESSMENT

When Asian American clients enter counseling, mental health practitioners must assess a number of factors in order to obtain a good understanding about the clients' background and their reasons for seeking treatment. In addition to the typical areas of assessment in counseling, such as the nature, severity, and duration of the problem, information about the factors related to clients' cultural backgrounds could lead to more relevant and helpful counseling interventions. Such factors for assessment include (1) acculturation and enculturation statuses, (2) experiences with oppression, (3) beliefs about the locus of problem etiology and related goal of counseling, (4) possible presence of culture-specific psychological disorders, (5) prevalence of psychosomatic symptoms, and (6) availability of indigenous sources of support.

As noted previously in this chapter, acculturation refers to the degree to which Asian Americans adhere to the norms of the U.S. culture, and enculturation refers to the extent to which Asian Americans have retained the norms of the traditional Asian culture. Along these two domains, a number of constructs can be assessed. B. S. K. Kim and Abreu (2001) noted that the dimensions that underlie acculturation and enculturation include cultural values, behaviors, knowledge, and identity. The researchers defined *cultural values* as attitudes and beliefs about social relations, cultural customs, and cultural traditions. *Cultural behaviors* were defined in terms of friendship choice, preferences for television program and reading, participation in cultural activities, language use, food choice, and music preference. *Cultural knowledge* was expressed through culturally specific information such as names of historical leaders and historical significance of cultural activities. *Cultural identity* was described as choice of one's cultural identification, attitudes toward the culture, and level of comfort toward people of the culture. The assessment of these constructs along the domains of both acculturation and enculturation can provide insights into the types of counseling interventions that may be effective with Asian American clients. To the extent that clients adhere to the norms of the indigenous culture, deviation from conventional modes of service may be necessary. On the other hand, to the extent that clients adhere to the norms of the U.S. culture, conventional modes of service can be effective.

Value enculturation and behavioral acculturation are orthogonal dimensions, and there is evidence to show that the former changes more slowly than the latter. A study by B. S. K. Kim et al. (1999) found that there were no differences on adherence to Asian cultural values among Asian Americans who were first-, second-, or third-generation Americans, whereas significant differences were found on their level of adherence to behavioral norms of the U.S. culture. This finding suggests that many Asian Americans retain their traditional Asian cultural norms after they have become behaviorally acculturated. Hence, the degree to which conventional modes of service need to be modified should be determined by an examination of both acculturation and enculturation statuses rather than only one of these dimensions.

Asian Americans, as a result of their minority status, are often victims of oppression by the dominant culture. As described in chapter 11, Asian Americans continue to suffer from discrimination and racism, which can have negative mental health outcomes. Hence, it is important to assess the extent to which clients have been exposed to oppression by the dominant group and whether clients' presenting issues might be related to oppression. Also, Asian Americans have been often labeled the "model minority" group, a myth that can divert attention away from psychosocial problems experienced by many Asian Americans, including discrimination and racism; see chapter 10. Hence, it is important for mental health practitioners to assess the degree to which clients have been negatively affected by the model minority notion.

After acculturation and enculturation and experiences with oppression have been assessed, it may be also useful to assess Asian Americans' belief about the locus of problem etiology and their goal of counseling. Atkinson, Thompson, and Grant (1993) developed a three-dimensional model of multicultural counseling (see chapter 16), which posits that the combinations of acculturation (high and low), locus of etiology (internal and external), and goal of counseling (prevention and remediation) necessitates eight different helper roles. For example, the model suggests that to help prevent the occurrence of a problem with an external cause for a client who is high in acculturation, the mental health practitioner should serve as a consultant who can offer useful information to the client to take appropriate preventive measures. A study by Atkinson, Kim, and Caldwell (1998) with Asian American college students reported initial support for the roles specified by the three-dimensional model.

Another important area of assessment is the possible presence of culture-specific psychological syndromes. Given the diversity of ethnicities represented among Asian Americans, there are numerous culture-specific forms in which psychological problems may be manifested. A list of culture-bound syndromes that reflect this variety and uniqueness within the Asian American population can be found in the *Diagnostic and Statistical Manual of Mental Disorders—Fourth Edition* (*DSM-IV;* American Psychiatric Association, 1994), a diagnostic tool commonly used by mental health professionals. These ailments specific to Asians, and by extension, Asian Americans, are *amok* (a dissociative disorder; found in Malaysia, Laos, and the Philippines), *dhat* (anxiety and hypochondriasis disorder; found in India), *hwa-byung* ("anger syndrome"; found in Korea), *koro* (anxiety about sex organ receding into the body and causing death; found in south and east Asia), *latah* (hypersensitivity to sudden fright; found in south and east Asia), *qi-gong psychotic reaction* (dissociative and paranoid symptoms; found in China), *shenjing shuairuo* (physical and mental fatigue symptoms; found in China), *shen-kui* (anxiety and panic symptoms; found in China and Taiwan), *shin-byung* (anxiety and so-matic symptoms; found in Korea), and *taijin kyofusho* (similar to social phobia; found in Japan); see chapter 11 for more complete descriptions of some these syndromes. It should be noted, however, that these syndromes may apply only to a very limited number of Asians or Asian Americans who hold traditional Asian beliefs and worldviews.

As described in chapter 11, traditional Asian Americans may tend to somati-cize their psychological distress. Mental health practitioners who work with Asian Americans could find it helpful to learn about their clients' beliefs about the effects of psychological problems on their physical health so that more holistic forms of service can be provided. For example, clinicians working with Asian American clients who are experiencing gastrointestinal problems as a result of stress from in-terpersonal discord might collaborate with the clients' physicians to treat the phys-ical symptoms while attending to the psychological difficulties. Certainly, treat-ment of the psychological ailments alone (or, more typically, the physical symptoms alone) may not lead to lasting relief from the psychological problems.

Mental health practitioners who work with Asian American clients will also want to assess for possible sources of indigenous support systems. Traditional Asian American clients may find it helpful to receive support from the extended family. In doing so, clients can continue to maintain valuable interpersonal con-nections with important persons in their lives. In addition, these connections could help clients not only to feel supported by their family but also to know that they still are integral members of the family. If Asian American clients who hold traditional values do not appear to have readily available sources of support from their families, mental health practitioners may do well to assess their clients' openness to receiving support from community agencies or organizations that serve Asian Americans (e.g., temples, churches, "mutual associations"). To this end, it would be helpful for practitioners to identify these agencies and organiza-tions in their communities and to maintain ongoing professional relationships with them.

POTENTIAL CONFLICT BETWEEN ASIAN AMERICANS' CULTURAL VALUES AND CONVENTIONAL COUNSELING

As noted earlier in this chapter, Asian American clients' enculturation level should be assessed because it may play an important role in counseling process and outcome. In particular, Asian American clients' cultural value orientation may significantly affect counseling process and outcome (B. S. K. Kim, Atkin-son, & Umemoto, 2001); refer to chapter 10 for a summary of cultural values commonly observed among Asian Americans. Multicultural counseling scholars have suggested that the match or mismatch among client's cultural values, coun-selor's cultural values, and the values inherent in the counseling interventions de-termines counseling process effectiveness and, distally, counseling outcome (Atkinson, Morten, & Sue, 1998; D. W. Sue & Sue, 1999). If interventions used by mental health practitioners ignore the values salient for Asian Americans and unknowingly promote ideals that conflict with these values to the extent that Asian American clients adhere to these values, the interventions may be irrelevant at best and harmful at worst.

Several examples can be generated in which a mismatch between conventional counseling approaches and Asian American clients' cultural values can lead to negative counseling process and outcome. Some counseling theories (e.g., gestalt theory) posit the notion that emotional expressions are beneficial and even curative to clients' problems. However, for Asian Americans clients who adhere to traditional Asian values and believe that stoicism and reticence are signs of psychological strengths (i.e., adherence to the value dimension of *self-control and restraint*), being forced to express their emotions, especially negative ones, might leave them feeling embarrassed and vulnerable. Psychoanalytic theories posit the importance of an exploration of the underlying unconscious dynamics causing clients' problems, which often include unresolved issues with family members or other significant figures in one's early life. For traditional Asian Americans who value *avoidance of family shame,* such exploration may be threatening and leave them feeling disloyal to their family. Traditional Asian American clients who adhere to the value of *deference to authority figures* may look toward mental health practitioners to provide guidance and possible solutions to their problems. Being forced to treat the practitioners in an egalitarian manner, as is often called for by humanistic theories, may lead clients to feel discomfort in the relationship. Lastly, for clients who adhere to Asian values of *self-effacement,* having to openly describe their achievements and accomplishments perhaps as a way to dispute their negative self-concepts, as may be done in cognitive therapies, may be counterproductive and leave the clients feeling uncomfortable.

However, some of the interactions between conventional counseling approaches and cultural values salient among traditional Asian Americans may also lead to positive counseling process and outcome. For example, the value of *maintenance of interpersonal harmony* may lead clients to work just as hard as mental health practitioners to form an effective working alliance, a key ingredient in humanistic counseling theories. In addition, the value of *deference to authority figures* may allow practitioners to have increased credibility with which they can increase their helpfulness with Asian American clients. The presence of these types of values among Asian American clients may enhance compliance with treatment strategies that are used by clinicians. However, before mental health professionals can accept these ideas on the effects of values match and mismatch on counseling process and outcome, research is needed to study the extent to which these ideas are valid.

In summary, to anticipate whether Asian cultural values will play helpful or impeding roles in counseling, mental health practitioners should identify the cultural values that are salient to their clients. To facilitate this process, practitioners might present a list of Asian cultural values to their clients and ask the clients to talk about the salience of these values to them. In doing so, the clinicians also may be able to gain useful information about the clients' background and presenting problems that may be related to their cultural values. Once important cultural values have been identified, practitioners can formulate hypotheses about how these values may affect the counseling relationship and process and can implement interventions that address these potentialities. In turn, these interventions may enhance the counseling process and help ensure a positive outcome.

INDIGENOUS HEALING PRACTICES AS ALTERNATIVE METHODS OF MENTAL HEALTH TREATMENT

After reviewing the results of a formal assessment, mental health practitioners may consider one of two routes of treatment: (1) conventional counseling and psychotherapy that integrate culturally relevant and sensitive interventions, and (2) referral to practitioners of indigenous healing methods. If mental health practitioners determine that Asian American clients would not fare well in conventional forms of counseling and psychotherapy, even with the augmentation of culturally relevant and sensitive interventions, they may consider referring the clients to practitioners of indigenous healing practices. Although there is controversy about the validity of indigenous treatment methods, clear documentation that utilizes Western research paradigms indicates that many Asian clients find these methods to be beneficial. Because mental health practitioners should do their best to provide the necessary assistance for clients to overcome their difficulties, indigenous healing practices may need to be considered as viable alternatives to conventional mental health services.

Shamans may be helpful in treating traditional Asian Americans who are suffering from culture-specific syndromes as well as those persons who are suffering from ailments diagnosable through Western taxonomies but who lack culturally appropriate service providers (Walsh, 1994). Shamans in anthropological terms are referred to as witches, witch doctors, wizards, medicine men or women, and sorcerers. It is believed that these individuals possess the power to enter an altered state of consciousness that leads them to cures for various psychological ailments. Shamans can be individuals who were identified at birth to hold magical powers and who are then trained to become master shamans. Shamans are often called to service when persons experience psychological ailments that are believed to be caused by displeased spirits who have possessed the individuals. It is believed that shamans have the power to exorcise the individuals of the spirits. There is some research evidence on the effectiveness of employing shamans for psychological problems among Asians (e.g., Kendall, 1988; Walters, 2001; Yi, 2000).

In addition to shamans, traditional Asian American also may turn to other forms of treatment that are deemed to be effective for resolving psychological difficulties. Two popular treatments are acupuncture and tai chi chuan. Acupuncture treatments are based on principles of Chinese medicine in which health and illness are viewed in terms of a balance between the yin and the yang forces (Meng, Luo, & Halbreich, 2002). It is believed that the balance largely depends on the proper circulation of the vital energy *chi* along energetic pathways. Acupuncture involves the insertion of small pins into specific points on the body to improve the proper circulation of this energy, which may be associated with psychological difficulties. It is believed that the pins help to restore curative energies that are spread to the rest of the body. Acupunctures have been used to treat depression, anxiety disorders, alcoholism, and substance abuse (see Meng et al., 2002).

In contrast to acupuncture, tai chi chuan is a form of moderate exercise that induces relaxation and meditation (Koh, 1981). It involves a complex pattern of slow movements in the arms and legs. For example, one form of tai chi chuan includes a sequence of 25 complex movements that can be further broken down into 148 gestures (i.e., changes in arm or leg position). There has been some research on the effects of tai chi chuan on the mental health among its practitioners. A study reviewing the extant literature found that tai chi chuan may enhance overall psychological well-being, including improvements in mood (Sandlund & Norlander, 2000). However, the authors noted that it is not clear whether the positive effects of tai chi chuan are due solely to its relaxation and meditation components or whether they are the consequence of various peripheral factors such as the fact that participants are engaging in an activity that is pleasurable and satisfying. Whatever the mechanism, it seems clear that tai chi chuan can have positive effects on the mental health of those who practice it.

Although the use of indigenous healing methods may offer significant help to clients, mental health practitioners should be advised that the healing practices are only applicable to a limited number of Asian Americans who hold traditional values and who have not been exposed to contemporary mental health practices in either their home or host country. Clinicians also should be cautioned that they should not try to provide these indigenous healing practices themselves unless they are indoctrinated in the indigenous culture. To facilitate referral of clients to the practitioners of these types of services, clinicians should work with local agencies and organizations that serve Asian Americans and that can identify the practitioners of indigenous healing methods.

MODIFICATION OF CONVENTIONAL FORMS OF COUNSELING TO MEET CULTURAL NEEDS

If the formal assessment results show that Asian American clients can benefit from conventional forms of counseling and psychotherapy, care must be taken to augment the treatment with culturally relevant and sensitive strategies. A number of research studies have been done on counselor types and counseling interventions that may be effective with Asian American clients. In general, the findings suggest that Asian American clients favor ethnically similar counselors over ethnically dissimilar counselors (Atkinson, Maruyama, & Matsui, 1978; Atkinson & Matsushita, 1991; Atkinson, Poston, Furlong, & Mercado, 1989; Atkinson, Wampold, Lowe, Matthews, & Ahn, 1998) and favor counselors with similar attitudes, more education, and similar personality and who are older (Atkinson et al., 1989; Atkinson, Wampold, et al., 1998). Asian American clients also favor a logical, rational, and directive counseling style to a reflective, affective, and nondirective one (Atkinson et al., 1978), especially if the counselor is an Asian American (Atkinson

& Matsushita, 1991). The findings also suggest that Asian American clients view culturally sensitive counselors as being more credible and culturally competent than less sensitive counselors (Gim, Atkinson, & Kim, 1991), and clients judge culturally responsive counselors as more credible than culturally neutral counselors (Zhang & Dixon, 2001). Asian Americans also prefer counselors who use the consultant helping role when the presenting problem has an external etiology (e.g., racism) and who take the role of the facilitator of indigenous support systems when the problem has an internal etiology (e.g., depression; Atkinson, Kim, & Caldwell, 1998). Furthermore, research suggests that bicultural Asian Americans perceive counselors as being more attractive than do Western-identified participants (Atkinson & Matsushita, 1991). In addition, a study by Merta, Ponterotto, and Brown (1992) suggests that acculturated Asian international student clients view authoritative peer counselors as being more credible than collaborative peer counselors. A limitation of this latter study, however, was that those participants deemed to be highly acculturated had only an average of 1 year and 9 months of residence in the United States and reported only adequate proficiency in English.

Although these findings provide some insights into what might comprise effective counseling strategies when mental health professionals treat Asian American clients, none of the studies, except for Merta et al. (1992), employed actual clients who were engaged in a realistic counseling situation. Instead, the studies utilized either surveys or audiovisual analogue designs, which rely on the ability of participants to accurately assume the role of clients based on reading counseling scripts, listening to audiotapes, or watching videotapes. As a result, it can be questioned whether the findings have external validity to actual counseling sessions. Pope-Davis, Liu, Toporek, and Brittan-Powell (2001), after a review of extant literature on multiculturally competent counseling strategies, recommended that "Research on clients' experiences in counseling should try to replicate real counseling" (p. 132).

There have been some efforts to study counseling process using Asian American clients in actual counseling sessions. The results of this type of research suggest that Asian American clients who have high adherence to Asian cultural values perceive counselors more positively than do clients low in adherence to Asian values (B. S. K. Kim, Li, & Liang, 2002), especially if the counselors also are Asian Americans (B. S. K. Kim & Atkinson, 2002). These findings are consistent with the notion that the cultural value of *deference to authority figures,* which is held by many Asian Americans, may cause these clients to give favorable ratings to their counselors (Atkinson et al., 1990; Gim et al., 1990). In terms of research on counseling strategies, the findings suggest that clients in a single session of counseling favor immediate resolution of the problem over exploration of the problem to gain insight (Kim et al., 2002) and directive style over nondirective style (Li & Kim, 2002). These findings are consistent with past results based on analogue designs and suggest that Asian American clients prefer a high degree of structure in their sessions and some form of guidance from their counselors. It should be noted, however, that these research findings offer only initial insights into counseling strategies that are effective with Asian American clients. Certainly, more research that employs actual clients and counseling sessions are needed.

In general, many of these research findings are consistent with S. Sue and Zane's (1987) notion of *gift giving*. The authors theorized that for mental health practitioners to be perceived as culturally responsive and to reduce clients' premature termination, practitioners should focus on helping clients to experience immediate and concrete benefits of counseling in the initial sessions; the authors termed this strategy *gift giving*. Examples of gifts are in general a resolution of a presenting problem and in particular anxiety reduction, depression relief, cognitive clarity, normalization, and skills acquisition. S. Sue and Zane pointed out that ethnic minorities in general and Asian Americans in particular have the need to attain some type of meaningful gains early in counseling and that "Gift giving demonstrates to clients the direct relationship between working in therapy and alleviation of problems" (p. 42). The current research literature on the counseling of Asian Americans provides support for these ideas and suggests that mental health practitioners may do well to provide immediate and concrete benefits to Asian American clients at an early onset of counseling. In doing so, practitioners may prevent these clients from terminating prematurely and, ultimately, help the clients resolve all the presenting issues.

ADDITIONAL SOURCES OF MENTAL HEALTH SUPPORT

To the extent that clients can benefit from additional support, mental health practitioners in both treatment situations (i.e., conventional counseling and psychotherapy, and a referral to a practitioner of indigenous healing methods) might consider referring the clients for adjunctive support services to agencies or organizations that serve Asian Americans. For example, it has been well documented that Korean Americans are overrepresented in churches in comparison to other ethnic groups and that they tend to seek support from church priests and other parishioners (H. Kim, 1977; Park, 1989). Mental health practitioners working with traditional Korean American clients may do well to help establish connections between their clients and their clients' churches so that the systems of support available in the churches can be utilized by the clients. Similarly, traditional Vietnamese American clients might be referred to temples in which priests can provide supportive services. One benefit of these existing sources of support found within the ethnic communities is that service providers may be able to speak the native languages of the clients. However, although culture-based sources of support may be useful, care should be taken so that the clients will not experience shame and embarrassment, which may occur if other members of the community learn that these individuals suffer from psychological difficulties. To avoid such situations, mental health practitioners should work closely with their clients to identify support sources with which clients feel comfortable.

A couple of research studies support the use of these sources of support. Atkinson, Kim, and Caldwell (1998) found that Asian American college students endorsed the use of indigenous support systems when Asian American clients experience problems that are internal in nature (e.g., depression). Indigenous support systems include culturally compatible religious or community centers designed to serve Asian American clients. In a study utilizing a qualitative method, B. S. K. Kim, Brenner, Liang, and Asay (2002) found that although Asian American participants had negative attitudes toward seeking help from counselors and psychologists, participants tended to seek emotional support from community organizations such as churches. To be able to make these referrals, it is critical for mental health practitioners to be in contact with ethnic organizations in their communities and to be aware of the types of resources that are available.

TREATMENT RECOMMENDATIONS

Although more research on effective ways to serve Asian Americans is needed, the empirical literature to date offers some guidance. Based on this literature, the following treatment recommendations can be made.

1. To meet the psychological needs of Asian Americans and to increase their utilization of counseling services, mental health practitioners need to conduct more outreach services. In addition, practitioners need to attend to possible feelings of shame and embarrassment by Asian Americans who seek treatment.

2. During initial assessment of Asian American clients, mental health practitioners should assess their clients' levels of acculturation and enculturation to determine the degree to which conventional modes of counseling and psychotherapy will be relevant to the clients.
    a. To the extent that the clients are highly acculturated, conventional modes of treatment may be effective.
    b. To the extent that the clients are highly enculturated, conventional modes of treatment need to be altered to infuse increased levels of cultural relevancy and sensitivity.

3. Mental health practitioners should gather information about clients' experiences with oppression (discrimination and prejudice) and about family and peer relationships. This information may provide insights about the level of credibility ascribed to practitioners, cross-cultural relationships that may be associated with the presenting problems, and important and potentially useful sources of emotional support.

4. After assessing clients' acculturation level, locus of problem etiology, and goal of counseling, mental health practitioners may refer to Atkinson et al.'s (1993) three-dimensional model of multicultural counseling to determine appropriate helper roles for their Asian American clients.

5. For traditional Asian American clients (i.e., those with high enculturation and low acculturation), especially those who are mistrustful of conventional treatment providers, mental health practitioners might consider making referrals to cultural resources within the community, practitioners of indigenous healing methods, or both.

6. When counseling traditional Asian American clients, mental health practitioners may be more effective when

a. they are ethnically similar. Hence, an effort should be made to assign Asian American clients to ethnically similar practitioners.
b. they use directive, logical, rational counseling style.
c. they focus on providing immediate and concrete benefits of counseling, especially during the early stages of the counseling relationship. As mentioned in this chapter, gift giving (S. Sue & Zane, 1987) can be an important mechanism by which mental health practitioners can ensure that clients will return for subsequent sessions. The use of gift giving also may increase the likelihood that clients comply with subsequent treatment interventions.

7. In addition to these strategies, non-Asian American practitioners may enhance their credibility with Asian American clients by acknowledging that they are from a different cultural background and that the difference may impact the counseling relationship and effectiveness. Mental health practitioners also may enhance their credibility by attending to cultural influences on the presenting issues. Clinicians also might inform their clients that they are open to learning as much as possible about the clients' cultural background so that they can increase their helpfulness to the clients; they can then invite the clients to share relevant cultural information. Throughout the counseling process, mental health practitioners should inquire about the cultural appropriateness of their interventions and make adjustments based on client feedback.

Exercises

1. You are a counselor at a community mental health center, and you have been assigned to assess a 50-year-old Asian American female client who complains about being severely depressed because she is mistreated by her coworkers, all of whom are non-Asian Americans.
   a) Identify all the culture-related factors you would need to consider during your initial assessment session to obtain a good understanding of this client's functioning.
   b) How would these cultural factors guide your treatment of this client?
   c) If you deem that you will need additional culture-specific forms of support for this client, which community agencies in your area would you consider as possible sources of referral?

2. You are a counselor at the counseling center of a local college, which is predominantly comprised of European American students. A 20-year-old Asian American male student, who immigrated to the United States at the age of 15, seeks your assistance because he is dealing with issues related to career uncertainty.
   a) How might you develop a working alliance with this client? What are some cultural barriers you might encounter?

b) What factors in the client's life would you consider to be important in the exploration of his career choice? (Hint: Consider relevant cultural values.) How would these factors be different if the client is highly acculturated?

c) As you work with the client, it becomes apparent to you that he also is experiencing serious interpersonal problems with his parents. What cultural factors might you consider before proposing a change to the counseling goal so that you and the client can attend to the familial conflict?

REFERENCES

American Psychiatric Association. (1994). *Diagnostic and statistical manual of mental disorders* (4th ed.). Washington, DC: Author.

Atkinson, D. R., & Gim, R. H. (1989). Asian-American cultural identity and attitudes toward mental health services. *Journal of Counseling Psychology, 36,* 209–212.

Atkinson, D. R., Kim, B. S. K., & Caldwell, R. (1998). Ratings of helper roles by multicultural psychologists and Asian American students: Initial support for the three-dimensional model of multicultural counseling. *Journal of Counseling Psychology, 45,* 414–423.

Atkinson, D. R., Lowe, S. M., & Matthews, L. (1995). Asian-American acculturation, gender, and willingness to seek counseling. *Journal of Multicultural Counseling and Development, 23,* 130–138.

Atkinson, D. R., Maruyama, M., & Matsui, S. (1978). The effects of counselor race and counseling approach on Asian Americans' perceptions of counselor credibility and utility. *Journal of Counseling Psychology, 25,* 76–83.

Atkinson, D. R., & Matsushita, Y. J. (1991). Japanese-American acculturation, counseling style, counselor ethnicity, and perceived counselor credibility. *Journal of Counseling Psychology, 38,* 473–478.

Atkinson, D. R., Morten, G., & Sue, D. W. (1998). *Counseling American minorities* (5th ed.). Boston: McGraw-Hill.

Atkinson, D. R., Poston, W. C., Furlong, M. J., & Mercado, P. (1989). Ethnic group preferences for counselor characteristics. *Journal of Counseling Psychology, 36,* 68–72.

Atkinson, D. R., Thompson, C., & Grant, S. (1993). A three-dimensional model for counseling racial/ethnic minorities. *The Counseling Psychologist, 21,* 257–277.

Atkinson, D. R., Wampold, B. E., Lowe, S. M., Matthews, L., & Ahn, H. (1998). Asian American preference for counselor characteristics: Application of the Bradley-Terry-Luce model to paired comparison data. *The Counseling Psychologist, 26,* 101–123.

Atkinson, D. R., Whiteley, S., & Gim, R. H. (1990). Asian-American acculturation preferences for help providers. *Journal of College Student Development, 31,* 155–161.

Berry, J. W. (1980). Acculturation as varieties of adaptation. In A. M. Padilla (Ed.), *Acculturation: Theory, models, and some new findings* (pp. 9–25). Boulder, CO: Westview Press.

Berry, J. W., Poortinga, Y. H., Segall, M. H., & Dasen, P. R. (1992). *Cross-cultural psychology: Research and application.* New York: Cambridge University Press.

Gim, R. H., Atkinson, D. R., & Kim, S. J. (1991). Asian-American acculturation, counselor ethnicity and cultural sensitivity, and ratings of counselors. *Journal of Counseling Psychology, 38,* 57–62.

Gim, R. H., Atkinson, D. R., & Whiteley, S. (1990). Asian-American acculturation, severity of concerns, and willingness to see a counselor. *Journal of Counseling Psychology, 37,* 281–285.

Herskovits, M. J. (1948). *Man and his works: The science of cultural anthropology.* New York: Knopf.

Kendall, L. (1988). Healing thyself: A Korean shaman's afflictions. *Social Science and Medicine, 27,* 445–450.

Kim, B. S. K., & Abreu, J. M. (2001). Acculturation measurement: Theory, current instruments, and future directions. In J. G. Ponterotto, J. M. Casas, L. A. Suzuki, & C. M. Alexander (Eds.), *Handbook of multicultural counseling* (2nd ed., pp. 394–424). Thousand Oaks, CA: Sage.

Kim, B. S. K., & Atkinson, D. R. (2002). Asian American client adherence to Asian cultural values, counselor expression of cultural values, counselor ethnicity, and career counseling process. *Journal of Counseling Psychology, 49,* 3–13.

Kim, B. S. K., Atkinson, D. R., & Umemoto, D. (2001). Asian cultural values and the counseling process: Current knowledge and directions for future research. *The Counseling Psychologist, 29,* 570–603.

Kim, B. S. K., Atkinson, D. R., & Yang, P. H. (1999). The Asian values scale: Development, factor analysis, validation, and reliability. *Journal of Counseling Psychology, 46,* 342–352.

Kim, B. S. K., Brenner, B. R., Liang, C. T. H., & Asay, P. A. (in press). A qualitative study of adaptation experiences of 1.5-generation Asian Americans. *Cultural Diversity and Ethnic Minority Psychology.*

Kim, B. S. K., Li, L. C., & Liang, C. T. H. (2002). Effects of Asian American client adherence to Asian cultural values, session goal, and counselor emphasis of client expression on career counseling process. *Journal of Counseling Psychology, 49,* 342–354.

Kim, B. S. K., & Omizo, M. M. (in press). Asian cultural values, attitudes toward seeking professional psychological help, and willingness to see a counselor. *The Counseling Psychologist.*

Kim, H. (1977). The history and role of the church in the Korean American community. In H. Kim (Ed.), *The Korean diaspora: Historical and sociological studies of Korean immigration and assimilation in North America* (pp. 47–63). Santa Barbara, CA: ABC Clio.

Koh, T. C. (1981). Tai chi chuan. *American Journal of Chinese Medicine, 9,* 15–22.

Leong, F. T. L. (1994). Asian Americans' differential patterns of utilization of inpatient and outpatient public mental health services in Hawaii. *Journal of Community Psychology, 22,* 82–96.

Leong, F. T. L., Wagner, N. S., & Tata, S. P. (1995). Racial and ethnic variations in help-seeking attitudes. In J. G. Ponterotto, J. M. Casas, L. A. Suzuki, &

C. M. Alexander (Eds.), *Handbook of multicultural counseling* (pp. 415–438). Thousand Oaks, CA: Sage.

Li, L., & Kim, B. S. K. (2002). *Effects of counseling style and Asian American client adherence to Asian cultural values on career-focused counseling process.* Manuscript submitted for publication.

Meng, F., Luo, H., & Halbreich, U. (2002). Concepts, techniques, and clinical applications of acupuncture. *Psychiatric Annals, 32,* 45–49.

Merta, R. J., Ponterotto, J. G., & Brown, R. D. (1992). Comparing the effectiveness of two directive styles in the academic counseling of foreign students. *Journal of Counseling Psychology, 39,* 214–218.

Park, K. (1989). "Born Again": What does it mean to Korean-Americans in New York City? *Journal of Ritual Studies, 3/2,* 287–301.

Pope-Davis, D. B., Liu, W. M., Toporek, R. L., & Brittan-Powell, C. S. (2001). What's missing from multicultural competency research: Review, introspection, and recommendations. *Cultural Diversity and Ethnic Minority Psychology, 7,* 121–138.

Sandlund, E. S., & Norlander, T. (2000). The effects of Tai Chi Chuan relaxation and exercise on stress responses and well-being: An overview of research. *International Journal of Stress Management, 17,* 139–149.

Segall, M. H., Dasen, P. R., Berry, J. W., & Poortinga, Y. H. (1990). *Human behavior in global perspective: An introduction to cross-cultural psychology.* New York: Pergamon Press.

Snowden, L. R., & Cheung, F. H. (1990). Use of inpatient mental health services by members of ethnic minority groups. *American Psychologist, 45,* 347–355.

Sue, D. W. (1990). Culture-specific strategies in counseling: A conceptual framework. *Professional Psychology: Research and Practice, 21,* 424–433.

Sue, D. W., & Sue, D. (1999). *Counseling the culturally different: Theory and practice* (3rd ed.). New York: Wiley.

Sue, S. (1977). Community mental health services to minority groups: Some optimism, some pessimism. *American Psychologist, 32,* 616–624.

Sue, S., Fujino, D. C., Hu, L., Takeuchi, D. T., & Zane, N. W. S. (1991). Community mental health services for ethnic minority groups: A test of the cultural responsiveness hypothesis. *Journal of Consulting and Clinical Psychology, 59,* 533–540.

Sue, S., & Morishima, J. K. (1982). *The mental health of Asian Americans.* San Francisco: Jossey-Bass.

Sue, S. & Zane, N. (1987). The role of culture and cultural techniques in psychotherapy: A critique and reformulation. *American Psychologist, 42,* 37–45.

Tata, S. P., & Leong, F. T. L. (1994). Individualism-collectivism, social-network orientation, and acculturation as predictors of attitudes toward seeking professional psychological help among Chinese Americans. *Journal of Counseling Psychology, 41,* 280–287.

U.S. Bureau of the Census. (2002). *The Asian population: 2000.* Retrieved November 10, 2002, from http://www.census.gov/prod/2002pubs/c2kbr01-16.pdf

Walsh, R. (1994). The making of a shaman: Calling, training, and culmination. *Journal of Humanistic Psychology, 34,* 7–30.

Walters, G. D. (2001). The Shaman effect in counseling clients with alcohol problems. *Alcoholism Treatment Quarterly, 19,* 31–43.

Yi, K. Y. (2000). Shin-byung (divine illness) in a Korean woman. *Culture, Medicine, and Psychiatry, 24,* 471–486.

Zhang, N., & Dixon, D. N. (2001). Multiculturally responsive counseling: Effects on Asian students' ratings of counselors. *Journal of Multicultural Counseling and Development, 29,* 253–262.

Part V THE HISPANIC
AMERICAN CLIENT

CHAPTER 13   *¡Somos!* Latinas
and Latinos in
the United States

Alberta M. Gloria and Theresa A.
Segura-Herrera, University of
Wisconsin–Madison

Identified as *la raza cósmica* or the cosmic race (Comas-Díaz, 2001), Latinas and Latinos comprise one of the youngest, largest, most culturally diverse, and fastest-growing racial and ethnic groups in the United States. In understanding the complexities of a heterogeneous group, it is necessary to gain a contextualized and culturally grounded understanding of the multifaceted influences and characteristics of Latinas and Latinos in the United States (Gloria & Rodriguez, 2000).

In providing an overview, the information presented in this chapter is not intended to be a complete description of Latinas and Latinos. Instead, the following information is presented as a knowledge base from which those who work with Latinas and Latinos can understand the complexities that form their psychosociocultural realities (Gloria & Rodriguez, 2000). Specifically, this chapter addresses demographic and psychosociocultural variables such as terminology and self-referents, population estimates, geographic representation, immigration, and generational statuses of Latinas and Latinos. Next, specific group issues such as age, language, employment, income, education, and health will be examined. More personal issues such as religion and spirituality, sexuality and sexual orientation, and phenotype are also discussed. Brief overviews of sociopolitical histories of different subgroups, social perceptions, and cultural values will also be presented. Topics are addressed independently; however, there is considerable overlap and interconnection among the social, historical, and cultural realities of Latinas and Latinos.

DEMOGRAPHIC AND
PSYCHOSOCIOCULTURAL VARIABLES

Great diversity exists among Latinas and Latinos. The following sections reveal some of the diversity in self-referents, demographic variables, and psychosociocultural variables.

Terminology and Self-Referents

Attempts to identify the most inclusive and least offensive term to describe millions of racially, ethnically, and culturally diverse Latinas and Latinos have resulted in widespread criticism and inadequate terminology, particularly because self-identifying terms vary by generational status, geography, nationality, and personal preference. Although the term *Hispanic* is widely used by government agencies and within the public sector, it homogenizes millions of individuals of different races, classes, languages, national origins, genders, and religions (Oboler, 1995) and has colonial implications and cultural heritage to Spain (Comas-Díaz, 2001).

The term *Latino* first appeared on the 2000 U.S. census form, and the 1970 census was the first to include a separate question asking about an individual's Hispanic origin. Prior to the 1970 census, Hispanic origin was indirectly determined via Spanish surname or report of Spanish as one's native tongue (Guzmán, 2001). Use of the term *Latina* or *Latino* also causes parameter concerns because it excludes Europeans (e.g., Spaniards), it masks between-group differences, and it creates misguided assumptions that there is a "typical Latino" (Gloria, 2001) or that "all Latinos are alike" (Garcia-Preto, 1996). Further, the terms *Latina* and *Latino* identify gender, whereas the term *Hispanic* is nongendered. Another important issue is that neither term takes into consideration generational status or place of birth. For example, a person who has resided in Texas for the past 60 years and a person who immigrated from Mexico two weeks ago would both be considered Latino or Hispanic, yet their realities and experiences are quite different.

Although individuals often choose self-referents that affirm national origin (e.g., Cuban, Peruvian) or ethnic identity (e.g., Xicano, Boricuas; Comas-Díaz, 2001), a critical consideration regarding the choice of a self-identifier is that of personal agency. That is, the personal choice and meaning ascribed to the self-identifiers of each individual or community of individuals are primary to the social and cultural "politics" of the label itself (Gloria, 2001). Ultimately, however, a unifying identifier generates social and political power (Garcia-Preto, 1996).

The terms *Latina* and *Latino* will be used for purposes of this chapter because they connote gender. Further, in the context of this chapter, the term *Latinas* will refer to females and the term *Latinos* will refer only to males.

Population Estimates

Approximately one in every eight persons in the United States is Latina or Latino (Therrien & Ramirez, 2001). Currently comprised of more than 35 million persons (excluding the Commonwealth of Puerto Rico and U.S. island areas), the Latina and Latino population has grown 61% between 1970 and 1980, 53% between 1980 and 1990 (U.S. Department of Commerce, 1993), and 57.9% from 1990 (22.4 million) to 2000 (35.3 million; Guzmán, 2001). The recent growth rate is more than four times the increase in the total U.S. population (13.2%), and as a result, Latinas and Latinos are projected to constitute the nation's largest minority group by 2005 (U.S. Department of Commerce News, 2000a).

Non-U.S.-born individuals represent 10.4% of the total U.S. population (38.4 million people), and more than half (51%) of these individuals are from Latin American countries (Lollock, 2001). In particular, Central Americans (including Mexicans) accounted for 34.5% of the non-U.S.-born Latinas and Latinos and about one third of the total non-U.S.-born individuals in the United States. As of 2000, 80.4% of those who arrived before 1970 obtained U.S. citizenship, compared to only 8.9% of those who arrived between 1990 and 1999 (Lollock, 2001). Political influence is compromised, however, because 39.1% of the voting-age population of Latinas and Latinos are not U.S. citizens (Jamieson, Shin, & Day, 2002).

The proportional representation of specific ethnic groups within the Latina and Latino population has dramatically changed since 1990. By subgroup, Latinas and Latinos who are classified as "other" (e.g., South and Central American, Dominican, individuals who did not identify a specific ethnic background) had the largest population growth, increasing almost 100% (5.1 to 10.0 million) compared to Mexicans (59%; 13.5 to 20.6 million), Puerto Ricans (24.9%; 2.7 to 3.4 million), and Cubans (18.9%; 1.0 to 1.2 million; Guzmán, 2001). Approximately 4.8% and 3.8% of the total Latina and Latino population is comprised of, respectively, Central Americans (particularly Salvadorans, 1.9%) and South Americans (particularly Colombians, 1.3%; Guzmán, 2001).

Geographic Representation

Although Latinas and Latinos live in every U.S. state, more than three fourths (76.8%, or 27 million) are geographically concentrated in seven states (i.e., California, Texas, New York, Florida, Illinois, Arizona, and New Jersey), and more than half live in California and Texas. Almost half of Latinas and Latinos live in metropolitan areas (46.4%), particularly New York City, Los Angeles, Chicago, Houston, and San Antonio (Guzmán, 2001). Mexicans are concentrated in the western (56.8%) and the southern (32.6%) United States (Therrien & Ramirez, 2001), living primarily in Los Angeles, Chicago, Houston, San Antonio, and Phoenix (Guzmán, 2001). The majority of Puerto Ricans (63.9%) are located in the northeastern United States (Therrien & Ramirez, 2001) in New York, Chicago, and Philadelphia (Guzmán, 2001). Most Cubans (80.1%) reside in the southern United States (Therrien & Ramirez, 2001), particularly Florida (Guzmán, 2001). Finally, South and Central Americans are most often located in the southern (34.6%), northeastern (32.3%), and western (28.2%) United States (Therrien & Ramirez, 2001).

Immigration

Although difficult to estimate, there are approximately 3.2 million illegal immigrants in the United States, and more than half enter the United States legally as tourists, students, or temporary or migrant workers (Simon, 1995). The majority of Latina and Latino immigrants come to the United States with proper documentation and become "illegal" when their paperwork permitting travel expires.

Further, many undocumented immigrants enter the United States by plane, whereas less than half come on foot (Ramos, 2000).

The motives for Latina and Latino migration to the United States vary, ranging from those who seek occupational or educational opportunities to those who flee political persecution and socioeconomic oppression. Nonetheless, Latina and Latino immigrants often share common migration experiences as they enter a country that has a different culture and as they navigate unexpected obstacles of poverty, discrimination, language, and ambiguous immigration or legal status. Physically, many are uprooted from familiar people and places. Socially, immigrants are disjointed from the intimacy of their immediate family, friends, and hometown community, often leaving behind children and spouses (Zea, Diehl, & Porterfield, 1997). Culturally, immigrants are disconnected from their customary ways of living, thinking, and doing (Falicov, 1998). For example, the stressors associated with feeling uprooted are magnified for Latinas and Latinos who are survivors of war-related violence (Zea et al., 1997). Trauma, such as experiencing state-sponsored violence, witnessing the razing of their village, viewing mutilated corpses, witnessing or being tortured, and having loved ones disappear, frequently leads to higher reports of post-traumatic stress disorder symptoms and other adjustment difficulties (Zea et al., 1997).

Generational Status

Generational status can vary from days to centuries depending on the origins and immigration histories of Latinas and Latinos. For example, variability in generational status is indicated by those Latinas and Latinos who are fifth-generation descendants of Spanish colonists compared to those who are recently arrived immigrants. Generational status is often used as a single indicator of the degree to which cultural values and traditions are adhered to and practiced, and it varies by self-identification (G. Marín & Marín, 1991). For example, individuals who are of Mexican descent and who are first-generation (i.e., non-U.S.-born individuals who migrated to the United States) often prefer to be identified as Mexican, whereas those who are second generation prefer to be called Mexican American.

Age

More than one third (35%) of the U.S. Latina and Latino population is 18 years of age or younger compared to one quarter (25.7%) of the total U.S. population (Guzmán, 2001). With a median age of 25.9 years (35.3 years for the general U.S. population), Latinas and Latinos are substantially younger than any U.S. racial or ethnic group. The age gap between Latinas and Latinos and the general U.S. population is expected to widen given the increased number of Latina and Latino infants born over the past 10 years (Ramos, 2000) and the continued migration of younger individuals (Falicov, 1998). Mexicans had the lowest median age (24.2), followed by Puerto Ricans (27.3), Central American (29.2), Dominicans (29.5), South American (33.1), and Cubans (40.7) (Guzmán, 2001). Further, 75% of Latinas and Latinos in the United States are under the age of 39, compared with 60% of the total U.S. population (García & Marotta, 1997).

Language

Spanish is spoken by nearly half of all non-English speakers in the United States (U.S. Department of Commerce, 1993). Although Latina and Latino ethnic groups are interconnected through language, they have dialect differences and linguistic nuances (Gloria, Rodriguez, & Castillo, in press). For example, the different ethnic uses of everyday words (e.g., corn, *maiz, elote,* or *choclo*) can create language barriers. As a result of language differences and a lack of bilingual services, Latinas and Latinos experience inappropriate physical and mental health diagnoses and treatment (Echeverry, 1997) and are discriminated against in educational settings (Mestre & Royer, 1991).

English proficiency is a pressing social and educational issue vital to the economic and social advancement of Latinas and Latinos (Gonzalez, 2000). The importance of English proficiency is exemplified by Latina and Latino immigrants who need English language skills in order to carry out daily activities or to work in the United States (Gloria et al., in press). Despite the need for English proficiency, more than three quarters of all Latinas and Latinos speak Spanish at home (Garcia & Marotta, 1997). Nevertheless, 70% of Latina and Latino immigrant children are predominantly English-speaking (Gonzalez, 2000).

Gloria et al. (in press) warned that the level of English proficiency used to carry out daily activities, however, may not be sufficient to convey emotional content and underlying cultural meanings for Latinas and Latinos. As a result, Spanish may be used when discussing emotions or disclosing past experiences. Likewise, English may be the preferred language to communicate culturally stigmatized feelings, behaviors, and topics (e.g., sexual issues; Green, 1997).

Employment

The majority of occupations and types of employment held by Latinas and Latinos help maintain the economically stable lifestyle of the United States, because many take dangerous low-paying jobs (such as harvesting fruits and vegetables and butchering livestock) that do not provide health insurance or other benefits or paid time off (Ramos, 2000). For example, Ramos posited that without Mexicans in the workforce for just one day, millions of dollars would be lost in the orange, lettuce, avocado, and grape industries. Further, the sewing industry as well as hotels, restaurants, stores, and gasoline stations would be immobilized.

Latinos participate in the labor force at a higher rate (78.4%) than White men (74.3%), whereas Latinas engage in the labor force at a lower rate (55.8%) than White women (60.3%; Ramirez, 2000). Latinas and Latinos are more likely to work in service-oriented occupations and twice as likely to be employed as operators and laborers than Whites are (Therrien & Ramirez, 2001). Frequently, the service-oriented jobs are hazardous and low-paying and often do not provide health care, vacation time, or other benefits (Ramos, 2000). Occupational safety for Latinas and Latinos, therefore, is a serious concern, particularly because immigrant workers accounted for 50% of job-related deaths. Further, there was an 11.6% increase in job-related fatalities for Latino workers (U.S. Department of

Labor, 2002). These figures are likely underestimated because companies often do not report critical job incidents for fear of being fined for hiring illegal immigrants. In addition, many undocumented workers are unaware of their rights to safe working environments and choose not to report unsafe work conditions for fear of deportation or termination (U.S. Department of Labor, 2002).

Puerto Ricans have the highest unemployment rates (8.1%), followed by Other Latinas and Latinos (7.8%), Mexicans (7.0%), Cubans (5.8%), and Central (5.1%) and South Americans (5.1%; Therrien & Ramirez, 2001). The unemployment rate for Latinas and Latinos aged 16 years and older was 6.7% compared to 3.6% for Whites (Ramirez, 2000). Many of those Latinas and Latinos who were not employed in 2000 did not work in order to care for children or others (42%) or experienced chronic illness or disability (17.2%; Weismantle, 2001).

Income

Latinas and Latinos have a lower income ($12,306) than Whites ($23,415), Blacks ($15,197), and Asian/Pacific Islanders ($22,352). As a result, one in four Latinas or Latinos lives in poverty, and they are three times more likely to be living below the poverty level than are Whites (U.S. Department of Commerce News, 2000b). Of those Latinas and Latinos who live in poverty, almost half (47.5%) are children under 18 years of age (Ramirez, 2000). As a matter of tradition and economic necessity, Latina and Latino family members pool their individual incomes. The median family income of Latinas and Latinos in 2000 was the highest ever at $33,447, a 5.3% increase from 1999 (DeNavas-Walt, Cleveland, & Roemer, 2001). However, this figure masks variation in family income across ethnicity and sex. For example, 26.7% of Puerto Rican families, 24.4% of Mexican families, 18.5% of Central and South American families, and 11% of Cuban families live below the poverty level (Ramirez, 2000). For Latina-headed households, the poverty rate was 34.2% compared to 16.9% for White female-headed households (Dalaker, 2001).

For full-time workers, only 20.6% of Mexicans have annual earnings of $35,000 or more, followed closely by Central and South Americans (24.5%) and Puerto Ricans. Full-time Cuban workers (34.4%) are most likely to earn $35,000 or more compared to 49.3% for Whites. Only 9.6% of Latinas and Latinos earn $50,000 or more compared to 27.4% of Whites. Mexicans (7.7%) are least likely to earn $50,000 or more (Therrien & Ramirez, 2001).

Education

Latinas and Latinos continue to be undereducated. Comprising the largest percentage of elementary- and secondary-level children, Latinas and Latinos do not proportionally enter high school and college (National Center for Education Statistics [NCES], 2000a). The high school dropout rate for Latinas and Latinos who are 16 to 24 years old has been consistently higher than those of other races and ethnicities for almost 30 years; as a result, approximately 30% of Latinas and Latinos are not in school or lack a high school credential (NCES, 2000b). In particular, there is a 44% dropout rate for immigrant Latinas and Latinos; later generation individuals have a 15% to 16% dropout rate (NCES, 2002).

The rates of dropouts or stop outs (those who take a temporary leave from school with the intention of returning) illustrate the educational challenges that many Latinas and Latinos have to contend with, such as limited educational resources, few bilingual teachers, low academic expectations from teachers, misplacement into special education, educational tracking, and few teachers who integrate culture into classroom curricula (President's Advisory Commission of Educational Excellence for Hispanic Americans, 1996). The undereducation of Latinas and Latinos perpetuates cycles of segregation and underemployment, because they are isolated from social, economic, and political opportunity and advancement (Aguirre & Martinez, 1993).

Educational attainment, however, varies by ethnic group. Specifically, Mexicans are least likely to have a high school education (51.0%), followed by Puerto Ricans and Central and South Americans (64.3% each). Cubans are most likely to have earned a high school degree (73%; Therrien & Ramirez, 2001). The trends for college completion rates are similar: Mexicans have the lowest rate of college completion (5%) and Cubans have the highest (20%). Puerto Ricans and Central and South Americans have college completion rates of 10% and 16% respectively (Aguirre & Martinez, 1993).

Educational attainments also vary by gender; Latinas tend to have more stressful educational experiences (Gándara & Osugi, 1994) and tend to drop out or stop out of college at higher rates than Latinos (Vásquez, 1982). The need for Latinas ages 25 to 34 to pursue advanced education is important, because those who had 9 to 11 years of schooling earned 30 % less than did Latinos with a high school diploma. Also, Latinas who earned a bachelor's degree earned 82% more than did Latinas with a high school education (NCES, 1995).

Religion and Spirituality

Although Catholicism is the predominant religion of many Latinas and Latinos, no single denomination encompasses their diverse religious and spiritual practices (Gloria et al., in press). Beginning with the Spanish conquest of the Americas in the sixteenth century, Catholicism became the prominent religion as *conquistadores* and priests forced the conversion of indigenous peoples from their native religions to Catholicism (Zea, Mason, & Murguía, 2000).

Because Latinas and Latinos vary in their adherence and practice of the Catholic faith, opposition to the Roman Catholic church's stance on social issues such as divorce, abortion, homosexuality, and premarital sex is evident (Zea et al., 2000). Similarly, conversions to other religious denominations (e.g., the Evangelical, Mormon, Anglican, Baptist, or Jewish religions) or preferences for practicing native traditions are common. For example, many Puerto Ricans, Mexicans, and Cubans practice *Espiritismo, Curanderismo,* and *Santeria,* respectively. Each spiritual tradition developed independently as result of the integration of folk Catholicism with indigenous spiritual practices (Koss-Chioino, 1995).

Sexuality

The topic of sexual behavior or sexuality has traditionally been considered taboo for Latinas and Latinos. Whether influenced by traditionality, cultural norms, or religiosity, Latinas and Latinos tend not to discuss sexuality (B. V. Marín & Gómez, 1997). "Sexual silence" (Diaz, 1997) is the inability to verbalize and acknowledge oneself as a sexual being to others and is often the culturally accepted norm when Latinas and Latinos address issues of sexuality. Open disclosure about one's sexual behavior, particularly in same-sex relationships, violates cultural expectations of *respeto* (e.g., respecting family members, particularly elders, and setting a "good" example for those who are younger) and female gender roles (e.g., to not engage in pleasurable sexual behavior; Green, 1997). For example, many Latinas and Latinos would consider it disrespectful and even confrontational for a person (particularly if that person was lesbian, gay, bisexual, or transgendered—LGBT) to discuss his or her sexuality with family members (B. V. Marín & Gómez, 1997). Sexual silence and the complex interplay among cultural constructs explain why some Latinas and Latinos are uninformed about sex and sexuality (Amaro, Messinger, & Cervantes, 1996).

Also, many LGBT Latinas and Latinos must manage multiple cultural identities across and within LGBT, ethnic minority, and White cultures and communities (Fukuyama & Ferguson, 2000; Green, 1997). The challenge of having multiple identities is one factor that places LGBT Latinas and Latinos at an increased risk for isolation, anxiety, confusion, and depression (Fukuyama & Ferguson, 2000).

Because family is a central value, LGBT Latinas and Latinos are often pressured to marry and have children, and same-sex relationships are overlooked to maintain family stability (Fukuyama & Ferguson, 2000). As a result, homosexuality is often considered a threat to gender roles and familial expectations. Important to note, however, is that Latinos who have sex with men are often not stigmatized as gay if they assume the active role rather than the passive or receptive role (Zamora-Hernandez & Patterson, 1996).

Phenotype

A salient aspect of heterogeneity among Latinas and Latinos is phenotype. Variation in physical appearance often depends on ancestral origin, ranging from Native indigenous, to criollo (White European), to African, to a blend of these origins (*mestizaje* [Native and European] or *mulata* or *mulatto* [African and European]). Historically, skin color, hair texture, and facial features are distinguishing physical features associated with race, ethnicity, and status (Gomez, 2000).

Differences in statuses associated with phenotypes, particularly skin color, have been attributed to the Spanish colonization of the Americas. White European conquistadores exerted their dominance and power by consciously and subconsciously proclaiming their culture and phenotype superior to that of indigenous and African peoples, who comprised the dark-skinned, subordinate, and conquered group (Arce, Murguia, & Frisbie, 1987). The enduring effects of European colonists who ascribed White superiority over darker-skinned indigenous and African people continue today as these same distinguishing physical qualities continue to perpetuate racial and power inequities (Gomez, 2000). For example, Latino and Latina parents encourage their children to stay out of the sun when playing outside, hoping that their children's skin will not physically resemble a more indigenous, darker phenotype.

Darker skin tones have also been associated with increased depressive symptoms, lower educational attainment, and lower economic and social status (such as farm workers who are darker-skinned from working *de sol a sol* [sunup to sundown]; Arce et al., 1987; Codina & Montalvo, 1994). Conversely, light-skinned Latinas and Latinos who resemble European ancestry (who can "pass" for being White) tend to have higher levels of socioeconomic status and experience fewer discriminatory labor market practices (e.g., decreased hourly wages) than their darker-skinned counterparts (Gomez, 2000).

SOCIOPOLITICAL HISTORIES

Like the heterogeneity of subgroups, the sociopolitical histories of Latinas and Latinos are diverse. Because of abject poverty, foreign debt, and progressively deteriorating standards of living in Latin America (Gonzalez, 2000), migration to the United States provides a sense of hope and opportunity for many Latinas and Latinos. When the potential for economic progress is assessed (e.g., earnings for one hour of work in the United States compared to earnings for an entire day or more in one's homeland), the risk of migrating (either legally or illegally) is often an enticing and necessary option. Beyond economic benefits, many Latinas and Latinos also migrate to avoid political tyranny and the consequences of war (e.g., communism, state-sponsored violence). Very brief overviews of the sociopolitical histories of different Latina and Latino ethnic groups are provided in the following sections.

Individuals of Mexican Descent—Mexicanos

Latinas and Latinos of Mexican descent are the only ethnic group comprised of both early settlers and recent immigrants (Gonzalez, 2000). Up until the mid-1800s, Mexicans freely migrated to and from the land that now forms Texas (Gonzalez, 2000). The settlement of Anglo, Irish, and German immigrants along a predominantly Mexican-owned strip of land led to disputes over land-grazing ownership, which triggered the Mexican War in 1846 (Gonzalez, 2000). The 1848 Treaty of Guadalupe Hidalgo ended the war and marked the annexation of Texas (the originally disputed territory), Arizona, California, Colorado, Nevada, New Mexico, Utah, and Wyoming to the United States (Falicov, 1998). As a result, more than 75,000 Mexican residents of these regions suddenly became U.S. citizens (Falicov, 1998). Anglo settlers viewed these new citizens as barriers toward progress, and violence against them was common (Gonzalez, 2000). In order to survive, many Mexicans (i.e., new U.S. citizens) became poorly paid workers on the land that they once owned (Falicov, 1998).

U.S. policy toward Mexican immigration has been contradictory and largely dependent on economic conditions. For example, the 1993 North American Free Trade Agreement allowed Mexican workers (who provide inexpensive labor) to enter the United States. Nevertheless, public dissatisfaction with Mexican immigration has instigated deportation raids and other anti-immigration tactics (e.g., Operation Wetback of 1954, California's Proposition 187 in 1994; Gonzalez, 2000).

Individuals of Puerto Rican Descent—Puerto Riqueños

The United States acquired Puerto Rico when Spain was defeated in the Spanish-American War in 1898 and was perceived as an asset for its strategic military position and fertile coffee and sugar plantations (Falicov, 1998). Puerto Ricans initially welcomed U.S. promises to stop Spanish colonialism and to provide islanders the autonomy to maintain their own laws and practices. Within two years, however, the Foraker Act (Organic Act of 1900) and the Jones Act of 1917 made the island a U.S. territory with an appointed governor and administrative staff. Soon thereafter, a compulsory military service law drafted 20,000 islanders into World War I as American soldiers.

The Foraker Act also facilitated the expropriation of Puerto Rican–owned lands by American-owned sugar companies (Gonzalez, 2000). Because of the exploitation of workers on sugar, tobacco, and coffee plantations, frequent strikes and anti-American violence erupted in the 1930s, and Puerto Rico rapidly earned the reputation of being the "poorhouse of the Caribbean" (Gonzalez, 2000). In the 1940s, the United States established military bases on the island of Vieques, taking over a large portion of the island. By the 1950s, post–World War II congressional approval allowed islanders to elect their own governor and create the Puerto Rican Commonwealth. In response to the island's increasingly high unemployment during the 1950s, some residents of rural areas flocked to larger cities and many others migrated to the United States (Gonzalez, 2000). Although migration began as early as the 1920s, more than 40,000 Puerto Ricans fled to New York City during the 1950s economic crisis (Gonzalez, 2000). As a result, an estimated 2.8 million Puerto Ricans live in the United States, and 3.8 million live on the island (Gonzalez, 2000). Because of citizenship, ease of travel, and political and economic connections, the migration pattern for Puerto Ricans is circular (Vazquez, 1997).

Individuals of Cuban Descent—Cubanos

Cuban migration is characterized by multiple migratory waves that date back to the late 1800s. At that time, prosperous cigar factories and steam liner businesses fostered close economic ties between Cuba and the United States (Gonzalez, 2000). Although a small number of Cubans would travel and vacation in the United States, they rarely sought permanent U.S. residence (Gonzalez, 2000). The Cuban Revolution of 1959, which established Castro's political and economic reforms, triggered the migration of almost 215,000 Cubans who sought refuge in the United States (Gonzalez, 2000). These immigrants were from upper- and upper-middle class backgrounds with wealth and entrepreneurial skills, higher levels of education, the privilege of white skin, and a passionate opposition to Castro and communism (Falicov, 1998).

Between 1960 and 1962, Operation Pedro Pan enabled more than 14,000 unaccompanied Cuban children to enter the United States, many of whom were placed in foster homes. Limitations during the cold war prevented many individuals from being reunited with family for years (Triay, 1998). Under the 1966 Cuban Adjustment Act, refugees received automatic eligibility for public assistance, Medicaid, food stamps, free English classes, educational scholarships, low-interest college loans, and cash allowances for families (Gonzalez, 2000). Similar support, however, has not been offered to any other Latina and Latino immigrants.

Another wave of more than 125,000 Cubans entered the United States during the *Mariel* flight in the 1980s (Gonzalez, 2000). *Marielitos* were significantly different from other immigrant waves in that they were comprised of predominantly poor, dark-skinned, and uneducated Cubans, some of whom were mentally ill, dangerous (i.e., criminals), or "less desirable" (Gonzalez, 2000). Unlike previous migration waves, the arrival of the *Marielitos* generated an anti-immigrant fervor and eventually led to the Immigration Reform Act of 1995, which encouraged the detainment and deportation of illegal immigrants. The *Balceros* (individuals who use small handmade boats to flee Cuba) are the most recent wave of Cuban refugees. Those who are caught before reaching U.S. soil are detained (oftentimes for years) in tent cities at the Guantanamo base.

Individuals of Central American Descent—Centro Americanos

Immigrants from Guatemala, El Salvador, and Nicaragua are the most recently arrived Latina and Latino ethnic groups within the United States. The Refugee Act granted political asylum to those fearing or experiencing political persecution, which allowed all Central Americans to be eligible for refugee status. Since the 1980s, individuals of Central American descent have migrated as a result of poverty, substandard living conditions, lack of employment and education, and the violence and terror of civil wars that were often militarily and financially supported by the United States.

The majority of these immigrants originated from countries that had civil war fatalities five times greater than U.S. losses in the Vietnam War (Gonzalez, 2000). Specifically, war fatalities in Guatemala, El Salvador, and Nicaragua cumulatively surpassed one quarter of a million in 1989 (140,000, 70,000, and 60,000, respectively). As many immigrants flee the destruction of war by leaving their countries and entering the United States on foot through Mexico, they contend not only with Spanish dialect differences but also with threats of sexual and physical violence (Ramos, 2000). Although these migratory experiences were not addressed by the U.S. government, the opportunity of political asylum symbolized progress to U.S. immigration policy (Ramos, 2000).

Individuals of South American Descent—Sud Americanos

Because of their diverse geographies, climates, races, languages, and ethnicities, immigrants who originate from South American countries (e.g., Colombia,

Venezuela, Ecuador, Peru) introduce a cultural complexity like no other Latina or
Latino subgroup (Garcia-Preto, 1996). Like other Latina and Latino immigrants,
South Americans have migrated to the United States for several reasons, includ-
ing religious or political persecution, natural disasters, civil wars, and extreme
poverty (Gonzalez, 2000; Ramos, 2000). South Americans, however, have a his-
tory of economic and political arrangements with the United States rather than a
history of colonization (Santiago-Rivera, Arredondo, & Gallardo-Cooper, 2002).
South American immigrants tend to be bilingual, bicultural, and educated (Flores
& Carey, 2000), which has made their transitional experiences to the United
States somewhat easier.

   Despite characteristics that make for a somewhat easier transition, South
American immigrants often change their surname in their attempt to fit in (via their
language skills) or "pass" for Black or White Americans (via their phenotype). Because of their smaller population size within the United States in comparison to
other Latina and Latino groups, South Americans are often aggregated with Central
Americans, thereby negating their history and experiences (Garcia-Preto, 1996).

SOCIAL PERCEPTIONS

Stereotypes have historically influenced public perception of Latinos and Latinas.
Negative stereotypes, a form of psychological and sometimes physical violence
that impacts all aspects of Latino and Latina lives, are perpetuated (implicitly and
explicitly) in the media and in economic and social systems (Utsey, Bolden, &
Brown, 2001).

Media

Media portrayals of Latinas and Latinos influence their regard and treatment by
the general public, which in turn affects their quality of life and well-being (e.g.,
inferior wages, substandard work conditions, sense of self; Niemann, 2001). For
example, film and television productions perpetuate negative stereotypes when
Latinas and Latinos continuously are portrayed as maids, janitors, drug lords,
gang members, or criminals. Further, Latinas and Latinos are frequently and
stereotypically depicted as uneducated, underpaid, lazy, and immoral (National
Latino Children's Institute, 1997).

Economy

A plethora of negative stereotypes and confusing facts about Latina and Latino immigrants also have guided anti-Latino immigrant laws and public policy (e.g., California's Proposition 187). Because immigration remains controversial, the media
represent undocumented Latina and Latino immigrants as numerically extant, criminal, and promiscuous. Immigrants are further portrayed as costly to the United
States because of their assumed "dependency" on social services and "unwillingness
to work" (Cowan, Martinez, & Mendiola, 1997). Recently immigrated Latinas and

Latinos, however, tend to be healthier (needing fewer public health expenditures) and to be more productive workers than U.S.-born citizens and those who have lived in the United States for 10 years or more (Simon, 1995). Also, many people erroneously believe that Latina and Latino immigrants take jobs from other U.S. citizens. However, U.S. cities with more immigrants experience growths in employment opportunities, declines in low-wage industries (where immigrants typically find employment), and overall job advancement for less-skilled citizens (Simon, 1995).

Illegal Latina and Latino immigrants are also thought to drain government resources (e.g., welfare, education), yet their tax-dollar contributions are often distributed to federal and not local systems (Gonzalez, 2000). For example, illegal immigrants residing in Los Angeles County contributed $3 billion in taxes; however, more than half (56%) of the tax dollars were relegated to federal budgets, and the remaining monies provided services (e.g., education, health care, law enforcement) to local residents (Gonzalez, 2000). Despite consistent findings by economists that both legal and illegal immigrants make an important contribution to the economy, polls demonstrate that a vast majority of U.S. citizens want less immigration (Simon, 1995).

Education

Stemming from a deficit model perspective, myths about Latina and Latino students' educational attainment add to current levels of undereducation (Retish & Kavanaugh, 1992). For example, it is often believed that Latina and Latino cultural values discourage educational achievement. Instead, Latina and Latino families have consistently been identified as a source of educational support and encouragement (Aguirre & Martinez, 1993). Another prominent myth is that Latinas and Latinos are intellectually inferior, as evidenced by lower IQ scores and poor standardized test scores. Systematic and cultural test bias for Latinas and Latinos continues, particularly for those whose second language is English (Mestre & Royer, 1991).

The idea that the quality of education for Latina and Latino students is equivalent to that of other students is also a common myth (Retish & Kavanaugh, 1992). Unlike their counterparts, Latinas and Latinos contend with numerous educational barriers, including limited educational resources, low academic expectations from teachers, educational tracking, and misplacement into special education (President's Advisory Commission of Educational Excellence for Hispanic Americans, 1996). In explaining the educational experiences of Latinas and Latinos, Secada et al. (1998) suggested that U.S. school environments often "push out" Latina and Latino students. Overall, negative educational mistruths about Latina and Latino students shed light on their educational status of underrepresentation at all levels of education.

CULTURAL VALUES

The values presented here are intended only as a brief introduction. Cultural values vary as a function of ethnic identity, acculturation, and enculturation for each individual Latina and Latino. Therefore, assumptions should not be made about the degree to which individual Latinas and Latinos adhere to these cultural values.

Familismo

A profound sense of family, *familismo,* is a core aspect of Latina and Latino culture (G. Marín & Marín, 1991); *todo para la familia* (everything for the family) is a common mantra. *Familismo* is characterized by strong feelings of loyalty, unity, solidarity, reciprocity, interdependence, and cooperation (Falicov, 1996). As a result, family needs take precedence over individual needs. Family is also physically manifested through kinship systems that include nuclear, extended, and nonrelated family members (Comas-Díaz & Griffith, 1988). For Latinas and Latinos, family is a natural support system that provides physical, emotional, and social support and also has the durability to endure change and the flexibility to expand and include new members. For example, children become part of the family (*hijos e hijas de crianza*) by virtue of being taken care of by adult members of the family (Fox, 1996). Flexibility of roles within the family, however, is typically not a valued attribute among Latinas and Latinos (Paniagua, 1994).

Personalismo

A style of communication that emphasizes personal interactions, *personalismo* represents an orientation in which people are more important than the tasks at hand (Santiago-Rivera et al., 2002). This orientation values dignity of self and others and the reciprocity of respect for others regardless of personal (e.g., gender) or social status (Bracero, 1998). Interactions are characterized by personal warmth and genuineness that may take the form of *platicando,* or "personal small talk" (Santiago-Rivera et al., 2002, p. 116).

Simpatía

Related to *personalismo, simpatía* emphasizes harmonious and pleasant interpersonal relationships (Santiago-Rivera et al., 2002). The value of *simpatía* promotes behaviors that are respectful of others and that maintain interpersonal harmony (Triandis, Marín, Lisansky, & Betancourt, 1984). Latinas and Latinos are likely to adhere to *simpatía* when talking with friends and family even if they will be late for an appointment or when sacrificing their needs to attend a family function instead. As a result, interactions may be indirect and detail-specific, and direct argument or contradiction is considered rude (Santiago-Rivera et al., 2002).

Cariño

Cariño, the personal quality of being affectionate, refers to the expression of verbal and nonverbal endearments (Santiago-Rivera et al., 2002). Being *cariñoso* or *cariñosa* is a highly valued act that expresses a close relationship with others. Latinas and Latinos often manifest *cariño* by kissing on the cheek or hugging when greeting a person or by touching a person on the shoulder or arm when talking. Similarly, using language that is diminutive with others (e.g., using nouns with the suffix of *ito* or *ita—mi'ja* to *mi'jita* ["my daughter" to "my little daughter"]) reflects a deeper and more intimate form of communication (Santiago-Rivera et al., 2002).

Respeto

A show of respect in interpersonal interactions acknowledges an individual's personal power regardless of the degree of power held (G. Marín & Marín, 1991). More specifically, *respeto* is appropriate deferential behavior based on age, social or economic status, or sex (Paniagua, 1994). A Latino who shows proper respect for an elder would be considered *una persona bien educada,* or a person who was taught by his parents the importance of respect within personal relationships. In contrast, a Latino who is *mal educado,* or poorly educated, is often believed to be someone who was not properly taught how to treat others, particularly those in positions of authority (Paniagua, 1994), something that would be considered *una falta de respeto* (a lack of respect).

Confianza

Confianza is the development of trust, intimacy, and familiarity within a relationship (Bracero, 1998; Santiago-Rivera et al., 2002). *Confianza* allows the expression of intimacy based on mutual understanding and appreciation (Delgado, 1983). When *confianza* is established, Latinas and Latinos often interact and speak knowing that others *son de confianza* (can be trusted; Santiago-Rivera et al, 2002). Moreover, *confianza,* identified as "optimal relatedness," is the standard by which all social relationships (e.g., familial, personal, professional) are measured (Bracero, 1998).

Machismo, Hembrismo, and Marianismo

Although transformed over time, traditional gender roles continue (Vega, 1995). Being *macho* (literally meaning "male") or the value of *machismo* have both positive and negative connotations yet are most often negatively defined. At one extreme, macho Latinos promote strict gender roles (that cause distress to their families), drink large amounts of alcohol, are sexually ready and available, are extremely authoritarian, or dominate women psychologically or physically (Abreu, Goodyear, Campos, & Newcomb, 2000). In contrast, the positive aspects of machismo refer to Latinos who support and protect their families, provide structure to family relationships, and are responsible to their family, friends, and community (Morales, 1996).

Hembra (meaning "female") or the value of *hembrismo* (femaleness) indicates that Latinas are expected to competently fulfill multiple roles in and out of the home (Comas-Díaz, 1989) while displaying strength, perseverance, and flexibility (Gloria, 2001). *Marianismo* reveres the Virgin Mary, indicating that Latinas must be morally and spiritually superior to men, selfless or *aguantar* (able to endure or tolerate adversity), and nurturing (Lopez-Baez, 1999). Many Latinas are expected to live cultural contradictions by maintaining traditional values (Gloria, 2001) while assuming traditional Latino gender roles (e.g., serving as heads of households because of changing economics and acculturation) and fulfilling cultural roles to maintain psychological ties to their native culture or homeland (Santiago-Rivera et al., 2002).

¡SOMOS EL PASADO, EL PRESENTE, Y EL FUTURO!
[WE ARE THE PAST, PRESENT, AND FUTURE!]

Extensive data and literature are outlined in this chapter, and the question that may surface is, *¿Todo esto y que?* that is, what use is all of this information? First, the information provided here is culturally and contextually based and can be used to dispel inaccurate assumptions and stereotypes about Latinas and Latinos. Second, this chapter highlights the central role that Latinas and Latinos have had and will continue to have in the economic, social, and cultural development of the United States. Third, although the commonalities of immigration, education, linguistics, and culture of Latinas and Latinos are illustrated, this chapter also emphasizes the need for unique considerations based on distinctive characteristics and experiences. Fourth, despite the need to aggregate information about Latinas and Latinos, clearly a universal Latina or Latino does not exist. Finally, an explanation of ethnic group similarities and differences provides implications for culturally appropriate and relevant social service programming and service provision. Service providers need to acknowledge cultural values, affirm similarities and differences, and debunk misinformed stereotypes about Latinas and Latinos, particularly because they are an integral part of the past, present, and future of the United States. *¡Somos!* We are!

Exercises

1. Esteban is a 16-year-old Salvadoran refugee who is dark-skinned and has been in the United States for nine months. Soon after his father's disappearance and the increased financial hardship for his family, his mother arranged for Esteban to join her brother in Miami. As a result of his limited English proficiency and his need to work full-time, he is experiencing difficulty in high school. Because he knows few people outside his uncle's family and his Pentecostal church, Esteban has been unable to discuss his questioning of his sexual orientation.
   a) Given Esteban's demographics, what issues will he need to contend with in the United States?
   b) What characteristics will Esteban share and not share with other Latino and Latina groups and subgroups?
   c) What familial considerations might Esteban need to contend with?
2. Lillian is a 40-year-old second-generation Chicana who is a certified public accountant. Lillian and her husband have two children, and all four are bilingual, are light-skinned, and have lived in Chicago all their lives. Despite her educational and professional accomplishments, Lillian has continually been passed over for promotion. As a result, she sought consultation from a *curandera* and her parish priest.
   a) Given Lillian's demographics, what issues will she need to contend with in the United States?
   b) What characteristics will Lillian share and not share with other Latino and Latina groups and subgroups?
   c) What social perception issues will Lillian most likely encounter?

REFERENCES

Abreu J., Goodyear, R. K., Campos, A., & Newcomb, M. (2000). Ethnic belonging and traditional masculinity ideology among African Americans, European Americans, and Latinos. *Psychology of Men and Masculinity, 1*(2), 75–86.

Aguirre, A., Jr., & Martinez, R. O. (1993). *Chicanos in higher education: Issues and dilemmas for the 21st century.* ASHE-ERIC Higher Education Report No. 3. Washington, DC: The George Washington University, School of Education and Human Development.

Amaro, H., Messinger, M., & Cervantes, R. (1996). The health of Latino youth: Challenges for disease prevention. In M. Kagawa-Singer, P. A. Katz, D. A. Taylor, & J. H. M. Vanderryn (Eds.), *Health issues for minority adolescents* (pp. 80–115). Lincoln: University of Nebraska Press.

Arce, C. H., Murguia, E., & Frisbie, W. P. (1987). Phenotype and life chances among Chicanos. *Hispanic Journal of Behavioral Sciences, 19*(1), 19–32.

Bracero, W. (1998). Intimidades: Confianza, gender, and hierarchy in the construction of Latino-Latina therapeutic relationship. *Cultural Diversity and Mental Health, 4,* 264–277.

Codina, G. E., & Montalvo, F. F. (1994). Chicano phenotype and depression. *Hispanic Journal of Behavioral Sciences, 16* (3), 296–306.

Comas-Díaz, L. (1989). Culturally relevant issues and treatment implication for Hispanics. In D. R. Koslow & E. Salett (Eds.), *Crossing cultures in mental health* (pp. 31–48). Washington, DC: Society for International Education, Training, and Research.

Comas-Díaz, L. (2001). Hispanics, Latinos, or Americanos: The evolution of identity. *Cultural Diversity and Ethnic Minority Psychology, 7,* 115–120.

Comas-Díaz, L., & Griffith, E. E. H. (1988). *Clinical guidelines in cross-cultural mental health.* New York: Wiley.

Cowan, G., Martinez, L., & Mendiola, S. (1997). Predictors of attitudes toward illegal Latino immigrants. *Hispanic Journal of Behavioral Sciences, 19*(4), 403–415.

Dalaker, J. (2001). *Poverty in the United States: 2000.* Current Population Reports, P60-214. Washington, DC: U.S. Census Bureau.

Delgado, M. (1983). Activities and Hispanic groups: Issues and suggestions. *Social Work With Groups, 6,* 85–96.

DeNavas-Walt, C., Cleveland, R. W., & Roemer, M. I. (2001). Money income in the United States: 2000. Current Population Reports, P60-213. Washington, DC: U.S. Census Bureau.

Diaz, R. M. (1997). Latino gay men and psychocultural barriers to AIDS prevention. In M. P. Levin, P. M. Nardi, & J. H. Gagon (Eds.), *In changing times: Gay men and lesbians encounter HIV/AIDS* (pp. 221–244). Chicago: University of Chicago Press.

Echeverry, J. J. (1997). Treatment barriers: Accessing and accepting professional help. In J. G. García & M. C. Zea (Eds.), *Psychological intervention and research with Latino populations* (pp. 94–107). Boston: Allyn and Bacon.

Falicov, C. J. (1996). Mexican families. In M. McGlodrick, J. Giordano, & J. Pearce (Eds.), *Ethnicity and family therapy* (pp. 169–182). New York: Guilford Press.

Falicov, C. J. (1998). *Latino families in therapy: A guide to multicultural practice.* New York: Guilford Press.

Flores, M. T., & Carey, G. (2000). *Family therapy with Hispanics: Toward appreciating diversity.* Boston: Allyn and Bacon.

Fox, G. (1996). *Hispanic nation: Culture, politics, and the constructing of identity.* Tucson: University of Arizona Press.

Fukuyama, M. A., & Ferguson, A. D. (2000). Lesbian, gay, and bisexual people of color: Understanding cultural complexity and managing multiple oppressions. In R. M. Perez, K. A. DeBord, & K. J. Bieschke (Eds.), *Handbook of counseling and psychotherapy with lesbian, gay, and bisexual clients* (pp. 81–105). Washington, DC: American Psychological Association.

Gándara, P., & Osugi, L. (1994). Educationally ambitious Chicanas. *The NEA Higher Education Journal: Thought and Action, 10,* 7–35.

García, J. G., & Marotta, S. (1997). Characterization of the Latino population. In J. G. García & M. C. Zea (Eds.). *Psychological interventions and research with Latino populations* (pp. 1–14). Needham Heights, MA: Allyn and Bacon.

Garcia-Preto, N. (1996). Latino families: An overview. In M. McGoldrick, J. Giordano, & J. K. Pearce (Eds.), *Ethnicity and family therapy* (pp. 141–154). New York: Guilford Press.

Gloria, A. M. (2001). The cultural construction of Latinas: Practice implications of multiple realities and identities. In D. B. Pope-Davis & H. L. K. Coleman (Eds.), *The intersection between race, gender, and class: Implications for multicultural counseling* (pp. 3–24). Thousand Oaks, CA: Sage.

Gloria, A. M., & Rodriguez, E. R. (2000). Counseling Latino university students: Psychosociocultural issues for consideration. *Journal of Counseling and Development, 78,* 145–154.

Gloria, A. M., Rodriguez, E. R., & Castillo, E. M. (in press). Counseling Latinos and Latinas: A psychosociocultural approach. In P. S. Richards & T. Smith (Eds.), *Practicing multiculturalism: Internalizing and affirming diversity in counseling and psychology.* Boston: Allyn and Bacon.

Gomez, C. (2000). The continual significance of skin color: An exploratory study of Latinos in the Northeast. *Hispanic Journal of Behavioral Sciences, 22*(1), 94–104.

Gonzalez, J. (2000). *Harvest of an empire: A history of Latinos in America.* New York: Penguin Press.

Green, B. (1997). Ethnic minority lesbians and gay men: Mental health and treatment issues. In B. Green (Ed.), *Ethnic and cultural diversity among lesbians and gay men* (pp. 216–239). Thousand Oaks, CA: Sage.

Guzmán, B. (2001). *The Hispanic population.* Current Population Reports, C2KBR/01-3. Washington, DC: U.S. Census Bureau.

Jamieson, M., Shin, H. B., & Day, J. (2002). *Voting and registration in the election of November 2000.* Current Population Reports, P20-542. Washington, DC: U.S. Census Bureau.

Koss-Chioino, J. D. (1995). Traditional and fold approaches among ethnic minorities. In J. Aponte, R. Rivers, & J. Wohl (Eds.), *Psychological interventions and cultural diversity* (pp. 145–163). Boston: Allyn and Bacon.

Lollock, L. (2001). *The foreign-born population in the United States: March 2000.* Current Population Reports, P20-534. Washington, DC: U.S. Census Bureau.

Lopez-Baez, S. (1999). Marianismo. In J. S. Mio, J. E. Trimble, P. Arredondo, H. E. Cheatham, & D. Sue (Eds.), *Key words in multicultural interventions: A dictionary* (p. 183). Westport, CT: Greenwood.

Marín, B. V., & Gómez, C. A. (1997). Latino culture and sex: Implications for HIV prevention. In J. G. García & M. C. Zea (Eds.), *Psychological interventions and research with Latino populations* (pp. 73–93). Boston: Allyn and Bacon.

Marín, G., & Marín, B. V. (1991). *Research with Hispanic populations.* Thousand Oaks, CA: Sage.

Mestre, J. P., & Royer, J. M. (1991). Cultural and linguistic influences on Latino testing. In G. D. Keller, J. R. Deneen, & R. J. Magallán (Eds.), *Assessment and access: Hispanics in higher education* (pp. 39–66). Albany: State University of New York Press.

Morales, E. (1996). Gender roles among Latino gay and bisexual men: Implications for family and couple relationships. In J. Laird & R. J. Green (Eds.), *Lesbians and gays in couples and families: A handbook for therapists* (pp. 272–297). San Francisco: Jossey-Bass.

National Center for Education Statistics. (2000a). *The condition of education 2000.* NCES 2000-062. U.S. Department of Education. Washington, DC: U.S. Government Printing Office.

National Center for Education Statistics. (2000b). *The educational progress of Hispanic students.* NCES 95-767. U.S. Department of Education. Washington, DC: U.S. Government Printing Office.

National Center for Education Statistics. (2002). *The condition of education 2002.* NCES 2000-025. U.S. Department of Education. Washington, DC: U.S. Government Printing Office.

National Latino Children's Institute. (1997). Who's on the air? Latino representations in the media. *El Futuro: Newsletter.* Retrieved November 2, 2002, from http://www.nlci.org/press/Past%20articles/whosontheair.htm

NCES (1995). *Findings from the Condition of Education 1995: The Educational Progress of Hispanic Students.* U.S. Department of Education, Office of Educational Research and Improvement, 95–767.

Niemann, Y. F. (2001). Stereotypes about Chicanas and Chicanos: Implications for counseling. *The Counseling Psychologist, 29,* 55–90.

Oboler, S. (1995). *Ethnic labels, Latino lives: Identity and the politics of (re)presentation in the United States.* Minneapolis: University of Minnesota Press.

Paniagua, F. A. (1994). *Assessing and treating culturally diverse clients: A practical guide.* Thousand Oaks, CA: Sage.

President's Advisory Commission of Educational Excellence for Hispanic Americans. (1996). *Our nation on the fault line: Hispanic American education—A report to the President of the United States, the nation, and the Secretary of Education.* Washington, DC: Department of Education.

Ramirez, R. R. (2000). *The Hispanic population in the United States: Population characteristics.* Current Population Reports, P20-527. Washington, DC: U.S. Census Bureau.

Ramos, J. (2000). *La otra cara de América: Historias de los immigrantes latinoamericanos que están cambiando a Estados Unidos.* Mexico, DF: Gijalbo.

Retish, P., & Kavanaugh, P. (1992). Myth: America's public schools are educating Mexican American students. *Journal of Multicultural Counseling and Development, 20,* 89–96.

Santiago-Rivera, A. L., Arredondo, P., & Gallardo-Cooper, M. (2002). *Counseling Latinos and la familia: A practical guide.* Thousand Oaks, CA: Sage.

Secada, W. G., Chavez-Chavez, R., Garcia, E., Munoz, C., Oakes, J., Santiago-Santiago, I., & Slavin, R. (1998). *No more excuses: The final report of the Hispanic dropout project.* Washington, DC: U.S. Department of Education.

Simon, J. L. (1995). *Immigration: The demographic and economic facts.* Washington, DC: Cato Institute and the National Immigration Forum.

Therrien, M., & Ramirez, R. R. (2001). *The Hispanic population in the United States: March 2000.* Current Population Reports, P20-535. Washington, DC: U.S. Census Bureau.

Triandis, H. C., Marín, G., Lisansky, J., & Betancourt, H. (1984). Simpatía as a cultural script of Hispanics. *Journal of Personality and Social Psychology, 47,* 1363–1375.

Triay, V. A. (1998). *Fleeing Castro: Operation Pedro Pan and the Cuban children's program.* Gainesville: University Press of Florida.

U.S. Department of Commerce. (1993). *We the American . . . Hispanics.* Economics and Statistics Administration. U.S. Bureau of the Census. WE-2R.

U.S. Department of Commerce News. (2000a). *Census bureau projects doubling of nation's population by 2100.* CB00-05. Washington, DC: U.S. Census Bureau.

U.S. Department of Commerce News. (2000b). *Census bureau updates profile of nation's Latino groups.* CB00-38. Washington, DC: U.S. Census Bureau.

U.S. Department of Labor. (2002). *Occupational Safety and Health Administration's efforts to protect immigrant workers.* Statement of John L. Henshaw, Assistant Secretary of Labor for Occupational Safety and Health before the Subcommittee on Employment, Safety and Training Committee on Health Education, Labor and Pensions, United States Senate, February 27, 2002. http://www.osha.gov/pls/oshaweb/owasrch.search_form?p_doc_type=TESTIMONIES

Utsey, S. O., Bolden, M. A., & Brown, A. L. (2001). Visions of revolution from the spirit of Frantz Fanon: A psychology of liberation from counseling African Americans confronting societal racism and oppression. In J. G. Ponterotto, J. M. Casas, L. A. Suzuki, & C. M. Alexander (Eds.), *The handbook of multicultural counseling* (2nd ed., pp. 311–336). Thousands Oaks, CA: Sage.

Vásquez, M. J. T. (1982). Confronting barriers to the participation of Mexican American women in higher education. *Hispanic Journal of Behavioral Sciences, 4,* 147–165.

Vega, W. A. (1995). The study of Latino families: A point of departure. In R. E. Zambrana (Ed.), *Understanding Latino families: Scholarship, policy, and practice* (pp. 3–17). Thousand Oaks, CA: Sage.

Weismantle, M. (2001). *Reasons people do not work: Household economic studies.* Current Population Reports, P70-76. Washington, DC: U.S. Census Bureau.

Zamora-Hernandez, C. E., & Patterson, D. G. (1996). Homosexually active Latino men: Issues for social work practice. In J. F. Longres (Ed.), *Men of color: A context for service to homosexually active men* (pp. 69–91). New York: Harrington Park Press.

Zea, M. C., Diehl, V. A., & Porterfield, K. S. (1997). Central American youth exposed to war violence. In J. G. García & M. C. Zea (Eds.), *Psychological interventions and research with Latino populations* (pp. 73–93). Boston: Allyn and Bacon.

Zea, M. C., Mason, M. A., & Murguía, A. (2000). Psychotherapy with members of Latino/Latina religions and spiritual traditions. In P. S. Richards & A. E. Bergin (Eds.), *Handbook of psychotherapy and religious diversity* (pp. 397–419). Washington, DC: American Psychological Association.

CHAPTER 14

Physical and Mental
Health Concerns
of Hispanics

José M. Abreu and Hiroshi M. Sasaki,
University of Southern California

The purpose of this chapter is to highlight some of the health issues that affect the Hispanic population in the United States. Whenever possible, we will identify health problems that are specific to Hispanic subgroups (e.g., Mexican Americans, Puerto Ricans), although identification is oftentimes difficult because health and epidemiological reports typically provide data that aggregate all U.S. Hispanics into a single group (see chapter 13). The chapter is organized under two broad sections. The first section focuses on the physical health concerns that affect Hispanics and highlights specific diseases that afflict this population. Although physical health concerns are not traditionally within the purview of mental health practitioners, we included this section because unhealthy lifestyles, which involve cognitions, emotions, and behaviors, can trigger the onset of physical ailments. The second section focuses on Hispanic mental health concerns, including the risks posed by inordinately high levels of stress due to discrimination, adaptation to U.S. culture, and poverty. One major issue is whether these stresses lead to unique patterns of mental health concerns for this population.

PHYSICAL HEALTH CONCERNS

Some afflictions, such as cardiovascular diseases and cancer, rank high as leading causes of death among Hispanics, although the mortality rates of Whites and Blacks who suffer from these diseases actually exceed that of Hispanics. For example, the National Vital Statistics Report from the Centers for Disease Control and Prevention (CDC; 2002b) indicated that although heart disease, cancer, and cerebrovascular disease ranked among the top five leading causes of death in 2000 across all ethnic groups included in the CDC data, the percentages of total deaths for Hispanics (24.1%, 19.7%, 5.8% respectively) were actually lower than for Whites (30.3%, 23.4%, 7.1%) or Blacks (27.1%, 21.7%, 6.7%) for each of these three afflictions. Other afflictions, such as diabetes and AIDS, however, have much higher prevalence and morbidity rates among Hispanics compared to other ethnic groups; these specific diseases are the focus of this section.

For diabetes, the proportion of deaths and incidence rates for Hispanics are several times that of Whites. Among Mexican Americans, for example, the incidence rate of diabetes is three to five times that of the general U.S. population (Brown, Becker, Garcia, Barton, & Hanis, 2002). In some Mexican American communities, the incidence rate for diabetes is at 50% or higher (Brown, Upchurch, Garcia, Barton, & Hanis, 1998). With regard to HIV infection and AIDS, the *American Journal of Public Health* (Klevens, Diaz, Fleming, Mays, & Frey, 1999) stated that nearly half a million AIDS cases were reported to the CDC between 1991 and 1996. Of these, an alarming 19% were of Hispanic origin; compared to Whites, Hispanics were three to five times as likely to be diagnosed with AIDS.

A more general but related issue is the quality of treatments received by Hispanics compared to Whites; evidence indicates that the former are treated with a lower quality of care than are the latter, *regardless* of the reasons for treatment. For example, a newly released survey (Smedley, Stith, & Nelson, 2002) reported that with income, age, insurance status, and severity of condition held constant, ethnic minorities still receive substandard medical treatment. The basis for this disparity in treatment care has been ascribed to cultural biases and stereotypes held by medical practitioners as well as language and cultural barriers that impede the communication process between patients and their physicians.

Diabetes

In the year 2000, about 10% of the total U.S. Hispanic population (approximately 30 million) people had been diagnosed with diabetes (National Diabetes Information Clearinghouse, 2002). On the average, Hispanics are nearly twice as likely as Whites to have diabetes. Mexican Americans are three to five times as likely as Whites to be afflicted by diabetes; in some communities, the prevalence rates are alarmingly high (Haffner et al., 1990). For example, in Starr County, Texas, "50% of the Hispanic population [of which over 90% trace their ancestry to Mexico] over the age of 35 either have diabetes or are first-degree relatives of someone with diabetes" (Hanis et al., 1983, p. 659). Risk factors for diabetes include genetic susceptibility (this risk factor is not yet well understood, but a family history of diabetes increases the chance that people will develop the disease) as well as lifestyle behaviors. Obesity is a major risk factor for type 2 diabetes (adult-onset), and Hispanics are more likely than Whites to be overweight. (Whereas 32% and 33% of White men and women in the United States are considered overweight, comparable statistics for Hispanic men and women are 35% and 47%.) Lack of physical exercise is another risk factor. The Third National Health and Nutrition Examination Survey (NHANES III; Harris et al., 1998) found that 65% of Mexican American men and 74% of Mexican American women reported that they participated in little or no physical activity.

Serious health complications are associated with diabetes. Diabetic retinopathy is a deterioration of the blood vessels in the eye caused by high blood sugar, leading to vision loss and blindness. Diabetes is the leading cause of kidney failure, which can lead to lifelong dependence on dialysis treatment and eventual death. Peripheral neuropathy, a degenerative disease that affects nerve endings and that leads to amputation of anatomical extremities, is also caused by diabetes. NHANES III reported that the prevalence rates for diabetic retinopathy, kidney failure, and peripheral neuropathy among Mexican Americans were at least twice that of Whites (Harris et al., 1998). Since diabetes and obesity are risk factors for stroke and related cardiovascular conditions, Hispanics would be expected to suffer from higher prevalence rates for these diseases. However, the opposite is in fact the case. For example, although heart disease is the most common cause of death among people with both types of diabetes (type 1: childhood-onset; type 2: adult-onset), Mexican Americans actually have *lower* rates of myocardial infarctions than do Whites.

According to the Diabetes Control and Complications Trials Research Group (1993), educational interventions can reduce the risk and complications of diabetes by one third. However, these interventions have been developed for middle-class European Americans, and the cultural relevance of these interventions vis-à-vis non-Whites has not been taken into account (Brown et al., 2002). Not surprisingly, traditional interventions have proven ineffective in preventing and treating Hispanics (Brown & Hanis, 1999). In fact, health practitioners tend to label Hispanics as being noncompliant patients, unable or unwilling to follow preventive protocols, especially dietary practices (Brown et al., 2002). As a result, some providers don't even attempt to prescribe lifestyle changes that promote positive behavioral changes and instead rely on insulin as the mode of treatment (Haffner et al., 1990).

HIV and AIDS

The number of deaths claimed by the human immunodeficiency virus (HIV) increased steadily from 1980 to 1995 (CDC, 1997). This surge began to recede for the first time in 1996, with an even greater decline the following year (CDC, 1998b). However, since 1989, the rate of AIDS has been higher among Hispanics than among Whites (Selik, Castro, Pappaioanou, & Buehler, 1989), and in 1995 HIV infection was the leading cause of death among Hispanics between 25 and 44 years of age (Anderson, Kochanek, & Murphy, 1997). Early studies (Selik et al., 1989; Diaz, Buehler, Castro, & Ward, 1993) reported that whereas Hispanic men with AIDS who were born in Puerto Rico were more likely to have contracted the disease through injection drug use, those born in Mexico, Cuba, and Central and South America were more likely to have been exposed to HIV through same-sex intercourse. For the year 1996, the incidence rates for AIDS per 100,000 population were 73.6, 20.4, and 1.1 for Hispanic men, women, and children, respectively. Comparable statistics for White men, women, and children were 22.5, 2.9, and .02, respectively (Klevens et al., 1999). Klevens et al. also found a trend of increasing AIDS cases among foreign-born Hispanic men and women and among heterosexual U.S.-born Hispanics. Declines occurred among U.S.-born injection drug users and men who have sex with men.

A more recent report (CDC, 2002a) indicates that whereas Hispanics represented 13% of the U.S. population in the year 2000, they accounted for 19% of new AIDS cases reported for that year. This incidence rate is three times the rate documented for Whites. Although males accounted for 81% of AIDS cases among Hispanics, the proportion of females appears to be increasing (overall prevalence rate was 19% but the incidence rate for the year 2000 was 23%). The CDC report puts the cumulative total number of AIDS cases among Hispanic men at 114,019. In terms of mode of HIV infection, about 42% of cases involved men having sex with men, 35% were injection drug users, and 6% contracted the disease through heterosexual contact. Among Puerto Rican men, however, the proportion of injection drug user cases was greater than the cases involving men having sex with men. For Hispanic women, heterosexual contact accounted for the highest number of cases (47%), followed by injection drug use (40%).

The CDC report (2002a) also highlights the need for comprehensive approaches to AIDS prevention and treatment among Hispanics, which not only should address underlying social and economic conditions that cross ethnic boundaries (poverty, access to medical insurance) but also must be consistent with the values and beliefs of this diverse population. For example, the use of "shooting galleries" (in which injection drug users share needles) is considered a very high-risk behavior for HIV infection. Because this practice is apparently more prevalent among Hispanics of Puerto Rican ancestry, prevention strategies should emphasize programs for drug users that provide the information, skills, and support needed to reduce both drug-related and HIV risks. In addition, or alternatively, established substance abuse and AIDS prevention programs need to be better integrated so as to create a synergistic thrust that takes advantage of multiple opportunities for intervention. For Hispanics born in Mexico, Cuba, and Central and South America, CDC data indicate that the primary mode of transmission is through sexual practices. Thus, prevention efforts targeting these populations must address attitudes about sexuality and condom use, which may differ from those of other populations at high risk for infection.

Health Concerns Due to Work-Related Discrimination

Although it is difficult to collect data concerning discrimination against Hispanic workers, two specific high-risk industries offer vivid examples of how workplace discrimination greatly increases health risk for undocumented Hispanics: meatpacking and farmwork, areas in which most newly hired workers are Hispanic (Migration Dialogue, 2000). In *Fast Food Nation,* investigative journalist Eric Schlosser (2001) exposes big meatpacking companies that have moved toward less skilled labor and increasingly faster slaughterhouse lines, which has resulted in a workforce largely consisting of undocumented and uninsured Hispanic laborers subjected to extremely high risk. Schlosser found that approximately one out of three of the roughly 150,000 documented meatpacking workers sustains an injury each year that requires medical care beyond first aid, an injury rate three times higher than average factories; in addition, the rate of cumulative trauma injuries (repetitive motion, carpal tunnel, etc.) is 35 times higher than in any other U.S. industry. Because they fear losing their employment, Hispanic undocumented workers experience more pressure than do documented laborers to avoid reporting injuries or unsafe conditions or practices. Furthermore, the sanitation workers (many of whom are undocumented) who clean the slaughterhouses at night represent those with highest risk for occupational infections from contaminated animal products and waste.

Farmwork represents another area of high risk for Hispanics. The American Thoracic Society (1998), in collaboration with the National Institute for Occupational Safety and Health, recently compiled a comprehensive analysis of respiratory health hazards in agriculture. It notes that the majority of workers are migrant or seasonal (e.g., up to 80% in some areas of California). Although Schlosser (2001) found that Hispanics account for 70% of the seasonal workforce nationwide, this number is most likely quite conservative because of underreporting by undocumented laborers. Exposure to hazards such as dust, microorganisms, microbes, decomposition and silo gases, pesticides, disinfectants, fertilizers, and so on substantially increase risk for airway disorders (e.g., asthma, chronic airway disease), interstitial lung disease (e.g., organic dust toxic syndrome, interstitial fibrosis), and respiratory infections.

Other Physical Health Concerns

As stated earlier in this chapter, cancer, heart problems, and cardiovascular afflictions represent the leading causes of death for Hispanics, although these diseases pose an even greater threat to members of other ethnicities (African Americans and European Americans) and will not be discussed in this chapter (for a comprehensive review of racial/ethnic discrimination through the unequal treatment of these diseases, see Smedley et al., 2002). Aside from diabetes, HIV, and work-related illnesses, however, there are other medical concerns to which Hispanics are especially prone, including cirrhosis of the liver, hepatitis A, and lung cancer, all of which are triggered by unhealthy lifestyles or choices.

Cirrhosis   Cirrhosis is a liver disease that causes many complications, including accumulation of fluid in the abdomen, bleeding disorders, increases in blood pressure, brain disorders, and death. Alcohol abuse is the leading cause of cirrhosis in the United States. A National Institute on Alcohol Abuse and Alcoholism report (2002; National Institute of Health, 2001) indicated that cirrhosis death rates were higher among Hispanic males than any other ethnic group (including Whites). Styles of drinking (binge consumption), poverty, alcohol availability (e.g., number of neighborhood liquor stores), and lack of access to medical care are factors that may contribute to this disparity across ethnicities.

Hepatitis A   A recent study by the University of California, Los Angeles Center for the Study of Latino Health and Culture (2002) found that Hispanic children in California are six times more likely than White children to be diagnosed with Hepatitis A. This disease poses a significant health risk for this population because Hispanic children account for nearly half of all children living in California, a proportion that is increasing rapidly. Hepatitis A is a viral infection of the liver that spreads through personal contact with infected individuals or through the consumption of contaminated food and water. Symptoms include mild flu-like illness, yellow skin or eyes, tiredness, severe stomach pains or diarrhea, loss of appetite, or nausea. Although this disease can be easily prevented by vaccination, it poses a problem for many Hispanic families who do not have easy access to medical care. People can also prevent the infection by washing their hands after using the toilet and before preparing or eating food.

Lung Cancer   Smoking is responsible for approximately 90% of the lung cancer deaths in the United States. Overall, lung cancer is the leading cause of cancer deaths among Hispanics, especially Cuban American men (CDC, 1998a). In 1997, 26.2% of Hispanic men smoked, compared with 27.4% of White men. The smoking rate among Hispanic women was 14.3 %, compared with 23.3% among White women. Statistics indicate that although Hispanic adults are the racial or ethnic group *least* likely to smoke, Hispanic adolescents are now the group *most* likely to smoke. For example, Hispanic 8th graders are more likely to be current smokers (18.3%) than are their White (17.8%) or Black (6.6%) counterparts.

Unequal Medical Treatment Issues

Health problems affecting Hispanics are exacerbated by racial/ethnic biases and prejudices among medical practitioners. Commenting on the Institute of Medicine's new book, *Unequal Treatment: Confronting Racial and Ethnic Disparities in Health Care* (Smedley et al., 2002), former president of the American Medical Association Alan Nelson wrote:

> Disparities in the health care delivered to racial and ethnic minorities are real and are associated with worse outcomes in many cases, which is unacceptable. The real challenge lies not in debating whether disparities exist, because the evidence is overwhelming, but in developing and implementing strategies to reduce and eliminate them. (National Academies, 2002, p. 1)

This book, which represents an exhaustive review of hundreds of studies reported in the medical literature on health care disparities between ethnic minorities and Whites, shows that with few exceptions these differences exist consistently across a range of illnesses and health care services. Data collected in this review indicate that ethnic minorities face various obstacles to health care, including language and cultural barriers as well as lack of access to insurance coverage. For example, African Americans, Asian Americans, and Hispanics experience language difficulties when interacting with doctors. For these and other reasons, members of minority groups claim to feel disrespected by physicians and believe that the health care received would be better if they were White.

Smedley et al. (2002) provide ample evidence that these subjective perceptions of inequality are real; their research indicates that even if income, age, insurance status, and severity of condition are held constant, ethnic minorities receive substandard medical treatment. Differences in treatment were attributed to biases and other forms of prejudice as well as lack of cultural or linguistic competence. Specifically, Smedley et al. review evidence that a difference in medical treatment contributes to increased severity of disorders and to higher mortality rates. For example, minorities with diabetes are less likely to be recommended for kidney transplants and to receive dialysis than are nonminorities. Minorities with HIV are less likely to receive each of the following: retroviral therapy, protease inhibitors, or prophylaxis for pneumocystis pneumonia. One study of 6-year mortality rates in patients hospitalized for HIV-related illness revealed that Hispanics have twice the risk of dying than do non-Hispanic White patients.

MENTAL HEALTH CONCERNS

Although the literature suggests that Hispanics are generally less prone to develop psychological disorders compared to the general population (Vega et al., 1998), there are marked within-group differences indicating that sociocultural factors (e.g., acculturation) may lead to increased risk of psychopathology. This section reviews the epidemiological and clinical literature on Hispanic mental health.

Psychiatric Diagnosis and Psychopathology

In general, epidemiological studies suggest that there are few ethnic differences in psychopathology (e.g., Huertin-Roberts, Snowden, & Miller, 1997; R. Roberts & Sobhan, 1992). Whether Hispanics differ from non-Hispanics in prevalence rates and types of mental health concerns has been the topic of several investigations, which have produced, at best, mixed results. For example, some studies have reported higher rates of psychological disorders among Hispanics compared to members of other ethnic groups (e.g., R. Roberts & Vernon, 1984), other studies report the opposite (e.g., Vernon & Roberts, 1982). In reviewing this literature, several authors have highlighted the inconsistency of findings (Guarnaccia, Good, & Kleinman, 1990; Moscicki, Locke, Rae, & Boyd, 1989; Nagayama, Bansal, & Lopez, 1999; Rogler, 1989; Shrout, Canino, Bird, & Rubio-Stipek, 1992), and most reviewers point to differences in measures and measuring methods across studies as its source. Rogler noted that studies reporting high levels of psychopathology among its Hispanic participants tended to use number of symptoms as a dependent variable, whereas studies reporting little or no differences between Hispanics and other ethnic groups were likely to use discrete diagnoses as the variable of interest. Commenting on Rogler's finding, Shrout et al. speculated that because diagnoses take into account the functional disruption caused by symptoms, it could be the case that although Hispanics may experience higher levels of symptomatology (compared to members of other ethnic groups), these symptoms may not be sufficiently disruptive to warrant a diagnosis. The mixed findings may also reflect the heterogeneity among U.S. Hispanics; some are foreign-born in countries that pose various types of stressors, whereas others are U.S.-born and not only have little connection to their ancestral country of origin but also have differing experiences as members of a U.S. minority group. Another problem is bias in clinical judgment against ethnic minority clients that may lead to misdiagnoses that over- or under-pathologize clients (Abreu, 1999; Garb, 1997; Snowden & Cheung, 1990).

The most recent and comprehensive investigation of ethnic differences in psychopathology (Nagayama et al., 1999) was based on a meta-analytic review of 31 years of comparative research on the Minnesota Multiphasic Personality Inventory (MMPI/MMPI-2). In discussing their findings, the authors concluded that differences among European Americans, African Americans, and Latino Americans were trivial. For instance, the small effect sizes that were found for all MMPI/MMPI-2 scales constituted less than five T-score points on any particular scale, a difference that is not clinically significant. The largest difference was found between Latinos and European Americans on scale 5, with male Latinos scoring lower on the scale (less than five T-score points—a small effect size). Scale 5 is not a clinical scale, however, because it taps differences in preferences for gender-related behaviors. Low scores indicate an interest for stereotypically masculine preferences in work, hobbies, and other activities. The authors interpreted the findings as an indication of no apparent differences in self-reported psychopathology *across* the ethnic groups that participated, which represented educational, employment, medical, and psychiatric settings, but they emphasized the notion that differences may exist *within* ethnic groups. They also point out that any given MMPI/MMPI-2 score may have different implications in European American versus non–European American social contexts.

Sociocultural Factors: Acculturation and Acculturative Stress

In spite of what epidemiological and clinical studies may indicate regarding the prevalence of psychopathology among Hispanics, historical and sociocultural factors affecting this ethnic group would suggest a high need for mental health services. Stressors such as low educational and economic status, trauma experienced in home countries plagued by political instability, adaptation to U.S. culture, and perceived discrimination are likely precursors to mental health problems (Cervantes, Padilla, & Salgado de Snyder, 1991). Although these factors may not lead to a syndrome of symptoms associated with a mental disorder, they may induce a level of discomfort that affects daily functioning, such as culturally patterned forms of distress and disorder (U.S. Department of Health and Human Services, 2001). Time spent in the United States, for example, appears to be a mental health risk factor for Hispanics. Robins and Regier (1991) found that Mexican Americans and Whites had similar levels of psychological disorders; however, U.S.-born Mexican Americans had higher levels of depression and phobias compared to their counterparts born in Mexico. In a similar study (Vega et al., 1998) based on a large sample of Mexican Americans from Fresno County, California, Mexican immigrants reported remarkably lower levels of psychopathology (25% had some form of disorder) compared to U.S.-born Mexican Americans (48% had some form of disorder). Vega et al. also found higher rates of psychopathology among immigrant participants whose length of stay in the United States was greater than 13 years than among participants who had lived in the United States fewer than 13 years. Further, a comparison of the Canino, Rubio-Stipek, Shrout, and Bravo (1987) study based on samples of Puerto Rican participants from the island and the Moscicki et al. (1989) study based on samples of Puerto Rican participants from New York indicates that island Puerto Ricans had lower rates of depression (4.6%) than did those from New York (9%).

Although these findings have led some writers to suggest that U.S. acculturation poses a mental health risk for Hispanics (Escobar, Nervi, & Gara, 2000; Ortega, Rosenheck, Alegria, & Desai, 2000), it is not yet clear which aspects of acculturation (e.g., negative experiences with U.S. institutions; losing native-culture practices) may be responsible for such risks (see B. S. K. Kim & Abreu, 2001). Rather than focusing on acculturation as a process, some writers have turned their attention to the *effects* of this process (Cervantes et al., 1991; Saldana, 1994; Smart & Smart, 1995). For example, Smart and Smart defined *acculturative stress* as "the psychological impact of adaptation to a new culture" (p. 25), with likely deleterious effects on physical health and self-esteem. With regard to physical health, it may be that acculturative stress leads to psychological discomfort that is expressed in terms of somatic complaints (Arce & Torres-Matrullo, 1982; Smith, 1985) or may actually pave the way to physical illness (Cleghorn & Streiner, 1979). Hispanic self-esteem may be undermined by pervasive stereotypes deeply ingrained in U.S. culture; these stereotypes tend to describe Hispanics in negative, simplistic, and demeaning ways (Finch, Hummer, Kolody, & Vega, 2001).

Life experiences involving rapid changes in norms, institutions, and belief systems are likely to become sources of stress for Hispanics who have experienced immigration or frequent migration events. In these cases, any prior socialization may be insufficient to provide adequate coping resources (Argueta-Bernal, 1990). Ybarra (1982), for example, found that Hispanic households are often disrupted when males are absent for extended periods of time because of distant work locations. These types of situations lead to feelings of being out of control among fathers and pose role conflicts for mothers, especially those who must work outside the home. The acculturation process also causes increased conflict between first-generation Hispanic parents and their U.S.-born children (M. Kim, 2001). Spanish may be spoken at home when children are young, but once they are of school age, language conflicts are likely to occur, because children may prefer English while parents may prefer Spanish. In some cases, communication between parents and their children becomes severely strained, because the former may speak little English and the latter may retain little fluency in Spanish. The issues can extend beyond language problems; parents may also preserve the values and beliefs of the native culture, whereas their children are more likely to adopt U.S. customs and norms. This generation rift exacerbates parent-child conflicts, especially during adolescence, a time when conflicts are normatively acute.

Although the actual consequences of acculturative stress are not well known (Myers & Rodriguez, 2003), recent studies provide some evidence of acculturative stress as a possible precursor of psychological problems. Cabrera Strait (2001), who surveyed a sample of Hispanic youths averaging 16 years of age, found that those who experienced more acculturative stress drank more than their counterparts and that acculturative stress predicted drinking beyond individual acculturation level. Substance use was also positively related to other maladaptive behavior, such as criminal activity. Hovey and Magana (2002) reported that Mexican migrant farmworkers who experience elevated acculturative stress were susceptible to the development of anxiety-related disorders. In one other study (Finch et al., 2001), perceived discrimination (as a result of living in the United States) among a sample of Mexican Americans was directly related to physical health problems, which were mediated by depression.

Children and Youth

Clinical studies focusing on children and adolescents indicate that Hispanics are more likely than Whites to experience mental health problems. Using the Childhood Behavior Checklist, Achenbach et al. (1990) reported a higher proportion of "problem cases" among a sample of youths from Puerto Rico (36%) than among a sample of primarily White youths from the U.S. mainland (9%). Vazsonyi and Flannery (1997) found more delinquency-type problems among Hispanic sixth and seventh graders from a Southwestern city than among White students. A similar study (Glover, Pumariega, Holzer, Wise, & Rodriguez, 1999), based on a sample of Texas middle school students, reported more anxiety-related problem behaviors among Mexican American students than among White students.

Studies focusing on depression have also shown that Hispanic youths seem more at risk than their White counterparts. R. E. Roberts, Roberts, and Chen (1997), for example, reported that Mexican American middle school students sampled from the Houston, Texas, area were twice as likely to be diagnosed with major depression than were White students. Two other studies focusing on affective symptoms expressed by Mexican American and White adolescents found higher rates of depression among members of the former group compared to the latter (R. Roberts & Sobhan, 1992; R. E. Roberts & Chen, 1995). Another study, based on a survey of Mexican American adolescents on both sides of the Mexico-Texas border, revealed high rates of depression, drug use, and suicide (Swanson, Linskey, Quintero-Salinas, & Pumariega, 1992). In this last study, living in the United States was apparently a risk factor, because U.S. participants had higher rates of all three measures of interest than did their Mexican counterparts.

Refugees

An estimated 2 million immigrants fleeing civil wars in Nicaragua, El Salvador, and Guatemala have made their way to Mexico, the United States, and Canada. The pervasiveness of systematic human rights violations in these politically unstable countries has put many of its citizens at risk for post-traumatic stress disorder (PTSD) and depression. In a study of Central American immigrants in Los Angeles, California, Cervantes, Salgado de Snyder, and Padilla (1989) found that half their participants reported symptom clusters consistent with a PTSD diagnosis. A similar immigrant study reported prevalence rates for PTSD of 60% among adult Central Americans (Michultka, Blanchard, & Kalous, 1998).

Culture-Bound Syndromes

Hispanics use several labels to describe psychological syndromes, for example, *susto* (fright), *mal de ojo* (evil eye), *nervios* (nerves), and *ataques de nervios* (attack of nerves). *Ataques de nervios* is an especially interesting syndrome, because it may include dissociative experiences, aggression, fainting or seizure, crying, trembling, and suicidal gestures (Guarnaccia, De La Cancela, & Carrillo, 1989). In a study implemented in Puerto Rico, Guarnaccia, Canino, Rubio-Stipec, and Bravo (1993) found that up to 14% of the sample reported having an *ataque*. The concept of *nervios* is also a general descriptor used by Hispanics to describe distress associated with anxiety and depression (Salgado de Snyder, Diaz-Perez, & Ojeda, 2000) and delusions or hallucinations (Jenkins, 1988). Recognizing culture-bound syndromes such as *ataques* and *nervios* is valuable because this awareness may lead clinicians to identify the existence of distress and illness that does not conform to *DSM-IV-TR* (American Psychiatric Association, 2000) nomenclature.

CONCLUSION

Hispanics are just as likely as or less likely than other ethnic groups to suffer from some physical health concerns, such as cancer and heart disease. For other diseases, such as diabetes, HIV, and AIDS, however, Hispanics have higher prevalence rates when compared to other groups. Given the documented prevalence of unequal treatment of ethnic minorities (including Hispanics) by medical practitioners, the medical establishment needs to address issues regarding the role of stereotypes and language as barriers to effective practices. With regard to mental health concerns, Hispanics as a group are less likely than Whites to suffer from most diagnosable psychiatric disorders. However, sociocultural factors such as acculturation and acculturative stress lead to a series of psychological problems affecting Hispanic children, adults, and communities. These problems include anxiety, depression, and alcohol use. Hispanic children and adolescents appear to be particularly at risk to acculturative stress. In addition, PTSD and other anxiety disorders are highly prevalent among Hispanic immigrants fleeing politically unstable Central American countries. Lastly, culture-bound labels such as *ataques* and *nervios* describe syndromes that do not conform to *DSM* categories but need to be recognized as indications of psychological distress.

Exercises

1. Felicia is a 35-year-old woman who recently immigrated to the United States from El Salvador. She now lives in East Los Angeles in a predominantly Hispanic neighborhood. She joined her husband, Pablo, who immigrated to the United States with the couple's three children five years earlier. Lencha is Pablo's mother and an active member of her local Catholic parish. Lencha noticed that her daughter-in-law had been acting strange; a case of *nervios,* she told her priest. The priest, Father McGowan, encouraged Lencha to take Felicia to the Catholic Social Services (CSS) office located behind the rectory. Assume that you are a staff counselor at CSS and are assigned to work with Felicia. Describe the information that you solicited *and* obtained during the initial intake interview. Then, on the basis of this information, design an appropriate intervention.
2. Tomás Guzman is from Michoacan, Mexico. He has worked as a migrant worker in the United States for 15 years, picking grapes, strawberries, avocados, lettuce, and other fruits and vegetables. He is now a resident of Los Angeles, California, and lives with his wife and three school-age children who recently immigrated from Michoacan to join Mr. Guzman. He currently works in a restaurant and likes this type of work. He came to your social work office asking for help. Because he now has to pay rent for a three-bedroom apartment and because of the high cost of living in California, he is having difficulty making ends meet. He is also concerned about his family's health; he says that Mrs. Guzman and the children seem to get sick a lot. As his case worker, you decide that it would be a good idea to refer the entire Guzman family for a medical workup. To write a thorough referral request, you need to ask the Guzman family some questions. In a follow-up appointment, you meet with the entire Guzman family. On the basis of the information presented in this chapter relative to physical health concerns likely to affect Hispanics, provide a description of the information you would seek from the Guzmans.

REFERENCES

Abreu, J. M. (1999). Conscious and nonconscious African American stereotypes: Impact on first impression and diagnostic ratings by therapists. *Journal of Consulting and Clinical Psychology, 67,* 387–393.

Achenbach, T., Bird, H. R., Canino, G., Phares, V., Gould, M., & Rubio-Stipec, M. (1990). Epidemiologic comparisons of Puerto Rican and U.S. mainland children: Parent, teacher, and self-reports. *Journal of the American Academy of Child and Adolescent Psychiatry, 29,* 84–93.

American Psychiatric Association (2000). *Diagnostic and Statistical Manual of Mental Disorders (4th ed., text rev.).* Washington, DC: American Psychiatric Association.

American Thoracic Society. (1998). Respiratory health hazards in agriculture. *American Journal of Respiratory and Critical Care Medicine, 158,* S1–S76.

Anderson, R. N., Kochanek, K. D., & Murphy, S. L. (1997). Report of final mortality statistics, 1995. *Month Vital Statistics Report, 45*(suppl 2), 52–54.

Arce, A. A., & Torres-Matrullo, C. M. (1982). Application of cognitive behavioral techniques in the treatment of Hispanic patients. *Psychiatric Quarterly, 54,* 230–236.

Argueta-Bernal, G. A. (1990). Stress and stress-related disorders in Hispanics: Biobehavioral approaches to treatment. In F. C. Serafica, A. J. Schwebel, R. K. Russell, P. D. Isaac, & L. B. Myers (Eds.), *Mental health of ethnic minorities* (pp. 202–221). New York: Praeger.

Brown, S. A., Becker, H. A., Garcia, A. A., Barton, S. A., & Hanis, C. L. (2002). Measuring health beliefs in Spanish-speaking Mexican Americans with type 2 diabetes: Adapting an existing instrument. *Research in Nursing and Health, 25,* 145–158.

Brown, S. A., & Hanis, C. L. (1999). A border health initiative for Mexican Americans with type 2 diabetes. *Diabetes, 48,* 159.

Brown, S. A., Upchurch, S., Garcia, A., Barton, S. A., & Harris. C. (1998). Symptom related self care of Mexican Americans with NIDDM: Preliminary findings of the Starr County Diabetes Education Study. *The Diabetes Educator, 24,* 331–339.

Cabrera Strait, S. (2001). An examination of the influence of acculturative stress on substance use and related maladaptive behavior among Latino youth. *Dissertation Abstracts International: Section B. The Sciences and Engineering, 62* (5-B), 2532.

Canino, G. J., Rubio-Stipek, M., Shrout, P. E., & Bravo, M. (1987). Sex differences and depression in Puerto Rico. *Psychology of Women Quarterly, 11,* 443–459.

Centers for Disease Control and Prevention. (1997). Update: Trends in AIDS incidence, deaths, and prevalence—United States, 1996. *Morbidity and Mortality Weekly Report, 46*(8). Retrieved November 23, 2002, from ftp://ftp.cdc.gov/pub/Publications/mmwr/wk/mm4608.pdf

Centers for Disease Control and Prevention. (1998a). *Hispanics and tobacco.* Retrieved November 23, 2002, from http://www.cdc.gov/tobacco/sgr/sgr_1998/sgr-min-fs-hsp.htm

Centers for Disease Control and Prevention. (1998b). New data show continued decline in AIDS deaths. Retrieved November 23, 2002, from http://www.cdc.gov/od/oc/media/pressrel/r990831.htm

Centers for Disease Control and Prevention. (2002a). *HIV/AIDS among Hispanics in the United States.* Retrieved November 23, 2002, from http://www.cdc.gov/hiv/pubs/facts/hispanic.htm

Centers for Disease Control and Prevention. (2002b). *National Vital Statistics Report, 50*(16). Retrieved November 23, 2002, from http://www.cdc.gov/nchs/fastats/pdf/nvsr50_16tb2.pdf

Cervantes, R. C., Padilla, A. M., & Salgado de Snyder, N. S. (1991). The Hispanic Stress Inventory: A culturally relevant approach to psychosocial assessment. *Psychological Assessment, 3,* 438–447.

Cervantes, R. C., Salgado de Snyder, N. S., & Padilla, A. M. (1989). Post-traumatic stress in immigrants from Central America and Mexico. *Hospital and Community Psychiatry, 40,* 615–619.

Cleghorn, J. M., & Streiner, B. J. (1979). Prediction of symptoms and illness behavior from measures of life change and verbalized depressive themes. *Journal of Human Stress, 5,* 16–23.

Diabetes Control and Complications Trials Research Group. (1993). The effect of intensive treatment of diabetes on the development and progression of long-term complications in insulin-dependent diabetes mellitus. *New England Journal of Medicine, 329,* 977–986.

Diaz, T., Buehler, J. W., Castro, K. G., & Ward, J. W. (1993). AIDS trends among Hispanics in the United States. *American Journal of Public Health, 83,* 504–509.

Escobar, J. I., Nervi, C. H., & Gara, M. A. (2000). Immigration and mental health: Mexican Americans in the United States. *Harvard Review of Psychiatry, 8,* 64–72.

Finch, B. K., Hummer, R. A., Kolody, B., & Vega, W. A. (2001). The role of discrimination and acculturative stress in the physical health of Mexican-origin adults. *Hispanic Journal of Behavioral Sciences, 23,* 399–429.

Garb, H. N. (1997). Race bias, social class bias, and gender bias in clinical judgment. *Clinical Psychology: Science and Practice, 4,* 99–120.

Glover, S. H., Pumariega, A. J., Holzer, C. E., III, Wise, B. K., & Rodriguez, M. (1999). Anxiety symptomatology in Mexican-American adolescents. *Journal of Child and Family Studies, 8,* 47–57.

Guarnaccia, P. J., Canino, G., Rubio-Stipec, M., & Bravo, M. (1993). The prevalence of ataques de nervios in the Puerto Rico Disaster Study: The role of culture in psychiatric epidemiology. *Journal of Nervous and Mental Disease, 181,* 157–165.

Guarnaccia, P. J., De La Cancela, V., & Carrillo, E. (1989). The multiple meanings of ataques de nervios in the Latino community. *Medical Anthropology, 11,* 47–62.

Guarnaccia, P. J., Good, B. J., & Kleinman, A. (1990). A critical review of epidemiological studies of Puerto Rican mental health. *American Journal of Psychiatry, 147,* 1449–1456.

Haffner, S. M., Stern, M. P., Dunn, J., Mobley, M., Blackwell, J., & Bergman, R. N. (1990). Diminished insulin sensitivity and increased insulin response in nonobese, nondiabetic Mexican-Americans. *Metabolism, 39,* 842–847.

Hanis, C. L., Ferrell, R. E., Barton, S. A., Aguilar, L., Garza-Ibarra, A., Tulloch, B. R., Garcia, C. A., & Schull, W. (1983). Diabetes among Mexican-Americans in Starr County, Texas. *American Journal of Epidemiology, 118,* 659–668.

Harris, M. I., Flegal, K. M., Cowie, C. C., Eberhardt, M. S., Goldstein, D. E., Little, R. R., Wiedmeyer, H. M., & Byrd-Holt, D. (1998). Prevalence of diabetes, impaired fasting glucose, and impaired glucose tolerance in U.S. adults: The Third National Health and Nutrition Examination Survey (NHANES), 1988–94. *Diabetes Care, 21,* 518–524.

Hovey, J. D., & Magana, C. G. (2002). Psychosocial predictors of anxiety among immigrant Mexican migrant farmworkers: Implications for prevention and treatment. *Cultural Diversity and Ethnic Minority Psychology, 8,* 274–289.

Huertin-Roberts, S., Snowden, L., & Miller, L. (1997). Expressions of anxiety in African Americans: Ethnography and the epidemiological catchment area studies. *Culture, Medicine, and Psychiatry, 21,* 337–363.

Jenkins, J. H. (1988). Ethnopsychiatric interpretations of schizophrenic illness: The problem of nervios within Mexican-American families. *Culture, Medicine, and Psychiatry, 12,* 301–329.

Kim, B. S. K., & Abreu, J. M. (2001). Acculturation measurement: Theory, current instruments, and future directions. In J. G. Ponterotto, J. M. Casas, L. A. Suzuki, & C. M. Alexander (Eds.), *Handbook of multicultural counseling* (2nd ed., pp. 394–424). Thousand Oaks, CA: Sage.

Kim, M. (2001). Marital conflict, parent-child interaction, and children's social adjustment: An examination of Mexican-American families. *Dissertation Abstracts International: Section B. The Sciences and Engineering, 62*(6-B), 2974.

Klevens, R. M., Diaz, T., Fleming, P. L., Mays, M. A., & Frey, R. (1999). Trends in AIDS among Hispanics in the United States, 1991–1996. *American Journal of Public Health, 89,* 1104–1106.

Michultka, D., Blanchard, E. B., & Kalous, T. (1998). Responses to civilian war experiences: Predictors of psychological functioning and coping. *Journal of Traumatic Stress, 11,* 571–577.

Migration Dialogue. (2000). Meat, poultry, and migrants. *Rural Migration News, 6*(3). Retrieved November 21, 2002, from http://migration.ucdavis.edu/rmn/Archive_RMN/jul_2000-01rmn.html

Moscicki, E. K., Locke, B. Z., Rae, D. S., & Boyd, J. H. (1989). Depressive symptoms among Mexican Americans: The Hispanic Health and Nutrition Examination Survey. *American Journal of Epidemiology, 130,* 348–360.

Myers, H. F., & Rodriguez, N. (2003). Acculturation and physical health in racial and ethnic minorities. In K. M. Chun & P. B. Organista (Eds.), *Acculturation: Advances in theory, measurement, and applied research* (pp. 163–185). Washington, DC: American Psychological Association.

Nagayama, G. C., Bansal, A., & Lopez, I. R. (1999). Ethnicity and psychopathology: A meta-analytic review of 31 years of comparative MMPI/MMPI2 research. *Psychological Assessment, 11*(2), 186–197.

National Academies. (2002). *Minorities more likely to receive lower-quality health care, regardless of income and insurance coverage.* News release page maintained by the National Academies Office of News and Public Information. Retrieved August 5, 2002, from http://www4.nationalacademies.org.

National Diabetes Information Clearinghouse. (2002). *Diabetes in Hispanic Americans* (NIH Publication No. 02-3265). Retrieved November 23, 2002, from http://www.niddk.nih.gov/health/diabetes/pubs/hispan/hispan.htm#c

National Institute on Alcohol Abuse and Alcoholism. (2002). Alcohol and minorities: An update. *Alcohol Alert, 55.* Retrieved November 23, 2002, from http://www.niaaa.nih.gov/publications/aa55.htm

National Institutes of Health. (2001). NIAAA analysis reveals increased risk for liver cirrhosis death among Hispanic Americans. Retrieved November 23, 2002, from http://www.nih.gov/news/pr/aug2001/niaaa-14.htm

Ortega, A. N., Rosenheck, R., Alegria, M., & Desai, R. A. (2000). Acculturation and the lifetime risk of psychiatric and substance use disorders among Hispanics. *Journal of Nervous and Mental Disease, 188,* 728–735.

Roberts, R., & Sobhan, M. (1992). Symptoms of depression in adolescence: A comparison of Anglo, African, and Hispanic Americans. *Journal of Youth and Adolescence, 21,* 639–651.

Roberts, R., & Vernon, S. (1984). Minority status and psychological distress reexamined: The case of Mexican Americans. *Research in Community and Mental Health, 4,* 131–164.

Roberts, R. E., & Chen, Y. (1995). Depressive symptoms and suicidal ideation among Mexican-origin and Anglo adolescents. *Journal of the American Academy of Child and Adolescent Psychiatry, 34,* 81–90.

Roberts, R. E., Roberts, C. R., & Chen, Y. R. (1997). Ethnocultural differences in prevalence of adolescent depression. *American Journal of Community Psychology, 25,* 95–110.

Robins, L. N., & Regier, D. A. (1991). *Psychiatric disorders in America: The epidemiological catchment area study.* New York: Free Press.

Rogler, L. H. (1989). The meaning of culturally sensitive research in mental health. *American Journal of Psychiatry, 146,* 296–303.

Saldana, D. H. (1994). Acculturative stress: Minority status and distress. *Hispanic Journal of Behavioral Sciences, 16,* 116–128.

Salgado de Snyder, V. N., Diaz-Perez, M. J., & Ojeda, V. D. (2000). The prevalence of nervios and associated symptomatology among inhabitants of Mexican rural communities. *Culture, Medicine, and Psychiatry, 24,* 453–470.

Schlosser, E. (2001). *Fast food nation: The dark side of the all-American meal.* Boston: Houghton Mifflin.

Selik, R. M., Castro, K. G., Pappaioanou, M., & Buehler, J. W. (1989). Birthplace and the risk of AIDS among Hispanics in the United States. *American Journal of Public Health, 79,* 836–839.

Shrout, P. E., Canino, G. J., Bird, H. R., & Rubio-Stipek, M. (1992). Mental health status among Puerto Ricans, Mexican Americans, and non-Hispanic Whites. *American Journal of Community Psychology, 20,* 729–752.

Smart, J. F., & Smart, D. W. (1995). Acculturative stress: The experience of the Hispanic immigrant. *The Counseling Psychologist, 23,* 25–42.

Smedley, B. D., Stith, A. Y., & Nelson, A. R. (2002). *Unequal treatment: Confronting racial and ethnic disparities in health care.* Washington, DC: National Academy Press. Retrieved November 21, 2002, from http://www.nap.edu/catalog/10260.html

Smith, E. M. J. (1985). Ethnic minorities: Life stress, social support, and mental health issues. *The Counseling Psychologist, 13,* 537–579.

Snowden, L. R., & Cheung, F. K. (1990). Use of inpatient mental health services by members of ethnic minority groups. *American Psychologist, 45,* 347–355.

Swanson, J. W., Linskey, A. O., Quintero-Salinas, R., & Pumariega, A. J. (1992). A binational school survey of depressive symptoms, drug use, and suicidal ideation. *Journal of the American Academy of Child and Adolescent Psychiatry, 31,* 669–678.

University of California, Los Angeles. (2002). Hepatitis A rate among California's Latino children at epidemic level: Nearly half of children in state are Latino. Retrieved November 23, 2002, from http://www.newsroom.ucla.edu/page.asp?menu=fullsearchresults&id=3147

U.S. Department of Health and Human Services. (2001). *Mental health care for Hispanic Americans: A report of the Surgeon General.* Washington, DC: U.S. Department of Health and Human Services, Centers for Disease Control and Prevention.

Vazsonyi, A. T., & Flannery, D. J. (1997). Early adolescent delinquent behaviors: Associations with family and school domains. *Journal of Early Adolescence, 17,* 271–293.

Vega, W. A., Kolody, B., Aguilar-Gaxiola, S., Alderete, E., Catalano, R., & Caraveo-Anduaga, J. B. (1998). Lifetime prevalence of *DSM-III-R* psychiatric disorders among urban and rural Mexican Americans in California. *Archives of General Psychiatry, 55,* 771–778.

Vernon, S., & Roberts, R. E. (1992). Prevalence of treated and untreated psychiatric disorders in three ethnic groups. *Social Science and Medicine, 16,* 1575–1582.

Ybarra, L. (1982). When wives work: The impact on the Chicano family. *Journal of Marriage and the Family, 44,* 169–178.

CHAPTER 15 # Treatment Issues with Hispanic Clients

José M. Abreu, University of Southern California; Andrés J. Consoli, San Francisco State University; and Scott J. Cypers, University of Southern California

Hispanics are the fastest growing minority group in the United States (see chapter 13 for details). High rates of fertility and continued immigration within the last decade have produced a dramatic growth rate estimated in the 60% range. Island Puerto Ricans and undocumented residents not included, more than 35 million Hispanics currently live in the United States. This statistic is expected to increase to 100 million or more by 2050. As a group, Hispanics face a multitude of risk factors, including poverty (one third meets poverty criteria) and its related consequences such as homelessness or inadequate housing; unsafe neighborhoods characterized by crime, violence, disease, and pollution; high rates of single-parent homes; high unemployment and underemployment; low educational attainment; lack of health insurance and limited health care access; higher prevalence rates of HIV infection and diabetes; discrimination and acculturative stress. The purpose of this chapter is to highlight some of the treatment issues affecting Hispanics such as patterns of utilization, acculturation, and counseling approaches.

MENTAL HEALTH UTILIZATION

There is a sizable, persistent unmet need for treatment in people suffering from mental disorders. Overall, it is estimated that about 50 million adults in the United States need mental health care at any given time, yet only one third to one fifth, or even fewer, receive the needed care (Robins & Regier, 1991). The gap in services holds true even among people who are experiencing substantial distress and impairment and among those who acknowledge needing help (Katz et al., 1997; Wells, Golding, Hough, Burnam, & Karno, 1988). Among ethnic minorities, the proportion receiving the care needed is even lower (Swartz et al., 1998).

Many studies indicate that ethnic minorities are underrepresented among those who use mental health services (Diala et al., 2000; Vega, Kolody, Aguilar-Gaxiola,

Partial work for this chapter was supported by NIMH grant # 3 R24 MH61573-01A1S1 awarded to the second author. We thank Maria Moore and Enjolie Lafaurie for their assistance in compiling the references for this chapter.

& Catalano, 1999)—particularly outpatient services such as psychotherapy (Olfson & Pincus, 1994a, 1994b)—and those who seek services drop out of treatment at higher rates than Whites do (Sue, 1977, 1988, 1998). For example, the 1987 National Medical Expenditure Survey indicated that ethnic minorities were dramatically underrepresented among long-term users of psychotherapy (e.g., over 21 sessions), with Caucasians accounting for 93.5% of these users (Olfson & Pincus, 1994b). These findings suggest problems of differential access, effectiveness, or both (Sledge, 1994). Some studies, however, have challenged the belief that ethnic minorities underuse mental health services (Goodman & Siegel, 1978), and others have documented a significant improvement over time (Sue, 1977, contrasted with O'Sullivan, Peterson, Cox, & Kirkeby, 1989).

Patterns of Utilization Among Hispanics

Data addressing the utilization patterns of Hispanics indicate that this topic is a complex one. For example, Padilla, Ruiz, and Alvarez (1975) reported evidence of serious underuse by Hispanics, whereas Karno and Morales (1971) reported overutilization. Investigations focusing specifically on Mexican American utilization of mental health services are also mixed; some report underuse (Jaco, 1960; Karno & Edgerton, 1969; Keefe, Padilla, & Carlos, 1978; Padilla & Ruiz, 1973; Torrey, 1972), and others show use consistent with community representation (Andrulis, 1977; S. López, 1981; Sánchez, Acosta, & Grosser, 1979; Trevino & Bruhn, 1977; Trevino, Bruhn, & Bunce, 1979). Cheung and Snowden (1990) reported that Hispanic utilization rates varied according to type of service available and that Hispanics overutilized community-based facilities. Generally, these conclusions corroborate the results of an earlier study (Sue, 1977). S. López (1981) addressed the inconsistencies in these findings by pointing to methodological problems associated with utilization research, including the basis on which comparisons are made, that is, nationwide versus community-wide ethnic representation, and failure to take into account mental health services need. In addition, Hispanics have been significantly underrepresented in applied psychology research (Case & Smith, 2000), particularly in psychotherapy studies (see Miranda et al., 1996).

Studies based on large population samples typically provide some evidence indicating low rates of mental health service utilization. For example, in the Los Angeles Epidemiological Catchment Area site, Hough and collaborators (Hough et al., 1987) found that Mexican Americans were only half as likely as non-Hispanic Whites to have made a mental health visit, and the researchers reported a significantly lower number of general medical or mental health visits (approximately three visits by Mexican Americans compared to more than six visits by non-Hispanic Whites). Vega and collaborators (Vega et al., 1999) surveyed a probability sample ($N = 3,012$) of Fresno County, California, and found that among those diagnosed with a mental disorder, only about one fourth had accessed services. Significant differences in use were found between Mexican immigrants and Mexican Americans born in the United States. The use by the former (15.4%) was two fifths that by the latter (37.5%). Furthermore, the most educated, urban population had the highest utilization of mental health services whereas the least educated, rural population had the highest use of informal care providers. Most recently, Vega and López (2001) argued that total utilization rates of public mental health systems by Hispanics in California point to persistent underutilization: Although Hispanics represent 29% of the population in California, they received 15.4% of inpatient or residential care, 19.7% of outpatient care, and 16.9% of partial day care.

Reasons for Underutilization

Several writers have identified acculturation as a critical factor contributing to the probability of mental health service use by Mexican Americans (Sánchez & Atkinson, 1983; Wells et al., 1988). Additionally, some studies have documented that ethnic minorities may be more likely to seek services in the general care sector than in the mental health sector (Cooper-Patrick, Crum, & Ford, 1994; Cooper-Patrick et al., 1999; Ford, Kamerow, & Thompson, 1988; Gallo, Marino, Ford, & Anthony, 1995; Olfson et al., 2000). In fact, a significant proportion of mental health care is provided by professionals outside the mental health field, mostly by general medical practitioners followed by human services professionals and voluntary support networks, a state of affairs described as a "de facto mental health system" (Regier et al., 1993, p. 85).

Conflicts between values reflected in counseling theories and practices and Hispanic values comprise another possible reason for underutilization. Simoni and Pérez (1995) and Zea, Quezada, and Belgrave (1994) argue that Hispanic values such as familism, interdependence, family and community centeredness, well-defined gender roles *(machismo/marianismo)*, *simpatía* (smooth and pleasant social relationships), power distance (societal support for power differentials leading to obedience and conformity), *personalismo* (personable demeanor), *respeto* (deference based on power differentials such as wealth, age, prestige), linearity (an emphasis on the role of authority in solving problems), present-time orientation, *dignidad* (dignity, worthiness), *confianza* (trust), spirituality (fatalism), and a collectivistic worldview play a role in attitudes toward mental health services. Indeed, tension between individualism and collectivism seems to be quite prevalent when mental health researchers compare and contrast "traditional" theories of psychotherapy and more contemporary theories, including but not limited to those with a multicultural emphasis.

Other cultural factors may pose further barriers to treatment. Some writers have singled out language or location of services as dimensions that affect treatment utilization (Cheung & Snowden, 1990; Flaskerud, 1986; O'Sullivan & Lasso, 1992). Relatedly, other investigators point to ethnic matching between client and mental health practitioner as a significant factor (Abreu & Gabarain, 2000; Atkinson, Poston, Furlong, & Mercado, 1989; three studies in S. R. López, López, & Fong, 1991). For example, analogue studies examining Mexican American preferences for practitioner ethnicity have reported clear preferences for an ethnic match, that is, a mental health practitioner who is ethnically similar to the client (S. R. López et al., 1991). However, in a subsequent study that examines

the role of possible confounds in Mexican American practitioner preference analogue research, Abreu and Gabarain found that social desirability might play a
role in the reported findings (expressing a preference for an ethnically dissimilar
practitioner is less socially desirable than stating a preference for an ethnically
similar practitioner).

Although expressed preference for an ethnically similar mental health practitioner may be partially a function of social desirability, this preference should not
be interpreted as evidence that practitioner ethnicity is unimportant to prospective
Mexican American or other Hispanic clients. Preference for mental health practitioner ethnicity very likely plays a major role in ethnic minority utilization of mental health services regardless of whether it is based on social desirability or pre-
sumptions about the practitioner's cultural values, knowledge, or skills. It may be
that prospective clients expect to be better understood by a mental health practitioner who, by virtue of being ethnically similar, may have had comparable life experiences and faced interrelated problems. For example, a Hispanic mental health
practitioner may be assumed to have experienced certain culture-specific events,
such as speaking Spanish at home and English in school, the influences of *padri-
nos/madrinas* (godparents), *quinceañeras,* or other such occurrences that foster a
sense of affinity toward the practitioner. Or more generally, Hispanic clients may
feel better able to identify with and trust a Hispanic mental health practitioner because of the common experiences of surviving and managing a social milieu characterized by prejudice and biases. It is also possible that a client may be better able
to express certain feelings in Spanish than English and that the prospect of seeing
a Hispanic helper may involve *expectations* that he or she would be better able to
understand these expressions. Some empirical evidence supports the speculation
that Hispanic preference for a Hispanic practitioner involves a priori expectations.

For example, in a study based on a sample of Mexican American college students, Abreu (2000) found that expectations about mental health practitioners and
the counseling process were more positive when the practitioner was Mexican
American rather than European American. In discussing his findings, Abreu argued that to the extent that counseling expectations interact with decisions to seek
help (Tinsley, Brown, de-St-Aubin, & Lucek, 1984), the obtained finding is consistent with reports indicating that Mexican American utilization rates of mental
health services vary depending on availability of community-based bilingual and
bicultural services (Cheung & Snowden, 1990). This finding is congruent, at least
in principle, with Sue and Zane's (1987) proposition that the lack of *ascribed*
credibility attributed to nonminority practitioners may be the primary reason for
ethnic minority underutilization of mental health services.

Although favorable counseling expectations of an ethnically similar mental
health practitioner by Hispanic clients is consistent with strategies that seek to
match practitioners and clients on ethnicity, unrealistically *high* expectations of performance could put some Hispanic practitioners at a disadvantage, and they may
need to assess their clients' expectations carefully when formulating treatment
goals. By the same token, European American practitioners exceeding relatively
low client expectations of performance are likely to be perceived in a positive light
by their Hispanic clients. There is some empirical evidence for this phenomenon.

Atkinson, Casas, and Abreu (1992), for example, reported higher Mexican American ratings of cross-cultural competence for a European American practitioner portrayed as culturally sensitive than for a Mexican American practitioner also portrayed as culturally sensitive. From a practical standpoint, it would be reasonable to speculate that practitioner behaviors that are responsive to the counseling expectations of Hispanic clients may improve the effectiveness of Hispanic as well as non-Hispanic practitioners assigned to work with this population. This speculation is consistent with Sue and Zane's (1987) position that although ascribed mental health practitioner credibility may be related to initial decisions to seek (or not seek) help, *achieved* practitioner credibility determines treatment termination or persistence among those minority clients who choose to seek help.

Enabling resources, such as health insurance coverage, are also considered important factors that influence access to mental health services. Some surveys estimate that approximately 35% of Hispanics in the United States lack health insurance. Although health insurance may account for some of the underuse described in this chapter, it does not explain the whole picture. While acknowledging the need to address the role of lack of insurance as a barrier to mental health care for Mexican Americans, Vega, Kolody, and Aguilar-Gaxiola (2001) pointed out that even among those who are insured there is a need for "education and more effective referral from other sectors . . . to encourage use of these services" (p. 133). These findings suggest a strong role for sociological, psychological, and cultural dimensions to influence access beyond enabling resources.

Finally, a number of other barriers to Hispanic use of mental health services have been articulated but have not been empirically supported. Specifically, alternative resources, such as *curanderos* and *herbalistas* (Mexican Americans) and *espiritistas* (Puerto Ricans and Cuban Americans) have been cited as substitutes for conventional mental health services (Atkinson, Abreu, Ortiz-Bush, & Brewer, 1994; Padilla, Carlos, & Keefe, 1976). Additional dimensions as barriers to access and use may include negative attitudes toward the seeking of services (e.g., social stigma or shame) and anti-immigrant policies.

TREATMENT ISSUES: PREVENTIVE APPROACH

In defining culturally sensitive mental health services for Hispanics, Rogler, Malgady, Costantino, and Blumenthal (1987) affirm that treatment approaches need to take into account Hispanic norms and values. A sound multicultural perspective honors not only a person's individuality and collectivity but also the centrality of context and circumstances in which any given behavior is embedded. In other words, a person's comportment is rendered comprehensible when a practitioner carefully integrates subjective and personal explanations with intersubjective and interpersonal ones. In this vein, Bohart (2000) identified the client as the most important "common factor," further arguing that a true holistic or integrative approach needs to honor and facilitate the self-healing capacities of clients.

Congruent with these views, the role of the mental health practitioner can be conceived as that of a change agent who seeks to provide the necessary services not only to treat those diagnosed with an illness or disorder but also to proactively engage others in a range of activities destined to promote physical and mental health via the fostering of protective factors and the reduction of risk factors. We believe strongly that much of the potential and actual contributions that mental health practitioners have to offer are not only at the tertiary treatment level but also at the preventive and maintenance level, especially with regard to physical health concerns affecting Hispanics. To underscore our position that counseling activities can respond to a model that focuses on primary as well as secondary and tertiary treatments, we offer the following discussions, introduced in chapter 14, about HIV and AIDS and diabetes and how they affect Hispanic populations.

HIV and AIDS

Because HIV (and by extension, AIDS) is not partial to the race and ethnicity of its recipients, effective prevention and treatment are clearly behaviorally based. The statistics noted in chapter 14, for example, show that HIV transmission via sexual contact and intravenous substance abuse accounts for most of the AIDS cases reported in the year 2000. In the fight against AIDS, not only has HIV *testing* proven to be a valuable tool in the effective management of HIV disease, but it has also brought about much-needed public awareness regarding the role of risk behaviors and prevention. Recent research, for example, indicates that people who are tested for HIV tend to respond by reducing their sexual risk behaviors (Alwano-Edyegu & Marum, 1999; Denning, Nakashima, Wortley, & Shas Project Group, 1999). With regard to timely treatment, the International AIDS Society–USA Panel indicated that HIV testing improves the clinical prognosis through early detection and antiretroviral treatment (Carpenter et al., 1998). In addition, Quinn et al. (2000) found that early treatment makes HIV-infected individuals less infectious.

Although previous studies indicated that the lapse of time between HIV infection and testing (which is critical for effective interventions) was much longer for Hispanics than for Whites (Sabogal & Catania, 1996; Scwarcz et al., 1997), a more recent study indicates that this disparity may be narrowing (Fernández, Perrino, Royal, Ghany, & Bowen, 2002). In this survey study, more than 1,000 Hispanic men who trace their origin to one of several Latin American countries were recruited from gay and non-gay venues (i.e., bars, gyms) in South Florida and were interviewed with regard to risk behaviors and HIV testing. Results show that overall testing rates were high (76% compared with 66% for the general U.S. population), especially among those at high risk for HIV infection. Fernández et al. found that men who had a higher number of sexual partners, who had sex with men, and who were worried about sexually transmitted diseases were more likely to be tested (unfortunately, injection drug use as a risk was not assessed); these findings indicate that self-assessment of risk behaviors was a likely motivator for men to seek help. Men who had never been tested were more likely to identify themselves as heterosexual than as men who have sex with men. Consequently, the authors argue that

> there is a need to examine further the behaviors associated with testing among heterosexual men and to identify their motivating factors. Persuading high risk

heterosexual men to recognize their risk for infection and the importance of HIV testing may be our next challenge. (p. 383)

Organized efforts to address the threat of AIDS among Hispanics has taken the form of community planning groups, an outgrowth of the belief that responses to local HIV prevention priorities and needs is best carried out through local participatory planning. To this end, two national conferences (Community Planning Leadership Summit in Houston, Texas, and Capacity Building for HIV Prevention in Atlanta, Georgia) and a regional meeting (*Enlace:* Skills Building for the Latino Community in El Paso, Texas) were held in 2001, at which various topics and themes were raised and discussed. On the basis of their experience in working with Hispanics, participating health officials and staff generated the following suggestions:

- Assist clinical staff to recognize the risk and stigma among Hispanics associated with homosexuality (*rechazo,* or rejection), with having AIDS, or with a nondocumented immigration status
- Get to know the impact of AIDS on Hispanic communities
- Acknowledge interlinked issues of religion, fatalism, *machismo* or gender (e.g., difficulty negotiating condom use), and denial ("AIDS doesn't happen to us!")
- Address barriers to AIDS prevention or treatment program attendance: child care, transportation, cost, multiple jobs, incentives, meeting times, location of meetings
- Avoid generalizations of Hispanics (lack of recognition and awareness of different national backgrounds)
- Generate Spanish-language materials that are culturally targeted to the local Hispanic groups (i.e., Mexican, Puerto Rican, Cuban, Dominican, etc.)
- Establish outreach to migrant and seasonal farmworkers, injection drug users, people living with HIV and AIDS, and men who self-identify as non-gay but who have sex with men

Whereas a competent mental health practitioner will help HIV-positive Hispanics process their diagnosis, treatment, and prognosis (tertiary treatment), a culturally competent practitioner will conceptualize and implement culturally relevant strategies such as the ones just listed to redress the spread of HIV (VanOss Marín, 1994).

Diabetes

On the average, Hispanics are nearly twice as likely to have diabetes as Whites are. Mexican Americans are three to five times more likely than Whites to be afflicted by diabetes; in some communities, the prevalence rates are alarmingly high (Brown, Becker, Garcia, Barton, & Hanis, 2002). Health beliefs have long been considered an important component to diabetes management (Given, Given, Gallin, & Condon, 1983). Studies have shown that health beliefs have direct and indirect effects on diabetes metabolic control (Brown & Hedges, 1994), especially beliefs related to a sense of agency or control over the disease (Surgenor, Horn, Hudson, Lunt, & Tennent, 2000). Health beliefs relative to control issues are especially important to members of ethnic minority groups (Fitzgerald et al., 2000). For example, in the Brown et al. (2002) study, which was implemented among the residents of Starr County, Texas (a community that is nearly 100% Hispanic), researchers found that the high prevalence rates of diabetes apparently led to the belief among community residents that one could not control diabetes and that everyone eventually would get the disease.

One of the main goals to any diabetes prevention or treatment program is to encourage individuals to prevent or control diabetes by making healthy food choices. In order to bring this message to Hispanic communities, key organizations (such as the National Council of La Raza and the National Hispanic Council on Aging) could be contacted to help distribute culturally appropriate diabetes education messages through established community channels. Another resource is the National Diabetes Information Clearinghouse, which provides many fact sheets and pamphlets about diabetes and its management in easy-to-read formats in English and Spanish.

Food is an integral part of family gatherings and community celebrations in the Hispanic culture. Diabetes prevention and treatment campaigns need to encourage Hispanic families to consider how much and how often they eat and how they prepare their food. They should not be told that they have to give up favorite foods when making dietary decisions, because this approach has been shown to be ineffective at best (National Coalition of Hispanic Health and Human Services Organizations, 1998). This problem is highlighted by the question raised by a Hispanic woman reacting to written materials that promoted a healthy diet: *"¿Qué es un bagel?"* ["What's a bagel?"]. The message should be that people can continue to eat the foods they love and that they simply need to consider making a few small changes in portion sizes and in how favorite dishes are prepared. Cooking with olive oil instead of lard and limiting salt intake by using fresh herbs and spices like cilantro to season foods are just two examples of ways that Hispanics can prepare healthier foods without sacrificing taste. Similar recipe guides can also offer suggestions on how to make other healthy ingredient substitutions and how to alter preparation of traditional foods to preserve flavor but reduce added fat, high-fat meats, and salt. It is also important to disseminate information regarding control issues. That is, individuals, not doctors or nurses, control diabetes prevention and treatment. The message here is that individuals can assume control over their health by making *small* lifestyle changes (Brown et al., 2002).

General Approach to Address Other Concerns

Aside from HIV and AIDS and diabetes, chapter 14 highlighted other concerns affecting Hispanic health (e.g., work-related illnesses, hepatitis). We would like to suggest the following approaches as a general strategy for mental health practitioners working with Hispanic populations:

- To earn the *confianza* (trust) of a targeted community, find out who is respected in the community. Ask clients, staff, business owners, clergy, members of the media, teachers, and so on to identify the respected leaders and agencies that serve the community's needs. This takes time; be patient.

- Learn (or remember) the value of *personalismo*. Go to local leaders and ask for their opinions about what people in the community need the most. Don't assert your agenda; instead, listen to the community's agenda and assign your priorities based on their needs.
- Develop culturally relevant media and materials to convey your message; target whole families, not individuals. Persons developing such media and materials should be familiar with the literacy level and culture of specific target groups.
- Remember that the purpose of any intervention is to improve health by changing the cultural and environmental factors that support unhealthy behaviors (e.g., tobacco commercials that target young Hispanics).

TREATMENT ISSUES: SECONDARY AND TERTIARY APPROACHES

The treatments of Hispanic mental health problems have been conceptualized from a variety of sociological, psychosociological, and psychiatric perspectives. One common denominator across these points of view is the fundamental assumption that acculturation poses a risk for Hispanic health, an assumption with some empirical support (Burnam et al., 1987; Cabrera Strait, 2001; Hovey & Magaña, 2002), as discussed in chapter 14.

Acculturation, Stress, and Approach to Counseling

Alderete, Vega, Kolody, and Aguilar-Gaxiola (2000) identified four interrelated etiological explanations relative to acculturation processes affecting Hispanic mental health: acculturative stress, social learning or deculturation, social marginality, and identity disintegration. A variant of the general social stress model (Pearlin, Menaghan, Lieberman, & Mullan, 1981), *acculturative stress* theory is based on the assumption that adaptation (acculturation) to U.S. culture produces social conflict, including intergenerational friction (Gil & Vega, 1996; Rogler, Cortes, & Malgady, 1991). Personal resources such as psychological and emotional coping skills as well as external social networks are taxed, resulting in various forms of mental health concerns. The other side of acculturation is *deculturation,* that is, as new patterns of U.S. values, behaviors, and customs are learned, native culture might be weakened, and individuals may lose natural protective or coping factors inherent in the indigenous cultural milieu, such as familistic values, cultural traditions, and social support (Rumbaut, 1977; Suarez-Orozco & Suarez-Orozco, 1995). Increases in drug and alcohol use, interpersonal violence, and lowered expectations of personal attainment are likely outcomes, especially among Hispanic adolescents (Swanson, Linskey, Quintero-Salinas, & Pumariega, 1992). *Social marginality* refers to Hispanic integration into low-income communities riddled with social pathologies and a long history of discrimination and social neglect. Social marginality may explain why "years of living in U.S." is apparently a risk factor for Hispanic health (Vega et al., 1998). *Identity disintegration* refers to the destruction of cultural referents that give meaning to self-identity; it has been used as an etiological explanation of psychopathology among Mexican Indians.

Although these four broad categories have been used as a heuristic to conceptualize the effects of acculturative stress on Hispanic psychosocial functioning, as of yet little empirical data validate or tie these categories with outcome or process measures. Nonetheless, we would like to suggest several approaches that are based on the acculturation literature (Comas-Diaz & Minrath, 1987; Rogler et al., 1991; Smart & Smart, 1995; Vargas-Willis & Cervantes, 1987; Padilla, 1980) and that are likely to be effective in the prevention and treatment of this source of psychosocial stress among Hispanics.

Because the sociopolitical factors that catalyze Hispanic immigration to the United States differ from those that affect Asians, Europeans, and other groups (see chapter 13), several issues warrant special consideration from mental health practitioners who work with Hispanic clients.

Discrimination and Racial Identity   In Latin American countries, people are used to being around and are accepting of individuals who represent a wide variety of skin color without the pervasive dichotomization of "White" versus "non-White" that is so prevalent in the United States. Although Latin American countries are far from impervious to prejudice and discrimination based on skin color, immigrants adjusting to U.S. culture are likely to become confused in a sociopolitical environment so attuned to race rather than ethnicity. For example, Hispanic immigrants with African ancestry often have to contend with being perceived as African American rather than as immigrants from a Latin American country. In some cases, these individuals or their children may choose to identify as African American. Mental health practitioners working with Hispanics need to be sensitive to these sources of stress by assessing how their clients identify themselves (e.g., by nationality, race, or ethnicity) and whether their clients, through this identification, feel discriminated against. In this vein, one of the objectives of counseling could be to help clients develop a sense of pride about their unique features (skin color, Spanish accent) in spite of prevalent stereotypes that denigrate these characteristics; this approach may be especially helpful for clients suffering from depressive symptoms. Likewise, mental health practitioners can facilitate their clients' sense of empowerment as they become more aware of societal stressors. For example, a practitioner could help a first-generation client articulate the types of social injustices or discrimination experienced in his or her country of origin and then help the client compare and contrast them with experiences of inequality while living in the United States. This approach could help the client foster a sense of empowerment as well as a political and social consciousness within which to make sense of the stress involved in acculturating to U.S. culture (La Roche, 2002).

Discrimination against Hispanics relative to biased treatment in employment, education, housing, and other human services is common (Padilla, 1980), especially for undocumented Hispanics, who live in constant fear of deportation and are often subjected to work exploitation. Mental health practitioners working with undocumented clients need to understand basic immigration laws and develop an appreciation for the acculturative stress (which may be experienced as depression or anxiety) that undocumented status imposes on Hispanic immigrants. More generally, discrimination experienced by Hispanics is a likely precursor to poor psychological functioning. For example, Finch, Hummer, Kolody, and Vega (2001) surveyed a large sample of Mexican Americans ($N = 3,012$) living in California and found that discrimination was related to poor physical health and depression. Mental health practitioners working with depressed Hispanic clients would do well to explore the possible link between their clients' symptoms and stress caused by discrimination.

Language Use   As U.S. immigrants, Hispanics have demonstrated a remarkable commitment to the Spanish language. Even in cases where second- or third-generation individuals lose the use of Spanish almost completely, certain Spanish words are retained and used in the company of other Hispanics. In fact, many Hispanics speak "Spanglish" with each other, a combination of Spanish and English mingled together. The sociopolitical histories relative to the colonial and Mexican hegemony plus perennial waves of immigration from Latin American countries have left a legacy of Spanish-language culture in U.S. geographical areas such as the West Coast, Southwest, and south Florida. Names of towns and cities, broadcast and printed media, cuisine, and historical sites speak to these legacies. Because language is so central to the counseling process, bilingual services are a must when Spanish is a client's preferred language. Second- (or subsequent) generation clients who may prefer English to Spanish would still benefit from a mental health practitioner who has at least a working knowledge of Spanish. Because Spanish is typically the first language that second-generation Hispanics learn, many early emotions and thoughts are likely encoded in Spanish rather than English. A practitioner who can understand Spanish may facilitate awareness of thoughts and emotions held outside of consciousness, which the client may be able to express more freely in the language in which they were encoded (Santiago-Rivera & Altarriba, 2002).

Spanish *dichos* (used generally in Latin American folklore) or *refranes* (used in Mexican folklore) may also prove helpful to mental health practitioners working with Hispanic, Spanish-speaking clients. *Dichos* and *refranes* are sayings or proverbs that capture folk wisdom relative to various human situations (Zuñiga, 1991). Aviera (1996) facilitated a *dichos* therapy group with hospitalized Spanish-speaking patients and reported that his intervention effectively facilitated rapport building, decreased defensiveness, enhanced motivation, stimulated exploration and articulation of feelings, and improved insight and self-esteem. Similarly, Constantino, Malgady, and Rogler (1986) developed an approach to therapy based on Spanish language folklore. Constantino et al. designed and implemented what they termed *cuento,* or folklore therapy, to assist Puerto Rican second-generation children in a mental health clinic at risk of mental health disorders because of family conflicts involving acculturation differences. The therapy was facilitated by bilingual therapists who read folktales (in Spanish and

English) to the children and then led group discussions on the meaning of the stories. In subsequent sessions, the children were asked to role-play the various characters in the *cuentos* and then to discuss the role-playing activities in relation to their own personal problems. The authors report that this intervention successfully reduced level of trait anxiety among participants.

Generation Status and Family Structure   Hispanic families comprised of first- and second-generation individuals experience intergenerational cultural stress, especially adolescent members. Throughout this phase of development, normative conflicts arise between parents and their children, and intergenerational acculturation differences are likely to exacerbate this process. Conflict within Hispanic families can cause a sense of alienation between parents and children, leading the latter to engage in high-risk behaviors such as dropping out of school and using alcohol and drugs.

At a more general level, there is typically a high degree of interdependence between Hispanic parents and their children (Marín & Triandis, 1985). In Hispanic culture, emphasis is placed on social relationships and group goals rather than on individuality. Hispanics learn behavioral expectations for self and others through scripts (cultural scripts are an essential component of the meaning system of any cultural group) passed down from parents to their children (La Roche, 1999). Such scripts include *personalismo* (personal rather than institutional relationships), *familismo* (family orientation), *respeto* (deferential behaviors toward others based on age, sex, and authority), *simpatía* (friendly interpersonal attitude that eschews conflict), and allocentrism (a cultural value predicated on the notion that individuals understand themselves through others). Mental health practitioners working with Hispanic families need to take these cultural factors into account to better understand family dynamics and to develop appropriate treatment plans.

For example, when working with Hispanic families wherein parents speak only Spanish and their children are bilingual, non-Spanish-speaking clinicians who rely on the children to translate need to be careful not to insult parents. For such mental health practitioners, it may seem natural to face the children while speaking to them, then to wait while the children translate to their parents. Because the parents (especially the father when present) may perceive such interaction as lacking *respeto,* it is best for practitioners to face parents and speak to them rather than to the children. Mental health practitioners working with Hispanic adolescents at risk of dropping out of school or engaging in other problem behaviors would benefit from a family approach that takes into account Hispanic family values and intergenerational conflicts caused by acculturation differences.

Assessment

Acculturation is a very salient factor of the Hispanic experience, a process associated with stress and a likely precursor to other psychosocial concerns. Therefore, assessment of acculturation should be one of the first objectives among mental health practitioners working with Hispanic clients (readers interested in Hispanic assessment for *DSM-IV* diagnostic purposes can see Cuellar, 1998).

A measurement model frequently cited by researchers of acculturation was developed by John Berry and his colleagues (Berry, 1990, 1994; Berry & Kim, 1988; Berry, Kim, Power, Young, & Bajaki, 1989; Berry, Trimble, & Olmeda, 1986), who proposed four acculturation attitudes (integration, assimilation, separation, and marginalization). These attitudes express the combined level of adherence to host and indigenous cultures, with each culture represented by a separate continuum. *Integration* occurs when an individual sustains an active interest in the indigenous culture while maintaining daily interactions with members of the dominant or host group. Thus, a person with this acculturation attitude desires to become proficient in the culture of the dominant group and yet retains proficiency in the indigenous culture; this attitude represents biculturalism and is believed to be the most adaptive. *Assimilation* occurs when an individual maintains daily interactions with members of the host group but has no interest in remaining conversant with the native culture; an assimilated individual absorbs the culture of the dominant group while rejecting the indigenous culture. *Separation* occurs when much value is placed on the culture of origin and its members, but contact with members of the host culture is avoided. An individual with a separation attitude is not interested in learning the culture of the dominant group and only wants to maintain and perpetuate the culture of origin. Finally, *marginalization* represents the attitude of an individual with no interest in maintaining or acquiring proficiency in any culture, native or host. Marginalization is perhaps the most problematic of the four acculturation attitudes because, by definition, a marginalized individual would generally not be expected to relate well to others. To the extent that individuals may not always have the freedom to choose how they want to acculturate and that their choices are inevitably influenced if not constrained by the dominant group, mental health practitioners ought to thoughtfully consider the context in which acculturation choices are made. The terms *pluralism, conformity, segregation,* and *discrimination* may describe the attitudes of a dominant group that, in turn, may influence the individual choices of integration, assimilation, separation, and marginalization respectively (Berry, 1997).

Mental health practitioners working with Hispanics can choose from a wide variety of tests developed to measure acculturation. Currently, there are at least 23 instruments developed to measure Hispanic acculturation, 8 of which were designed to be used with Hispanics in general, 3 with Cuban Americans, 11 with Mexican Americans, and 1 with Puerto Rican Americans. Although a description of extant instruments tapping Hispanic acculturation is beyond the scope of this chapter (an exhaustive review of acculturation instruments is provided by Kim and Abreu, 2001), we will provide a brief description of one such measure.

The Bidimensional Short Acculturation Scale for Hispanics (BSASH; Marín & Gamba, 1996) is a 24-item instrument derived from an initial set of 60 items (30 for Hispanic domain and 30 for non-Hispanic domain) measuring language use, media preference, participation in cultural activities, and ethnicity of social relations. The final instrument was derived from the results of a factor analysis, and it measures language use, linguistic proficiency, and preferences for electronic media on two subscales, each representing a continuum on the use of Spanish and English. The BSASH has adequate internal consistency for both subscales

and evidence of criterion, convergent, and face validity. It follows the acculturation model that was described in this section; high English but low Spanish scale
scores are indicative of an assimilation attitude, and the reverse pattern of scores
indicates a separation attitude. High scores on both Spanish and English scales
represents an integration attitude, whereas low scores on each scale represents
marginalization. The Short Acculturation Scale for Hispanic Youth (Barona &
Miller, 1994) is a 12-item instrument for children and adolescents that is similar
in construction to the BSASH.

Using Alderete et al.'s (2000) model of acculturation as an etiological dimension of Hispanic mental health, practitioners can utilize BSASH scores (or
scores from other acculturation measure) to help determine the likely source of
acculturation stress that their Hispanic clients are experiencing. Given the importance of *familismo* and allocentrism in Hispanic culture, assessment of acculturation should focus on the members of an entire family unit whenever possible.

Culture-Bound Syndromes

As discussed in chapter 14, Hispanics use several labels to describe psychological syndromes such as *susto* (fright), *mal de ojo* (evil eye), *nervios* (nerves), and
ataques de nervios (attack of nerves). Guarnaccia, Canino, Rubio-Stipec, and
Bravo (1993) reported that up to 14% of a sample of Puerto Ricans reported having an *ataque*. The concept of *nervios* is also used more generally by Hispanics
to describe distress associated with anxiety and depression (Salgado de Snyder,
Diaz-Perez, & Ojeda, 2000) and with delusions or hallucinations (Jenkins, 1988).
Knowledge of these syndromes should help clinicians working with Hispanics to
identify distress and illness in their clients that may be manifested in ways that
may not conform to *DSM* nomenclature.

CONCLUSION

The utilization patterns of Hispanic mental health services are complex, but research data indicate that overall this ethnic group tends not to take advantage of
services as readily as European Americans do. The reasons for this apparent underutilization are complicated, and several explanations have been offered: the
use of health care professionals outside of mental health; value conflicts between
Hispanic culture and conventional psychological principles; acculturation and
language issues; lack of Hispanic mental health practitioners; and the difficulties
that Hispanics have in accessing care due to lack of insurance and for other structural reasons. Preventive approaches to health concerns of Hispanics, such as diabetes and HIV diseases, were discussed as were treatments of mental health concerns that focus on the Hispanic experience in the United States. This focus
includes issues generally related to acculturative stress, such as discrimination,
language use, generational status, and family structure. Lastly, an assessment approach based on acculturation was presented.

Exercises

1. You have been commissioned by the National Coalition of Hispanic Health and Human Services Organizations to develop and implement culturally sensitive programs that address (1) HIV-AIDS or (2) diabetes prevention and treatment among Hispanics. Based on the information presented in this chapter, provide an outline for the development and implementation of such a program focusing on HIV-AIDS or diabetes (choose one).

2. A mental health agency serving a largely Hispanic clientele hires you to develop and implement a culturally sensitive training program for its mental health staff (e.g., psychologists, counselors, social workers). Based on the information provided in this chapter, provide an outline detailing a training program that incorporates issues and concepts related to "acculturation and stress," "discrimination and racial identity," "language use," "family structure," and "clinical assessment."

REFERENCES

Abreu, J. M. (2000). Counseling expectations among Mexican American college students: The role of counselor ethnicity. *Journal of Multicultural Counseling and Development, 28,* 130–143.

Abreu, J. M., & Gabarain, G. (2000). Social desirability and Mexican American counselor preferences: Statistical control for a potential confound. *Journal of Counseling Psychology, 47,* 165–176.

Alderete, E., Vega, W. A., Kolody, B., & Aguilar-Gaxiola, S. (2000). Effects of time in the United States and Indian ethnicity on DSM-III-R psychiatric disorders among Mexican Americans in California. *Journal of Nervous and Mental Disease, 188,* 90–100.

Alwano-Edyegu, M. G., & Marum, E. (1999). *Knowledge is power: Voluntary HIV counseling and testing in Uganda.* Geneva: UNAIDS.

Andrulis, D. P. (1977). Ethnicity as a variable in the utilization and referral patterns of a comprehensive mental health center. *Journal of Community Psychology, 5,* 231–237.

Atkinson, D. R., Abreu, J. M., Ortiz-Bush, Y., & Brewer, S. (1994). Mexican American and European American ratings to four alcoholism treatment programs. *Hispanic Journal of Behavioral Sciences, 16,* 265–280.

Atkinson, D. R., Casas, A., & Abreu, J. M. (1992). Mexican-American acculturation, counselor ethnicity and cultural sensitivity, and perceived counselor competence. *Journal of Counseling Psychology, 39,* 515–520.

Atkinson, D. R., Poston, W. C., Furlong, M. J., & Mercado, P. (1989). Ethnic group preferences for counselor characteristics. *Journal of Counseling Psychology, 36,* 68–72.

Aviera, A. (1996). "Dichos" therapy group: A therapeutic use of Spanish language proverbs with hospitalized Spanish-speaking psychiatric patients. *Cultural Diversity and Mental Health, 2,* 73–87.

Barona, A., & Miller, J. A. (1994). Short acculturation scale for Hispanic youth (SASH-Y): A preliminary report. *Hispanic Journal of Behavioral Sciences, 16,* 155–162.

Berry, J. W. (1990). Psychology of acculturation: Understanding individuals moving between cultures. In R. W. Brislin (Ed.), *Applied cross-cultural psychology* (pp. 232–253). Newbury Park, CA: Sage.

Berry, J. W. (1994). Acculturation and psychological adaptation: An overview. In A. Bouvy, F. J. R. van de Vijver, P. Boski, & P. Schmitz (Eds.), *Journeys into cross-cultural psychology* (pp. 129–141). Amsterdam, Holland: Swets and Zeitlinger.

Berry, J. W. (1997). Acculturation and health. In S. Kazarian & D. Evans (Eds.), *Cultural clinical psychology* (pp. 39–57). New York: Oxford.

Berry, J. W., & Kim, U. (1988). Acculturation and mental health. In P. R. Dasen, J. W. Berry, & N. Sartorius (Eds.), *Health and cross-cultural psychology: Toward applications* (pp. 207–236). Newbury Park, CA: Sage.

Berry, J. W., Kim, U., Power, S., Young, M., & Bajaki, M. (1989). Acculturation attitudes in plural societies. *Applied Psychology: An International Review, 38,* 185–206.

Berry, J. W., Trimble, J. E., & Olmeda, E. L. (1986). Assessment of acculturation. In W. J. Lonner & J. W. Berry (Eds.), *Field methods in cross-cultural research* (pp. 291–324). Newbury Park, CA: Sage.

Bohart, A. C. (2000). The client as active self-healer: Implications for integration. *Journal of Psychotherapy Integration, 10,* 127–149.

Brown, S. A., Becker, H. A., Garcia, A. A., Barton, S. A., & Hanis, C. L. (2002). Measuring health beliefs in Spanish-speaking Mexican Americans with type 2 diabetes: Adapting an existing instrument. *Research in Nursing and Health, 25,* 145–158.

Brown, S. A., & Hedges, L. V. (1994). Predicting metabolic control in diabetes: A pilot study using meta-analysis to estimate a linear model. *Nursing Research, 43,* 362–368.

Burnam, M. A., Hough, R. L., Karno, M., Escobar, J., & Telles, C. A. (1987). Acculturation and lifetime prevalence of psychiatric disorders among Mexican Americans in Los Angeles. *Journal of Health and Social Behavior, 28,* 89–102.

Cabrera Strait, S. (2001). An examination of the influence of acculturative stress on substance use and related maladaptive behavior among Latino youth. *Dissertation Abstracts International: Section B. The Sciences and Engineering, 62*(5-B), 2532.

Carpenter, C. C., Fishl, M. A., Hammer, S. M., Jacobsen, D. M., Katzenstein, D. A., Montaner, J. S., Richman, D. D., Saag, M. S., Schooley, R. T., Thompson, M. A., Vella, S., Yeni, P. G., & Valberding, P. A. (1998). Antiretroviral therapy for HIV infection in 1998: Updated recommendations of the International AIDS Society–USA panel. *Journal of the American Medical Association, 280,* 78–86.

Case, L., & Smith, T. B. (2000). Ethnic representation in a sample of the literature of applied psychology. *Journal of Consulting and Clinical Psychology, 68,* 1107–1110.

Cheung, F. K., & Snowden, L. R. (1990). Community mental health and ethnic minority populations. *Community Mental Health Journal, 26,* 277–291.

Comas-Diaz, L., & Minrath, M. (1987). Psychotherapy with ethnic minority borderline clients. *Psychotherapy, 225,* 418–426.

Constantino, G., Malgady, R., & Rogler, L. (1986). Cuento therapy: A culturally sensitive modality for Puerto Rican children. *Journal of Consulting and Clinical Psychology, 54,* 639–645.

Cooper-Patrick, L., Crum, R. M., & Ford, D. E. (1994). Characteristics of patients with major depression who received care in general medical and specialty mental health settings. *Medical Care, 32,* 15–24.

Cooper-Patrick, L., Gallo, J. J., Powe, N. R., Steinwachs, D. S., Eaton, W. W., & Ford, D. E. (1999). Mental health service utilization by African Americans and Whites: The Baltimore Epidemiologic Catchment Area follow-up. *Medical Care, 37,* 1034–1045.

Cuellar, I. (1998). Cross-cultural clinical psychological assessment of Hispanic Americans. *Journal of Personality Assessment, 70,* 71–86.

Denning, P., Nakashima, A., Wortley, C., & Shas Project Group. (1999). *High-risk sexual behaviors among HIV infected adolescents and young adults.* Paper presented at the sixth conference on retroviruses and opportunistic infections, Chicago, IL.

Diala, C., Muntaner, C., Walrath, C., Nickerson, K. J., LaVeist, T. A., & Leaf, P. J. (2000). Racial differences in attitudes toward professional mental health care and in the use of services. *American Journal of Orthopsychiatry, 70,* 455–464.

Fernández, M. I., Perrino, T., Royal, S., Ghany, D., & Bowen, G. S. (2002). To test or not to test: Are Hispanic men at higher risk for HIV getting tested? *Aids Care, 14,* 375–384.

Finch, B. K., Hummer, R. A., Kolody, B., & Vega, W. A. (2001). The role of discrimination and acculturative stress in the physical health of Mexican-origin adults. *Hispanic Journal of Behavioral Sciences, 23,* 399–429.

Fitzgerald, J. T., Gruppen, L. D., Anderson, R. M., Funnell, M. M., Jacober, S. J., Grunberger, G., & Aman, L. C. (2000). The influence of treatment modality and ethnicity on attitudes in type 2 diabetes. *Diabetes Care, 23,* 313–318.

Flaskerud, J. H. (1986). The effects of culture-compatible intervention on the utilization of mental health services by minority clients. *Community Mental Health Journal, 22,* 127–141.

Ford, D. E., Kamerow, B. D., & Thompson, J. W. (1988). Who talks to physicians about mental health and substance abuse problems? *Journal of General and Internal Medicine, 3,* 363–369.

Gallo, J. J., Marino, S., Ford, D., & Anthony, J. C. (1995). Filters on the pathway to mental health care: II. Sociodemographic factors. *Psychological Medicine, 25,* 1149–1160.

Gil, A. G., & Vega, W. A. (1996). Two different worlds: Acculturation stress and adaptation among Cuban and Nicaraguan families. *Journal of Social and Personal Relationships, 13,* 435–456.

Given, C. W., Given, B. A., Gallin, R. S., & Condon, J. W. (1983). Development of scales to measure beliefs of diabetic patients. *Research in Nursing and Health, 6,* 127–141.

Goodman, A. B., & Siegel, C. (1978). Differences in white-nonwhite community mental health center service utilization patterns. *Journal of Evaluation and Program Planning, 1,* 51–63.

Guarnaccia, P. J., Canino, G., Rubio-Stipec, M., & Bravo, M. (1993). The prevalence of ataques de nervios in the Puerto Rico Disaster Study: The role of culture in psychiatric epidemiology. *Journal of Nervous and Mental Disease, 181,* 157–165.

Hough, R. L., Landsverk, J. A., Karno, M., Burnam, A., Timbers, D. M., Escobar, J. I., & Regier, D. A. (1987). Utilization of health and mental health services by Los Angeles Mexican Americans and non-Hispanic whites. *Archives of General Psychiatry, 44,* 702–709.

Hovey, J. D., & Magaña, C. G. (2002). Psychosocial predictors of anxiety among immigrant Mexican migrant farmworkers: Implications for prevention and treatment. *Cultural Diversity and Ethnic Minority Psychology, 8,* 274–289.

Jaco, E. G. (1960). Mental health of the Spanish American in Texas. In M. K. Opler (Ed.), *Culture and mental health: Cross-cultural studies.* New York: Macmillan.

Jenkins, J. H. (1988). Ethnopsychiatric interpretations of schizophrenic illness: The problem of nervios within Mexican-American families. *Culture, Medicine, and Psychiatry, 12,* 301–329.

Karno, M., & Edgerton, R. B. (1969). Perception of mental illness in a Mexican-American community. *Archives of General Psychiatry, 20,* 233–238.

Karno, M., & Morales, A. (1971). A community mental health service for Mexican Americans in a metropolis. *Comprehensive Psychiatry, 12,* 116–121.

Katz, S. J., Kessler, R. C., Frank, R. G., Leaf, P., Lin, E., & Edlund, M. (1997). The use of outpatient mental health services in the United States and Ontario: The impact of mental morbidity and perceived need for care. *American Journal of Public Health, 87,* 1136–1143.

Keefe, S. E., Padilla, A. M., & Carlos, M. L. (1978). Emotional support systems in two cultures: A comparison of Mexican Americans and Anglo Americans. *Spanish Speaking Mental Health Research Center Occasional Paper* (No. 7). Los Angeles: University of California Press.

Kim, B. S. K., & Abreu, J. M. (2001). Acculturation: Theory, measurement, research, and future directions. In J. G. Ponterotto, J. M. Casas, L. A. Suzuki, & C. M. Alexander (Eds.), *Handbook of multicultural counseling* (2nd ed., pp. 394–424). Thousand Oaks, CA: Sage.

La Roche, M. J. (1999). Culture, transference, and countertransference among Latinos. *Psychotherapy, 36,* 389–397.

La Roche, M. J. (2002). Psychotherapeutic considerations in treating Latinos. *Harvard Review Psychiatry, 10,* 115–122.

López, S. (1981). Mexican American usage of mental health facilities: Underutilization considered. In A. Baron, Jr. (Ed.), *Exploration in Chicano psychology.* New York: Praeger.

López, S. R., López, A. A., & Fong, K. T. (1991). Mexican Americans' initial preferences for counselors: The role of ethnic factors. *Journal of Counseling Psychology, 38,* 487–496.

Marín, G., & Gamba, R. J. (1996). A new measurement of acculturation for Hispanics: The bidimensional acculturation scale for Hispanics (BAS). *Hispanic Journal of Behavioral Sciences, 18,* 297–316.

Marín, G., & Triandis, H. C. (1985). Allocentrism as an important behavior of Latin-Americans and Hispanics. In R. Diaz-Guerrero (Ed.), *Cross-cultural and national studies in social psychology.* Amsterdam, New York: North-Holland.

Miranda, J., Azocar, F., Organista, K. C., Muñoz, R. F., & Lieberman, A. (1996). Recruiting and retaining low-income Latinos in psychotherapy research. *Journal of Consulting and Clinical Psychology, 64,* 868–874.

National Coalition of Hispanic Health and Human Services Organizations. (1998). *Delivering preventive health care to Hispanics: A manual for providers.* Washington, DC: Author.

O'Sullivan, M. J., & Lasso, B. (1992). Community mental health services for Hispanics: A test of the culture compatibility hypothesis. *Hispanic Journal of Behavioral Sciences, 14,* 455–468.

O'Sullivan, M. J., Peterson, P. D., Cox, G. B., & Kirkeby, J. (1989). Ethnic populations: Community mental health services ten years later. *American Journal of Community Psychology, 17,* 17–30.

Olfson, M., & Pincus, H. A. (1994a). Outpatient psychotherapy in the United States: I. Volume, costs, and user characteristics. *American Journal of Psychiatry, 151,* 1281–1288.

Olfson, M., & Pincus, H. A. (1994b). Outpatient psychotherapy in the United States: II. Patterns of utilization. *American Journal of Psychiatry, 151,* 1289–1294.

Olfson, M., Shea, S., Feder, A., Fuentes, M., Nomura, Y., Gameroff, M., & Weissman, M. M. (2000). Prevalence of anxiety, depression, and substance use disorders in an urban general medicine practice. *Archives of Family Medicine, 9,* 876–883.

Padilla, A. M. (1980). *Acculturation: Theory, models, and some new findings.* Boulder, CO: Westview.

Padilla, A. M., Carlos, M. L., & Keefe, S. E. (1976). Mental health services utilization by Mexican Americans. In M. Miranda (Ed.), *Psychology for the Spanish Speaking* (Monograph No. 3). Los Angeles: Spanish Speaking Mental Health Research Center.

Padilla, A. M., & Ruiz, R. A. (1973). *Latin mental health: A review of the literature* (DHEW Publication No. HSM 73-9142). Washington, DC: U.S. Government Printing Office.

Padilla, A. M., Ruiz, R. A., & Alvarez, R. (1975). Community mental health services for the Spanish-speaking/surnamed population. *American Psychologist, 30,* 892–905.

Pearlin, L. I., Menaghan, E. G., Lieberman, M. A., & Mullan, J. T. (1981). The stress process. *Journal of Health and Social Behavior, 22,* 337–356.

Quinn, T. C., Wawer, M. J., Sewankambo, N., Serwadda, D., Li, C., Wabwire-Mangen, F., Meehan, M. O., Lutalo, T., & Gray, R. H. (2000). Viral load and heterosexual transmission of HIV type I. *Journal of the American Medical Association, 342,* 921–929.

Regier, D. A., Narrow, W. E., Rae, D. S., Manderscheid, R. W., Locke, B. Z., & Goodwin, F. K. (1993). The de facto U.S. mental and addictive disorders service system: Epidemiologic catchment area prospective 1-year prevalence rates of disorders and services. *Archives of General Psychiatry, 50,* 85–94.

Robins, L. N., & Regier, D. A. (1991). *Psychiatric disorders in America: The epidemiological catchment area study.* New York: Free Press.

Rogler, L. H., Cortes, D. E., & Malgady, R. G. (1991). Acculturation and mental health status among Hispanics. *American Psychologist, 46,* 585–597.

Rogler, L. H., Malgady, R. G., Costantino, G., & Blumenthal, R. (1987). What do culturally sensitive mental health services mean? The case of Hispanics. *American Psychologist, 42,* 565–570.

Rumbaut, R. D. (1977). Life events, change, migration, and depression. In W. E. Fann, I. Karocan, A. D. Pokorny, & R. L. William (Eds.), *Phenomenology and treatment of depression* (pp. 115–126). New York: Spectrum.

Sabogal, F., & Catania, J. A. (1996). HIV risk factors, condom use, and HIV antibody testing among heterosexual Hispanics: The National AIDS Behavioral Survey. *Hispanic Journal of Behavioral Sciences, 18,* 367–391.

Salgado de Snyder, V. N., Diaz-Perez, M. J., & Ojeda, V. D. (2000). The prevalence of nervios and associated symptomatology among inhabitants of Mexican rural communities. *Culture, Medicine, and Psychiatry, 24,* 453–470.

Sánchez, A. R., Acosta, R., & Grosser, R. (1979). *Mental health services to ethnic minorities in Colorado.* Denver: Division of Mental Health, Department of Institutions, State of Colorado.

Sánchez, A. R., & Atkinson, D. R. (1983). Mexican American cultural commitment, preference for counselor ethnicity, and willingness to use counseling. *Journal of Counseling Psychology, 30,* 215–220.

Santiago-Rivera, A. L., & Altarriba, J. (2002). The role of language in therapy with the Spanish-English bilingual client. *Professional Psychology: Research and Practice, 33,* 30–38.

Scwarcz, S. K., Spitters, C., Ginsberg, M. M., Anderson, L., Kellogg, T., & Katz, M. H. (1997). Predictors of HIV counseling and testing among sexually transmitted disease clinic patients. *Sexually Transmitted Diseases, 24,* 347–352.

Simoni, J. M., & Pérez, L. (1995). Latinos and mutual support groups: A case for considering culture. *American Journal of Orthopsychiatry, 65,* 440–445.

Sledge, W. H. (1994). Psychotherapy in the United States: Challenges and opportunities. *American Journal of Psychiatry, 151,* 1267–1270.

Smart, J. F., & Smart, D. W. (1995). Acculturative stress: The experience of the Hispanic immigrant. *The Counseling Psychologist, 23,* 25–42.

Suarez-Orozco, C., & Suarez-Orozco, M. M. (1995). *Transformations: Immigration, family life, and achievement motivation among Latino adolescents.* Stanford, CA: Stanford University Press.

Sue, S. (1977). Community mental health services to minority groups: Some optimism, some pessimism. *American Psychologist, 32,* 616–624.

Sue, S. (1988). Psychotherapeutic services for ethnic minorities: Two decades of research findings. *American Psychologist, 43,* 301–308.

Sue, S. (1998). In search of cultural competence in psychotherapy and counseling. *American Psychologist, 53,* 440–448.

Sue, S., & Zane, N. W. S. (1987). The role of culture and cultural techniques in psychotherapy: A critique and reformulation. *American Psychologist, 42,* 37–45.

Surgenor, L. J., Horn, J., Hudson, S. M., Lunt, H., & Tennent, J. (2000). Metabolic control and psychological sense of control in women with diabetes mellitus. *Journal of Psychosomatic Research, 49,* 267–273.

Swanson, J. W., Linskey, A. O., Quintero-Salinas, R., & Pumariega, A. J. (1992). A binational school survey of depressive symptoms, drug use, and suicidal ideation. *Journal of the American Academy of Child and Adolescent Psychiatry, 31,* 669–678.

Swartz, M. S., Wagner, H. R., Swanson, J. W., Burns, B. J., George, L. K., & Padgett, D. K. (1998). Comparing use of public and private mental health services: The enduring barriers of race and age. *Community Mental Health Journal, 34,* 133–144.

Tinsley, H. E., Brown, M. T., de-St-Aubin, T. M., & Lucek, J. (1984). Relationship between expectancies for a helping relationship and tendency to seek help from a campus help provider. *Journal of Counseling Psychology, 31,* 149–160.

Torrey, E. F. (1972). *The mind game: Witch doctors and psychiatrists.* New York: Bantam Books.

Trevino, F. M., & Bruhn, J. G. (1977). Incidence of mental illness in a Mexican community. *Psychiatric Annals, 7,* 33–51.

Trevino, F. M., Bruhn, J. G., & Bunce, H. (1979). Utilization of community mental health services in a Texas-Mexico border city. *Social Science and Medicine, 13A,* 331–334.

VanOss Marín, B. (1994). La cultura latina y la sexualidad: Implicaciones para la prevención del VIH/SIDA [The Latin culture and sexuality: Implications for the prevention of HIV and AIDS]. *Revista de Psicología Social y Personalidad, 10,* 171–183.

Vargas-Willis, G., & Cervantes, R. C. (1987). Consideration of psychological stress in the treatment of the Latina immigrant. *Hispanic Journal of Behavioral Sciences, 9,* 315–329.

Vega, W., Kolody, B., & Aguilar-Gaxiola, S. (2001). Help seeking for mental health problems among Mexican Americans. *Journal of Immigrant Health, 3,* 133–140.

Vega, W. A., Kolody, B., Aguilar-Gaxiola, S., Alderete, E., Catalano, R., & Caraveo-Anduaga, J. B. (1998). Lifetime prevalence of DSM-III-R psychiatric disorders among urban and rural Mexican Americans in California. *Archives of General Psychiatry, 55,* 771–778.

Vega, W., Kolody, B., Aguilar-Gaxiola, S., & Catalano, R. (1999). Gaps in service utilization by Mexican Americans with mental health problems. *American Journal of Psychiatry, 156,* 928–934.

Vega, W. A., & López, S. R. (2001). Priority issues in Latino mental health services research. *Mental Health Services Research, 3,* 189–200.

Wells, K. B., Golding, J. M., Hough, R. L., Burnam, A., & Karno, M. (1988). Factors affecting the probability of use of general and medical health and social/community services for Mexican Americans and non-Hispanic whites. *Medical Care, 26,* 441–452.

Zea, M. C., Quezada, T., & Belgrave, F. Z. (1994). Latino cultural values: Their role in adjustment to disability. *Journal of Social Behavior and Personality, 9,* 185–200.

Zuñiga, M. E. (1991). "Dichos" as metaphorical tools for resistant Latino clients. *Psychotherapy: Theory, Research, Practice, and Training, 28,* 480–483.

Part VI IMPLICATIONS FOR MINORITY GROUP/CROSS-CULTURAL COUNSELING

CHAPTER 16

Current Issues
and Future Directions
in Counseling Ethnic
Minorities

As the title implies, this chapter discusses both the current status of and possible future trends in multicultural counseling. More specifically, it focuses on ethics, competencies, and models and theories pertaining to counseling ethnic minorities. It documents the advancements that mental health professionals and organizations have made in this area in recent decades, but it also points out the need for future progress.

ETHICAL CONSIDERATIONS IN COUNSELING ETHNIC MINORITIES

In the late 1960s ethnic minority psychologists and counselors began expressing concern that counseling an ethnically different client without proper training and experience was unethical. This view received a major boost in 1973 when the American Psychological Association (APA) Vail Conference Follow-Up Commission declared that

> the provision of professional services to persons of culturally diverse backgrounds by persons not competent in understanding and providing professional services to such groups shall be considered unethical; that it shall be equally unethical to deny such persons professional services because the present staff is inadequately prepared, that it shall be the obligation of all service agencies to employ competent persons or to provide continuing education for the present staff to meet the service needs of the culturally diverse population it serves. (Korman, cited in Midgette & Meggert, 1991, p. 139)

Although most training programs now incorporate multicultural experiences and content in their curriculum, professional competence remains the quintessential ethical issue for mental health practitioners working with ethnic minority clients (Lefley, 2002).

Current Ethical Codes

Nondiscrimination and the need for multicultural competence are codified in the ethical standards of the APA and the American Counseling Association (ACA).

The most recent edition of the APA's *Ethical Principles of Psychologists and Code of Conduct* (American Psychological Association, 2002a) was ratified by the Council of Representatives at the 2002 national convention and became effective June 1, 2003. Although the entire APA code has implications for multicultural counseling, the following points relate directly to multicultural counseling practice, training, and research, and they merit reprinting in this book:

- Psychologists respect and protect human and civil rights. (Preamble)
- Psychologists recognize that fairness and justice entitle all persons to access to and benefit from the contributions of psychology and to equal quality in the processes, procedures, and services being conducted by psychologists. Psychologists exercise reasonable judgment and take precautions to ensure that their potential biases, the boundaries of their competence, and the limitations of their expertise do not lead to or condone unjust practices. (Principle D: Justice)
- Psychologists are aware of and respect cultural, individual, and role differences, including those based on age, gender, gender identity, race, ethnicity, culture, national origin, religion, sexual orientation, disability, language, and socioeconomic status and consider these factors when working with members of such groups. Psychologists try to eliminate the effect on their work of biases based on those factors, and they do not knowingly participate in or condone activities of others based upon such prejudices. (Principle E: Respect for People's Rights and Dignity)
- Psychologists provide services, teach, and conduct research with populations and in areas only within the boundaries of their competence. (Standard 2.01a)
- Where scientific or professional knowledge in the discipline of psychology establishes that an understanding of factors associated with age, gender, gender identity, race, ethnicity, culture, national origin, religion, sexual orientation, disability, language, or socioeconomic status is essential for effective implementation of their services or research, psychologists have or obtain the training, experience, consultation, or supervision necessary to ensure the competence of their services, or they make appropriate referrals. (Standard 2.01b)
- Psychologists planning to provide services, teach, or conduct research involving populations, areas, techniques, or technologies new to them undertake relevant education, training, supervised experience, consultation, or study. (Standard 2.01c)
- In their work-related activities, psychologists do not engage in unfair discrimination based on age, gender, gender identity, race, ethnicity, culture, national origin, religion, sexual orientation, disability, socioeconomic status, or any basis proscribed by law. (Standard 3.01)
- Psychologists do not knowingly engage in behavior that is harassing or demeaning to persons with whom they interact in their work based on factors such as those persons' age, gender, gender identity, race, ethnicity, culture, national origin, religion, sexual orientation, disability, language, or socioeconomic status. (Standard 3.03)

- Psychologists use assessment instruments whose validity and reliability have been established for use with members of the population tested. (Standard 9.02b)
- Psychologists use assessment methods that are appropriate to an individual's language preference and competence, unless the use of an alternative language is relevant to the assessment issues. (Standard 9.02c)
- Psychologists using the services of an interpreter obtain informed consent from the client/patient to use that interpreter, ensure that confidentiality of test results and test security are maintained, and include in their recommendations, reports, and diagnostic or evaluative statements, including forensic testimony, discussion of any limitations on the data obtained. (Standard 9.03c)
- When interpreting assessment results, including automated interpretations, psychologists take into account the purpose of the assessment as well as the various test factors, test taking abilities, and other characteristics of the person being assessed, such as situational, personal, linguistic, and cultural differences, that might affect psychologists' judgments or reduce the accuracy of their interpretations. (Standard 9.06)

Similarly, the entire 1995 *Code of Ethics and Standards of Practice* of the ACA is applicable to counseling, teaching, and conducting research with ethnic minority individuals, but in the interest of space, only those sections most directly relevant are cited:

- Association members recognize diversity in our society and embrace a cross-cultural approach in support of the worth, dignity, potential, and uniqueness of each individual. (Preamble)
- Counselors do not condone or engage in discrimination based on age, color, culture, disability, ethnic group, gender, race, religion, sexual orientation, marital status, or socioeconomic status. (Section A.2.a)
- Counselors will actively attempt to understand the diverse cultural backgrounds of the clients with whom they work. This includes, but is not limited to, learning how the counselor's own cultural/ethnic/racial identity impacts her/his values and beliefs about the counseling process. (Section A.2.b)
- Counselors are aware of their own values, attitudes, beliefs, and behaviors and how these apply in a diverse society, and avoid imposing their values on clients. (A.5.b)
- Counselors will demonstrate a commitment to gain knowledge, personal awareness, sensitivity, and skills pertinent to working with a diverse client population. (C.2.a)
- [Counselors] take steps to maintain competence in the skills they use, are open to new procedures, and keep current with the diverse and/or special populations with whom they work. (C.2.f)
- Counselors do not discriminate against clients, students, or supervisees in a manner that has a negative impact based on their age, color, culture, disability, ethnic group, gender, race, religion, sexual orientation, or socioeconomic status, or for any other reason. (C.5.a)

- Counselors, as either employers or employees, do not engage in or condone practices that are inhumane, illegal, or unjustifiable (such as considerations based on age, color, culture, disability, ethnic group, gender, race, religion, sexual orientation, or socioeconomic status) in hiring, promotion, or training. (D.1.i)
- Counselors recognize that culture affects the manner in which clients' problems are defined. Clients' socioeconomic and cultural experience is considered when diagnosing mental disorders. (E.5.b)
- Counselors are cautious when selecting tests for culturally diverse populations to avoid inappropriateness of testing that may be outside of socialized behavioral or cognitive patterns. (E.6.b)
- Counselors are cautious in using assessment techniques, making evaluations, and interpreting the performance of populations not represented in the norm group on which an instrument was standardized. They recognize the effects of age, color, culture, disability, ethnic group, gender, race, religion, sexual orientation, and socioeconomic status on test administration and interpretation and place test results in proper perspective with other relevant factors. (E.8)
- Counselors design and conduct research that reflects cultural sensitivity appropriateness. (G.1.a)
- Counselors are sensitive to diversity and research issues with special populations. They seek consultation when appropriate. (G.1.f)
- Counselors respect diversity and must not discriminate against clients because of age, color, culture, disability, ethnic group, gender, race, religion, sexual orientation, marital status, or socioeconomic status. (Standard of Practice - 1)

Criticisms of the APA and ACA Ethical Codes

Although these ethical codes make it clear that psychologists and mental health practitioners are not to discriminate against clients, students, and research subjects based on their race, ethnicity, or culture and are to use culturally appropriate tests and obtain appropriate training to adequately serve diverse clients, they have been criticized for promoting values antithetical to multicultural counseling. Although this book went to press before criticisms of the 2003 version of the APA code appeared in print, some of the same criticisms of the 1992 versions still apply, for example, Payton's (1994) criticism that the 1992 version limits its aspirations and principles to psychologists' work-related activities. In several places in the 2003 version the admonitions against discriminating on the basis of diversity are qualified because the admonition is limited to work-related activities, which implies that a psychologist could eschew racism at work while embracing it outside the office.

Other concerns have also been raised with specific aspects of the APA and ACA ethical codes. Ethical codes define principles (i.e., obligations) for professionals that are arrived at by consensus of an ethics committee and the membership of the organization. It can be argued that the APA and ACA ethical codes (as well as the codes of other mental health professional organizations) reflect the values of middle-class European Americans and not those of ethnic minorities (DuBose, Hamel, & O'Connell, 1994; Ibrahim, 1996; Pedersen, 1995). As such, they typically reflect the values of the society and culture in which they are established. In particular, these codes have been criticized for placing a heavy emphasis on autonomy and individualism, whereas many ethnic minority cultures place greater emphasis on community and collectivism. For example, both the 2003 APA and 1995 ACA codes make it clear that each individual client retains sole ownership of any personal information disclosed in psychotherapy. In collectivistic cultures, however, "it would be highly inappropriate not to involve the family in all matters concerning a patient's health and welfare" (Lefley, 2002, p. 12). Paradoxically, professional ethical codes allow mental health practitioners to provide strangers (i.e., insurance representatives) with intimate information about their clients but to withhold the same information from family members most directly involved with clients' care and welfare.

Meara, Schmidt, and Day (1996) argue that concerns about the shortcomings of *principle ethics*—that is, obligatory behaviors—can best be addressed through the adoption of an approach to counseling based on *virtue ethics.* Rather than defining obligations, virtue ethics set forth a set of ideals to which professionals aspire. Although Meara et al. acknowledge that virtue ethics, like principle ethics, can vary from culture to culture, they cite the following reasons why virtue ethics may enhance the practice of counseling in a multicultural society:

> First, the stating of virtues fosters self and other-awareness by making explicit what is often implicit. Such awareness could reduce ethnocentrism and increase cross-cultural understanding. Second, explicit statement of virtues provides a frame of reference for asking whether and how other cultures are similar or different. Cultures may differ in the virtues they espouse, in the relative importance placed on different virtues, or in the ways particular virtues such as prudence, integrity, respectfulness, and benevolence are defined and expressed in the common-sense practices of everyday life. Third, once questions about other virtues or ways of being virtuous are considered, we can evaluate what virtues (if any) are appropriate for the profession in this time and place and decide if and how we might want to develop them. (p. 54)

While accepting the premise that virtue ethics may provide a more culturally sensitive approach than principle ethics do, Ibrahim (1996) takes Meara et al. (1996) to task for framing their discussion of principle and virtue ethics within the mainstream cultural values of the United States. Drawing on Pedersen's (1995) discussion of relativism, absolutism, and universalism in ethics, Ibrahim argues that what is needed is a universalist approach to ethics in professional psychology. The relativist position examines the ethics of each culture separately, the absolutist position applies the ethics of the dominant culture to all cultures, and the universalist position looks for ethical guidelines common across cultures while acknowledging those that are unique to each culture (Pedersen, 1995, pp. 35–36). According to Ibrahim, psychology needs to develop an ethical code that reflects both the shared worldview and the unique cultural values of the public it serves.

It is hoped that these criticisms of the current ethical standards will encourage revisions that will make future versions even more applicable across diverse ethnic groups. The increasingly multicultural nature of this society calls for mental health practitioners to continually reexamine the virtues to which they and the members of the communities they serve aspire (Meara et al, 1996). Ibrahim (1996) also makes an important point that the profession should strive to identify universal values. Being a mental health practitioner in a multicultural society demands sensitivity to ethical issues beyond those directly addressed by a rigid set of professional ethical standards. In particular, the heavy stress on individual autonomy found in the ethical codes of professional mental health organizations may need to be moderated when working with ethnic minority clients.

These arguments about the applicability of the ethics codes for multicultural counseling notwithstanding, the underlying ethical concern when working with ethnic minority clients remains as it was at the Vail Conference in 1973, namely the competence to practice. As is true in psychological practice in general, in multicultural counseling it is far more difficult to identify competence than it is to identify incompetence. For this reason, defining multicultural competence has become the *raison d'être* of the multicultural counseling movement. The next section discusses various attempts to define multicultural competence and concerns raised by those attempts.

ISSUES IN DEFINING AND OPERATIONALIZING MULTICULTURAL COUNSELING COMPETENCE

Pope-Davis, Reynolds, Dings, and Ottavi (1994) offered the following definition of multicultural competence:

> an appreciation of and sensitivity to the history, current needs, strengths, and resources of communities and individuals who historically have been underserved and underrepresented by psychologists . . . Specifically, these competencies entail the following: an awareness of one's own biases and cultural assumptions, content knowledge about cultures different from one's own culture, an accurate self-assessment of one's multicultural skills and comfort level, an appropriate application of cultural knowledge to the counseling process, and an awareness of the cultural assumptions underlying the counseling process. (p. 466)

More recently, Constantine and Ladany (2001) contended that multicultural counseling competence consists of six dimensions: (a) counselor self-awareness, (b) general knowledge abut multicultural issues, (c) multicultural counseling self-efficacy, (d) understanding of unique client variables, (e) en effective counseling working alliance, and (f) multicultural counseling skills. Both these definitions (and, indeed, all definitions to date) lean heavily on the work of a series of professional committees charged with identifying what is meant by multicultural counseling competence.

Multicultural Counseling: Competencies or Guidelines?

The first formal attempt to codify specific multicultural counseling competencies was undertaken by the Educational and Training Committee (chaired by Derald

Wing Sue) of APA Division 17 in the early 1980s. The E and T Committee made public in 1981 a position paper (D. W. Sue et al., 1982) that stated three purposes. First, the committee wanted to demonstrate that multicultural competencies could be specified for the purposes of training and practice. Second, they wanted to begin defining cross-cultural counseling/therapy. Third, they recommended that APA adopt the resulting competencies and incorporate them in the organization's accreditation criteria.

In their position paper, the committee identified consciousness raising (attitudes and beliefs), knowledge, and skills as three important curriculum areas for a cross-cultural counseling program. Under attitudes and beliefs they listed four competencies that a cross-cultural counselor should have. The culturally skilled counseling psychologist:

1. has moved from being culturally unaware to being aware and sensitive to his or her own cultural heritage and to valuing and respecting differences.
2. is aware of his or her own values and biases and how they may affect minority clients.
3. is comfortable with differences that exist between the counselor and client in terms of race and beliefs.
4. is sensitive to circumstances that may dictate referral of the minority client to a member of his or her own race or culture (D. W. Sue et al., 1982, p. 50).

The committee also identified four types of knowledge that a cross-cultural counselor should have. The culturally skilled counseling psychologist:

1. will have a good understanding of the sociopolitical systems operation in the United States with respect to its treatment of minorities.
2. must possess specific knowledge and information about the particular group he or she is working with.
3. must have a clear and explicit knowledge and understanding of the generic characteristics of counseling and therapy.
4. is aware of institutional barriers that prevent minorities from using mental health services (D. W. Sue et al., 1982, p. 50).

Finally, the committee identified three skills that a cross-cultural counselor should have. The culturally skilled counseling psychologist:

1. is able to generate a wide variety of verbal and nonverbal responses.
2. is able to send and receive both verbal and nonverbal messages accurately and "appropriately."
3. is able to exercise institutional skills on behalf of his or her client when appropriate. (D. W. Sue et al., 1982, pp. 50–51)

Ten years later the Professional Standards Committee (PSC, also chaired by Derald Wing Sue) of the Association for Multicultural Counseling and Development (a division of the American Association for Counseling and Development, or AACD, precursor to the American Counseling Association) updated and expanded the competencies identified by the earlier APA committee. The purpose of the PSC position paper was to (a) develop a rationale for multicultural counseling, (b) identify specific multicultural counseling competencies, and (c) challenge AACD to develop multicultural standards. The PSC position paper (D. W. Sue, Arredondo, & McDavis, 1992) identified 31 multicultural counseling strategies (hereafter referred to as the Competencies) that many counselors and psychologists consider the most valid, comprehensive set of competencies to date. The Competencies are printed in their entirety in the appendix following this chapter in recognition of the important role that they have played in defining multicultural counseling competence.

Several attempts were subsequently made to refine and expand on the Competencies identified by D. W. Sue et al. (1992). In 1996, Arredondo et al. published an article in which they identified a number of "explanatory statements" for each of the 31 Competencies; the purpose of the explanatory statements was to operationalize the 1992 Competencies by providing concrete examples of how counselors could implement them. In 1998, D. W. Sue and other members of a joint task force (APA Divisions 17 and 45) published *Multicultural Counseling Competencies: Individual and Organizational Development,* which added 3 more competencies to the 31 identified by D. W. Sue et al. (1992). Although numerous other efforts have been made by individual scholars to develop multicultural competencies, as of the fall of 2002 neither APA or ACA committees were engaged in any formal efforts to further expand or refine the efforts of earlier professional committees (D. W. Sue, personal communication, September 5, 2002).

One of the concerns about identifying a list of multicultural counseling competencies is that the term *competence* implies a minimal, measurable standard of practice (Constantine & Ladany, 2001). Ideally, standards of practice are linked to outcome data demonstrating the efficacy of each standard. Although most of what mental health practitioners do in their professional practice has yet to be supported unequivocally by research, some leaders within the multicultural counseling movement began advocating for the development of multicultural counseling guidelines, the rationale presumably being that the larger professional membership might more readily accept guidelines than competencies. In the late 1990s, a joint committee of APA Divisions 17 and 45 began working on a set of multicultural guidelines. At the first National Multicultural Conference and Summit (NMCS) held in January 1999 in Newport Beach, California, participants unanimously adopted a resolution calling on the APA to adopt and implement multicultural competency guidelines that could be used in the training of psychologists (D. W. Sue, Bingham, Porche-Burke, & Vasquez, 1999). This goal was accomplished during the 2002 APA national convention when the APA Council of Representatives endorsed the Guidelines on Multicultural Education, Training, Research, Practice, and Organizational Change for Psychologists (American Psychological Association, 2002b).

In summary, the D. W. Sue et al. (1982) and D. W. Sue et al. (1992) multicultural counseling competencies and the APA guidelines (American Psychological Association, 2002b) have received important endorsements from professional organizations. The D. W. Sue et al. (1992) Competencies have been endorsed by three divisions (17, 35, 45) of the APA and five divisions (ACES, AADA, AGLBIC, ASCA, ASGW, IAMFC) of the ACA (D. W. Sue, personal communication, August 26, 1997). Moreover, the Competencies are now reflected in the

APA and ACA codes of ethics and accreditation manuals. The guidelines were recently (August 2002) approved by the APA Council of Representatives. Very clearly, the Competencies and guidelines have had a major impact on professional psychology and counseling. Concerns have been raised, however, that the Competencies, in particular, lack empirical validation.

Challenges to Multicultural Counseling Competence

Atkinson and Israel (in press) reviewed the history of the multicultural counseling competence movement and cited evidence that it has become a mainstream, significant force in professional counseling and psychology. In particular, they pointed to the impact the movement has had on professional codes of ethics, accreditation criteria, training program curricula, and scholarly publications as evidence that the fields of counseling and psychology have endorsed multicultural counseling competence. At the same time, these authors suggest that without a strong research base, the multicultural counseling competence movement could face a struggle in the future to maintain its position of influence.

Of particular concern is the fact that the Competencies have never been empirically validated (Constantine & Ladany, 2001). Atkinson and Israel (in press) blamed this lack of empirical validation, paradoxically, on the highly positive reception given the D. W. Sue et al. (1982) and D. W. Sue et al. (1992) multicultural counseling competencies and the instruments developed to measure them; in essence they were accepted by the counseling profession without question. "Ironically, the fact that these two publications (Sue et al. 1982; Sue et al., 1992) were so widely endorsed and embraced may have contributed to our current lack of empirical support for MCCs because researchers were not motivated to either look further for additional competencies or validate those identified in Sue et al. (1982) or Sue et al. (1992)" (Atkinson & Israel, in press). The influence of these two publications has been so pervasive that it is almost impossible for researchers to conduct research on multicultural counseling competence without being biased by the Competencies (Pope-Davis, Liu, Toporek, & Brittan-Powell, 2001). In addition to calling for research to determine the validity of the Competencies, which were developed by committee consensus, Atkinson and Israel urged researchers to empirically identify new multicultural counseling competencies and to develop new instruments to assess multicultural counseling competence.

Other concerns have been raised regarding the Competencies. Their status as a set of unique competencies, distinct from general counseling competencies, has been called into question. Coleman (1998) examined differences between the two types of competence and concluded that "general and multicultural counseling competence are so highly correlated that they may be a single construct" (p. 154). Also, the Competencies have been challenged for being too narrowly conceived. Pope-Davis et al. (2001) pointed out that the Competencies were developed by professionals and that client views concerning counselor multicultural competence have yet to be taken into account. Perhaps the most caustic challenge to the Competencies came from Weinrach and Thomas (2002). Responding specifically to the Arredondo et al. (1996) version, Weinrach and Thomas charged that the

Competencies were obsolete, unreliable, and invalid, and they argued strongly against adoption by the ACA umbrella organization.

The fact that multicultural counseling competencies have not been empirically identified or validated has not deterred researchers from looking at associations between measures of multicultural counseling competence and other variables. Using various instruments developed to measure multicultural counseling competence, researchers have examined the relationships between self- and other-reported competencies and counselor demographic variables (Ottavi, Pope-Davis, & Dings, 1994; Pope-Davis & Ottavi, 1994; Pope-Davis, Reynolds, Dings, & Nielson, 1995), racial identity development (Ladany, Inman, Constantine, & Hofheinz, 1997; Ottavi et al., 1994), and training experiences (D'Andrea, Daniels, & Heck, 1991; Neville et al., 1996; Ottavi et al., 1994; Pope-Davis et al., 1995; Pope-Davis et al., 1994; Sodowsky, Kuo-Jackson, Richardson, & Corey, 1998). Most of these studies have resulted in equivocal or unremarkable findings. However, it is somewhat disconcerting that despite the lack of empirical validation, the Competencies (or instruments based on them) have served as dependent variables in studies that could affect the selection and training of counselors and psychologists.

Problems with Assessing Multicultural Competence

In addition to Arredondo et al.'s (1996) attempt to operationalize multicultural competence, efforts by researchers to develop measures of multicultural competence have, in effect, operationalized multicultural competence. By the mid-1990s, four instruments purporting to assess multicultural competence had appeared in the professional literature: the Cross-Cultural Counseling Inventory–Revised (CCCI–R; LaFromboise, Coleman, & Hernandez, 1991), the Multicultural Counseling Awareness Scale–Form B (MCAS; Ponterotto, Sanchez, & Magids, 1991), the Multicultural Counseling Inventory (MCI; Sodowsky, Taffe, Gutkin, & Wise, 1994), and the Multicultural Awareness-Knowledge-and-Skills Survey (MAKSS; D'Andrea et al., 1991). All four of these instruments reflect the three multicultural competency domains (awareness, knowledge, and skills) identified by D. W. Sue et al. (1982). Three of the four instruments (MCAS, MCI, MAKSS) require each respondent to judge his or her own multicultural attitudes, knowledge, and skills; one (CCCI–R) requires an observer to rate the subject's multicultural competency.

However, the validity of all four instruments has been questioned in several studies and reviews of research. Based on their review of all four instruments, Ponterotto, Rieger, Barrett, and Sparks (1994) recommended that "none of them be incorporated in counseling training for any purpose other than research and continuing validation" (p. 321). Furthermore, Ponterotto et al. concluded that none of the factor analyses of data on these four instruments provided support for the three dimensions of multicultural competence identified by D. W. Sue et al. (1982), dimensions that have become the cornerstones of multicultural practice, training, and research. Pope-Davis and Dings (1995) reviewed the same four instruments and determined that "it is unclear not only what each instrument measures but also to what extent two measures can be considered in any way inter-changeable" (p. 309). After examining the internal structure and interinstrument and subscale correlations of the MCAS, MAKSS, and Survey of Graduate Students' Experiences with Diversity (Talbot, 1992), Kocarek, Talbot, Batka, and Anderson (2001) reached a similar conclusion: "although many subscales (across the instruments) have similar names, they seem to be measuring different aspects of the constructs or slightly different constructs altogether" (p. 494). Furthermore, Pope-Davis and Dings questioned whether self-report is an appropriate method for measuring multicultural counseling competence, given that mental health practitioners and other respondents may report anticipated rather than actual behaviors and attitudes, select socially desirable responses, and interpret items differently than the authors intended.

Recent research has provided empirical evidence that self-report instruments may be measuring social desirability and self-efficacy for multicultural competence and not multicultural competence per se. Several studies examining the validity of these measures reported that when social desirability is accounted for, there is no relationship between multicultural counseling competence scores and multicultural case conceptualization ability (Constantine & Ladany, 2001; Ladany et al., 1997). Worthington, Mobley, Franks, and Tan (2000) examined the relationship among a self-report instrument (MCI), an other-report instrument (CCCI–R), and a social desirability scale. They found little evidence of a relationship between the MCI and CCCI–R scores but a strong relationship between MCI scores and social desirability scores. Worthington et al. concluded that self-report instruments measure self-efficacy for multicultural counseling competence, not multicultural counseling competence.

The concerns raised about the use of self-report instruments to measure multicultural counseling competence suggest that more appropriate methodology is needed to assess awareness, knowledge, and skills in this area. In their review of instruments designed to assess multicultural counseling competence, Pope-Davis and Dings (1995) suggested that awareness items are too transparent in the existing instruments and that awareness could be measured less transparently by criterion-keyed responses to various statements. They also pointed out that direct assessment methods, such as multiple-choice or essay achievement tests, would be more appropriate than self-report instruments to measure multicultural knowledge. With respect to multicultural counseling skill, these authors suggested that performance assessment by clients or supervisors or both would be more appropriate than self-reports.

Several other authors have suggested alternatives to the self-report methodology for assessing multicultural counseling competence. Coleman (1996) proposed that a multicultural portfolio, roughly analogous to the artist's portfolio, could be used for this purpose. He suggested that mental health practitioners could include self-selected evidence of their multicultural awareness, knowledge, and skills in their portfolio. Portfolio submissions might include written work, audiotapes, and videotapes and that the portfolio itself might be an expandable file folder, a CD-ROM, or some other means of storing data. The portfolio concept holds promise, despite the heavy time and proficiency demands it places on supervisors when they evaluate each practitioner's unique materials.

A more efficient method of measuring one multicultural competence domain was developed by Ruelas (2000). She operationalized multicultural counseling skill as the ability to match counselor role with the client's level of acculturation, problem etiology, and goal of counseling. Ruelas provided mental health practitioners with vignettes in which these client characteristics were specified along with a list of eight different counselor roles, and she asked respondents to identify the appropriate counselor role. Appropriate counselor roles for each vignette were those specified in the three-dimensional model of multicultural counseling (Atkinson, Thompson, & Grant, 1993; to be discussed later in this chapter). Thus, Ruelas was able to use a multiple-choice methodology to assess multicultural competence.

Future of the Multicultural Counseling Competence Movement

Very clearly, the multicultural counseling competence movement has had a major impact on psychology and counseling. Furthermore, it is self-evident that mental health practitioners need special awareness, knowledge, and skills when working with ethnic minority and other diverse clients. It would be an error to conclude that just because the validity of self-report instruments designed to measure multicultural counseling competence has been questioned, the Competencies themselves are invalid. Nonetheless, Atkinson and Israel (in press) have predicted that the movement will wane in the future unless existing competencies are validated, new competencies are developed, and new, more objective instruments are created that operationalize validated competencies. They suggested that researchers need to go back to the drawing boards and do the nitty-gritty work needed to identify and validate multicultural counseling competence. They also urged academics to generate a larger pool of young researchers interested in examining the role of ethnicity and culture in counseling competence.

THEORIES AND MODELS THAT GUIDE MULTICULTURAL COUNSELING PRACTICE

With the growing interest in multicultural counseling has come professional pressure for the development of multicultural counseling theory. The demand for theory to guide practitioner, educator, and research behavior is perfectly understandable; mental health practitioners and psychologists have been schooled in the importance of theory in understanding human behavior. However, very little of what has been written about multicultural counseling (or counseling in general for that matter) to date qualifies as theory in the formal sense. According to Patterson (1966), a formal theory includes a set of stated assumptions that are internally consistent and related to one another in clearly stated ways. Also, the concepts of the theory are clearly defined and the definitions relate the concepts to observable data, thereby making possible the empirical verification of the theory. In short, the theory should lead to testable hypotheses that, if supported, validate the theory.

Although some authors have embraced the term *multicultural theory*, others have been reluctant to suggest that the assumptions, relationships, concepts, and hypotheses they are putting forth constitute a formal theory. For this reason, some of the theories described in this section were originally identified as models of or approaches to multicultural counseling theory. Nonetheless, two review chapters, one in the *Handbook of Counseling Psychology* (Ponterotto, Fuertes, & Chen, 2000) and one in the *Handbook of Multicultural Counseling* (Fuertes & Gretchen, 2001) have identified a total of 16 theories or emerging theories of multicultural counseling. In the interest of space, only four of the most promising theories are presented here. Readers are encouraged to consult Ponterotto, Fuertes, and Chen (2000), Fuertes and Gretchen (2001), and the original publications cited by these authors for more detailed discussion of multicultural counseling theory.

Helms's Interactional Model

The Helms's Black/White Interaction model (Helms 1990, 1995) was one of the first models of cross-cultural counseling to appear in the professional counseling literature. This model grew out of Helms's work with Black racial identity development (see chapters 2 and 4) and White racial identity development (Helms, 1984, 1990). Helms (1990) postulates that White racial identity formation is a two-phase developmental process in which "Phase 1, the abandonment of racism, begins with the Contact stage and ends with the Reintegration stage. Phase 2, defining a positive White identity, begins with the Pseudo-Independent stage and ends with the Autonomy stage" (p. 55). In the contact stage the individual is oblivious to his or her own racial identity. This stage is followed by the disintegration stage, in which the individual first acknowledges his or her White identity. The individual then moves to the reintegration stage, in which he or she idealizes Whites and denigrates Blacks. In the subsequent Pseudo-Independent stage, the individual begins to question the attitude that Blacks are innately inferior to Whites. As the individual searches for a more positive attitude toward Blacks, he or she enters the Immersion/Emersion stage and begins an honest appraisal of racism and what it means to be White. In the final stage, Autonomy, the individual assumes a multicultural identity and a nonracist attitude (Helms, 1990, pp. 51–52).

Although a full discussion of Helm's Black/White Interaction model is beyond the scope of this text, a key concept is that the relationship between the counselor and the client stage of racial identity development (rather than racial similarities or differences per se) is predictive of counseling outcome. According to Helms (1995), the basic premises of the racial identity interaction model are

> (a) racial identity statuses structure people's reactions to one another as well as to external events, (b) people form harmonious or disharmonious alliances with one another based on the tenor of their expressed racial identity, (c) racial reactions occur within the context of direct or vicarious interpersonal activities, and (d) patterns of reactions within an interpersonal context can be classified according to quality. (p. 191)

Four types of relationships are possible for same-race and cross-race dyads: parallel, crossed, progressive, and regressive. In a *parallel* relationship, the counselor and client share similar racial attitudes about Blacks and Whites. In a *crossed* relationship, the counselor and client hold opposing racial attitudes about Blacks and Whites. "A *progressive* relationship is one in which the counselor's stage of racial consciousness is at least one stage more advanced than the client's; a *regressive* relationship is one in which the client's stage of development is at least one stage more advanced than the counselor's" (Helms, 1990, p. 141, italics added). Examples of each type of relationship are presented in Table 16.1; however, be aware that numerous other combinations within each type are possible.

Although a few studies have been conducted on Helms's Black/White Interaction model, more research is needed to determine its validity and whether it can be generalized to racial/ethnic groups other than Blacks and Whites. Assuming that the model is supported by future research, it will have important implications for the practice of counseling and the training of counselors (to be discussed in the next section). With respect to counseling practice, it is clear that for both ethnically similar and ethnically dissimilar counseling dyads, progressive relationships are likely to be most productive and regressive relationships likely to be least productive (and perhaps even harmful). Mental health practitioners should assess their own and their client's racial identity development and refer the client to a more appropriate practitioner in the case of a regressive counseling relationship. Practitioners, Black or White, at higher levels of racial identity development will be able to establish productive relationships with more clients than will those at the preencounter (Black practitioner) or contact (White practitioner) stages of development.

Three-Dimensional Model for Counseling Racial/Ethnic Minority Clients

A second model for multicultural counseling involves a reassessment of the roles of the mental health practitioner. In chapter 3 it was noted that a great deal of criticism has been directed at the conventional counseling role of psychotherapy. Time-bound, space-bound, cathartic psychotherapy may be irrelevant to the life experiences and needs of many ethnic minorities, especially recent immigrants. Rather than demanding that the client adapt to the mental health practitioner's culture, critics argue that the practitioner should adjust to and work within the client's culture. In particular, they have suggested that practitioners need to engage in viable alternatives to the conventional counseling and psychotherapy roles (Atkinson et al., 1993).

The following alternatives to the traditional counseling and psychotherapy roles are discussed in the sections that follow: (a) advocate, (b) change agent, (c) consultant, (d) adviser, (e) facilitator of indigenous support systems, and (f) facilitator of indigenous healing methods. There is considerable overlapping of these six role functions, but each includes some aspects that make it different from the other roles and from the conventional counseling and psychotherapy roles. A brief description of each role is offered here, followed by a brief discussion of how conventional counseling and conventional psychotherapy can be applied more effectively with ethnically diverse clients than they have been in the past. Finally, a three-dimensional model is introduced that mental health practitioners can use to

TABLE 16.1 Examples of the Four Types of Counseling Relationships Based on Racial Identity Stages

STAGES OF IDENTITY			COUNSELING PROCESS		
Counselor's	Client's	Type of Relationship	Common Affective Issues	Counselor/Strategies	Counseling Outcome
			Black Dyads		
1. Preencounter	Preencounter	Parallel	Anger about being assigned to a Black person. Guilt about negative feelings.	Both will use strategies designed to deny and avoid issues to reinterpret whatever happens in a manner consistent with perceived negative stereotypes.	Client terminates with little symptom remission. Counselor "pushes" client out of counseling.
2. Immersion	Preencounter	Crossed (Progressive)	Counselor may feel angry and rejecting; client feels fearful and intimidated.	General non-acceptance of one another; counselor may be low in empathy, use much advice giving; client is passive and tries not to become involved in the process.	If counselor can act as positive role model, client may develop positive feelings about Blackness; self-esteem is enhanced.
3. Preencounter	Immersion	Regressive (Crossed)	Counselor shares White society's fear, weariness and anxiety; client displaces anger.	Client attempts to reform counselor; counselor attempts to avoid issues.	Short relationships; client's anger may be enhanced, counselor's anxiety may be increased.
4. Encounter	Preencounter	Progressive	Counselor feels excited and apprehensive about working with Black client; client feels angry and apprehensive and distrusting.	Social discussion in which counselor tries to prove he/she is Black; client tries to prove he/she isn't.	Long relationships if counselor uses enthusiasm to engage client; limited symptom remission if counselor avoids doing therapy.

TABLE 16.1 Examples of the Four Types of Counseling Relationships Based on Racial Identity Stages—*Continued*

STAGES OF IDENTITY			COUNSELING PROCESS		
Counselor's	Client's	Type of Relationship	Common Affective Issues	Counselor/Strategies	Counseling Outcome
			White Dyads		
1. Contact	Contact	Parallel	Counselor and client exhibit curiosity and naivete about racial issues.	Information sharing, avoidance of negative affect related to racial matters.	Discussion of racial issues is aborted because neither knows how to resolve them.
2. Contact	Reintegration	Crossed (Regression)	Mutual dislike because they don't empathize with one another's racial attitudes.	Argumentative attempts to reeducate each other.	Premature termination; client's symptoms may be aggravated because he/she doesn't respect counselor.
3. Autonomous	Disintegration	Progressive	Counselor may be empathic and accepting; client needs to deal with self-concept issues and confused feelings.	Counselor attempts to encourage self-awareness and understanding of racial dynamics.	Potential for client insight and knowledge acquisition is good.
4. Disintegration	Autonomous	Regressive	Friction: low levels of empathy and understanding.	Counselor attempts to protect and nurture client inappropriately.	Premature termination; client perceives counselor as inexpert.

TABLE 16.1 Examples of the Four Types of Counseling Relationships Based on Racial Identity Stages—*Continued*

| | STAGES OF IDENTITY | | | COUNSELING PROCESS | |
	Counselor's	Client's	Type of Relationship	Common Affective Issues	Counselor/Strategies	Counseling Outcome
				Mixed Dyads		
1. Preencounter		Reintegration	Parallel	Mutual anxiety: counselor wants to prove competence; client displaces anger previously denied.	Abusive relationship; client tests and manipulates; counselor is unassertive and task oriented.	Relationship may be long-lasting because it reinforces stereotypes; little symptom remission.
2. Immersion		Reintegration	Crossed	Direct overt expression of hostility and anger by both.	Debates; refusal to become involved with one another.	Short-lived; leaves both feeling frustrated about original beliefs.
3. Internalization		Disintegration	Progressive	Client's self-concept issues, feelings of confusion, and helplessness are the focus.	Counselor attempts to model positive adjustment and to elicit denied feelings.	Potential for client cross-racial skill development and improved self-confidence is good.
4. Disintegration		Internalization	Regressive	Counselor experiences pain and/or anxiety about cross-racial issues.	Counselor interacts with undue reserve, uneasiness, and incongruence; client senses counselor's discomfort.	Premature termination client will seek counselor more in tune with her/his needs.

Note: From *Black and White Racial Identity: Theory, Research, and Practice* (pp. 142–143) by J. E. Helms, 1990, New York: Greenwood Press. Copyright 1990 by J. E. Helms. Reprinted with permission.

help determine which of the eight roles (six alternative roles plus conventional counseling and psychotherapy) is most appropriate in a particular situation involving a racial/ethnic minority client.

Advocate   All ethnic minority individuals by definition are oppressed to some degree by the dominant society. Some ethnic minority individuals and groups have developed skills that help them deal with discrimination. Others, particularly recent immigrants, may lack the English-speaking skills and economic power to confront or deflect oppressive environments. In these situations the client or clients may need an advocate rather than a psychotherapist.

In this role the mental health practitioner represents a client or group of clients who have brought a particular form of discrimination to the practitioner's attention. Being an empathic practitioner who suggests alternative ways of coping with discrimination may not be enough. Instead, the practitioner also may need to actively pursue alternative courses of action with or for the client, including serving as a spokesperson for the client overwhelmed by bureaucracy. As an advocate, the mental health practitioner speaks on behalf of the client, often confronting the institutional sources of oppression that are contributing to the client's problems. Not infrequently the injustice involves the institution employing the practitioner (such as when an ethnic minority client is assigned to group rather than individual therapy as a cost savings, whereas European American clients typically receive individual therapy). If the client's goals are in conflict with those of the institution, the practitioner must decide to represent the client and not the institution or the system, presumably within ethical restrictions imposed by the profession. The practitioner need not represent a particular client or group of clients; rather, the entire minority culture experiencing an injustice may function as the client (such as when ethnic minority students are placed in academic tracks according to ethnic stereotypes). Because an ethnic minority client is involved, the practitioner has the added responsibility of making certain that the client can benefit fully from the social and economic resources of the majority culture without losing what is unique and valued in his or her own culture.

The advocate role is extremely important for counselors in ethnically diverse schools (Esquivel & Keitel, 1990), particularly those with recent immigrants. The National Coalition of Advocates for Students (1988) has developed a number of recommendations for advocacy on behalf of immigrant students. School counselors (and other school personnel) are urged to advocate that their school: (a) ensure that all school personnel understand that immigrant children have a legal right to free, appropriate public education; (b) restructure those policies and practices that sort immigrant students into programs that prepare them for inferior futures; (c) ensure that immigrant students (and all students) experience a school environment free of victimization, harassment, and intergroup conflict; and (d) ensure a more equitable allocation of resources to those (typically inner-city) schools that serve immigrant students.

Change Agent   According to Egan (1985), "change agent refers to anyone who plays an important part in designing, redesigning, running, renewing, or improving any system, subsystem, or program" (p. 12). As a change agent, the mental health practitioner attempts to change the social environment that oppresses racial/ethnic minorities and helps the client identify both the external sources of his or her problem and methods of resolving the problem. Rather than encouraging the client to "own the problem," the practitioner helps the client become aware of the oppressive forces creating the problem. Together the practitioner and client develop a strategy for eliminating or reducing the effects of the oppression on the client's life, often by facilitating the formation of racial/ethnic minority political groups. Through political power, racial/ethnic minorities and other disenfranchised groups are able to bring about change in their social and physical environment. The mental health practitioner serving as a change agent frequently assumes a low-visibility profile, often finding it useful to mobilize other influential persons in the offending institution to bring about change (Waltz & Benjamin, 1977).

Lewis and Lewis (1977) identified four ways the mental health practitioner can serve as a change agent: (a) by assessing community needs, (b) by coordinating activities and resources, (c) by providing training in skill building, and (d) by advocating change. Ponterotto (1987) has described a multimodal approach to counseling Mexican Americans that includes a change agent component and that appears equally applicable to other ethnic groups. The change agent component involves identifying the social, environmental, and institutional factors that are oppressing the client but that are external to his or her control. The mental health practitioner helps the client organize a plan for confronting the situation and identify agencies that could facilitate elimination of the problem.

As a change agent, the mental health practitioner also can work directly with majority clients in an attempt to move them toward the goal of reducing racist attitudes. Katz and Ivey (1977) described a racism-awareness training program that involves a reeducation process designed "to raise [the] consciousness of White people, help them identify racism in their life experience from which their racist attitudes and behaviors have developed, and move them to take action against institutional and individual racism" (p. 487). The six phases of the program are designed to help participants to:

1. Increase their understanding of racism in society and themselves.
2. Confront discrepancies existing between the myths and reality of American ideology and behavior.
3. Sort through some of their feelings and reactions that were triggered by phases 1 and 2.
4. Confront the racism in the White culture that their own actions support.
5. Understand and accept their Whiteness.
6. Develop specific action strategies to combat personal and institutional racism. (p. 487)

Katz and Ivey's suggestion that racism is a White problem and that White mental health practitioners should assume a major role in dealing with it makes sense. European American practitioners are, in some respects, in the best position to confront the majority population with their own stereotypic attitudes and behaviors.

The first National Multicultural Conference and Summit reaffirmed the need for psychologists to function as change agents when working with culturally diverse clients. According to D. W. Sue et al. (1999),

> The NMCS reasserted the importance of having psychologists (a) develop an awareness of how policies and practices of our profession and society, although well-intentioned, may harm culturally different groups in our society; (b) realize the role psychology and psychologists may play in perpetuating injustice; and (c) suggest ways that our profession and psychologists must respond to alleviate injustice and oppression arising from a monocultural psychology. (p. 1067)

Consultant   According to Hansen, Himes, and Meier (1990), consultation involves a collegial relationship between the consultant and the consultee (or client), who work together to affect the behavior of a third party. A distinction between the change agent role and the consultant role is that a primary goal of the former is to alleviate existing problems whereas a primary goal of the latter is to prevent the problems from developing.

In the consultant role, mental health practitioners can help ethnic minority clients learn skills needed to interact successfully with the dominant society. For example, some minority clients lack assertiveness skills. According to Wood and Mallinckrodt (1990),

> members of many ethnic minority groups have values about assertive responding that differ markedly from those of the dominant culture. The resulting inability to perform skills valued by the dominant culture may place ethnic minority persons at a significant disadvantage for coping in the majority society. (p. 5)

LaFromboise and Rowe (1983) proposed social skills training as a strategy for helping American Indians learn to relate to non-Indians. They suggested that a skills training approach is particularly applicable to American Indian clients because: (a) "it is less culturally biased than alternative approaches stemming from the academic tradition" (p. 591); (b) it can be used to prevent as well as remediate problems; (c) it involves the use of modeling in small group settings, a procedure compatible with American Indian methods of transmitting knowledge; (d) it has been found to be more effective than alternative treatments; and (e) it is applicable to the kinds of problems American Indians are currently experiencing.

Adviser   Some ethnic minority individuals, particularly recent immigrants, simply are not aware of the kind of discrimination they may face or the kinds of problems they may encounter as a result of overt or covert racism. In this case the mental health practitioner may be of most assistance by advising these individuals about the problems they or their families may encounter; the goal is to prevent problems. The consultant role differs from the adviser role in that in the consultant role the client (often high in acculturation) initiates contact with the practitioner to seek help in preventing a problem, whereas in the adviser role the practitioner initiates contact with the client (often low in acculturation) to advise him or her of unanticipated problems.

The role of adviser has been eschewed historically by the counseling profession. For the past four decades the counseling literature has criticized advice giving while promoting such alternative counselor behaviors as listening, facilitating, and supporting. In reality, however, advice may be exactly what recent immigrants need to prevent problems before they develop. An example of advice giving is for a practitioner to advise recent immigrants of the discrimination they will face on the job market and that their children may face in school. Further, the mental health practitioner should advise recent immigrants as to what they and their children might do to reduce the impact of such discrimination.

Facilitator of Indigenous Support Systems   It is probably accurate to state that every culture in the world has developed some form of social support to help prevent and remediate psychological and relationship problems. According to Lefley (2002), families are the major support systems for individuals around the world. Counseling as a social support system evolved in the United States as this country's economic base shifted from agriculture to industry to technology and as people became more mobile and removed from their family support systems (Tyler, 1961). Like counseling, social support systems often provide a medium for advice giving, consultation, modeling, catharsis, reinforcement, and advocacy. Thus, social support systems serve many of the same functions as professional counseling but are more socially acceptable within many cultures.

When people began immigrating to the United States in large numbers from any country, as they did from Vietnam in 1975 and as they do from Central America currently, their indigenous social support systems are often in disarray and nonfunctional. However, these preexisting social support systems frequently can be adapted to fit the new situation, or new support systems can emerge in the context of the new cultural milieu. Examples of indigenous social support systems that play an important role in many ethnic minority communities are extended ethnic community centers, family networks, neighborhood social networks, ethnic churches, and ethnic advocacy groups.

Mental health practitioners can facilitate the development of indigenous support systems by publicly acknowledging the important role they play, by supporting government and private funds to build ethnic community centers, and by encouraging ethnic organizations (e.g., ethnic churches, ethnic service organizations) to provide such services. Practitioners can also facilitate the use of indigenous support systems by referring clients to them.

Facilitator of Indigenous Healing Methods   In their review of intervention and treatment research with ethnic minorities, Kurasaki, Sue, Chun, and Gee (2000) concluded that "culture-specific treatment should be available to ethnic clients, especially those who are unacculturated or who hold very traditional ethnic values that are discrepant from Western values" (p. 246). Just as all cultures have developed support systems to help prevent psychological and relationship problems, all cultures have developed methods of intervening with these problems once they develop. Although the psychological healing methods of various cultures may have common elements (Torrey, 1972; Tseng & McDermott, 1975), each has evolved within a cultural context and is effective because members of that culture believe in its efficacy. According to Wohl (2000), "If the explanatory models [beliefs about problem etiology and treatment] of the clinician and the patient are far apart and the distance between them is not negotiated, treatment will flounder" (p. 81). Individuals who believe in a healing regimen are likely to follow it and invest themselves in making it successful.

Conventional counseling may be ineffective for someone who believes that his or her psychological problems are the result of an "evil eye" or an inappropriate diet. For this reason, Cayleff (1986) suggests that

> When counseling ethnic and racial minorities, certain belief systems of the client must be considered if quality care is to be given. This entails understanding and honoring folk belief systems such as (a) the humoral hot-cold theory of physical and mental disease . . . , (b) *curanderismo* . . . and belief in folk disease . . . , and (c) religious healing rituals and practices. (p. 345)

Understanding and honoring folk belief systems does not mean that the mental health practitioner must begin incorporating these healing methods in his or her own practice. It does mean that the practitioner must accept that healing methods from the client's culture are more likely to be effective with the client than are conventional psychotherapeutic strategies from the dominant culture (Berthold, 1989). According to Cayleff (1986), practitioners violate the ethical principle of beneficence (doing good) if they fail to honor the client's belief system.

Frequently, mental health practitioners are unaware of or are disdainful of these procedures and prefer to engage the client in the very counseling process so heavily criticized by minority representatives. Practitioners may best serve their minority clientele by attempting to facilitate rather than discourage the use of indigenous support systems. For those still concerned that indigenous healers may harm their clients, Lefley (2002) points out that (a) alternative healers can and do make appropriate referrals to the biomedical system, (b) clients using alternative healers often do so concurrently with their use of mental health professionals, and (c) the combination of folk healers and mental health workers often results in enhanced treatment compliance.

The mental health practitioner can facilitate indigenous healing methods by (a) referring the client to an indigenous healer and (b) incorporating the healing methods of the indigenous culture in his or her counseling practice. Referring the client to an indigenous healer requires that the practitioner be familiar with healers from various cultures and their credibility within the racial/ethnic community. Incorporating the healing methods of various cultures into a counseling practice is more problematic. First, individual practitioners are unlikely to become skilled in the healing methods of numerous cultures, especially without proper training and indoctrination by indigenous healers. Second, and most important, healing methods from various cultures can involve beliefs about the causes of and solutions to mental health problems that conflict with those of the practitioner. It is doubtful that mental health practitioners can appropriately implement healing methods that conflict with their own personal beliefs. Furthermore, clients are likely to become aware of the conflicting values and raise questions about the practitioners' integrity.

Conventional Counselor   Counseling has been defined as:

> a process in which clients learn how to make decisions and formulate new ways of behaving, feeling and thinking. Counselors focus on the goals their clients wish to achieve. Clients explore their present level of functioning and the changes that must be made to achieve personal objectives. Thus counseling involves both choice and change, evolving through distinct stages such as exploration, goal setting, and action. (Gladding, 1996, p. 8)

This definition of counseling suggests that mental health practitioners help clients establish goals and change the way they feel, think, and behave. In the process, practitioners help clients remediate existing problems, prevent problems, and make decisions. The remediation of existing problems is a healing function that will be discussed in the next section, titled "Conventional Psychotherapist." This section focuses on the practitioner's role of helping clients make decisions and prevent problems.

Helping clients make decisions is a universal process that applies across the various cultures within the United States. Mental health practitioners engage the client in listing alternatives, considering the possible consequences of each alternative, weighing the probability of each alternative, and choosing an alternative. In helping racial/ethnic minority clients make decisions, however, the mental health practitioner must be sensitive to cultural values and to oppressive forces that may impinge on decision making. It is also essential for the practitioner to be aware of his or her own cultural biases that may be influencing the client's decision making and to acknowledge these biases to the client.

Because both nuclear and extended families are so important to many ethnic minorities, preventive family counseling may be particularly relevant for African Americans, American Indians, Asian Americans, and Hispanics (Lefley, 1994). Lefley suggests that family psychoeducation may be particularly useful but cautions that although "communication skills, behavior management techniques, and problem-solving strategies are needed by all families, . . . they must be geared to the conceptual framework of a particular culture" (p. 232). For example, she suggests that egalitarian problem-solving techniques, culturally biased assessment of enmeshment, and inadequate attention to spiritual factors may be problematic and in need of adjustment when practitioners work with ethnic minority clients.

Conventional Psychotherapist   Although the exclusive use of psychotherapy as the intervention of choice with racially/ethnically diverse clients is inappropriate, the elimination of psychotherapy as a counseling tool with special populations would be equally ill-advised (Wohl, 2000). Ethnically diverse clients can experience the same mental disorders that afflict nonminority clients. Further, many ethnically diverse clients are bicultural and feel comfortable with conventional forms of psychotherapy. Thus, when the goal of counseling is to remediate an existing psychological problem, the mental health practitioner may want to provide psychotherapy if the client is bicultural and if the problem is no longer being maintained by external sources of oppression.

When psychotherapy is provided for racial/ethnic minority clients, counselor credibility may be more important than knowledge of the client's indigenous culture per se, particularly for highly acculturated clients. S. Sue and Zane (1987) have suggested that although knowledge of a client's culture and techniques generated by this knowledge are important when a mental health practitioner works with ethnically diverse clients, their primary importance in psychotherapy may be to establish the practitioner's credibility. These authors argue that knowledge of a client's culture and culturally specific forms of intervention may be distal to therapeutic outcome. More directly related to therapeutic outcome, they argue, are practitioner credibility and giving, two processes particularly relevant in work with ethnically diverse clients. Credibility is a function of ascribed status and achieved status. Ascribed status is assigned by others; achieved status is primarily a function of the practitioner's skills. S. Sue and Zane suggest that three factors are significantly linked to achieved status:

1. *Conceptualization of the problem.* If the client's problems are conceptualized in a manner that is incongruent with the client's belief systems, the credibility of the therapist is diminished.
2. *Means for problem resolution.* If the therapist requires from the client responses that are culturally incompatible or unacceptable, the achieved credibility of the therapist is diminished.
3. *Goals for treatment.* If the definitions of goals are discrepant between therapist and client, credibility of the therapist is diminished. (p. 41)

Wohl (2000) points out the importance of addressing resistance in conventional psychotherapy with culturally different clients, but he cautions against misinterpreting as clinical resistance any wariness on the part of ethnic minority clients that is due to past discrimination. He also suggests that therapists must be aware of their own countertransference tendencies. These tendencies include avoiding racial/ethnic issues out of fear of offending the client and offending the client by communicating conscious and unconscious racist attitudes. Wolf points out that in "interethnic, intercultural situations, one must pay much more attention to the work of establishing the basis for a communicative relationship than in those where this factor is not evident" (p. 80). Regarding the acknowledgment of race/ethnicity as a factor in interracial psychotherapy, Wohl suggests that there are several alternatives:

> One would have therapists introduce the topic of race and its possible impact on the therapeutic relationship openly at the outset of psychotherapy. Presumably this would lead to an exploration of the patient's attitudes about and difficulties with ethnic conflict and ethnic identity . . . The other position holds that therapists should be willing to discuss racial issues but provides no specific technical guidance about how they are to be introduced and by which participant . . . The fine line in this instance, then, is to balance out readiness to deal with a problem that is believed to be a part of the therapeutic interaction against the sense that generally it is better to wait until one has evidence that the issue exerts sufficient pressure within the patient that would make dealing with it fruitful. Above all, it is important to avoid the comfort of an intellectualized discussion of race and the evils of racism. (p. 86)

After reviewing research on ethnic minority treatment and intervention, S. Sue et al. (1994) concluded that (a) having a bilingual therapist is vital to an ethnic minority client not proficient in English, (b) having an ethnically similar therapist may be advantageous to an ethnic minority client, (c) therapists who are not familiar with the cultures of their ethnic minority clients should consult with mental health professionals who are, and (d) pretherapy intervention may be important for ethnic minority clients who are not familiar with the psychotherapy process.

Selection of an Appropriate Role   Selecting from among these various roles the most appropriate one for a particular client and a particular problem can be a difficult and confusing task. Atkinson et al. (1993) have addressed this problem by suggesting that at least three factors need to be taken into account in the selection of an appropriate role: (a) locus of problem etiology, (b) client's level of acculturation, and (c) goal of counseling. Locus of problem etiology refers to a continuum of problem causes that range from external to internal. Externally caused problems are those imposed on the client by the environment; in the case of racial/ethnic minority clients, these externally imposed problems are often a function of oppression. Job discrimination based on racial/ethnic bias is an example of an externally imposed problem. Mood swings, irrational fear, and weak impulse control are examples of problems assumed to have an internal source. Although some psychologists (e.g., behaviorists) might argue that all client problems have an external source, most client problems are treated by psychologists as if they have an internal etiology.

Level of acculturation refers to the extent to which the client has adopted the culture of the mainstream, dominant society. Recent immigrants are often low in acculturation, although even third- and fourth-generation immigrants may have avoided adopting dominant cultural values. Persons high in acculturation have adopted the attitudes, values, and behaviors of the dominant society. They may have retained cultural values from their indigenous culture (and are therefore bicultural), or they may have lost most of their ancestral cultural values.

The goals of counseling also can be portrayed as a continuum that ranges from preventive on one end to remedial on the other. Atkinson et al. (1993) suggested that mental health practitioners can determine the best role to use with an ethnic minority client by conceptualizing the etiology, acculturation, and goals continua as a cube or three-dimensional model, as presented in Figure 16.1. The intersections of these three continua form the corners of the cube, and each corner is associated with one of eight roles that a practitioner might assume when working with a racial/ethnic minority client.

Atkinson et al. (1993) cautioned against using the three-dimensional model as a cookbook for role determination. In reality, clients and their problems are seldom identified with the extremes of these continua, and therefore no single role is clearly most appropriate. Atkinson et al. also expressed concern that mental health practitioners not interpret the model as a justification for ignoring minority cultural background when the client is highly acculturated. Highly acculturated individuals may still retain strong ties to their indigenous culture. Also, as racial/ethnic minorities they cannot escape the oppression and discrimination of a racist society. Given these caveats, however, the three-dimensional model can

FIGURE 16.1   Three-Dimensional Model of Multicultural Counseling

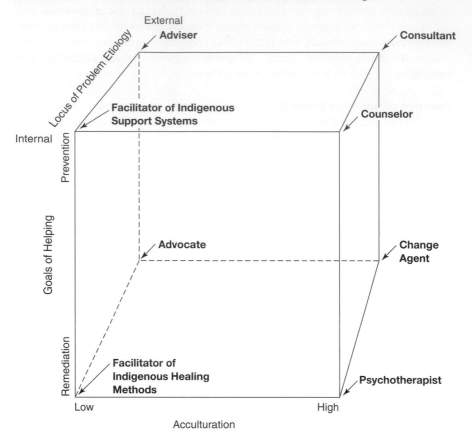

be a useful way to conceptualize racial/ethnic minority clients and their problems and can help mental health practitioners determine the best role or combination of roles to use when working with them.

   There is some research support for the validity of the three-dimensional model. Atkinson, Kim, and Caldwell (1998) reported the results of two studies in which respondents were given vignettes describing an ethnic minority person with high or low acculturation who was experiencing or about to experience a problem with either an internal or external etiology. In the first study, 103 members of APA who were interested in ethnic minority issues rated the helpfulness of helper activities that depicted the eight counselor roles. A role identified by the three-dimensional model to be most appropriate for a given vignette was considered to be validated when respondents gave a significantly higher mean rating to it than to the mean for the other seven roles. Six of the eight roles (facilitator of indigenous support systems, consultant, counselor, facilitator of indigenous healing methods, change agent, and psychotherapist) were validated in the first study. In the second study, 183 Asian American students rated the helpfulness of each role for each of the vignettes. This study validated the roles of facilitator of the indigenous support systems, consultant, and change agent and also found that Asian American students consistently preferred the facilitator of indigenous support systems and consultation roles. Taken collectively, the results of these two studies provided strong support for selecting and emphasizing counseling roles on the basis of a minority client's level of acculturation, problem etiology, and goal of counseling.

Ruelas (2000) also provided criterion-related validity for the three-dimensional model. A national sample of psychologists who were members of APA and who had a self-reported interest in multicultural issues was given brief vignettes that described level of acculturation, goal of counseling, and problem etiology for an ethnic minority individual. A significant relationship was found between respondents' ability to identify appropriate helping strategies (as determined by the three-dimensional model) and the hours of multicultural supervision they had received. A strong relationship was also found between the respondents' ability to identify appropriate strategies and their multicultural research experience.

Theory of Multicultural Counseling and Therapy

As multicultural counseling and therapy (MCT) became increasingly influential in the mental health professions, a number of scholars expressed the need to develop theories to organize the burgeoning literature in the field (Ivey, Ivey, & Simek Morgan, 1993; Pedersen, 1994; Ponterotto & Casas, 1991; D. W. Sue & Sue, 1990). These scholars noted that work in multicultural counseling was often based on inconsistent formulations and lacked a conceptual framework to guide practice considerations. Furthermore, they pointed out that current theories of counseling and therapy originate from a European American context, are culture-bound, and are inadequate to describe and explain the richness and complexity of culturally different populations in the United States. These theories strongly influenced mental health practitioners' conceptualizations of normality and abnormality, which in turn determined the nature of helping techniques and strategies. Therefore European American orientations (psychodynamic, existential/humanistic, and cognitive/behavioral) potentially neglect or trivialize Asian, African, and other non-Western contributions (D. W. Sue, 1995).

Attempting to critically integrate research and work in multicultural psychology, D. W. Sue, Ivey, and Pedersen (1996) recently proposed a theory of MCT that operates from six major propositions and 47 corollaries. A few of the assumptions underlying MCT theory are summarized here. Any attempt to briefly describe the theory does not do it justice. The interested reader is encouraged to seek out the original sources for a more critical analysis.

1. One of the primary assumptions guiding the MCT theory is that culture is central to all theories of normal and abnormal development and that failure to acknowledge this reality leads to inaccurate diagnosis and treatment. The APA and ACA ethical codes and standards of practice place high value on autonomy and individualism. It is clear, however, that many culturally different

groups value collectivism and interdependence. An unenlightened therapist who equates autonomy with maturity may unknowingly and inaccurately label traditional Asian American clients as "overly dependent" if they seek parental or family input before making decisions.

2. European American conceptions of mental health must be balanced by non-Western perspectives. Theories of counseling and therapy arise from European American culture and reflect the values, mores, customs, philosophies, and language of that group. As such, they represent worldviews embedded in a particular cultural context. Non-Western worldviews of helping, indigenous to other cultures, must be seen as equally legitimate. Failure to acknowledge and adjust counselor practice accordingly may deprive racial/ethnic minority clients of culturally relevant services or result in cultural oppression (D. W. Sue, 1978).

3. MCT theory offers a both-and rather than an either-or view of theory and practice. In other words, diverse theories and counseling practices provide different perspectives of the same phenomenon. For example, humanistic/existential approaches emphasize the "feeling self"; cognitive approaches, the "thinking self"; and behavioral approaches, the "behaving self." MCT theory views the totality of human existence to be comprised of not only biological, thinking, feeling, and behaving selves but also social, cultural, and political ones as well. Thus, a holistic view of counseling means that all these various selves can exist under the same umbrella. MCT theory is a metatheory of counseling and psychotherapy and offers an organizational framework for the numerous helping approaches developed by humankind.

4. Human development is embedded in *multiple levels* of experiences—individual, group, and universal—and in *multiple contexts,* including individual, family, and cultural milieu. In other words, people (a) are unique, (b) share commonalities with their reference groups (race, culture, ethnicity, gender, sexual orientation, etc.), and (c) share many universal qualities by virtue of being *Homo sapiens.* Traditional counseling and therapy have historically tended to relate to clients at only the *individual* or *universal* levels, thereby negating group identities. Likewise, the totality of contexts (individual, family, and society) must be the focus of any effective treatments. Remedial work aimed only at the client addresses merely the individual context and may fail to acknowledge that the source of problems potentially resides in systemic forces.

5. The effective MCT practitioner is one who uses modalities and defines goals consistent with the life experiences and cultural values of the client. No single approach is equally effective across all populations and life situations. The ultimate goal of the helping professions must be to expand the repertoire of helping responses available to the mental health practitioner regardless of theoretical orientation. As a result, MCT theory also stresses the importance of multiple helping roles developed by many culturally different groups and societies. The conventional practitioner role is seen as only one of many available to the helping professional.

MCT theory as proposed by D. W. Sue et al. (1996) is an attempt to lay the groundwork for a systematic theory of multicultural helping. From their theory, these authors attempt to derive research, training, and practice implications for the mental health profession. Some of these derivations challenge traditional mental health practices and appear quite revolutionary. However, because this theory is so recent, there has been no direct formal testing of its propositions and corollaries. Although the theory was formulated from the existing research literature on multicultural psychology, it appears that the future impact of MCT theory will ultimately reside in the validity of its underlying assumptions.

Common Factors Approach to Multicultural Counseling

Although most of the research and writing on multicultural counseling has focused on the identification of specific treatments and development of a unique theory for counseling ethnic minorities (S. Sue, Zane, & Young, 1994), Fischer, Jome, and Atkinson (1998) have suggested that multicultural counseling is best conceptualized pragmatically and theoretically within the common factors framework. A brief discussion of the common factors approach to counseling and psychotherapy and an overview of the conflict between this approach and the empirically supported treatment (EST) approach will be presented, followed by an examination of the implications of this approach for counseling ethnic minorities.

Common Factors Approach to Counseling and Psychotherapy   Proponents of the common factors approach argue that although each psychotherapy theory identifies specific ingredients that presumably account for its effectiveness, the comparable effectiveness across theories is the result of underlying factors common to all of them. This theory has a long history (e. g., Frank, 1961, 1973, 1982; Rosenzweig, 1936). Rosenzweig was one of the first authors to suggest that common factors accounted for the comparable treatment effectiveness of divergent psychotherapies. However, it was not until Frank published *Persuasion and Healing* in 1961 that the common factors approach gained widespread attention. Since then numerous books and articles have appeared that proclaim the importance of common factors in the helping relationship.

Recently Fischer et al. (1998) identified two lines of scholarship on common factors. One line is closely allied with the psychotherapy integration movement and focuses on psychotherapy process and outcome. The other comes out of transcultural work aimed at identifying the factors common to all psychological and spiritual healing (Frank, 1961, 1973, 1982; Torrey, 1972, 1986). The transcultural efforts to identify common factors are particularly relevant to multicultural counseling, given that many ethnic minorities are recent immigrants.

Although every author and researcher seems to have come up with his or her own set of, or labels for, common factors, the therapeutic alliance (relationship) appears on almost everyone's list (Wampold, 2001). Basically, the therapeutic alliance refers to the trusting relationship that has been established between the mental health practitioner and the client. Examples of other common factors are the therapeutic qualities of the practitioner, client expectation for improvement, the practitioner's investment in treatment effectiveness, client perceptions of the practitioner's expertness, and shared beliefs between the practitioner and client about the causes of and solutions for the problem.

Although the common factors explanation for counseling and psychotherapy has been around for a long time, it has not gained widespread acceptance by mental health practitioners. In part this lack of acceptance may be because most counselors and psychologists are trained in graduate programs that espouse one particular theoretical orientation. It may also be due in part to greater success on the part of specific ingredient advocates in getting their case across to practitioners and educators. Whatever the reason in the past, the debate between common factors and special ingredients advocates became highly politicized in the 1990s.

EST Versus Common Factors   The search for specific treatments that are empirically validated or supported has a long history in counseling and psychology (e.g., Paul, 1967). However, the EST movement galvanized as a political force in the early 1990s in response to efforts by health maintenance organizations (HMOs) to identify specific, reimbursable treatments for mental disorders. Because drug companies had generously funded research on psychopharmacological treatments for mental disorders while psychotherapy researchers had to compete for grants to fund their research, HMO guidelines initially tended to promote psychopharmacological treatments over psychotherapeutic treatments (Crits-Christoph, Chambless, Frank, Brody, & Karp, 1995). Furthermore, HMO guidelines tended to favor drug treatments because psychotherapy outcomes are often less obvious and less immediate than psychopharmacological effects.

In 1993, the president of the Division of Clinical Psychology (Division 12) of the APA formed the Task Force on Promotion and Dissemination of Psychological Procedures (hereafter referred to as the Task Force), which published its first report in 1995 in *The Clinical Psychologist*. The Task Force identified the political nature of the task with which it was confronted by urgently appealing to members of Division 12 for support: "If clinical psychology is to survive in this heyday of biological psychiatry, APA must act to emphasize the strength of what we have to offer—a variety of psychotherapies of proven efficacy" (Task Force, 1995, p. 3). The main goal of the Task Force was to "consider methods for educating clinical psychologists, third party payers, and the public about effective psychotherapies" (Task Force, 1995, p. 3). Since the initial Task Force report appeared in 1995, subsequent reports have been published by Division 12 (Chambless et al., 1998; Chambless et al., 1996), Division 29 (Norcross, 2001), and others (e.g., Hahlweg, Fiegenbaum, Frank, Schroeder, & Von Witzleben, 2001; Sanderson & Rego, 2002) that identify specific ESTs for use with specific types of problems. Also, Division 12 has since appointed two additional task forces to work on ESTs. In 2001, Chambless and Ollendick reported that 108 ESTs had been identified for adults and 37 for children.

However, the EST movement has been subjected to considerable criticism. For example, Atkinson, Bui, and Mori (2001) cited concerns about (a) the assumptions underlying ESTs; (b) the criteria used to establish ESTs; (c) the lack of consideration of client, therapist, and relationship variables (indeed, treatment manuals are intended to minimize these variables); and (d) the failure to acknowledge ethnic/cultural factors.

The most important criticism of the EST movement, however, is that meta-analyses of treatment comparison research support the effectiveness of common factors, not specific treatments. Wampold (2001) reviewed the research support for both common factors and specific ingredients in a book appropriately titled *The Great Psychotherapy Debate* and found strong support for common factors and little support for specific ingredients. In particular, Wampold cites the results of a series of meta-analyses (Shapiro & Shapiro, 1982; Smith & Glass, 1977; Smith, Glass, & Miller, 1980; Wampold et al., 1997) that all lead to the same conclusion: When confounds and statistical chance are accounted for, all types of treatment are uniformly efficacious. Furthermore, the findings of meta-analytic studies examining research on just one of the common factors, the working alliance (Horvath & Symonds, 1991; Martin, Garske, & Davis, 2000), found that treatment type accounts for about 1% of the variance in treatment outcome whereas the working alliance accounts for 5% or more. Assuming that other common factors also contribute to the variance in treatment outcome, researchers would be better advised to begin identifying empirically supported common factors than to waste more time on identifying ESTs (Wampold, 2001)! For a thorough discussion of the common factors versus specific ingredients debate, as well as a detailed analysis of the empirical support for both, see Wampold (2001).

Common Factors in a Cultural Context   According to Fischer et al. (1998), if common factors are more effective than specific ingredients in counseling, then the most important task of a mental health practitioner working with a culturally different client is to develop *"culturally relevant versions* of these 'universal' processes in therapy" (p. 542). By " 'universal' processes," Fisher et al. were referring to factors common to all therapy and not the universalistic or generic approaches to multicultural counseling advocated by some authors. The universalistic approach assumes that one specific counseling theory can be applied with uniform success across all ethnic groups. Instead, Fischer et al. were arguing for utilizing knowledge of the client's culture to optimize the effectiveness of the factors common to all counseling theories and interventions.

Fischer et al. (1998) reviewed the literature on common factors, identified four that were empirically supported and appeared to have particular relevance to multicultural counseling, and provided theoretical and empirical support from the multicultural counseling literature for each. The four common factors identified were the therapeutic relationship (or working alliance), a shared worldview, client expectations, and a ritual or intervention. Fischer et al. point out that the four factors are neither mutually exclusive nor independent. Furthermore four factors are not exhaustive; future research may reveal other factors that are common to all effective cross-cultural therapy.

Optimizing the common factors effect, especially with culturally different clients, is much more complex than following a treatment manual for an EST. First of all, it requires the mental health practitioner to possess a thorough knowledge of both the client's culture and the common factors. It further requires the practitioner to optimize each common factor to fit the client's cultural characteristics (e.g., level of acculturation, ethnic identity status, socioeconomic level, unique personal characteristics). Counseling with a culturally different client is essentially a process in which mental health practitioners use their knowledge of and experience with the client's culture to build relationships, develop shared worldviews, raise the client's expectations that therapy will be helpful, and implement interventions that make sense to the client. The common factors approach to counseling and psychotherapy does not deny the importance of an intervention strategy (or ritual). Rather, it attempts to put the particular strategy into perspective as one of a number of common factors that contribute to counseling process and outcome. The EST and culturally specific approaches to multicultural counseling have both placed too much stress on the importance of specific, highly structured interventions. Instead of following the manualized version of an EST or the strict dictates of a culture-specific intervention, the mental health practitioner should meld his or her knowledge of the client's culture and common factors to create an intervention customized to fit the client's specific cultural characteristics.

Fischer et al. (1998) cite a number of studies involving ethnic minority participants that lend credibility to the common factors approach to multicultural counseling. However, more research is needed on building a therapeutic relationship, sharing worldviews, raising client expectations, and customizing interventions in a multicultural context. Also, training programs will need to place greater emphasis on enhancing common factors with culturally different clients if future mental health practitioners are to benefit fully from this approach to multicultural counseling.

CONCLUSION

Multicultural counseling has come a long way since the early 1970s, when little attention was being given to the counseling needs of ethnic minorities. This chapter reviews the progress that has been made in three areas important to the practice of counseling ethnic minorities: ethics, competence, and theory. It is gratifying that professional organizations have included nondiscrimination policies in their codes of ethics, but concerns about built-in ethnocentrism still remain, and critics undoubtedly will raise other ethical concerns about the limitations of the codes for counseling and psychotherapy with ethnic minority clients. The multicultural competence movement that culminated in the APA Council of Representatives' endorsement of the Guidelines on Multicultural Education, Training, Research, Practice, and Organizational Change for Psychologists (American Psychological Association, 2002b) has enjoyed considerable success in recent years, but questions are being raised by detractors within the professional literature. In order to address these criticisms, advocates will need to provide empirical evidence to support multicultural counseling competencies. With regard to theory, a tension exists between proponents of specific techniques and common factors approaches to multicultural counseling, a debate that is likely to go on for decades. This debate also can best be resolved through future research on multicultural counseling.

REFERENCES

American Counseling Association. (1995). *Code of ethics and standards of practice.* Alexandria, VA: Author.

American Psychological Association. (2002a). *Ethical principles of psychologists and code of conduct 2002.* Retrieved November 22, 2002, from http://www.apa.org/ethics/homepage.html

American Psychological Association. (2002b). *Guidelines on multicultural education, training, research, practice, and organizational change for psychologists.* Washington, DC: Author. Retrieved November 5, 2002, from http://www.apa.org/pi/multiculturalguidelines.pdf

Arredondo, P., Toporek, R., Brown, S. P., Jones, J., Locke, D. C., Sanchez, J., & Stadler, H. (1996). Operationalization of the multicultural counseling competencies. *Journal of Multicultural Counseling and Development, 24,* 42–78.

Atkinson, D. R., Bui, U., & Mori, S. (2001). Multiculturally sensitive empirically supported treatments—An oxymoron? In J. G. Ponterotto, J. M. Casas, L. A. Suzuki, & C. M. Alexander (Eds.), *Handbook of multicultural counseling* (pp. 542–574). Thousand Oaks, CA: Sage.

Atkinson, D. R., & Israel, T. (in press). The future of multicultural counseling competence. In D. Pope-Davis (Ed.), *The handbook of multicultural competencies.* Thousand Oaks, CA: Sage.

Atkinson, D. R., Kim, B. S. K., & Caldwell, R. (1998). Ratings of helper roles by multicultural psychologists and Asian American students: Initial support for the three-dimensional model of multicultural counseling. *Journal of Counseling Psychology, 45,* 414–423.

Atkinson, D. R., Thompson, C. E., & Grant, S. K. (1993). A three-dimensional model for counseling racial/ethnic minorities. *The Counseling Psychologist, 21,* 257–277.

Berthold, S. M. (1989). Spiritualism as a form of psychotherapy: Implications for social work practice. *Social Casework, 70,* 502–509.

Cayleff, S. E. (1986). Ethical issues in counseling gender, race, and culturally distinct groups. *Journal of Counseling and Development, 64,* 345–347.

Chambless, D. L., Baker, M. J., Baucom, D. H., Beutler, L. E., Calhoun, K. S., Crits-Christoph, P., Dainto, A., De Rubeis, R., Detweiler, J., Haaga, A. F., Johnson, S. B., McCurry, S., Mueser, K. T., Pope, K. S., Sanderson, W. W., Shoham, V., Stickle, T., Williams, D. A., & Woody, S. R. (1998). An update on empirically validated therapies II. *The Clinical Psychologist, 51,* 3–16.

Chambless, D. L., & Ollendick, T. H. (2001). Empirically supported psychological interventions: Controversies and evidence. *Annual Review of Psychology, 52,* 685–716.

Chambless, D. L., Sanderson, W. C., Shoham, V., Johnson, S. B., Pope, K. S., Crits-Christoph, P., Benjamin, M. B., Woody, S. R., Sue, S., Beutler, L., Williams, D. A., & McCurry, S. (1996). An update on empirically validated therapies. *The Clinical Psychologist, 49* (2), 5–18.

Coleman, H. L. K. (1996). Portfolio assessment of multicultural counseling competency. *The Counseling Psychologist, 24,* 216–229.

Coleman, H. L. K. (1998). General and multicultural counseling competency: Apples and oranges? *Journal of Multicultural Counseling and Development, 26,* 147–156.

Constantine, M. G., & Ladany, N. (2001). New visions for defining and assessing multicultural counseling competence. In J. G. Ponterotto, J. M. Casas, L. A. Suzuki, & C. M. Alexander (Eds.), *Handbook of multicultural counseling* (2nd ed., pp. 482–498). Thousand Oaks, CA: Sage.

Crits-Christoph, P., Chambless, D. L., Frank, E., Brody, C., & Karp, J. F. (1995). Training in empirically validated treatments: What are clinical psychology students learning? *Professional Psychology: Research and Practice, 26,* 514–522.

D'Andrea, M., Daniels, J., & Heck, R. (1991). Evaluating the impact of multicultural counseling training. *Journal of Counseling and Development, 70,* 143–150.

DuBose, E. R., Hamel, R. P., & O'Connell, L. J. (Eds.). (1994). *A matter of principles? Ferment in U.S. bioethics.* Valley Forge, PA: Trinity Press International.

Egan, G. (1985). *Change agent skills in helping and human service settings.* Monterey, CA: Brooks/Cole.

Esquivel, G. B., & Keitel, M. A. (1990). Counseling immigrant children in the schools. *Elementary School Guidance and Counseling, 24,* 213–221.

Fischer, A. R., Jome, L. M., & Atkinson, D. R. (1998). Reconceptualizing multicultural counseling: Universal healing conditions in a culturally specific context. *The Counseling Psychologist, 26,* 525–588.

Frank, J. D. (1961). *Persuasion and healing.* Baltimore, MD: Johns Hopkins University Press.

Frank, J. D. (1961). *Persuasion and healing* (Rev. ed.). Baltimore, MD: Johns Hopkins University Press.

Frank, J. D. (1982). Therapeutic components shared by all psychotherapies. In J. H. Harvey & M. M. Parks (Eds.), *The master lecture series: Vol. I. Psychotherapy research and behavior change* (pp. 5–37). Washington, DC: American Psychological Association.

Fuertes, J. N., & Gretchen, D. (2001). Emerging theories of multicultural counseling. In J. G. Ponterotto, J. M. Casas, L. A. Suzuki, & C. M. Alexander (Eds.), *Handbook of multicultural counseling* (2nd ed., pp. 509–541). Thousand Oaks, CA: Sage.

Gladding, S. T. (1996). *Counseling: A comprehensive profession.* Englewood Cliffs, NJ: Prentice Hall.

Hahlweg, K., Fiegenbaum, W., Frank, M., Schroeder, B., & Von Witzleben, I. (2001). Short- and long-term effectiveness of an empirically supported treatment for agoraphobia. *Journal of Consulting and Clinical Psychology, 69,* 375–382.

Hansen, J. C., Himes, B. S., & Meier, S. (1990). *Consultation's concepts and practices.* Englewood Cliffs, NJ: Prentice Hall.

Helms, J. E. (1984). Toward a theoretical explanation of the effects of race on counseling: A Black and White model. *The Counseling Psychologist, 12,* 153–165.

Helms, J. E. (1990). *Black and White racial identity: Theory, research, and practice.* Westport, CT: Greenwood.

Helms, J. E. (1995). An update of Helms's White and people of color racial identity models. In J. G. Ponterotto, J. M. Casas, L. A. Suzuki, & C. M. Alexander (Eds.), *Handbook of multicultural counseling* (pp. 181–198). Thousand Oaks, CA: Sage.

Horvath, A. A., & Symonds, B. D. (1991). Relation between working alliance and outcome in psychotherapy: A meta-analysis. *Journal of Counseling Psychology, 38,* 139–149.

Ibrahim, F. A. (1996). A multicultural perspective on principle and virtue ethics. *The Counseling Psychologist, 24,* 78–85.

Ivey, A. E., Ivey, M. B., & Simek-Morgan, L. (1993). *Counseling and psychotherapy: A multicultural perspective.* Boston: Allyn and Bacon.

Katz, J. H., & Ivey, A. (1977). White awareness: The frontier of racism awareness training. *Personnel and Guidance Journal, 55,* 485–489.

Kocarek, C. E., Talbot, D. M., Batka, J. C., & Anderson, M. Z. (2001). Reliability and validity of three measures of multicultural competency. *Journal of Counseling and Development, 79,* 486–496.

Kurasaki, K. S., Sue, S., Chun, C., & Gee, K. (2000). Ethnic minority intervention and treatment research. In J. F. Aponte & J. Wohl (Eds.), *Psychological interventions and cultural diversity* (pp. 234–249). Boston: Allyn and Bacon.

Ladany, N., Inman, A. G., Constantine, M. G., & Hofheinz, E. W. (1997). Supervisee multicultural case conceptualization ability and self-reported multicultural competence as functions of supervisee racial identity and supervisor focus. *Journal of Counseling Psychology, 44,* 284–293.

LaFromboise, T. D., Coleman, H. L. K., & Hernandez, A. (1991). Development and factor structure of the Cross-Cultural Counseling Inventory–Revised. *Professional Psychology: Research and Practice, 22,* 380–388.

LaFromboise, T. D., & Rowe, W. (1983). Skills training for bicultural competence: Rationale and application. *Journal of Counseling Psychology, 30,* 589–595.

Lefley, H. P. (1994). Service needs of culturally diverse patients and families. In H. P. Lefley & M. Wasow (Eds.), *Helping families cope with mental illness* (pp. 223–242). Langhorne, PA, England: Harwood Academic Publishers.

Lefley, H. P. (2002). Ethical issues in mental health services for culturally diverse communities. In P. Backlar & D. L. Cutler (Eds.), *Ethics in community mental health care: Commonplace concerns* (pp. 3–22). New York: Kluwer Academic/Plenum Publishers.

Lewis, M. D., & Lewis, J. A. (1977). The counselor's impact on community environments. *Personnel and Guidance Journal, 55,* 356–358.

Martin, D. J., Garske, J. P., & Davis, M. K. (2000). Relation of the therapeutic alliance with outcome and other variables: A meta-analytic review. *Journal of Consulting and Clinical Psychology, 68,* 438–450.

Meara, N. M., Schmidt, L. D., & Day, J. D. (1996). Principles and virtues: A foundation for ethical decisions, policies, and character. *The Counseling Psychologist, 24,* 4–77.

Midgette, T. E., & Meggert, S. S. (1991). Multicultural counseling instruction: A challenge for faculties in the 21st century. *Journal of Counseling and Development, 70,* 136–141.

National Coalition of Advocates for Students. (1988). *New voices: Immigrant students in U.S. public schools.* Boston, MA: Author. (ERIC Document Reproduction Service No. ED 297 063).

Neville, H. A., Heppner, M. J., Louie, C. E., Thomson, C. E., Brooks, L., & Baker, C. E. (1996). The impact of multicultural training on White racial identity attitudes and therapy competencies. *Professional Psychology: Research and Practice, 27,* 83–89.

Norcross, J. C. (2001). Purposes, processes, and products of the task force on empirically supported therapy relationships. *Psychotherapy: Theory, Research, Practice, Training, 38,* 345–356.

Ottavi, T. M., Pope-Davis, D. B., & Dings, G. (1994). Relationship between White racial identity attitudes and self-reported multicultural counseling competencies. *Journal of Counseling Psychology, 41,* 149–154.

Patterson, C. H. (1966). *Theories of counseling and psychotherapy.* New York: Harper and Row.

Paul, G. L. (1967). Strategy of outcome research in psychotherapy. *Journal of Consulting Psychology, 31,* 109–118.

Payton, C. R. (1994). Implications of the 1992 ethics code for diverse groups. *Professional Psychology: Research and Practice, 25,* 317–320.

Pedersen, P. B. (1994). *Culture-centered counseling: A search for accuracy.* Newbury Park, CA: Sage.

Pedersen, P. B. (1995). Culture-centered ethical guidelines for counselors. In J. G. Ponterotto, J. M. Casas, L. A. Suzuki, & C. M. Alexander (Eds.), *Handbook of multicultural counseling* (pp. 34–49). Thousand Oaks, CA: Sage.

Ponterotto, J. G. (1987). Counseling Mexican Americans: A multimodel approach. *Journal of Counseling and Development, 65,* 308–312.

Ponterotto, J. G., & Casas, J. M. (1991). *Handbook of racial/ethnic minority counseling research.* Springfield, IL: Charles C Thomas.

Ponterotto, J. G., Fuertes, J. N., & Chen, E. C. (2000). Models of multicultural counseling. In S. D. Brown & R. W. Lent (Eds.), *Handbook of counseling psychology* (3rd ed., pp. 639–669). New York: Wiley.

Ponterotto, J. G., Rieger, B. P., Barrett, A., & Sparks, R. (1994). Assessing multicultural counseling competence: A review of instrumentation. *Journal of Counseling and Development, 72,* 316–322.

Ponterotto, J. G., Sanchez, C. M., & Magids, D. M. (1991, August). *Initial development and validation of the Multicultural Counseling Awareness Scale (MCAS).* Paper presented at the annual meeting of the American Psychological Association, San Francisco, CA.

Pope-Davis, D. B., & Dings, J. G. (1995). The assessment of multicultural counseling competencies. In J. G. Ponterotto, J. M. Casas, L. A. Suzuki, & C. M. Alexander (Eds.), *Handbook of multicultural counseling* (pp. 287–311). Thousand Oaks, CA: Sage.

Pope-Davis, D. B., Liu, W. M., Toporek, R. L., Brittan-Powell, C. S. (2001). What's missing from multicultural competency research: Review, introspection, and recommendations. *Cultural Diversity and Ethnic Minority Psychology, 7,* 121–138.

Pope-Davis, D. B., & Ottavi, T. M. (1994). Examining the association between self-reported multicultural counseling competencies and demographic variables among counselors. *Journal of Counseling & Development, 72,* 651–654.

Pope-Davis, D. B., Reynolds, A. L., Dings, J. G., & Nielson, D. (1995). Examining multicultural counseling competencies of graduate students in psychology. *Professional Psychology: Research and Practice, 26,* 322–329.

Pope-Davis, D. B., Reynolds, A. L., Dings, J. G., & Ottavi, T. M. (1994). Multicultural competencies of doctoral interns at university counseling centers: An exploratory investigation. *Professional Psychology: Research and Practice, 25,* 466–470.

Rosenzweig, S. (1936). Some implicit common factors in diverse methods in psychotherapy. *American Journal of Orthopsychiatry, 6,* 412–415.

Ruelas, S. (2000). *Multicultural counseling competencies* (Doctoral dissertation, University of California, Santa Barbara, 2000). *Dissertation Abstracts International, 62*(5), 2499.

Sanderson, W. C., & Rego, S. A. (2002). Empirically supported treatment for panic disorder: Research, theory, and application of cognitive behavioral therapy. In R. L. Leahy & E. T. Dowd (Eds.), *Clinical advances in cognitive psychotherapy* (pp. 211–239). New York: Springer.

Shapiro, D. A., & Shapiro, D. (1982). Meta-analysis of comparative therapy outcome studies: A replication and refinement. *Psychological Bulletin, 92,* 581–604.

Sodowsky, G. R., Kuo-Jackson, P. Y., Richardson, M. F., & Corey, A. T. (1998). Correlates of self-reported multicultural competencies: Counselor multicultural social desirability, race, social inadequacy, locus of control racial ideology, and multicultural training. *Journal of Counseling Psychology, 45,* 256–264.

Sodowsky, G. R., Taffe, R. C., Gutkin, T. B., & Wise, S. L. (1994). Development of the Multicultural Counseling Inventory: A self-report measure of multicultural competencies. *Journal of Counseling Psychology, 41,* 137–148.

Smith, M. L., & Glass, G. V. (1977). Meta-analysis of psychotherapy outcome studies. *American Psychologist, 32,* 752–760.

Smith, M. L., Glass, G. V., & Miller, T. I. (1980). *The benefits of psychotherapy.* Baltimore: Johns Hopkins University Press.

Sue, D. W. (1978). Eliminating cultural oppression in counseling: Toward a general theory. *Journal of Counseling Psychology, 25,* 419–428.

Sue, D. W. (1995). Toward a theory of multicultural counseling and therapy. In J. A. Banks & C. A. McGee Banks (Eds.), *Handbook of research on multicultural education* (pp. 647–659). New York: Macmillan.

Sue, D. W., Arredondo, P., & McDavis, R. J. (1992). Multicultural counseling competencies/standards: A call to the profession. *Journal of Multicultural Counseling and Development, 20,* 64–88.

Sue, D. W., Bernier, J. E., Durran, A., Feinberg, L., Pedersen, P., Smith, E. J., & Vasquez-Nuttal, E. (1982). Position paper: Cross-cultural counseling competencies. *The Counseling Psychologist, 10*(2), 45–52.

Sue, D. W., Bingham, R. P., Porche-Burke, L., & Vasquez, M. (1999). The diversification of psychology: A multicultural revolution. *American Psychologist, 54,* 1061–1069.

Sue, D. W., Ivey, A. E., & Pedersen, P. B. (1996). *A theory of multicultural counseling and therapy.* Pacific Grove, CA: Brooks/Cole.

Sue, D. W., & Sue, D. (1990). *Counseling the culturally different* (2nd ed.). New York: Wiley.

Sue, S., & Zane, N. (1987). The role of culture and cultural techniques in psychotherapy: A critique and reformulation. *American Psychologist, 42,* 37–45.

Sue, S., Zane, N., & Young, K. (1994). Research on psychotherapy with culturally diverse populations. In A. E. Bergin & S. L. Garfield (Eds.), *Handbook of psychotherapy and behavior change* (4th ed., pp. 783–817). New York: Wiley.

Talbot, D. M. (1992). *A multimethod study of the diversity emphasis in master's degree programs in college student affairs.* Unpublished doctoral dissertation. University of Maryland, College Park.

Task Force on the Promotion and Dissemination of Psychological Procedures. (1995). Training in and dissemination of empirically validated psychological treatments: Report and recommendations. *Clinical Psychologist, 48,* 1, 3–23.

Torrey, E. F. (1972). *The mind game: Witch doctors and psychiatrists.* New York: Emerson-Hall.

Torrey, E. F. (1986). *Witchdoctors and psychiatrists: The common roots of psychotherapy and its future.* New York: Harper and Row.

Tseng, W. S., & McDermott, J. F., Jr. (1975). Psychotherapy: Historical roots, universal elements, and cultural variations. *American Journal of Psychiatry, 132,* 378–384.

Tyler, L. E. (1961). *The work of the counselor* (2nd ed.). New York: Appleton-Century-Crofts.

Waltz, G. R., & Benjamin, L. (1977). *On becoming a change agent.* Ann Arbor, MI: Eric Counseling and Personnel Services Information Center.

Wampold, B. E. (2001). *The great psychotherapy debate.* Mahwah, NJ: Erlbaum.

Wampold, B. E., Mondin, G. W., Moody, M., Stich, F., Benson, K., & Ahn, H. (1997). A meta-analysis of outcome studies comparing bonafide psychotherapies: Empirically, "All must have prizes." *Psychological Bulletin, 122,* 203–215.

Weinrach, S. G., & Thomas, K. R. (2002). A critical analysis of the Multicultural Counseling Competencies: Implications for the practice of mental health counseling. *Journal of Mental Health Counseling, 24,* 20–35.

Wohl, J. (2000). Traditional individual psychotherapy and ethnic minorities. In J. F. Aponte & J. Wohl (Eds.), *Psychological interventions and cultural diversity* (pp. 75–91). Boston: Allyn and Bacon.

Wood, P. S., & Mallinckrodt, B. (1990). Culturally sensitive assertiveness training for ethnic minority clients. *Professional Psychology: Research and Practice, 21,* 5–11.

Worthington, R. L., Mobley, M., Franks, R. P., & Tan, J. A. (2000). Multicultural counseling competencies: Verbal content, counselor attributions, and social desirability. *Journal of Counseling Psychology, 47,* 460–468.

Appendix
Cross-Cultural Counseling
Competencies:
A Conceptual Framework

Counselor Awareness of Own Assumptions, Values, and Biases

Beliefs and Attitudes

1. Culturally skilled counselors have moved from being culturally unaware to being aware and sensitive to their own cultural heritage and to valuing and respecting differences.
2. Culturally skilled counselors are aware of how their own cultural background and experiences, attitudes, and values and biases influence psychological processes.
3. Culturally skilled counselors are able to recognize the limits of their competencies and expertise.
4. Culturally skilled counselors are comfortable with differences that exist between themselves and clients in terms of race, ethnicity, culture, and beliefs.

Knowledge

1. Culturally skilled counselors have specific knowledge about their own racial and cultural heritage and how it personally and professionally affects their definitions and biases of normality-abnormality and the process of counseling.
2. Culturally skilled counselors possess knowledge and understanding about how oppression, racism, discrimination, and stereotyping affect them personally and in their work. This allows them to acknowledge their own racist attitudes, beliefs, and feelings. Although this standard applies to all groups, for White counselors it may mean that they understand how they may have directly or indirectly benefitted from individual, institutional, and cultural racism (White identity development models).

From Derald Wing Sue, Patricia Arredondo, and Roderick J. McDavis, Multicultural Counseling Competencies and Standards: A Call to the Profession, *Journal of Counseling and Development,* vol. 70 (March/April 1992): 481–483.

3. Culturally skilled counselors possess knowledge about their social impact upon others. They are knowledgeable about communication style differences, how their style may clash or facilitate the counseling process with minority clients, and how to anticipate the impact it may have on others.

Skills

1. Culturally skilled counselors seek out educational, consultative, and training experiences to enrich their understanding and effectiveness in working with culturally different populations. Being able to recognize the limits of their competencies, they (a) seek consultation, (b) seek further training or education, (c) refer out to more qualified individuals or resources, or (d) engage in a combination of these.
2. Culturally skilled counselors are constantly seeking to understand themselves as racial and cultural beings and are actively seeking a nonracist identity.

Understanding the Worldview
of the Culturally Different Client

Beliefs and Attitudes

1. Culturally skilled counselors are aware of their negative emotional reactions toward other racial and ethnic groups that may prove detrimental to their clients in counseling. They are willing to contrast their own beliefs and attitudes with those of their culturally different clients in a nonjudgmental fashion.
2. Culturally skilled counselors are aware of their stereotypes and preconceived notions that they may hold toward other racial and ethnic minority groups.

Knowledge

1. Culturally skilled counselors possess specific knowledge and information about the particular group that they are working with. They are aware of the life experiences, cultural heritage, and historical background of their culturally different clients. This particular competency is strongly linked to the "minority identity development models" available in the literature.
2. Culturally skilled counselors understand how race, culture, ethnicity, and so forth may affect personality formation, vocational choices, manifestation of psychological disorders, help-seeking behavior, and the appropriateness or inappropriateness of counseling approaches.
3. Culturally skilled counselors understand and have knowledge about sociopolitical influences that impinge upon the life of racial and ethnic minorities. Immigration issues, poverty, racism, stereotyping, and powerlessness all leave major scars that may influence the counseling process.

Skills

1. Culturally skilled counselors should familiarize themselves with relevant research and the latest findings regarding mental health and mental disorders of

various ethnic and racial groups. They should actively seek out educational experiences that enrich their knowledge, understanding, and cross-cultural skills.

2. Culturally skilled counselors become actively involved with minority individuals outside the counseling setting (community events, social and political functions, celebrations, friendships, neighborhood groups, and so forth) so that their perspective of minorities is more than an academic or helping exercise.

Developing Appropriate Intervention Strategies and Techniques

Attitudes and Beliefs

1. Culturally skilled counselors respect clients' religious and/or spiritual beliefs and values about physical and mental functioning.
2. Culturally skilled counselors respect indigenous helping practices and respect minority community intrinsic help-giving networks.
3. Culturally skilled counselors value bilingualism and do not view another language as an impediment to counseling (monolingualism may be the culprit).

Knowledge

1. Culturally skilled counselors have a clear and explicit knowledge and understanding of the generic characteristics of counseling and therapy (culture bound, class bound, and monolingual) and how they may clash with the cultural values of various minority groups.
2. Culturally skilled counselors are aware of institutional barriers that prevent minorities from using mental health services.
3. Culturally skilled counselors have knowledge of the potential bias in assessment instruments and use procedures and interpret findings keeping in mind the cultural and linguistic characteristics of the clients.
4. Culturally skilled counselors have knowledge of minority family structures, hierarchies, values, and beliefs. They are knowledgeable about the community characteristics and the resources in the community as well as the family.
5. Culturally skilled counselors should be aware of relevant discriminatory practices at the social and community level that may be affecting the psychological welfare of the population being served.

Skills

1. Culturally skilled counselors are able to engage in a variety of verbal and nonverbal helping responses. They are able to *send* and *receive* both *verbal* and *nonverbal* messages *accurately* and *appropriately*. They are not tied down to only one method or approach to helping but recognize that helping styles and approaches may be culture bound. When they sense that their helping style is limited and potentially inappropriate, they can anticipate and ameliorate its negative impact.

2. Culturally skilled counselors are able to exercise institutional intervention skills on behalf of their clients. They can help clients determine whether a "problem" stems from racism or bias in others (the concept of healthy paranoia) so that clients do not inappropriately blame themselves.
3. Culturally skilled counselors are not averse to seeking consultation with traditional healers or religious and spiritual leaders and practitioners in the treatment of culturally different clients when appropriate.
4. Culturally skilled counselors take responsibility for interacting in the language requested by the client; this may mean appropriate referral to outside resources. A serious problem arises when the linguistic skills of the counselor do not match the language of the client. This being the case, counselors should (a) seek a translator with cultural knowledge and appropriate professional background or (b) refer to a knowledgeable and competent bilingual counselor.
5. Culturally skilled counselors have training and expertise in the use of traditional assessment and testing instruments. They not only understand the technical aspects of the instruments but are also aware of the cultural limitations. This allows them to use test instruments for the welfare of the diverse clients.
6. Culturally skilled counselors should attend to as well as work to eliminate biases, prejudices, and discriminatory practices. They should be cognizant of sociopolitical contexts in conducting evaluations and providing interventions, and should develop sensitivity to issues of oppression, sexism, and racism.
7. Culturally skilled counselors take responsibility in educating their clients to the processes of psychological intervention, such as goals, expectations, legal rights, and the counselor's orientation.

Credits

Text and Line Art Credits

P. 16 "politically correct" Entry from *Webster's New World® College Dictionary,* Third Edition. Copyright © 1996 Wiley Publishing, Inc. All rights reserved. Reproduced here by permission of the publisher.

Fig. 2.1 From W. J. Lonner and J. W. Berry, *Field Methods in Cross-Cultural Research,* Sage, 1986. Copyright © 1986 Sage Publications, Inc. Reprinted by permission of Sage Publications, Inc.

Fig. 7.1 From M. T. Garrett and E. F. Pichette, "Red as an Apple: Native American Acculturation and Counseling with or without Reservation," *Journal of Counseling and Development,* 78, 3–13, 2000. Reprinted with permission from the American Counseling Association.

T 7.1 From M. T. Garrett, "Understanding the 'Medicine' of Native American Traditional Values: An Integrative Review," *Counseling and Values,* 43, 84–98, 1999. Reprinted with permission from the American Counseling Association.

Pp. 160–161 From D. McLaughlin, "Critical Literacy for Navajo and other American Indian Learners," *Journal of American Indian Education,* 33, 1994, 47–59. Reprinted with permission from the publisher.

P. 342 From 2002 "Ethical Principles of Psychologists and Code of Conduct," *APA,* 2002, 57, 1060–1073. Copyright © 2002 by the American Psychological Association. Reprinted with permission.

P. 343 From *ACA Code of Ethics and Standards of Practice,* 1995. Reprinted with permission from the American Counseling Association.

P. 347 From "APA Educational Training Committee Position Paper," 1982 by Derald Wing Sue et al., *The Counseling Psychologist,* Vol. 10. Copyright © 1982 Sage Publications, Inc. Reprinted with permission from Sage Publications, Inc.

T 16.1 From *Black and White Racial Identity: Theory, Research and Practice,* Greenwood Publishing Group, 1990, Table 9.1. Copyright © 1990 by J. E. Helms. Reprinted with permission from the publisher.

Fig. 16.1 From D. R. Atkinson, C.E. Thompson, S. Grant, "A Three-Dimensional Model for Counseling Racial/Ethnic Minorities," *The Counseling Psychologist,* Fig. 1. Reprinted with permission from Sage Publications, Inc.

Appendix From Derald Wing Sue, Patricia Arredondo and Roderick J. McDavis, "Multicultural Counseling Competencies and Standards: A Call to Profession," *Journal of Counseling and Development,* Vol. 70, March /April 1992, pp. 481–483. Reprinted with permission from the American Counseling Association.

Photo credits

Page 1: © John Henley/Corbis
Page 81: © Index Stock Imagery, Inc
Page 145: Robert Huntzinger/Corbis
Page 215: © Mike Douglas/The Image Works
Page 277: © Zephyr Picture/Index Stock Imagery, Inc.
Page 339: © Nathaniel Antman/The Image Works

Author Index

Abramowitz, S. I., 74
Abreu, J. M., xxi, 31, 34, 35, 36, 70, 260, 263, 293, 300–310, 317–330
Achenbach, T., 309
Acosta, R., 318
Adams, E. M., 37
Adams, J. Q., 5
Adams, P. F., 111
Adebimpe, V. R., 59, 64, 68, 115
Aderibigbe, Y. A., 247
Adler, N. E., 106, 114, 116
Aguilar, L., 301
Aguilar-Gaxiola, S., 306, 307, 317–318, 321, 325, 326, 330
Aguirre, A., Jr., 285, 291
Ahler, J. G., 159
Ahn, H., 268, 371
Ajamu, A., 105, 109, 116
Alderete, E., 306, 307, 325, 326, 330
Alegria, M., 308
Alexander, G. A., 241
Alipuria, L. L., 181
Allen, B. P., 5
Allen, J., 199, 200
Alonzo, W., 5
Altarriba, J., 327
Alvarez, R., 318
Alvidrez, J., 64
Alwano-Edyegu, M. G., 322
Aman, L. C., 324
Amaro, H., 286
American Cancer Society, 90, 242
American Council on Education, 87
American Counseling Association, 341, 343
American Psychiatric Association, 71, 246, 247, 264, 310
American Psychological Association, 57, 341, 342, 348, 372
American Thoracic Society, 304
Ancis, J., 133
Anderson, L., 322
Anderson, M. J., 183
Anderson, M. Z., 351
Anderson, N. B., 97
Anderson, R. M., 324
Anderson, R. N., 110, 111, 302
Andrulis, D. P., 318
Antal, E., 246
Anthony, J. C., 319
Arani, D., 90
Arce, A. A., 308
Arce, C. H., 286, 287
Arellano, L. M., 241
Argueta-Bernal, G. A., 308
Arias, E., 110

Arnold, B., 36
Arnold, F., 225
Arnold, M. S., 201, 202
Arredondo, P., 290, 292, 293, 294, 348, 349, 350
Asay, P. A., 271
Asian American Students Association of Brown University, 227
Atkinson, D. R., xxi, 36, 49, 61, 66, 68, 95, 232, 259, 260, 261, 263, 264, 265, 268, 269, 270, 271, 319, 321, 349, 352, 354, 365, 366, 369, 370, 371, 372
Attneave, C. L., 162, 194, 206
Au, J. K. D., 227
Audette, D., 5, 7
Auger, S., 197, 198
Augustine, D. S., 135
Aviera, A., 327
Avison, W. R., 244
Ayers, W., 90
Azocar, F., 318

Bach, P. B., 90
Bachman, R., 181
Bachu, A., 2
Bajaki, M., 32, 329
Baker, C. E., 350
Baker, F. M., 70, 117, 126, 127, 135
Baker, M. J., 370
Baldwin, J. A., 92
Bansal, A., 306, 307
Barber, M., 121
Barnes, M., 64
Barona, A., 330
Barresi, C. M., 7
Barrett, A., 350
Barrett, P. M., 96
Barton, S. A., 301, 302, 323, 324
Baruth, L. G., 178, 182, 184
Bastian, L. A., 128
Batka, J. C., 351
Baucom, D. H., 370
Beauboeuf-Lafontant, T., 135
Beauvais, F., 180
Becker, A., 114
Becker, H. A., 301, 302, 323, 324
Begg, C. B., 90
Belgrave, F. Z., 319
Bell, C. C., 117, 126, 127, 135
Belleroe, E., 153
Benjamin, L., 359
Benjamin, M. B., 370
Ben-Jochannan, U., 135
Bennett, S. K., 195
Benson, K., 371
Berglund, P., 64
Bergman, R. N., 301, 302

I

Berlin, J. A., 90
Bernal, M. E., 7
Bernier, J. E., 347, 348, 349, 350
Bernstein, L., 241
Berry, B., 39
Berry, J. W., 8, 30, 31, 32, 32f, 33, 195, 260, 329
Berryhill-Paapke, E., 148
Berthold, S. M., 362
Betancourt, H., 127, 292
Beutler, L., 370
Bichsel, R. J., 195
BigFoot-Sipes, D. S., 195
Bingham, C. R., 74
Bingham, R. P., 19, 348, 360
Binion, V. J., 127
Bird, H. R., 306, 309
Blackwell, J., 301, 302
Blanchard, E. B., 309
Blank, M. B., 61
Blow, F. C., 74
Blumberg, E., 226
Blumenthal, R., 321
Bobo, L., 83
Boesch, R., 130
Bohart, A. C., 321
Bolden, M. A., 290
Bonacich, E., 220, 225
Bonilla-Silva, E., 89
Bosworth, H. B., 128
Bourjolly, J. N., 98
Bourne, M. L., 127
Bowen, G. S., 322
Bowen-Reid, T. L., 98
Bowie, J. V., 95
Boyd, J. H., 306, 308
Boyd-Franklin, N., 135
Boyer, L. B., 187
Boykin, A. W., 135
Bracero, W., 292, 293
Bravo, M., 307, 310, 330
Brendtro, L. K., 153
Brenner, B. R., 271
Brewer, S., 321
Brinkley, D. F., 61
Brittan-Powell, C. S., 269, 349
Brodie, R. E., II, xxi, 90, 105–121
Brody, C., 370
Brokenleg, M., 153
Broken Nose, M. A., 197, 206
Brooks, L., 350
Brotherton, D., 155
Brown, A. L., 290
Brown, C., 127
Brown, M. T., 320
Brown, R. D., 269
Brown, S. A., 246, 301, 302, 323, 324
Brown, S. P., 348, 349, 350
Browne, L., 96
Bruchac, J., 187
Bruhn, J. G., 318
Buchwald, D., 243
Buehler, J. W., 302
Bui, U., 68, 370
Bulhan, H. A., 126
Bunce, H., 318
Bunzel, J. H., 227
Bureau of Labor Statistics, 86
Burgess, E. W., 30
Burke, J., 90

Burnam, A., 317, 318, 319
Burnam, M. A., 325
Burns, B. J., 64, 128, 317
Butcher, J. N., 199
Butler, E. M., 98
Butterfield, M. I., 128
Byrd-Holt, D., 301, 302

Cabrera Strait, S., 308, 325
Cachola, S., 241
Caldwell, C. H., 65, 129
Caldwell, R., 264, 269, 270, 366
Calhoun, K. S., 370
Cameron, M. C., 193, 195, 196, 201
Campos, A., 293
Canino, G., 330
Canino, G. J., 306, 307, 309, 310
Cannon, M. S., 73
Caraveo-Anduaga, J. B., 306, 307, 326
Carey, G., 290
Carey, P., 242
Carino, B., 225
Carlin, A. S., 251
Carlos, M. L., 318, 321
Carpenter, C. C., 322
Carr, L. G., 246
Carrillo, E., 310
Carroll, J., 161, 208
Carter, R. T., 39
Casas, A., 321
Casas, L. A., 367
Case, L., 318
Cass, V. C., 37
Cassidy, R. C., 2, 6
Castillo, E. M., 283, 285
Castillo, R. J., 247
Castro, K. G., 302
Catalano, R., 306, 307, 317–318, 318, 326
Catania, J. A., 322
Cayleff, S. E., 362
Celano, M., 105
Census Bureau. See U.S. Census Bureau
Centers for Disease Control and Prevention (CDC),
    300, 302, 303, 305
Cervantes, R., 286, 307, 308, 309
Cervantes, R. C., 326
Chambless, D. L., 127, 370
Chan, K. K., 246
Chan, N., 242
Chan, S., 218, 219, 220, 221, 222, 223, 226,
    229, 231
Chapa, J., 17
Chatters, L. M., 129
Chavez, E. L., 180
Chavez-Chavez, R., 291
Chavous, T. M., 92
Chee, K. T., 249
Chen, E. C., 353
Chen, M. S., 242
Chen, Y., 309
Cheng, L., 220
Cheung, F., 247
Cheung, F. H., 259
Cheung, F. K., 64, 69, 73, 306, 318, 319, 320
Cheung, M., 73
Chew, M., 29
Chin, D., 250
Chin, V., 234
Choe, J., 251

Choney, S. K., 148
Christensen, M., 206
Chun, C., 28, 29, 75, 361
Chun, C.-A., 249
Chun, K. M., 244, 247
Chung, R. C., 69
Cimbolic, P., 130
Clark, R., 97
Clark, V. R., 97
Clarke, J. H., 135
Clegg, L., 111
Cleghorn, J. M., 308
Cleveland, R. W., 48, 284
Coalition for Asian American Children and
    Families, 251
Cobbs, P. M., 49
Codina, G. E., 287
Coiro, M. J., 119
Cokley, K. O., 38
Coleman, H., 206, 207
Coleman, H. L. K., 155, 349, 350, 351
Coleman, M. N., 96
Coleman, V. D., 204
Collins, C., 129
Collins, P. H., 90
Colmant, S. A., 207
Comas-Díaz, L., 279, 280, 292, 293, 326
Committee of 100, 249
Condon, J. W., 323
Consoli, A. J., xxi, 317–330
Constantine, M. G., 39, 346, 348, 349, 350, 351
Constantino, G., 327
Cook, D. A., 38
Cooper-Patrick, L., 319
Copeland, L. A., 74
Corbiere, M., 46
Corbine, J. L., 148, 150, 156, 184, 186, 194, 205
Corey, A. T., 350
Cornelius, J. R., 115
Cornelius, M. D., 115
Cornell, G. R., 180
Cortes, D. E., 325, 326
Cose, E., 96
Costantino, G., 321
Cowan, G., 290
Cowie, C. C., 301, 302
Cox, C. I., 37
Cox, G. B., 318
Cox, O. C., 6
Cramer, L. D., 90
Crits-Christoph, P., 68, 370
Crocker, J., 46, 92
Cross, W. E., Jr., 37, 38, 41, 91, 93, 94
Crum, R. M., 319
Cuellar, I., 36, 328
Curry, R. H., 108, 109
Cushman, P., 126, 128
Cypers, S. J., xxi, 317–330

Dahlstrom, W. G., 199
Dainto, A., 370
Dalaker, J., 284
Dana, R. H., 182
D'Andrea, M., 350
Daniels, J., 350
Darity, W., 107, 108, 110, 111, 112, 113
Dasen, P. R., 260
Dauphinais, P., 195
D'Avanzo, C., 244

Davis, A., 89
Davis, F. J., 131
Davis, K., 244, 245
Davis, M. K., 371
Day, J., 281
Day, J. D., 345, 346
de Anda, D., 35
DeBuono, B. A., 90
Deffenbacher, J. L., 180
De La Cancela, V., 310
Delgado, M., 293
Deloria, V., Jr., 149, 150
DeNavas-Walt, C., 48, 284
Denning, P., 322
Department of Health and Human Services (DHHS),
    58, 60, 61, 62, 74, 193, 241,
    243, 307
De Rubeis, R., 370
Desai, R. A., 308
Des Roches, C., 244, 245
de-St-Aubin, T. M., 320
DeTurk, P. B., 110
Detweiler, J., 370
Diabetes Control and Complications Trials Research
    Group, 302
Diala, C., 128, 317
Diaz, R. M., 286
Diaz, T., 301, 302
Diaz-Perez, M. J., 310, 330
Diehl, V. A., 282
Dinges, N. G., 180
Dings, G., 350
Dings, J. G., 346, 350, 351
Dinh, K. T., 251
Dixon, D. N., 269
Dodson, J., 129
Doheny, V., 61
Doherty, W. J., 138
Downing, N. E., 37
Dube, R., 90
DuBose, E. R., 345
DuBray, W. H., 148, 152
Dudley, J. Iron Eye, 150
Dufrene, P. M., 150, 204
Dunn, J., 301, 302
Dupey, P., 157, 204
Duran, G., 96
Durran, A., 347, 348, 349, 350
Dynneson, V. V., 195

Eagleton, T., 7
Eastman, K. L., 244, 247
Eaton, W. W., 319
Eberhardt, M. S., 301, 302
Echeverry, J. J., 283
EchoHawk, M., 181
Eder, J., 149
Edgerton, R. B., 318
Edlund, M., 64, 317
Edman, J. L., 248
Edwards, B. K., 111
Egan, G., 358
Eisner, M. P., 111
Ellis, R., 183
Emery, J., 251
Epps, E. G., 11
Escarce, J. J., 90
Escobar, J., 325
Escobar, J. I., 308, 318

Esenber, J. M., 90
Espiritu, Y. L., 232
Esquivel, G. B., 65, 68, 358
Ethnomed, 242, 248
Evans, L., 89

Fabrega, H., 72, 115
Fairchild, H. H., 5
Fairchild, H. P., 10
Falconer, J. W., 96
Falicov, C. J., 282, 287, 288, 289, 292
Farley, R., 30
Favreau, O. E., 16
Fawcett, J., 225
Feagin, J. R., 7, 83, 89
Feder, A., 319
Feeny, N. C., 126
Feinberg, L., 347, 348, 349, 350
Feldman, P., 106, 114, 116
Fenton, S., 9
Ferguson, A. D., 286
Fernández, M. I., 322
Fernando, S., 7
Ferrell, R. E., 301
Fhagen-Smith, P. E., 38, 93, 94
Fiegenbaum, W., 370
Finch, B. K., 308, 309, 327
Fischer, A. R., 93, 369, 371, 372
Fish, J. M., 4, 5, 128
Fisher, A. R., 46
Fishl, M. A., 322
Fisk University Social Science Institute, 223
Fitzgerald, J. T., 324
Fitzgibbons, L. A., 126
Flannery, D. J., 309
Flannery-Schroeder, E. C., 126
Flaskerud, J. H., 319
Flegal, K. M., 301, 302
Fleming, P. L., 301, 302
Flores, M. T., 290
Foa, E. B., 126
Fong, K. T., 319
Fong, T. P., 218, 220, 224, 225, 226, 227, 228, 229, 231, 234, 235
Fontana, A., 63, 126
Ford, D., 319
Ford, D. E., 319
Ford, R. C., 37
Foucault, M., 126
Four Worlds Development Project, 150
Fox, G., 292
Fraga, E. D., 66
Frank, E., 370
Frank, J. D., 369
Frank, M., 370
Frank, R. G., 317
Franklin, J. H., 135
Franks, R. P., 351
Freedle, R., 37
Freire, P., 135
Frey, R., 301, 302
Friedman, S., 59, 70, 126
Frisbie, W. P., 286, 287
Fritz, J., 187
Frye, B. A., 244
Fu, P., 246
Fuentes, M., 319
Fuertes, J. N., 353
Fujino, D. C., 49, 64, 128, 259

Fukuyama, M. A., 286
Funnell, M. M., 324
Furlong, M. J., 268, 319

Gabarain, G., 319
Gallardo-Cooper, M., 290, 293, 294
Gallin, R. S., 323
Gallo, J. J., 319
Gamba, R. J., 329
Gameroff, M., 319
Gándara, P., 285
Gara, M. A., 308
Garb, H. N., 306
Garcia, A., 301
Garcia, A. A., 301, 302, 323, 324
Garcia, C. A., 301
Garcia, E., 291
García, J. G., 282, 283
Garcia, R. L., 159
Garcia-Preto, N., 280, 290
Gardner, R., 225
Garrett, J. T., 148, 150, 152, 154, 155, 157, 158, 159, 160, 185, 198
Garrett, M. T., xxi–xxii, 147–166, 151t, 159f, 184, 185, 186, 194, 197, 198, 203, 204, 208
Garrett, M. W., 207
Garske, J. P., 371
Garwick, A., 197, 198
Garza-Ibarra, A., 301
Gay, G., 37
Gee, K., 28, 29, 75, 361
George, L. K., 317
Gerard, P. A., 39
Gersh, B. J., 90
Gerton, J., 155
Ghany, D., 322
Ghee, K. L., 17
Gil, A. G., 325
Gillespie, J. V., 119
Gim, R. H., 261, 269
Ginsberg, M. M., 322
Given, B. A., 323
Given, C. W., 323
Gjerdingen, D. K., 242
Gladding, S. T., 363
Gladstone, G., 249
Glass, G. V., 371
Gloria, A. M., xxii, 279–294
Glover, C. S., 241
Glover, S. H., 309
Goldberg, E., 89
Golding, J. M., 317, 319
Goldstein, D. E., 301, 302
Gomez, C., 286, 287
Gómez, C. A., 286
Gomez, J. P., 127
Gonzalez, C. A., 58
Gonzalez, J., 283, 287, 288, 289, 290, 291
Good, B. J., 72, 306
Goodman, A. B., 318
Goodwin, F. K., 319
Goodyear, R. K., 293
Gordon, M. M., 11
Gottesfeld, H., 63
Gould, M., 309
Graham, J. R., 199
Graham, T. L. C., 206
Grant, S., 264, 271
Grant, S. K., 352, 354, 365

Gray, B. A., 58
Gray, R. H., 322
Green, B., 283, 286
Greene, R. L., 64, 68
Gregg, J., 108, 109
Gretchen, D., 353
Grieco, E. M., 2, 6
Grieger, I., 202
Grier, W. H., 49
Griffith, E. E. H., 58, 129, 292
Grosser, R., 318
Grunberger, G., 324
Gruppen, L. D., 324
Guarnaccia, P. J., 306, 310, 330
Gurland, B., 70
Gutierres, S. E., 208
Gutkin, T. B., 350
Guttman, M. A. J., 207
Guzmán, B., 280, 281, 282

Haaga, A. F., 370
Haffner, S. M., 301, 302
Hagedorn, J., 233
Hahlweg, K., 370
Hahn, R. A., 67
Halbreich, U., 267, 268
Hall, W. S., 37
Hamel, R. P., 345
Hammer, S. M., 322
Hammerschlag, C. A., 185
Hanis, C., 301
Hanis, C. L., 301, 302, 323, 324
Hankey, B. F., 111
Hanley, C. P., 37
Hanley, T. C., 37
Hannan, E. L., 90
Hansen, J. C., 360
Hardison, C. B., 129
Harless, W., 90
Harman, C. P., 128
Harrell, J. P., 98
Harris, G. J., 121
Harris, M. I., 301, 302
Hatch, M. L., 59, 70, 126
Hathue, N., 246
Haviland, M. G., 195
Hawkins, J. M., 127
Hawks, B. L., 242
Hayes-Bautista, D. E., 17
Healthy People 2010, 90
Heck, R., 350
Hedges, L. V., 323
Hee, S. J., 228, 229
Heilbron, C. L., 207
Heiman, J. R., 251
Heinrich, R. K., 148, 150, 156, 184, 186, 194, 205
Helms, J. E., 6, 28, 37, 38–39, 49, 65, 92–93, 95, 116,
    127, 134, 138, 354, 355t–357t
Hendershot, G. E., 111
Henkin, L. B., 244
Henwood, K. L., 13
Heppner, M. J., 350
Hernandez, A., 350
Herring, R. D., xxii, 150, 158, 159, 171–189, 203
Herskovits, M., 30
Herskovits, M. J., 260
Hetts, J. J., 83
Highlen, P. S., 37
Hildsheim, A., 241

Hill, C. E., 130
Hill, P. C., 98
Himes, B. S., 360
Hirschfelder, A., 150
Ho, D. Y. F., 28
Hodgkinson, H. L., 147
Hofheinz, E. W., 350
Holditch-Davis, D., 119
Holmes, D., 70, 96
Holzer, C. E., III, 309
hooks, b., 135
Hooton, T. M., 243
Hoover, R. N., 241
Horn, J., 324
Hornig, C. D., 59
Horn-Ross, P. L., 241
Horswill, R. K., 195
Horvath, A. A., 371
Horwath, E., 59
Hough, R. L., 317, 318, 319, 325
Hovey, J. D., 309, 325
Hoyert, D. L., 110
Hu, L., 49, 64, 128, 259
Hu, T., 62, 65, 74
Hudson, S. M., 324
Huertin-Roberts, S., 306
Hughes, C. C., 182, 183
Hughes, D. L., 243
Huh-Kim, J., 245
Huisman, K. A., 250
Human Rights Watch, 88
Humes, K., 49
Hummer, R. A., 308, 309, 327
Hwang, J. S., 248
Hyer, M. B., 241

Ibrahim, F. A., 345, 346
Indian Health Services, 173, 193, 196
Inman, A., 351
Isaac, K., xxii, 125–139
Israel, B., 114
Israel, T., 349, 352
Ivey, A., 359
Ivey, A. E., 367, 368
Ivey, M. B., 367
Iwamasa, G. Y., 72

Jackson, B., 37
Jackson, J., 114
Jackson, J. C., 242
Jackson, J. S., 64, 65, 68, 107, 108, 109, 127,
    128, 129
Jackson, M. L., 19
Jaco, E. G., 318
Jacober, S. J., 324
Jacobsen, D. M., 322
James, S. A., 114
Jamieson, M., 281
Jamin, D., 243
Jenkins, J. H., 310, 330
Johnson, A. G., 15
Johnson, C. A., 194, 200, 206
Johnson, D. L., 194, 200, 206
Johnson, F., 206
Johnson, J., 59
Johnson, J. L., 193, 195, 196, 201
Johnson, M. E., 195
Johnson, P., 189
Johnson, R. C., 248

Johnson, S. B., 370
Johnson, S. D., Jr., 9
Jome, L. M., 369, 371, 372
Jones, B. E., 58
Jones, J., 348, 349, 350
Jones, J. M., 12, 135
Jones-Webb, R. J., 59
Jones-Wilson, F. C., 106, 111, 112
Juntunen, C. L., xxii–xxiii, 193–208

Kaemmer, B., 199
Kagawa-Singer, M., 180
Kales, H. C., 74
Kallen, H. M., 11
Kalous, T., 309
Kameoka, V. A., 248
Kamerow, B. D., 319
Karno, M., 317, 318, 319, 325
Karp, J. F., 370
Kashubeck, S., 250
Katz, J. H., 359
Katz, M. H., 322
Katz, P. A., 109, 113
Katz, S. J., 64, 317
Katzenstein, D. A., 322
Kavanaugh, P., 291
Keck, P. E., 127
Keefe, S. E., 30, 318, 321
Keitel, M. A., 65, 68, 358
Kellogg, T., 322
Kendall, L., 267
Kendall, P. C., 126
Kerner, J. F., 90
Kessler, R., 64
Kessler, R. C., 59, 317
Key, C. R., 241
Kim, A. U., xxiii, 217–236
Kim, B. S. K., xxiii, 31, 34, 35, 36, 232, 258–272,
    308, 329, 366
Kim, G., 251
Kim, H., 270
Kim, M., 308
Kim, P. S., 226
Kim, R., 195
Kim, S. J., 261, 269
Kim, U., 31, 32, 33, 329
Kimbarow, M. L., 126
King, A., 118
Kirkeby, J., 318
Kirmayer, L. J., 72
Kiselica, M. S., 201, 203
Kleinman, A., 72, 306
Klevens, R. M., 301, 302
Klonoff, E. A., 34, 49, 114
Kluckhohn, C., 8
Kocarek, C. E., 351
Kochanek, K. D., 302
Kodras, J. E., 59
Koh, T. C., 268
Kolody, B., 306, 307, 308, 309, 317–318, 321, 325,
    326, 327, 330
Kolonel, L. N., 241
Kosary, C. L., 111
Koss-Chioino, J. D., 67, 68, 285
Kramer, J., 241
Krieger, N., 85
Kriepe de Montano, M., 150
Kroeber, A. L., 8
Krug, M., 10

Kumanyika, S. K., 180
Kumar, D., 90
Kung, W. W., 249
Kuniyuki, A., 242
Kunjufu, J., 120
Kuo-Jackson, P. Y., 350
Kuper, A., 8
Kurasaki, K. S., 361

Ladany, N., 346, 348, 349, 351
LaFromboise, T., 67, 155, 172, 184, 195, 196, 198,
    204, 208
LaFromboise, T. D., 350, 360
Lake, M. G., 156, 185
Landrine, H., 34, 49, 114
Landsverk, J. A., 318
Lane, P., Jr., 175
Lantiqua, R., 70
La Roche, M. J., 326, 328
Larrabee, A. L., 72
Lashley, K. H., 195
Lasso, B., 319
Lau, J. K., 246
LaVeist, T. A., 95, 128, 317
Leaf, P., 317
Leaf, P. J., 128, 317
Lee, C. C., 201
Lee, P. A., 248
Lee, R. M., 96, 251
Lee, S., 249
Lee, S. A., 198, 205
Lee, W. H., 235
Lefley, H. P., 8, 59, 65, 341, 345, 361,
    362, 363
Leo, R. J., 70, 74
Leong, F. T. L., 58, 64, 65, 66, 68, 69, 258, 259,
    260, 261
Lesser, I. M., 247
Levin, J. S., 98
Lew, S., 36
Lewis, G. B., 226
Lewis, J. A., 201, 202, 359
Lewis, M. D., 359
Lex, B. W., 180
Li, C., 322
Li, L., 269
Liang, C. T. H., 269, 271
Lichtenberg, P. A., 126
Lieber, E., 250
Lieberman, A., 318
Lieberman, L., 5
Lieberman, M. A., 325
Liff, J. M., 241
Light, I., 225
Lilly, R. L., 93, 96
Lin, E., 64, 317
Lin, K., 69, 72
Lin, K.-M., 246, 247
Linskey, A. O., 309, 325
Linton, R., 30
Lippincott, J. A., 66
Lisansky, J., 292
Little, R. R., 301, 302
Littlefield, A., 5
Little Soldier, L., 150
Liu, J. F., 244
Liu, W. M., 269, 349
Locke, B. Z., 73, 306, 308, 319
Locke, D. C., 348, 349, 350

Locust, C., 149, 156, 184
Loftin, J. D., 149
Lollock, L., 281
Longworth, S. L., 244
Lonner, W. J., 8, 31, 32f
López, A. A., 319
Lopez, I. R., 306, 307
López, S., 318, 319
Lopez, S. R., 127
Lopez-Baez, S., 294
Louie, C. E., 350
Lowe, S. M., 61, 268
Lucek, J., 320
Luhtanen, R., 46, 92
Lum, D., 179, 180, 188
Lum, J. L., 250
Lum, O. M., 244
Lunt, H., 324
Luo, H., 267, 268
Lutalo, T., 322

Mabunda, L. M., 106, 111, 112
MacAskill, R. L., 73
MacPhee, D., 187
Madonia, M. J., 127
Magana, C. G., 309
Magaña, C. G., 325
Magids, D. M., 350
Maher, P. J., 115
Maldonado, R., 36
Malgady, R., 327
Malgady, R. G., 321, 325, 326
Mallinckrodt, B., 195, 360
Malone, J. L., 194
Manderscheid, R. W., 73, 319
Manning, M. L., 178, 182, 184
Manson, S., 206
Manson, S. M., 72, 180, 199
Manyfingers, B., 206, 207
Maples, M. F., 157, 204
Marano, M. A., 111
Marín, B. V., 282, 286, 292, 293
Marín, G., 35, 282, 292, 293, 328, 329
Marino, S., 319
Markides, K. S., 180
Markstrom-Adams, C., 231
Marotta, S., 282, 283
Martin, D. J., 371
Martín-Baró, I., 128
Martinez, L., 290
Martinez, R. O., 285, 291
Marum, E., 322
Maruse, K., 29
Maruyama, M., 268
Mason, M. A., 285
Matsuda, K., 246
Matsui, S., 268
Matsushita, Y. J., 268, 269
Matthews, L., 268
Mays, M. A., 301, 302
Mays, V. M., 129
McCarthy, D. M., 246
McCormick, R. M., 206
McCurry, S., 370
McDavis, R. J., 117, 348, 349
McDermott, J. F., Jr., 361
McElroy, S. L., 127
McIntosh, P., 14–15
McIntyre, L. M., 128

McKinnon, J., 49
McLaughlin, D., 161
McLemore, S. D., 11
Meara, N. M., 345, 346
Meehan, M. O., 322
Meggert, S. S., 341
Meier, S., 360
Mellow, A. M., 74
Menaghan, E. G., 325
Mendiola, S., 290
Meng, F., 267, 268
Mercado, P., 268, 319
Merritt, R. D., 72
Merta, R. J., 269
Messinger, M., 286
Meston, C. M., 251
Mestre, J. P., 283, 291
Mezzich, J., 115
Mezzich, J. E., 72
Michalek, C., 70, 74
Michultka, D., 309
Midgette, T. E., 341
Mierzwa, J. A., 66
Migration Dialogue, 303
Milazzo-Sayre, L. J., 73
Milbrodt, T., 194, 208
Miles, M. S., 119
Miller, B. A., 111, 241
Miller, P. J. A., 330
Miller, J. G., 127
Miller, L., 306
Miller, T. I., 371
Miller-Heyl, J., 187
Min, P. G., 225, 227
Minino, A. M., 112
Mink, I. T., 250
Minn, J. Y., 244
Minrath, M., 326
Mintz, L. B., 250
Mio, J. S., 57
Miranda, J., 318
Mobley, M., 301, 302, 351
Mohatt, G. V., 196, 198, 205, 208
Moldoveanu, M., 243
Mondin, G. W., 371
Montalvo, F. F., 287
Montaner, J. S., 322
Moody, M., 371
Moradi, B., 46, 93
Morales, A., 318
Morales, E., 293
Mori, S., 68, 370
Morin, P. M., xxiii, 193–208
Morishima, J. K., 259
Morris, D. R., 57
Morris, P., 126
Morrison, T., 136
Morrow, C. A., 178, 187
Morten, G., 37, 39, 259, 260, 265
Moscicki, E. K., 306, 308
Moss, A. A., Jr., 135
Moss, N. E., 85
Mueser, K. T., 370
Mullan, J. T., 325
Munday, C., 127
Munoz, C., 291
Muñoz, R. F., 318
Muntaner, C., 128, 317
Murguía, A., 285

Murguia, E., 286, 287
Murphy, S. L., 110, 302
Murray, H. A., 200
Murray, J., 74
Myers, H. F., 180, 308
Myers, J. E., 157, 204
Myers, L. J., 37

Nagata, D. K., 224
Nagayama, G. C., 306, 307
Nagel, J., 7
Nakashima, A., 322
Narayan, D. A., 70, 74
Narikiyo, T. A., 248
Narrow, W. E., 319
National Academies, 305
National Advisory Mental Health Council Workgroup
    on Racial/Ethnic Diversity in Research Training
    and Health Disparities Research, 60, 74
National Cancer Institute, 241
National Center for Education Statistics (NCES),
    284, 285
National Center for Health Statistics (NCHS),
    106–107, 111, 112, 240
National Coalition of Advocates for Students, 358
National Coalition of Hispanic Health and Human
    Services Organizations, 324
National Diabetes Information Clearinghouse, 301
National Health and Nutrition Examination Survey
    (NHANES), 301
National Institute of Health, 304
National Institute on Alcohol Abuse and
    Alcoholism, 304
National Latino Children's Institute, 290
National Population Projections, 2
National Science Foundation, 226
National Women's Health Information Center,
    240, 241
Native American Leadership Commission on Health
    and AIDS, 174
NCES. See National Center for Education
    Statistics
NCHS. See National Center for Health Statistics
Neidert, L. J., 30
Neighbors, H. W., 59, 64, 65, 68, 127, 128
Nelson, A. R., 301, 304, 305
Nelson, E. S., 12
Nervi, C. H., 308
Neufeldt, V., 16
Neville, H. A., xxiii, 83–99, 125, 130, 131, 133, 135,
    350
Newcomb, M., 293
Ngo, V., 251
Nguyen, L. T., 244
Nguyen, S. D., 249
NHANES. See National Health and Nutrition
    Examination Survey
Nickerson, K. J., 49, 65, 95, 128, 317
Nielson, D., 350
Niemann, Y. F., 290
Nihira, K., 250
Noh, S., 244
Nomura, M. M. Y., 241
Nomura, Y., 319
Norcross, J. C., 370
Norlander, T., 268
Northrup, J., 147, 165
Norton, I. M., 200
Novak, M., 31

Nuccio, I., 246
Nutt Williams, R., 130

Oakes, J., 291
Oberg, K., 33
Oboler, S., 280
O'Connell, J. J., 195
O'Connell, L. J., 345
O'Connell, M., 2
Oddone, E. Z., 128
Oetting, E. R., 180
Ojeda, V. D., 310, 330
Okazaki, S., 244
Okonji, J. M. A., 130
Olfson, M., 318, 319
Olmeda, E., 32
Olmeda, E. L., 329
Olmedo, E. L., 30
Omi, M., 136
Omizo, M. M., 261
Ong, P., 220, 226, 228, 229
Organista, K. C., 318
Ortega, A. N., 308
Ortiz-Bush, Y., 321
Osborne, L. W., 207
Osborne, W. L., 157, 186
Ososkie, J. N., 130
Ostrove, J. M., 106, 114, 116
Osugi, L., 285
O'Sullivan, M. J., 318, 319
Oswalt, W. H., 149
Ottavi, T. M., 346, 350

Padgett, D. K., 64, 128, 317
Padilla, A. M., 34, 35, 307, 308, 309, 318,
    321, 326
Pandurangi, A. K., 247
Paniagua, F. A., 178, 292, 293
Panwala, S., 243
Pappaioanou, M., 302
Paradis, C. M., 59, 70, 126
Parham, T. A., 28, 39, 93, 105, 109, 116, 117
Park, E., 250
Park, K., 270
Park, R. E., 30, 31, 223
Parker, E., 114
Parker, G., 249
Parron, D. L., 72
Parsey, K. S., 128
Patrick, C., 64
Patterson, C. H., 352
Patterson, D. G., 286
Patterson, S., 196, 197
Paul, G. L., 370
Payton, C. R., 344
Pearlin, L. I., 325
Pedersen, P., 347, 348, 349, 350
Pedersen, P. B., 345, 367, 368
Penn, N. E., 241
Peregoy, J. J., 204
Pérez, L., 319
Perlo, V., 89
Perrino, T., 322
Perron, J., 46
Peterson, P. D., 318
Pewewardy, C., 172
Phan, L. T., 157, 204
Phares, V., 309
Phelps, R. E., 39

Phillips, P., 246
Phinney, J. S., 9, 29–30, 46, 92, 181
Pichette, E. F., 155, 159, 159f, 160
Pierce, W., 90
Pike, M. C., 241
Pincus, H. A., 318
Piran, N., 250
Plank, G. A., 150
Poland, R. E., 246, 247
Pollock, D., 70, 74
Ponterotto, J. G., 37, 202, 269, 350, 353, 359, 367
Poortinga, Y. H., 260
Pope, K. S., 370
Pope-Davis, D. B., 269, 346, 349, 350, 351
Porche-Burke, L., 19, 348, 360
Porterfield, K. S., 282
Portman, T. A. A., 182
Poston, W. C., 268, 319
Poston, W. S. C., 37
Powe, N. R., 319
Power, S., 32, 329
Preisser, A. B., 250
President's Advisory Commission of Educational
    Excellence for Hispanic Americans, 285, 291
Pulos, S., 130
Pumariega, A. J., 309, 325

Quezada, T., 319
Quinn, T. C., 322
Quintero-Salinas, R., 309, 325

Rae, D. S., 306, 308, 319
Rafii, S., 90
Ramirez, M., 70
Ramirez, R. R., 48, 280, 281, 283, 284, 285
Ramos, J., 282, 283, 289, 290
Ramos-Sanchez, L., 36, 66
Redfield, R., 30
Red Horse, J. G., 150, 152, 180
Reed, W., 107, 108, 110, 111, 112, 113
Reedy, R., 205
Regier, D. A., 307, 317, 318, 319
Rego, S. A., 370
Reich, C. A., 1
Retish, P., 291
Reyhner, J., 149
Reynolds, A. L., 37, 346, 350
Reynolds, L. T., 5
Richardson, M. F., 350
Richardson, T. Q., 6
Richman, D. D., 322
Rickard-Figueroa, K., 36
Rieger, B. P., 350
Ries, L. A. G., 111
Rivera, G., 67, 69
Rivers, R. Y., 178, 187
Robbins, R. R., 148
Roberson, N., 107, 108, 110, 111, 112, 113
Roberts, C. R., 309
Roberts, J. S., 74
Roberts, R. E., 306, 309
Robins, L. N., 307, 317
Robinson, M., 201, 203
Rodriguez, E. R., 279, 283, 285
Rodriguez, M., 309
Rodriguez, N., 308
Rodriguez, R., 1, 9, 18
Roemer, M. I., 48, 284
Rogler, L., 327

Rogler, L. H., 306, 321, 325, 326
Root, M. P. P., 5
Rose, P. I., 3
Rosenbeck, R., 126
Rosenheck, R., 63, 308
Rosenstein, M. J., 73
Rosenthal, J. F., 241
Rosenzweig, S., 369
Roush, K. L., 37
Rowe, W., 195, 360
Rowley, S. A. J., 92
Royal, S., 322
Royer, J. M., 283, 291
Rubio-Stipec, M., 309, 310, 330
Rubio-Stipek, M., 306, 307
Ruelas, S., 352, 367
Ruelas, S. R., 36, 66
Ruiz, A. S., 37
Ruiz, R. A., 318
Rumbaut, R. D., 325
Rushton, J. P., 4
Russell, G., 147, 148, 162, 163

Saag, M. S., 322
Sabogal, F., 322
Sahay, S., 250
Saldana, D. H., 308
Salgado de Snyder, N. S., 307, 308, 309
Salgado de Snyder, V. N., 310, 330
Samaan, R. A., 120
Sanborn, T. A., 90
Sánchez, A. R., 318, 319
Sanchez, C. M., 350
Sanchez, J., 348, 349, 350
Sanderson, W. C., 370
Sanderson, W. W., 370
Sandlund, E. S., 268
Santiago-Rivera, A. L., 290, 292, 293, 294, 327
Santiago-Santiago, I., 291
Sarason, B. R., 251
Sarason, I. G., 251
Sarata, B. P. V., 117, 118
Sasaki, H. M., xxiii, 300–310
Sax, K. W., 127
Schaefer, R. T., 5, 7
Schlesinger, H. J., 64, 128
Schlosser, E., 303, 304
Schmidley, D., 1, 2
Schmidt, L. D., 345, 346
Schoen, C., 244
Schooley, R. T., 322
School of Cooperative Individualism, 87
Schroeder, B., 370
Schulberg, H. C., 127
Schull, W., 301
Schulman, K. A., 90
Schultz, A., 114
Schwabe, A. M., 59
Scwarcz, S. K., 322
Sears, D. O., 83
Secada, W. G., 291
Segall, M. H., 8, 31, 260
Segura-Herrera, T. A., xxiv, 279–294
Selik, R. M., 302
Sellers, R. M., 92
Sellers, S. L., 107, 108, 109
Serwadda, D., 322
Sewankambo, N., 322
Shapiro, D., 371

Shapiro, D. A., 371
Sharma, S., 90
Shas Project Group, 322
Shea, S., 319
Shea, S. H., 246
Shear, M. K., 127
Shekhdar, A., 244, 245
Shelton, J. N., 92
Sheppard, H. L., 1
Sherry, C., 70, 74
Shin, H. B., 281
Shoen, C., 245
Shoham, V., 370
Shrout, P. E., 306, 307
Sidanius, J., 83
Siegel, C., 318
Silver, S., 70
Simek-Morgan, L., 367
Simon, J. L., 281, 291
Simoni, J. M., 319
Simons, R. C., 182, 183
Sistrunk, S., 90
Siu, P. P. C., 225
Skinner, J. F., 241
Skorikov, V. B., 46
Slater, J., 90
Slavin, R., 291
Sledge, W. H., 318
Smart, D. W., 308, 326
Smart, J. F., 308, 326
Smedley, A., 125
Smedley, B. D., 301, 304, 305
Smith, B. L., 110, 112
Smith, E. J., 37, 347, 348, 349, 350
Smith, E. M. J., 308
Smith, G. G., 105
Smith, H. O., 61
Smith, M. A., 92
Smith, M. L., 371
Smith, R., 246
Smith, T. B., 318
Snowden, L., 306
Snowden, L. H., 62, 64, 65, 74
Snowden, L. R., 59, 64, 69, 73, 98, 128, 244, 259, 306, 318, 319, 320
Sobhan, M., 306, 309
Sodowsky, G. R., 189, 350
Sodowsky, M. L., 350
Song, Y. I., 250
Spanierman, L., 133
Sparks, R., 350
Special Populations Task Force of the President's Commission on Mental Health, 57
Speight, S. L., 37
Spencer, M., 231
Spitters, C., 322
Stadler, H., 348, 349, 350
Stark, C., 16
State Population Projections, 2
Stechuchak, K. M., 128
Steinwachs, D. S., 319
Stern, M. P., 301, 302
Stich, F., 371
Stickle, T., 370
Stiffarm, L. A., 175
Stith, A. Y., 301, 304, 305
Stone, D., 90
Stonequist, E. V., 31, 39
Strakowski, S. M., 127

Streiner, B. J., 308
Su, T., 246
Suarez-Orozco, C., 325
Suarez-Orozco, M. M., 325
Substance Abuse and Mental Health Services Administration, 246
Sue, D., xxiv, 37, 39, 42, 45, 187, 188, 198, 240–251, 259, 260, 265, 367
Sue, D. W., 19, 37, 40, 42, 45, 58, 65, 66, 73, 187, 188, 198, 249, 259, 260, 265, 347, 348, 349, 350, 360, 367, 368
Sue, S., 9, 28, 29, 40, 49, 61, 62, 64, 75, 128, 130, 244, 247, 259, 270, 272, 318, 320, 321, 361, 363, 364, 369, 370
Suinn, R. M., 36
Sumner, W. G., 12
Surgenor, L. J., 324
Surgeon General's Report, 244
Sutherland, M., 121
Sutton, C. T., 197, 206
Swanson, G. M., 241
Swanson, J. W., 309, 317, 325
Swartz, M. S., 317
Swinomish Tribal Mental Health Project, 183
Sydell, E. J., 12
Sylvester, J. L., 106, 107, 109, 110
Symonds, B. D., 371
Syzmanski, D., 133

Taffe, R. C., 350
Takagi, D., 226, 227
Takaki, R., 132, 218, 223, 225, 227
Takeuchi, D., 128
Takeuchi, D. T., 49, 62, 64, 73, 259
Talbot, D. M., 351
Taleghani, C. K., 90
Talleyrand, T. Q., 6
Tamir, A., 241
Tan, J. A., 351
Tang, J., 226
Tansey, B., 226
Tashima, N., 29
Task Force on the Promotion and Dissemination of Psychological Procedures, 370
Tata, S. P., 58, 65, 66, 68, 69, 258, 260, 261
Tate, C., 5, 7
Tatum, B. D., 13
Tatum, E., 180
Taylor, D. A., 109, 113
Taylor, J. D., 39
Taylor, M. J., 180
Taylor, R. J., 98, 129
Taylor, V. M., 242
Tellegen, A., 199
Telles, C. A., 325
Templeton, A. R., 5
Tennent, J., 324
Teresi, J. A., 70
Terrell, F., 49, 65, 95
Terrell, F. N., 49
Terrell, S., 49
Terrell, S. L., 95
Tetrick, F. L., 61
Teyber, E., 137
Therrien, M., 48, 280, 281, 283, 284, 285
Thomas, K. R., 148, 150, 156, 184, 186, 194, 205, 349
Thomason, T. C., 148, 150, 198
Thompson, C., 264, 271

Thompson, C. E., xxiv, 49, 95, 125–139, 352, 354, 365
Thompson, E., 65
Thompson, J. W., 319
Thompson, M. A., 322
Thompson, S. E., 127
Thomson, C. E., 350
Thorn, G. R., 117, 118
Timbers, D. M., 318
Tinsley, H. E., 320
Tinsley-Jones, H. A., 13, 14
Toarmino, D., 249
Tolman, A., 205
Toporek, R., 348, 349, 350
Toporek, R. L., 269, 349
Torres-Matrullo, C. M., 308
Torres-Rivera, E., 157, 204
Torrey, E. F., 318, 361, 369
Tran, L., 243
Trapnell, P. D., 251
Treadwell, K. R. H., 126
Tremblay, C., 46
Trevino, F. M., 17, 318
Triandis, H. C., 292, 328
Triay, V. A., 289
Trieweiler, S. J., 127
Trimble, J., 32
Trimble, J. E., 196, 198, 204, 208, 329
Troiden, R. R., 37
Tsai, J. L., 248
Tseng, W. S., 361
Tugrul, K. C., 127
Tulloch, B. R., 301
Turner, L. W., 121
Tyler, L. E., 361

Uba, L., 231
Ullman, J. B., 114
Umemoto, D., 232, 265
University of California, Los Angeles Center for the Study of Latino Health and Culture, 304
Unrau, Y. A., 206, 207
Upchurch, S., 301
U.S. Bureau of Indian Affairs, 148
U.S. Census Bureau, 47, 48, 63, 84, 85, 86, 87, 106, 108, 112, 113, 147, 148–149, 178, 217, 228, 229, 241, 258
U.S. Department of Commerce, 280, 283, 284
U.S. Department of Health and Human Services. See Department of Health and Human Services
U.S. Department of Labor, 283–284
U.S. Surgeon General's Report, 126, 127, 129
Utsey, S. O., 290

Valberding, P. A., 322
Van Bockern, S., 153
Van Dijk, T. A., 12
Vandiver, B., 93, 94
Vandiver, B. J., 38, 93
Vangel, S. J., 126
VanOss Marín, B., 323
van Ryn, M., 90
van Uchelen, C., 67
Vargas-Willis, G., 326
Varvin, S., 205
Vasquez, M., 19, 348, 360
Vásquez, M. J. T., 285, 288
Vasquez-Nuttal, E., 347, 348, 349, 350
Vazsonyi, A. T., 309

Vega, W. A., 293, 306, 307, 308, 309, 317–318, 319, 321, 325, 326, 327, 330
Velasquez, R. J., 241
Vella, S., 322
Vera, H., 83, 89
Vereen, L., 157, 204
Vernon, S., 306
Vigil, P., 36
Vodracek, F. W., 46
Vontress, C. E., 37
Von Witzleben, I., 370

Wabwire-Mangen, F., 322
Wagner, H. R., 317
Wagner, N. S., 58, 65, 66, 68, 69, 258, 260
Waldron, E. E., 132
Wall, T. L., 246
Waller, M. A., 196, 197
Walrath, C., 317
Walrather, C., 128
Walsh, R., 267
Walters, G. D., 267
Walters, J. M., xxiv, 83–99, 125, 130
Waltz, G. R., 359
Wampold, B. E., 68, 268, 369, 371
Wang, G. C. S., 244, 247
Wang, P. S., 64
Ward, J. W., 302
Warren, J. L., 90
Washington, E. A., 106, 108, 109, 110, 111, 112
Waters, M., 5
Watkins, C. E., 49, 95
Watts, L. K., 208
Wawer, M. J., 322
Weaver, H. N., 188
Weinrach, S. G., 349
Weismantle, M., 284
Weissman, M. M., 319
Weizmann, F., 5
Wells, K. B., 317, 319
West, D., 241
West, D. W., 241
West, S. A., 127
Westermeyer, J. J., 183
Whaley, A. L., 49, 50, 65, 70, 95, 130
White, J. L., 105, 109, 116, 135
White, W., 132
Whiteley, S., 261, 269
Wicker, L. R., xxiv, 90, 105–121
Wiedmeyer, H. M., 301, 302
Wilbur, M. P., 154, 155, 184
Willging, C. E., 198
Williams, D., 114
Williams, D. A., 370
Williams, D. R., 85, 97, 116, 117, 118, 129
Williams, J. P., 241
Williams, K. E., 127
Williams, S., 90
Williams-Morris, R., 116, 117, 118
Wilson, J. W., 39
Winant, H., 136
Winkelman, M., 33
Wirth, L., 17
Wise, B. K., 309
Wise, S. L., 350
Wohl, J., 68, 361, 363, 364
Wood, P. S., 360
Woodson, C. G., 135
Woody, S. R., 370

Worrell, F., 93, 94
Worrell, F. C., 38
Worthington, R., 49, 95
Worthington, R. L., 133, 351
Wortley, C., 322
Wu-Williams, A. H., 241
Wyatt, G. E., 5

Yang, P. H., 36, 232, 261, 263
Yasui, Y., 242
Ybarra, L., 308
Yee, A. H., 5
Yee, B. W. K., 241
Yeh, M., 62
Yeh, Y.-Y., 248
Yeni, P. G., 322
Yi, J. K., 242
Yi, K. Y., 267
Ying, Y., 249
Ying, Y.-W., 248

Yoo, J.-H., 243
Yoshioka, R. B., 29
Young, J. L., 129
Young, J. L., Jr., 241
Young, K., 128, 130, 364, 369
Young, M., 32, 329

Zamora-Hernandez, C. E., 286
Zanbe, N. W. S., 49
Zane, N., 9, 61, 128, 130, 270, 272, 363, 364, 369
Zane, N. W. S., 64, 245, 259, 320, 321
Zea, M. C., 282, 285, 319
Zhang, A. Y., 244
Zhang, N., 269
Zhao, S., 59
Zia, H., 217, 220, 222, 230, 232, 234, 235
Ziegler, R. G., 241
Zoellner, L. A., 126
Zuckerman, M., 4, 5
Zuñiga, M. E., 327

Subject Index

AA. *See* Alcoholics Anonymous
AACD. *See* American Association for Multicultural
    Counseling and Development
ABPsi. *See* Association of Black Psychologists
ACA. *See* American Counseling Association
Accessibility of mental health services, 61–63
Acculturation, 11
    of American Indians, 34, 158–160, 159*f,* 195
    of Asian Americans, 36, 260–262
    dimensions of, 34
    vs. enculturation, 260
    and help-seeking behavior, 195
    of Hispanic Americans, 35–36, 307–309,
        325–330
    levels of, 159, 159*f*
    measuring, 35–37
    psychological, 31–35, 32*f*
    and role of counselor, 365, 366*f*
    theories of, 31–35
Acculturation attitudes, 32–33
Acculturative stress, 33, 308–309, 325, 327
Acupuncture, 267–268
Adolescents
    African American
        death rates for, 113
        pregnancy in, 113
    American Indian
        pregnancy in, 177–178
        suicide in, 181
    Asian American
        mental illness in, 244–245
        substance abuse in, 245–246
    Hispanic American
        acculturative stress in, 308–309
        mental health needs of, 309
        smoking in, 305
Advisers, 360–361, 366*f*
Advocacy counseling, for American
    Indians, 201–204
Advocates, 358, 366*f*
Affordability of mental health services, 62–63
African American, use of term, 17
African American Acculturation Scale, 49
African Americans, 83–139. *See also* Children, African
    American; Men, African American; Women,
    African American
    acculturation of, 34

adolescents
    death rates for, 113
    pregnancy in, 113
and alternative sources of help, 68
cultural mistrust in, 49–50, 65, 94–95, 134
demography of, 84–85
diagnostic bias and, 69–70, 127
education of, 47, 87, 116–117, 120
fertility rate of, 2
and health disparities, 90–91
life expectancy for, 110
mental health needs of, 58–60, 114–120
physical health needs of, 106–113
in prison, 87–89, 118
racial categorization of, 5
racial identity development in, 37–39, 92–94
racism and, 131–136
religion and, 129
socioeconomic status of, 47–48, 85–87, 119
    and mental health, 114
    and physical health, 106–107
and stigma of mental illness, 65, 115
treatment bias and, 73
treatment of, 125–139
unemployment of, 86, 116
and use of mental health services, 63–65, 115, 128
within-group differences of, 29, 47–48, 49,
    95–96
Afrocentric type, 94
Aguantar, 294
AIDS
    in African Americans, 111–112, 119
    in American Indians, 174–175
    in Hispanic Americans, 302–303, 322–323
Alaska Natives, 171
Alcohol abuse
    in American Indians, 179–181, 183, 204
    in Asian Americans, 245, 246–247
    in Hispanic Americans, 304, 308–309
Alcoholics Anonymous (AA), 208
Alcohol use disorder, 246–247
Alternative sources of help, 68–69, 267–268
American Association for Multicultural Counseling
    and Development (AACD), 347–348
American Counseling Association (ACA), 57, 202
    ethical codes of, 343–344
    criticisms of, 344–346

American Indian Religious Freedom Act (1978),
    149, 163
American Indians, 147–208. *See also* Men, American
    Indian; Women, American Indian
  acculturation of, 34, 158–160, 159*f*, 195
  adolescents
    pregnancy in, 177–178
    suicide in, 181
  alcohol use in, 179–181, 183, 204
  and alternative sources of help, 68
  children, 152–153
  communication style of, 158, 197–198
  and community, 197, 207–208
  conventional *vs.* traditional native counseling for,
    196–199
  cultural mistrust in, 194–195
  cultural-related syndromes in, 182–183
  definition of, 148–149
  demography of, 173–174
  diversity of, 147–148
  Eagle feathers and, 157, 207–208
  ethnic identity conflicts in, 181–182
  and family, 151, 152, 156, 197, 206–207
  humor and, 157–158, 204
  Indian Health Service and, 172–173
  life expectancy for, 178
  mental health needs of, 171–172, 178–182
  mental health providers and, 161–162, 184,
    195–196
  physical health needs of, 171–172, 174–178
  psychological assessment of, 199–200
  racial categorization of, 5
  racism and, 149–150, 172
  social and political issues for, 162–166
  socioeconomic status of, 174
  and spirituality, 154–157, 184–186, 204–205
  terms applied to, 149
  traditions of, 150–158, 151*t*, 196–198
  treatment of, 193–208, 360
  unemployment rate for, 172
  and use of mental health services, 64, 193–196
  within-group differences of, 48, 49
"Americanization," 11
American Psychological Association (APA), 57–58
  ethical codes of, 342–343
  criticisms of, 344–346
Amok, 247–248, 264
Anglo American, use of term, 18
Antimiscegenation laws, 223
APA. *See* American Psychological Association
ARSMA II, 36
Asian American, use of term, 17, 217
Asian Americans, 217–272. *See also* Adolescents,
    Asian American
  acculturation of, 36, 260–262
  additional sources of mental health support for,
    270–271
  and alternative sources of help, 68–69, 267–268
  cultural values of, 232–233
    vs. conventional counseling, 265–267
    and perceptions of mental health services and
      providers, 261–262
    and psychological assessment, 263–265
  culture-bound syndromes in, 247–248, 249,
    264–265
  demography of, 217–218
  education of, 226–227, 228–229
  employment of, 224–226, 228–229
  ethnic identity conflicts in, 249–250

  and family, 232, 233, 250–251, 266
  fertility rate of, 2
  health practices and beliefs of, 242–243, 248
  immigration history of, 218–222
  life expectancy for, 240
  men, cancer in, 241
  mental health needs of, 243–251, 259–260
  mental health providers and, 259–263, 268–270,
    366–367
  as "model minority," 227–230, 264
  physical health needs of, 240–243
  psychological assessment of, 263–265
  racial identity in, 230–232
  racial self-hatred in, 40
  racism and, 222–227, 224–227, 231, 264
  salaries of, 226, 228–229
  and stigma of mental illness, 65–66, 248, 260
  substance abuse in, 245–247
  suicide in, 244
  treatment of, 258–272
  and use of mental health services, 64, 259
  within-group differences of, 29, 48, 49
  women
    cancer in, 241, 242
    suicide in, 244
Asian Indians, 217, 219, 229
Asian Values Scale (AVS), 36, 261
Assimilated American Indian, 159
Assimilation, 11, 33, 329
  attitudes toward, 27, 28
  cultural, 11
  models of, 30–31
  structural, 11
Association for Multicultural Counseling and
    Development, 57, 347
Association of Black Psychologists
    (ABPsi), 97–98
Ataques de nervios, 183, 310
Authority figures, deference to, 261, 266, 269
Autonomy stage of racial identity development,
    353, 356*t*
Availability of mental health services, 61–62
AVS. *See* Asian Values Scale
Awareness, cultural, 34

Balceros, 289
Behavioral treatment, for African Americans, 126–127
Behavior shift, 33
Being, 154
Bereavement, 117
Bicultural American Indian, 159
Biculturalism, 33, 34–35
Bidimensional Short Acculturation Scale for Hispanics
    (BSASH), 329–330
Bilinear model of acculturation, 36
Bilingual counseling, 327
Bilingual education, 11, 33
Bilingual voting ballots, 33
Biological definition of race, 4–5
Black, use of term, 17
Black Racial Identity Attitude Scale
    (RIAS-B), 39
Black Racial Identity Development (BRID), 39
Blacks. *See* African Americans
Black Student Psychological Association, 57–58
Black/White Interaction model, 353–354, 355*t*–357*t*
Black Women's Health Project (BWHP), 97–98
Blood quantum, 148, 162, 181
"Brain drain," 220

Breast cancer
    in American Indians, 174
    in Asian Americans, 241
BRID. *See* Black Racial Identity Development
Brown University, 226–227
BSASH. *See* Bidimensional Short Acculturation Scale
    for Hispanics
Bureau of Indian Affairs, 150
BWHP. *See* Black Women's Health Project

California, 2
Cambodia, 221
Cancer
    in African Americans, 110–111
    in American Indians, 174
    in Asian Americans, 241, 242
Cardiovascular diseases
    in African Americans, 110
    in American Indians, 175
Cariño, 292–293
Casinos, 165–166
Catholicism, 285
Caucasian American, use of term, 18
CCCI-R. *See* Cross-Cultural Counseling Inventory-
    Revised
Census Bureau
    on fertility rates, 2
    projections by, 2
    racial categorization by, 6, 230–231
    on socioeconomic status, 62–63
Center for Epidemiological Studies Depression (CES-
    D), 199
Centers for Disease Control and Prevention
    (CDC), 300, 303
Centro Americanos, 289
    age of, 282
    AIDS in, 302
    demography of, 281
    education of, 285
    income of, 284
Cervical cancer
    in American Indians, 174
    in Asian Americans, 241, 242
CES-D. *See* Center for Epidemiological Studies
    Depression
Change agents, 358–360, 366*f*
Child abuse, among Asian Americans, 251
Children
    African American
        AIDS in, 112
        education of, 120
        lead poisoning in, 113
        mental health needs of, 120
        sickle cell anemia in, 113
        teenage pregnancy in, 113
    American Indian, 152–153
    Hispanic, mental health needs of, 309
    school counseling for, 358
Chinese Americans
    diversity of, 231
    employment of, 225
    and family problems, 250, 251
    health practices and beliefs of, 243
    immigration of, 217, 218–219
    somatization in, 249
    substance abuse in, 245, 246
Chinese Exclusion Act (1882), 11, 219
Cirrhosis, 304
Citizenship Act (1924), 149

Civil Liberties Act (1988), 224
Class, definition of, 85
CMI. *See* Cultural Mistrust Inventory
Cold illness, 183
Collective Self-Esteem Scale (CSES), 46
Collectivism, 232, 345, 368
Color-blind racial ideology, 95–96
Common factors approach to multicultural counseling,
    369–372
Communication, and American Indians, 158, 197–198
Community, and American Indians, 197, 207–208
Community context, and mental health needs, 59–60
Concrete expression, 136
Confianza, 293, 319, 324–325
Conformity stage of minority identity development,
    40–41, 41*t,* 45
Conformity status of racial identity, 38, 92
Consultants, 360, 366*f*
Contact stage of racial identity development,
    353, 356*t*
Control, locus of, 109
Counseling. *See also* Mental health services;
    Treatment
    advocacy, 201–204
    bilingual, 327
    conventional, 362–363, 366*f*
        vs. Asian Americans' cultural values,
            265–267
        vs. traditional native, 196–199, 362
    definition of, 362–363
    ethical considerations in, 341–342
    family, 206–207, 363
    goals of, and role of counselor, 365, 366*f*
    group, 207–208
    individual, 204–208
    MID model for, 44–47
    multicultural. *See* Multicultural counseling
    at school, 358
Counselors. *See* Mental health service providers
Cross-cultural counseling, 19. *See also* Multicultural
    counseling
Cross-Cultural Counseling Inventory-Revised
    (CCCI-R), 350, 351
Crossed relationship, 354, 355*t*–357*t*
Cross Racial Identity Scale (CRIS), 93–94
Cross's model of racial identity development, 37–38,
    91, 93
CSES. *See* Collective Self-Esteem Scale
Cuban Adjustment Act (1966), 289
Cubanos, 288–289
    age of, 282
    AIDS in, 302
    demography of, 281
    education of, 285
    income of, 284
    lung cancer in, 305
    and religion, 285
Cuban Revolution (1959), 288
Cuento, 327
Cultural assimilation, 11
Cultural awareness, 34
Cultural barrier theory, 66
Cultural behaviors, 263
Cultural conformity, 28
Cultural factors, and physical health, 108–109
Cultural identity, 263
Cultural identity development, 37–47
Cultural knowledge, 263
Culturally deprived, 9–10

Culturally disadvantaged, 9–10
Cultural mistrust, 49–50, 65
  in African Americans, 49–50, 65, 94–95, 134
  in American Indians, 194–195
Cultural Mistrust Inventory (CMI), 49
Cultural pluralism, 11–12
Cultural racism, 12
Cultural-related syndromes. *See* Culture-bound
  syndromes
Cultural values
  of Asian Americans, 232–233
  vs. conventional counseling, 265–267
  and perceptions of mental health services and
    providers, 261–262
  and psychological assessment, 263–265
  definition of, 263
  of Hispanic Americans, 291–294, 319
Culture, 7–10
  definition of, 7–8
  race and, 131–136
Culture-bound syndromes
  in Americans Indians, 182–183
  in Asian Americans, 247–248, 249, 264–265
  in Hispanic Americans, 310, 330
"Culture shock," 33
Curanderos, 69

Deculturation, 195, 325
Deference to authority figures, 261, 266, 269
Demography
  of African Americans, 84–85
  of American Indians, 173–174
  of Asian Americans, 217–218
  of Hispanic Americans, 280–281
Dental sealants, 177
Dental services, for American Indians, 177
Dhat, 264
Diabetes
  in African Americans, 111
  in American Indians, 175
  in Hispanic Americans, 301–302, 323–324
Diabetes Control and Complications Trials Research
  Group, 302
Diabetic retinopathy, 301
Diagnostic and Statistical Manual of Mental Disorders
  (DSM), 71–73
Diagnostic bias, 69–73, 127, 306
Dichos, 327
Dietetics programs, for American Indians, 176–177
Dignidad, 319
Directions of existence, 185
Discriminatory attitude, 40–41. *See also* Racism
Disintegration, identity, 326
Disintegration stage of racial identity development,
  353, 356t, 357t
Dissonance stage of minority identity development,
  41–42, 41t, 45
Dissonance status of racial identity, 38, 92
Domestic violence, among Asian
  Americans, 250–251
Dropout patterns, 64
*DSM. See Diagnostic and Statistical Manual
  of Mental Disorders*

Eagle feathers, 157, 207–208
ECA. *See* Epidemiological Catchment Area
Education
  of African Americans, 47, 87, 116–117, 120
  of Asian Americans, 226–227, 228–229

bilingual, 11, 33
  of Hispanic Americans, 284–285, 291
Educational and Training Committee, 346–347
Ego status, 38
Elderly, and American Indians, 152–154
El Salvador, 289
Emersion status of racial identity, 38, 92–93
Empirically supported treatments (ESTs), 68, 370–371
Employment
  of Asian Americans, 224–226, 228–229
  of Hispanic Americans, 283–284, 291, 303–304
Employment Division of Oregon v. Smith, 163
Encounter stage of racial identity development,
  37, 355t
Enculturation, 32, 260
Epidemiological Catchment Area (ECA), 58–59, 64
Essentialism, 133, 134
ESTs. *See* Empirically supported treatments
Ethical codes
  of American Counseling Association, 343–344
  of American Psychological Association, 342–343
  criticisms of, 344–346
Ethical considerations in counseling, 341–342
Ethnic diversification
  in California, 2
  forces of, 1–2
  predictions for, 2
Ethnic Heritage Studies Bill (1973), 11
Ethnic identity conflicts, 181–182, 249–250
Ethnic identity development, 37–47
Ethnicity, 7–10
  definition of, 7
  vs. race, 8–9
Ethnicity-specific mental health programs,
  61–62, 74
Ethnic loyalty, 34
Ethnic minorities. *See also* specific minorities
  definition of, 17
  mental health needs among, 58–60
  socioeconomic status of, 62–63
  within-group differences of. *See* Within-group
    differences
Ethnic minority counseling, 19–20
Ethnocentrism, 12
European American, use of term, 18
European Americans
  cultural mistrust of, 49–50, 65, 94–95, 134
  diagnostic bias and, 70
  fertility rate of, 2
  and individualism, 345, 367–368
  life expectancy for, 110
  mental health needs of, 58–60
  racial identity development in, 353
  treatment bias and, 73
  and use of mental health services, 63–64
  and White privilege, 14–15
  women, and use of mental health services, 64
Existence, directions of, 185
External locus of control, 109

Facilitators of indigenous healing methods,
  361–362, 366f
Facilitators of indigenous support systems, 361
Familismo, 292, 328, 330
Family
  American Indians and, 151, 152, 156, 197, 206–207
  Asian Americans and, 232, 233, 250–251, 266
  Hispanic Americans and, 292, 328
  as support system, 361

Family counseling, 206–207, 363
Family Preservation Services (FPS), 206–207
Family reunification, 220, 221
Fast Food Nation (Schlosser), 303–304
Federal Glass Ceiling Commission, 225
Fertility rate, 2
Filipinos, 217, 219, 229, 230, 232, 245, 248
Folk healers, 68–69
Folklore
    and American Indians, 186–187
    counselor accepting, 362
    and Hispanic Americans, 327–328
Foraker Act (1900), 288
Four directions of existence, 185
FPS. *See* Family Preservation Services

Gaming, 165–166
Gays, 286, 322–323
Generosity, 153
Genetic predisposition, 109
Gentlemen's Agreement (1907), 219
Ghost sickness, 183
Gift giving, 270
Glass ceiling, 225–226
Grave desecration, 165
Greater Circle of Life, 153
Grief, 117
Group-appreciating attitude, 41, 42, 43, 44
Group counseling, 207–208
Group-depreciating attitude, 40, 42, 43
Guatemala, 289

Harmony, 156
Hate crimes, 234
Healing beliefs, 184–186, 205, 207
Health disparities, 90–91
Health insurance, 63, 107, 241
Heart disease
    in African Americans, 110
    in American Indians, 175
Helms's Interactional model, 353–354, 355t–357t
Helms's model of racial identity, 38–39, 92–93
Hembrismo, 293
Hepatitis A, 304–305
Hepatitis B, 241, 242
Hispanic American, use of term, 17–18, 280
Hispanic Americans, 5, 279–330. *See also*
    Adolescents, Hispanic American; Men, Hispanic
    American; Women, Hispanic American
    acculturation of, 35–36, 307–309, 325–330
    age of, 282
    alcohol use in, 304, 308–309
    and alternative sources of help, 68, 69
    cultural values of, 291–294, 319
    culture-bound syndromes in, 310, 330
    demography of, 280–281
    diagnostic bias and, 306
    education of, 284–285, 291
    employment of, 283–284, 291, 303–304
    family and, 292, 328
    fertility rate of, 2
    and folklore, 327–328
    generational status of, 282
    immigration of, 281–282
    income of, 284
    language of, 283
    mental health needs of, 306–310
    mental health providers and, 319–321
    phenotype of, 286–287

physical health needs of, 300–306
prevention programs for, 321–325
racial categorization of, 6
racism and, 305–306, 326–327
religion and, 285
sexuality of, 286
social perceptions of, 290–291
sociopolitical histories of, 287–290
and stigma of mental illness, 65, 66
treatment of, 317–330, 359
and use of mental health services, 64, 65, 317–321
within-group differences of, 48, 49
HIV/AIDS
    in African Americans, 111–112, 119
    in American Indians, 174–175
    in Hispanic Americans, 302–303, 322–323
Homosexuality, 286, 322–323
Hospitalization, involuntary, 73
Hot-cold belief, 242
Humility, 153
Humor, American Indians and, 157–158, 204
Hwa-byung, 248, 264
Hypodescent, 5

Identity disintegration, 326
IHS. *See* Indian Health Service
Immersion-emersion anti-White type, 94
Immersion-emersion intense Black involvement
    type, 94
Immersion stage of minority identity development,
    41t, 42–43, 45
Immersion stage of racial identity development, 37,
    353, 355t, 357t
Immersion status of racial identity, 38, 92–93
Immigration
    and American culture, 10–11
    of Asian Americans, 218–222
    of Hispanic Americans, 281–282
    increase in, 1
    and marginalization, 31
    sources of, 1–2
Immigration Act (1924), 219
Immigration Act (1965), 219–220
Immigration Reform Act (1995), 289
Incarceration. *See* Prison
Indian Health Service (IHS), 172–173, 196
Indian Health Service Injury Prevention
    program, 176
Indigenous healing methods, facilitators of,
    361–362, 366f
Indigenous support systems, facilitators of,
    361, 366f
Individual counseling, for American Indians,
    204–208
Individualism, 345, 367–368
Individual racism, 12
Infant mortality
    of African Americans, 112
    of American Indians, 175–176
Institute of Medicine, 305
Institutional racism, 12, 107–108, 114
Integration, 33, 329
Integrative awareness status of racial
    identity, 38
Intergenerational transference of wealth, 86
Internalization biculturalist type, 94
Internalization-commitment stage of racial
    identity development, 37
Internalization commitment status of racial identity, 93

Internalization multiculturalist inclusive type, 94
Internalization nationalist type, 94
Internalization stage of racial identity
    development, 37, 38, 357*t*
Internalization status of racial identity, 38, 93
Internalized racism, 13, 116
Internal locus of control, 109
International AIDS Society-USA Panel, 322
Internment, 223–224
Interpersonal harmony, 232, 266
Intervention
    disparities in quality of, 73–74
    network therapy as, 208
Introspection stage of minority identity development,
    41*t*, 43–44, 46
Involuntary hospitalization, 73

Japanese Americans
    and ethnic identity, 231
    immigration of, 217, 219
    internment of, 223–224
    mental health practices and beliefs of, 248
    substance abuse in, 245, 246
Jones Act (1917), 288

Kidney failure, 301–302
Korean Americans, 219, 232, 243, 246,
    250, 270
Koro, 247, 264

Laos, 221
Latah, 247, 264
Latina, use of term, 280
Latinas and Latinos. *See* Hispanic Americans
Latino, use of term, 17 18, 280
Lead poisoning, 108, 113
Lesbian, gay, bisexual, transgendered individuals
    (LGBT), 286
Life expectancy
    for African Americans, 110
    for American Indians, 178
    for Asian Americans, 240
    for European Americans, 110
Lifestyle factors, and physical health, 108–109
Liver cancer, in Asian Americans, 241
Locus of control, 109
Loyalty, ethnic, 34
Loyalty tests, 224
Lung cancer, 305
*Lying, Secretary of Agriculture, et al v.
    Northwest Indian Cemetery Protective
    Association,* 163

Machismo, 293, 319, 323
MAKSS. *See* Multicultural Awareness-
    Knowledge-and-Skills Survey
Mal de ojo, 310
Mal puesto, 183
Marginal American Indian, 159
Marginality, social, 325–326
Marginalization, 31, 33, 329
Marginal person, 31, 35
Marianismo, 293–294, 319
Marielitos, 289
Mascot issues, 165, 202
Maternal mortality rate, for American Indians,
    175–176
MCAS. *See* Multicultural Counseling
    Awareness Scale

McCarren-Walter Act (1952), 219
MCI. *See* Multicultural Counseling Inventory
MCT. *See* Multicultural counseling
    and therapy
Media portrayal, of Hispanic Americans, 290
Medicine, 154, 155–156, 157
MEIM. *See* Multigroup Ethnic
    Identity Measure
Melting pot, 10–11, 30–31
Men
    African American
        cancer in, 111
        HIV/AIDS in, 112
        mental health needs of, 117–118
        in prison, 87–89, 118
        and violence, 110
    American Indian
        heart disease in, 175
        HIV in, 175
        suicide in, 181
    Asian American, cancer in, 241
    Hispanic American
        gender roles of, 293
        HIV/AIDS in, 303
        smoking in, 305
Mental health needs, 58–60
    of African Americans, 58–60, 114–120
    of American Indians, 171–172, 178–182
    of Asian Americans, 243–251, 259–260
    of Hispanic Americans, 306–310
Mental health research, disparities in, 74–75
Mental health service providers
    as advisers, 360–361, 366*f*
    as advocates, 358, 366*f*
    and American Indians, 161–162, 184,
        195–196
    and Asian Americans, 259–263, 268–270,
        366–367
    aware of own assumptions, values, and biases,
        379–380
    as change agents, 358–360, 366*f*
    as consultants, 360, 366*f*
    as conventional counselors, 362–363, 366*f*
    as conventional psychotherapists, 363–365, 366*f*
    credibility of, 36, 363–364
    developing appropriate strategies, 381–382
    and diagnostic bias, 69–73
    ethnically similar, 61–62, 130, 195, 268–269,
        319–321
    as facilitators of indigenous healing methods,
        361–362, 366*f*
    as facilitators of indigenous support systems,
        361, 366*f*
    and Hispanic Americans, 319–321
    multicultural sensitivity of, 16
    and racism, 13–14, 15
    selecting appropriate role, 365–367
    understanding worldview of culturally different
        client, 380–381
Mental health services. *See also* Counseling;
    Treatment
    disparities in access to, 61–63
    disparities in quality of, 69–75
    disparities in use of, 63–69
Mental illness
    in Asian Americans, 244–245
    Asian beliefs about, 65–66, 248, 260
    conflicting views about, 66–68
    social stigma of, 65–66, 115

Mexicanos, 287–288
acculturation of, 34, 36
age of, 282
AIDS in, 302
and alternative sources of help, 69
change agents for, 359
demography of, 281
diabetes in, 301, 302, 323
education of, 285
income of, 284
and religion, 285
and stigma of mental illness, 66
and use of mental health services, 318–321
Mexican War (1846), 287
Minnesota Multiphasic Personality Inventory
(MMPI), 307
Minority, definition of, 16–17
Minority Identity Development (MID), 39–47, 41*t*
Mistrust. *See* Cultural mistrust
"Model minority," 227–230, 264
Modern racism, 12–13
Modesty, 153
Multicultural Awareness-Knowledge-and-Skills Survey
(MAKSS), 350, 351
Multicultural counseling and therapy (MCT)
of Asian Americans, 260–261, 265
common factors approach to, 369–372
definition of, 19
models of, 352–367
theory of, 367–369
Multicultural Counseling Awareness Scale (MCAS),
350, 351
Multicultural counseling competence, 346–349
assessment of, problems with, 350–352
challenges of, 349–350
conceptual framework for, 379–382
future of, 352
Multicultural Counseling Inventory (MCI), 350, 351
Multicultural sensitivity, 16
Multidimensional theories of acculturation, 34–35
Multigroup Ethnic Identity Measure (MEIM), 46

National Asian Pacific American Legal
Consortium, 234
National Association for the Advancement of Colored
People (NAACP), 132
National Coalition of Advocates for Students, 358
National Comorbidity Survey (NCS), 59
National Health and Nutrition Examination Survey
(NHANES), 301
National Institute for Occupational Safety
and Health, 304
National Institute of Mental Health (NIMH), 58,
72, 73
National Medical Expenditure Survey, 318
National Multicultural Conference and Summit
(NMCS), 19, 348, 360
National Survey of Black Americans (NSBA), 128
Native Americans. *See* American Indians
Native Hawaiians, 241, 245
NCS. *See* National Comorbidity Survey
Negro to Black Conversion model, 37–38, 91, 93
Nervios, 310
Network therapy, 208
Neurasthenia, 248, 249
Neutralism, 133, 134
New racism, 12–13
NHANES. *See* National Health and Nutrition
Examination Survey

Nicaragua, 289
Nigrescence model, 37–38, 91, 93
NIMH. *See* National Institute of Mental Health
9/11 terrorist attack, and hate crimes, 234
NMCS. *See* National Multicultural Conference
and Summit
Nonverbal communication, and American Indians, 158,
197–198
North American Free Trade Agreement, 288
*Northwest Indian Cemetery Protective Association,
Lying, Secretary of Agriculture, et al v.,* 163
NSBA. *See* National Survey of Black Americans
Nutrition programs, for American Indians, 176–177

Obesity, in Hispanic Americans, 301
Occupational safety, 283–284, 303–304
Office of Management and Budget (OMB), racial
categorization by, 6
1.5 generation, 230
Operation Pedro Pan, 289
Opposites, rule of, 204
Organ donation, among African Americans, 112
Organic Act (1900), 288
Osteoporosis, in Asian Americans, 241

Pacific Islanders
mental health needs of, 243–251
physical health needs of, 240–243
within-group differences of, 48
Pantraditional American Indian, 159
Parallel relationship, 353–354, 355*t*–357*t*
Parent-child conflicts, 308, 328
Patience, 154
"Pensionados," 219
People of Color Racial Identity (PCRI), 38–39
Peripheral neuropathy, 302
Personalismo, 292, 319, 325, 328
Phenotypes, 4
Physical differences, 4, 5
Physical health needs
of African Americans, 106–113
of American Indians, 171–172, 174–178
of Asian Americans, 240–243
of Hispanic Americans, 300–306
PIC. *See* Prison industrial complex
Picture-story tests, 200
Platicando, 292
Pluralism, cultural, 11–12
Political correctness, 16
Political issues, for American Indians, 162–166
Post-traumatic stress disorder (PTSD), 309
Preencounter assimilation type, 94
Preencounter miseducation type, 94
Preencounter (racial) self-hatred type, 94
Preencounter stage of racial identity development, 37,
38, 355*t*, 357*t*
Pregnancy, teenage. *See* Teenage pregnancy
Prevention programs
for American Indians, 176
for Hispanic Americans, 321–325
Principle ethics, 345
Prison, African Americans in, 87–89, 118
Prison industrial complex (PIC), 89
Problem etiology, and role of counselor, 365, 366*f*
Professional Standards Committee (PSC), 347–348
Progressive relationship, 354, 355*t*–357*t*
Pseudo-independent stage of racial identity
development, 353
Psychological acculturation, 31–35, 32*f*

Psychotherapists, conventional, 363–365, 366*f*
PTSD. *See* Post-traumatic stress disorder
Public health nursing visits, for American Indians, 177
Puerto Riqueños, 288
　age of, 282
　AIDS in, 302
　demography of, 281
　education, of, 285
　income of, 284
　and religion, 285

Qi-gong psychotic reaction, 264

Race, 3–7
　biological definition of, 4–5
　and culture, 131–136
　vs. ethnicity, 8–9
　social definition of, 6–7
Racial identity
　in American Indians, 162–163
　in Asian Americans, 230–232
　unhealthy, 115–116
Racial identity development, 37–47
　in African Americans, 37–39, 92–94
　in American Indians, 159, 159*f*
　in European Americans, 353
Racial ideology, color–blind, 95–96
Racism, 12–14
　and African Americans, 131–136
　and American Indians, 149–150, 172
　and Asian Americans, 222–227, 224–227, 231, 264
　cultural, 12
　and diagnostic bias, 71, 306
　effects of, 13
　and Hispanic Americans, 305–306, 326–327
　individual, 12
　institutional, 12, 107–108, 114
　internalized, 13, 116
　new, 12–13
　persistence of, 83
Reburial, 165
Rechazo, 323
Referral, disparities in, 73
Refranes, 327
Refugees, mental health needs of, 309
Regressive relationship, 354, 355*t*–357*t*
Reintegration stage of racial identity development, 353, 356*t*, 357*t*
Religion
　and African Americans, 129
　and American Indians, 149, 154–157, 163–164
　and Hispanic Americans, 285
Repatriation, 165
Research
　American Indians in, 199–200
　disparities in, 74–75
Resistance stage of minority identity development, 41*t*, 42–43, 45
Respeto, 293, 319, 328
RIAS-B. *See* Black Racial Identity Attitude Scale
Rule of opposites, 204

Sacred sites, 164
Salaries, of Asian Americans, 226, 228–229
Sanitation services, for American Indians, 177
School counselors, 358
Self-actualization, 39
Self-appreciating attitude, 42, 43, 44
Self-concept, 39

Self-control, 232, 266
Self-depreciating attitude, 40, 42
Self-effacement, 232, 266
Self-esteem, 39, 308
Self-hatred, 37–38, 94, 116
Sensitivity, multicultural, 16
Separation, 33, 329
Sexuality, of Hispanic Americans, 286
Sexual silence, 286
Shamans, 267
Sharing, American Indians and, 198
Shenjing shuairuo, 248, 249, 264
Shen-kui, 264–265
Shin-byung, 265
Sickle cell anemia, 108, 109, 113
Simpatía, 292, 319, 328
SL-ASIA. *See* Suinn-Lew Asian Self-Identity Acculturation Scale
Smith, Employment Division of Oregon v., 163
Smoking, 305
Social action approach to counseling. *See* Advocacy counseling
Social definition of race, 6–7
Social issues, for American Indians, 162–166
Social justice approach to counseling. *See* Advocacy counseling
Social marginality, 325–326
Social stigma of mental illness, 65–66, 115
Social support systems, 361
Socioeconomic status
　and access to mental health services, 62–63
　of African Americans, 47–48, 85–87, 119
　　and mental health, 114
　　and physical health, 106–107
　　women, 85–86
　of American Indians, 174
　　and children's mental health, 120
　of Hispanic Americans, 284
　and mental health needs, 59–60
Socioeconomic within-group differences, 47–49
Somatization, 248, 249
Southeast Asia, immigration from, 220–221
"Spanglish," 327
Spanish-American War, 288
Spanish language, 283, 308, 327–328
Spirituality, and American Indians, 154–157, 184–186, 204–205
Spying, 235
Stomach cancer, in Asian Americans, 241
Storytelling, 158
Stress, acculturative, 33, 308–309, 325, 327
Structural assimilation, 11
Substance abuse
　in African Americans, 112
　in American Indians, 179–181, 183, 204
　in Asian Americans, 245–247
　in Hispanic Americans, 304, 308–309
Sud Americanos, 289–290
　age of, 282
　AIDS in, 302
　demography of, 281
　education of, 285
　income of, 284
Suicide
　in American Indians, 181
　in Asian Americans, 244
Suinn-Lew Asian Self-Identity Acculturation Scale (SL-ASIA), 36
Support systems, 361

Survey of Race Relations, 223
Susto, 310
Sweat lodge ceremony, 185–186, 205, 207
Synergistic stage of minority identity development, 41*t*, 44, 46

Tai chi chuan, 268
Taijin kyofusho, 247, 265
Talking circle, 186, 207
Task Force on Promotion and Dissemination of Psychological Procedures, 370
Teenage pregnancy
   in African Americans, 113
   in American Indians, 177–178
Thailand, 221
Thematic apperception tests (TAT), 200
Therapists. *See* Mental health service providers
Three-dimensional model for counseling, 354–367, 366*f*
Time, American Indians and, 154, 198–199
Traditional American Indian, 159
Traditions
   of American Indians, 150–158, 151*t*, 196–198
   of Asian Americans, 242–243
Trauma, 282, 309
Treatment. *See also* Counseling; Mental health services
   of African Americans, 125–139
   of American Indians, 193–208, 360
   of Asian Americans, 258–272
   of Hispanic Americans, 317–330, 359
Treatment bias, 73–74
Treaty of Guadalupe Hidalgo (1848), 287
Treaty rights, 163
Tribal-specific interventions, 161–162
Tribes, 150–152, 163
Tuberculosis
   in African Americans, 109
   in Asian Americans, 241
Tuskegee Experiment, 65
Tydings-McDuffie Act (1934), 219

Underemployment, 229
Unemployment rates
   for African Americans, 86, 116
   for American Indians, 172
Unequal Treatment: Confronting Racial and Ethnic Disparities in Health Care (Smedley, Stith, Nelson), 305
Unilinear measurement of acculturation, 36
U.S. Bureau of the Census. *See* Census Bureau
Utilization of mental health services, 63–69, 128

   by African Americans, 63–65, 115, 128
   by American Indians, 193–196
   by Asian Americans, 64, 259
   by Hispanic Americans, 64, 65, 317–321

Vietnam, 221
Vietnamese Americans, 231–232, 242, 243, 250, 251
Violence, injuries and death from, 110
Virtue ethics, 345
Vision quest, 186, 205
Voting ballots, bilingual, 33

Wacinko, 183
War Brides Act (1945), 219
"War on drugs," 88
Wealth, of African Americans, 86–87
White, use of term, 18
White privilege, 14–15
Whites. *See* European Americans
Wind illness, 183
Within-group differences, 27–50
   acculturation and, 30–37
   of African Americans, 29, 47–48, 49, 95–96
   cultural mistrust and, 49–50
   racial/ethnic identity development and, 37–47
   socioeconomic, 47–49
Women
   African American
      cancer in, 111
      and death from violence, 110
      enhancing health status of, 97–98
      and health disparities, 90
      HIV/AIDS in, 112, 119
      mental health needs of, 119
      in prison, 88
      socioeconomic status of, 85–86, 119
      unavailability of same-race male partners for, 119
      and use of mental health services, 64
   American Indian
      cancer in, 174
      maternal mortality rate for, 175–176
      and mental health providers, 195–196
   Asian American
      cancer in, 241, 242
      suicide in, 244
   European American, and use of mental health services, 64
   Hispanic American
      and folk healers, 69
      gender roles of, 293–294
      HIV/AIDS in, 303
      smoking in, 305
      and use of mental health services, 64